International Relations:
Geopolitical and Geoeconomic
Conflict and Cooperation

International Relations: Geopolitical and Geoeconomic Conflict and Cooperation

William Nester
St. John's University
Jamaica, New York

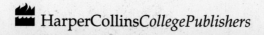
HarperCollins*CollegePublishers*

Acquisitions Editor/Executive Editor: Leo Wiegman
Cover Illustration: Ruttle Graphics, Inc./Trevor Moo-Young
Electronic Production Manager: Angel Gonzalez Jr.
Publishing Services: Ruttle Graphics, Inc.
Electronic Page Makeup: Ruttle Graphics, Inc.
Printer and Binder: R R Donnelley & Sons Company
Cover Printer: The Lehigh Press

**INTERNATIONAL RELATIONS: GEOPOLITICAL AND GEOECONOMIC
CONFLICT AND COOPERATION**

Library of Congress Cataloguing-in-Publication Data
Nester, William R., 1956–
        International relations: geopolitical and geoeconomic conflict and cooperation / William Nester.
                p.   cm.
        Includes bibliographical references and index.
        ISBN 0-673-99305-1
        1. International relations. 2. International economic relations. 3. Geopolitics. I. Title.
    JX1395.N387 1995
    327.1'09'04—dc20   94-32955
                                                            CIP

95 96 97 9 8 7 6 5 4 3 2 1

With deepest Love
to my darling nieces,
Kayde and Sarah

BRIEF TABLE OF CONTENTS

TABLE OF CONTENTS

LIST OF MAPS, CHARTS, AND TABLES

PREFACE

THE NEW WORLD ORDER

Recent revolutionary events have dramatically changed the world. The Cold War is over. The Soviet empire has collapsed. Communist and other authoritarian regimes are being overthrown around the globe. The White House and Kremlin have agreed to deep cuts in nuclear and conventional forces. A comprehensive Middle East peace settlement between Israel and the Arab states now seems imminent following the dramatic August 1993 agreement between Israel and the Palestinian Liberation Organization (PLO). In recent years, the United Nation (UN) has managed geopolitical conflicts that were formerly decided by the immediate participants. UN peacekeeping forces now patrol around twenty countries. In the Persian Gulf War (1990-1991), the UN sanctioned an American-led coalition that drove Iraqi forces from Kuwait, and subsequently sent in technicians to dismantle Iraq's chemical and nuclear weapons program.

With the Cold War's demise, Middle East peace settlements, and UN assertion of collective security, governments can now focus greater attention on dealing with a range of worsening economic, environmental, and humanitarian problems that afflict the world. In June 1992, representatives of 178 countries gathered at the Earth Summit in Rio de Janeiro to debate and sign several treaties pledging themselves to alleviate the world's worsening environmental crises. In other international forums, governments implemented agreements to combat terrorism and the illicit drug trade, and to regulate the flow of refugees. The European Union's (the current name since January 1, 1993 for the former European Community) twelve nations are struggling to forge tighter economic and political ties. Washington, Ottawa, and Mexico City are developing a North American Free Trade Association (NAFTA) that unites 380 million people. Led by Japan, the Newly Industrializing Countries (NICs), and China, the Pacific basin is surpassing the Atlantic basin as the world's most economically dynamic area. Although the United States, Japan, and the European Union continue to attempt to manage the global economy carefully, they clash frequently over conflicting interests. Meanwhile, much of humanity remains scourged by disease, poverty, exploitation, and violence, while wars ravage the former Yugoslavia, Angola, the Sudan, Peru, and elsewhere. All these forces shape and are shaped by international relations.

More than ever, the reality of international relations is quite different from the traditional emphasis on war and peace. Not only are most states at peace most of the time, but only a tiny fraction of the relations between the world's over 190 states contain even the hint of violence. The diminishing threat or reality of war between states, however, does not mean that international relations are conflict-free. Although geopolitical issues dominate the headlines, it is geoeconomic disputes over trade, investments, immigration, pollution, deforestation, foreign aid, drug smuggling, and technology which largely shape international relations. As with geopolitical issues, states cooperate as much as they confront each other in geoeconomic conflicts. But cooperation usually comes only after hard bargaining and the wielding of power by participants. And while nation-states remain the primary actors, their power in different issues is increasingly constrained or enhanced by global economic forces, international laws, regimes, and organizations, multinational corporations, and international mass media and public opinion.

Students like to be challenged and stimulated. They want to learn more about the world and themselves. Few subjects are more fascinating or relevant than international relations. But by using textbooks and hearing lectures that emphasize geopolitics, students receive a distorted view of the real world. Many professsors recognize this and are searching for an international relations textbook that provides a balanced, in-depth analysis of the way the world really is. But can any one international relations textbook be all things to all professors?

A NEW APPROACH TO TEACHING INTERNATIONAL RELATIONS

Scholars strive to keep up with the changes in their field. Sometimes the cumulative weight of new information and perspectives calls for a new way of analyzing the discipline.

International Relations: Geopolitical and Geoeconomic Conflict and Cooperation will attempt to redress the traditional imbalance in favor of geopolitics at the expense of geoeconomics. International relations is not a Hobbesian "war of all against all" in which countries are either preparing for or engaging in war. In reality, most states are at peace most of the time. Although states remain the primary actors in international relations and conflict is endemic, most states are primarily motivated by and engaged in geoeconomic rather than geopolitical struggles, and the parameters of those conflicts are shaped by a continually evolving global political economy. State sovereignty itself is increasingly at bay. The sovereign state's central role in international relations continues, but it is being challenged by such ever more powerful forces as international law and morality, governmental and private international organizations, multinational corporations, and the thickening web of complex geoeconomic interdependence.

This will not be a traditional international relations textbook with an emphasis on war and peace. Although some chapters will necessarily emphasize one more than the other, overall a balanced view of geopolitics and geoeconomics, and their interrelationship is provided.

More specifically, this text will differ from most in ten ways:

1. Most international relations texts follow one of three broad approaches to the subject—theoretical, historical, or contemporary issues and case studies. This text integrates all three approaches in a balanced, comprehensive presentation.

2. It remedies the traditional neglect of international political economy (IPE) or geoeconomics (a more succinct and increasingly popular term that balances the concept of geopolitics) by weaving the theme throughout each chapter as appropriate.

3. It provides a balanced analysis of geopolitics and geoeconomics, and their interrelationship, rather than emphasizing one or the other.

4. Altogether there are nine chapters which emphasize their interrelationship, four which emphasize geopolitics and five geoeconomics.

5. It opens with two succinct chapters on the global political economy's evolution, giving students a broad overview of the interrelated economic, political, technological, military, social, cultural, and power changes and continuities over the past five centuries, within which to understand the more specific concepts, subjects, and case studies of the sixteen following chapters.

6. It analyzes the "interdependent" relations among the industrialized countries in two chapters, and the "dependent" relations between industrialized and less developed countries in three other chapters.

7. An important theme in all of the geoeconomic chapters is the relationship between internal and external forces in shaping a nation-state's development or underdevelopment, and the subsequent impact on national interests, policies, power, and international relations.

8. It offers important sections on political and economic regionalism, with an emphasis on the European Union and North American Free Trade Association.

9. It devotes a chapter to global environmental crises and international attempts to manage them.

10. Throughout, it analyzes the role of perceptions and misperceptions (image and reality) in shaping conflicts, interests, policies, and power.

ELABORATION OF THE TEXT'S THEMES

This text explores geopolitics with rigor and depth, with a particular focus on the balance of power, crisis management, imperialism, arms races, arms control, the Cold War, conventional and nuclear warfare, regional conflicts, terrorism, ideology, and counterinsurgency. It will also deal with more recent geopolitical issues and questions. Did ideological conflict really end with the Cold War? Has nationalism replaced international ideologies as the driving force in international relations? Although the emphasis is on the Cold War and international wars, an important section will discuss the role of civil wars and independence struggles in international relations. Most textbooks concentrate on geopolitics and generally present this subject very well.

Yet geopolitical struggles occur within a global economy, a complex relationship which most textbooks do not explain. Politics and economics are inseparable. Economic alliances, like the European Union and OPEC, can shape international relations as profoundly as do military alliances like NATO and the former Warsaw Pact. Although the global economy is supposed to be based on principles of free trade, governments continually hurl accusation of unfair trade, investment, technology, financial, or industrial policy practices against each other. Democratic industrial countries joust with each other, and individually or collectively against less developed countries.

This book addresses liberal and neomercantilist theories and policies and offers clear explanations. One chapter focuses on macroeconomic, industrial, trade, and technology policy. Another evaluates the GATT, IMF, World Bank, OECD, and other international economic organizations. Two others analyze, respectively, the conflicts and cooperation among the industrialized states, and between them and the less developed states.

Another important related theme I explored is regionalism. While nationalism is tearing some states apart, internationalism is uniting others. In just forty years, the European Union has evolved into a highly unified economic and political system encompassing 340 million people. Meanwhile the United States is attempting to forge a North American common market. In November 1993, during the Asia Pacific Economic Council (APEC) summit, the fifteen attending heads of state agreed to work toward turning their organization into a free trade zone spanning the Pacific basin.

Major themes of this book are interdependence and the international efforts to create formal political and economic integration and cooperation. The world is knit by an increasingly dense network of international organizations and law. According to the United Nations Charter, international politics and individual states should be governed by the ideals of human rights and morality. International relations will be increasingly bound by the formal channels of international organizations, regimes, and law, as well as a range of informal economic, social, political, cultural, moral, psychological, and environmental ties.

Whether the issue is geopolitical or geoeconomic, how do states determine their national interests in conflicts? How is foreign policy made and implemented? This book carefully examines all levels of policy making, including the roles of individual psychology, group decision-making processes, bureaucratic politics, perceptions, interest groups, formal political systems, public opinion, culture, history, and the international system itself.

Some nations have developed rapidly while others have stagnated. What accounts for a nation's ability to develop? Are development and underdevelopment explained primarily by internal or international forces? What links are there between economic and political development? Many of the world's authoritarian regimes are being swept away or challenged by a wave of popular democratic revolutions. How enduring will these changes be? How do the recent democratic revolutions compare to the communist revolutions of the earlier twentieth century? What causes revolutions? This book explores the relationship between political and economic development. It takes a fresh look at questions of modernization, development, and dependence with a particular emphasis on the Third World.

We cannot understand the present unless we understand the past. One problem with many texts is that they give the student slices of history without showing how they all connect. Nor can we study, let alone understand, any subject in a vacuum; politics pervade all human pursuits. This book will remedy this deficiency by providing an analysis in the first two chapters of the global political economy's development from the late Middle Ages through today. Elsewhere throughout the text the emphasis is on the world since 1945. All along politics will be the core concept for exploring the dynamic interrelationship among such international forces as trade, war, technology, the nature and policies of government, development, underdevelopment, ideology, culture, ecology, and psychology. Succinct case studies, many from the last few years, will illuminate these related themes.

Approaching an old subject from a new and more comprehensive perspective will be a challenge. Yet this exploration of geopolitics and geoeconomics is not only workable, but will help professors and students gain a deeper understanding of international relations well into the twenty-first century.

ABOUT THE AUTHOR

Dr. William Nester is Assistant Professor in the Department of Government at St. John's University. He has previously served as Lecturer at the School of Oriental and Asian Studies at the University of London. He received his Ph.D. in 1987 from the University of California at Santa Barbara and has written six scholarly books on Japanese political economy, numerous journal articles on different aspects of international political economy and the novel, *Ends of the Earth* (Northwest Publishing). For five consecutive years, Dr. Nester has received a Faculty Merit Award at St. John's.

Development of the Global Political Economy

Anarchy, Order, and the Changing Nature of International Relations

Key Terms and Concepts

Authoritarianism
Biodiversity
Cold War
Deforestation
Dependence
Desertification
Dumping
Fascism
Free Trade
General Agreement on
    Trade and Tariffs
    (GATT)
Geoeconomics

Geopolitics
Greenhouse Effect
Hegemon
Hobbesian
Human Rights
Imperialism
Intercontinental Ballistic
    Missiles (ICBM)
Interdependence
Liberal Democracy
Multinational Corporation
New World Order

North Atlantic Treaty
    Organization (NATO)
Organization of Petroleum
    Exporting Countries
    (OPEC)
Ozone Layer Depletion
Population Explosion
Sovereignty
Totalitarianism
Trade War
Warsaw Pact

President George Bush, during his 1991 State of the Union address, argued that international relations were fundamentally changing into a "new world order" in which "diverse nations are drawn together in common cause to achieve the universal aspirations of mankind: peace and security, freedom and the rule of law." Is a new world order emerging as the President declared, and does the new world order imply the existence of an old world order? Or is the international system inherently anarchic with all states engaged in a perpetual war of all against all? Are international politics characterized by order or anarchy?

Clearly, there is no world government that issues laws, regulates behavior, and punishes violators. International relations are shaped by the countless actions of over 190 nation-states which, by definition, enjoy *sovereignty*—the freedom to answer to no higher authority than themselves and to act in no other interest than their own.

SOVEREIGNTY AT BAY?

Yet sovereignty is more a concept than a reality; international relations is more than a Hobbesian "war of all against all;" and the world is more than a tower of Babel with everyone speaking and acting at cross-purposes. There is a world order or system. Governments, corporations, international organizations, and individuals act within the paramaters of the global political economy's rules and power distribution. Most states behave and clash within relatively orderly channels which are shaped formally with thousands of international organizations, regimes, and laws and informally through international customs and morality. All states obey the global system's rules most of the time, some of course much more consistently than others. The strands of that world order in which states act are constantly being knit into an increasingly elaborate web of economic, political, military, nuclear, legal, organizational, ecological, social, psychological, and cultural ties. Complex interdependence has dramatically changed the traditional manifestations of global power and relations.

Although most would agree that the world is becoming increasingly interdependent, do these increased ties between countries and people represent a completely new world order? Not necessarily. A world political economy or order has evolved since the first Portugese and Spanish adventurers set sail for the world's far corners over five hundred years ago. Until recently, the development of that world order was slow. Although countries increasingly traded, allied, and negotiated with each other, the divisions between them far outweighed the ties, and nations often settled their conflicts with war or the threat of war. However, since 1945, despite or more likely because of the Cold War, the interdependent world order has developed rapidly and profoundly. Today every human lives under the shadow of potential nuclear and ecological extinction, and nearly all humans are tied to all others through their country's membership in the United Nations and countless political and economic international organizations, and the benefits of global trade, telecommunications, and travel.

Why is interdependence important to us? Interdependence means that any major international event can affect us one way or another, and likewise every major American public issue is, to varying degrees, an international issue. When the General Agreement on Tariffs and Trade (GATT) talks break down, when the Organization of Petroleum Exporting Countries (OPEC) raises oil prices, when tropical forests are destroyed, when the ozone layer is eaten away, when the Tokyo stock market plunges, we, in tiny and usually unobservable ways, are affected. Likewise, when Washington imposes tariffs or fails to reduce the budget deficit, when pollution drifts across to Canada, when the Defense Department builds new weapons systems, when the economy expands or contracts, we affect the world. The differences between international and domestic issues are increasingly blurred.

GEOPOLITICAL AND GEOECONOMIC RELATIONS

Yet, are relations between states today fundamentally different than they were half a century ago? International politics spans *geopolitical* and *geoeconomic* (or political economic as it is sometimes known) conflict. Geopolitics includes disputes over territory, beliefs, behaviors, or some other issue in which those involved might well consider using some sort of violence to resolve that conflict. Territorial expansion, human rights, arms races, drug smuggling, refugees, and ideological strife are a few prominent geopolitical conflicts. Geoeconomics includes those issues which can be managed by any means short of violence. Disputes over trade, intellectual property, economic development, multinational corporations, industrial policy, and the environment are several important geoeconomic issues.

Geopolitical conflicts almost invariably have some geoeconomic basis. Sometimes geoeconomic conflicts are the primary reasons states either threaten to or actually do go to war. The trade wars of the early 1930s, for example, plunged the world into a severe depression which fueled the rise of *fascism* and *imperialism* in Japan, Germany, and Italy. Each of those states sought security in creating a largely autarkic empire. When participants in a geoeconomic conflict consider using violence, it stops being geoeconomic and becomes geopolitical.

Undoubtedly, the life and death issues of geopolitics are more dramatic and pressing. In geopolitics, a nation's security is sometimes decided through war. In geoeconomics, a nation's security is determined by the sum of countless economic policies and negotiations: prosperity or deprivation for individuals, industries, and national economies are shaped by thousands of cuts and parries rather than one decisive blow.

In many geopolitical and geoeconomic conflicts there are distinct aggressors and defenders. Military assaults by one state on another are easily chronicled. On August 2, 1990, Iraq clearly violated international law when it invaded and conquered Kuwait. The United States received United Nations approval to organize and lead a military alliance against Iraq if it did not withdraw from Kuwait by a January 15, 1991, deadline. The deadline passed with Iraq still in Kuwait. The alliance then attacked and expelled Iraq's army from Kuwait.

Clear aggressors and defenders in geoeconomic struggles are less easy to determine, although there are some cases. For example, Japanese corporations have been particularly notorious for *dumping,* or selling below production cost, their goods in other countries to capture market share from their foreign rivals. International law prohibits dumping and allows governments to retaliate against the dumping firms. The United States, the European Union, and other countries have imposed penalties against Japanese and other firms found guilty of dumping.

But in most geopolitical and geoeconomic conflicts, it is difficult and sometimes impossible to determine which side is at fault and which is the aggrieved. Take the geopolitical conflict over four tiny islands north of Japan, occupied by Russia, and claimed by both Russia and Japan. Both Moscow and Tokyo provide in depth legal and moral arguments for ownership of the disputed islands, and the issue remains deadlocked. Or what about the geoeconomic question of whether *multinational corporations* (MNCs) give more than they take from a poor nation's development. Again there are compelling arguments either way.

THE PRIMACY OF GEOECONOMICS IN INTERNATIONAL RELATIONS

Is geopolitics or geoeconomics more prevalent in international relations? Geopolitical issues certainly make the headlines. In the early 1990s, Iraq's invasion of Kuwait and the American-led coalition that ejected Iraq from Kuwait; fighting between India and Pakistan, Yugoslavia and Bosnia, Azerbaijan and Armenia; civil wars in Peru, Angola, and

Sudan; North Korea's nuclear weapons program; conflict between Israelis and Palestinians; or coups in Haiti, Guatemaula, and Peru were all distinctly geopolitical conflicts in which some potential and often actual use of violence was present within and/or between states.

Yet, while geoeconomic issues are more often relegated to a newspaper's back pages if reported at all, they are much more common. Most states are at peace most of the time. States rarely have their vital interests threatened or threaten the vital interests of others. Every day the world's 190 plus states conduct thousands of negotiations over thousands of issues in either bilateral or multilateral forums. The vast majority of these issues, however, directly involve the security of influential interest groups rather than the entire nation. In June 1991, after tough and often bitter negotiations, the United States and Japan signed an agreement whereby Tokyo promised to allow greater access for American semiconductor makers in Japan's markets. In April 1992, the United States and Chile began discussing the possibility of forming a free trade agreement. In May 1992, the European Community (renamed the European Union since January 1, 1993,) agreed to cut back its agricultural subsidies if the United States and Japan would do the same. In November 1992, Washington threatened to launch a trade war against the European Community if it did not agree to cut back its farm subsidies. These four examples were typical geoeconomic issues whose impact beyond the interest groups immediately involved was unnoticeable. Nonetheless, these issues involve vital questions of power, wealth, employment, income, technology, and national security.

Some geoeconomic issues, however, are potentially as devastating as war. The *greenhouse effect,* in which pollution traps heat in the atmosphere and may cause global temperatures to rise as much as nine degrees Fahrenheit over the next century, could lead to widespread crop failures, desertification, and the flooding of sea-level land. The result could be starvation, malnutrition, and misery for most people on the planet.

WAS THE COLD WAR THE WAR TO END ALL WARS?

Like World War I, the Second World War ended with the great promise that it would be the war to end all wars. By September 1945, the attempts by the totalitarian governments of Japan, Germany, and Italy to conquer the world were decisively defeated. Henceforth, it was hoped, all the world's nations would settle all conflicts peacefully and justly through the United Nations. Never again would the world's economy break down into trade wars and depression as it did in the 1930s. Instead, a global free trade system would be created and carefully managed by networks of international trade and finance organizations. All the world's peoples would realize their national and human rights to be free as promised by the Atlantic and United Nations charters.

These dreams proved to be short-lived. The wartime alliance between the United States and Soviet Union broke down into nearly five decades of geopolitical conflict known as the Cold War and fueled by diametrically opposed ideologies, security needs, and threat perceptions between American and Soviet-led blocs. The Cold War is now over, with the Soviet empire dismembered and communism renounced almost everywhere except in China, Cuba, and North Korea. The Cold War ended partly from four decades of an American-led containment of the Soviet Union, and partly by communism's inability to satisfy even the most basic economic let alone political needs of the people under its grip.

Some argue that the world is converging politically. During the 1980s, outright liberal democracies or quasi-democracies replaced *authoritarian* governments around the world, not just in the former Soviet empire, but from Taiwan to Nicaragua, and Nepal to South Korea. Today, according to the human rights organization Freedom House, around 40 percent of the world's countries have *liberal democratic* constitutions, including every country in the western hemisphere except Cuba, Haiti, and Peru. However, another *human rights* organization, Amnesty International, pointed out that in 1992 the governments of 142 countries systematically abused human rights. Although Freedom House emphasizes the progress toward human rights and Amnesty International the continuing abuses, both note a steady improvement. Monthly, it seems, another country or two sheds the more outrageous forms of political oppression and adopts the trappings and sometimes the institutions and values of liberal democracy. There is clearly a correlation between economic and political development. The demands for political representation and rights grow along with a middle class.

Assuming that this general trend toward democratization will continue, what impact will it have on international relations? War, many argue, is history's engine. Liberal democracies have never fought each other. The more liberal or quasi-liberal countries, the fewer the international wars.

Yet war will continue to plague humanity. Liberal democratic states will continue to fight authoritarian states, and authoritarian states will continue to fight each other. But the number of international wars will likely diminish as all countries become so bound by the ever growing matrix of global economic and cultural ties that the use of force to settle international conflicts becomes increasingly costly if not unthinkable. Complex interdependence and the slow spread of liberal democracy have reduced the relative number of geopolitical conflicts and increased the relative number of geoeconomic conflicts.

War will increasingly be within, rather than between, sovereign states. While the world unites in many ways, parts of it are rapidly disintegrating into civil war and anarchy. Nationalism, rather than internationalism, is the driving force behind the independence struggles of scores of suppressed peoples around the world. Although the Eastern European states and the former Soviet republics won a largely bloodless independence from the Soviet Union, Kurds and Shi'ites still struggle for independence from Iraq, Tibetans from China, Tamils from Sri Lanka, Sikhs from India, Bantus from South Africa, Palestinians from Israel, and Slovenes, Croats, and Bosnians from Yugoslavia, to name a few.

There is more hope, however, for demobilizing most of the vast arsenals and military forces facing each other across international borders. The Cold War's nuclear and conventional arms races created stockpiles capable of destroying the planet. Global military spending in 1990 alone was a mind-boggling $950 billion, of which the United States and Soviet Union accounted for half. The planet groans under the weight of over 50,000 nuclear bombs, many of them resting atop *intercontinental ballistic missiles* (ICBM).

Yet, even during the Cold War's height, Washington and Moscow did try to reign in the arms race and did succeed in signing several agreements capping the deployment of certain nuclear weapons types. In 1987, Washington and Moscow signed the first treaty which actually eliminated a class of nuclear weapons. With the Cold War's demise, the superpowers and their allies have announced treaties and unilateral promises to pare their nuclear and conventional forces even more sharply. Moscow's *Warsaw Pact,* through which it simultaneously threatened Western Europe and subjugated Eastern Europe, was dismantled in June 1991, and the troops are being sent home. Although *NATO* remains intact, the organization is trying to find a *raison d'être* in the New World Order. Meanwhile, Washington will halve the number of American troops stationed in Europe to 100,000 and pare its military budget by 25 percent by the mid-1990s. The United States, Russia, and other states will undoubtedly continue to reduce their nuclear and conventional forces until they reach minimal levels of deterence. Similar arms control agreements are possible in regional geopolitical conflicts elsewhere.

THE RISE AND FALL OF GREAT POWERS

During the 1980s and into the 1990s, there were tremendous shifts in the global military and economic power balances. The costs of winning the Cold War for the United States were exorbitant. In the late 1940s, the United States was wealthy enough to single-handedly finance the reconstruction of Western Europe and Japan, a bill that surpassed $20 billion, or $225 billion in today's dollars, between 1947 and 1952! However, in 1985, the United States was transformed from the world's greatest creditor to worst debtor nation. Japan inherited America's position as the world's banker, as well as that of the leading technological and manufacturing power. Today, although the United States is the world's unchallenged military power, it cannot afford all of its foreign or even domestic commitments. During the recent Persian Gulf War (1990–1991), for example, Washington had to pass the financial hat to its allies to pay for the war.

What led to America's rapid decline from the world's financier to penny pincher? What accounts for the rise of Japan and the European Union into global economic superpowers? Many argue that by concentrating most of its human, material, and technological resources in its global geopolitical struggle against the Soviet Union, the United States lost a geoeconomic struggle against Japan, and, to a lesser extent, the European Union. If the new world order is anything, it is shaped largely by economic rather than military competition, a reality most Americans are only slowly beginning to understand.

Regardless of whether Washington can arrest America's relative decline, it is unlikely that either Japan or the European Union will emerge as the economic *hegemon* of the twenty-first century. There will most likely be a stable geoeconomic power balance between Tokyo, Brussels, and Washington. In an increasingly interdependent world, the prosperity of one great power depends on that of the others. None of the three great geoeconomic powers will jeopardize their own prosperity by going over the brink of a *trade war.* Conflicts will remain numerous and bitter, but they will continue to be managed so that the global economy continues to develop steadily.

GLOBAL RELATIONS AND THE WRETCHED OF THE EARTH

What about the world's real economic losers? Four of five people in the world are poor; one of five in the world exists in abject poverty. What can or should be done about the world's poor? Can every country in the world successfully develop? Or are economic winners and losers not only inevitable but is the success of some actually built on the exploitation, *dependence,* and continued poverty of others? Is the failure to develop largely a result of internal or external forces? Will these issues become more or less prominent in the post-Cold War era?

INTERNATIONAL RELATIONS AND GLOBAL ENVIRONMENTAL CATASTROPHES

As the nuclear shadow hanging over the world's fate wanes, another menacing shadow of global environmental catastrophe thickens, born of the worsening and interrelated greenhouse effect, *ozone layer depletion, population explosion, desertification, deforestation,* and air and water pollution.

Governments increasingly recognize these threats to humanity and have begun working together to overcome them. The most impressive effort to date occured in June 1992, when the representatives of 178 nations gathered in Rio de Janiero to sign two treaties, one in which participants agreed to impose limits on greenhouse emissions and the other to protect *biodiversity.* Remarkable as this achievement seemed, political differences led to both treaties becoming watered-down versions of the orginal proposals. Protesting what the Bush administration claimed were the treaty's anti-growth measures, the White House succeeded in blocking any timetables or pollution reduction standards, thereby rendering the greenhouse treaty's importance symbolic at best. Citing similar concerns, the White House pointedly refused even to sign the biodiversity treaty. A proposed treaty limiting tropical deforestation was scuttled by Brazil and others who argued that the countries in temperate climates should impose similar restrictions on their own logging. Meanwhile, India led the poorer countries in demanding that the richer countries transfer technology and funds so the Third World can comply with the treaties; no agreement was reached on any burden-sharing. Despite the disappointment of the Rio de Janiero conference, increasing numbers of governments recognize the vital necessity of dismantling the environmental time bomb before it is too late and are actively taking steps to alleviate those problems. But many fear that national and special interest groups will derail any international attempts to address the world's environmental crises systematically.

A NEW APPROACH TO INTERNATIONAL RELATIONS

Clearly the world and the relations which govern it have changed greatly over the past five centuries, particularly since 1945. While conflict remains endemic to international relations, the nature of those conflicts and the means to manage them have changed profoundly. The global interdependence of problems and organized attempts to overcome those problems are steadily increasing, and the global agenda today contains issues like the environment, economic competition, and human rights that were not priorities a generation ago. The world is converging politically, economically, and culturally, and that integration is abetted by the proliferation of international organizations and laws. Yet all this represents not a truly new world order, but the latest stage in global development.

This book analyzes the changes and continuities in international relations over the past five hundred years with an emphasis on the geopolitical and geoeconomic struggles since 1945. The book's central theme is that international relations takes place in a global political economy which has been developing since the fifteenth century. In a sense, the world order is synomous with the structure and most pressing conflicts and issues of the global political economy whose characteristics have changed dramatically over the last five centuries. The global system's structure is shaped by and shapes the distribution of geopolitical and geoeconomic power, the relationship between geopolitical and geoeconomic power and conflicts, and the growing impact of international organizations, law, and other non-state forces.

Section I explores the development of the global political economy and how the manifestation of political and economic power in international relations has changed over time.

Section II focuses on the nation-state, revealing how governments create and implement policies, and the types of power they can weild to promote their national interests in a competitive and often outright hostile world.

Section III explores other increasingly important forces and actors shaping international relations, including international law, organizations, and morality.

Section IV concentrates on geopolitical issues of war and peace, the Cold War, arms races and disarmament, and nuclear, conventional, and unconventional warfare.

Section V analyzes economic strategies, conflict, and cooperation among the industrialized world while Section VI does so between the industrialized world and Third World.

Section VII explores the interrelated global environmental crises that all humans ultimately face, and the attempts by nation-states and international organizations to address them.

Development of the Modern World: From Florence to the Marne

Key Terms and Concepts

Civilization	Imperialism	Nationalism
Democracy	Industrial Revolution	Reformation
Economic Liberalism	Liberalism	Renaissance
The Enlightenment	Mercantilism	Social Darwinism
Feudalism	Modernization	Sovereignty

International relations take place in the modern world, and cannot be understood apart from the matrix of modern forces which shape them. *Modernization* began in Europe over five hundred years ago, born of and an umbrella term for a series of inter-related and endless intellectual, political, economic, technological, religious, sociological, and psychological revolutions. These revolutions originated in small corners of Europe, spread over the continent and then eventually, via Western imperialism, the world. Today, either superficially or pervasively, all the world's countries and most of its individuals are modern and modernizing.

Modernization, however, is a relative rather than absolute concept. The standards by which we judge an individual's or nation's degree of modernization are continually changing. What was considered modern yesterday is often dismissed as obsolete today. Indeed, modernization's essence is revolutionary change—for the better, although that might not be apparent to those experiencing its effects. Sometimes the survivors may envy the dead. There were an estimated 25 million people in Mexico before the Spanish conquest in 1521; within a century, disease and exploitation had reduced the population to less than 2 million. The Spanish soldiers had conquered for gold and the priests for converts. Neither group understood that forces we now label as modernization were insidiously eating away the Medieval world in which they thought and acted, and they would have been terrified if they had known. Nonetheless, the unforseen and unwanted long-term result of the conquest was modernization. Today Mexico's population is soaring past 90 million and is expected to double within a generation. Although most Mexicans remain poor, virtually all lead more comfortable and longer lives than their pre-Cortés ancestors. Most importantly, they perceive themselves and the world through largely modern rather than traditional minds. Yet Mexico may be successfully modernizing by early rather than late 20th century standards. Countries with unbridled population and pollution growth are now considered modernization laggards rather than leaders.

Modernization entails revolutionary changes in outlook, technology, and organization that transform every aspect of a society. But the countries which have modernized

11

most successfully have experienced those changes slowly over centuries rather than gen-erations; the revolution of modernization is best achieved through evolution. Yet, there is no one modernization pattern. Every country must find its own modernization path. The paths advocated by some of modernization's prophets, however, clearly lead to dead ends. Lenin asserted confidently that his modernization vision entailed taking one step back for every two forward; Stalin argued just as confidently that you have to break eggs to make omlettes. Many governments attempted to follow the Soviet moderniza-tion model of central planning, state ownership of production, and political oppression. While the Soviet model did achieve some gains in mass education, industrialization, and science, it largely failed to develop a complex modern economy and proved devastating by most human, material, and ecological measures. In the late 1980s and into the 1990s, anti-communist revolutions destroyed one Leninist regime after another, and liberal political economic systems are emerging from the ruins.

In 1914, few Mexicans or Russians were modern by any measurement, and both countries were mired in social, economic, and political feudalism. It was in Western Eu-rope and North America that modernization had seemingly triumphed. The West had experienced waves of revolutionary progressive changes since the Renaissance, and by the early twentieth century its inhabitants enjoyed unprecedented wealth and opportu-nities. Then, in August 1914, the modernization revolution which started in Florence took a very wrong turn at the Marne. Europe plunged into a four year war which gutted the continent psychologically and materially, and unleashed political, economic, tech-nological, and ideological forces which have shaped international relations throughout this century and into the next.

What is modernity?[1] Why did modernity begin in Europe? How did Europe im-pose itself and sow modernization's seeds in virtually every corner of the globe? This chapter will analyze the development of the modern global political economic system, first by examining further the concept of modernization, and then by detailing the in-terplay of those revolutionary changes over the past five centuries up through World War I.

MODERNITY

Modernization is first of all a state of mind—only modern minds can create modern worlds. Modernity thus began with the intellectual revolution of the Renaissance, which in turn eventually spawned a range of other revolutions—political, economic, indus-trial, sociological, psychological, and cultural. Modernity is conveyed through mass institutions—corporations, schools, bureaucracies, transportation, media, communica-tions, laboratories, and metropolises. But without a modern outlook, the vast complex bundle of modern techniques and institutions is unworkable.

Although the modern mind has evolved from the Renaissance through today, its essence is a belief that human reason rather than a transcendant god is the master of humanity's fate, and that individuals should freely pursue their material, emotional, and spiritual needs. Modern societies are politically, economically, and socially mobile, and modernity empowers individuals to transform themselves, to satisfy their craving to do—know, and become. More recently, modernity allows individuals to simply be. Self-transformation and changing the world are interrelated, one cannot exist without the other. Modern individuals change, in usually minute ways, the world and thus themselves, through both thoughts and actions, and can remake themselves in their own images or those of others. An individual's power, position, and opportunities in a modern society thus depends less on ancestry and more on personal abilities and ambitions. Freedom, however, is not absolute. Choices are ultimately limited, and modern individuals must take responsibility for the choices they make and do not make. Authentic choices are made rationally, skeptically, scientifically. The United States Marines' challenge to recruits "to be all that you can be" could be the motto for the modern age.

Modernity's essence is rapid change. "All is flux, nothing stays still," Heraclitus said of reality, and that particularly characterizes the world during the past five centuries. Modernity is an endless, accelerating process of creative destruction in which traditions, institutions, buildings, communities, and even people are retained only as long as they can be justified, usually in monetary terms. The obsolete, the functionless are discarded and replaced with something more appropriate, more modern. Modernization never ends. Modernization's only constant is change.

There is some continuity amid the change. Although we are all modernizing, in different depths and ways, even in the most modern societies, traces of tradition are embedded in virtually all individuals, and we are all torn, to greatly varying extents, between modern and traditional urges.

Modernity has had its discontents. Modernity's mad pace and bewildering array of choices can be profoundly distressing and alienating for many. In the nineteenth century, even the transcendentalist Thoreau admitted that "most men lead lives of quiet desperation."[2] Karl Marx and Max Weber provided more in-depth analyses of modernity, with Marx decrying the alienation of human beings from community, work, and self, and Weber asserting that modernity imprisons humanity within complexes of omnipotent and unyielding bureaucracies he called "iron cages."[3] In the early twentieth century, Freud and his followers argued that civilization itself springs not from noble dreams but from the sublimation of humanity's most base hungers.[4] Franz Kafka provided the same bleak vision more poetically in his short stories and the novels "The Castle" and "The Trial."[5] During the postwar era, poets and philosophers have continued exploring modern human's fate. In his most famous poem T.S. Eliot declared: "We are the hollow men," while Herbert Marcuse maintained that we are "one dimensional men."[6] Michel Foucault wholeheartedly agreed and explored how humanity is trapped in "total institutions."[7] More recently, Alvin Toffler described Man's alienation "future shock."[8]

Few individuals are more modern than modernity's critics. Modern minds question everything, examine everything under a microscope, and in so doing strip most things of their aura, their remoteness, and in the case of religions, their claims to solely represent truth and salvation. "God is dead," Nietzsche triumphantly declared.[9] Or as Marx put it, the:

constant revolutionizing of production, uninterrupted disturbance of all social relations, everlasting uncertainty and agitation, distinguish the bourgeois epoch from earlier times. All fixed, fast-frozen relations, with their train of ancient and venerable prejudices and opinions, are swept away, all new-formed ones become antiquated before they can ossify. All that is solid melts into air, all that is holy is profaned, and men at last are free to face . . . the real conditions of their lives and their relations with their fellow men.[10]

Modern literature is filled with metaphors for modernization perils and paradoxes. Mary Shelley's "Frankenstein" and Walt Disney's Mickey Mouse cartoon, "The Sorcerer's Apprentice" explore the consequences of technologies originally created for humanity's sake that eventually mastered and imperiled humanity. As Marx put it, "Modern bourgeois society, a society that has conjured up such gigantic means of production and exchange, is like the sorcerer who is no longer able to control the powers of the underworld that he has called up by his spells."[11] Goethe's "Faust" is the quintessential modern man. Faust sells his soul to Mephistopheles for the power to modernize the world, but in so doing destroys as much as he creates.

How do individuals achieve meaning or salvation in a godless universe? While some individuals search for meaning amidst a world of constant chaos and upheaval, most in advanced industrial societies simply accept the routine of office and television. From the Romantic movement of the late eighteenth and early nineteenth centuries to the New Age movement of the 1980s, many others have sought refuge from modernity's excesses in the spiritual serenity of temples or wilderness or creativity. The responsibilities that accompany freedom, particularly the imperative to strip away one's illusions and see the world as it really is, are overwhelming to many. Confronted with this negation of their basic beliefs, many find salvation in totalitarian, political, or religious movements. The fascism of Japan, Germany, and Italy during the 1930s, the communist fervor that gripped millions throughout the twentieth century until recently, and the Islamic fundamentalism that engulfed Iran in 1979 were all built upon a popular rejection of the turmoil, uncertainty, and responsibilities of modern life. Adherents immersed themselves in a sea of humanity led by charismatic leaders like Hitler, Castro, or the Ayatollah, and tolemic symbols like the swastika, sickle and hammer, or crescent.

THE RISE AND FALL OF CIVILIZATIONS

While modernity is relatively new, international relations are as old as civilization. Although human beings have existed for almost two hundred thousand years, until the last ten thousand years they all wandered the earth in small groups hunting, gathering edible plants, and attempting to survive threats from other humans, beasts and harsh weather. Although they warred, traded, allied, and avoided other groups, and thus had relations, whether or not these groups can be described as "nations" and their relations "international" is problematic and will not be addressed here.

Eventually some groups settled down in river valleys and began sowing and reaping crops. Over centuries some of these settlements developed into complex "civilizations" which included most of the following components: the mastery of agriculture; domestication of animals; complex, hierarchial political, social, economic, and religious institutions; the use of metals, the wheel, and writing systems; clearly defined territories; and trade with other peoples. The first civilization emerged in Mesopotamia around 5,000 B.C., and for the next six thousand years, great civilizations there and elsewhere rose, extended their rule over vast areas, then collapsed for a variety of interrelated political, technological, economic, and ecological reasons.

During the fifteenth century, beyond Christian Europe, advanced and powerful civilizations sprawled across vast stretches of the globe: Ming China, Aztec Mexico, Inca Peru, Benin Africa, Mogul India, Ashikaga Japan, and Ottoman Asia Minor. In Southeast Asia alone, there was a patchwork of smaller civilizations like the Khmer, Thai, Vietnamese, Burmese, and Javanese. All of these non-European civilizations were ruled by centralized bureaucracies and had achieved enormous advances in technology, the arts, philosophy, and wealth. Elsewhere humans were largely organized in small hunter-gather groups or primitive farm communities. However, despite their dazzling achievements, none of the non-European civilizations developed the intellectual, organizational, and technological prerequisites for modernity and global conquest.[12]

China had the most potential to modernize. The huge Chinese empire was economically and technologically rich, had dynamic cities, extensive trade throughout East, Southeast, and West Asia, rich agriculture, a highly developed port, communications, and transportation infrastructure, a large, literate merchant class, advanced technology like gunpowder, cannon, ocean-going ships, printing, highly refined products like steel, porcelin, and the use of credit and paper money. The Ming Dynasty ruled China's 100–130 million inhabitants through a professional bureaucracy and a unifying political philosphy, Confucianism. Militarily, the Chinese had over 1 million men under arms and a 1,350 ship navy. Between 1405 and 1433, Admiral Cheng Ho led seven naval, trade, and exploration expeditions which reached as far as the Persian Gulf and East Africa. The Chinese could have "discovered" Europe rather than the Europeans China.

Yet, the Ming Dynasty retreated from the brink of becoming a global power. The naval expeditions were not only discontinued but the emperor also forbade any further construction of ocean-going ships. Geopolitics partly explains this withdrawal. Ming China shifted from an offensive to defensive stance in response to a failed attempt to defeat Annan Vietnam, and the aggression of Mongols along China's vulnerable northern frontier and Japanese pirates along the coast. Philosophical and political reasons reinforced the geopolitical imperative to withdraw. Confucianism celebrated the scholar-bureaucrats who ran China and denegrated merchants and soldiers alike. The Court may have feared that its military and merchant classes were gaining too much wealth and power from their naval expeditions, while those very expeditions may have drained China's wealth with no real return at a time of northern and eastern military threats. Not only did the Ming retreat from the world but they also failed even to maintain China's canals, ports, and industries. In 1644, the Manchurians conquered the Ming and ruled China until 1911.

Ironically, the Western European states set sail for the West at a time when Europe was threatened with an invasion from the East. Seven centuries after Islamic Arab armies had overrun the southern Mediterranean and Iberia, new Muslim armies, led by several Turkish and Persian nations, overran all of the Middle East and Southeast Europe, and much of South and Southeast Asia.

Of these imperial nations, the Ottoman Turks directly threatened Europe, and seemingly possessed enormous potential for becoming a global power. The Ottomans captured Constantinople in 1453, carved out an empire in the Balkans and eastern Mediterranean, and would seriously threaten Europe for the next three hundred years, twice marching to the gates of Vienna itself (1529, 1683). Like the previous Arab empire, the Ottoman empire had well-run cities, universities and libraries, a vigorous intellectual class, excelled in advanced science and such technologies as cannon and musket production, and possessed a well-organized bureaucracy, well-trained, tough, and loyal armies, and vast fleets of fast maneuverable galleys. The capital, Constantinople, had a population of half a million, far larger than any European city, and the empire included 14 million people.

What limited the Ottomans' expansion and prevented their modernization? Imperial overstretch and a succession of incompetent rulers eventually brought the Ottomans' expansion to a halt and long decline. The Ottomans failed to keep up with advances in weapons, ships, and arms developed in West Europe. Essentially, the Ottoman Empire failed to generate the wealth and innovations necessary to fulfill its ambitions and commitments. Islam, like Confucianism, tended to inhibit individual initiative. Similar problems plagued Muslim empires elsewhere, particularly the Mogul empire of northern India and Pakistan. Although other great civilizations existed in the fifteenth century, all but Europe's failed to develop into modern civilizations and project their power worldwide.

THE TRANSITION FROM FEUDAL TO MODERN EUROPE

We cannot understand the emergence of modernity in Europe without exploring what preceded it. For over five centuries, the Roman Empire had cloaked most of Europe and the Mediterranean basin with a common government, law, and market. Long before Rome was sacked in 476, the empire itself had collapsed under the weight of political corruption and inefficiency, economic decline, and waves of foreign invasions. A united market from England to Syria and Gibralter to the Rhine disappeared with the Roman Empire.

What followed was a millenium of European history from around 450 to 1450 called the Middle Ages. The loss of Roman law and administration meant that everyone had to fend for him or herself. At first the population declined from pestilence and the sword. The survivors fled into the countryside and even the greatest cities dwindled into towns and most towns became overgrown fields and woods again. Although slavery disappeared with Rome's fall, few peasants retained their own land. Eventually most peasants sold out to the local strongman and his warriors, who protected them often in return for half of their production.

Thus, during this time Europe was fragmented politically into hundreds of small fiefdoms, a political system known as *feudalism*. The local strongmen became lords, and their followers knights. Few lords remained completely independent. Most lords allied with other lords under the distant authority of the greatest lord of all, the king. There were no nations. The identity of most serfs centered on their village. Languages like

French, German, Italian, or Spanish were so fractured into dialects that often people from nearby valleys or even villages had trouble understanding each other. Latin was Europe's lingua franca.

Feudal Europe came to be composed of four interdependent classes—priests, nobles, serfs and artisans, and merchants. There was virtually no movement between classes. With *primogeniture,* a noble's eldest son inherited the property, forcing other sons to look for employment elsewhere. The vast majority of people—80 to 90 percent—were serfs who tilled the land of nobles. The clergy was the most open class, with peasants as well as nobles often entering monasteries.

The least populous were the merchants and artisans who organized themselves into craft guilds for protection and promotion. The guilds were monopolies which determined the producers, production, and price of a particular good, as well as the civic obligations of the guild members. Each profession—mason, silversmith, armourer, shipwright, weaver, and so on—had its own exclusive guild. Prices were fixed, and the primary goal was order rather than profit.

For most of the Middle Ages, the kings were weak, and most controlled little more than the lands immediately surrounding their castles. Lords supplied their kings with no more than thirty days of military service a year and a portion of the production seized from their serfs. By the fifteenth century, however, the kings of England, France, Portugal, Castile, and Catalonia had amassed considerable power over their lords. Elsewhere in central and eastern Europe, kings remained weak or nonexistent and local lords were largely independent.

The foundation of European civilization was Christianity, and Europe's political as well as spiritual leader was the pope who ruled from Rome. Only the Pope possessed sovereignty which, according to the great Medieval theologian Thomas Aquinas, was the complete power to determine one's fate. As God's earthly emissary, the pope's sovereignty extended over all within Christendom. All Christian lords ultimately bowed to Rome. The power to excommunicate and thus deny the sacraments allowed popes to keep recalcitrant kings and lords in line. Faced with being condemned to an eternity in hell, more than one medieval king found himself crawling literally on his hands and knees to the Pope to seek forgiveness.

Rome's powers were economic as well. The Catholic Church inhibited trade by imposing the notion of a just price, which meant selling something only for what it cost. Thomas Aquinas called it "wholly sinful to practice fraud for the purpose of selling a thing for more than its just price."[13] The Church also condemned lending money for interest (usury) as a mortal sin. Usurers were excommunicated and sometimes even tried as heretics. Jews thus became the Medieval world's chief money-lenders, although some Christian institutions like the Knights Templars also lent money at interest to Medieval kings and lords. With most people forbidden to enjoy a profit motive, trade expanded slowly.

What then enabled Europe to break free of the massive bonds of religious, economic, political, and social feudalism? Ironically, the Church's attempts to free the Holy Land from the infidel Muslims unleashed forces that eventually cracked open the Medieval world and allowed the seeds of modernity to be planted in its crevices. For almost two hundred years (1095–1291), Rome issued papal bulls or orders calling on all knights to gather in Crusades for the Middle East and Iberian peninsula. Although the

Figure 2.1
Europe after the Peace of Westphalia, 1648

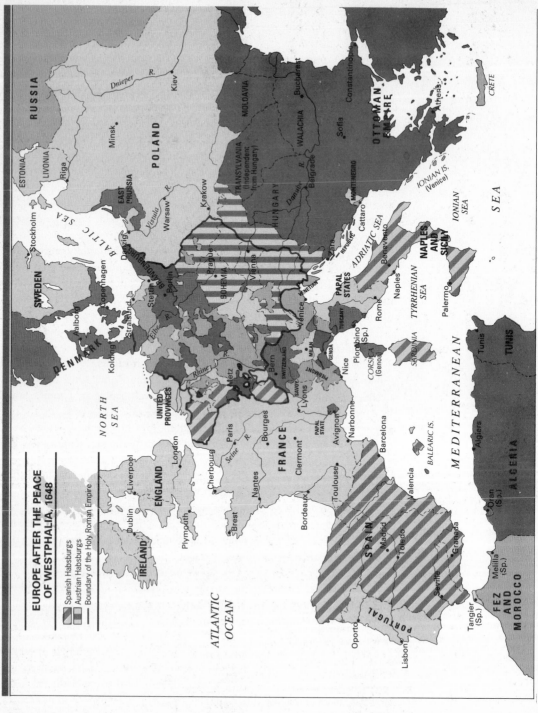

Source: T. Walter Wallbank, et al. *Civilization: Past and Present.* New York: HarperCollins, 1992, p. 463.

Crusades failed dismally in their mission, they proved to be a vital boost to Europe's development. Crusades took enormous resources to organize, launch, and sustain, and they stimulated enormous strides in production, trade, and finance. The Crusades also exposed the Medieval world to the philosophical, technological, artistic, and Sybaritic world of the Arab and Byzantine empires, as well as the northern Italian cities. The primary beneficiaries were Venice and the other city-states of northern Italy, which prospered enormously as the dealers between the eastern Mediterranean and northern Europe.

Despite the Crusade's stimulus, trade revived slowly. Although the fiefs were self-sufficient in food and clothing, most had to obtain armour, tools, and weapons elsewhere. But with little money in circulation, most trade was conducted through the barter of one fief's surplus production for that of another, and the trade occurred in local villages or annual country fairs. Each fief imposed its own taxes on merchants, creating virtually insurmountable trade barriers. There were, for example, 60 toll stations on the Rhine River alone.[14]

Despite these constraints, each kingdom and all of Europe were slowly knit together into a slowly expanding network of trade routes and small cities. Europe's diverse climate and natural resources allowed the creation of a range of products. Many navigable rivers and proximity to the sea further enhanced trade. The exchange of bulk items like grain, lumber, wool, and wine made regions interdependent, and large numbers of people prosperous. The invention of double entry bookkeeping in 1494 was in many ways as revolutionary a development as Columbus' discovery of America two years earlier. Trade was increasingly conducted with money and even credit rather than barter. More people became free to rise or fall in the world largely according to their own ambitions and skills. The guilds were unable to control the expansion of trade, and the prices of increasing amounts and types of goods were shaped by supply and demand. A society of law and contract began to replace a society of status. Huge banking houses emerged to finance kings and merchants alike. The Fuggers of Augsburg and Medicis of Florence had financial empires with bank branches across Europe. Genoese bankers financed both the Middle East and Atlantic trades. The Hanseatic League was a trading alliance of city-states bordering the North and Baltic seas.

Medieval kings and the growing merchant or bourgeois class shared a common interest. The kings needed the bourgeois for money and goods while the bourgeois needed the king for trade protection and promotion. Only the king could cut through the web of local trade restrictions, while his patronage stimulated the mass production of tapestries, armour, furniture, paintings, and the like. The wealthier the king and his nobles, the greater the patronage, which encouraged the further creation of production and wealth. Increasingly dependent on merchants for loans and luxury goods, kings and princes competed fiercely with each other to promote trade. In return for a percentage of the profits, kings and queens licensed huge trading companies to explore and exploit foreign lands and negotiate with foreign powers.

Closely related to the expansion of trade was the expansion of cities. Modernity is an urban phenomenon. The growth in the size and number of cities during the Middle Ages was an extremely slow process. Cambridge, for example, expanded at the rate of one house a year between 1086 and 1279, while all together about one thousand towns, or only one a year, emerged during the Middle Ages.[15] Crossroads, hamlets, castles and monasteries gradually became trade centers and towns. As towns grew in population, status, and economic vitality, they gradually obtained more freedom from the local lord, and began minting their own money and establishing laws. As cities grew in wealth and population, they demanded more goods and services, which in turn created more wealth and population. Countryside and city were increasingly linked economically, socially, and politically, with cities leading development.

Despite the revival of trade and cities, Europe remained largely agrarian. Ninety percent of the population were peasants who toiled endlessly in the fields and lived from one day to the next on what little that was not confiscated by their lords. Production was hand-crafted rather than mass produced. Most people continued to be paid in kind rather than wages for their labor.

Ultimately, modernity began in the minds of a few men. During the late Middle Ages, universities emerged in the cities to replace the monasteries as the centers of learning. At the universities one could study not just the Scriptures but ancient Greek, Roman, Arab, and Byzantine texts as well, many of which were filled with startling new and often heretical ideas. Europe's intellectual revolution, however, did not truly begin until movable type was perfected in the 1440s, inaugurating an explosion in the amount and types of books, literacy, and knowledge. According to Kirkpatrick Sales, "by 1500 there were over 110 places on the subcontinent, from Toledo to Stockholm, with at least one printing press and some with three or four. Within the relatively short period of half a century—from 1454 to 1501 . . . there were, by one estimate, 20 million books printed, in at least 40,000 separate editions."[16] For the first time in human history, learning and knowledge was no longer the priviledge of a few but available to anyone with the ability to read.

The dynamic interplay between these intellectual, commercial, and political revolutions led to what became known as the *Renaissance,* or rebirth of rational learning and new ideas in philosophy, the arts, and technology. The Renaissance emerged from two clusters of city-states. Starting in the late fourteenth century, the Italian states of Florence, Venice, Genoa, Milan, Urbino, and Modena, to name some of the more prominent, became powerful centers of trade, philosophy, and the arts. This northern Italian Renaissance was further stimulated in 1453 when the fall of Constantinople to the Turks unleashed a flood of merchants, nobles, and intellectuals fleeing to those city states. During the fifteenth century, similar forces blossomed in the northern European cities of Amsterdam, Antwerp, and Deft.

Modernity's central pillar rests on the shift from a God-centered universe in which individuals devoted themselves to fulfilling their class role, to a human-centered universe in which individuals were largely free to fulfill their creative and economic potential. People, or more importantly their rational minds, became the measure of all things. A universal person was skilled in all of the fine arts, philosophy, etiquette, languages, history, science, and music. There was not just a toleration but a celebration of new ideas and ways of seeing the world.

Artists increasingly explored secular as well as religious themes. Portraits of smug, well-fed and -clothed financiers and merchants replaced holy trinities and madonna and child as dominant artistic themes. And the religious themes of artists like Micheangelo, Leonardo Da Vinci, or Botticelli, to name a few, were explored through distinct styles and perspectives that made the anonymous Medieval paintings seem wooden and shallow in comparison.

The shift from a god-centered to human-centered world was symbolized by the gradual replacement of Latin by the local language as the language of discourse and literature. Dante's "Divine Comedy" and Machiavelli's "The Prince" were written in Italian rather than Latin. The Age of Reason emerged alongside, competed with, and eventually overwhelmed the Age of Faith.

WESTERN IMPERIALISM'S FIRST WAVE

Imperialism, or the conquest of one people by another, is as old as humankind. Yet even the greatest past conquerers never dreamed of subduing the entire world. How did Europe succeed in spreading its power and influence around the globe?

There were two waves of European imperialism, the Age of Sail (1450–1850) and the Age of Steam (1850–1950). Each of these imperialist waves was stimulated by a dynamic mix of technological, political, economic, and intellectual changes. During the first phase, the same forces which began to transform Europe from feudalism to modernity also stimulated a global quest among Europeans for wealth, power, and discovery. The immediate catalyst for European imperialism was the Ottoman conquest of the Middle East which disrupted the flow of Southeast Asian spices to Europe. During the 1450s, the first Portugese caravels sailed south along the African coast trying to find a direct route to the Spice Islands.

Europe's division into a half dozen large centralized kingdoms and hundreds of smaller fiefdoms, and the incessant warfare and rivalry among them, was perhaps the ultimate reason for Europe's eventual domination of the world. The rivalry bred new innovations in technology, military tactics, weapons, ship designs, and the creation of wealth. Kings understood the relationship between wealth and power. With money, kings could build up armies and navies with which to seize more wealth. Kings followed a strategy of *mercantilism* in which they tried to maximize exports and minimize imports, thus increasing the amount of availiable money. Trade was seen as a zero-sum war in which one nation's gains were losses for all the other nations.

Europeans could never have sailed to the world's far ends without new navigational devices like the compass and sextant, and new ship and rigging designs. The need to navigate tempestuous waters like the North Sea, Bay of Biscay, and even the Atlantic Ocean by hardy fishermen bound for the Newfoundland fishing banks, required tough, well-built ocean-going ships which could carry large loads. The invention of new metal alloys allowed for the development of lighter weight yet powerful cannon and muskets. These revolutionary technological advances launched an arms race among the European states which gave them virtually uncontested seapower against non-European states. In contrast, the slender, oared Ottoman and Venetian galleys may have been swifter and more maneuverable, but were fragile on the open ocean and held limited cannon, freight, and supplies. The Western European three-masted ships evolved into floating, ocean going gun platforms that could blast any Ottoman galley, Arab dhow, or Chinese junk out of the water, and if necessary sail for months without replenishment of supplies.

The perennial insecurity, which bred strength among European states, contrasted with the security of other great civilizations, which bred complacency. Without the constant threat of war, the Chinese, Turks, Mogols, and other great empires had no compelling reason to innovate technologically, organizationally, or economically. Thus despite enormous advantages in manpower, the other great civilizations were inevitably beaten by superior European military technology and tactics.

Europe's first wave of imperialism also depended on the revival of trade and the emergence of huge merchant and banking corporations which financed most of the voyages of discovery and conquest. Private corporations were given royal charters, which entitled them to conquer and colonize foreign lands in the king's name. The conquistadors were more entrepreneurs than royal servants and were driven by visions of gold, spices, silver, and slaves. After the colonies were established, other commodities, such as sugar, indigo, rice, tobacco, timber, furs, hides, and cotton became the most important products.

How did the Europeans justify their conquest of other peoples and lands? Essentially, Europeans considered the non-Christian world "terra nullis," which meant that it belonged to no one and thus could be taken by anyone. Whether it was the king of a civilization thousands of years old or the head of a wandering band of hunter-gatherers, non-European leaders could gain legitimacy in Eurpean eyes only if they were formally recognized by Europeans as the rightful rulers. In this way, Europeans completely remade the world in their own image. It was this outlook which allowed the Pope to issue a bull in 1494 which divided the entire world between Spain and Portugal!

Within one hundred years of the first Portugese expeditions, the globe was clearly being integrated into one vast trade system. In 1522, the remnants of the Magellan expedition sailed back to Cádiz after circumnavigating the globe. By the mid-1550s the Spanish and Portugese had conquered virtually all of Central and South America, while the British, French, and Dutch had launched their own exploration and trade expeditions across the Atlantic and around Africa. The trans-Atlantic trade grew eightfold between 1510 and 1550, and a further threefold between 1550 and 1610.[17]

The influx of silver from the mines of Peru and Mexico vastly stimulated Europe's economic development and shifted the power balance, but ironically, it was the northern Europeans rather than the Iberians who gained the most. Rather than investing their wealth into productive enterprises which would create yet more wealth, the Spanish simply bought luxury items produced elsewhere in Europe. Between 1520 and 1650, prices rose 200 to 400 percent throughout Europe as American gold and silver flooded local markets, and eventually found its way into the coffers of French, Dutch, and English merchants and manufacturers. Europe was enriched by more than silver. New crops like maize, potatoes, and tomatoes expanded diets, while the incessant international rivalries stimulated rapid scientific and technological advances in all fields.

THE EMERGENCE OF SOVEREIGN NATION-STATES

Meanwhile, the intellectual revolution which sparked the Renaissance reached a new stage called the *Reformation*. Few acts in history were as revolutionary as when Martin Luther nailed his "95 Theses" to the door of Wittenburg Cathedral in 1517, condemning a corrupt papacy that sold indulgences and practiced usury. Luther's act tapped into a deep well of resentment against the Church's corruption and hypocrisy and, in so doing, launched the Reformation (1517–1648). Other religious revolutionaries emerged to found the different sects of what became known as Protestantism, named for their adherent's "protests" against Catholicism. The Protestants' central message was that individuals could reach God directly by their own faith rather than through "good works" sold to them by a corrupt church or by the priest's transformation of the host.

One of the most prominent Protestants, John Calvin (1509–1564), preached a harsh doctrine in which most people were predestined for hell. Slender as the chance was, some might be saved by singlemindedly focusing their lives on fulfilling their calling or profession. Calvinists exalted rather than condemned the merchants and moneylenders. Profit, interest, and wealth were created for God's glory as well as one's earthly comfort. The Calvinist work ethic may not have had as major a role in Europe's development as is commonly believed. Calvinism's theological justification for making money reflected attitudes that had been developing within Europe's cities and trade routes over hundreds of preceding years. Thus Calvinism did not create a new value system so much as it legitimized an existing one.

The Protestant revolution could not have survived had it not been championed by kings and princes. In 1534, Henry VIII became the first king to declare his independence from Rome, and others followed suit. For the next one hundred and twenty years until 1648, Europe was torn apart by religious warfare with a largely Catholic southern Europe attempting to conquer a largely Protestant northern Europe. These religious wars were aimed at either converting or killing the enemy's population, and they culminated with the Thirty Years War (1618–48), in which Catholic and Protestant lords and kings devastated most of central Europe in their struggle for supremacy.

The religious wars finally ended with the Treaty of Westphalia in 1648. As early as 1586, the French legal philosopher Jean Bodin, in his "Six Books on the State" had rejected the notion of papal *sovereignty* and instead argued that every king was sovereign, although his powers were restricted by his kingdom's laws. Bodin's principle formed the Treaty's basis. Henceforth, every lord could decide for himself his realm's religion, each state would be considered independent from and equal to all others, and no state had the right to interfere in the internal affairs of others. Westphalia thus marked the end of papal and the beginning of national sovereignty.

The period from 1648 to 1789 was known as the age of absolute monarchs, epitomized by Louis XIV's remark "L'état, c'est moi" (I am the state). During the sixteenth and seventeenth centuries, the balance of power between kings and lords shifted decisively in favor of the former. The king's power flowed from several sources. Kings and bankers formed alliances in which the kings would grant protection and privileges to the bankers in return for huge loans which augmented the royal tax receipts. This financial power allowed kings to build professional armies and bureaucracies with which to subjugate the lords and protect the state. Despite this vast accumulation of power, the king's rule was never truly absolute; there were always some administrative and cultural constraints on royal power.

Technology aided this transition from Medieval feudalism to absolute monarchy. Gunpowder enabled kings to batter down the thin castle walls of rebellious princes and unify the realm. The nature of warfare changed markedly after 1648 as the waging and goals of warfare became more limited. Untrained, undisciplined feudal levies were abandoned, and armies were composed of highly professional mercenaries. Bayoneted muskets replaced pikes as the dominant infantry weapon. Campaigns and battles were fought with chessboard-like strategies in which casualties were relatively limited and most of the population was untouched.

The nobility became increasingly superfluous in a world of professional armies and bureaucracies. They produced nothing and lived off of society, no longer protecting it as they had during the Middle Ages. The income from their fiefs was steadily eroded by the inflation that swept Europe after the colonization of the Americas. Louis XIV constructed elaborate court rituals and ranks just to give the nobles something to do and keep them quiescent and obedient. Louis XIV's court became the model for the other European monarchies of Prussia, Austria, Russia, and Spain, and the scores of smaller ones in Central Europe and Italy.

Meanwhile, the money-making bourgeois class surpassed the nobility in numbers, income, and, increasingly, status. By the seventeenth century, Europe's economy ran predominantly on cash or credit and most urban dwellers labored for wages rather than in kind or tenancy. The interrelated processes of increased trade, urbanization, and monetization in Great Britain, and to a lesser extent elsewhere, were boosted by the enclosure movement in which lords enclosed pastures which had previously been common land for all. By the early nineteenth century nearly half of Britain had been enclosed. Unable to graze their flocks, the peasants drifted off to the towns to find new livelihoods. This population movement eroded the feudal society and economy of countryside and town alike. Not only did the lords find fewer peasants under their sway, but the guilds could not control the influx of emigrants to the cities as newcomers refused to join. The result was a greater agricultural efficiency and production to feed growing cities, increased competition among craft producers, greater social mobility, and a growing bourgeois class.

POLITICAL REVOLUTION

The age of absolute monarchy was short-lived. Europe's intellectual revolution, which had passed through its Renaissance and Reformation phases, now entered the *Enlightenment* (1648–1789) period which, among other things, marked the transcendence of northern Europe, particularly France, Great Britain, and Holland, as Europe's dynamic intellectual core. Great Britain's Hobbes, Hume, Locke, and Newton; France's Descartes, Rousseau, and Voltaire; and Holland's Leibnitz, Erasmus, and Spinoza created a vast range of seminal works in science and political philosophy. While the major issues of the Renaissance were intellectual and artistic freedom, and for the Reformation religious freedom, for the Enlightenment, it was political freedom. Although a few philosophers like Thomas Hobbes reinforced the notion of absolute monarchy, most championed the concept of popular sovereignty, better known as *democracy*.

This notion of popular sovereignty fueled revolutions in Great Britain (1642–88), the United States (1775–91), and France (1789–1804), exemplified by the words of America's "Declaration of Independence" from Great Britain in 1776:

We hold these truths to be self-evident: That all men are created equal; that they are endowed by their Creator with certain unalienable rights, and among these are the rights of life, liberty, and the pursuit of happiness; that, to secure these rights, governments are instituted among men, deriving their just powers from the consent of the governed; that whenever any government becomes destructive of these ends, it is the right of the people to alter or to abolish it, and to institute new government.

Nationalism and *liberalism* marched hand-in-hand. During the independence struggles of the Netherlands and the United States most people transferred their predominant loyalty and identity from their village to their nation-state. Although America's independence struggle against Britain is the most famous, Holland's war of liberation from Spanish Habsburg rule lasted eighty years, from the 1560s to 1648!

The period from the storming of the Bastille (1789) to Napoleon's defeat at Waterloo (1815) dramatically changed both national and international politics. From the French Revolution emerged the idea of a radical "left" striving to overthrow the status quo and a conservative "right" attempting to maintain it. Anticipating the Bolsheviks by over a century, the French leaders attempted to export revolution and overthrow monarchs across Europe. Robespierre and the other revolutionary leaders also created Europe's most elaborate police state to date, using "terror" and mass executions as a means of destroying their opponents. With its "levée en masse," Paris mobilized all of its citizens against the counter-revolutionary armies of Austria, Prussia, Russia, and Britain. Wars were once again fought over ideas rather than just territory. Warfare changed as French conscripts and Spanish guerrillas presented organizational and tactical innovations.

France's revolution was short-lived. In 1794, Robespierre and 21 other leaders were deposed and executed by a conservative coalition which ruled France for the rest of the decade until it yielded power to Napoleon in 1800. Napoleon assumed dictatorial powers and in 1804 had himself crowned emperor. The coalition of European powers which eventually defeated and exiled Napoleon met at the Congress of Vienna in 1815 and attempted to return Europe to its pre-1789 status quo. In 1817, Austria, Prussia, and Russia formed the "Holy Alliance," a year later joined by France, to put down any revolutions that challenged the divine right of kings. From 1815 through 1848, attempts at revolution flared across Europe and were invariably crushed by one or more of the great powers.

Yet, the revolutionary ideals of "liberty, equality, and fraternity," along with nationalism, lived on, eventually swept the world, and remain perhaps the most powerful force in international relations. This process "began in Europe itself, as the advanced ways of western Europe descended, irresistibly and at a fast clip down the cultural slope into central, southern, southeastern, and eastern Europe, into the fringe lands of the continent, as it also spilled overseas into the non-European world."[19] In Europe, Napoleon's armies marched from Lisbon to Moscow and left the seeds of liberty and nationalism in their bootsteps. In the early nineteenth century, precocious Germans, Italians, Poles, and Hungarians were among the first to conceive their respective nations, although the cultural boundaries were often hazy. Pan-Germanism and Pan-Slavism preceded Pan-Africanism and Pan-Asianism by a century. After long struggles, Italy was unified in 1861 and Germany in 1871, but the nationalist aspirations of the Poles, Serbs, Hungarians, Czechs, and others would remain suppressed until 1919.

Elsewhere, liberalism and nationalism were conveyed from the United States, Great Britain, France, and Holland by example as well as conquest. Political exiles in

London, Amsterdam, New York, or Paris carried back to their subjugated lands the ideals of the American Declaration of Independence and French Declaration of the Rights of Man. But the largely unwitting global champions of these ideals were Great Britain and France, whose troops, gunboats, and colonial administrators carried with them the flames of liberty and nationalism. Intellectuals throughout Latin America increasingly rallied around the liberal and nationalist ideals expressed by the American and French revolutions. In 1804, Haiti became the second country in the western hemisphere to win its independence, and by 1824 virtually all of Latin America had been liberated and divided into a score of nation-states. Although most of these states started out with liberal constitutions often modeled after that of the United States, the new regimes usually collapsed and were replaced by authoritarian governments. From 1775 through 1825 alone, 95 colonial relationships were severed, mostly in Europe and the western hemisphere.[20]

ECONOMIC REVOLUTION

In the late eighteenth century, the notion of popular economic sovereignty arose to reinforce that of popular political sovereignty. Throughout the early modern era, governments followed mercantilist policies in which they attempted to maximize exports and minimize imports to garner as much wealth in their own realm as possible. Trade was seen as a zero-sum rivalry in which one nation's gain was the others' loss. Although Louis XIV's Finance Minister Jean-Baptiste Colbert most systematically formulated and implemented mercantilist policies, his predecessors, most notably Henry IV's minister, Maximilien Bethune, the Duke of Sully, had adopted similar measures.

Adam Smith (1723–1790) developed a philosophy of economics diametrically opposed to *mercantilism*. In some respects, the publication of Smith's "Wealth of Nations" in Britain in 1776 was as revolutionary as the Declaration of Independence that year on the other side of the Atlantic. Smith called for *economic liberalism* in which everyone could produce and consume what they wanted, and celebrated the laws of supply and demand, the division of labor, and mass production. If everyone did what they did best and traded their production or wages for everything else, everyone would be better off. Prosperity springs from everyone being free to fulfill their respective self-interests.

Other thinkers expanded on Smith's thesis. In 1817, David Ricardo argued that every nation, like every individual, had certain natural or comparative advantages in production. Ricardo illustrated this concept by comparing Great Britain and Portugal, in which Great Britain had a natural advantage in raising sheep and Portugal in producing grapes. Wool can be developed into textiles and grapes into wine. Although Great Britain could try to grow grapes and Portugal raise sheep, the costs would be high. It thus makes much more sense for Great Britain and Portugal to produce what they naturally excel at and trade for everything else.

In the mid-nineteenth century, Great Britain championed the concept of free trade and began negotiating market opening agreements with other countries. Trade, however, was never completely free. Although there was a significant series of trade agreements and reductions of trade barriers between the leading European states during the late nineteenth century, significant barriers remained, and most imperial states prevented others from trading with their colonies.

These new concepts of economic liberty coincided with what has been perhaps the most important revolution of all—the *industrial revolution*. The industrial revolution marked the shift from small-scale, handmade craft production to large-scale assembly-line factory production which used inanimate energy sources like coal. The industrial revolution represented:

> *the transformation of an essentially commercial and agricultural society into one in which industrial manufacture became the dominant mode of organizing economic life . . . After 1850, the factory was not only the key economic institution of England, it was also the institution which shaped its politics, its social problems, and the character of its daily life, just as decisively as the manor or guild had done a few centuries earlier.*[21]

Marx vividly captured industrialization's vast changes and impact:

> *The bourgeoisie, in its reign of barely a hundred years, has created more massive and more collosal productive power than have all previous generations put together. Subjection of nature's forces to man and machinery, the application of chemistry to agriculture and industry, steam navigation, railways, electric telegraphs, the clearing of whole continents for cultivation, canalization of rivers, whole populations conjured out of the ground—what earlier century had even an intimation that such productive power slept in the womb of social labor.*[22]

Why did Great Britain lead the industrial revolution?[23] In Great Britain, as elsewhere, an agricultural revolution preceded the industrial revolution. The "enclosure movement" rationalized livestock production by squeezing out the small producers and allowing the landowners large scale production. Then, inspired by the theories of Jethro Tull and Lord Townsend, landowners applied such scientific methods as crop rotation, fertilizers, and improved seeds to agriculture. The increased farm production fed the increased population manning the shops and factories of the cities.

The industrial revolution was also preceded by a trade revolution, and here again Great Britain led the way. Mass industrial production could never have emerged without an existing network of national and international trade. British war and merchant ships dominated the global trade system. No country was better organized than Britain with its centralized administration and well-developed transportation and communications system. It also held considerable amounts of coal and iron ore which would form the basis of iron, steel, shipbuilding, railroads, bridges, and military weapons.

Finally, an intellectual revolution must precede an industrial revolution. No Europeans had a more positive attitude toward linking science, inventions, and business than the British. Journals like the *Gentlemen's Magazine* and groups like the Royal Society and Society for the Encouragement of the Arts and Manufacture, whose members were a dynamic mix of England's leading intellectuals, merchants, and inventors aided industrialization through the constant promotion and exchange of ideas and business. The government developed the patent system to promote and protect inventors.

Thus, Great Britain had all the prerequisites for successful industrialization: an enterprising, inventive, entreprenerual class; a mobile population; an expanding middle class; ample resources; a relatively efficient adminstration; a well-developed transportation and communications infrastructure; naval and trade surpremacy; and the advantage of being the world's wealthiest country.

In this very favorable setting, a number of entrepreneurs and tinkerers invented machines that were essential to industrialization. In 1769, Richard Arkwright invented the spinning jenny which revolutionized textile production; throughout the late eighteenth century, James Watt invented a series of increasingly efficient steam engines; Benjamin Huntsman more efficient methods of steel production; Josiah Wedgewood mass production techniques for china; John Wilkinson new methods for creating iron; James Maudslay the automatic screw machine. With mass production, goods were created more quickly, cheaply, and uniformly, while often including more interchangeable parts, which gave the manufacturer an enormous advantage over those who still relied on handcrafted production.

The increase in production was extraordinary. Between 1701 and 1781 raw cotton imports increased from 1 million to 5 million pounds, then skyrocketed to 60 million pounds by 1802! Pig iron increased from 68,000 tons in 1788 to 1,347,000 tons in 1839![24] By 1830, with only 10 percent of Europe's population and 2 percent of the world's population, Great Britain accounted for 67 percent of European industrial output, and 9.5 percent of global output, including 53 percent of the world's iron, 50 percent of its coal and lignite, and 50 percent of cotton consumption.[25] The second industrializing nation, France, was at least two generations behind Great Britain. Yet, between 1815 and 1845, France's pig iron production grew fivefold, its coal production, sevenfold, and imported goods tenfold! Great Britain remained the largest industrial power for most of the nineteenth century, with its share of global manufacturing rising from 1.9 percent in 1750 to 18.5 percent in 1900, while France's rose from 4.0 percent to 6.8 percent, Germany's from 2.9 percent to 13.2 percent, Japan's from 3.8 percent to 2.4 percent, and the United States from 0.1 percent to 23.6 percent.[26]

In the late nineteenth century, the United States surpassed Great Britain and became the world's dominant industrial power. America's Civil War revolutionized industry as Washington's demand for mass quantities of steel, ships, weapons, textiles, railroads, and canned foods, to name a few, transformed relatively small industries into vast mass production complexes. New wealth and economic dynamism were created amidst four years of destruction.

As in Great Britain, America's mass industrialization was led by entrepreneurs who combined revolutionary production techniques with ruthless business tactics, like Carnegie in steel, Vanderbilt in railroads, Rockefeller in oil, Ford in automobiles, Armour and Swift in meat packing, Frick in coke, McCormick in farm machinery, and J.P. Morgan in banking.[27] America's millionaires numbered 100 in 1880; 40,000 in 1916.[28] American industry was transformed from a collection of hundreds of small factories employing dozens to vast industrial complexes employing thousands. By the late nineteenth century, the "captains of industry" had become virtual industrial dictators with monopoly power over their respective sectors. Enormous political as well as economic power was concentrated in the hands of a few.

Figure 2.2
**World Industrial Production and Trade During the
Early Industrial Revolution**

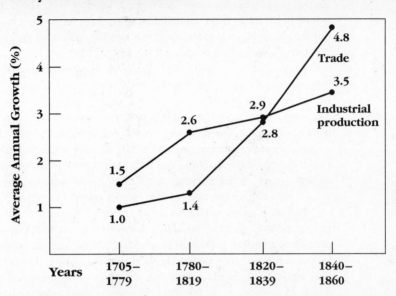

Source: Rostow (1978)

How did this political and economic concentration occur? The winner of price wars would buy out the opposition, acquiring more economic power with which to undercut the remaining competitors, while pouring money into the pockets of elected and appointed officials to tip the rules in his industry's favor. When there was a balance of power between two or more huge corporations in the same industry, they usually agreed to form an oligopoly and maintain high price levels. Mergers were organized into vast "trusts" in which the corporation and its stocks were controlled by a board of directors. For example, J.P. Morgan's banking empire included 341 directorships in 112 corporations whose total wealth was three times greater than the value of New England's total wealth![29] Although Washington attempted to reign in these monopolies by passing the 1890 Sherman and 1914 Clayton antitrust acts, they largely failed to check, let alone reverse, corporate concentration and power. Although the government used the Sherman Antitrust Act to break up the Standard Oil Trust in 1911, between 1909 and 1928, it failed to take action as the largest 200 corporations increased their gross assets 40 percent more rapidly than all other corporations to the point where they owned 85 percent of all corporate wealth.[30]

The result was the opposite of Adam Smith's free competition ideal: "a society in which production is governed by blind market forces is being replaced by one in which production is carried on under the ultimate control of a handful of individuals."[31] President Wilson clearly addressed the problem: "If monopoly persists, monopoly will always sit at the helm of government. I do not expect to see monopoly restrain itself. If there are men in this country big enough to own the government of the United States, they are going to own it."[32]

The agricultural and industrial revolutions had both positive and negative effects on the world. On one hand they allowed production to rise faster than population, raising the living standards of most people, while better hygiene, diet, medicine, and safety allowed people to enjoy longer and more productive lives. The high living standards and quality of life in the democratic industrial countries would not have been possible without the industrial revolution. Many other countries around the globe are currently passing through the different industrial revolution stages.

The horrors of the early industrialization age seemed to outweigh the benefits. The new manufacturing techniques and products created as much poverty as wealth by bankrupting obsolete industries and often underpaying the workers of new industries. And while industrialization brought tremendous wealth to the factory, mine, and shop owners, it imposed mass misery on the armies of men, women, and children who worked as much as sixteen hours a day, six days a week for subsistence wages. The machines claimed countless limbs and lives of the operators. Even Adam Smith had mixed feelings about the industrialists with their "mean rapacity, the monopolizing spirit . . . they neither are, nor ought to be, the rulers of mankind."[33]

Industrialization resulted in the alienation of many from their workplaces, communities, and even themselves. Under industrialization, virtually no one is a craftsman producing an entire product through idea, design, and manufacture; almost everyone produces just one tiny part of the final product. People themselves become machine-like, repeating the same simple task hundreds or thousands of times daily alongside hundreds and sometimes thousands of workers performing similar functions. The final product to which they have contributed becomes an abstraction, a source of imprisonment rather than pride. Smith deplored the effects of mass production in which the individual repeating the same motions "becomes as stupid and ignorant as it is possible for a human being to become."[34]

Finally, the industrial, technological, and medical revolutions resulted in a population explosion, as the birth rate exceeded the death rate. In the century from 1750 to 1850, Europe's population rose from 140 million to 266 million, and Asia's from 400 million to 700 million. Most of this new population was born into or migrated to cities. The world's population skyrocketed throughout the twentieth century, reaching 5.4 billion in 1992 and is expected to double by 2020! This population explosion is increasingly straining the earth's carrying capacity and has unleashed a range of global environmental problems that may eventually devastate the earth.

Industrialization's horrors caused many to seek economic reform or even revolution. As early as 1813, mobs of unemployed craftsmen or Luddites marched into factories and destroyed the machines which had taken their jobs. The pressure for reform rather than revolution was more common and came mostly from the workers themselves who organized into unions which lobbied both the factory owners and the government. In 1848, Karl Marx issued his "Communist Manifesto" which called for revolution: "Workers of the world unite! You have nothing to lose but your chains!" Inspired by the words of Marx and other radicals, socialist parties organized to overthrow governments across Europe.

The governments of most industrializing countries attempted to undercut these revolutionary forces by enacting reforms and coopting the more moderate opposition. Starting in 1802, London enacted a series of child labor laws that gradually eased the work hours and conditions in factories and mines and enacted similar laws for women and men. Other industrial countries experienced the same cycle of industrialization, political backlash, and reform. At first, the unions were outlawed and their leaders imprisoned. But after decades of struggle, unions were legalized in the democratic industrial countries, which then spawned political parties based largely on union membership and finance. Gradually, most workers rose from a subsistence existence to relatively comfortable lives while labor unions and socialist parties became accepted players in the political system.

WESTERN IMPERIALISM'S SECOND WAVE

Like its first wave, Western imperialism's second wave was stimulated by a mix of political rivalries, ideological excuses, economic imperatives, and technological advances. Economic reasons were perhaps the most important—the need for cheap and secure sources of food, raw materials, and minerals, captive markets, and the imperative to offset the expanding power of one's rivals. Nationalist rivalries and the prestige of empire were also important. Prime Minister Benjamin Disraeli captured the Zeitgeist when he asked publicly in 1872, "whether you will be content to be a comfortable England, modeled and moulded upon Continental principles . . . , or whether you will be a great country—an imperial country— a country where your sons, when they rise, rise to paramount positions, and obtain not merely the respect of their countrymen, but command the respect of the world."[35]

Great Britain in particular sought to continuously expand its global power in order to help check Germany's rising power in Europe. New powers like Germany, the United States, Japan, Italy, and Belgium joined the ranks of older imperial powers like Great Britain, France, and Russia, while others like Sweden and Austria did not get involved in overseas imperialism, and Holland, Spain, and Portugal clung to old conquests rather than attempting new ones.

Europe's great powers sublimated their ancient animosities and ambitions on the continent by conquering distant lands around the globe. Yet in doing so, Europe's conflicts were globalized and a final reckoning simply postponed. Benjamin Cohen writes:

> The imperial powers typically pursued their various interests overseas in a blatantly aggressive fashion. Bloody, one sided wars with local inhabitants of contested territories were commonplace: 'sporting wars,' Bismarck once called them. The powers themselves rarely came into direct military conflict, but competition among them was keen, and they were perpetually involved in various diplomatic crises. In contrast to the preceding years of comparative political calm, the period after 1870 was one of unaccustomed hostility and tension.[36]

The great powers largely cooperated in dividing much of humanity amongst themselves. At the Congress of Berlin in 1885, Great Britain, France, Germany, Portugal, Italy, and Belgium simply drew carefully negotiated lines across a map of West Africa and

Figure 2.3
The Partition of Africa to 1914

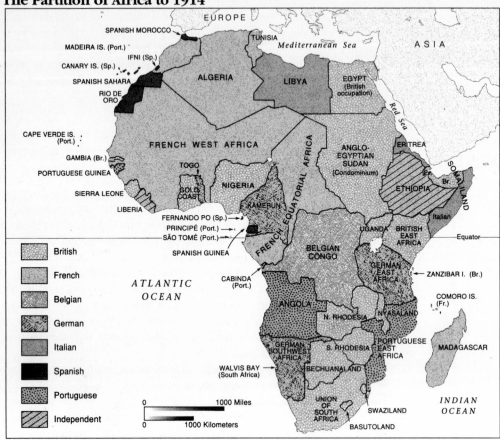

the Congo, thus carving it into separate empires. Likewise in China, the great powers negotiated different spheres of influence along the Chinese coast for their exclusive exploitation. During this second wave, most of Africa and Asia came under foreign rule. In 1800, Europeans controlled 35 percent of the earth's land surface. During Western imperialism's second wave the Europeans doubled their control to 67 percent of the world in 1878 and 84 percent by 1914!

How were the Europeans, Americans, and Japanese so successful? The industrial revolution gave Great Britain in particular, and the other great powers as well, a decisive advantage over the rest of the world. In 1750, the world's great civilizations may well have had roughly similar levels of industrialization. Britain's industrial revolution gave its manufacturers an enormous comparative advantage which, when combined with imperialism mascarading as free trade, wiped out vigorous industries in India, Turkey, China, Egypt and elsewhere, impoverishing millions. The British East India Company's export of cotton fabrics to India alone rose from 1 million yards in 1814 to 995 million in 1870. Europe's share of global manufacturing rose steadily from a mere 23.2 percent in 1750 to 62.0 percent in 1900, while the rest of the world's share plunged from 73.0 percent to 11.0 percent.[38]

Advances in military technology and tactics gave Europeans an invincible edge over other peoples. Then modern warfare blossomed to its full horrors during the American Civil War. Technology supplied railroads, the telegraph, rifles, long range cannons, and steam-fired iron-clad warships, allowing armies and navies unprecedented mobility and firepower. Meanwhile, major advances in medicine, nutrition, mass production, national and international credit, and sanitation enabled governments to supply and maintain armies in jungles, deserts, or mountains around the world. The conquest of Africa, for example, would not have been possible without medicines which safeguarded soldiers and administrators from the ravages of tropical diseases. The pen and sword were equally vital to the war effort. War was waged as much by armies of bureaucrats setting production quotas and moving supplies as it was by the soldiers in the field. And increasingly, war was fought not just against the uniformed enemy army, but against the entire enemy population. Thus, a handful of well-trained and equipped European troops or gunboats could humble vast civilizations. With only six gunboats in 1854, America's Commodore Perry forced Japan to open itself to the global trade system. At the battle of Omdurman in 1898, British troops killed over 11,000 Sudanese dervishes and lost only 48 of their own men.

These industrial, technological, and organizational advances allowed the Western powers and later Japan not only to conquer but to rule other peoples at a relatively small cost. By the late nineteenth century, Great Britain ruled a vast global empire on a shoe-string budget. From 1815 to 1880, Britain expended only 2 to 3 percent of GNP on defense. The British army actually decreased from 255,000 in 1816 to 248,000 in 1880.[39] Although London's expenditures on imperialism were relatively small, Britain did experience continual balance of payments problems as it invested more than it made overseas.

Japan and the United States were the two newest great powers. Japan embarked upon an ambitious imperial drive less than a generation after being forced by gunboats to open to the world economy. In 1868, a coup overthrew the decadent Tokugawa regime which had ruled Japan since 1600. The new regime embarked on a comprehensive attempt to create modern political, economic, industrialial, educational, military, and social institutions. Japan's leadership understood that the Western imperial powers only respected strength and embarked on a step-by-step conquest of northeast Asia. Japan took over the Ryukyu Islands in 1872, sent gunboats into Pusan Korea in 1876 to force the Korean King to open his realm to Japanese trade, acquired Taiwan and the Pescadore Islands after a successful war with China (1894–1895), and Korea after winning a war with Russia (1904–1905).

Although the United States expanded across the continent through a series of successful wars against and negotiations with the Native American nations, Mexico, Spain, and Great Britain, it did not become an overseas power until it defeated Spain in 1899 and acquired the Philippines, Puerto Rico, and several other Pacific and Carribean islands. Despite its original promise to aid the Filipino struggle against its colonial master Spain, the Americans reneged on their promise after defeating the Spanish and fought a bloody three year war to conquer the Philippines.

Imperialists justified their conquests of others by citing the "White Man's Burden" or civilizing mission. Thinkers like Great Britain's Herbert Spencer and Karl Pearson and America's Josiah Strong justified imperialism as a natural struggle among nations in which the fittest survive and subjugate the others by right of their natural superiority. According to *Social Darwinism,* as the biologist Pearson put it in 1901: "History shows . . . one way, and only one way in which the high state of civilization has been produced, namely, the struggle of race with race, and the survival of the physically and mentally fitter race."[40] Even Marx was ambiguous about Western imperialism, recognizing that it brought revolutionary advances as well as destruction in its wake: "England has to fulfill a double mission in India, one destructive, the other regenerative—the annihilation of the Asiatic society, and the laying of the material foundations of Western society in Asia."[41]

What impact did colonization have on its subjects? Colonization unleashed the same modernization processes among the oppressed peoples that had earlier occurred in Europe, but much more rapidly. Money replaced barter as the medium of exchange, and labor was paid with wages rather than in kind. Communal land became privatized in the hands of the few, while the many became tenants, and most people survived on a hand-to-mouth basis. Agriculture was organized into huge plantations producing cash crops like cotton, rubber, or coconuts, and these products were tied to the metropole's economy. New cities arose as trade or administrative centers, while even the most remote regions were linked with telegraph, railroads, steamships, and later airplanes and telephones. Modern medicine allowed people to lead longer, healthier lives thus causing rapid population growth. Mass school systems allowed for an increasingly high literacy rate, and, with it, an awareness of the world and one's place within it. Individuals began to transfer their identities and loyalties from their village to their nation. The Western liberal democratic concepts of freedom, equality, and representation mingled with Marxist notions of class struggle and national liberation in an increasing number of minds within the indigenous populations.[42] But all of these changes were enormously costly in lost lives and traditional ways of life.

WORLD WAR I

By 1914, nearly all of humanity had either achieved liberation from or remained directly ruled by Western imperialism, and even the world's most remote regions bore some imprint of Western culture. All the easy conquests were gone. In August 1914 Europe's great powers turned against each other and fought a four year war which destroyed virtually everything—the empires, ideologies, and economic order—that had been so carefully constructed since 1815.

Why did they do it? Although the imperial nations had largely cooperated in dividing much of the world among themselves, there were tensions that several times almost led to war. The imperial race was both stimulated by and fostered an arms race. Germany in particular expended enormous quantities of financial and human resources in efforts to build a fleet which could rival Great Britain's. By the early twentieth century, Europe's great powers had divided into two rigid alliance systems reinforced by a web of secret agreements concerning the division of spoils. Germany, Austro-Hungary, and Italy formed the Triple Alliance in 1882 which was balanced by the Dual Alliance of France and Russia in 1894. Britain continued to play its role as "balancer" and remained aloof from any entangling alliance until it signed a defense treaty with Japan in

1902, ententes with France in 1904 and Russia in 1907, and a naval agreement with France in 1912. The two alliances went to the brink of war over Morocco (1901, 1911, 1912) and the Balkans (1908–1909, and 1912–1913).

These alliances were on a hair-trigger. As the American Civil and Franco-Prussian Wars had shown, wars were won by speed, maneuver, and the attack of huge forces at the enemy's critical points. The general staff of each European army had devised elaborate railway schedules to mobilize and send their soldiers to the front. Because of the vast differences in their respective territories and railway systems, the mobilization time varied considerably between each power. Germany's mobilization would only take two weeks while Russia's lumbered along over six weeks. Thus, time was essential to victory. One nation's mobilization was as good as a war declaration.

The European powder keg was fused; all it needed was a spark to ignite it. The assasination of Austria's crown prince, the Arch-Duke Ferdinand, in Serbia in June 1914 sparked World War I. Austria used the assassination as an excuse to attack Serbia, Russia's ally. Austria had long feared that Serbian nationalism could serve as a model for national groups within its own polyglot empire. The result, however, was that Russia then declared war on Austria, Germany's ally, and Berlin then declared war on Russia and France. Germany felt compelled to move first to avoid fighting a two-front war against France and Russia. But its invasion of Belguim in August 1914 to flank French forces massed along the Rhine prompted Britain to enter the war. Without British troops at Mons and the Marne, the French army would have been overwhelmed as it was during the Franco-Prussian War of 1870, and Germany would have become Europe's unchallenged hegemon.

The anticipated quick war of maneuver and mass attacks that had characterized most conflicts for 400 years, however, gave way under the concentrated fire of massed machine guns and artillery to trench warfare in which gains were measured in yards at the expense of hundreds of thousands dead. Other powers entered the bloodbath. Turkey joined the Central powers in November 1914, Japan and Italy the Allies in 1915, Bulgaria the Central Powers, and China and Siam the Allies in 1917. But the stalemate was not broken until the United States joined the Allies in 1917. The weight of over 1 million American troops tipped the balance on the western front. On November 11, 1918, the guns finally fell silent.

STUDY QUESTIONS

1. What are modernization's central and interrelated characteristics? Which aspects of modernization change and which remain the same? What have been modernization's positive and negative effects?

2. Explain the political, social, economic, religious, and psychological characteristics of European feudalism.

3. What technological, economic, social, political, intellectual, and religious forces contributed to the breakdown of European feudalism and the rise of modernization?

4. Why did modernity begin in Europe? Why did modernization not emerge in other advanced non-western civilizations of the fifteenth and sixteenth century?

5. Analyze the major characteristics of the Renaissance, Reformation, and Enlightment, and their role in Europe's early modernization.

6. Analyze the technological, political, religious, economic, and social reasons for Europe's first wave of imperialism. What were the positive and negative effects of European imperialism for Europe and the conquered lands?

7. What is sovereignty? How has the focus of sovereignty shifted throughout the modern era?

8. Explain the characteristics of and differences between a feudal and absolute monarchy. What political, religious, economic, technological, social, and intellectual forces led to the transition from feudal to absolute monarchy in Europe?

9. What were the political, economic, intellectual, religious, technological, and social forces which led to the political revolutions in the United States and France in the late eighteenth century? What were the consequences of those revolutions for those two countries and the world?

10. What is nationalism? How is nationalism both stimulated by and a stimulate of modernization?

11. What is liberalism? Why did liberalism not take root in other countries experiencing revolutions or independence struggles?

12. What are major tenets of economic liberalism? Who were its major philosophers? Why and how did Great Britain champion economic liberalism in the nineteenth century?

13. What social, technological, political, agricultural, intellectual, economic forces led to the industrial revolution? Why did it begin in Great Britain? How did industrialization spread elsewhere? What were the positive and negative consequences of the industrial revolution in the nineteenth century?

14. Analyze the technological, political, religious, economic, intellectual, and social reasons for the second wave of European (along with American and Japanese) imperialism in the nineteenth and early twentieth century. What were the positive and negative effects of this second imperial wave on both the conquerors and conquered?

ENDNOTES

1. For a brilliant discussion of modernity which has inspired much of the following discussion, see Marshall Berman, *All That Is Solid Melts Into Air: The Experience of Modernity* (New York: Simon and Schuster, 1982). For an excellent analysis of the premodern features of non-Western states, see Janet Abu-Lughod, *Before European Hegemony* (New York: Oxford University Press, 1989).

2. Henry David Thoreau, *Walden and Civil Disobedience* (New York: Norton, 1966).

3. See Robert Tucker, ed., The Marx-Engels Reader, 2nd ed.(New York: Norton, 1978), 475–476; W.G. Runciman, ed., Max Weber: Selections in Translation (New York: Cambridge University Press, 1978).

4. Sigmund Freud, *Civilization and Its Discontents* (New York: Norton, 1962).

5. Franz Kafka, *The Trial* (New York: Vintage Books, 1974); *The Castle* (Avon, Conn.: Limited Editions, 1975).

6. T.S. Eliot, *The Waste Land* (New York: Chelsea House, 1986); Herbert Marcuse, *The One Dimensional Man* (Boston: Beacon Press, 1964).

7. Michel Foucault, *Politics, Philosophy, Culture* (New York: Routledge, 1988). Behavioralism, structuralism, and deconstructionism are the most prominent schools of thought which attack the notion of reason as the primary force in shaping individuals and the world.

8. Alvin Toffler, *Future Shock* (New York: Bantam Books, 1971).

9. See Friedrich Nietzsche, *Thus Spake Zarathustra: A Book for All and None* (New York: Penguin Books, 1978).

10. See Robert Tucker, ed., *The Marx-Engels Reader,* 2nd ed.(New York: Norton, 1978), 475–476.

11. Quoted in Berman, *All That Is Solid Melts Into Air: The Experience of Modernity* (New York: Simon and Schuster, 1982), 37.

12. For an excellent analysis of this question, see Paul Kennedy, *The Rise and Fall of the Great Powers* (New York: Random House, 1987).

13. Thomas Aquinas, "Summa Theologia," in A.E. Moore, ed., *Early Economic Thought* (Cambridge, Mass.: Harvard University Press, 1924), 54.

14. *Cambridge Economic History of Europe,* vol. 2 (Cambridge: Cambridge University Press, 1952), 134.

15. Robert Heilbronner, *The Making of Economic Society* (Englewood Cliffs, N.J.: Prentice-Hall, 1987), 45.

16. Kirkpatrick Sale, *The Conquest of Paradise* (New York: Knopf, 1990), 41.

17. Paul Kennedy, *The Rise and Fall of the Great Powers,* 27.

18. See Skinner and Wilson, *Essays on Adam Smith* (Oxford: Clarendon Press, 1975).

19. Theodore Von Laue, *The World Revolution of Westernization* (New York: Oxford University Press, 1986), p.38.

20. Albert Bergeson and Ronald Schoenberg, "Long Waves of Colonial Expansion and Contraction," 231–277, in Albert Bergeson, ed., *Studies of the Modern World System* (San Diego: Academic Press, 1980).

21. Robert Heilbronner, *The Making of Economic Society,* 77.

22. Quoted in Robert Tucker, ed., *The Marx-Engels Reader,* 2nd ed., 473–475.

23. See Phyllis Deane, *The First Industrial Revolution* (Cambridge: Cambridge University Press, 1965); David Landes, *Prometheus Unbound* (Cambridge: Cambridge University Press, 1969); Nathan Rosenberg and L.E. Birdsell, *How the West Grew Rich* (New York: Basic Books, 1986).

24. Robert Heilbronner, *The Making of Economic Society,* 78.

25. Paul Kennedy, *The Rise and Fall of the Great Powers,* 151.

26. A. Dunham, *The Industrial Revolution in France, 1815–1848* (New York: Exposition Press, 1955), 432; Paul Kennedy, *The Rise and Fall of the Great Powers,* 149.

27. For an excellent account, see Alfred D. Chandler, *The Visible Hand: The Managerial Revolution in American Business* (Cambridge, Mass.: Harvard University Press, 1977).

28. Robert Heilbronner, *The Making of Economic Society,* 105.

29. Robert Heilbronner, *The Making of Economic Society,* 113.

30. Robert Heilbronner, *The Making of Economic Society,* 115.

31. Berle and Means, *The Modern Corporation and Private Property* (New York: Macmillan, 1948), 46.

32. Quoted in Richard Hofstadter, *The Age of Reform* (New York: Knopf, 1955), 231.

33. Adam Smith, *The Wealth of Nations* (New York: The Modern Library, 1937), 460.

34. Adam Smith, *The Wealth of Nations,* 734.

35. T.E. Kebbel, ed., *Disraeli, Selected Papers of the Late Right Honorable the Earl of Beaconsfield,* vol. 2 (London: Macmillan, 1889), 534.

36. Benjamin Cohen, *The Question of Imperialism* (New York: Basic Books, 1973).

37. Paul Kennedy, *The Rise and Fall of the Great Powers* (New York: Random House, 1987), 150.

38. Paul Kennedy, *The Rise and Fall of the Great Powers,* 148-149.

39. Paul Kennedy, *The Rise and Fall of the Great Powers,* 153.

40. Karl Pearson, *National Life from the Standpoint of Science* (London: Dulau, 1901), 21.

41. Quoted in Theodore Von Laue, *The World Revolution of Westernization* (New York: Oxford University Press, 1986), 42.

42. For an excellent discussion of the relationship between economic, political and social development, see Barrington Moore, *The Social Origins of Dictatorship and Democracy* (Boston: Beacon Press, 1966).

The Development of the Modern World: From Versailles to Rio de Janeiro

Key Terms and Concepts

Authoritarianism
Bipolar World
Bretton Woods
Cold War
Communism
Containment
Democrazia
Detente
Domino Theory
Fascism
First World
Fourteen Points
General Agreement for Trade and Tariffs (GATT)
Glasnost
Global Containment

International Bank for Reconstruction and Development (IBRD)
International Monetary Fund (IMF)
League of Nations
Marshall Plan
Multipolar World
New Economic Policy
New International Economic Order (NIEO)
New World Order
Newly Industrialized Countries (NICs)
Nixon Doctrine

Organization of Petroleum Exporting Countries (OPEC)
Perestroika
Second World
Self-Determination
Strategic Arms Limitation Talks (SALT I and SALT II)
Totalitarianism
Truman Doctrine
United Nations (UN)
United Nations Conference on Trade and Development (UNCTD)
Versailles Treaty

Modernization's relentless pace accelerated during the twentieth century. For the previous four hundred years, the global political economy had expanded through the stimulus of European imperialism, trade, and industrialization. Then during the twentieth century, a range of new ideological, technological, military, political, economic, and social forces arose that threatened to tear the global political economy apart or drastically alter its power structure. If the nineteenth century (1815 to 1914) was the "age of optimism," the twentieth century (1914–1991) has been an "age of anxiety," if not downright pessimism, as one world war was followed, after a decade of relative prosperity, by global depression and an even more devastating world war, and then by a Cold War and nuclear arms race that threatened to destroy all humankind.

Yet enormous positive achievements flowed from the late 20th century: an expanding interdependent global economy in which an increasing percentage of humankind lived prosperous, stable lives, the breakup of the Western and Soviet empires resulting in the emergence of over 135 new countries, the toppling of one authoritarian regime after another around the world to be replaced by liberal democracies, and the development of new technologies and medicines that prolong and enhance our lives.

The twenty-first century really began a decade early, in 1991, with the Cold War's end, breakup of the Soviet empire, and communism's collapse. The 1990s and beyond could be an age of unprecedented international cooperation and peaceful management of most problems. The world is becoming increasingly knit together politically, economically, environmentally, and culturally. Yet the anxieties remain, with a still unresolved nuclear weapons and energy problem joined by the much more insidious threats of a worsening greenhouse effect, ozone layer depletion, unbridled population explosion, and desertification.

WORLD WAR I AND THE VERSAILLES SYSTEM

World War I and its settlement caused tidal waves of changes to sweep the world—changes whose effects we are still experiencing. The war left 20 million dead and Europe physically and psychologically devastated. It immediately destroyed four empires—the Austro-Hungarian Habsburg, German Hohenzollern, Russian Romanov, and the Turkish Ottoman—and eventually all others as each colonial power proved impotent against the growing nationalism in their possessions.

World War I marked the end of Europe's domination of the world, although this did not become apparent until later. The United States had become the world's largest economic power in the late nineteenth century and its entry into World War I tipped the balance in favor of the Allies. Yet, despite a promising beginning, the war did not mark the start of American hegemony. On January 8, 1918, President Wilson announced his *Fourteen Points* which were the ideals for which the United States was fighting, whose most important points were: the creation of a *League of Nations* which would attempt to settle disputes peacefully, *self-determination* for all peoples, the end of secret negotiations and treaties, freedom of the seas, free trade, and arms reduction. Although the *Treaty Versailles,* signed on June 28, 1919, rejected Wilson's notion of self-determination for all peoples, it did include the League of Nations. The Senate, however, refused to approve America's membership in the League of Nations, and the United States retreated into political isolationism.

To the victors went the spoils. The Versailles peace settlement conferred upon Britain and France the former Ottoman provinces in the Middle East as mandates to be prepared for eventual self-rule. Elsewhere, the German possessions in Africa were mandated to Britain and South Africa, and those in the Pacific to Japan. Finally, the French won control over the German industrial Saarland. The fallen East European empires were carved and then remolded into nine new states: Austria, Hungary, Czechoslovakia, Yugoslavia, Poland, Finland, Estonia, Latvia, and Lithuania.

Although declared the "war to end all wars," like many preceding peace settlements, the Versailles Treaty sowed the seeds of future conflicts. New totalitarian and expansionist ideologies like communism and fascism emerged, which led to a range of new rivalries, wars, and changes. But this would not be evident for another generation. At first, the world did appear to have abandoned old power balance norms and to have embraced internationalism as the guiding principle of international relations. The Washington Treaty of 1922 and London Treaty of 1930, led to great power

Figure 3.1
The Versailles Peace Settlement for Europe, 1919

THE VERSAILLES PEACE
SETTLEMENT FOR EUROPE, 1919

Newly Created States
Ceded Territories

Source: Wallbank/Taylor, Civilization: Past and Present, New York: HarperCollins, 1992, p. 787.

agreements capping the naval arms race, while the 1928 Kellog-Briand Pact outlawed wars of aggression.

The world economy grew rapidly during the 1920s. Few countries grew faster than the United States, which had been the world's leading economic power since the late nineteenth century, and its rapid growth stimulated the global boom. America's economy grew about 1.5 percent to 2 percent annually between 1874 and 1929, allowing a doubling of per capita income every twenty years. In 1911, America's per capita income was $368 compared to Britain's $250, Germany's $178, France's $161, and Italy's $108. In 1928, a year before the stock market crash, America's $541 per capita income overshadowed Britain's $293, Germany's $199, France's $188, and Italy's $96. America's per capita income had increased by 46 percent, while that of Britain and France by

33 percent, Germany by 25 percent, but Italy's actually declined.[1] America's economic development was enormously accelerated by World War I, with American firms selling to both sides of the conflict and capturing foreign markets from the hard-pressed European firms.

Although by refusing to join the League of Nations it seemed to relinquish its international political obligations, Washington did in fact take over London's role as global banker. In 1919, America's GNP surpassed that of all Europe, and New York had replaced London as the world's financial capital. The United States lent Germany the money to hand over to France and Britain as reparations, keeping all three great powers, and thus the world, afloat economically.

After leading the industrial revolution, why had Europe fallen behind the United States? Europe remained divided into a half dozen large nation-states and a dozen or more smaller ones, each competing fiercely with the others. With the populations of Europe's largest countries—Germany, France, Britain, Italy, and Austria—each one third to one quarter that of the United States, the industries of these states lacked the markets within which to achieve large scale production and profits. Traditionally, the Europeans attempted to alleviate their own limited markets by capturing others through colonialism and trade. But colonialism not only failed to create large enough markets, it imposed enormous financial costs on the imperial state as well. Rather than risk losing their industries to international competition, each state allowed its industries to organize into huge cartels which maintained high prices and low production. Thus, each European state was trapped in a vicious development cycle in which low growth meant low consumer spending which meant continued low growth.

The 1920s economic boom was fueled partly by a steadily expanding New York stock market. Between 1920 and 1929, the market expanded 4000 percent in value and over 10 million in new investors while industrial production itself grew only 45 percent. Then on Tuesday, October 29, 1929, investors dumped over 16 million shares and the market free fell, losing $30 billion in value over the next two weeks. America's economy became mired in a depression in which output dropped from $104 billion in 1929 to $56 billion in 1933, with 25 percent of the working population unemployed. The depression seemed to wipe out all the gains America had made during World War I and the 1920s. America's GNP was cut in half, its industrial output by 67 percent, and its trade, by 75 percent. The United States' share of global manufacturing plunged from 43.3 percent in 1929 to 28.7 percent in 1938![2]

Why did the New York stock market and global economy crash? The stock market sky-rocketed from speculation and a "get rich quick" psychology to the point where it no longer reflected any genuine production value. There were no government restraints on the speculative bubble. Stocks and bonds of dubious value were traded to enormous heights, and often traded on credit. The stock market rise hid severe problems in America's economy, with the farm sector in particular lagging far behind. Four out of ten farmers were tenants by 1929, and the average farmer made only 30 percent of the average urban wages. Perhaps the major reason for the farm depression was low productivity brought about by exhausting the soil with obsolete plowing, fertilizer, and seed technology. So the farm economy was already depressed when the stock market collapsed.

With the world's most productive economy and wealthiest population, and because of global economic interdependence, when America's economy collapsed it pulled the rest of the world down with it. American bankers recalled their foreign loans, which caused widespread foreign bankruptcies. Although other states struck first by erecting huge trade barriers and sparking a global trade war, Washington exacerbated these problems with its Smoot-Hawley legislation in 1930, mandating tariff hikes of 50 percent. Other countries boosted their tariff barriers and engaged in competitive currency devaluations to expand exports and repel imports. The result was a global depression with world trade and production cut to half its peak, and the armies of unemployed and impoverished people threatening all countries with political instability.

TOTALITARIANISM: THE RISE OF COMMUNISM AND FASCISM

The most disturbing development of the inter-war era was the emergence of *totalitarianism* Communist and Fascist governments. Mussolini coined the word "totalitarian" to express the state's role of personifying the "immanent spirit of the nation," but the word has come to mean the state's total control of politics, economics, and society. In this sense, totalitarianism has been more nearly a *Communist* than *Fascist* phenomenon. Fascist Italy, Germany, and Japan all allowed some economic and social freedoms, and perhaps only in Japan was political rule "total" in the sense that there was no opposition, and virtually all Japanese were prepared to sacrifice themselves for the state.

Totalitarianism is modernity's step-child, fueled by the mass reaction to the economic and political failures of many democratic regimes, and made technically possible on a national scale through modern mass communications and transportation which allow mass mobilization, surveillance and repression. Mussolini's Minister of Justice, Alfredo Rocco, could have been describing communism or fascism when he called for the necessity "of sacrifice, even up to the total immolation of individuals, in behalf of society . . . For Fascism, society is the end, individuals the means, and its whole life consists in using individuals as instruments for its social ends."[3] Adherents of totalitarian creeds believed they possessed a transcendent truth whose pursuit and fulfillment justified any action. Communism and fascism are secular religions whose disciples must blindly follow and sacrifice everything to its dictates. Marx, Lenin, Hitler, Mussolini, and Hirohito became messiahs who would supposedly liberate the masses from the evils of contrary beliefs and practices and lift them above all other nations.

Perhaps the most important result of World War I was the Russian Revolution. Vladimir Lenin, the Bolshevik Party (later renamed the Communist Party) leader, differed with Marx in several key areas. While Marx thought revolution would break out in the most advanced industrial states, Lenin argued that the late industrializing states like Russia were the ripest for revolution because industrialization's worst excesses had not yet been softened by reform. While Marx organized mass socialist movements, Lenin advocated a "dictatorship of the proletariat" that would seize power and then mobilize the masses.

In 1917, Russia certainly teetered on the brink of revolution. Over the previous two decades, the Russian Imperial government had been thoroughly discredited. First, in 1905 Moscow lost the Russo-Japanese War and massacred over a thousand protesters in front of the imperial palace in St. Petersburg. Then it refused to enact anything more than cosmetic political or economic reforms, which completely failed to address the rising pressure for a constitutional monarchy and popular representation, and alleviation of wretched factory and field work conditions, and the vast gap between a small rich class and the masses of poor. Finally, the imperial government sent millions of Russians to their deaths and suffered repeated defeats during World War I. On February 28, 1917, the Tsar finally abdicated and allowed the creation of a popularly elected national assembly. But the progressive Kerensky government, which took power, upheld its pledge to its allies to remain in a vastly unpopular war while it refused to redistribute land, and it soon lost legitimacy as well.

Contrary to popular image, the Bolsheviks took power via a carefully planned and executed coup d'état rather than the mass protests that toppled East European dictatorships in the late 1980s. When Bolshevik "Red Army" units seized key administrative posts in St. Petersburg and Moscow on October 24, 1917, they encountered little opposition. With the cry of "bread and peace," the Bolsheviks gained support and consolidated power by distributing food and land, thus satisfying the basic needs of most peasants and workers, and by promising to hold elections and sign a peace treaty with the Germans. But the Bolsheviks received only 9 million of 36 million votes cast during the election of November 25, so on January 19, 1918, the Red Army dissolved the National Assembly, arrested the representatives, and formed a dictatorship. The result was civil war. In order to gain popular support and to concentrate on defeating their opponents, the Bolsheviks signed the Brest-Litovsk Treaty with Germany on March 3, 1918, in which they surrendered the western part of the Russian empire. But it took three more years of brutal civil war before the communists were able to defeat the counter-revolutionary forces which had been aided by British, French, American, and Japanese troops and supplies.

Like most revolutionaries, the Bolsheviks were brilliant conspirators but administrative neophytes. Leninism, like Marxism, critiqued the old society and devised a means of overthrowing it, but failed to provide a blueprint for the new society. When once asked the revolution's guiding principles, Lenin replied "Soviets (popular councils) plus electricity." In 1921, after the Civil War had been largely won and with the need for reconstruction increasingly pressing, Lenin announced his New Economic Policy (NEP), which allowed market forces relative freedom.

Whether the Soviet Union might have eventually become a mixed economic system presided over by the communist party will never be known. Lenin died in 1924, and over the next four years Joseph Stalin succeeded in eliminating all the other communist leaders and emerged as the Soviet Union's totalitarian dictator. How did Stalin do it? After becoming the party's general secretary in 1922, Stalin used his position to fill the party's ranks with his own followers. Then, by using his majority in the party congresses, he adroitly played off the more moderate "right wing" communists against the radical "left wing" led by Trotsky. By 1927, Stalin succeeded in eliminating both groups of opponents and asserting total power over the Soviet Union. In 1928, he embarked on a massive collectivization campaign to nationalize all private businesses and farms and to control all aspects of the Soviet economy. To achieve total power, Stalin had an estimated 20 million people murdered either directly through execution or indirectly through starvation or being worked to death. Von Laue captures Stalin's total power: "he was the state; his security was state security; his will constituted sovereignty;

his power created the distinction between right and wrong; his personality set the style for the heroic Soviet experiment that was to complete Lenin's vision."[4] Communist parties that have seized power since the Russian Revolution have carefully emulated Stalin's "democratic centralist" model.

While Stalin was methodically destroying his opponents and creating a totalitarian political, economic, and social system, an extreme form of nationalism and *authoritarianism* was emerging in Italy, Japan, and Germany. There were significant variations among these three national socialist or fascist states in the government's ability to mobilize the nation's human and material forces, with Japanese fascism clearly exerting the most powerful grip over the population, followed by Germany, and then Italy. Yet all three governments promoted an ideology which proclaimed their nation superior to all others, and the devotion of all individuals to the state. Fascism exalted the nation, state, and war; the state was the instrument which expressed national culture and waged war. Individuals achieved their identity and meaning, and fulfilled national culture by serving the state and basking in its glories. Conquest and empire were the state's most sublime achievements.

Benito Mussolini originally was a radical socialist who became an ardent nationalist during World War I. He founded his own party in March 1919 based on demands for social justice and national vigor, and for the next three years the Fascist Party developed a national following. In November 1922 Mussolini threatened to march on Rome with his small army of Blackshirts. Rather than arrest Mussolini, the King, army generals, and leading power brokers agreed to offer him the prime ministership. As prime minister, Mussolini suspended many civil liberties and forged a government-business alliance which succeeded in rapidly expanding Italy's industrial power and middle class. Mussolini's totalitarianism was actually an authoritarian state which actively developed the economy and maintained political stability.

Adolf Hitler, like Mussolini, fought in World War I and, after the war founded his own party, the National Socialist (Nazi) Party, which combined ideas of socialism and nationalism. The Nazi Party's popularity rose slowly over the next decade from its founding in 1922. But in 1933, the National Socialists won the largest share of seats in the Reichstag, and thus Hitler was named prime minister. Like Mussolini, Hitler retained his popularity through his boundless charisma, appeals to German nationalism, and ability to develop the economy successfully. Unlike Italian or Japanese fascism, however, Hilter's fascism also scapegoated Jews and other "undesirable" minorities as the cause of all Germany's problems, rounded them up into huge concentration camps, and eventually murdered over 6 million of them.

Japanese fascism grew not from one individual but from many, and its imperialism during the 1930s was simply the second stage of an expansion that began in the 1870s and continued through World War I. Prime Minister Tanaka expressed his nation's grand strategy for expansion clearly in 1927:

> *The way to gain actual rights in Manchuria and Mongolia is to use this region as a base and under the pretense of trade and commerce penetrate the rest of China. Armed by the rights already secured we shall seize the resources all over the country. Having China's entire resources at our disposal we shall proceed to conquer India, the Archipelago, Asia Minor, Central Asia, and even Europe.[5]*

Like Italy and Germany, during the 1920s Japan had a liberal democracy that was badly discredited by corruption, inefficiency, and an indifference to mass poverty and other social problems. Small ultra-nationalist groups began assassinating Japan's political and economic elite and advocating the system's overthrow and replacement with an imperial state in which the emperor would enjoy total power. During the 1930s, the government gradually co-opted many of the ultra-nationalist ideas and in 1940 dissolved all political parties, unions, and other organizations and merged them into the Imperial Rule Assistance Association (IRAA), whose power to mobilize the Japanese population into sacrificing themselves for the state far exceeded that of the fascist governments of Germany and Italy and perhaps even Stalin's Soviet Union.

Communist totalitarianism differs from fascist totalitarianism in two important ways. First, Communist power is far more "total." Under the concept of "democratic centralism," the Communist party controlled not just all political relationships, but all economic, social, religious, and cultural ones as well; fascist totalitarianism tolerated no political opposition but did allow some limited economic, social, religious, and cultural freedoms. Secondly, communism is theoretically a universalistic ideology which applies to all humanity; fascism is a nationalistic creed.

THE ANTI-COLONIALISM STRUGGLE

World War I, Wilson's plea for self-determination, and the global depression greatly encouraged existing anti-imperial movements. As early as 1885, western-educated Indian nationalists founded the Indian National Congress to lobby Great Britain for home rule and later independence. The first Pan-African Conference was held in 1900, and in 1914, responding to World War I's outbreak, a Pan-African Congress leader wrote with incredible foresight that:

> We can only watch and pray. Unarmed, undisciplined, disunited we cannot strike a blow, we can only wait the event. But whatever that may be, all the combatants, the conquerors and conquered alike, will be exhausted by the struggle, and will require years for their recovery, and during that time much may be done. Watch and wait! It may be that the non-European races will profit by the European disaster.[6]

W.E.B. Dubois offered a bleaker vision in 1915: "The colored peoples will not always submit to foreign domination . . . . These nations and races, composing as they do the vast majority of humanity, are going to endure this treatment as long as they must and not a moment longer. Then they are going to fight and the War of the Color Line will outdo in savagery any war this world has yet seen. For colored folk have much to remember and they will never forget."[7]

The most important independence agents were the imperial countries themselves. Nationalist leaders in the colonies took up President Woodrow Wilson's call for self-determination for all nations. France and Great Britain had used colonial labor and taxes to help fight the war, and the hundreds of thousands of Africans, Chinese, Vietnamese, and Indians who served behind the lines in Europe took home liberal and socialist ideas.

During the inter-war years, what had been mostly small conspiratorial independence groups in Asia and Africa became mass movements. Great Britain responded positively to the more organized of these movements, granting colonial assemblies for India in 1917, and for West Africa in 1919, while in 1935, America's Tydings-McDuffy Act promised the Philippines' independence in 1945. However, elsewhere the colonial powers brutally suppressed these movements and arrested the leaders.

The most successful anti-imperial struggle of the inter-war era was in China. The western powers and Japan had carved spheres of influence from its coastal regions during the late nineteenth century. In 1905, Sun Yatsen founded the Nationalist Party (Kuomingtang, KMT) based on the "Three Principles" of national independence, democracy, and socialism. In 1911, the KMT and other forces rebelled openly against the Manchurian dynasty, which abdicated the following year, and Yuan Shikai became president of the new republic. The KMT was not powerful enough to unite China, which had broken up into autonomous states lead by warlords. In 1915 Tokyo took advantage of the war among the western powers and anarchy in China by imposing its infamous "21 Demands," which allowed Japan the premier imperial position in China. Yuan's government in Nanjing was powerless to resist the Japanese demands. Chinese resentment at Japanese imperialism grew, culminating with the 1919 "May Fourth Movement," in which there were mass Chinese protests against Tokyo's imperialism and boycotts of Japanese goods.

China's internal divisions were complicated further by the founding of the Chinese Communist Party (CCP) in 1921, which formed a shaky alliance with the KMT in 1924. The Soviets supplied advisors and aid to the two parties and helped forge a united front between them against the warlords during the mid-1920s. In 1927, however, KMT Generalissimo Chiang Kaishek launched a sneak attack against the CCP and wiped out the cadres in most of the cities. The remnants fled into the countryside, rallied, and continued to fight against the KMT. In 1934, Chiang launched a new offensive against the communist stronghold in Jiangxi and eventually drove the communists on an 8,000 mile retreat. The communist remnants of the "long march" took refuge around Yenan in the vast arid lands of northern China. It was here that Mao Zedong took undisputed leadership of the CCP and imposed a new revolutionary philosophy based on peasant, rather than proletariat, power. With the Japanese invasion of China in 1937, the KMT and CCP once again formed a united front. Although foreign powers were finally expelled from China in 1945, the KMT and CCP would fight bitterly for another 4 years before the Communists' victory.

WORLD WAR II AND AMERICAN HEGEMONY

World War II was caused by Japanese, German, and Italian imperialism. By 1941, all the world's great powers and many of its smaller states were at war. The war might not have become global if Great Britain, France, and the United States had intervened earlier, but the leadership of all three democratic industrial powers was hobbled by the political and economic isolationism of their electorates during the 1930s.

Japan conquered Manchuria in 1931. The League of Nations dispatched the Lytton Commission to investigate and, acting on the findings, condemned Japan's aggression in 1933. The League, however, failed to threaten Japan with economic or military sanctions. Tokyo responded by withdrawing from the League, and continued to penetrate north China economically and politically. In 1937, the Japanese attacked China and overran most of its northern and eastern regions. The League did not even condemn Japan's attack. The League of Nations did condemn Italy in 1935 for its attack on Ethiopia, but failed to halt the German army's march into the demilitarized Rhineland the following year.

The great powers, Great Britain and France, also failed to block Germany's takeover of the neutral Rhineland in 1936 or merger with Austria in 1938, and actually acquiesced to Germany's takeover of Czechoslovakia's Sudetenland in 1938. It was only when Germany and the Soviet Union conquered Poland in September 1939 that France and Great Britain declared war on Germany. Meanwhile, the Japanese took over northern Indochina in 1940 and southern Indochina in 1941. The war became global on December 7, 1941, when the Japanese attacked American forces in Hawaii and the Philippines and Great British forces throughout Southeast Asia. As in World War I, the mobilization of America's vast economic and military power proved the deciding factor in World War II. After three years of devastating warfare, the American-led Allies finally crushed Germany in May 1945 and Japan in August 1945.

In many ways, the Second World War was as cataclysmic a watershed in American history as the Civil War. For 170 years the United States had prospered in relative geographic and political isolation, its leaders obeying President Washington's admonition to avoid entangling alliances while its merchants gathered wealth from the world's markets. Washington's diplomacy and its wars with Great Britain (1812–1815), Mexico (1846–1948), and the various Indian nations, were almost solely to promote America's expansion to the Pacific Ocean. America's global power increased with its territorial, industrial, and population growth. Victory over Spain in 1899 won America a small overseas empire, encompassing the Philippines, Puerto Rico, and a scattering of small Pacific Islands, and thus made the United States a minor "great power"; intervention in World War I made the United States one of the Big Three powers at the Versailles peace conference. Yet, the United States turned its back on the responsibility that accompanies power; it rejected membership in the League of Nations and returned to political isolationism. The "business of America is business," President Coolidge dourly declared, and America's foreign policy remained mercantilist. In the early 1930s, America's isolationism became economic as well when Smoot Hawley helped topple the global trade system.

All this began to change with Franklin Roosevelt's election to the presidency in 1932. Roosevelt understood that the United States could no longer afford to turn its political or economic back on the world. In an increasingly interdependent world, America's prosperity depended on global prosperity, and as the world's largest economy, the United States had the chief responsibility for reviving and nurturing the global economy. The Roosevelt administration first began to fulfill this mission after Congress passed the 1934 Reciprocal Trade Act, which authorized the president to conduct trade negotiations with other countries. Although the White House signed several trade agreements up through the early 1940s, these had a relatively limited effect on alleviating the global depression and trade wars. The Japanese attack on Pearl Harbor and across Southeast Asia in December 1941 gave Roosevelt the national emergency necessary to justify the mobilization of America's vast potential economic and military power toward defeating the fascist powers and reviving the global economy.

Roosevelt sought to succeed where his predecessor Wilson had failed in creating a lasting and just global peace and its accompanying prosperity. This vision would rest on two pillars: an improved version of the League of Nations—the *United Nations* (UN)—which would keep the peace, and a network of international organizations to rebuild the global economy. In 1944 at a conference at the *Bretton Woods* resort in New Hampshire, representatives from 44 countries joined to create the *International Monetary Fund* (IMF) and *International Bank for Reconstruction and Development* (IBRD, World Bank) which were designed to reconstruct those countries devastated by war, revive their economies and trade, and fix all currencies to the dollar and gold. In 1945, 50 nations met in Washington to sign the United Nations Charter, which embodied the ideals of a new world order, calling for all nations to work toward achieving peace, human rights, gender equality, national self-determination, political liberty, and economic development.

By 1945, the United States had clearly accepted the crown of global leadership, and the policies it pursued in that role reflected its liberal democratic values and institutions, sense of cultural superiority, and belief in progress. The world would be a far better place, so the American outlook went, if its countries would just discard their corrupt and inefficient institutions and practices and adopt those of America. From now on the United States would lead, not as in the past by providing a distant model, but by plunging into the complex world of international politics and convincing others to follow. Former President Wilson perhaps captured this vision best when he declared: "Sometimes people call me an idealist. Well, that is the way I know I am an American. America is the only idealistic country in the world."[8]

The United States could easily afford the burdens of global leadership. American wealth and power grew enormously during World War II. Even in 1938 the United States had 54 percent of the world's gold and financial reserves compared to 11 percent each for France and Great Britain.[9] Then from 1939 to 1945 America's GNP increased from $88.6 billion to $135 billion. America's gold reserves of $20 billion were two-thirds of the world total, and its industrial output was half the world total.

Yet the creation of the IBRD and IMF in 1944 and the *General Agreement for Trade and Tariffs* (GATT) in 1947 was not enough to revive the global economy. Western Europe and Japan were stalled in a vicious development cycle. They were devastated and impoverished by the war, and they desperately needed food, medicine, and clothing for themselves and equipment to revive their industries. The Americans could supply all of these goods, but the Europeans and Japanese had no way to pay for them. Thus, the world economy remained stagnant, and by 1947 many feared it would slide into another depression.

THE COLD WAR AND THE BIPOLAR WORLD

Despite the White House's internationalist policies and America's vast power, the public was ambiguous over the country's postwar role, with many calling for a return to political if not economic isolation. It was the outbreak of the Cold War with the Soviet Union which tipped the balance decisively between the isolationists and internationalists to the latter and stimulated the global economy's revival.

Someone once said that the only way to stir and mobilize the American public from their isolationist lethargy was to scare the hell out of them and, thus, the struggle with the Soviet Union was depicted in the most apocalyptic of images. Containment policy maker, George Kennan, publicly argued in 1947 that:

> *Today we Americans stand as a lonely, threatened power on the field of world history. Our friends have worn themselves out and have sacrificed their substance in the common cause. Beyond them—beyond the circle of those who share our tongue and our traditions—we face a world which is at worst hostile and at best resentful. A part of that world is subjugated and bent to the service of a great political force intent on our destruction. The remainder is by nature merely jealous of our material abundance, ignorant or careless of the values of our national life, skeptical as to our mastery of our own fate and our ability to cope with the responsibilities of national greatness.*[10]

Why did the wartime alliance between the United States and Soviet Union breakdown into nearly a half century of Cold War? Scholars have debated the question ever since the late 1940s and have yet to achieve a consensus. Some argue that the Soviet Union was clearly at fault.[11] After all, it was the Soviets which toppled one government after another throughout East Europe and imposed communist dictatorships in their place. Others argue that it was actually the United States which was at fault.[12] According to that view, a Cold War between the Soviet Union and the West has existed ever since the Bolshevik Revolution when British, French, American, and Japanese troops intervened in the civil war on the side of the counter-revolutionaries. Although the western powers set aside their containment of the Soviet Union during World War II, the United States soon resorted to anticommunism as an excuse to mobilize the American public behind the measures needed to revive the global economy.

However, most scholars conclude that the Cold War was inevitable and no one country was to blame.[13] With the Germans and Japanese devastated by defeat, and the British and French by victory, the United States and the Soviet Union were the world's only genuine great powers in 1945. That would have been grounds enough for conflict. Historically, great powers have always competed and frequently gone to war over vital and even superfluous issues. But this great power rivalry was exacerbated by the diametrically opposed ideologies that each power espoused—the United States liberal democracy and free markets; the Soviet Union one-party rule and the state control of all property and production.

Was the Soviet Union inherently expansionist? Answers to this question range from depicting the Soviet Union as an evil empire bent on global conquest to a peace-loving state which solely tried to defend itself. Most analysts, however, agree that the Soviet takeover of East Europe and attempts at expansion elsewhere were largely opportunistic rather than part of some grand design for global conquest. In 1945, the Soviet Red Army simply moved into the political vacuum left by Germany's defeat. The Soviet empire inherited the Russian empire's xenophobia and search for defensible borders. That expansionist mentality was primarily defensive, forged by a millenium of continual attacks by neighboring aggressors on a Russia exposed on the vast steppes. This traditional drive combined with and was often justified by the communist ideology of global revolution.

What was the point of this global rivalry? Why were trillions of dollars spent on activities which seemed to offer little, if any, concrete payback? George Kennan, an American diplomat in Moscow during the war years, was containment's architect. In 1946, he sent his famous "long telegram" to Washington warning of the Soviet threat, and in 1947 he anonymously published his even more famous "Mr. X article" in *Foreign Affairs,* the nation's most important foreign policy journal, carefully detailing the Soviet threat and what the United States must do to contain it.[14] According to Kennan, the Soviet threat was primarily ideological and political rather than military. The fear was not that Soviet tanks were going to burst across the West German border, but that Soviet backed Communist parties in Western Europe and elsewhere would take advantage of the pervasive postwar poverty, chaos, and uncertainty, and through both subversion and elections take over those governments. The result would be an enormous expansion of Soviet power and influence.

How could the United States counter this threat? Communism flourishes in societies in which a small wealthy class exploits poverty-stricken masses. If mass poverty were eliminated, communism's appeal would shrivel. Liberal democracy, in contrast, is nurtured best in a middle class society. Thus, Kennan urged Washington to extend massive economic and political aid to the world's most important industrial countries and regions. Washington should not, however, try to pour money into every country ripe for revolution. Many countries lacked geoeconomic or geopolitical importance, or their revolutions were primarily nationalist struggles against colonialism. The United States would simply throw away its money if it attempted to counter the tide of history in such countries. As long as West Europe and Japan were transformed into stable, prosperous liberal democracies, the Soviet threat would be contained, and the global balance of power would be preserved in America's favor. The rest of the world, whether communist or noncommunist, would have to trade with the United States, Western Europe, and Japan. According to Kennan, the Soviet threat itself would be relatively short-lived. Kennan understood that the Soviet's leadership expansionist energies would eventually dry up if they scored no great successes, while the Soviet Union itself would eventually collapse from communism's internal contradictions and inability to distribute anything other than poverty or provide any meaningful life for those unfortunate enough to live under its rule.

By early 1947, President Truman agreed to use the policy of containment to deal with Moscow's consolidation of power in East Europe and seeming attempts to expand that power elsewhere. In March he announced what became known as the *Truman Doctrine,* by which the United States would aid "free countries who are resisting attempted subjugation by armed minorities," and immediately dispatched economic and military aid to Greece and Turkey whose governments were attempting to squash communist-led revolts.[15] In June 1947, Secretary of State Marshall announced what became known as the *Marshall Plan,* by which the United States would extend billions of dollars in aid to Europe. Successfully waging the Cold War required special institutions. The Department of Defense (DOD), National Security Council (NSC), and

Central Intelligence Agency (CIA) were created in 1947 to plan and execute America's anti-Communist and anti-Soviet policies.

The Cold War escalated rapidly from its 1947 beginnings. The Soviets toppled a democratic government and imposed a communist government in Czechoslovakia in 1948, blockaded Berlin for nine months from 1948 through 1949 in an unsuccessful attempt to force the Allies out, and exploded an atomic bomb in 1949, thus seeming to give Moscow military parity with Washington. Elsewhere, the Chinese Communist Party defeated the Nationalist Party and in October 1949 took over all of China except Taiwan, Ho Chi Minh's communist forces battled French colonial forces in Vietnam, and communist guerrillas plagued governments throughout East and Southeast Asia. Even Japan had a growing communist party. The global balance of power seemed to be shifting steadily in Moscow's favor.

Although the United States has followed a containment policy toward the Soviet Union and other communist countries through 1991, by 1950 George Kennan's *selective containment* policy was replaced with Paul Nitze's *global containment* policy. In his NSC 68 report issued in early 1950, Nitze argued that the United States was engaged in a global struggle with the Soviet Union in which one side's gain was the other's loss. The United States had to mobilize and use every means possible, including military power, to defeat any Soviet advance. No corner of the world was unimportant.

Although Kennan and other selective containment advocates protested Nitze's vision as self-defeating and exaggerated, the global containment strategy seemed warranted after communist North Korea's attack on South Korea in June 1950. Until then, the Cold War had been played out mainly in Europe. The White House interpreted the North Korean attack as directly influenced by the Soviet Union, and thus represented a "hot" war in a remote region. Within 48 hours of the attack, the Truman administration decided not only to dispatch an American-led allied army under United Nations auspices to reinforce the South Korean army, but also to send the U.S. Seventh Fleet into the straits between China and Taiwan, thus saving the KMT from what would have been an inevitable Chinese communist conquest.

Henceforth, America's containment policy would be global. No country was considered too remote or economically insignificant to warrant being written off by Washington. Global containment operated under the logic of the *domino theory*—if one country in a region fell to communism, it would simultaneously weaken the resolve of noncommunist governments and strengthen communist forces in neighboring countries. Thus, the fall of one domino would bring down the rest. As President Johnson put it, "if we don't stop the communists in Vietnam, they'll march into Hawaii today, and San Francisco tomorrow."[16]

The United States protected the "free world" (which included dozens of highly authoritarian and repressive states) with a matrix of alliances, military bases, and billions in military and economic aid to anticommunist governments and movements. America's commitments were vast:

> *In 1970, the United States had more than 1,000,000 soldiers in 30 countries, was a member of four regional defense alliances and an active participant in a fifth, had mutual defense treaties with 42 nations, was a member of 53 international organizations, and was furnishing military or economic aid to nearly 100 nations across the face of the globe.[17]*

The United States and Soviet Union fought bitterly during the Cold War in scores of battlefields around the globe. But the warfare always stopped short of direct combat between American and Soviet troops. At times both sides did go to the brink of war. During the two Berlin crises (1948–1949, 1958–1961) and the Cuban missile crisis (1962), Americans and Soviets could very well have opened fire on each other, setting off a third world war. The war was instead fought through propaganda, coups, the funding of friendly and subversion of unfriendly guerrillas, political parties or governments, a steadily spiraling conventional and nuclear arms race, and, in countries like Korea, Vietnam, and Afghanistan, wars against the other side's allies.

With Western Europe, Japan, and other industrial countries achieving economic prosperity and political stability by the 1950s, the Cold Warriors shifted their battle to winning the hearts and minds of those in the less developed countries, many of which were just achieving their independence. Regional conflicts, some of which had been seething for generations and even centuries, were caught up in the Cold War ideological struggle. National leaders played Washington and Moscow off against each other and were in turn manipulated by the Americans and Soviets. Regional conflicts were globalized as the Soviets and Americans provoked arms races and coups, and manipulated politics and economies. For example, since the United Nations created Israel in 1948, conflict has been continual between Israel and shifting alliances of the surrounding Arab states. Eventually, the United States and the Soviet Union became deeply involved in this regional conflict.

Although the United States ultimately won the Cold War, it suffered some humiliating and debilitating defeats along the way. Fidel Castro's overthrow of the American-backed Batista regime in 1959 and declaration of a communist Cuba shortly thereafter unleashed a struggle between the United States and Castro for the allegiance of Cubans that has carried on into the post-Cold War world. Washington's efforts to topple the Castro regime, including eight assassination attempts, the invasion of anti-communist Cuban military forces at the Bay of Pigs in 1961, and a continuing economic embargo have all failed.

America's worst defeat was in Vietnam. France's colonial hold over Vietnam, was steadily undermined after 1945 and finally decisively defeated in 1954 at the battle of Dien Bien Phu by Ho Chi Minh and his communist army. The 1954 Geneva peace conference negotiated France's withdrawal and Vietnam's division into a communist north and non-communist south. As it had for the French in the late 1940s and early 1950s, Washington extended vast economic and military aid to South Vietnam's President Ngo Dinh Diem in his struggle against the communist Viet Cong insurgency. But the communists continued to gain ground despite American aid. In 1961, President Kennedy agreed to send in American military advisors, and by his death in 1963 the number had grown to 16,000. President Johnson accepted the Defense Department analysis that a major effort could destroy the Viet Cong. The excuse for making this effort came with reports, since proven false, of an attack by North Vietnamese gunboats on American ships operating in the Gulf of Tonkin. Johnson demanded and received a Congressional resolution which essentially empowered him to use virtually any means to defeat the Communist insurgency in South Vietnam. America's participation was then dramatically escalated from a predominantly advisory role to a massive combat one; by 1968 there were over 550,000 American troops in Vietnam, and the U.S. Air Force had already dropped more bomb tonnage than had all the forces in World War II.

Yet, America's vast military efforts succeeded in achieving only a battlefield stalemate, while a growing majority of the American population favored the war's end. The communists suffered a terrible military defeat but great political victory in their Tet offensive in early January 1968, as the American public saw on television Viet Cong attacking the American embassy. Many Americans reasoned that if the American army could not protect the American embassy then how could it defeat the Viet Cong elsewhere? The Vietnam War seemed unwinnable. Newly elected President Nixon began a slow withdrawal of American forces from Vietnam, the transfer of most fighting to the South Vietnamese army, and negotiations with North Vietnam. A peace treaty was signed in 1972, which supposedly allowed the United States to withdraw in "honor." North Vietnam conquered South Vietnam in 1975. The war in Indochina cost the United States $150 billion, 60,000 lives, several hundred thousand wounded, and a psychological trauma that remains unhealed today. For the Vietnamese, Laotians, and Cambodians it led to millions dead and the imposition of communist dictatorships.

DECOLONIZATION, DEVELOPMENT, AND STAGNATION

Over 135 countries have achieved independence since 1945. These predominantly poor countries, along with Latin-American and other countries which had already gained independence, became known as the *Third World,* in contrast to the *First World* of the democratic industrial countries and *Second World* of the communist countries. A trickle of newly independent states in the late 1940s and 1950s, including India (1947), Pakistan (1947), Burma (1948), Indonesia (1950), became a flood after the mid-1950s, as the rest of Asia and Africa became sovereign states.

Imperialism planted the seeds of its own destruction. The colonial process of creating an administrative region and exploiting it inevitably raised the cultural and political consciousness of its inhabitants, a consciousness that eventually swelled into an independence movement. Ironically, the more enlightened the rule, the more the indigenous elites received the formal and political education which allowed them to lead the independence struggle. It is no coincidence that the first independence movement arose in the relatively liberally governed British India, while the relatively tightly controlled Portugese colonies of Angola and Mozambique were among the last to achieve independence. Regardless of the colonial policies, a combination of the independence movements and growing international condemnation of colonialism inevitably convinced the imperial states to give up their holdings.

The path to independence and its aftermath were rarely peaceful. Some newly independent countries themselves experienced independence movements. Shortly after India achieved independence, a genocidal war broke out between Hindus and Muslims in which as many as 10 million people may have died. Most of the the Muslim regions broke away to form Pakistan, while 50 million Muslims remained under Indian rule. The violence of the independence struggles, however, varied considerably from the relatively peaceful independence of most of France's West African colonies to the bitter warfare that preceded independence in Vietnam, Malaysia, Indonesia, Algeria, and Kenya.

Few of the newly independent states were prepared for independence. One reason was that virtually all of these states were not nations but multi-nations. Each colony's borders had been drawn to satisfy the imperial state's political and economic needs, an important part of which was to discourage national unity. Thus, each colony became a crazy quilt of national fragments, many of which were linguistic, religious, cultural, or historic rivals.

The newly independent nation-states were just as divided between rulers and the ruled. The political and economic elites who had led the independence struggle were often educated in the imperial capital and acquired the colonial powers' values, manners, and even language. For example, although only 1 percent of the population speaks it, English is one of India's official languages because it provides a neutral means of communication and thus gives no single ethnic group an advantage.

As the Marxist theoretician Frantz Fanon said: "The colonized man is an envious man."[18] The rhetoric of the independence movements fueled a popular revolution of rising expectations for the political, economic, and social gains that would presumably accompany liberation. Most people were brutally disappointed. The independence leaders may have been skilled at leading an underground struggle, but few had any understanding of how to run a modern political economy. The revolution of rising expectations turned into rising frustrations when mismanagement and corruption often caused people's lives to worsen rather than get better.

Many new governments attempted to help legitimize their rule by creating official national creeds, such as Indonesian President Sukarno's "Five Principles" (Pantja Sila), which called for nationalism, humanitarianism, authoritarian democracy, social justice, and god; Egyptian President Nasser's "Philosophy of the Revolution" which described Egypt's role as the natural leader of the Arabs, Africa, and Islam; or Ghanian President Nkrumah's "I Speak of Freedom" which asserted a similar role for Ghana in Africa. Some leaders of the newly independent nations like Nasser, Nehru, and Nkrumah even claimed leadership over peoples beyond their respective national borders and became the heroes to millions throughout the developing world. Nkrumah declared in 1961 that: "All Africans know I represent Africa and that I speak in her name. Therefore no African can have an opinion that differs from mine."[19]

The governments of many newly independent countries espoused "socialism" as their state creed, and to that end began nationalizing industries and submitting five-year development plans. Yet few of these states ever came close to achieving the complete abolition of private property and a centrally planned economy. Regarding his government's first five-year plan, Nehru admitted: "We just took what was there and called it a plan."[20] Often socialism was simply used as an excuse to create a dictatorship. Nkrumah argued that:

> *Capitalism is too complicated a system for the newly independent states. Hence the need for a socialist society. But even a system based on social justice and a democratic constitution may need backing up, during the period following independence, by emergency measures of a totalitarian kind. Without discipline true freedom cannot survive.[21]*

As early as the mid-1950s, representatives of Third World states met to discuss their common problems and to present a united front to the democratic industrial and communist blocs alike. The first *nonaligned movement* was held in Belgrade in 1954, and was followed up by the larger Bandung Conference of April 1955 in which representatives of 20 countries swore to remain independent and forge a political economic alternative to the Cold War rivalry. Indonesian President Sukarno captured the conference's mood when he said: "We have been the unregarded, the peoples for whom decisions were made by others whose interests were paramount, the people who lived in poverty and humiliation. Then our nations demanded, nay fought for independence, and achieved indepedence, and with that independence came responsibility."[22] The non-aligned movement was reinforced by the emergence of regional organizations like the League of Arab States (1948), Organization of African Unity (1963, OAU), or Association of Southeast Asian Nations (1967, ASEAN), and the United Nations Group of 77 in the 1960s, which formed to promote shared political and economic goals.

Third World nonalignment and solidarity were more rhetorical than real. Few states actually watched the Cold War from the sidelines. The United States and the Soviet Union had client states throughout the less developed world. Conflicts between less developed states sometimes broke down into war. India and Pakistan fought three border wars, and other wars broke out between China and India, China and Vietnam, and Iraq and Iran. Most wars, however, were civil rather than international as suppressed and brutalized peoples fought for independence from the dominant ethnic group. Many governments in the less developed world displayed a double standard in denouncing "imperial exploitation" while often much more brutally exploiting their people whom they were supposed to represent. Tanzanian President Nyerere, for one, bravely decried "this tendency in Africa that it does not matter if an African kills other Africans . . . Being black is now becoming a certificate to kill fellow Africans."[23]

Third World unity reached a height during the 1960s and 1970s with the programs of *United Nations Conference on Trade and Development* (UNCTAD), and the *Organization of Petroleum Exporting Countries'* (OPEC) success in nationalizing oil production and quadrupling oil prices in 1973 and further doubling them in 1979. In 1974, the nonaligned movement espoused the *New International Economic Order* (NIEO) which asserted that:

> *the remaining vestiges of alien and colonial domination, foreign occupation, racial discrimination, apartheid and neo-colonialism in all its forms continue to be among the greatest obstacles to the full emancipation and progress of the developing countries . . . The benefits of technological progress are not shared equitably by all members of the international community. The developing countries, which constitute 70 percent of the world's population, account for only 30 percent of the world's income. It has proven impossible to achieve an even and balanced development of the international community under the existing international economic order. The gap between the developed and the developing countries continues to widen in a system which was established at a time when most of the developing countries did not even exist . . . which perpetuates inequality.*[24]

The nonaligned movement fell apart during the 1980s for several reasons. First, there was nothing "nonaligned" about the movement. Most of the members were openly aligned or sympathetic to the communist states, while many of the rest were openly aligned with the West. The movement was as split economically as it was politically. There was a large and widening gap between *newly industrializing countries* (NICs) like South Korea, Taiwan, Singapore, or Chile which had achieved rapid and equitable economic growth and the world's poorest countries like Haiti, Bangladesh, Burma, or Tanzania. Finally, the Cold War's end meant that less developed countries could no longer play the two superpowers against each other and would henceforth have to accommodate themselves to the industrial democracies.

THE COLD WAR AND THE MULTIPOLAR WORLD

Nixon's withdrawal from Vietnam was part of a global realignment of American power in accord with a world that had changed greatly since 1945. During the 1960s, the once tightly structured *bipolar world* centered around Soviet and American blocs broke up into a much more fluid multipolar ideological, military, and economic world. The non-aligned movement which emerged in the mid-1950s followed by the breakdown in Sino-Soviet relations during the late 1950s, and France's withdrawal from NATO in 1966 were significant steps toward a *multipolar world*. Meanwhile, the European Community and Japan grew enormously from the 1950s through the early 1970s and caught up to the United States in per capita income and economic dynamism.

The Nixon administration viewed the world's multipolarization as positive for American national interest, and tried to deepen it. In 1969, Nixon announced that henceforth the United States would not directly fight communist insurgencies, but would only aid those governments willing to protect themselves (the *Nixon Doctrine*). Meanwhile, the White House attempted to play the Soviets and Chinese off against each other by pursuing *detente* with both. As Kissinger put it, "the hostility between China and the Soviet Union served our purposes best if we maintained closer relations with each side than they did with each other."[25] In 1971, Nixon and Soviet leader, Leonid Brezhnev signed the *Strategic Arms Limitation Talks* (SALT I) which imposed limits on certain weapons systems; in 1978, President Carter and Brezhnev signed SALT II which expanded those limits.

Meanwhile, the global geoeconomic balance of power was shifting dramatically. In 1971, the United States suffered its first trade deficit since 1888! The burdens of containing communism and maintaining the global economy were becoming increasingly intolerable for the United States. On August 15, 1971, President Nixon announced his *New Economic Policy,* which proved as important a shift from past policy as his detente with the Soviet Union and China. Nixon imposed a temporary 10 percent surcharge on existing import tariffs and revoked the dollar's convertability into gold, thus essentially scraping the fixed exchange rate system which had been the world economy's central girder since 1944. Although the United States continued to encourage greater European unity and Japanese growth, Nixon urged them to take responsibility for a larger share of the common burden of defending and managing the global political economy.

Global economic power had decentralized from American hegemony during the 1940s and 1950s to a balance of geoeconomic power among the United States, Japan, and the European Community during the 1960s. But these great powers were unable to prevent the Organization of Petroleum Exporting Countries from boosting oil prices

Figure 3.2
Expanding World Trade (in dollars)*

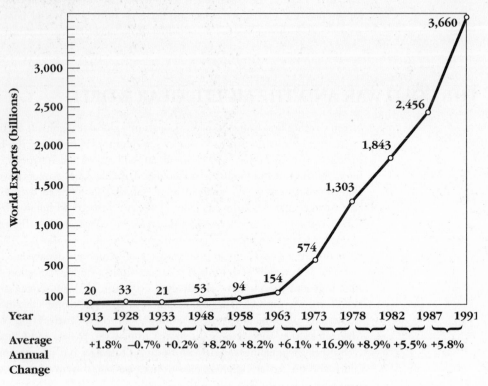

Source: 1913–58 figures are from Root (1973:24), the 1963–82 figures are from GATT (1983:126). The 1987 figure is from UN (1988:102). The 1988–91 figures are from IMF (1992) and World Bank (1992).

twice during the 1970s. In November 1973, using the Arab-Israeli Yom Kippur War as an excuse, OPEC quadrupled oil prices from $2.50 a barrel to $11.50 a barrel, which led to a dramatic shift in global economic power and dynamism. The industrial economies became hobbled by inflation and slow growth that persisted for a decade. Although the less developed nations initially cheered OPEC's actions, the poorer countries were the worst hit by the grossly inflated prices. The OPEC countries received huge financial windfalls: in 1974, an additional $70 billion; from 1975 through 1979 an annual $200 billion, and, after further doubling its prices that year, $500 billion![26]

What did OPEC do with all of this money? Since most of the oil rich countries could not absorb the money into their own economies, they ended up investing it in Western banks, which in turn lent it out to the poorer countries to help them pay for their own oil and other imports. The Third World's debts mounted rapidly and, with their economies stalled, they had difficulty paying off the interest let alone the principle. There was a very real danger that if the major Third World debtors like Mexico or Brazil defaulted on their loans, they would bankrupt the world's major banks, which in turn would cause the entire global economy to collapse.

As if the global economic crisis were not enough, the overthrow of the pro-United States Shah of Iran in early 1979 by a fundamentalist Islamic revolution and the takeover of the American embassy, followed by the Soviet invasion of Afghanistan in December 1979, led to a shift in the Persian Gulf's power balance and seemed to indicate the Cold War's revival. The interrelated global economic and political crises helped elect Ronald Reagan to the presidency in 1980 when he promised to revive America's flagging power by doubling the defense budget and asserting American military power throughout the world. During the next dozen years, the United States invaded tiny Grenada to destroy a Marxist-Leninist regime and Panama in 1990 to overthrow and extradite its president, Manuel Noriega, on drug charges to the United States. Then, in 1992 the United States led a United Nations sanctioned alliance that expelled an Iraqi army from Kuwait. Meanwhile, the United States funded anti-communist guerrilla armies in Afghanistan, Nicaragua, Angola, Ethiopia, and Kampuchea.

Yet, despite or because of these Reagan and Bush administration policies, America's relative economic decline accelerated. America's national debt quadrupled from $970 billion in 1981 to over $4 trillion in 1992, while its trade and payments deficits soared, leading to the nation's transformation from the world's banker to its greatest debtor. The economic growth of the United States hobbled along at rates lower than preceding decades, and average real per capita income continued to fall. Japan surpassed the United States as the world's leading banking, manufacturing, and technological power. Washington seemed increasingly impotent in the face of deepening global economic, political, and environmental challenges. What went wrong? Essentially the United States failed to adapt to revolutionary changes which had been active for decades in the global political economy and which by the late 1980s became known as the "New World Order."

THE NEW WORLD ORDER

What is the *New World Order?* Essentially, it is a complete reordering of international priorities, strategies, and values. Geoeconomic conflicts over trade, investments, and economic strategies have become the most important item on the international agenda, followed by international attempts to deal with the world's worsening and interrelated environmental crises. Geopolitical conflicts in the Middle East and elsewhere continue to make the headlines, but with the Cold War's end few of these conflicts merit the attention they once did. The bipolar world in which most countries were associated with one of the two superpowers has given way to a genuine multipolar world in which five great powers—the United States, Japan, Russia, China, and the European Community—cooperate on addressing most important issues. The world is converging politically and economically. Increasing numbers of states are being transformed from authoritarianism to liberal democracy, while most states are trying to emulate Japan by carefully managing their economies and picking industrial winners.

When did this New World Order begin? Perhaps 1985 was the most dramatic and symbolic year in which this long-term transformation of international relations became clear. In 1985, Japan inherited the throne as the world's most dynamic financial, technological, and manufacturing nation, while the United States free fell from being the world's largest creditor into the worst debtor nation. Meanwhile, the European Community agreed that year to dismantle all of its internal barriers by 1992, thus creating the world's largest unified market. Most importantly, in 1985, Mikhail Gorbachev became the Soviet communist party's Secretary General and began to formulate the reforms that would lead to the collapse of communism and the Soviet empire.

Kennan's predictions proved to be correct. During the late 1980s and early 1990s, the two Germanys were reunited, Eastern Europe was liberated, the Soviet Union broke up, and communist dictatorships were overthrown almost everywhere. How did this occur?

There are two long-term and one short-term reasons for the collapse of communism and the Soviet empire. The most important long-term reason was communism's internal contradictions. Communism was deeply flawed theoretically and, when applied, led at best to the massive exploitation of a population by a tiny well-organized elite which enjoyed what little wealth and privilege the system produced. At worst, as in the Soviet Union, China, and Kampuchea, to name a few, the result was genocide. State ownership and planning of the entire economy failed, often tragically, to achieve sustained economic development. Soviet statistics about becoming the world's largest producers of steel, for example, were often grossly inflated and actual production often grossly misallocated. Although the communist systems did succeed in achieving significant gains in literacy, health care, and safety, these gains could not balance the system's economic failings.

Although communism's collapse was inevitable, the rulers remained largely blind to their system's vast inadequacies. At the 1962 party congress, Khrushchev confidently predicted that the Soviet Union would economically surpass the United States by 1970 and achieve communism by 1980! Khrushchev had this in mind when he arrogantly declared at the United Nations in 1962 that he would "bury the United States." Communism's collapse was accelerated by America's containment policy. If Soviet-backed communist parties had taken power in the industrial powerhouses of West Europe and Japan, communism's demise would have been delayed immeasurably as those geoeconomically strategic regions became communist, rather than liberal democratic, showcases.

The short-term reason for the democratic revolutions that swept East Europe and the Soviet Union was Mikhail Gorbachev. It was Gorbachev's policies of restructuring (*perestroika*), openness (*glasnost*), and democracy (*democrazia*) which released the confined nationalist and democratic spirits. Why did Gorbachev follow these policies which eventually swept him and communism from power? In a sense, he had little choice, although he did not necessarily have to take the path he did. By the 1980s, even its most diehard supporters agreed that communism was experiencing a crisis. Gorbachev reasoned that if he could reform the system, he might be able to save it. But by emphasizing political rather than economic reforms, he created rising frustrations when people were able to participate more openly in politics without the majority of them achieving any material gains. While Russia may have achieved significant democratic political reforms, yet it remains in economic crisis.

While Soviet communism crumbled, China's "communist" rulers remained in power by following the opposite tack—they made sweeping economic reforms while maintaining tight political controls. Since 1978, Beijing has steadily reduced central planning and allowed ever more private property and production within relatively free markets. The result has been a steady rise in living standards. Ironically, China's rulers may be undermining their own legitimacy and power through these successful policies. In 1989, hundreds of students and other sympathizers occupied Tiananmen Square in Beijing and called for democracy. The government responded by massacring the pro- testers. China's democracy movement collapsed. But in the decades ahead, as China's middle class further widens, people will increasingly demand more political freedoms as they did in neighboring South Korea and Taiwan.

Some argue that there was yet another reason for the Soviet collapse—the Reagan adminstration's almost tripling of America's defense budget during the 1980s which, according to the Reagan supporters, forced the Soviet Union to collapse in its attempt to compete. Others counter that the defense buildup reinforced the Kremlin hardliners' position that Gorbachev's reforms were too risky, and thus prevented them from being implemented sooner and more comprehensively. Instead, by tripling America's national debt during the 1980s, the Reagan adminstration undermined American rather than Soviet power. Whether the Reagan buildup contributed to or delayed communism's collapse will remain a controversial question, but regardless it was a secondary factor at best.

The New World Order does not mean any lessening in the number or intensity of wars occuring around the world. The vast majority of these wars, however, will be in- ternal rather than international, with peoples tearing apart the often highly artificial na- tion-states imposed on them in decades past. Long suffering minorities, or in the case of black South Africans, majorities, will revolt against the dominant nationality.

Why are wars like Iraq's invasion of Kuwait and the subsequent international coali- tion against Iraq increasingly anacronistic? In an interdependent world, states can much more cheaply acquire through trade, diplomacy, and other means the security, wealth, and prestige that they formerly used to achieve through the use of force. The world's greatest military powers—the United States and Russia—are rapidly demobilizing their once vast conventional and nuclear forces, and other states are reducing their own bloated military budgets. Without the Cold War, militant states can no longer play the two superpowers against each other to receive huge amounts of economic and military aid.

Certainly, the world does appear to be moving into a new and unprecedented age of cooperation. By the hour the first bombs dropped on January 16, 1991, President Bush had rallied 40 nations to his alliance to liberate Kuwait from Iraq. In a richly sym- bolic sequence, the president first sought United Nations approval for an economic blockade and possible military attack on Iraq before asking Congress for a similar green light. Also telling was the White House's need to seek the aid of its allies to help pay for the war. The United States is no longer the economic superpower it was at the Cold War's beginning when it could single-handedly contribute $17 billion to West Europe and $2 billion to Japan to stimulate their reconstruction and prosperity, a combined fig- ure that in today's dollars would be over $225 billion!

The United Nations approved economic sanctions and a military alliance against Iraq to force it to withdraw from Kuwait and dismantle its nuclear weapons program. The United Nations is conducting more peace keeping forces than ever—in 1993, UN forces were patrolling 13 different conflicts, and only budget constraint prevented more missions. Yet, the international effort against Iraq is unlikely to become a model for the future policing of world conflicts. Although after the UN-Iraq War, most would-be aggressors would certainly hesitate before attacking a neighboring country, most international conflicts may not be so clear-cut as the various wars in the former Yugoslavia attest.

Geoeconomic struggles, meanwhile, are intensifying. While the United States and the Soviet Union harmed each other in their geopolitical struggle, the European Community, Japan, and Newly Industrializing Countries (NICs) have grown rapidly. Nearly all states are becoming more protectionist. Although continuing to profess an adherence to free trade ideals, the United States increasingly erected trade barriers throughout the 1980s. It also attempted to forge a North American trade bloc of 365 million consumers by signing a free trade agreement with Canada in 1988 and one with Mexico in 1990. The European Union (EU) has also changed its situation. In 1992, Brussels dismantled the last significant barriers to internal trade, bolstered many of its restrictions against Japanese goods, and signed a free trade agreement with the seven nation European Free Trade Association (EFTA), thus creating the world's largest trade bloc with 380 million consumers.

With only 120 million consumers, Japan would appear to be outnumbered in market size. But throughout the postwar era, Tokyo carefully constructed its own unofficial trade bloc in East and Southeast Asia. Japanese firms already have predominant trade, investment, and aid shares with virtually every nation in the region, and Japanese officials now work carefully with Southeast Asian national officials to tie their development policies closely to Japan's economy.

For the indefinite future, geoeconomic rather than geopolitical conflicts will shape most international relations. A breakdown of the global economy, however, is unlikely. International organizations like the GATT, IMF, and World Bank provide the global economy's major institutions, principles, and dispute forums, while representatives of the most powerful democratic industrial states meet frequently to iron out specific problems. International trade and investments, however, will be increasingly managed along the principle of reciprocity rather than free trade. Meanwhile, complex interdependence will deepen, and the United Nations and other international organizations will play an increasingly important role in managing international relations and conflicts.

The world's gravest challenge involves not trade or even war but the earth's ecological devastation. Although humanity remains shadowed by the threat of nuclear destruction, another Chernobyl rather than Hiroshima disaster is more likely. During the 1980s, increasing numbers of individuals and governments became aware of the calamitous nature of the greenhouse effect, ozone layer depletion, overpopulation, desertification, and deforestation. Some progress in addressing these problems has been made. In 1988, representatives of over 40 nations signed the Montreal Protocol, in which participants pledged to reduce ozone depleting chemicals by 2000. In June 1992, representatives of 178 nations gathered at Rio de Janeiro to sign treaties in which they pledged to achieve significant reduction in greenhouse pollution and to protect biodiversity. The United States played the spoiler in both treaties, refusing to ratify the biodiversity treaty and ensuring that there were no timetables or incentives for compliance with the greenhouse treaty. An international consensus was broken by other interests as well. A Brazil-led coalition of tropical forest countries succeeded in setting aside a proposed treaty that would have limited logging. Meanwhile India led the poorer countries in a demand that the world's wealthy countries transfer to them the finance and technology necessary for them to comply with the treaties. The rich countries were noncommital.

INTO THE TWENTY-FIRST CENTURY

Will these meager measures prove to be too little too late? The world's population is expected to double from 5.5 billion inhabitants in 1992 to 11.4 billion by 2050! Can the earth sustain this further doubling of population? Will the increased competition for scarce resources unravel the recent gains in international cooperation? Could the world descend once more into the maelstrom of global geopolitical conflicts? Will new ideologies arise to divide nations against each other and provoke them to war over real and perceived differences? Or will the world remain largely at peace while the global economy fragments into American, European, and Japanese trade blocs?

Or will these dire possibilities remain the realm of fiction? Has the nature of international relations and power changed fundamentally in an increasingly interdependent world? Will the collapse of communism and the Soviet empire prove to be the "end of history" as all states sooner or later adopt liberal democracy and relatively open economies? After all, liberal democratic states have never gone to war against each other since 1815.

Are nation-states themselves obsolete? Will they break apart into smaller cultural groups as in the Soviet Union and Yugoslavia? Or will they submerge their identities into even larger groupings like the European Union or North American free trade market? What role will the United Nations, other international organizations, and international law play in the new world order? Most states already obey international law most of the time, while all states are members of the United Nations, and most states enjoy membership in dozens of international organizations. Will this growing matrix of international organizations and law eventually develop into a world federation, in which states abandon their sovereignty and accept the decisions of a world government? How interdependent can we truly become? Will the world ever be united by a common government, let alone culture? Can diverse peoples ever truly understand and empathize with one another?

These questions can only be answered with time. One thing is certain, the nature of international relations and the world is rapidly changing.

STUDY QUESTIONS

1. What were the political, economic, balance of power, and psychological consequences of World War I and the Versailles Treaty?

2. Why did the global economy collapse into depression and trade wars during the 1930s, and what were the political consequences of that collapse?

3. What is totalitarianism? What accounted for the rise of totalitarian fascist and communist systems during the early twentieth century?

4. Why did a communist revolution occur in Russia in 1917? What were the major political, economic, and social characteristics of the communist system?

5. Compare and contrast the origins and development of fascism in Italy, Japan, and Germany.

6. What were the origins and political, economic, and balance of power consequences of World War II?

7. What was the purpose and significance of such international economic organizations as the IMF, World Bank, and GATT, and international political organizations like the UN? What was the American role in creating these institutions?

8. What was the Cold War? What were its major causes, phases, and consequences?

9. What were the differing American strategies during the Cold War?

10. What were the reasons for and consequences of the vast decolonization process which brought over 100 countries to independence following 1945?

11. What were the origins, aspirations, successes, and failures of the non-aligned movement?

12. What were the reasons for the shift in the global power balance from a bipolar to a multipolar alignment?

13. What were the reasons for and significance of President Nixon's "new economic" and "detente" policies?

14. What is OPEC? What were the reasons for and significance of OPEC's quadrupling of oil prices in 1973 and further doubling of prices in 1979? Why did OPEC's influence decline in the mid-1980s and after?

15. What were President Reagan's military and economic policies, and what effect did they have on the United States and the world?

16. Why were the long-and short-term reasons for the Cold War's end and collapse of communism and the Soviet empire?

17. What is the New World Order? What are the major international issues and challenges in the 1990s and beyond?

ENDNOTES

1. Robert Heilbronner, The Making of Economic Society (Englewood Cliffs, N.J.: Prentice-Hall, 1987), 168.

2. Paul Kennedy, *The Rise and Fall of the Great Powers* (New York: Random House, 1987), 330.

3. Quoted G. Mosse, *Masses and Man* (New York: Howard Fertig, 1980), 101.

4. Theodore Von Laue, *The World Revolution of Westernization* (New York: Oxford University Press, 1986), 109.

5. Quoted in Franz Schurmann and Orville Schell, eds., *The China Reader: Republican China* (New York: 1967), 184.

6. Immanuel Geiss, *The Pan-African Movement* (London: Macmillan, 1974), 229–230.

7. Immanuel Geiss, *The Pan-African Movement*, 230.

8. Quoted in Arthur Mann, *The One and the Many* (Chicago: University of Chicago Press, 1979), 69.

9. Paul Kennedy, *The Rise and Fall of the Great Powers*, 307.

10. George Kennan, *Memoirs 1925–1950* (Boston: Little Brown, 1967), 35.

11. Adam Ulam, *The Rivals: America and Russia Since World War II* (New York: Viking Press, 1971); John Spanier, *American Foreign Policy Since World War II, 1917-1965* (New York: Praeger, 1960); Desmond Donnelly, *Struggle for the World: The Cold War, 1917-1965* (New York: St. Martin's Press, 1965).

12. Denna Frank Flemming, *The Cold War and Its Origins: 1917–1960* (2 vols) (New York: Macmillan, 1961); Gabriel Kolko, *The Politics of War: The World and United States Foreign Policy* (New York: Pantheon Books, 1968); Thomas Patterson, *Soviet-American Confrontation: Postwar Confrontation and the Origins of the Cold War* (New York: Putnam, 1973); Daniel Yergin, *Shattered Peace: The Origins of the Cold War and National Security State* (New York: Penguin, 1977); Gar Alperovitz, *Atomic Diplomacy: Hiroshima and Potsdam* (New York: Vintage, 1965); Walter Lafeber, *America, Russia, and the Cold War* (New York: Wiley, 1990).

13. Vojtech Mastny, *Russia's Road to the Cold War* (New York: Columbia University Press, 1978); William Taubman, *Stalin's American Policy* (New York: Norton, 1981); John Gaddis, *Strategies of Containment* (New York: Oxford University Press, 1987).

14. See also George Kennan, *Memoirs 1925–1950*, 35.

15. Theodore Von Laue, *The World Revolution of Westernization*, 171.

16. Quoted in Walter Lafeber, *America, Russia, and the Cold War* (1990), 73.

17. Ronald Steel, *Pax Americana* (New York: Viking Press, 1977), 134.

18. Frantz Fanon, *The Wretched of the Earth* (New York: Grove Weidenfeld, 1963), 32.

19. Paul Johnson, *Modern Times: The World From the Twenties to the Eighties* (New York: HarperCollins, 1985), 513.

20. Hiranyappa Venkatasubbiah, *India's Economy Since Independence* (London: Macmillan, 1958), 287.

21. Kwame Nkrumah, *The Autobiography of Kwame Nkrumah* (Edinburgh: T. Nelson, 1957), X.

22. George McT.Kahin, *The Asian-African Conference, Bandung, Indonesia* (Ithaca, N.Y.: Cornell University Press, 1956), 42.

23. Paul Johnson, *Modern Times: The World From the Twenties to the Eighties,* 537.

24. *United Nations Yearbook,* 1974 (New York: U.N. Publishing, 1974), 324.

25. Quoted in John Gaddis, *Strategies of Containment,* 179.

26. Daniel Papp, *Contemporary International Relations* (New York: Macmillan, 1988), 380.

The Nation-State and International Relations

Nations, Nation-States, and Nationalism

Key Terms and Concepts

Culture	Irredentism	Socialization
Ethnic Group	Multinationalism	Sovereignty
Ideology	Nation-Building	State
Internationalism	Nation-State	Subculture

Nations, nation-states, and nationalism are largely modern concepts that have evolved in importance over the last several hundred years. Despite growing interdependence and the proliferation and power of international organizations, regimes, law, world opinion, and multinational corporations, the *nation-state* remains central to international relations. In 1945, there were 51 United Nations members; in 1993, there were 187! Within a decade another 20 or so countries may achieve independence.

Nationalism, nation-building, and *multinationalism* may well be the heart of geopolitical issues in the post-Cold War world. More established and newly independent states alike are faced with the problem of realizing "out of many, one" (E Pluribus Unum). A 1979 study found that only 9.2 percent of all the world's countries had populations 100 percent of one nation. In 18.9 percent the largest nationality accounted for 90 to 99 percent of the population, in 18.9 percent 75 to 89 percent, in 23.5 percent 50 to 74 percent, and in 29.5 percent less than 50 percent.[1] Of 166 nation-states in the mid-1980s, only 33 percent were considered homogenous in which 90 percent of the population was of one *ethnic group*. Of the multinational states, the dominant nation accounted for less than 70 percent of the total population in about 50 percent of those countries, and less than 50 percent in 25 percent.[2]

Governments from Nigeria to Malaysia and from Canada to Belgium are trying to promote a new cultural identity that spans sometimes dozens of distinct cultural identities. In many of these nation-states, people are forced to choose between loyalty to one's government and loyalty to one's culture, whether that culture be predominantly ethnic, racial, religious, or some combination thereof. These unification efforts often fail. Sometimes, as in Yugoslavia, Northern Ireland, Nigeria, Sri Lanka, Chad, Iraq, Lebannon, and Angola, to name a few, the nation-state dissolves into civil war as long suppressed and exploited minority cultures seek independence.

Thus, civil rather than international wars increasingly make the headlines as minorities sharing a common culture and heritage demand their own autonomous or independent state. For example, the Kurdish nation sprawls over large chunks of Iraq, Iran, Syria, and Turkey. For decades, the Kurds have been fighting for greater autonomy or outright independence in all of those states. Unlikely as it currently seems, a generation from now the Middle East might well include a new Kurdish nation-state, which could have a profound effect on the regional power balance. Hundreds of other nations may share similar aspirations. One study identified over 260 ethnic groups that could qualify for sovereignty, of which more than 50 had separatist movements and 20 were fighting for independence.[3]

The more states there are in the international system, the more potential problems, particularly if the new nation-states carry deep animosities toward the nation-states which formerly suppressed them. If so, in the future we could return full circle to an era of international wars.

To understand the forces of nationalism and multinationalism, we must understand the vessels which give them meaning—culture, ideology, nation, state, and nation-state. Although we tend to use these words interchangeably, they differ conceptually. A state is a political entity, a nation-state is a political entity with sovereignty, and a nation is primarily a population with a common culture, language, history, and ideals. Ideologies are systems of beliefs, behavior, and institutions which can span nations. This chapter will explore these concepts and their impact on international relations.

CULTURE

The word culture conjures up a host of images. The popular view of culture is one of symphony orchestras and art museums attended by wealthy, snobbish patrons. In every society, a few privileged people are "cultured," most are not. In reality, although culture is associated with museums, galleries, and concert halls, we are all constantly immersed in a culture, whether we are aware of it or not. Everyone is part of a predominant culture, and often partly shaped by many others as well. Culture shapes everything we see, do, think, feel, and even dream. Von Laue asserts that "culture, like the individual mind, is a complex universe of which the major part is hidden in the vast recesses of the subconscious."[4]

Culture is any group's distinct collective means of interpreting and interacting with the world and each other within a given environment. More specifically, culture is a group's integrated, distinct system of values, ethics, behavior patterns, history, and language which are in turn reflected in that group's social, economic, and political institutions. Cultures are not isolated. Every culture borrows from and lends to others; generally the more dynamic and successful a culture, the more it exchanges with other cultures. Yet, despite this exchange, a culture's essential values must remain largely unchanged in order for it to survive.

People are born into a culture and from birth are constantly socialized into that culture's values, ethics, behavior and so on. The family provides the individual's most important *socialization* experience. Babies join families with a certain socioeconomic level, composition (single- or two-parent, number of children, extended or nuclear),

Table 4.1
Nationalities of the Former Soviet Republics

Republic (Old Name)	Area (1,000 sq. mi.)	Population (millions)	National Groups* (2% or greater)	Heritage
Armenia	11.6	3.3	90% Armenian; 5% Azeri (Azerbaijani); 2% Russian, 2% Kurdish	Indo-European
Azerbaijan	33.6	.7.3	78% Azeri; 8% Russian; 8% Armenian	Turkic
Belarus (Byelorussia)	80.3	10.4	79% Belarussian; 12% Russian; 4% Polish, 2% Ukrainian	Slavic
Estonia	45.1	1.6	62% Estonian; 30% Russian	Finno-Karelian
Georgia	27.0	5.5	69% Georgian; 9% Armenian; 9% Russian; 5% Azeri; 3% Ossetian; 2% Abkhazian	Caucasus-Aryan
Kazakhstan	1,048.7	17.0	40% Kazakh; 38% Russian; 6% German, 6% Ukrainian; 2% Tatar	Turkic-Mongol
Kyrgyzstan (Kirghizia)	76.8	4.5	52% Kyrgyz; 22% Russian; 13% Uzbek; 3% Ukrainian; 2% German; 2% Tatar	Turkic-Mongol
Latvia	64.6	2.7	54% Latvian; 33% Russian; 5% Belarussian	Balt
Lithuania	65.2	3.8	80% Lithuanian; 9% Russian; 8% Polish	Balt
Moldova (Moldavia)	13.4	4.4	64% Moldovan; 14% Ukrainian; 13% Russian; 4% Gagauzi; 2% Bulgarian	Romanian
Russia	6,591.0	148.9	83% Russian; 4% Tatar; 3% Ukrainian	Slavic
Tajikistan (Tadzhikistan)	55.2	5.5	59% Tajik; 23% Uzbek; 10% Russian; 2% Tatar	Aryan-Persian
Turkmenistan	188.4	3.8	68% Turkmeni; 13% Russian; 9% Uzbek; 3% Kazakh	Turkic
Ukraine	233.1	52.0	74% Ukrainian; 21% Russian	Slavic
Uzbekistan	172.5	21.0	69% Uzbek; 11% Russian; 4% Kazskh; 4% Tajik; 4% Tatar; 2% Karakalpal	Turkic-Mongol

*Because of post-independence migrations, figures are approximate.

Data sources: Based on *Journal of Soviet Nationalities* (Spring 1990), pp. 150–53. *New York Times,* August 29, 1991, p. A19 and September 1, 1991, Section 4, p. 2; *Time,* September 9, 1991, pp. 18–19. Kegley, Wittkopf, *International Relations,* 1994.

ethnicity, religion, and set of values. Usually the family's belief system reflects society's prevailing culture. Other forces are important in deepening the individual's socialization, including the school, neighborhood, workplace, mass media, peers, and government.

Ideally all of these socialization forces work together to socialize individuals with the same or similar cultural values. Sometimes these socializing institutions represent different cultures, and the individual may be torn between conflicting values and expectations. People born into an immigrant family might receive both the culture of their parent's ancestry and that of the new country. Sometimes there is a discrepancy between a society's ideals and the behavior of its institutions and individuals. A culture's socializing forces can be offset by an individual's exposure to violence, injustice, corruption, socioeconomic exploitation, and unfulfilled expectations, or defeat in war which could discredit the institutions or even values of the dominant culture.

There are no truly monocultural nations. Even nation-states like Iceland, Portugal, Bangledesh, Korea, and Japan have some *subcultures*. For example, although Japan is considered a "homogenous" culture, there are ethnic subcultures such as the Okinawans, Koreans, Chinese, and Ainu which speak Japanese yet whose ancestry represents a different national culture, and social subcultures such as the untouchable class (burakumin), atomic bomb victims (hibakusha), and mixed race people (konketsujin) which the dominant culture has set aside and often discriminates against.

Although culture is most commonly used to distinguish between nations, we can talk about cultures that embrace several nations or are national subcultures. Examples of supranational cultures are "Western culture" or "Far Eastern culture," in which different nationalities share some basic values, ethics, institutions, and history, if not language. Likewise, a nation can have many subcultures which are variations of the national culture.

IDEOLOGY

Human behavior is shaped by ideals. We believe or do not believe certain things and then act accordingly. We are all, to varying degrees, prisoners of the belief systems which permeate, shape, and constrain our societies. As we have seen, cultures are, in part, belief systems.

Ideologies are more systematic belief systems which can transcend a given culture. Political philosophies like liberal democracy, communism, or fascism are ideologies, as are religions, nations, and cultures. The essence of every ideology is a value system which determines that society's prevailing patterns of behavior, organization, goals, and policies. Some ideologies prescribe relatively strict sets of ideals and behavior, such as communism and fascism, while others like liberal democracy are more permissive.

Individuals are not born with ideologies; as with cultures, individuals are socialized into an ideology. Individuals socialized the same way in the same ideology may vary considerably in how strong a hold that ideology has on them. Some individuals rigidly adhere to their world view and reject any information that runs counter to their beliefs, a condition known as "cognitive dissonance." Some individuals are relatively open-minded and can "empathize" with the situations and perspectives of others. Each individual is a unique mix of natural intelligence, aptitude, interests, humor, personality, ambitions, and experiences, all of which shape that individual's own version of his society's ideology, and sometimes result in the individual adopting a completely different ideology.

Why do ideologies, or any belief system, have such a strong hold on us? Our minds are not open enough to see the world, let alone understand it, as it really is. Instead, our minds are selective; they grab bits of reality and give us the illusion that we are seeing the whole picture rather than just simple impressions. Ideologies help our minds make that selection process. As a system of related values, attitudes, beliefs, and behavior, ideologies give individuals a systematic way to see the world and their place in it. Ideologies bring order to a chaotic world in which we are bombarded with thousands of bits of often conflicting information every conscious and subconscious second.

Yet, ideologies have their drawbacks. While they provide us with a systematic way of seeing the world, ideologies can also limit our ability to see the world in different ways or understand it as it really is. Individuals raised in a liberal democratic society, for example, have trouble understanding the world through a Communist's eyes, and vice versa. And ideologies like communism and fascism, whose values demand the subjugation of the individual to the state, are particularly susceptible to the abuse of power and sometimes even genocide.

A comprehensive ideology asks and then answers a set of important, interrelated questions.[5] 1) Human Nature: What is the nature of humans? Basically good, bad or mixed? Are we shaped mostly by nature or nurture? How does human nature affect politics?

2) Roles: What are the respective roles and responsibilities of government, society, and the individual? Which needs should take precedence—society's or the individual's?

3) Law: What is the nature and role of law in society? Are there some laws, such as the Constitution, that are fixed or is everything open to question and change?

4) Human Rights: What rights do individuals enjoy? How much liberty? How much equality? What limits if any should be placed on human rights?

5) Power: How is power organized? How is the power distribution justified? How powerful are the powerholders? How are leaders selected? What limits their power?

6) Justice: What is it? How does the system guarantee it?

7) Goals: What is the purpose of society? Of government? What are the society's ideals? How are those ideals best achieved?

8) Institutions: What are the best political, economic, and social institutions for fulfilling society's ideals?

NATION

What then is a nation? A nation is a people with a common culture, ideology, language, traditions, and history, or, as John Stoessinger put it "a people's sense of collective destiny through a common past and the vision of a common future."[6] The most important distinction between a nation and a culture is that a nation must be believed to be realized. One can be part of a culture and not be aware of it. To be part of a nation, the individual must recognize that relationship. People cannot be nationalistic if they are not aware they are part of a nation. Self-identity depends upon context. We define ourselves by what we are not and identify with those who share similar characteristics. In traditional societies the primary loyalty was to the village. Advanced communications and transportation allows individuals to identify with those sharing a similar culture over large areas. Thus, nationalism, the political assertion of one's national identity, independence, and interests, is a modern phenomenon, a result of a people with a common culture, language, ideology, tradition, and history becoming aware of that reality, and acting on that awareness. National identity can only occur after a people has achieved certain levels of socioeconomic, technological, and political development. Nations do not necessarily have to be included within the same territory or legally defined—in fact most are not. Where was the nation of Israel before the sovereign state was created in 1948? Where does the Palestinian nation exist today? The answer is in the minds of those two peoples.

The first nation-states which achieved mass national identity were Great Britain, the Netherlands, the United States, and France. During the 1820s, nationalism swept away Spanish and later Portugese rule from most of Latin America. During the mid-nineteenth century, political unification for Germany and Italy, and revolution in Japan succeeded in creating modern mass national states, while nationalism was fermenting in dozens of other nation-states in Europe and elsewhere. The 1919 Versailles Peace Conference and President Wilson's call for "national self-determination" stimulated nationalism among colonial peoples. The imperial powers were able to suppress these independence movements until after World War II, when one by one new countries emerged from the ruins of former empires.

Nationalism can be either a powerfully constructive or destructive force in international relations. Nationalism by definition means a unified, mobilized, loyal population which governments can deploy for development or aggression. Nationalism can be expressed either through liberal democracy in which the state's purpose is to guarantee individual rights and democratic processes, or statism in which the state personifies the nation's glories and all citizens are mobilized for the state. Nationalists are committed toward putting national interests ahead of all others—individual, group, or international. In identifying so powerfully with one's own national interests, individuals can be indifferent to the needs of other peoples. Nationalism often promotes feelings of superiority over or fear of others, which can damage international relations. At worst, nationalism can lead to the frenzied expansionism of fascist Japan, Germany, and Italy, which resulted in the deaths of over 50 million people between 1931 and 1945.

STATES, NATION-STATES, AND SOVEREIGNTY

States are almost as old as humankind and its cultures. The first states emerged from the first attempts of small groups of people to divide political responsibilites, establish formal rules, and designate leadership among themselves. Since then, as cultures became more complex and often encompassed other cultures, states have come in all shapes and sizes, from the city-states of the ancient Greeks and Renaissance Italy, to the huge empires of Rome, China, and Persia, to the democracy of Athens or many native American Indian tribes, to the depotism of Czarist Russia or Tokugawa Japan, to the religious and political responsibilites shared by the Roman Catholic Church and the Holy Roman Empire.

Nation-states are products of the modern world; while any political entity can be a state, nation-states must by definition be sovereign. The first nation-states emerged with the Treaty of Westphalia of 1648, which ended the Thirty Years War between Protestant and Catholic princes and kings. The Thirty Years War was the culmination of 130 years of religious warfare sparked by Martin Luther's rebellion against the Pope in 1517. Henceforth, according to the Westphalia Treaty, each prince had the sovereign right to decide his state's religious preferences (cuius regio eius religio), a principle that had first been articulated with the Peace of Augsburg in 1555, but was now made irrevocable. The 1,200 year religious and secular power of Rome was destroyed along with the feudal world of decentralized power beholden to a far away ruler with limited but ultimate secular power (suzerainty). Through imperialism, diplomacy, and decolonization, Europe's nation-state system was eventually extended throughout the world.

Sovereignty thus depends on a government having the highest authority within a clearly defined territory encompassing a population, and that authority is recognized as legitimate by both its inhabitants and other sovereign governments. Sovereign states are considered equal in status according to international law, and have basic rights and responsibilities. One basic right according to international law is that every nation-state should be free to run its internal affairs as its government sees fit. This right is also a responsibility in that no nation-state can interfere in the internal affairs of others. Regardless of whether a nation-state's inhabitants are citizens or residents, they must all follow that government's laws. As Hedley Bull put it, sovereignty includes both "internal sovereignty, which means supremacy over all other authorities within that territory and population . . . and external sovereignty, by which is meant not supremacy but independence of outside authorities."[7]

Throughout the modern era, political philosophers, rulers, and politically active people have agreed that sovereignty is the right to assert supreme authority over a realm. Where that sovereignty lies, however, has been hotly debated. A succession of political philosophers—Jean Boudin (1530–1596), Hugo Grotius (1583–1645), and Thomas Hobbes (1588–1679)—explored the concept of sovereignty and argued that sovereignty, or the highest authority, should reside in the king. In 1571, Jean Boudin defined sovereignty as "surpreme power over citizens and subjects, unrestrained by law."[8] Later political philosophers John Locke (1632–1704), Charles Louis Montesquieu (1689–1755), Jean Jacques Rousseau (1712–1778), Thomas Paine (1737–1809), Thomas Jefferson (1743–1826), and others—rejected the concept of a monarchy with absolute sovereign powers and instead argued that sovereignty should be based in the people. Despite their differences, starting with Hobbes' *Leviathan* (1651), all these political philosophers shared the idea that the state resulted from a "social contract" between ruler and ruled, in which the latter granted authority to the former in return for security and justice. Thus, the state is a legal abstraction like a corporation in which its citizens or subjects are shareholders, as well as a concrete reality. The concept of popular sovereignty has become universal. Today, in virtually every country, sovereignty theoretically lies with the people who are "citizens" rather than "subjects." Each nation-state has a constitution which articulates the political system's sovereign purpose, values, and organization.

Once recognized, however, sovereignty is not absolute. Traditionally, a state was considered sovereign only if it could defend itself. Thus, imperialism—the conquest of one state by another—was considered just. Sovereign Poland was conquered and divided among Russia, Prussia, and Austria in 1796. The European powers, later joined by the United States and Japan, used this principle to justify conquering hundreds of nations around the world throughout the modern era.

States could gain as well as lose their sovereignty through armed struggle. Starting with America's War of Independence against Great Britain in 1776, increasing numbers of states achieved their independence through revolt. After 1945, although some colonies continued to win their freedom through bloodshed, most have achieved it by the imperial power voluntarily granting it in the face of mass political movements within the colony, international pressure, and the growing liability of maintaining an empire. Between 1989 and 1991, the sovereign states of Yugoslavia and the Soviet Union disintegrated into many.

Just because a state is recognized as sovereign by some, does not mean that it is recognized by all. For example, a state's membership in the United Nations depends on the Security Council and a majority in the General Assembly recognizing that state's sovereignty. Some states appear to have the prerequisites for sovereignty yet are not recognized by other nation-states. For instance, although Moscow and Pretoria created "republics" within their respective countries, virtually no other countries recognized them as such. The governments of the fifteen Soviet "Republics" and six South African "Homelands" were clearly not the highest authority—real power resided in Moscow and Pretoria, respectively.

Revolutionary change in which a government is overthrown and a new regime installed sometimes poses problems of international recognition. Many countries may favor waiting for a while before they extend diplomatic recognition to the new regime. For example, after the 1949 communist revolution in China, the United States continued to recognize the government in exile in Taiwan rather than the Communist government which ruled all of the mainland. In 1971, the United States established informal relations (de facto) with China, and in 1979 granted full legal recognition (de jure) to the Beijing regime. In contrast to the United States, Great Britain follows a policy of recognizing whatever regime is in power, regardless of whether or not it is politically or morally compatible. Thus, London officially recognized the Communist Party as China's legitimate government in January 1950.

In a world of sovereign states, international relations are by definition anarchical. If not a constant "war of all against all," international relations are certainly shaped by constant conflict as each state pursues its selfish interests often to the detriment of other nation-states. Each nation-state is solely responsible for its own protection, often leading to a "security dilemma" in which the military and other preparations a nation-state takes to protect itself from potential aggressors in turn potentially threatens the security of other states, thus leading them to take similar precautions and exacerbating the arms race. Steps taken to ensure the security of one nation-state may lead to the insecurity of others.

Theoretically all nation-states enjoy independence and equality. In reality, no nation-states are equal in status, power, or even rights, and the sovereign power of nation-states to act as they will within their borders, to varying extents, is severely eroded. Sovereign power is not enough. Although nation-states are theoretically equal they differ profoundly in power and its territorial, population, economic, technological, financial, cultural, and military components. The more powerful a country, and the more skillfully a government wields its nation's power, the more easily it can safeguard and expand its national interests. Likewise, although the international norm of sovereignty theoretically empowers states with independence, in an anarchical world states must ultimately defend themselves. Without a world police force, the stronger nation-states can often get away with exploiting the weaker nation-states.

Nation-states vary in population size from such behemoths as China and India with 1.2 billion and 875 million people, respectively, to such microstates as Nauru with 7,000 people. They vary in territory from continental sized powers like Russia, the United States, and Canada to tiny states like once again Nauru, Vanuatu, or the Cook Islands. Thirty-eight nation-states, or one-fifth of the world's total, have a combined population of only 10,668,000. Many of these microstates have given up some of their sovereignty in return for economic and political security. For example, the Republic of the Marshall Islands and the Federated States of Micronesia have signed a Compact of Association with the United States, giving Washington responsibility for their defense and foreign affairs. Monaco and Liechtenstein have granted to France and Switzerland, respectively, the rights to manage their defense and diplomacy.

Sovereignty means one country cannot interfere in another's internal affairs. In reality, despite the conceptual persistence of sovereignty and the lack of a world government, there are numerous and expanding webs of constraints on a state's foreign and domestic policies. The growing body of international law imposes clear restraints on a government's action not only toward other nation-states but even within its own borders. International law condemns both a government's aggression against other nation-states and against its own people. Iraqi President Saddam Hussein was cited not just for ordering his armies to invade neighboring Kuwait, but for his brutal repression of Kurdish and Shi'ite separatists within Iraq itself. The United Nations sanctioned international forces led by the United States to expel Iraq from Kuwait, and later to extend security and humanitarian aid to the Kurds and Shi'ites.

MULTINATIONALISM

Although the United States is often seen as a vast mosaic of diverse ethnic, racial, and cultural groups, it is actually one of the world's most unified nations. Like the United States, all of the five largest European countries—France, Great Britain, Germany, Italy, and Spain—have distinct racial, linguistic, ethnic, and religious minorities. London, Berlin, and Paris are just as much a mosaic of different subcultures as New York. Which country is more ethnically divided—the United States or France with its large Breton and Corsican minorites, Great Britain with its Welsh, Scots, and Irish, or Spain with its Basques? The American South, Southwest, California, and New England have distinct regional identities, although none today is separatist, and all mesh within a common American culture. Contrast America's relative regional unity with the immense regional, linguistic, and cultural differences between north and south Italy and Germany, or between Catalonia and the rest of Spain. Countries like Great Britain, the United States, Spain, Germany, and France are considered multiethnic rather than multinational. These nations have a range of distinct subcultures, some of which originated in another nation but have largely assimilated or blended into the values, language, behavior, and so on of the dominant culture.

However, about 90 percent of existing nation-states actually are multinational states, including such advanced industrial states as Canada, Belgium, and Switzerland and less developed states like Nigeria, India, Mexico, and Fuji, to name a few. Many believe that ideally every nation should have its own sovereign state. The United Nations enshrines the ideal of "self-determination for all peoples" whether its members choose to recognize a particular people or not. In 1992, the United Nations General Assembly passed a "Declaration of Rights of Indigenous Peoples," to help protect the estimated 300 million indigenous peoples living in more than 70 countries. Indigenous peoples are the original inhabitants of a land which was invaded and conquered by another people. Self-determination does not necessarily mean separation, but the right of those peoples to pursue their traditional way of life without interference from the culture.

Some multinational nation-states have stayed together while others have been torn apart by civil war. Switzerland, Belgium, and Canada are examples of multinational nation-states which have, to date, remained intact despite intranational conflicts. The glue that holds diverse peoples together consists of many ingredients. The same ingredients that form a cohesive nation can shape a cohesive multination—a shared history, culture, economy, language, ideals, government, laws, and goals.

Governments attempt to create a common identity out of many different nationalities. In multinational nation-states people's loyalties often become divided between their national identity and the supranational identity promoted by the nation-state. For example, with what culture does a French-Canadian identify more—Québécois, French, or Canadian? The answer would vary considerably from one French-Canadian to the next. Although there is a separatist movement, only 41.4 percent of voters in the 1980 referendum favored an independent Quebec. In 1992, Canadians voted "no" in a referendum which would have granted more autonomy to Quebec and some other regional and ethnic groups.

How do you create a new identity without destroying old ones? One way is to stress common purpose and values. There is a close relationship between policy, stability, and prosperity. The more politically stable a country, the more prosperous and vice versa. Countries cannot enjoy political economic development without constructive, farsighted government policies designed to create and distribute wealth and power as equitably as possible both among and within the nations it rules.

Since the early 1950s, Western Europeans have attempted to create an ever more integrated economic and political union with a capital at Brussels. There are now 12 nation-states and 345 million people in the European Union. In addition to deepening these political and economic institutions, Brussels is attempting to build a European "nation." These efforts have brought a mixed success. Although surveys indicate that over the past forty years increasing numbers of Europeans are identifying with the concept of being European, few seem willing to abandon their national identity. Throughout 1992, each of the Union's member states voted on whether or not to ratify a new treaty which would give them one currency and central bank by 1999 at the latest. Denmark's vote against the treaty in June caused a crisis which Brussels only overcame by allowing Denmark to accede to the treaty, but to opt out of some objectionable measures. Europeans are evenly divided on the question of greater economic unity, and few are willing to exchange their primary loyalty to the nation they were born into for the more abstract "nation" of Europe. At best, Europeans will increasingly accept European identity as secondary to their real nation.

The nation-building problems for newly independent countries are often much more severe than those of Europe. European identity is shaped by widespread literacy, high living standards, and mass media which help different nationalities empathize with each other and search for a common identity. Newly independent underdeveloped countries lack the mass literacy, high living standards, and mass media with which to forge another identity.

Language is one of the more important sources of common identity and purpose, and is a divisive force in multinations. English or French remains the official language for several scores of countries around the world long after they have achieved independence. Why do these countries not adopt one of their native languages as their official language rather than retain the colonial master's tongue? The answer is the neutrality of English or French.

Nigeria and India have both chosen to retain English as their official language. With 90 million people, Nigeria is Africa's most populous country. Although there are over 260 dialects spoken, Nigeria's different cultures can be grouped into Yoruba, Hausa, and Ibo. Seven years after Nigeria achieved independence in 1960, the Ibo nation tried to gain independence and form the Republic of Biafra. Over the next 3 years of civil war, 1.5 million people died from fighting and starvation. The Biafran independence movement was finally crushed in 1970.

India has 14 major language groups and 1,600 dialects! Although 85 percent of the population is Hindu, there are large, concentrations of Muslims (12 percent of population) and Sikhs (1 percent) which have demanded either outright separation as in Muslim Kashmir and Assam, or increased autonomy as in Sihk Punjab. If India adopted one of the 14 languages spoken in the country to be official it would offend the hundreds of millions of speakers of the other 13 languages which were not official. Those who spoke the one official language would have a political, economic, and social advantage over those who do not. Large parts of India are already torn by religious and ethnic strife. To make one native language official could well tear India apart.

Independence movements gain adherents when minority national groups feel they are being discriminated against or exploited by the majority. Like communism's collapse, the Soviet Union's breakup in 1990 and 1991 was inevitable, the only question was when. The Soviet Union was simply another name for the Russian empire; the 14 non-Russian Soviet "republics" were in effect Moscow's colonies. Russians were exactly 50 percent the Soviet population, with another 20 percent Slavic Ukranians and Belorussians, 20 percent Muslim Kazakhs, Azerbaijanis, Kirghiz, Turkmen, Uzbeks, Tadjiks, and others, about 3 percent Christian minorities like the Baltic Estonians, Latvians, and Lithuanians, and Caucasus Georgians and Armenians, and 1 percent Romanian Moldavians. In addition, there were hundreds of much smaller cultures.

A vast totalitarian state apparatus and communist ideology allowed the Russian Empire (as the USSR) to remain intact generations after other great empires—the Austro-Hungarian, Ottoman, British, French, and others—had crumbled. Moscow's totalitarian political, economic, and social controls had steadily loosened and its communist ideology had become increasingly discredited over the forty years following Stalin's death in 1953. It took President Gorbachev's policies of openness (Glasnost), restructuring (Perestroika), and democracy to finally topple the tottering empire. But unlike the breakup of other empires, Moscow's received its death blow when Russian President Boris Yeltsin declared his republic's independence from the Soviet empire, and the other republics followed suit.

Nationalism has replaced communism as the raison d'être of the new nation-states. Yet, independence has not solved a range of political, economic, ethnic, and environmental problems. Like other fallen empires, the broken pieces of the Soviet Union remain economically interdependent, the products of seven decades of centralized economic planning. Twelve of the former fifteen republics remain loosely tied through the Commonwealth of Independent States (CIS). Another problem is the Russian diaspora. Over 60 million Russians are scattered across the other former Republics, and the newly independent states are debating how to fit the Russians into their political, economic, and social life. Estonia arrived at a harsh solution. With nearly half of its population Russian, Estonia's government has ruled that only Estonians or those of other cultures who settled in the country before 1940 are allowed to be citizens. The law disenfranchises most of Estonia's Russian population. Russia and Ukraine are squabbling over who owns the Crimean Peninsula. Stalin handed over the Crimea from Russia to Ukraine in 1946, and now the Russians want it back from independent Ukraine.

Irredentism, or the problem of nations scattered among two or more nation-states, is often connected with the multinationalism problem. There are three types of irredentism. One pattern is when the government of one united nation claims that its compatriots in another state should be joined to it. For example, during the 1930s, Hitler followed an irredentist policy of uniting Germans living in surrounding countries like Austria, Czechoslovakia, and Poland with the Germans of Germany. The result of Hitler's ambitions, of course, was World War II.

More commonly, a nation divided among several nation-states desires its own sovereign state. The Kurdish people are scattered across parts of Turkey, Iraq, Iran, and Syria, and they have been struggling for independence for decades. Although the governments of the Middle East are bitterly opposed on virtually all issues, they are united in opposing any Kurdish independence. Likewise the Palestinians are divided across Israel, Lebanon, Syria, Jordan, and Egypt, while there are exiles in a dozen other countries. The Palestinian Liberation Organization (PLO) was founded in 1964 and dedicated to Palestinian independence. Originally the PLO favored the destruction of Israel and creation of a Palestinian state on its ruins. More recently, it has settled for a Palestine encompassing the West Bank of the Jordan River and Gaza Strip of lands occupied by Israel since the 1967 War. Israel's Likud Party, which ruled from 1975 to 1991, was adamantly opposed to any Palestinian autonomy let alone independence. When the Labor Party was elected in June 1991, it favored some Palestinian autonomy as part of its "land for peace" policy.

Finally, there is the Cold War problem where one previously united nation has been divided between communist and non-communist halves, and the halves want to become whole again, as in East and West Germany, East and West Austria, North and South Korea, and North and South Vietnam. The allies agreed to temporarily divide Germany, Austria, and Korea into occupation zones after the defeat of Germany and Japan. These divisions solidified with the Cold War and the fears of Moscow and Washington that reunification could lead to a government which joined the other side.

Vietnam was divided at the 17th parallel between a communist North and non-communist South at the Geneva Convention of 1954 where France granted the country independence.

After tough negotiations between the occupying powers, East and West Austria were rejoined in 1955 on the stipulation that the nation-state be neutral. Following Washington's advice, which feared a communist takeover, South Vietnam's government rejected holding elections as stipulated by the Geneva Convention. For two decades, South Vietnam battled a growing Communist insurgency backed by North Vietnam. The country was reunified in 1975 after the Saigon regime was conquered by North Vietnam. In 1986, Gorbachev renounced the Brezhnev Doctrine which justified Soviet military intervention in Communist countries experiencing a democratic revolution; in 1989, he allowed the Berlin Wall to be destroyed; and in 1990 he allowed East Germany to be reunited with West Germany. During the late 1980s, the governments of South and North Korea began negotiating their countries' reunification, but to date have made no progress. Reunification is unlikely unless one of the two Koreas experiences a revolution which brings to power a government similar to that in the other half. Most analysts say a revolution in either Seoul or Pyongyang is unlikely.

In no region are irredentist claims more possible than in Africa, in which only 1 of the 64 countries, Somalia, is not multinational. Tanzania President Julius Nyerere recognized this problem when he said that "African boundaries are so absurd that they need to be recognized as sacrosanct." He meant of course that Western imperialism had so arbitrarily and thoroughly divided African nations that any attempt to reorganize the continent along a "one-state, one-nation" principle would only result in chaos and war. The Organization of African States (OAS) has attempted to defuse any potential irredentist claims by declaring that Africa's present boundaries are inviolable. Somalia's claim to being one nation is no guarantee of order. In 1992, the country was torn apart by civil war and famine as rival groups fought for spoils and supremacy. It took the intervention of 20,000 soldiers in a UN peace keeping force to restore order and prevent genocide from starvation and murder.

NATIONALISM AND INTERNATIONALISM

Since the seventeenth century, nation-states have been the central players in international relations. In a world knit by thousands of international organizations and multinational corporations, is the nation-state becoming obsolete? Will nation-states become just one player among many on the global stage?

As we saw with Europeans, just because people are becoming more interdependent does not mean they are becoming more international. Individuals identify primarily with their respective nations rather than with humanity, and governments continue to put their perceived national interests before international interests, even though it is becoming increasingly difficult to distinguish between the two.

In the contemporary world, nationalism and *internationalism* both powerfully affect the world system. On the one hand, regions like Europe, North America, and Southeast Asia are attempting to forge closer international ties. People of different nationalities are becoming increasingly tied through foreign travel, television and radio, and the growth of problems like the greenhouse effect and ozone layer depletion which affect us all.

Elsewhere, nationalism is growing. While there are many nations in the world, few are synonymous with the nation-states in which they reside. Most of the world's nation-states are multinational. Nation-building has become the modern world's version of the philosopher's stone. The world's last great empire, the Russian, crumbled as much from growing nationalism as communism's failures. Yugoslavia is being torn apart as Croats, Slovenes, and Bosnians seek independence from the Serbian majority.

Interdependence will continue, although it is clear that nationalism will add more independent nation-states to the global system. The nation-state will remain the world system's most important unit. World government is unlikely for the foreseeable future.

STUDY QUESTIONS

1. What is culture?

2. What is an ideology?

3. What is a nation?

4. What is a nation-state?

5. What is socialization?

6. What is sovereignty, and how has the concept changed throughout the modern era? Why is sovereignty more an ideal than a reality?

7. How have nation-states coped with the problems of multinationalism?

8. What are the types of irredentism, and what are examples of irredentist conflicts?

9. In an increasingly interdependent world, is the nation-state becoming obsolete? Are there any viable alternatives?

ENDNOTES

1. Walter Connor, "Nation-building or Nation-destroying," in Fred Sondemann et al., eds. *The Theory and Practice of International Relations* (Englewood Cliffs, N.J.: Prentice-Hall, 1979).

2. John Clements, *Clements' Encyclopedia of World Governments,* vol. 7 (Dallas: Political Research, Inc., 1986); See such earlier similar studies as Walter Connor, "Nation-building or Nation-destroying," *World Politics,* vol. 24 1972, 319–355.

3. Ted Gurr and James R. Scarritt, "Minorities at Risk: A Global Survey," *Human Rights Quarterly,* vol. 11, 1989, 375–405; See also Ted Gurr, "Ethnic Warfare and the Changing Priorities of Global Security," *Mediterranean Quarterly,* vol. 1, 1990, 81–98.

4. Theodore Von Laue, *The Revolution of Westernization* (New York: Oxford University Press, 1987), 375.

5. Lyman Sargent, *Contemporary Political Ideologies* (Pacific Grove, Calif.: Brooks/Cole Publishing, 1990), 10–11.

6. John Stoessinger, *The Might of Nations* (New York: Random House, 1989), 10.

7. Hedley Bull, *Anarchical Society* (London: Macmillan, 1977), 8; See also Charles Tilly, *The Formation of Nation-states in Western Europe* (Princeton, N.J.: Princeton University Press, 1975); William H. McNeil, *The Pursuit of Power* (Chicago: University of Chicago Press, 1982); Hedley Bull and Adam Watson, ed., *The Expansion of International Society* (Oxford: Clarendon Press, 1984); Alan James, *Sovereign Statehood* (London: Allen & Unwin, 1986); Michael Mann, *States, War and Capitalism* (Oxford: Basil Blackwell, 1988); Yale Ferguson and Richard Mansbach, *The State, Conceptual Chaos, and the Future of International Relations* (Boulder, Colo.: Lynne Reiner Publishers, 1989); Charles Tilly, *Coercion, Capital, and European States, A.D. 990—1990* (Oxford: Basil Blackwell, 1990); Charles Gochman and Alan Ned Sabrosky, eds. *Prisoners of War? Nation-states in the Modern Era* (Lexington, Mass.: D.C. Heath, 1990).

8. For an interesting discussion, see George Sabine, *A History of Political Theory* (Hinsdale, Ill.: Dryden Press, 1973), chapter 21.

The Power and Wealth of Nations

Key Terms and Concepts

Balance of Power
Bipolar World
Compellence
Coordinating Committee
  on Export Controls
  (COCOM)
Defense
Dependence
Deterrence
Dumping
Economic Sanctions
Exchange Rate Comparison
  Method

Great Power
Gross National Product
  (GNP)
Gunboat Diplomacy
Imperial Overstretch
Intangible Power
Intelligence
Interdependence
Middle-Ranking Power
Multipolar World
Mutually Assured
  Destruction (MAD)
Neomercantilism

People's War
Per Capita Income
Politics
Power
Prestige
Propaganda
Purchasing Power Parity
  (PPP)
Security Dilemma
Small Power
Superpower
Tangible Power

Over five centuries of modernization, the manifestations of power have changed dramatically with new technologies, ideologies, political economic development and strategies, and various interdependencies. What aspects of power have changed and which have remained the same?

Hans Morgenthau maintained that: "International politics, like all politics, is a struggle for power. Whatever the ultimate aims of international politics, power is always the immediate aim."[1] Is Morgenthau right? Are all global politics essentially power struggles? Is the nature of power and international relations eternally fixed, or are their manifestations and patterns much more complex, subtle, and varied? Just what is *politics?* What is *power?* And what is the relationship between the two?

Politics and power are inseparable, but they are not synonymous. The essence of politics is conflict and the ways in which participants assert their respective interests in that conflict. Politics exists wherever the interests of two or more people or groups clash. Power, its distribution and the skill with which each side wields it, determines whether a conflict is resolved, managed, or deadlocked. Trade-offs, compromises, and cooperation are inevitable even in the most acrimonious or imbalanced of power relationships. Politics and power thus decide "who gets what, why, when, and how."[2] Political systems, whether on a local, national, or international level, are devised to manage politics and power.

Every political scientist seems to have his or her own definition of power. According to Morgenthau, power "may comprise anything that establishes and maintains control of man over man."[3] Robert Dahl calls power simply "the ability to shift the probability of outcomes."[4] Kenneth Waltz agrees partly with Dahl but adds that "politics is preeminently the realm of unintended and unexpected consequences . . . one is powerful to the extent that he affects others more than they affect him."[5] Karl Deutsch analyzes power in terms of its domain, range, and scope, in which a state's power domain includes both internal tangible and intangible resources as well as international contraints and opportunities on those power resources; its power range includes the spectrum and severity of coercion and persuasion a state could employ against its opponent; and power scope encompasses just what the state wishes to achieve, and the domain and range of power which it wields to achieve those goals.[6]

Power, essentially, can be two things: (1) the ability of an individual or group to mobilize appropriate resources to get others to do things that they otherwise would not do or refrain from doing things they intended to do (Morgenthau, Dahl, Deutsch); and (2) the inadvertent impact of individuals or groups on others (Waltz).

Power is often described as a type of currency. States want something and they use power to "buy" it, which can simply be more power. Some countries spend their power wisely, investing it in ways that enhance their abilities and goals; others dissipate it in wasteful consumption or projects; and yet others miserly accumulate it while rarely using it.

Power is relative. The power of one individual, group, nation, or alliance depends on that of others with which it has conflicting interests. Mexico is economically and militarily weak when compared to the United States and economically and militarily strong when compared to Guatemala. National power varies widely from one issue to the next. Every state faces a different distribution of power and interests for every different issue with which it is involved. The distribution of power is ever-changing. The United States has continued to grow economically, but at a much slower rate than its rivals, and thus America's power has declined accordingly. Finally, power is relative to a government's perception of and ability to achieve its nation's interests. If a government is too ambitious and wants, for example, a massive expansion of territory or economic growth and cannot get it, then it is relatively powerless. States with far less ambitious but easily obtainable goals can be considered relatively powerful. Even the smallest of states in territory, population, wealth, natural resources, or military forces can be considered powerful if it achieves its goals.

How is power asserted? To many, power's bottom line is simply the ability to hurt others more than they can hurt you or, in international terms, the ability to successfully wage war. Yet the most obvious assertions of power—holding a gun to another's head and demanding money or marching an army to another's frontier and demanding territory—are the least common. Power is manifested in many ways, of which military force is perhaps the least cost effective in advancing national interests. Most power is wielded much more subtly. Power spans everything from rational or emotional persuasion to the most brutal forms of coercion and violence. Power is the ability to give as well as to take away. States can offer others incentives—alliances, open markets, economic aid, technology, etc.—to change their behavior.

And sometimes the assertion of power is unintended, as when an economic recession in the United States causes depression in poorer countries economically dependent on the United States. In this chapter we will concentrate on power consciously deployed by states to achieve goals.

Logic, bribes, and threats are the three ways in which power can be wielded.[7] Logic involves persuading the one side to concede through the force of argument or emotion. Bribes are given to other sides to change their behavior. Threats are made and sometimes acted upon to force the opponent to give in. The more of these means a state employs in a conflict, the greater its chance of prevailing. For example, Washington's efforts to rebuild the global political economy during and after World War II involved logic, bribes, and threats. Washington used the logic of liberal economic theory to convince the West Europeans that it was in everyone's interest for them to slowly liberalize and integrate their economies, and it sweetened that logic with the bribe of the Marshall Plan which dispensed over $14 billion in economic aid to help rebuild the continent. Finally, the United States used military threats to deter the Soviet Union from disrupting or possibly invading West Europe.

States can use threats to defend, deter, or compel others, in which:

> *compellence is an attempt to force someone to give up something he or she values. Deterrence is designed to convince someone not even to try to engage in compellence, owing to the adverse consequences that such an effort would create. Defense is an action taken to protect oneself when an opponent ignores or fails to understand one's deterrent efforts and initiates the act of compellence anyway. Under such circumstances, defense usually centers on the ability to defeat the opponent in a trial of strength.*[8]

Thus, in a conflict in which threats are made, one side attempts to compel and the other side attempts to deter, and if that fails, defend against that compellence.

It is relatively easy to tell when defense or compellence succeeds. It is difficult to evaluate deterrence, which demands that the status quo be maintained, and the claims for its success "must rest on assertions about why something did not happen."[9] For example, the United States created NATO and built up its conventional and nuclear forces to deter a possible Soviet attack on West Europe. Did America's deterrence strategy against the Soviet Union succeed? Certainly, the Soviets never attacked West Europe. But maybe Moscow never intended to do so even if West Europe were defenseless. In that case, the United States and NATO deterred nothing.

Every assertion of power must include several ingredients to increase the chance of success. A state must clearly communicate what it wants in a conflict, and the means by which it intends to get what it wants, whether that be logic, bribes, and/or threats. A state has a greater chance of success if its demands require its opponent to make relatively minor rather than major changes. In order to be taken seriously, a state must demonstrate both the capacity and will to employ the power it claims to possess. Obviously, the greater a state's relative capacity to punish another state, and the more determined it seems to use that capacity, the more credible its potential power. Finally, the credibility of a state's capacity and will must be communicated in a way that weakens rather than strengthens the opponent's resolve on the issue.

For example, in July 1990, Iraq threatened to invade Kuwait. The United States warned Iraq not to do so. On August 2, Iraqi armies invaded and quickly conquered Kuwait. Why did Baghdad disregard Washington's warning? The reasons are complex but essentially, although Baghdad surely understood Washington's military capacity to defeat Iraq, it judged that the United States did not have the will to back up its warning.

The U.S. Ambassador to Iraq, April Glaspie, made a vague, ambiguous, last-minute statement to President Hussein, which was interpreted as meaning that the United States valued its relationship with Iraq over anything Iraq did to Kuwait. Thus, the White House's attempts to deter an Iraqi attack were undermined by poor communication, which in turn damaged the credibility of America's threat. After deterrence failed, the Bush administration then had to attempt to compel Iraq to withdraw from Kuwait. Even then, after a six month buildup of American-led Coalition forces which eventually numbered over half a million troops, Hussein believed that Bush was bluffing and refused to withdraw until after the Coalition destroyed and forced the surrender of his army in Kuwait.

Power is both a means and an end. Ideally, each participant in a conflict marshals all the means at its disposal to protect or augment its respective interests. The winners often have their power enhanced so that they have a better chance of realizing their interests in future conflicts. Thus, states use power to win a struggle and attempt to enhance their power by their victory. The increased power might include a legal precedent, territorial gain, reparation, or reduction of the other side's power resources.

Power and wealth are virtually inseparable. Wealth is power's bottom line. The great powers have always been the great economic powers, although the distribution and source of that economic power has varied greatly. The wealthier a state, the more easily it can achieve its geopolitical and geoeconomic interests.

How is power measured? Power is rarely absolute; it is almost always offset by other powers. There is often a wide gap between a state's human and material resources and its ability to achieve its goals. States rarely mobilize all the resources at their disposal in any one conflict. A state's potential power may differ greatly from the power it actually employs in a conflict. Power cannot be truly measured until it is used.

Despite these difficulties, many analysts have tried to measure power.[10] Most equate economic and military size with potential power. Some analysts have devised more sophisticated comparative methods. Ray, for example, combined total population, urban population, steel production, energy consumption, military personnel, and military budget to rank the eight leading countries every five years from 1900 to 1985.[11] Sawyer measured 236 variables among 82 countries to determine whether a country was developed or developing, had an open or closed political economy, and was a large or small country, all of which helped determine that country's power.[12] The significance of such number crunching may be as difficult to determine as power itself. And the analysts only attempt to measure a state's potential power; the results tell nothing about how governments wield their resources to protect or enhance national interests.

THE PREREQUISITES OF NATIONAL POWER

Tangible Sources of Power

National power is based on a range of tangible or "hard" resources like relative GNPs, military forces, and technology, and intangible or "soft" factors like leadership, national cohesion, and political will. It is the intangible power sources that often decide the winner in a conflict between forces with relatively evenly matched tangible power. Yet, when many people think of power, they often think of tangible sources of power and believe bigger or more is better. Take population for example. If all other power factors are equal (which, of course, they never are), then one could argue that the most populous state is the most potentially powerful. The quality of a population, however, is more important than its quantity. China and India have the world's first and second largest populations, respectively, but their vast, poverty-stricken, poorly-educated peoples are a liability rather than an asset. There are simply too many people for the available land and resources, and both countries would be better off with half the number of people.

While one of every 5 people in the world is Chinese, Americans are only 1 in 20. Yet which country more consistently and decisively shapes the world's fate? The great powers have not necessarily been the most populous states. Portugal, the Netherlands, and Great Britain became leading European powers despite having populations well below those of France or Spain. However, for those nation-states with educated, prosperous, skilled populations, the larger the better. With 250 million and 125 million people, respectively, the United States and Japan enjoy huge markets within which their industries can achieve large scale production, profits, and wealth.

One might also think that the more natural resources a nation has, the better. But as with anything else, it depends. Fertile land bountiful enough to support one's population is always an important pillar of power. Traditionally and throughout the early modern era, nations with more natural resources usually had at least one advantage over those with less. Imperialism has often been motivated by the attempt of one state to seize the resources of another.

But the importance of directly owning vast realms of natural resources diminishes as the world becomes more interdependent. Many richly endowed countries concentrate on extracting rather than refining their resources. Often, as in Zaire, Indonesia, or Papua New Guinea, to name a few, the result is a capital intensive mining sector which brings great wealth to a few while much of the population remains mired at a subsistence level. In the short run, the mining, logging, or energy wealth can be used to support the rest of the economy. But over the long term those nonrenewable resources will inevitably become depleted. And even in more advanced countries like Germany and Belgium, coal or iron ore mining corporations can use their political clout to gain huge government subsidies long after their mines' viability has ended. As a result, the nation's competitiveness is weakened because its industries are required to buy the more expensive domestic resource rather than find the cheapest international source. For example, although Japanese complain frequently of their country's dearth of natural resources, Japanese industries actually benefit because they can search the world for the cheapest possible sources, which helps bring down their product's final costs. Armed with this enormous comparative advantage, Japanese firms can undercut their foreign rivals and reap enormous wealth for their country. Hanrieder captured very concisely the shift in how states view territory and resources: "access rather than acquisition, presence rather than rule, penetration rather than possession have become the important issues."[13]

A nation-state's location, topography, and climate can all enhance or detract from power. Size is important. A small state like Kuwait is easily overrun by enemies, while the vast lands of Russia and China have swallowed up most foreign invaders. Size, however, does not matter geoeconomically. Hong Kong and Singapore are small city-states with populations of only 5.5 million and 2.5 million, respectively. Yet both have prospered, while China and Russia have remained economic cripples. A country's terrain can affect a nation's power as well. Vast deserts or mountains, or extremes of heat and cold, or humidity and dryness can simultaneously impede potential invaders and national development. Simple accidents of topography can help seal the fate of nations. The shallow seas on the Netherland's coast prevented the Dutch navy from adopting the huge warships that might have enabled it to win its naval wars against Great Britain in the mid-seventeenth century.

A state's location is clearly important, but there is no consensus on what location is the most advantageous. Sir Halford Mackinder asserted that "he who rules Eastern Europe commands the Heartland of Eurasia; who commands the Heartland rules the World Island of Europe, Asia, and Africa; and who rules World Island commands the World."[14] The naval historian Alfred Mahan argued the opposite, that naval supremacy was the key to global power. Mahan wrote:

> if a nation be so situated that it is neither forced to defend itself by land nor induced to seek extension of its territory by way of land, it has, by the very unity of its aim directed upon the sea, an advantage as compared with a people whose boundaries are continental.[15]

Nicholas Spykman agreed with Mahan and argued that the industrialized rimland of Europe, the Middle East, and South and East Asia were the world's most important regions.[16] Spykman's theory, in turn, greatly influenced George Kennan's containment policy. History supports the Mahan rather than Mackinder thesis.

Geography has often protected the most powerful states. The power of England, Japan, the United States, Portugal, Spain, and Russia has clearly been enhanced by their existence on the fringe of power systems, either outright protected by an ocean moat or enjoying mountain ranges or vast steppes upon which to defend themselves or launch an attack. As island nations, Great Britain and Japan have natural moats protecting them from foreign invaders. With oceans east and west, and weak neighbors north and south of a vast territory, the United States has been blessed geopolitically and geoeconomically. In order to even contemplate invading the United States, an aggressor would need complete navy and air superiority; to march inland and occupy the United States would require millions of troops. Geoeconomically the United States benefits greatly from being the centerpiece of both the Atlantic and Pacific basin trade systems.

Intangible Sources of Power

"Soft" or intangible power like one's national cohesion and determination, culture, institutions, and world view can be as important as the "hard power" of tanks and missiles in achieving one's goals. While population, resources, and geography are power's raw materials, it is leadership and political economic systems which give them shape and purpose, and it is strategy and will which deploy and unleash them. History is filled with examples of states disadvantaged in population, resources, or geography besting much larger states. Israel, for example, with only a fraction of the land, people, and resources of its neighbors, has defeated alliances of surrounding Arab states in five wars.

Do individuals make history or does history make individuals? When many people think about history, the faces, words, and actions of famous leaders first come to mind. What would have been the world's fate if Churchill rather than Chamberlain were prime minister when Hitler marched into the demilitarized Rhineland in 1936 or demanded Czechoslovakia's Sudetenland in 1938? Leadership clearly can be a decisive factor. Yet, even the greatest leaders are prisoners of their time and place, shaped and limited by historic forces far beyond their control.

In any struggle, the balance of will may be more important than the balance of tangible resources. All other things being equal, a contest will go to the side which has more to lose and is more willing to sacrifice to prevent that loss.[17] The Venetian Republic was fourteenth century Europe's most dynamic power. But Venice's power declined rapidly after its access to Southeast Asian spices disappeared when the Ottoman Turks closed the land route through the Middle East. Why did Venice not emulate the Portugese, Spanish, and other powers which built and dispatched oceangoing ships to Southeast Asia via the route around Africa? Certainly Venice possessed the economic and technological skills to do so. What was missing, however, was the recognition of the threat to Venice's wealth and the political will to marshal all of its power to overcome that threat.

Power begins in the mind; its essence is psychological rather than material. Thus, power is best wielded through psychological rather than physical manipulation. The most effective use of power is the ability to get others to obey one's dictates unquestioningly. In national crises, people tend to set aside their internal conflicts and rally around the flag against the external threat. Governments have been known to provoke international conflicts just to divert internal conflicts. Why do most people tend to march off to war without wondering whether their government's position was right or wrong? Governments exert enormous education, mass media, and other resources to socialize a deep and unquestioning loyalty in their population toward the country and leadership.

However, the loyalty of populations to their government and country varies considerably. During World War II, when faced with imminent defeat, Japanese soldiers charged in vast human wave attacks and were often cut down by the defenders to the man, while at home Japanese women, old men, and children were armed with bamboo spears and grenades and trained to charge any American invaders. During the Persian Gulf War (1990–1991), the Iraqi army also faced with imminent defeat, deserted or surrendered by the thousands while large segments of the population rose in revolt against the Hussein government. In retrospect, however, the willingness of Japanese soldiers and civilians to toss away their lives without any chance of victory did not prevent Japan's defeat any more than Iraq's disloyal soldiers and civilians caused Iraq's defeat. Other power factors in both wars were much more important.

Prestige is having something few or no others have but want. Prestige involves both symbols and concrete accomplishments, and is both a sign and source of power. It is a reputation for success, for doing things most others cannot do. Prestige can come to countries which win wars; negotiate peace settlements; build nuclear bombs; put a person on the moon; enjoy high economic growth, productivity, literacy, and longevity, and low crime, inflation, and unemployment; or develop new technologies and products.

While prestige is clearly a sign of power, how is it a source? Prestige breeds prestige. States with less prestige are more likely to give in or not challenge states with more. A state with the capability and resolve to defend its interests will rarely be challenged. The power to deter is also the power of prestige. The perception by some states that another is powerful can become a self-fulfilling prophecy. The more powerful a state is perceived to be, the less likely others will challenge it and the more likely they will bow before it. It is often said that military power does not have to be used to be useful. Threatening a country with war can be enough to force concessions.

Yet, prestige can also be a constraint on power. The more prestige a state has to lose, the more careful a government will be in avoiding sticky situations where it can be easily lost. The United States lost enormous prestige, as well as 58,000 lives and $650 billion, in Vietnam. Resolved to avoid any further loss of prestige, the Pentagon has pressured presidents to avoid any wars in which the United States might be defeated militarily or politically.

Power ultimately may lie in the ability to affect how others see and act in the world. Setting the agenda and terms of the debate can be as important in helping to achieve one's goals as any other "power" one brings to the table. In 1920, a British historian, J.F.C. Fuller predicted that as mass communications improve warfare characterized by mass violence and death may eventually give way to:

a purely psychological warfare, wherein weapons are not even used or battlefields sought . . . but rather the corruption of the human reason, and dimming of the human intellect, and the disintegration of the moral and spiritual life of one nation by the influence of the will of another is accomplished.[18]

Fuller's vision has yet to be fulfilled. Totalitarian states have succeeded in destroying the will of others and replacing it with their own, but only against their own people and not against foreigners.

Education presents all sides of an issue; propaganda presents only one side. The most effective *propaganda* should not seem like propaganda. Propaganda based on facts is obviously more effective in the long-run than that based on falsehood, since outright lies can be disproved. The ability of governments to use powerful radio and television stations to beam propaganda to any spot on the globe is not a source of power if the message is rejected. To be effective, a message must appeal to an individual's identity, beliefs, and conscience. Eygptian President Nasser achieved ascendancy in the Arab world, in part by skillfull use of the "transistor revolution" to beam the message of Arab nationalism and unity under his leadership to surrounding states.

Traditionally, diplomats and government leaders met and negotiated only with their counterparts. Today and into the future, diplomats and government leaders can use the electronic and print media to directly address foreign populations. Government propaganda or public relations, is a vital part of international relations. Virtually all governments try to promote a favorable image of themselves and an unfavorable one of their foes. Much of the Cold War was a propaganda war. The United States Information Agency (USIA) was created in 1953 to help Washington win the public relations front of the Cold War. Washington has spent billions of dollars transmitting news and commentaries to communist countries through the Voice of America, Radio Liberty, and Radio Free Europe. To promote its own views and undermine those of the United States. The Soviet Union not only had Radio Moscow but bankrolled innumerable scholarly and news conferences, demonstrations, publications, advertisements, labor unions, student groups, and peace movements, to name the more prominent. Mass media includes not only the obvious means like newspapers, television, radio, journals, and magazines, but also posters, films, fliers, billboards, murals, monuments, museums, postage stamps, street names, and even rumors.[19]

Every government must have some means of gathering and analyzing information vital to understanding the capabilities and intentions of other states. Ideally, the better the *intelligence,* or understanding of what one's foes are doing, the better the policies to deal with those foes. By knowing another state's plans, a government can take measures to counteract those plans. While popular films and novels tend to focus on the real and imagined paramilitary activities of intelligence organizations like the CIA or KGB, the primary function of any intelligence organization is intelligence. Information, however, must often be obtained by illegal or unethical means, which often includes getting foreigners to betray their respective countries. Intelligence gathering and assessment is a difficult and risky business. Even the best funded and trained intelligence organizations equipped with the latest satellites and computers have trouble gathering and assessing all important information. And it is much easier to count weapons and military units than to assess motivations and plans. During the 1970s and 1980s, the CIA was criticized for failing to predict such important international events as the Iranian revolution in 1979, East European and Soviet revolutions starting in 1989, or the Iraqi invasion of Kuwait in 1990. Intelligence organizations must address all of the important threats and challenges which a country faces. During the 1990s, the CIA began to shift from its almost total emphasis on geopolitical conflict to an increasing attention to geoeconomic and environmental conflicts.

Religious or political ideals can be a vital power resource. Joseph Stalin once scornfully dismissed the Roman Catholic Church by asking how many divisions the Pope had. Yet, spiritual power can play a role in international politics. In 1979, fundamentalist Muslims dramatically shifted the power balance in the Persian Gulf when they overthrew the Shah and erected an Islamic theocracy. To varying extents, fundamentalist Muslim forces threaten every state in the Middle East and southwest and central Asia. The fundamentalists are fiercely anti-Western, and their possession of oil rich Persian Gulf states might dramatically affect the global economy.

Although many around the world do so, the French are particularly fond of condemning what they call "American cultural imperialism." Although there is no evidence of a secret Washington agency which forces peoples around the world to listen to Madonna or Michael Jackson, drink Coca-Cola, watch "Raiders of the Lost Ark," or injest other icons of American pop culture, their popularity can subtly aid the United States' pursuit of its overseas interests. Von Laue argues that:

> *cultural understanding is a matter of raw power; who has the power to make his own understanding prevail? Similarly, in all cross-cultural comparison, the question is: who compares himself to whom on whose terms? Who has the power to impose their own terms in the comparison? Who provides the premises of comparison?*[20]

In other words, when one state accepts willingly, unwittingly, or by force another state's cultural values and symbols, it makes itself vulnerable to the culturally more powerful state. For over five hundred years, international relations have been shaped by Western culture and power. The West has imposed its values and institutions on the rest of humanity. Since 1945, American mass culture has penetrated virtually every society around the world, providing a common language with which states interpret and negotiate their respective interests.

America's most potent source of cultural power, however, has not been its pop culture but its political philosophy. "Liberty," Paul Nitze wrote, "is the most contagious idea in history."[21] No country has more deeply explored or attempted to fulfill the concept of liberty than the United States. It was Washington which was largely responsible for ensuring that the Western conception of human rights was enshrined in the United Nations Charter and the 1948 Declaration of Human Rights, which every United Nations member is pledged to uphold. Traditionally, however, despite the United Nations' clear human rights standard, most countries scorned it. Recently, the elite and mass acceptance of human rights is growing and serves as an increasingly powerful check on state behavior. In response to international moral pressure, countries as diverse as Nicaragua, the Philippines, and Kampuchea have held United Nations sponsored elections, while South Africa eradicated apartheid and the Soviet Union allowed more Jewish emigration. The power balance between liberal democratic and authoritarian states is tipping decisively in favor of the former, and with it will come increased international cooperation, peace, and more subtle ways of wielding power.

GLOBAL WEALTH AND POWER

Modern history records a parade of great military powers whose reach was, for a while, global: Portugal, Spain, the Netherlands, France, Great Britain, the United States. What caused the rise, dominance, and fall of these great powers?

Paul Kennedy argues that national power is rooted ultimately in economic, technological and organizational prowess:

> there exists a dynamic for change, driven chiefly by economic and technological developments, which then impact upon social structures, political systems, military power, and the position of individual states and empires. The speed of this global economic change has not been a uniform one, simply because the pace of technological innovation and economic growth is itself irregular . . . different regions and societies across the globe have experienced a faster or slower rate of growth, depending not only upon the shifting patterns of technology, production, and trade, but also upon their receptivity to the new modes of increasing output and wealth . . . military power rests upon adequate supplies of wealth, which in turn derive from a flourishing productive base, from healthy finances, and from superior technology . . . major shifts in the world's military-power balances have followed alterations in the productive balances.[22]

Thus, military victory, more often than not, rests ultimately on which side can devise, build, and sell a better mousetrap.

Imperial overstretch ultimately defeated one great power after another. There are interesting parallels between the respective declines of Spain and the United States.

Between the 1560s and 1648, Spain fought continually to crush the Netherlands's independence, an effort that proved as debilitating to Madrid as Washington's much shorter venture in Vietnam. By the early 1600s, Spain had exhausted itself financially and psychologically from the costs of conquering and holding its American empire and defending its European territories. With the 1648 Treaty of Westphalia, Spain not only signed away its claims to European territory beyond the Pyrenees but largely withdrew from European affairs and concentrated its efforts on administering and exploiting the Americas.

Why did Spain cling to its possessions long after it was clear that they were economic liabilities rather than benefits? Spain's Philip IV argued that:

although the war which we have fought in the Netherlands has exhausted our treasury and forced us into debts that we have incurred, it has also diverted our enemies in those parts so that, had we not done so, it is certain that we would have had war in Spain or somewhere nearer.[23]

Madrid feared that if it lost Flanders it would inevitably lose its German, Italian, and even American possessions. For decades, Spain's Army of Flanders cost one quarter of Madrid's budget.[24] Yet, the costs did not seem exorbitant because Spain could always pay them with American silver—at least until the mines began to be exhausted in the 1630s. This outlook differed little from the domino theory that led the United States into the quagmire of Vietnam. President Johnson succinctly captured the domino theory: "If we don't stop the Reds in South Vietnam, tomorrow they will be in Hawaii, and next they will be in San Francisco."[25]

Kennedy argues that, debilitating as these endless wars were, "at the center of Spanish decline . . . was the failure to recognize the importance of preserving the economic underpinnings of a powerful military machine."[26] Ironically, in 1492, the same year it financed Columbus' voyage, Spain expelled the Jews from its kingdom. Through their financial and commercial ventures, the Jews had contributed enormous wealth to Spain and expelling them crippled Spain's economic vitality.[27] Spain failed to reinvest the great wealth it extracted from its American empire into productive industries within Spain, which would create new wealth long after the American mines were depleted.

Yet, American silver paid only one quarter of Spain's budget; the rest had to be extracted from the peasants and merchants. Lacking and not interested in nurturing skilled craftsmen and entrepreneurs which could establish viable industries, Spain imported virtually all its finished goods, and thus suffered perennial and severe trade deficits. What little production occurred in Spain was further inhibited by internal customs barriers which drove up prices and quelled initiative. Agriculture remained backward, and Spain increasingly had to import grain. Although its vast sheep herds did produce wool, Spain imposed heavy taxes on wool exports for their revenues and thus ended up importing woolen goods from Great Britain and elsewhere. Madrid even allowed its once vast merchant fleet to rot away. By 1640, three-quarters of Spain's trade was carried in Dutch ships. Spain's international debt and the percentage of its national budget which paid interest on that debt steadily increased. Madrid attempted to service the debt by raising taxes, but that only further stifled individual initiative and wealth. Spain's bureaucracy was inefficient, corrupt, and incapable of understanding, let alone addressing, the range of severe, interrelated national problems. Most kings after Charles V and Philip II were weak leaders.

Does any of this sound familiar? Although the particulars differ, like Spain, the United States has diverted far too many resources into building and maintaining the world's greatest military machine and deploying it in far-flung commitments, while failing to reinvest in commercial technology and production. Meanwhile, Japan has leapfrogged the United States to become the world's most dynamic economic superpower.

Although all nations ultimately benefit from technological advances, most benefits accrue to the state which best capitalizes on those advances. Generally, the state which benefits is the state in which the new technology was invented and commercially applied. There are, of course, exceptions. Japan's rise into an economic superpower has been based in part on its ability to commercialize the research efforts of others. And then there are states which invent but fail to utilize their technology fully and thus decline relative to more dynamic states. Ming China had the technology to become a global power—gunpowder, ocean-going ships—but failed to exploit it. Among other things, the United States has failed to mobilize all its vast technologies and science laboratories into production, and thus it has fallen technologically, financially, and industrially behind.

States which face geopolitical challenges must walk a tightrope between expending too much and too little wealth on the military. The diversion of too much wealth into military power will ultimately weaken a nation's economic vitality and power; the diversion of too little wealth into military power in a world filled with militarily powerful rival states can leave that nation vulnerable to foreign aggression. As Kennedy warns: "A large military establishment may, like a great monument, look imposing to the impressionable observer; but if it is not resting upon a firm foundation (in this case a productive economy), it runs the risk of future collapse."[28]

Great powers decline because, according to Kennedy, their reach has exceeded their grasp. In other words, they lack the economic capacity to fulfill their defense commitments. If not enough human and material resources are reinvested in the creation of wealth, the state's economy eventually breaks down under the defense burden, and its economic position in the world is overtaken by others.

GEOPOLITICAL POWER

The Hierarchy and Reality of Geopolitical Power

We can distinguish between superpowers, great powers, middle-ranking powers, and small powers. The distinction concerns each state's ability to project military power beyond its borders. During the Cold War, the two superpowers, the United States and Soviet Union, had enough nuclear and conventional power to fight virtually anywhere. The great powers—Great Britain, France, China, and Israel—have nuclear and conventional forces but have a limited power to fight overseas. Regional or middle-ranking powers have large conventional military forces in a regional context, but lack the power to project it outside the region. Two middle ranking powers—Germany and Japan—

have relatively large conventional militaries, but are constitutionally limited in projecting that power abroad. We can also distinguish between middle-ranking powers with the dominant power in their region such as Vietnam, India, Nigeria, and South Africa, and those whose power is either balanced or overshadowed by others in the region. North and South Korea balance each other and are overshadowed by Russia, China, and Japan; Pakistan, Iran, Iraq, and Saudi Arabia balance each other; Syria, Egypt, and Libya balance each other and are overshadowed by Israel; and Argentina, Brazil, and Chile in southern Latin America balance each other. Small powers include all the other countries which have military forces mostly to maintain internal order and as a minimum deterrent against foreign invasion.

The military power of the countries within each of these categories can be ranked by comparing the size of their national military budgets and personnel. Those which spend the most do not necessarily have the largest military forces. In 1989, during the last year of the Cold War, in terms of sheer expenditure, the United States spent $307.7 billion on the military, followed by the Soviet Union with $299.8 billion, France with $36.0 billion, West Germany with $35.1 billion, Great Britain with $34.7 billion, Japan with $28.9 billion, and China with $21.3 billion. Measured by the number of people in military uniforms, China was first with 3.90 million, followed by the Soviet Union with 3.78 million, the United States with 2.25 million, India with 1.36 million, Vietnam with 1.10 million, and Iraq with 1.00 million. Of the other great powers, France ranked eleventh with 560,000, West Germany twelfth with 500,000, Great Britain nineteenth with 320,000, and Japan twenty-fifth with 180,000.[29]

But these categories and rankings are inadequate; they merely measure a state's potential military power. Military power, like all power, can only be ultimately measured according to whether or not it is successfully used. Factors other than military budget and personnel size are often decisive. For example, after 1945, despite America's vast military expenditures and soldiers, the United States suffered a series of humiliations by countries with much smaller forces. American and other allied forces were fought to a standstill in Korea; the United States lost the Vietnam War; a communist government seized and continued to maintain power in Cuba despite enormous American efforts to overthrow it; in 1968 the North Koreans seized the U.S. spy ship Pueblo and held it for nearly a year; and in 1979, Iranians overran the American embassy and held its 56 employees hostage for 444 days. Why did the United States lose these geopolitical conflicts? Essentially, Washington did not have the political will to use the overwhelming force that might have allowed the United States to prevail in these conflicts. There may have been good reasons for that prudence. The escalation of any of those conflicts could well have started World War III.

Other countries thought to be more powerful have been humbled by their lessers. The Soviet military machine failed to subject Afghanistan; after nearly a decade of bitter guerrilla fighting Moscow was forced into a humiliating retreat. The Chinese army invaded northern Vietnam in 1979 to retaliate for Vietnam's invasion of Cambodia. China's supposedly crack divisions were repulsed by supposedly second-rate Vietnamese units. In 1982, Great Britain had difficulty mustering enough troops and ships to fight Argentina after it invaded Great Britain's Falkland (Malvinas) Islands, and Great Britain might have lost had not Washington shared important intelligence concerning Argentina's fleet movement with London. Thus raw power—the number of troops,

Figure 5.1
Leading Military Powers, 1988

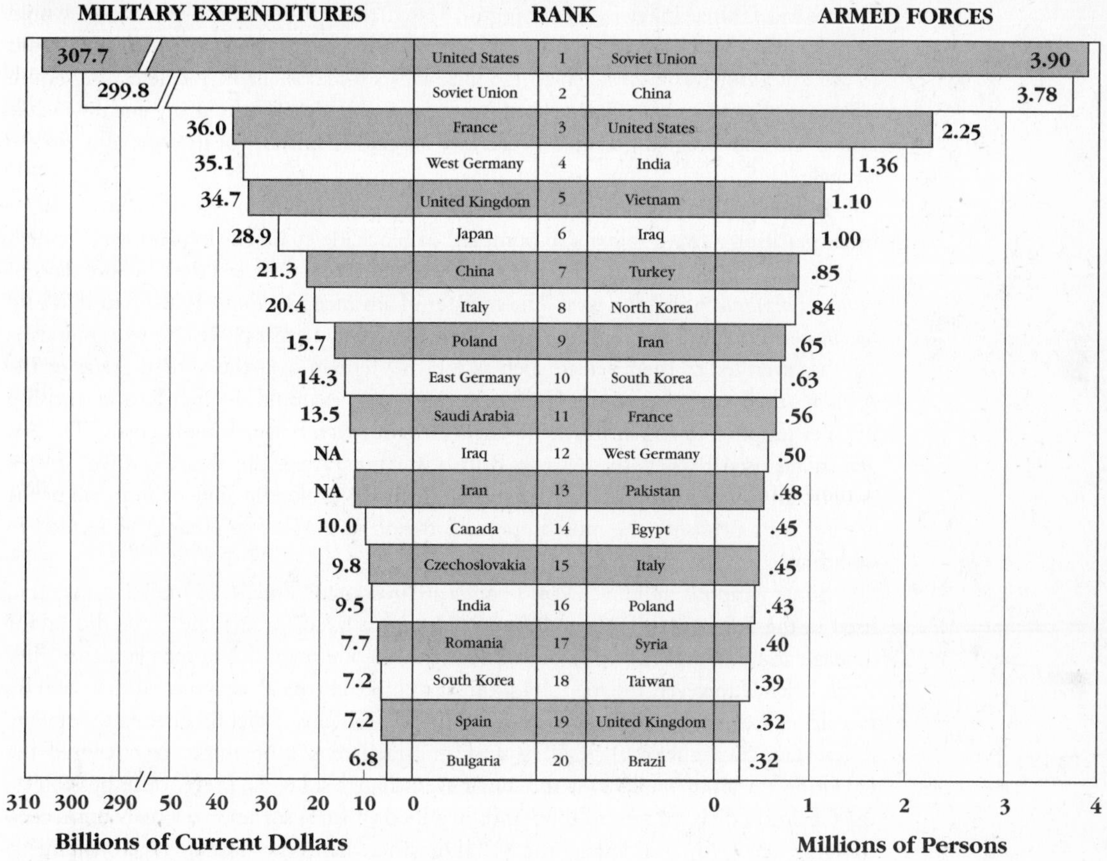

MILITARY EXPENDITURES		RANK		ARMED FORCES
307.7	United States	1	Soviet Union	3.90
299.8	Soviet Union	2	China	3.78
36.0	France	3	United States	2.25
35.1	West Germany	4	India	1.36
34.7	United Kingdom	5	Vietnam	1.10
28.9	Japan	6	Iraq	1.00
21.3	China	7	Turkey	.85
20.4	Italy	8	North Korea	.84
15.7	Poland	9	Iran	.65
14.3	East Germany	10	South Korea	.63
13.5	Saudi Arabia	11	France	.56
NA	Iraq	12	West Germany	.50
NA	Iran	13	Pakistan	.48
10.0	Canada	14	Egypt	.45
9.8	Czechoslovakia	15	Italy	.45
9.5	India	16	Poland	.43
7.7	Romania	17	Syria	.40
7.2	South Korea	18	Taiwan	.39
7.2	Spain	19	United Kingdom	.32
6.8	Bulgaria	20	Brazil	.32

310 300 290 50 40 30 20 10   0   0   1   2   3   4

Billions of Current Dollars   **Millions of Persons**

Source: U.S. Arms Control and Disarmament Agency, *World Military Expenditures and Arms Transfers 1989*
(Washington, D.C.: U.S. Government Printing Office, 1990), p. 3.

tanks, and bombs a state holds—tells nothing about how skilled a government is in brandishing that power.

Given all this, can we identify a decisive factor in a military struggle? Scholars differ over whether the side with the larger military usually prevails or not. One study compared 32 wars between 1816 and 1965 and found that the side with the largest forces won only 21 times.[30] In contrast, a much more comprehensive study of 164 conflicts between 1816 to 1976, most of which were resolved peacefully, found no correlation between military size and victory.[31]

Other factors are often much more decisive. History is filled with instances of armies with smaller numbers defeating far larger forces. With less than 35,000 men, Alexander conquered most of the Middle East and defeated armies many times superior in numbers all the way to the Indus River. The United States, despite its vast material advantage, lost its war with North Vietnam because it lacked the political will to win by either invading the north or by using nuclear weapons. The United States was inhibited both by international and domestic moral constraints on the use of nuclear weapons, and the fear that it could provoke a nuclear war with North Vietnam's allies, the Soviet Union and China. Likewise, Washington feared that an invasion of the north would bring China into the war, and ultimately force the United States to use nuclear weapons to win. Washington even failed to mobilize all its forces available for defending South Vietnam, at most, only 0.25 percent of America's population fought at any one time while North Vietnam seemed prepared to sacrifice an endless number of its population in the struggle.[32]

In the nineteenth century, the great powers could humble large but backward states by dispatching a few gunboats to bombard or blockade coastal cities, and well-trained, armed, and equiped infantry to defeat native armies many times larger. Those days of *gunboat diplomacy* are long past. The transfer of advanced weapons to the Third World has undermined the ability of the superpowers and other great powers to win militarily, and has even led to their defeat, such as North Vietnam over the United States or the Afghan rebels over the Soviet Union. Recently, for example, French Exocet antiship missiles supplied to Argentina made Great Britain's victory much more costly. The Argentinians used Exocets to sink two British warships. American shoulder-fired Stinger antiaircraft missiles supplied to Afghanistan guerrillas broke the Soviet command of the air and were probably the most important reason that Moscow eventually decided to withdraw from that country.

Some weapons in Third World hands are overrated. The SCUD missiles that Iraq used in the Persian Gulf War (1990–1991) against Saudi Arabia and Israel did minor damage and may have actually been inferior to the German V-2 bombs launched fifty years earlier. However, the mere Iraqi threat to place chemical weapons on their SCUD missiles caused the Coalition enormous political problems. Israel threatened to retaliate if Iraq launched chemical SCUDs, and an Israeli retaliation might have caused the Coalition's Arab members to withdraw or even change sides. To prevent this possibility, the Coalition diverted tens of thousands of Allied air force sorties in a largely unsuccessful effort to search and destroy the SCUDs rather than other more dangerous targets.

In addition to advanced weapons, the effective use of nationalism, modern arms, the mass media, and international organizations like the United Nations has empowered Third World countries to successfully resist Great Power intervention. The diffusion of military technology to the Third World and the ability to mobilize entire populations behind *People's Wars* makes the costs of Great Power intervention excruciatingly painful and ultimately fruitless. For example, Washington stood largely impotent in the 444 days following the seize of the American embassy in Iran in 1979. The rescue attempt resulted in disaster. Nye points out that in 1953 Washington used covert means to restore the Shah to power in Iran, then asks "how many troops would have been needed to restore the Shah in the socially mobilized and nationalistic Iran of 1979."[33]

Balance of Power

Regardless of the reasons for victory or defeat, just what is the basis for most geopolitical struggles? The Morgenthau school of scholars argues that geopolitical conflict results from states attempting to assert their interests at the expense of others within the prevailing international balance of power.

The classic *balance of power* system operates on the rather simple notion that "the enemy of my enemy is my friend." Few concepts of international relations have been as thoroughly explored. In the premodern era, Thucydides, Kautilya, Lord Shang, Polybius, and Machiavelli all analyzed the concept in depth, and tried to apply it to government policy.[34] The classic system requires a half dozen or more states of relatively similar size and capabilities; limited geographical area; a shared political culture among national elites; no fixed alliances; the tendency for most states to combine to offset any aggressor states or coalitions of states. It also requires the absence of ideology as a motivation for expansion; the preservation of defeated states in the system; the recognition that it is in all their interests to maintain the system; relatively slow means of transportation and communication that inhibit rapid mobilization and attacks; relatively limited means of mass destruction; the absense of international organizations that inhibit the actions of states; and a consensus among the governments of each state as to the system's rules. Power is not balanced for all states. The great powers ally and fight with and preside over more numerous intermediate and small states.

Although there is a consensus over the classic model's attributes, there is considerable disagreement over what the balance of power actually is, let alone which periods of international relations it characterized.[35] Some like Organski argue that a balance can only exist with a half dozen states with relatively equal power (multipolarity); others like Morgenthau argue that the balance refers to alliances of states (bipolarity).[36]

Did the classic balance of power ever exist? Although the period of European history from 1648 through 1792 did exemplify the classic balance of power, analysts argue endlessly over whether or not the system characterized any period after 1792. The French Revolution of 1789 dramatically changed the stakes of Europe's geopolitical system. The Revolution's beheading of Louis XVI and declaration of a Republic challenged every European monarchy. In 1792, the first coalition of counter-revolutionary states attacked and was defeated by France. That same year, Austria, Prussia, and Russia departed from the classic rule that no states would be destroyed when they agreed to divide Poland amongst themselves. From then until 1815, the other European powers allied repeatedly to first destroy the revolutionary French government and later Napoleon's imperial rule.

From 1815 to 1890, there was a condominium rather than balance of European power. Unlike during the classic period, no general European war broke out each generation, and great powers fought each other on only three occasions—the Crimean War (1853–1854), the Austro-Prussian War (1866), and the Franco-Prussian War (1870). The major conflicts were not between the great powers but between the great powers and lesser states experiencing democratic revolution. Russia, Austria, Prussia, and France cooperated to squash any revolutionary threats to monarchs anywhere in Europe, while all the great powers colonized overseas conquests. As Organski put it, during "the nineteenth century, after the Napoleonic Wars, there was almost continuous peace. The balance of power is given a good share of the credit for this peaceful century, but . . . there was no balance at all, but rather a vast preponderance of power in the hands of England and France."[37]

The condominium of power ended with German Kaiser Wilhelm II's forced resignation of his prime minister, Otto von Bismarck in 1890. Wilhelm abandoned Bismarck's policy of retaining Europe's status quo after achieving German unification in

1871 and instead embarked upon a naval and army buildup designed to win German hegemony over Europe. Until then the great powers had sublimated their own conflicts into a largely cooperative effort in dividing up much of Africa and Asia amongst themselves. Afterwards Europe became divided into two rigid alliances that before 1914 went to the brink of war several times over disputes in the colonies and Balkans.

Was the 1890-1914 system a *bipolar* or *multipolar world* system? Those who measure power on an individual state basis would argue that the pre-1914 was multipolar, since there was a relatively equal distribution among the great powers. Those who measure power among alliances as well as among states would argue the opposite, that the pre-1914 system was bipolar since the great powers were locked into two diametrically opposed alliances of relatively equal power.

At the Versailles peace conference in 1919, France, Great Britain, and the United States attempted to reassert a condominium of power over Europe and the world system. But the condominium unraveled as the United States immediately returned to political, and in 1930, economic isolation, and France and Great Britain failed to check the imperialist ambitions of fascist Japan, Italy, and Germany during the 1930s. In 1941, a global balance of two alliances emerged, but with ideological differences at its core, it bore no resemblance to the classic system.

Likewise, the Cold War has represented a global power balance between two diametrically opposed ideologies, each represented by a military superpower with enough nuclear power to destroy the world several times. Analysts are divided over just what to call the post-1945 system. The dispute centers over determining whether a system is multipolar or bipolar, and here we return to the question of whether the power distribution should be determined by states or alliances.

One way to finesse this problem is to distinguish between polarity, which refers to the distribution of power among states, and polarization, which refers to the alliances among states.[38] Thus, the system can be bipolar in structure but multipolar in the power distribution among states, a framework that can be applied to both world wars and the Cold War. While the post-1945 system remained bipolar in polarization, the sytem's polarity became increasingly multipolar.[39] States ally against threats rather than power per se. For example, the United States continued to hold predominant power throughout the postwar era, but the West European states chose to ally themselves with Washington rather than offset America's power by allying with Moscow because the Soviet Union rather than United States posed the genuine threat.

Military Assets and Liabilities, the Security Dilemma, and Power

Military forces must not only be financed, they need a purpose. Governments often expend enormous treasure and human resources preparing for threats which do not exist, or they overspend for those that do, and thus ultimately undermine their total power. For example, what is the United States going to do with 250,000 cruise missiles or 4,000 battle tanks? Military budgets are often shaped by political rather than strategic demands. Politicians lobby for a military base or armaments factory because it brings jobs and money to their district, even though the resources might have been better invested elsewhere. The result is that a nation's potential power sources are squandered rather than invested.

And then there is the *security dilemma*. Ironically, the military buildup which one state undertakes to feel more secure often makes other states feel more insecure so they in turn build up their own forces. The original state then feels threatened so it further builds its forces to deter a perceived foreign threat. Other states do the same, and the result is an arms race, which may lead to a war that all sides would have preferred to avoid. The United States and Soviet Union were caught in just such an arms race from 1945 to 1991, a race which ultimately undermined the economic and thus total power of both countries.

How does nuclear power enhance or detract from a nation's total power? Theoretically nuclear weapons deter foreign attack, although we can never know if potential enemies would have attacked had there been no nuclear weapons. The knowledge that they would destroy each other in a nuclear war, known as *Mutually Assured Destruction* (MAD), may well have deterred a war between the United States and Soviet Union. Nuclear power is far more important as a prestige symbol than as a means to assert national interests.

Weighed against these factors, however, are the enormous financial, human, and technological resources which must be marshalled to build up and maintain a nuclear force, resources that could be invested much more profitably elsewhere. Like other forms of military power, nuclear weapons drain a nation's economy; unlike other military weapons, nuclear bombs, which are accidently or purposely exploded can kill millions and make a land uninhabitable for thousands and even millions of years. The constraints on the use of nuclear power largely eliminate its military function. International morality and an absence of vital interests at stake may well have prevented the two superpowers and other nuclear powers like China, France, Great Britain, and Israel from using their weapons in wars with smaller states. America's tens of thousands of nuclear weapons did not prevent OPEC from nationalizing its oil fields and quadrupling oil prices in 1973, North Vietnam from conquering South Vietnam in 1975, or the Soviets from invading Afghanistan in 1979.

GEOECONOMIC POWER

Military forces were traditionally considered the most important component of national power. As Machiavelli put it: "the sinews of war are not gold, but good soldiers; for gold alone will not procure good soldiers, but good soldiers will always procure gold."[40] No longer. Military power becomes increasingly irrelevant to most conflicts of an increasingly *interdependent* global political economy in which all states are ever more tightly bound as both the system's beneficiaries and prisoners. As Rosecrance points out, autarky is impossible for a modern country:

> *In the world economy of the 1990s, however, it would be much more difficult to conquer territories containing sufficient oil, natural resources, and grain supplies to emancipate their holder from the restraints of the interdependent economic system*

. . . . Such an aggressor would need the oil of the Middle East, the resources of
Southern Africa, and the grain and iron of Australia, Canada, and the American
Middle West. Too much dependence and too little strength make that list
unachievable.[41]

Most states are at peace most of the time. Of the over 20,000 possible bilateral relations between the over 190 states in the world, only a handful actually contain the possibility of war. Virtually all of the bilateral relations are friendly and a military clash unthinkable.

But a war free relationship is not necessarily conflict free. States bicker continually over a wide range of economic and other issues. And as in geopolitical conflicts, the side prevails which can best mobilize and assert all available power resources. In an interdependent world, nations still struggle to defend and expand national security and prosperity. Power flows, not out of gun barrels, but from bank vaults, laboratories, boardrooms, factory floors, and classrooms. Nations tip the balance of power in their favor, not with vast military forces, but with vast trade surpluses. Armies are equipped with business suits, calculators, and flowcharts rather than khaki, rifles, and tanks. Superpower rests on corporate rather than nuclear power.

Until recently, most of those who studied power thought of it largely in geopolitical rather than geoeconomic terms. But events over the last two decades have resulted in increased attention to geoeconomic power and conflicts in international relations. OPEC's quadrupling of oil prices in 1973 and further doubling in 1979; the relative decline of the United States and the rapid rise of Japan, and, to a lesser extent, the European Community in geoeconomic power; and the incessant trade, investment, and technology conflicts among all three; the rise of the newly industrializing countries (NIC's) of East Asia; the Soviet empire's collapse; and Iraq's brutal conquest of Kuwait all reinforced the realization that in an increasingly interdependent world geoeconomic conflicts and power were the most important.

Geoeconomic Power and Its Creation

According to Isaak, geoeconomic power or the "structural position (and relative independence or dependence) of states and multinational corporations in the world political economy is made up of at least five primary structures:

1. Security Structure: the maintenance of order both within the organization or state and outside—within the international system at large.

2. Money and Credit System: the stability and relative value of the currency and the sources and flexibility of short-and long-term finance.

3. Knowledge Structure: literacy rates, technological competitiveness, training systems, and the distribution of critical economic information and skills throughout the population.

4. Production Structure: the way resources are organized and the knowledge structure is utilized to determine what is produced.

5. Value Structure: a cluster of psycho cultural beliefs and ideological preferences that transcend and color "the rational"—what the people predominantly choose to learn."[42]

Each state follows its own policies for maximizing its economic power. Not every means of acquiring geoeconomic power is successful. As the United States and the former Soviet Union discovered, investing heavily in a huge military industrial complex may actually diminish rather than enhance national power in an increasingly interdependent world. Military power was traditionally used to seize wealth; today, most countries create wealth and then divert a fraction of it to acquire military power while investing most of it in enterprises which can create more wealth. In his book, *The Rise of the Trading State,* Richard Rosecrance argued that today economic rather than military means are the primary source of national power. He contrasted military states like the United States and the Soviet Union with trading states like Japan, and concluded:

> *Since 1945, a few nations have borne the crushing weight of military expediture while others have gained a relative advantage by becoming military free-riders who primarily rely on the security provided by others. While the United States spent nearly 50 percent of its research and development budget on arms, Japan devoted 99 percent to civilian production.*[43]

Throughout the modern era, the democratic industrial states have increasingly assumed a greater responsibility for regulating their economies to create and distribute wealth. In so doing, they have marched steadily away from the free market ideals of Adam Smith and David Ricardo formulated in the late eighteenth and early nineteenth centuries. In the last few years, most of those states which suffered communist revolutions or had communism imposed on them by Soviet imperialism, have thrown off the shackles of state ownership of all production and property for a more market oriented system. States are trying to find a sensible middle way between the extreme, unachievable, and flawed "liberal" (free market) and "Marxist-Leninist" (state ownership) models.

How does a state become the world's leading and most dynamic geoeconomic superpower? In their book, *Politics and Productivity: The Real Story of Why Japan's Economy Works,* Johnson, Zysman, and Tyson argue that first the United States and then Japan became political-economic superpowers by mastering a new means of production and innovation, or a "technoeconomic paradigm."[44] America's economic supremacy throughout most of the twentieth century resulted from its ability to create and then master two dynamic innovations: mass production and the hierarchial, multidivisional corporation. America led the world in manufacturing high quality, inexpensive products, and other industrial nations scrambled to emulate its system. Since 1950, Japan has mastered a technoeconomic paradigm which represents a fundamentally different, superior way of production and technological innovation and thus is leading a third industrial revolution which will guarantee its economic supremacy for the foreseeable future as thoroughly as Great Britain's mastery of steam power did throughout the nineteenth century and America's mass production did throughout much of the twentieth century.

No country has been more successful in creating, distributing, and securing wealth than Japan. Through protectionist and nurturing industrial, technology, and trade policies, Tokyo achieved growth rates as much as four times higher and an income distribution more equitable than that of the United States.[45] Many other states, including the United States, are trying to emulate Japan's success by adopting some of its strategies.

The Balance of Geoeconomic Power

Potential economic power, like military power, can be measured, although such measurements give an even less reliable idea of the outcome of a power struggle. Evaluating the economic power of states by their economic power provides a pyramid ranking similar to that of military power. *Gross national product* (GNP), *per capita income,* finance, technology, manufacturing, productivity, savings, investments, and income distribution, to name a few, are all aspects of raw economic power, which reveal nothing about how skilled governments are in using their economic power.

There are two great patterns of relationships in the global political economy. Interdependent relations are generally between countries of roughly equal development levels and/or economic size. Dependent relations are generally between countries of roughly unequal development levels and/or economic size. The difference between an interdependent and dependent relationship is one of power. In interdependent relationships there is generally a power balance; in dependent relationships, a power imbalance.

In dependent relationships, the poorer or economically smaller nation is more vulnerable to an economic slow down or erection of trade barriers in the richer or larger nation. Both Canada and Mexico are trade dependent on the United States, importing and exporting a far greater percentage of their GNP with the United States than vice-versa. Although the living standards of Canadians and Americans are similar, Canada's economy is only one-tenth the size of the United States, and thus would suffer far more if trade relations ended. Mexico's per capita income is about one-sixth that of the United States.

There are three economic superpowers—the United States, Japan, and the twelve nation Economic Union (EU).[46] In bulk consumption power, the Union's 345 million population far surpasses America's 251 million or Japan's 124 million, while the Union's combined GNPs account for about 22 percent of global GNP, slightly larger than America's 19 percent and much larger than Japan's 14 percent. The Big Four—Germany, France, Italy, and Great Britain—account for about 75 percent of the Community's population and 85 percent of its GNP. With 80 million people, Germany by far is the largest, followed by about 60 million for the other three. The other members vary in size from Spain with 39 million to tiny Luxembourg with 370,000.

In 1990, Europe's GNP was $6.01 trillion and its per capita income $18,324, compared to Japan's $2.94 trillion and $23,810, and America's $5.13 trillion and $20,414. Per capita income, which is GNP divided by population, is not considered an accurate guide to living standards because it does not account for living costs. The *purchasing power parity* (PPP) is a more accurate measure of relative living standards because it compares the costs of a collection of goods. The difference between per capita income and purchasing power parity can be significant. In 1989, Japan's per capita income of $22,889 far outstripped Germany's $19,463, France's $16,884, Italy's

$15,056, Great Britain's $14,485, and America's $20,768. According to comparative PPP, however, Japan's dropped to $15,555 compared to Germany's $15,310, France's $14,577, Italy's $13,968, and Great Britain's $14,272.

Yet, these indicators of economic power were derived from the *exchange rate method,* whereby each nation's production was measured in dollars. The problem with this method is that if a nation's currency is weak compared to the dollar then the entire economy will appear weak, even if that nation in fact produces and consumes much. The IMF and increasing numbers of other international organizations, governments, think tanks, and analysts are using another means of comparing economic power, which is believed to be more accurate—the PPP method. PPP measures the cost of the same "basket" of such goods as food, housing, transportation, clothing, and so on in different countries, and thus determines the relative purchasing power. The different results of the two methods are striking. China, for example, ranked number 10 in GNP and $350 per capita income by the exchange rate method and number 3 and $1,450 in per capita income by the PPP method.

There is a dynamic relationship between savings and investment— generally the more a nation saves the higher its investment rate. Nations can augment their savings and investments by borrowing foreign capital or contribute to foreign savings and investments by investing overseas. Europe's savings rates are comparable to Japan's. In 1990, Germany's household savings rate was 13.9 percent, France's 12.0 percent, Great Britain's 9.1 percent, and Italy's 15.6 percent, while Japan's was 14.3 percent and the United States a minuscule 4.7 percent.[47]

What is important, however, is not the savings but the investment rate. By virtually any measurement, Community investments have lagged far behind those of Japan and even the United States. Japan's growth in gross capital formation has continually outstripped that of both the Community and the United States. From 1969 to 1979, Japan's gross capital formation grew an annual average 4.9 percent compared to Europe's 1.9 percent and America's 2.7 percent, and from 1979 to 1987, Japan's grew an average 3.8 percent compared to the Community's dismal 0.5 percent and America's 2.4 percent. From 1985 to 1988, Japan's gross capital formation rate of 23.7 percent was more than double the Community's 11.0 percent or America's 11.3 percent. Japan's net government investment in infrastructure as a percentage of GDP from 1980–1989 also outstripped its rivals, averaging 5.7 percent compared to Germany's 3.7 percent, France's 2.7 percent, Great Britain's 2.0 percent, and Italy's 4.8 percent. During this "Reagan era," America's was a mere 0.3 percent![48] One major reason for Japan's extraordinarily high investment rate has been its extremely low prime lending rate, which in 1988 was 4.88 percent compared to America's 10.00 percent, Germany's 10.50 percent, France's 11.00 percent, Great Britain's 16.00 percent, and Italy's 14.00 percent.[49]

Productivity and investment rates are closely linked. Generally the more money a firm invests, the greater its productivity. Unfortunately, absenteeism, low productivity, inefficiency, and poor workmanship remain characteristic of most European industries. A 1989 Commission study revealed that average American and Japanese productivity in 11 industries were tied at 100, while Germany and France's productivity ranked only 65 and Great Britain's 42. With America's twelve industries valued at 100, Japanese productivity far surpassed that of Germany, Great Britain, and France in eight of the eleven industries, including: consumer electronics—Japan 236, Germany 43, France 47, Great Britain 28; office and data equipment—Japan 94, Germany 45, France 43, Great Britain 37; chemicals and pharmaceuticals—Japan 119, Germany 75, France 79, Great Britain 54; transport equipment—Japan 95, Germany 60, France 54, Great Britain 23; paper and printing—Japan 89, Germany 76, France 67, Great Britain 43; industrial and agricultural machinery—Japan 103, Germany 46, France 49, Great Britain 20; metal product—Japan 143, Germany 54, France 60, Great Britain 38; ferrous and nonferrous ores and metals—Japan 149, Germany 92, France 72, Great Britain 66. Japan's rank varied in the other three industries: food, beverages, and tobacco—Japan 37, Germany 47, France 73, Great Britain 56; textiles, leather, and clothing—Japan 53, Germany 71, France 62, Great Britain 59; nonmetallic minerals—Japan 43, Germany 71, France 64, Great Britain 40.[50]

In an interdependent world, a nation's corporate strength may be as important a pillar of national security as military strength is in a Hobbesian world. The Union's corporate strength is far surpassed by both Japan and the United States. In 1991, only 3 European firms were placed in the world's 25 largest firms in market value, compared to 11 each for the Americans and Japanese; and only 7 EU firms ranked among the top 50 while 19 Japanese and 23 American firms struggled within that ranking. The top 1,000 firms ranked by market value included only 239 EU firms with a combined market value of $1.334 trillion (19.8 percent of total assets) compared to 309 Japanese firms with a combined market value of $2.246 trillion (33.4 percent of the total assets) and 359 American firms with a combined market value of $2.559 trillion (38.0 percent of total assets).[51] Among the world's Fortune 500 firms over the last decade there has been a steady decline in the number of American corporations and an equally steady rise in the number of Japanese corporations, while the number of European firms has been virtually unchanged. Between 1978 and 1989, the number of Fortune 500 Japanese corporations rose from 67 to 111, while Europe's rose slightly from 139 to 143 and America's plummeted from 229 to 167.[52]

The world economy runs on money. National and corporate success in the global economy depends on those which have the greatest financial power. Over the past two decades, the shift in the global balance of banking power has been extraordinary. Between 1970 and 1988, of the world's 50 largest banks, Japan's share rose from 11 to 24, total assets from $89 billion to $4.662 trillion, and its percentage of assets from 18 percent to 59 percent. While Europe's number rose from 16 to 17, its assets from $156 billion to $2.258 trillion, its assets dropped from 31 percent to 29 percent. America's numbers plunged from 15 to 4 and percentage from 38 percent to 6 percent, while its assets rose from only $188 billion to $484 billion![53] In 1989, of the world's top 50 banks in deposits, the 6 largest, 8 of the top ten, and 22 of the top 50 were Japanese! The seventh and ninth largest banks, and 22 of the top 50 were Community banks. In stark contrast only 2 American banks were in the top 50. Between 1980 and 1989, Japan's share of the international lending market rose from 4 percent with $189 billion to 40 percent with $1.4 trillion![54] Japan's banking industry is incredibly concentrated. In 1988, there were only 87 Japanese commercial banks of which 13 held 55 percent of the total assets! In contrast, there were 2,112 European commercial banks, 1,435 savings banks, 4,730 cooperative banks, and 1,819 other credit firms. America's financial system was even more decentralized and weak. In 1987, there were 14,207 American banks, 3,147 savings and loans, and 14,335 credit unions![55]

Robert Gilpin clearly understands the expanded criteria for great power status and national security in an interdependent world:

> *Today Great Power status accrues only to those nations which are leaders in all phases of basic-research and which possess the financial and managerial means to convert new knowledge into advanced technologies. In the case of the two superpowers, eminence in science and technology go hand-in-hand, and it appears unlikely that any nation or group of nations can ever again aspire to a dominent role in international politics without possessing a strong, indigenous scientific and technological capability. International politics has passed from the era of traditional industrial nation states to one dominated by the scientific nation state.*[56]

Although Gilpin was referring to the United States and the Soviet Union as the two superpowers, today he would certainly replace the Soviet Union with Japan.

The Japanese have surpassed the Americans in high technology by most indicators, and both countries are far ahead of the Europeans. A 1991 Commerce Department study revealed that of 12 emerging technology sectors, Japan was leading in 10 and running neck and neck with the United States in the other 2.[57] A 1987 National Academy of Engineering study revealed that Japan had surpassed the United States in 25 of 34 key areas of high technology, including artificial intelligence, optoelectronics, and systems engineering and control, while of 25 key semiconductor technologies, Japanese producers led in 12, were equal in 8, and were rapidly closing the gap in 5.[58] One important indicator of a nation's technological potential is the number of new patents it issues. Japan's 76,984 new patents in 1990 far surpassed Germany's 17,643, Great Britain's 8,795, France's 7,672, the Netherlands's 5,737, Italy's 1,106, and Belgium's 330. The United States still led in patents with 104,541 registered.[59]

Of course, simply inventing new technologies is not enough. Nations must be able to adapt those technologies to new products—a process at which the Japanese excel. An important pillar of Tokyo's industrial policies has been extracting the most vital foreign technologies while limiting the access of foreigners to Japanese technology. Between 1950 and 1980, Japanese firms signed about 30,000 licensing agreements for foreign technology worth about $10 billion, which originally cost between $500 billion and $1 trillion to develop.[60] In 1988, Japan bought $2.263 billion and sold $1.785 billion worth of technology. A related indicator of the technology gap is the large difference between European scientists working in Japan and Japanese scientists working in Europe. In 1988, there were 4,773 Japanese scientists in France, 4,526 in Germany, and 1,487 in Great Britain, while there were only 694 French, 542 German, and 1,458 British scientists in Japan. Yet, Europe's scientific gap is nothing compared to America's—there were 52,224 Japanese scientists in the United States while only 4,468 American scientists studied in Japan.[61] The Japanese continue systematically to vacuum the world's laboratories for all potentially profitable technology despite the fact that they are already the world's leaders.

Trade prowess is yet another indicator of a nation's global political economic power. Over the long term there has been a profound shift in the balance of trade power. On the eve of World War I in 1913, Great Britain (29.9 percent) was the world's largest exporter of manufactured products, followed by Germany 26.5 percent),

Table 5.1
Exports of High-Technology Products

Shares of Global Exports of High-Technology Products, 1980 and 1989[42]			

Microelectronics

1980	1989
1 U.S. (18.3%)	1 Japan (22.1%)
2 Japan (13.2%)	2 U.S. (21.9%)
3 Singapore (10.1%)	3 Malaysia (8.9%)
4 Malaysia (8.9%)	4 S. Korea (7.4%)
5 W. Germany (8.4%)	5 W. Germany (5.8%)

Computers

1980	1989
1 U.S. (38.6%)	1 U.S. (24%)
2 W. Germany (11.5%)	2 Japan (17.5%)
3 U.K. (10.4%)	3 U.K. (9%)
4 France (8.6%)	4 W. Germany (6.9%)
5 Italy (6.6%)	5 Taiwan (5.8%)

Aerospace

1980	1989
1 U.S. (47.6%)	1 U.S. (45.8%)
2 U.K. (19.7%)	2 W. Germany (12.5%)
3 W. Germany (9.1%)	3 U.K. (10.9%)
4 France (6.0%)	4 France (10.2%)
5 Canada (4.4%)	5 Canada (4.4%)

Telecommunications Equipment

1980	1989
1 W. Germany (16.7%)	1 Japan (24.7%)
2 Sweden (15.3%)	2 W. Germany (9.5%)
3 U.S. (10.9%)	3 U.S. (8.8%)
4 Japan (10.3%)	4 Sweden (8.1%)
5 Netherlands (9.3%)	5 Hong Kong (6.3%)

Machine Tools & Robotics

1980	1989
1 W. Germany (25.8%)	1 Japan (23.3%)
2 U.S. (14.1%)	2 W. Germany (20.8%)
3 Japan (11.3%)	3 U.S. (12.1%)
4 Sweden (9.1%)	4 Italy (10%)
5 Italy (8.7%)	5 Switzerland (8.4%)

Scientific/Precision Equipment

1980	1989
1 U.S. (28.3%)	1 U.S. (25.2%)
2 W. Germany (18.1%)	2 W. Germany (18.5%)
3 U.K. (9.4%)	3 Japan (12.9%)
4 France (8.0%)	4 U.K. (9.6%)
5 Japan (7.1%)	5 France (5.6%)

Medicine & Biologicals

1980	1989
1 W. Germany (16.7%)	1 W. Germany (15.6%)
2 Switzerland (12.5%)	2 Switzerland (12.2%)
3 U.K. (12.0%)	3 U.S. (12.2%)
4 France (11.9%)	4 U.K. (11.8%)
5 U.S. (11.4%)	5 France (10.3%)

Organic Chemicals

1980	1989
1 W. Germany (19.1%)	1 W. Germany (17%)
2 U.S. (13.9%)	2 U.S. (15.5%)
3 Netherlands (10.9%)	3 France (8.7%)
4 France (10.7%)	4 Netherlands (8.1%)
5 U.K. (8.4%)	5 U.K. (8.4%)

Kennedy, Preparing for Twenty-first Century, 1993, p. 153.

France (12.9 percent), the United States (12.6 percent), and Japan (2.4 percent). Other manufacturers accounted for a mere 15.7 percent of global exports. On the eve of World War II in 1937, Great Britain (22.4 percent) and Germany (22.4 percent) shared the number one position, followed by the United States (19.6 percent), Japan (7.2 percent), France (6.4 percent), and Italy (3.6 percent), while the share of other manufacturers rose to 28.4 percent. Following World War II, the United States was the only great power to emerge with its industrial base not only intact, but enhanced by the conflict. By the early 1950s, however, the other great powers had rebuilt their industries and many other countries had developed export industries. In 1973, Germany (17.4 percent) was the world's leading exporter of manufactured products, followed by the United States (12.9 percent), Japan (10.0 percent), France (7.5 percent), Britain (7.4 percent), and Italy (5.4 percent), while manufactured exports from other countries (39.4 percent) continued to rise. A decade later in 1984, Japan (14.4 percent) had captured the number one position, followed by Germany (12.9 percent), the United States (12.5 percent), France (6.1 percent), Italy and Great Britain (5.5 percent each), and other countries (43.1 percent).[62]

Another measure of national power is the percentage of exports and imports to GNP. For the economic great powers, the smaller the percentage of trade to GNP, the less vulnerable that country is to reductions and the more potential power it has to trade access to its own markets for foreign concessions from more vulnerable countries. There is a clear relationship between the population size of an industrial country and its trade dependence. The larger the population, the lower its dependence on trade as a percentage of GNP, while the smaller the population the greater the trade dependence. In 1913, Great Britain exported 42 percent and imported 17 percent of its GNP, compared to Germany's 31 percent and 10 percent, France's 26 percent and 13 percent, Japan's 40 percent and 34 percent, and America's mere 5 percent and 3 percent. The economic nationalism of the 1930s forced all the countries to try to reduce their trade vulnerability. In 1937, Japan's exports were still a high 40 percent of GNP but it succeeded in reducing its imports to only 11 percent, compared to Great Britain's 21 percent and 10 percent, Germany's 15 percent and 3 percent, France's 12 percent and 7 percent, and America's 5 percent and 2 percent. The three European powers increased their trade dependence again following World War II, while America kept its low and Japan reduced its trade dependence as its huge population became more affluent and productive. In 1983, America's exports were only 8 percent and its imports 10 percent of GNP, and Japan's 14 percent and 5 percent, compared to Germany's 43 percent and 35 percent, Great Britain's 26 percent and 29 percent, and France's 27 percent and 26 percent.

Perhaps the most important indicator of industrial power is a nation's share of technology-intensive trade. In 1965, America's percentage was 27.5 percent, compared to Germany's 16.9 percent, Great Britain's 12.0 percent, and Japan and France's 7.3 percent. In 1984, the United States still led with a 25.2 percent share, but Japan had nearly tripled its trade to 20.2 percent, followed by Germany's 14.5 percent, Great Britain's 8.5 percent, France's 7.7 percent, and Italy's 3.6 percent.[63]

A bilateral trade account reveals much about the relative strength of the two partners. In 1992, Japan enjoyed an overall trade surplus of $132 billion, while the United States and the European Union suffered trade deficits of $64 billion and $47 billion, respectively. Japan enjoyed a trade surplus of $52 billion with the United States and $26 billion with the European Union.

The bilateral foreign investment balance is yet another important indicator of power and relative openness. There is almost an exact balance of direct foreign investments (DFI) between the United States and the Union. In 1988, accumulated American direct investments in Europe were $326.9 billion with sales of $620.0 billion, while the Union's in the United States were $328.8 billion, with sales of $606 billion! However, with 59.0 percent of its total DFI in the United States compared to only 38.7 percent of American DFI in Europe, the Union was much more dependent on the United States as an investment outlet.[64] Although one would think that American firms would be making major direct investments in Europe to take advantage of 1992s aftermath, it has actually been European firms which are investing in the United States. In 1989, European firms spent $34 billion acquiring American firms, while American firms, bought only $5.2 billion worth of European firms.[65]

In contrast to the balance of investments and economic opportunities between the EU and the United States, there is a severe imbalance of investments between the EU and Japan. As elsewhere, Japanese investments reinforce gains made through exports. From 1951 to 1988, Japan invested $30.16 or 16.2 percent of its total in the EU while EU members invested only $3.01 billion or 23.6 percent of its total in Japan. Two years later, in March 1990, Japanese investments in the EU had jumped to $42 billion. In the first half of 1990, Japanese corporations made 25.7 percent of their direct buyouts of firms in the European Community.[66] Of Japan's direct foreign investments, 37.6 percent were in Great Britain, 24.0 percent in the Netherlands, 12.8 percent in Luxembourg, a surprisingly low 8.2 percent in Germany, 6.9 percent in France, 3.7 percent in Spain, 3.2 percent in Belgium, and 3.6 percent in the other members. In 1991, Great Britain and France were hosts to the two largest concentrations of Japanese factories in Europe, 187 and 122, respectively.[67] About half of Japan's EU investments are in wholly owned, greenfield sites; in Great Britain about 70 percent. Rapid as Japan's growing direct investments in Europe are, they still remain only one quarter of the $164 billion in American investments.[68]

Corporate leaders are to economic conflict what generals are to military conflict. There is an imbalance in managerial training in Europe and Japan. While the Community's annual graduation of 3,000 MBAs is miniscule compared to America's 70,000, it is much larger than the hundred or so Japanese graduates. Europe's best and largest business school is the Institut Européen d'Administration des Affairs (INSEAD), which annually graduates 420 MBAs. However, given the widespread adulation of Japanese management techniques and the relentless expansion of Japan's economy, perhaps MBAs are superfluous at best and a business impediment at worst because of the emphasis on financial changes to improve the bottom line rather than long-term increases in productivity and the creation of new consumer products. Japan relies instead on in-house company management training. Only about 10 percent of Europe's firms provide in-company education compared to 20 percent of American firms and 80 percent of Japanese firms, in which about 30 percent of all employees are always engaged in some form of training.

The Use of Geoeconomic Power

How is economic power wielded? Knorr reminds us "just as army divisions per se are not military power, so GNP or national wealth per se is not economic power."[69]

According to Knorr, economic power is the ability of a state to enrich itself while harming others. National economic power is actualized when wealth and economic policy are used deliberately to modify the behavior or capabilities of other states. The ability to close down valuable markets, to preempt sources of supply, to stop investments, or reduce economic aid would constitute elements of national economic strength comparable to military strength. According to Knorr, economic power can be actualized in three ways: 1) A applies economic power directly; 2) A threatens B with economic attack; 3) B anticipates the threat and adjusts according to A's wishes.[70]

In an interdependent world, states often use "co-optive" rather than coercive power to achieve their foreign policy goals. According to Nye, co-optive power:

> *is the ability of a nation to structure a situation so that other nations develop*
> *preferences or define their interests in ways consistent with one's own nation . . .*
> *The international institutions that the United States helped to establish have not*
> *merely affected the way in which other states pursue their interests but also how*
> *they understand their own behavior and define their national interests.*[71]

For example, by opening the American market to foreign competition, extending economic aid, and persistently touting the theoretical virtues of free trade, Washington has succeeded in persuading many other countries to lower their trade and investment barriers.

The coercive use of geoeconomic power is more common than its co-optive use. The power to give is also the power to deny. *Economic sanctions* are the most obvious way in which states employ geoeconomic power. Sanctions were rare in international relations before the mid-twentieth century. Napoleon tried to force Great Britain to accept his European conquests by organizing an international trade boycott against Great Britain known as the "Continental System." The sanctions failed because many European states and merchants cheated while Britain itself depended more on its trade with the empire than Europe. And like many economic sanctions, the Continental System hurt its perpetrators as badly and perhaps worse than its object.

Between 1914 and 1990, there were 142 international economic sanctions, of which 129 have occurred since 1940.[72] By far the most common situation has been for developed states to impose sanctions on developing states, which accounted for 66 cases since 1940. During the same period, while democratic industrial states imposed sanctions on communist states 18 times, the reverse occured only 5 times.

The trouble with economic sanctions is that they rarely work. Sanctions always have their loopholes through which the targeted state can trade. Prices may rise and shortages occur, but overall few countries suffer greviously from economic sanctions. Perhaps no country has faced more systematic international sanctions than Iraq, and yet that country continues to defy the United Nations. The value of economic sanctions lies chiefly in that they offer states a face-saving alternative to war. States can act tough and punish others without resorting to mass destruction.

Often the economic sanctions hurt the country which imposes them worse than the target. The Kennedy administration imposed an embargo on Cuba after it embraced communism and the Soviet Union, the Carter administration a grain embargo on the Soviet Union after it invaded Afghanistan, the Reagan administration an embargo on machine tools and earthmoving equipment to West Europe and the Soviet

Union when the Europeans and Soviets agreed to build a gas pipeline across the continent, and the Bush administration an embargo on trade with Panama to force out dictator Manuel Noriega. In all of these examples, the United States suffered more because American business lost out to their foreign rivals as the targeted country simply switched suppliers and markets.

The longest-lasting economic sanctions have been imposed by the *Coordinating Committee on Export Controls* (COCOM), which was founded in 1948. It includes nearly all the democratic industrial countries, and it is organized to impede the export of high technology to communist countries. COCOM's efforts have had only a limited success. Moscow and the other communist states were usually able to find a western firm willing to cheat on the restrictions, and it redoubled its own research and development efforts to catch up to the West.

The most dramatic use of geoeconomic power was the Organization of Petroleum Exporting Countries' (OPEC) quadrupling of oil prices, nationalization of most oil production, and temporary boycott of sales to the United States, the Netherlands, and Japan in 1973, and further doubling of oil prices in 1979. Although OPEC succeeded in asserting its economic goals of higher prices and ownership of production, it failed in its political objective of isolating Irsael. Since the 12 OPEC members supplied nearly 85 percent of the world market's oil supply and worked toward complying with strict production quotas, they had the power to limit the world's oil supply and thus raise its price to virtually any level. All the Western alliance's vast array of geopolitical power was impotent in the face of OPEC. There were not enough forces to invade the 12 OPEC nations, and even if there were, the oil fields would probably have been blown up similar to what the Iraqis did when defeated in Kuwait. OPEC's power was diluted gradually as most other countries embarked on sweeping energy conservation and efficiency measures, non-OPEC countries increased their production, and the OPEC members themselves increasingly cheated by selling more than their quota. By the mid-1980s, the artificial oil shortage had become an oil glut, prices dropped to half their highest level, and oil prices today are cheaper than before 1973, when adjusted for inflation.

States can assert geoeconomic power in a variety of ways. *Neomercantilism* is the strategy whereby a state targets its most important industries with subsidies, import protection, and export incentives in order to capture wealth that otherwise would have flowed to more efficient overseas producers. A particularly effective neomercantilist strategy is for an industry to dump or sell below price its products in foreign markets in order to drive competitors out of business. After taking over the market, the industry will then raise prices to recoup earlier loses. But sometimes a government will attempt to protect its industry against a foreign *dumping* attack. For example, in 1986, the United States and Japan signed an agreement in which Tokyo pledged to stop the dumping by Japanese semiconductor firms in the United States and elsewhere and to guarantee American producers a 20 percent market share in Japan.

Another neomercantilist strategy is to refuse to sell or license technology to other countries. In his book, *The Japan That Can Say No,* one of Japan's most prominent political leaders, Shintaro Ishihara, bluntly advocated using America's growing high technology dependence on Japan to extract political concessions: if Japan sold "microprocessor chips to the Soviet Union and stopped selling them to the United States, this would upset the entire military balance . . . . The more technology advances the more the US and the Soviet Union will become dependent upon the initiative of the Japanese people."[73] Charles Ferguson consisely captures the dangers inherent in America's loss of technological leadership to Japan:

> *technological revolutions often contribute to shifts in wealth and geopolitical influence by changing the sources of industrial and military success . . . As this transformation progresses, the United States is being gradually but pervasively eclipsed by Japan . . . [a development which could lead to American] "decline and dependence on Japan . . . [and] major economic and geopolitical consequences . . . (W)hile Japan is a military ally . . . American policy must recognize that Japan is also a closed, highly controlled, and systematically predatory actor in the international economy . . . [and] a statist, strategically cohesive free rider in the world techological system . . . The simultaneous need to preserve the military-diplomatic alliance while responding to Japan's technoeconomic Prussianism will therefore prove a critical challenge for US policy . . . the United States must learn that the . . . issue of high technology and Japanese industrial policy, not just Soviet warheads, will determine the future national security of the United States.[74]*

Any nation that dominates the technology food chain's base—the components and manufacturing equipment industry—has the power to dominate all the other links up the chain. With Japan's takeover of these segments, American industries are increasingly dependent on Japanese corporations for their components. Japan's most blatant use of its technological power has been to withhold or delay selling key equipment to American manufacturers. For example, America's remaining supercomputer producer, Cray, is dependent on Japanese suppliers for most of its key components, and the Japanese have not hesitated to exploit this dependency: in 1986, Hitachi delayed shipping a key component that Cray had actually designed, giving its own computer group a one-year lead time in placing it into its own supercomputers.[75] American firms have been complaining about this practice for years, but quietly, for fear that the Japanese firms will withhold even more equipment. On May 6, 1991, Sematech, an American consortium of 14 chip and computer makers publicly denounced Japan's hoarding of essential equipment for as long as 6 to 18 months and then selling it at prices 20 to 30 percent higher than Japanese firms pay in an attempt to damage the American firms as much as possible.

There is a reciprocal relationship between economic power—the ability to capture markets; pit raw material, capital, and component suppliers against each other to extract the lowest possible price; and technologically leapfrog, financially outspending, underselling, and eventually bankrupting rivals—and political power. Money buys access to political power, which can then be used to promote policies favoring the buyer, which allows even greater resources with which to buy more political power. Pat Choate, in his book *Agents of Influence,* reveals that the Japanese spend over $400 million annually in the United States lobbying politicians at the national, state, and local levels for favorable policies, a sum greater than what American business lobby groups spend.[76] The result, according to Choate, is that America's political and policy process is increasingly distorted to conform to Japanese rather than American interests. Other writers dismiss this perspective, arguing that America's political and economic system is strengthened rather than weakened by foreign participation.[77]

CONCLUSION

Throughout history, thousands of analysts and practitioners have grappled with the concept of power. About the only thing that most agree on is that power is the ability to get others to do things they otherwise would not do. Power permeates all human relations and, as Morgenthau pointed out, can be asserted by any means "from physical violence to the most subtle of psychological ties by which one mind controls another."[78]

Stalin once allegedly said of Yugoslavia's independent communist president, "I shall shake my little finger and there will be no more Tito." Achieving one's desires with a mere gesture is the ultimate power, but one that does not exist in international relations or even within the most totalitarian of countries. There are always some constraints on power, whether the wielder be an individual, group, country, alliance, corporation, or international organization.

International relations have not fundamentally changed throughout history: states still use power to assert their interests with some and against other states. However, the means by which states assert power and interests has changed dramatically in just the last half century. A state was once deemed powerful or weak by the size and prowess of its military force relative to those of other states. No longer. States increasingly defend and enhance their interests through geoeconomic rather than geopolitical means.

STUDY QUESTIONS

1. Just what is politics? What is power? And what is the relationship between the two?

2. How is power relative?

3. In what ways can power be asserted?

4. What is the difference between and relationship among compellence, deterrence, and defense?

5. What is the relationship between power and wealth?

6. How is power measured?

7. What are the tangible sources of national power? How has the relative importance of different tangible power sources changed throughout history?

8. What are the intangible sources of national power? How has the relative importance of different intangible power sources changed throughout history?

9. Are all global politics essentially power struggles? Is the nature of power and international relations eternally fixed, or are there manifestations and patterns much more complex, subtle, and varied? Explain.

10. What is the role of public relations or propaganda in power?

11. How can culture be a source of power?

12. According to Paul Kennedy, why do nations rise and fall in relative power?

13. What are the different ways of categorizing and ranking the military power of states?

14. What is gunboat diplomacy, and why is it increasingly ineffective in the contemporary world?

15. What are the various ways of understanding the balance of power?

16. What is the security dilemma?

17. How does nuclear power enhance or detract from a nation's total power?

18. Why is military power increasingly unimportant in an ever more interdependent global economy?

19. What are the different ways of categorizing and ranking the economic power of states?

20. In what ways can geoeconomic power be wielded?

21. How effective are economic sanctions as a form of geoeconomic power?

ENDNOTES

1. Hans Morgenthau, *Politics Among Nations: The Struggle for Power and Peace* (New York: Knopf, 1973), 28.

2. Harold Laswell, *Politics: Who Gets What, When, and How* (New York: Smith, 1936, 1950).

3. Hans Morgenthau, *Politics Among Nations: The Struggle for Power and Peace,* 9.

4. Robert Dahl, "The Concept of Power," *Behavioral Science,* vol. 2, 1957, 202.

5. Kenneth Waltz, "America's European Policy Viewed in Global Perspective," in Wolfram Hanrieder, ed., *The United States and Western Europe,* 13–14.

6. Karl Deutsch, *Analysis of International Relations* (Englewood Cliffs, N.J.: Prentice-Hall, 1968), 21–39.

7. C.W. Maynes, "Logic, Bribes, and Threats," *Foreign Affairs,* vol. 60, Fall 1985, 111–129.

8. John Rothgeb, *Defining Power: Influence and Force in the Contemporary International System* (New York: St. Martin's Press, 1993), 141.

9. Robert Art and Kenneth Waltz, "Technology, Strategy, and the Use of Force," in Robert Art and Kenneth Waltz, Eds. *The Use of Force: International Politics and Foreign Policy* (Boston: Little, Brown, 1971), 6.

10. Among others, see R.J. Rummel, "Indicators of Cross-National and International Patterns," *American Political Science Review,* vol. 63, March 1969, 127–147. James Lee Ray and J. David Singer, "Measuring the Concentration of Power in the International System," *Sociological Methods and Research,* May 1973, 403–436; Ray

Cline, *World Power Trends and Foreign Policy for the 1980s* (Boulder, Colo.: West-view Press, 1980); Jacek Kugler and Richard Arbetman, "Choosing Among Measures of Power: A Review of the Empirical Record," and Richard Merritt and Dina Zinnes, "Alternative Indexes of National Power," in Richard Stoll and Michael Ward, eds. *Power in World Politics* (Boulder, Colo.: Rienner, 1989); David Baldwin, *Paradoxes of Power* (New York: Basil Blackwell, 1991); Michael Sullivan, *Power in Contemporary International Politics* (Columbia: University of South Carolina Press, 1990); Ken Booth, ed., *New Thinking About Strategy and International Security* (London: Unwin Hyman Academic, 1991).

11. James Ray, *Global Politics* (Boston: Houghton Mifflin, 1990).

12. Jack Sawyer, "Dimensions of Nations: Size, Wealth, and Politics," *American Journal of Sociology,* vol. 73, September 1967, 145–172.

13. Wolfram Hanrieder, ed. *Comparative Foreign Policy: Theoretical Essay* (New York: McKay, 1971), 1280.

14. Halford Mackinder, *Democratic Ideals and Reality* (New York: Holt, 1919), 150.

15. Alfred T. Mahan, *The Influence of Seapower Upon History, 1660–1783* (Boston: Little, Brown, 1965), 29.

16. Nicholas Spykman, *America's Strategy in World Politics* (New York: Harcourt Brace, 1942), 472.

17. Steven Rosen, "War Power and the Willingness to Suffer," in Bruce Russet, ed., *Peace, War, and Numbers* (Beverly Hills: Sage Publications, 1972).

18. J.F.C. Fuller, *Tanks in the Great War, 1914–1918* (London: Murray, 1920), 320.

19. Paul Smith, *On Political Warfare* (Washington, D.C.: National Defense University Press, 1988).

20. Theodore Von Laue, *The World Revolution of Westernization* (New York: Oxford University Press, 1986), 376.

21. Quoted in Theodore Von Laue, *The World Revolution of Westernization,* 338.

22. Paul Kennedy, *The Rise and Fall of the Great Powers* (New York: Random House, 1987), 439.

23. Quoted in Geoffrey Parker, *Europe in Crisis, 1559–1659* (London: Macmillan, 1979), 238.

24. Paul Kennedy, *The Rise and Fall of the Great Powers,* 53.

25. Thomas Paterson, J. Gary Clifford, and Kenneth Hagan, *American Foreign Policy: A History,* vol. 2 (Lexington, Mass.: D.C. Heath, 1983), 245.

26. Paul Kennedy, *The Rise and Fall of the Great Powers,* 55.

27. Paul Kennedy, *The Rise and Fall of the Great Powers,* 49–55.

28. Paul Kennedy, *The Rise and Fall of the Great Powers,* 440.

29. U.S. Arms Control and Disarmament Agency, *World Military Expenditures and Arms Transfers, 1989* (Washington, D.C.: U.S. Government Printing Office, 1990), 3.

30. Cynthia Cannizzo, "The Costs of Combat: Death, Duration, and Defeat," in J. David Singer, ed., *The Correlates of War II: Testing Some Realpolitik Models* (New York: Free Press, 1980).

31. Zeev Moaz, "Resolve, Capabilities, and Interstate Disputes," In A.F.K. Organski and Jacek Kugler, eds. *The War Ledger* (Chicago: University of Chicago Press, 1980).

32. Andrew Mack, "Why Big Nations Lose Small War: The Politics of Asymmetrical Conflict," *World Politics,* vol. 27, January 1975, 197.

33. Joseph Nye, *Hawks, Doves, and Owls: An Agenda for Avoiding Nuclear War* (New York: Norton, 1985), 55.

34. For a discussion of the balance of power in history, see Quincy Wright, *A Study of International Relations* (New York: Appleton, 1955); See also Claude Inis, *Power and International Relations* (New York: Random House, 1962).

35. For a good critique, see Ernst Haas, "The Balance of Power: Prescription, Concept, or Propaganda?" *World Politics* , vol. 5, July 1953, 442–477.

36. See A.F.K. Organski, *World Politics* (New York: Knopf, 1968), 294; Hans Morgenthau, *Politics Among Nations: The Struggle for Power and Peace* (New York: Knopf, 1973), 213.

37. A.F.K. Organski, *World Politics* (New York: Knopf, 1968), 294.

38. James Lee Ray, *Global Politics* (Boston: Houghton Mifflin, 1990), 538.

39. David Rapkin, William Thompson, and Jon Christopherson, "Bipolarity and Bipolarization in the Cold War Era: Conceptualization, Measurement, and Validation," *Journal of Conflict Resolution,* vol. 23, June 1979, 261–296.

40. Niccolo Machiavelli, *The Prince and the Discourses* (New York: Modern Library, 1950), 310; Some of the following discussion and statistics were culled from William Nester, *American Power, the New World Order and the Japanese Challenge,* (New York: St. Martin's Press, 1993), and William Nester, *European Power and the Japanese Challenge* (New York: New York University Press, 1993).

41. Richard Rosecrance, *The Rise of the Trading State: Commerce and Conquest in the Modern World* (New York: Basic Books, 1986), 310.

42. Robert Isaak, *International Political Economy: Managing World Economic Change* (Englewood Cliffs, N.J.: Prentice-Hall, 1991), 30–31.

43. Richard Rosecrance, *The Rise of the Trading State: Commerce and Conquest in the Modern World* (New York: Basic Books, 1986), 13; Aaron Friedberg, "The Changing Relationship Between Economics and National Security," *Political Science Quarterly,* vol. 106, Summer 1991, 265–276; Ethan Kapstein, *The Political Economy of National Security: A Global Perspective* (New York: McGraw-Hill, 1992); Clyde Prestowitz, Ronald Morse, and Alan Tonelson, eds. *Powernomics: Economics and Strategy after the Cold War* (Lanham, Md.: Madison Books, 1991).

44. Chalmers Johnson. John Zysman, and Laura Tyson, *Politics and Productivity: The Real Story of Why Japan's Economy Works,* 43–50.

45. See William Nester: *American Power, the New World Order, and the Japanese Challenge; Japanese Industrial Targeting: the Neomercantilist Path to Economic Superpower* (New York: St. Martin's Press, 1992); *Japan and the Third World: Patterns, Power, Prospects* (New York: St. Martin's Press, 1992); *The Foundation of Japanese Power: Continuities, Changes, Challenges* (Armonk, N.Y.: M.E. Sharpe, 1991); *Japan's Growing Power Over East Asia and the World Economy: Ends and Means* (New York: St. Martin's Press, 1991); *European Power and the Japanese Challenge.*

46. Unless otherwise indicated, all statistics have been culled from various issues of *Japan: An International Comparison* (Keizai Koho Center, Nippon: Jetro Business Facts and Figures); IMF Direction of Trade. Parts of this section have been taken from William Nester, *European Power and the Japanese Challenge* (New York: New York University Press, 1993).

47. *New York Times,* 27 January, 1992.

48. *New York Times,* 27 January, 1992.

49. Sypros Makridakis, "Competition and Competition," in Makridakis et al., *Single Market Europe* (San Francisco: Jossey-Bass, 1991), 47, 50.

50. Sypros Makridakis, "Competition and Competition," in Makridakis et al. *Single Market Europe.*

51. *Businessweek* , 15 July 1991.

52. Sypros Makridakis, "Competition and Competition," in Makridakis et al., *Single Market Europe,* 59.

53. Gary Hufbauer, "An Overview," in Gary Hufbauer ed., *Europe 1992: An American Perspective* (Washington, D.C.: The Brookings Institute, 1990), 47.

54. *Moody's Bank and Finance Manual,* 1991; *New York Times, 2 June 1992.*

55. Carter H. Golembe and David Holland, "Banking and Securities," in Gary Hufbauer, *Europe 1992: An American Perspective* (Washington, D.C.: The Brookings Institute, 1990), 83–85.

56. Robert Gilpin, *France in the Age of the Scientific State* (Princeton N.J.: Princeton University Press, 1968), 25.

57. *New York Times,* 20 March, 1991.

58. National Academy of Engineering, *Strengthening U.S. Engineering Through International Cooperation: Some Reconsiderations for Action* (Washington, D.C.: National Academy Press, 1987); Clyde Prestowitz, *Trading Places: How We Lost to the Japanese* (New York: Basic Books, 1988), 37.

59. *New York Times,* 28 May, 1991.

60. Robert Reich, "The Quiet Path to Technological Preeminence," *Scientific American,* October 1989, 43.

61. *New York Times,* 28 April, 1991.

62. Francois Duchene and Geoffrey Shepherd, "Western Europe: A Family of Contrasts," in Francois Duchene and Geoffrey Shepherd, eds., *Managing Industrial Change in Western Europe* (London: Frances Pinter, 1987), 24.

63. Francois Duchene and Geoffrey Shepherd, "Western Europe: A Family of Contrasts," in Francois Duchene and Geoffrey Shepherd, eds. *Managing Industrial Change in Western Europe,* 36.

64. Gary Hufbauer, *Europe 1992: An American Perspective* (Washington, D.C.: The Brookings Institute, 1990), 24–25.

65. Douglas Rosenthal, "Competition Policy," in Gary Hufbauer, *Europe 1992: An American Perspective,* 315.

66. *Far Eastern Economic Review,* 27 June, 1991.

67. *New York Times,* 10 May 1991.

68. *Economist,* 20 April, 1991.

69. Klaus Knorr, *The Power of Nations, the Political Economy of International Relations* (New York: Basic Books, 1975), 3.

70. Klaus Knorr, *The Power of Nations, the Political Economy of International Relations,* 4–5.

71. Joseph Nye, *Hawks, Doves, and Owls: An Agenda for Avoiding Nuclear War.*

72. G.C. Hufbauer, et al., *Economic Sanctions Reconsidered: History and Current Policy* (Washington, D.C.: Institute for International Economics, 1990).

73. Shitaro Ishihara and Akio Morita, *The Japan That Can Say "No,"* (New York: Simon & Schuster, 1991), 18.

74. Charles Ferguson, "America's High Tech Decline," *Foreign Policy,* Spring 1989, 123, 125, 129.

75. Clyde Prestowitz, Ronald Morse, and Alan Tonelson, eds. *Powernomics: Economics and Strategy after the Cold War,* 11, 27.

76. Pat Choate, *Agents of Influence: How Japan's Lobbyists in the United States Manipulate America's Political and Economic System* (New York: Knopf, 1990).

77. See the work of Gary Saxonhouse and other leading neoclassical economists.

78. Hans Morgenthau, *Politics Among Nations: The Struggle for Power and Peace,* 5th ed., 9.

Foreign Policy Making and Implementation

Key Terms and Concepts

Chicken
Cognitive Dissonance
Crisis Decision-Making
Crisis Management
Foreign Policy
Groupthink
Interest Group
Intermestic Policy

Iron Triangle
Military Industrial
   Complex
Mirror Image
National Interests
Operational Code
Policy
Policy Cluster

Policy-Making
Realist School
Revisionist State
Satisfice
Standard Operating
   Procedures
Status Quo State

Foreign policy making is as old as the first organized states and their conflicts with other states. Throughout the modern era, the issues, means, and ends of foreign policy making for nation-states have proliferated and changed significantly.

The popular image of foreign policymaking is a council of wise people carefully and rationally choosing among alternatives until they find the one best able to fulfill national interests. In reality, policymaking is a messy, imprecise process which varies considerably from one issue, time, and government to the next. There are as many different *policy-making* processes as there are issues.

Policymaking is thus a multi-stranded tug of war between different and often diametrically opposed experts, interest groups, and public emotions. There are as many policymakers as there are individuals and groups interested in that particular issue. However, some individuals and groups are obviously much more influential in shaping foreign policy than others.

Although it is perhaps more accurate to speak of a nation's foreign policies than *policy,* most nations do have a broad set of national goals and strategies which guide the formulation of specific policies affecting specific issues. For example, America's foreign policies from 1947 through 1990 generally operated under the guidelines of "containment." The *foreign policy* ends of many Third World states are development and nonalignment, although the means to attain those ends vary considerably.

A nation's foreign policy includes the specific goals that leaders pursue in the global system, the values that shape those goals, and the means by which those goals are achieved. This chapter will explore the concept of national interests upon which governments base their policies, some flawed foreign policy models, the "level of analysis matrix" which enables analysts to gain an in depth understanding of why countries do what they do, and, finally, several policy types.[1]

NATIONAL INTERESTS

Why do governments do the things they do and do not do the things they seemingly could do? The answer is usually *national interests*. Governments follow policies which they believe protect or enhance their nation's interests. When Winston Churchill was asked for an explanation of Soviet behavior, he replied: "I cannot forecast to you the action of Russia. It is a riddle wrapped in a mystery inside an enigma; but perhaps there is a key. That key is Russian national interests."

National interests are evoked to justify virtually every act of state, from generosity to genocide. And, of course, some states follow policies that in retrospect undermine rather than enhance national interests. The imperialism of Germany, Japan, and Italy during the 1930s and 1940s, or Iraq's invasion of Kuwait in August 1990 were justified by the leaders of those countries as being in the nation's interests. But imperialism left those nations in ruins. Virtually all analysts agree that the United States was weakened economically, politically, militarily, and morally by its war in Vietnam. Yet the various administrations continually attempted to justify America's long involvement in Vietnam in terms of national interests. In evaluating a nation's policies, the first rule is that they should be achievable. Paul Kennedy's *Rise and Fall of the Great Powers* shows how great powers eventually declined because their ambitions—their declared national interests—exceeded their capabilities.[2]

All states share some common interests—political independence, economic growth, cultural preservation, peace. The most obvious national interest is self-preservation, and the greatest threat to that basic interest is for another state to invade and conquer it. The threat of foreign invasion, however, is increasingly rare in international relations. Three other "core national values" in diminishing importance are the enhancement of a nation's economic development, independence from the interference of foreigners in one's domestic affairs, and preservation of the nation's "way of life," or culture.

Other national interests are less concrete. Governments often pursue policies that enhance national prestige, or the acknowledgement by other states of one's economic, social, political, technological, military, or cultural achievements. This "interest" is particularly difficult to measure, and its achievement may well conflict with other more concrete national interests. For example, in the interests of national prestige, many developing and smaller nations have their own national airlines, even though they cost an enormous amount to create and often run at a loss. The proposed U.S. space station is estimated to cost anywhere from $80 billion to $180 billion, a sum that will never pay off economically. Many analysts argue that the same experiments designed for the space station could be conducted at a fraction of the cost on earth. Yet, its advocates continually justify the project for national prestige reasons. Is the prestige generated by the space station worth a minimum of $80 billion?

Another problem for policy makers is when national interests conflict with each other. For example, for almost fifty years, American policy makers and the public agreed that American interests were best served by the interrelated goals of containing the Soviet Union and developing and defending the global political economy. These policies were enormously successful. The Soviets were contained and communism eventually crumbled. The world economy is increasingly prosperous and dynamic. In the 1980s, however, increasing numbers of Americans wondered whether in achieving these national interests, other interests were neglected. The Soviet Union's demise and a secure, prosperous world economy does not automatically mean a secure, properous American economy. In expending enormous amounts of treasure, expertise, and blood developing and defending the global system, the United States neglected to maintain its own economic vitality and security. The United States today is the world's greatest debtor nation, has one of the lowest growth rates of any industrial democracy, runs huge trade deficits, is second now to Japan as a manufacturing, technological, and financial power, and is beset by a range of socioeconomic ills including poverty, crime, homelessness, crumbling infrastructure, and racism.

There can sometimes be trade-offs between a nation's short-term and long-term interests. For example, the United States has an interest in political stability and open markets in all foreign countries. The question is, how is this national interest best achieved? In the case of Nicaragua, Washington sent in the Marines on five occasions earlier in this century to maintain order and protect American investments. After 1930, Washington helped the Somoza dictatorship take and maintain power. Yet, American support for the increasingly corrupt and brutal Somoza regime contributed to anti-Americanism and revolutionary conditions which eventually resulted in the regime's overthrow in 1979 and the establishment of the Communist Sandinista government. The United States continued to intervene in Nicaragua by arming and training the "contras" or anti-communist guerrillas. In 1989, the Sandinistas lost power in an election to a coalition of forces which reopened the country to foreign trade and investment.

Were America's economic interests in Nicaragua worth the billions of dollars the United States spent over the past century in maintaining or reinstating friendly governments? It can be argued that Washington's interventionist policy served not the American public, but only that tiny number of businesses which traded or invested in Nicaragua. And even then, the interventionist policy may have protected those American business interests over the short-term, while failing to do so over the long-term since it contributed to the Sandinista revolution. However, those who have advocated an interventionist policy throughout the century have justified it not in dollars and cents, but in its balance of power and domino effects. A communist victory in Nicaragua, it was argued, may not be important in itself, but could lead to communist victories throughout Central America, which would threaten the Panama Canal and the regional power balance.

Who defines the nation's interests? The answer varies from one country and time to the next. National interests may be articulated by a dictator, a council of experts, or by the give-and-take of countless interest groups and public opinion.

In democratic countries, one political party's definition of national interests may differ markedly from other parties, and thus foreign policy may shift with each change in leadership. For example, Israel's conservative Likud party, which was in power from 1975 to 1991, refused to give back to Syria the Golan Heights that Israel seized in the 1967 War or grant more autonomy for Palestinians, even if it meant a continued military stand off with the potential for war. The Labor party, which won election in 1991, has favored trading land for peace with the Arabs and increased autonomy for Palestinians. Both parties claim that their policies best safeguard Israel's interests.

National interests are often defined by special *interest groups,* and the policies followed to achieve those special interests often largely benefit those groups. In the United States it was once said that "as GM goes so goes the nation," meaning that as long as GM was prosperous the country would be too. During the 1980s and into the 1990s, America's automobile industry was severely battered by cheaper, better quality Japanese imports, which captured 30 percent of the market. Although consumers benefited from the wider choices and cheaper prices that Japanese imports presented, America's automobile industry succeeded in pressuring the Reagan and Bush administrations to convince Tokyo to "voluntarily" restrict exports to 2.1 million vehicles a year, starting in 1982 since dropped to 1.6 million, and to build automobile factories in the United States to help employment here. These policies saved and revived America's automobile industry. Japan's market share had declined to 28 percent by 1994. If the Japanese had succeeded in bankrupting America's industry, America's economy would have suffered severely because of the loss of millions of high paying jobs and profits to Japan, while the Japanese automobile makers could have taken advantage of their oligopolistic power and raised prices.

Foreign policy debate is usually over means rather than ends. For example, although there was a national consensus on the perceived need to contain the Soviet Union and communism, there were considerable differences over just how to do so. Some like George Kennan advocated a "selective containment" in which only those areas like Europe, Japan, and the Middle East, with vital geopolitical and geoeconomic importance, would be defended. Others like Dean Acheson and John Foster Dulles pushed for "global containment" in which every government facing a communist rebellion must be supported for fear that its loss would result in a "domino effect" in which neighboring governments would also be overthrown by communists. The debate over America's war in Vietnam was essentially a debate over the best containment strategy. Advocates of selective containment maintained that Vietnam had no geopolitical or geoeconomic importance to the United States and thus should be avoided. Advocates of global containment countered that if Vietnam fell so would the rest of Southeast Asia and then the entire global power balance would shift against the United States. The global containers won the debate, and the United States became deeply involved in a war it eventually lost.

A vital national interest is preserving national ideals and culture, or ideology. How important is ideology in shaping a nation's foreign policy? Ideology often takes a back seat to other national concerns. During the Cold War the United States and the Soviet Union frequently proclaimed that their policies were based on their nations' ideals— liberal democracy and communism, respectively. However, neither country allowed its national ideals to interfere when other more concrete national interests were thought to be threatened. Despite its democratic ideals, the United States supported dozens of brutal anti-communist dictators around the world, and some administrations even suppressed political groups and information in the United States. Despite its ideal of communist party solidarity and self-proclaimed leadership of the global communist movement, the Soviet Union maintained close relations with governments like Iran, Egypt, and Iraq which purged the local communist party.

Ideology is often used to justify a particular policy. The Bush administration argued that its wars against Panama's President Manuel Noriega and Iraq's President

Saddam Hussein were democratic crusades against vicious dictators. Opponents countered that much less idealistic interests were at stake—Bush's virility in the Panama War and oil in the Persian Gulf War. In fact, American troops were committed in both countries for far more complex reasons than either its advocates or opponents argued.

Often what is important is not whether ideology guides policy in an objective sense. Instead, the belief that one's actions are based on the highest principles can be an enormous source of power. Idealism can allow a leader and his or her followers to cast aside the moral ambiguities and compromises that accompany most political decisions. Decisive action is more likely when a leader believes that he or she is acting on principle, and more importantly, is able to convince the political establishment and public that together they are embarked on a crusade to protect or expand their national ideals. Of course, ideological fervor can be a double-edged sword; it can lead to defeat and sometimes outright ruin as the Germans and Japanese, for example, discovered in 1945.

Raymond Aron explained the difficulties of defining national interests:

> *The plurality of concrete interests and ultimate objectives forbids a rational definition of national interest, even if the latter did involve, in itself, the ambiguity that attaches to collective interest in economic science. [Nation-states] are composed of individuals and groups, each of which seeks to maximize its resources, its share of the national income, or its position within the social hierarchy. The interests of those individuals and groups . . . added together . . . do not constitute a general interest.[3]*

The debate over national interests is unresolved. Some argue that national interests are ultimately subjective, defined by the specific interests, prejudices, and perceptions of each individual or group with a stake in the issue, and policy results from the conflicts between these different parochial interests. Others believe that while perceptions of national interests may vary according to parochial interest groups, there is an objective set of general national interests that all countries share, such as political economic development and security from military or political invasion, along with a set of specific interests for each country. If every nation has a set of interests, then there should be a clear set of policies which best protect those interests. The first view simply says politics shapes policy, and thus national interest is whatever the power balance or imbalance of parochial interests says it is; the second view acknowledges that while this reality may currently be true, there are genuine national interests, and we can evaluate the relative success or failure of a nation's policies by how it addresses those national interests.

Hans Morgenthau tried to bridge the gap between these two views by proposing that foreign policy makers evaluate an international issue by three criteria. First, policy makers should determine just what kind of issue was at stake—whether it involved the nation's physical safety, material well-being, political independence, and/or national cohesion. Secondly, they should distinguish between that issue's relative importance over the short-term and long-term, in which the latter should take precedence. Finally, they should figure out whether the issue is of primary or secondary importance to the country over both the short-term and long-term in relation to all other current issues. Thus, the nation's interests could be objectively determined.

FLAWED MODELS OF FOREIGN POLICY

How and why do governments follow certain policies and reject or not even consider others?[4] Analysts are deeply divided over this basic question, and have presented different models or theories to explain foreign policy behavior. Each model is provocative, but all fall short of providing an adequate understanding of the diversity and complexity of foreign policy making.

The "power balance" or *realist* explanation sees foreign policy as essentially shaped by one's relative power within the international system.[5] States are monolithic actors which simply react to shifts in the regional or global power balance. Domestic politics plays no significant role in shaping foreign policy. Democratic or authoritarian, communist or capitalist, the state's internal organization and ideology are unimportant in explaining why states do the things they do. The only important factor is power. States constantly try to increase their own power and offset the rising power of others in the international system. The behavior or policies of states thus change with shifts in the international power balance. The human beings which make foreign policy decisions are assumed to be "rational," have access to enough information to make rational decisions, and then choose that option which best advances their nation's interests within the prevailing power balance. The realist perspective is both an explanation of and a strategy for state behavior.

This "realist" view of global politics is not as realistic as it may appear. Although policy makers do consciously attempt to rationally make decisions, they can rarely do so. Real policy making is not a rational process. States are not unitary actors. They are composed of very human individuals and institutions which are incapable of flawlessly gathering and processing the information vital for every decision, and then rationally making and implementing the best decision for a given situation. Policy makers and institutions are forced to make dozens of important and routine decisions daily, and rarely have the time, information, or ability to rationally evaluate the options. And even when policy makers make a rational decision, they often lack the power to implement that policy as they wish. As Henry Kissinger put it, policy makers "are locked in an endless battle in which the urgent constantly gains on the important. The public life of every political figure is a continual struggle to rescue an element of choice from the pressure of circumstances."[6] A Kennedy advisor, Ted Sorensen, reveals that: "Each step cannot be taken in order. The facts may be in doubt or dispute. Several policies, all good, may conflict. Stated goals may be imprecise. There may be many intepretations of what is right, what is possible, and what is in the national interest."[7]

While realist theory offers a strategy for governments, it cannot explain why states do not always or even usually follow the dictates of power politics. For example, according to realist theory, Great Britain and France should have intervened against Hitler in 1936 when German troops marched into the demilitarized Rhineland, rather than waiting until Poland was attacked in 1939. Realist theory can only point out that Great Britain and France should have intervened, it cannot explain why they did not.

Another explanation of foreign policy is that states hold either a *status quo* or *revisionist* orientation toward the world and act accordingly. While all states strive to protect their national interests, most are content with the international status quo and their place in it. War is caused by a few trouble-makers who try to revise the power balance in their favor. For example, during the 1930s, ambitious, authoritarian governments in Japan, Germany, Italy, and the Soviet Union sought to expand their power and carve out huge empires in Europe, the Middle East, and Asia. At first, hobbled by an isolationist public, the status quo powers watched helplessly as Japanese, Italian, and German armies conquered one state after another. Eventually, however, the status quo states went to war—France and Great Britain after Germany attacked Poland, and the Soviet Union and the United States after they were directly attacked by Germany and Japan, respectively.

What causes a nation to be revisionist or status quo? Some argue that a nation's ideology is the most important factor, that democratic states are naturally peace-loving while authoritarian or revolutionary states are inherently aggressive. George Kennan argued that:

A democracy is peace-loving. It does not like to go to war. It is slow to rise to provocation. When it has once been provoked to the point where it must grasp the sword, it does not easily forgive its adversary for having produced this situation. The fact of the provocation then becomes itself the issue. Democracy fights in anger—it fights for the very reason that it was forced to go to war. It fights to punish the power that was rash enough and hostile enough to provoke it—to teach that power a lesson it will not forget, to prevent the thing from happening again. Such a war must be carried to the bitter end.[8]

Revolutionary states are naturally aggressive—they seek a "revolution without borders" in which their ideology is imposed everywhere. Revolutionary France, the Soviet Union, and Iran all dispatched their agents to foment revolution elsewhere. The classic expression of a revolutionary ideology affecting a nation's foreign policy was the 1793 declaration by France's revolutionary government that:

The French nation declares that it will treat as enemies every people who, refusing liberty and equality or renouncing them, may wish to maintain, recall, or treat with the prince and the privileged classes; on the other hand, it engages not to subscribe to any treaty and not to lay down its arms until the sovereignty and independence of the people whose territory the troops of the Republic shall have entered shall be established, and until the people shall have adopted the principles of equality and founded a free and democratic government.[9]

Eventually, though, the fires of revolutionary ardor burn out and the revisionist state becomes a status quo state. For example, Lenin had argued that in order for a revolution to succeed in Russia, it had to succeed everywhere. Thus, Lenin created and led the Communist International (Comintern) in 1918 as a secret organization which attempted to provoke revolutions abroad. By the late-1920s the failure of communist revolutions elsewhere and growing problems at home caused Stalin to shift to a "socialism in one state" policy. In 1956, Moscow adopted a policy of "peaceful coexistance" in which war between communist and capitalist countries was not inevitable, and in which both systems in fact could exist peacefully alongside each other as the capitalist countries slowly crumbled and were transformed by communism. Other revolutions have experienced similar transformations. The French were exhausted by a decade of revolution and eagerly accepted Napoleon's dictatorship in 1799, although that did not inhibit the emperor from attempting to conquer Europe. Similarly in Iran, a decade of revolution and foreign war has reduced the government and people's revolutionary fire. Following the death of Ayatollah Khomeini, the new leader, President Rafsanjani has reigned in his revolutionary agents and attempted to re-establish normal relations with other states.

Like the realist model, the "revisionist/status quo" foreign policy model is also limited. Few states in history have been revisionist in the revolutionary sense of trying to overthrow and change the entire world order. Virtually all states are revisionist in the sense that they want things from each other—territory, open markets, finance, and so forth. At times, governments believe that their interests in a conflict are worth going to war to protect or enhance. Some of these wars lead to sweeping changes in the power relations among states.

Does humankind make history or does history make humankind? Is history simply the sum of countless decisions made by unique individuals, or do leaders, even the most powerful, operate under enormous political contraints? Some argue that the character of those in power is decisive in shaping a nation's foreign policy. Leaders constantly face decisions. Their decisions reflect a complex mix of their personality, intelligence, knowledge, view of history, fears, and ambitions. Because all individuals are different, various individuals will make different decisions. Contrast the different positions of British Prime Minister Neville Chamberlain and Winston Churchill to Hilter's rise. During the Czechoslovakia crisis of 1938, while Churchill was advocating a strong British response, Chamberlain remarked: "How horrible, fantastic, incredible it is that we should be digging trenches and trying on gas-masks here because of a quarrel in a faraway country between people of which we know nothing!"[10] And what would have been the fate of Germany and the world had Hitler been killed rather than spared in World War I?

The "great individual explanation" is flawed as well. Clearly, great leaders do at times matter. Try to imagine the twentieth century without the birth of Lenin, Mao, or Hitler. Yet, of all the countless decisions made by a succession of national leaders, few dramatically change that nation's direction. We will, of course, never know how different leaders would have responded to the same situation. But every leader, even those with the most sweeping dictatorial powers, faces both domestic and international constraints. A leader is only as powerful in international relations as is his or her nation. For example, since coming to power in 1969, Libya's President Muammar Qadhafi has attempted to create a North African empire with himself at its head. His ambitions have been derailed repeatedly because his country lacks the strength, military prowess, finance, technology, and allies to take over the region. Other Arab states, the United States, and France have intervened to thwart his attempts to intimidate surrounding governments.

The "interdependence explanation" combines elements of international and national perspectives, and maintains that growing interdependence between states and democracy within states will bind them to the point where power politics becomes impossible. International relations will increasingly be shaped by shared interests and negotiation rather than force. Cordell Hull succinctly captured this internationalist perspective, although ironically he wrote it during the Cold War's early years: "there will no longer be need for spheres of influence, for alliances, balance of power, or any other of the special arrangements through which, in the unhappy past, the nations strove to safeguard their security or promote their interests."[11]

Clearly the world is becoming more economically interdependent, and an increasing number of states within the global system are becoming democratic. Yet, these trends do not erase the reality that every state has different power and interests in the system. Conflicts between states may well increase with interdependence, even if they are settled with diplomacy rather than force. The interdependence explanation cannot explain why states follow such different policies.

One of the most sophisticated attempts to analyze policy making was Graham Allison's "Essence of Decision." Allison explored the Kennedy adminstration's handling of the Cuban missile crisis through three decision making models.[12] The "rational model" assumed the decision maker sat down and carefully analyzed all the information and options affecting that issue and then chose that which best advanced national interests. The "organizational-process model" examines how different organizations with different missions filter information and options to decision makers that advance their own interests rather than provide an objective overview of the situation and national interests. The "bureaucratic politics model" focuses on how each advisor to the president represents his or her respective bureaucracy's interests. Allison reveals the flaws in each of these models. None of them alone provided an accurate understanding of what actually occurred.

THE LEVEL OF ANALYSIS MATRIX

Social scientists have found a theory of foreign policy elusive—the real world is too complex to be reduced to a few simple axioms. Yet, there are some similarities between countries in foreign policy making, and thus a basis for comparison.

In every sovereign state, there is a head of government who is responsible for making decisions. Yet the popular belief that a president or premier makes decisions after carefully and rationally weighing the alternatives is inaccurate. A leader's decision depends on and is shaped by five complex interrelated systems: (1) Leader's Psychological System—personality, character, intelligence, knowledge, experiences, aptitudes, interests, and world view; (2) Decision-making System—the leader's core group of advisors, and their respective psychological systems; (3) Political System—impact of revelant ministries, interests groups, mass media, and public opinion; (4) National System—the nation's history, traditions, ideology, and culture related to the immediate issue and similar issues; (5) International System—power balance affecting that issue, including how the five levels of analysis affect other states involved in the conflict.

These different levels all interact with each other, although their relative importance differs from one policy to the next. To examine the same decision from each different perspective would result in five different answers to the basic question of why the government acted as it did.

Leader's Psychological System

Many studies have examined how a leader's personality, character, and world view affect his or her policies.[13] How does a leader's psychology affect foreign policy? Every second we are bombarded with thousands of bits of sensory and cognitive information of which we must somehow make sense. It is impossible to understand this shifting world directly in its infinite complexity and ambiguity. Instead, we use mental maps or belief systems to screen out most of this flood of incoming information, while clinging to key elements. What actually happens is often not as important as what we think has, is, and will happen. These mental maps are formed by many forces. From birth, an individual's world view is shaped by a succession of interrelated environments, of which the family is the first and most important. Some people are much more psychologically open to new ways of understanding the world. Many people reject information that conflicts with their belief system, a process known as *cognitive dissonance*. Kenneth Boulding wrote that we do not:

> respond to the "objective" facts of the situation . . . but to [our] image of the situation. It is what we think the world is like, not what it is really like, that determines our behavior . . . we act according to the way the world appears to us, not necessarily according to the way it "is".[14]

In other words, facts do not exist until we create them.

Key events in a person's life also shape his or her world view. Generals and politicians alike often prepare psychologically and militarily for the last war, rather than carefully analyze and prepare for current and future challenges. Throughout the Cold War, American presidents continually compared Soviet with previous German and Japanese expansion. They were particularly sensitive to being accused of "appeasing" the Soviets like British Prime Minister Chamberlain had appeased Hitler during their meeting at Munich in 1938 by granting him the Sudetenland region of Czechoslovakia. For example, President Johnson justifed his escalation of America's involvement in Vietnam by arguing: "Everything I knew about history told me that if I got out of Vietnam . . . then I'd be doing exactly what Chamberlain did in World War II. I'd be giving a big fat reward to aggression . . . And so would begin World War III."[15]

What is important is not the real world but how it is perceived by those with the most power to shape it. Policymakers are no less prisoners of their respective mental maps of reality than anyone else. Every leader has an *operational code* or system of "general beliefs about fundamental issues of history and central questions of politics."[16] A leader's operational code gives him or her a means of evaluating information and problems, and making choices about them. A classic decision making study showed that Secretary of State John Foster Dulles interpreted and acted on all Soviet actions through his passionate belief that communism was a ruthless, godless system dedicated to world conquest and thus communists could never be trusted.[17]

Actors in conflicts are often trapped in a vicious cycle of misperceptions and corresponding actions. While both sides may have originally intended to remain defensive, they interpret the other side's action as aggressive and thus respond similarly. *Mirror images* occur when opponents view the other's actions as malevolent and aggressive and their own actions as innocent, just, and defensive. Throughout the Cold War, the United States and the Soviet Union held mirror images of each other, thus making any agreements difficult and reconciliation virtually impossible. President Jimmy Carter once said: "The hardest thing for Americans to understand is that they are not better than other people."[18] He might have added, that it was equally difficult for Americans during the Cold War to perceive the Soviet Union as anything less than an evil empire bent on world conquest.

There is a tendency to believe that the opponent is united behind a master plan in which the immediate issue is just one stage toward ultimate victory, while seeing one's own country as largely divided, weak, and defensive. As Kissinger put it: "The superpowers often behave like two heavily armed blind men feeling their way around a room, each believing himself in mortal peril from the other whom he assumes to have perfect vision . . . Each tends to ascribe to the other a consistency, foresight, and coherence that its own experience belies."[19]

A leader's physical and mental health, and ego and ambition all shape the ways in which he evaluates and decides policies. President Wilson suffered a stroke during the Versailles Peace Conference, which may have strongly affected his negotiating abilities with the other leaders at the time, and later to get the Senate to approve the treaty. President Franklin Roosevelt was only two months away from his death at the Yalta Conference with Stalin and Churchill in February 1945, and many argue that in his weakness he made unnecessary concessions to the Soviet Union in East Europe. A superinflated ego and ambition may be as self-defeating as a weak body and mind. Megalomaniacal leaders like Hitler or Hussein are inclined to embark their countries on aggressive wars against their neighbors, even when a rational analysis might show a significant chance of ultimate failure.

Decision Making System

But the leader's psychology alone does not explain foreign policy. The mix of a leader's immediate advisors and ministry heads have a profound impact on policy. Leaders vary considerably in the advisors they choose. Some leaders pick their decision makers more often than not for their loyalty rather than expertise, and for their willingness to mirror rather than challenge the leader's assumptions and perspectives.

Groups can become just as mired in a narrow view of reality as individuals, a phenomenon known as *groupthink*.[20] Individuals are pressured to be "team players" and not "rock the boat" with options or information that counter the prevailing assessment. Those who do dissent are often left out of the "policy loop" by the other policy makers, as Defense Secretary McNamara was during the Vietnam War when he began to express doubts over the Johnson administration's policies, or Secretary of State Vance was during the Iranian hostage crisis when he objected to the Carter plans for a rescue attempt. This is particularly common in a crisis situation, where information and time are limited and the stakes are crucial. Leaders and advisors collectively fall back on stereotypes to evaluate the situation and standard operating procedures or pre-existing plans to deal with it. For example, the Carter administration decided to attempt the rescue of American hostages held by Iran despite the mission commander's belief that the chance of success was virtually nil, and the CIA's assessment that at least 60 percent of the hostages would be killed.

Groupthink does not affect most policies. Whether the advisor was chosen to be a "yes man" or "devil's advocate," his positions often reflect the ministry or agency he or she represents, thus following the maxim that "where you stand depends on where you sit." There are, of course, always exceptions to this rule.[21] Advisors quickly learn how to best pitch an idea to their leader. Some leaders are known for following the advice of the last person they talked to, so advisors scramble to be last in line. President Ronald Reagan was particularly susceptible to colorful one page synopses or even short films on complex issues, so his advisors tried to make their presentations as Hollywood-like as possible.

Political System

To truly understand a government's decisions, the analyst must explore the endless maze of a state's domestic politics. Governments interpret and act on international threats and opportunities within the context of a complex domestic political situation. Every state has its own distinct policy-making system. Generally speaking, democracies and dictatorships do have significantly different policy making processes. But policy making systems clearly differ between democratic countries and between authoritarian countries. The number of groups that affect policy would obviously be vastly more numerous in a liberal democracy than in a communist dictatorship. Yet even in totalitarian systems like the Soviet Union under Stalin, there were distinct interest groups involving heavy industry, light industry, agriculture, technology and science, and military industry that battled each other, albeit it subtly, for a greater share of the budget and other resources. Each issue in each system elicits a different constellation of bureaucracies, interest groups, public opinion, and, in democratic countries, political parties.

While the leader handpicks his or her decisionmakers, he or she inherits an army of career bureaucrats whose primary loyalty is to themselves and then their organization. Although each bureaucracy has its own mission, they share the imperative of expanding their respective power, responsibilities, and personnel, often at the expense of their rivals. Each organization in the bureaucracy is a distinct interest group with its own values and priorities. Like any other interest group it confuses its interests with national interests, and presents its narrow view to the leadership. The result in every political system is a constant, behind-the-scenes struggle among different bureaucracies over their different interests on different issues. When a bureaucracy presents options, it may package one reasonable one—the one it wants chosen—along with several unreasonable ones, while leaving out other viable alternatives.

A vital role of bureaucrats is to collect information with which to evaluate old policies and propose new ones. As information is collected and passed up through the system, some is highlighted and much discarded. Information is often provided by those below according to what they believe their superiors want to hear. The result of this filtering process for decision-makers is often a narrow set of options and distorted view of the issue. For example, for years intelligence reports on Vietnam presented a rosy view that victory was just around the corner, that with more troops, firepower, and bombing the communists would be defeated. The reality was just the opposite. How did this intelligence distortion develop? President Lyndon Johnson made it clear through his statements and actions that this was the result he wanted, and thus key officials at different levels in the intelligence community filtered out any information that ran counter to what the administration wanted to hear. The Navy and Air Force in particular deliberately exaggerated the effectiveness of their respective bombing campaigns, with each hoping the president would favor one branch of the military over the other. But the chief effect of these exaggerations may have been to convince President Johnson that he could win the war through bombing.[22] It was said that Reagan administration CIA chief William Casey, "does not ask us for a review of an issue or a situation. He wants material he can use to persaude his colleagues, justify controversial policy, or expand the agency's involvement in covert action."[23]

Finally, bureaucracies shape decisions when they are responsible for implementing them. Ronald Reagan once lamented that, "one of the hardest things [about being president] is to know that down there is a permanent structure that's resisting everything you're doing." Or, as Harry Truman put it just before he handed the White House over to Dwight Eisenhower, "Poor Ike, he's used to having orders carried out and he'll sit in the Oval Office and no one will do want he wants."

Graham Allison's analysis of the Cuban missile crisis provides many cases of bureaucracies continuing to pursue their own narrow interests while the nation's interests hung in the balance. For example, the missiles could have been revealed sooner had the Defense Department and CIA not squabbled for five days over who should be responsible for flying over Cuba. The Defense Department won, but its overflight failed to provide the necessary intelligence. Negotiations resumed and it was finally decided to allow Air Force pilots to fly the CIA U-2 spyplanes. Another five days were then spent training the Air Force pilots to fly the U-2's. During the crisis itself, adhering to its "standard operating procedures," the Navy refused to obey President Kennedy's order that they move their blockade from 800 to 500 miles from Cuba to give the Soviets more time to consider the consequences. Fortunately, Khrushchev ordered his ships carrying missiles to reverse course before they reached the American blockade. In addition, the Navy forced Russian submarines to the surface without presidential authorization. The Air Force also acted contrary to instructions, sending a U-2 spy plan over Soviet territory after Kennedy's order not to commit any provocative acts.

While bureaucracies play an important role in policy making everywhere, the role of political parties varies greatly from one political system to the next, depending on the relative importance of a state's legislature in the system. Obviously parties play no role in those countries in which they are outlawed, and their importance varies from one one-party state to the next. In communist party states the party and government are synonymous, and thus the party plays the central role in policy making. In communist countries, policy results from the tug-of-war among a range of ideological and personal factions splitting the party. The Communist parties of the Soviet Union and China are particularly known for their divisions between ideological hard-liners who want to maintain confrontation with the West and pragmatists who seek detente. In noncommunist one-party states, the party's role may be purely symbolic. The legislature's purpose is simply to rubber stamp the executive's decisions without dissent, while elsewhere the party is used to mobilize the population behind government decisions.

The role of political parties in foreign policy is often constrained even in liberal democracies. In parliamentary systems, the prime minister is chosen by the majority party or coalition of parties in the legislature. While the majority party may be divided on issues and harshly debate them, once a decision is reached the party generally votes as a bloc.

In contrast, there is no party discipline in the United States Congress; every Representative and Senator votes for his or her own interests regardless of the postion the party leaders desperately try to encourage. Groups of like-minded legislators representing powerful interests can have an enormous impact on policy. Because of its constitutional powers involving trade and the declaration of war, Congress leads as much as it follows in foreign policy. Frequently there is a Republican president and Democratic Congress, and the result can be either consensus or deadlock depending on the issue and the president's skills.

Interest groups actively lobby the government for decisions favoring themselves. Although bureaucracies and political parties can both be considered interest groups in the broad sense of the term, interest groups are generally considered to be composed of private citizens rather than public officials. Interest groups can be broad based, such as business federations, labor groups, ethnic, and racial groups which may have an opinion on a range of issues, or those which focus on one or a few issues like disarmament or support for Israel.

Perhaps no country has more formal interest groups than the United States—in 1992, there were over 40,000 lobbyists registered in Washington. In America's open political system, foreign interest groups often play an important role in policy. Pat Choate's book, *Agents of Influence* reveals that Japan's government and businesses spend over $400 million annually in the United States trying to influence laws and policies in Japan's interests.[24] In the 1970s, the "Koreagate scandal" revealed huge bribes paid by South Korean agents to politicians to swing their votes on issues affecting South Korea. Many American bureaucrats resign their positions and to go to work for foreign interest groups, using their understanding of and access to America's political system to great advantage for their foreign employers.

To greatly varying extents, public opinion plays a role in every state's foreign policy-making process. Clearly, the more democratic the country, the more leaders make decisions with one eye glued to public opinion polls. Public opinion's influence on policy, in turn, varies from one democratic country to the next. A study of four liberal democracies found that public opinion had the greatest impact on foreign policy in the United States, followed by Germany, Japan, and France.[25]

Public opinion is not a monolithic bloc, but it reflects all the divisions of a nation's political spectrum. One study identified four major public opinion groups in the United States and Western Europe, with the relative strength of each bloc varying considerably among Europeans and Americans. A slightly greater percentage of Americans (24 percent) than Europeans (21 percent) were "Cold War Warriors" who took a hardline against the Soviet Union and favored higher military spending. Conversely, more Europeans (34 percent) than Americans (28 percent) were "internationalists" who favored open markets and increased social and cultural ties. More Americans (26 percent) than Europeans (20 percent) were "accommodationists" who favored international economic and social ties but little military activity. Almost exactly a quarter of the population on both sides of the Atlantic were "isolationists", Europeans (25 percent) and Americans (24 percent).

There is a dynamic relationship between governments and public opinion, in which each shapes the other's view. For example, America's opinion of the Soviet Union shifted markedly between 1989 and 1990. In April 1989, half of Americans believed the Soviets sought to dominate the world, a percentage which fell to 29 percent by May 1990. This view undoubtedly reflected Gorbachev's revolutionary policies which liberated Eastern Europe and democratized the Soviet Union. But how much did public opinion shift to reflect the Bush administration's increasingly conciliatory policies toward the Soviet Union and how much did it encourage the Bush administration to become more conciliatory?

American public opinion is usually only important on emotional issues of American involvement in wars, famine relief, and trade disputes that result in lost American jobs. Although, like peoples elsewhere, Americans tend to rally around the flag in crises, throughout the twentieth century, but particularly since Vietnam, American presidents have become increasingly careful about how and when they commit American troops to combat. For example, President Bush spent six months carefully building American support for the Persian Gulf coalition, as well as nurturing international opinion and actually winning UN backing of his plans before he sought Congressional approval.

Public opinion can be contradictory and fickle. All along the public gave President Bush mixed messages about the proper policy in the Persian Gulf. Between August 1990, when Iraq's invasion occurred and the beginning of fighting in January 1991, 67 percent to seventy-five percent of the public consistently favored sending troops to the region, even though 80 percent thought that the result would be war. Yet a majority were against sending any troops to the Persian Gulf if it cost any American lives or was simply to keep oil prices low. Fearing to inflame public opinion, President Bush did not explain to the American people that America's interest in the Persian Gulf was to keep oil flowing at low prices, and the best means of achieving that was to not allow any one country to dominate the region. He also did not explain that in order to achieve American interests, the United States had to protect Kuwait and Saudi Arabia, which had highly authoritarian political systems. Instead, he justified America's involvement by describing Iraqi President Hussein as another Hitler, bent on regional conquest and genocide and was committing genocide with his invasion of Kuwait, and therefore the United States had a moral mission to protect "democracy and freedom" in the region. Before the Coalition forces went to war against Iraq in January 1991, the American people were almost evenly divided over whether or not war in the Persian Gulf was justified. However, as soon as the bombs began to drop those who approved of the war, increased to nearly 80 percent!

Often coalitions of bureaucrats, representatives, and interest groups form to promote their collective interests on specific issues. An example of one of these *iron triangles* is the *military industrial complex* composed of the Defense Department, Representatives from districts with military bases or factories, and military contractors who collectively succeed in gaining more money, programs, and power from the political system. President Eisenhower coined the term, "military industrial complex" in his farewell speech in 1960, and he warned Americans that its continued growth threatened democracy itself.

Often there are iron triangles with opposing interests which check each other's power. Perhaps a more accurate way to understand policy making is to think of *policy clusters* which, along with either iron or loose triangles, include prominent journalists and academics, public opinion, and foreign interest groups which share an interest in the policy.

National System

A nation's heritage can profoundly affect its foreign policy. Culture and ideology provide a value system for evaluating present conflicts, dilemmas, and choices. History offers "lessons" from similar past situations to apply to contemporary ones. A nation's geographic position, development level, and natural and human resources all affect national interests and policies.

For example, many scholars have argued that Soviet foreign policy is simply a continuation of traditional Russian foreign policy which sought to expand national territory to defensible natural borders, dominate either directly or indirectly Eastern Europe, and achieve great power status and equality with the West. That policy of territorial, military, and political expansion, in turn, was shaped by the vulnerability of the Russian people on the vast steppes to foreign invasion. During Russia's 1,000 year history it suffered over 250 invasions of various magnitudes. Different leaders have advocated different strategies for achieving those goals. Slavophiles from Ivan the Terrible to Stalin have emphasized the importance for Russia to carve out a vast empire and act as the political and cultural leader of the Slavic peoples, while shunning the West. Westerners from Peter the Great to Gorbachev have argued that Russia can best achieve its security through adopting advanced Western technology and organization and maintaining good relations with the West.

History, however, is often an unreliable guide to present circumstances. American leaders learned from the 1930s policy toward Japan, Germany, and Italy that appeasement only stimulates the desire of dictators for more conquests. Hence, after 1945, vowing "no more Munichs," the United States refused to compromise on virtually every conflict with the Soviet Union and assumed that every Soviet move was part of some grand design to conquer the world. It can be argued that this uncompromising stance may have wrecked any possibility of reconciliation and deepened Cold War animosities. In 1949, the communists overthrew the American-backed Chiang Kaishek regime. The question "Who lost China?" soon reverberated through America's political system, a cry that may have influenced Presidents Eisenhower, Kennedy, and Johnson to do anything not to lose Vietnam.

People often judge others by their past rather than present behavior. For example, in the 50 years since World War II ended, Japan has developed into not only the world's most dynamic economic superpower but also into a highly democratic nation with an excellent human rights record and mass antiwar sentiment. For East and Southeast Asians, however, memories of Japan's brutal aggression and occupation of their nations remain vivid and shape their perceptions of Japan's policies toward them and the world. Because of this fear of Japanese domination and exploitation, a formal East and Southeast Asian Community, patterned after the European Community or North American Free Trade Association, is unlikely to emerge soon, if at all.

Ideology is important in helping to define the ends and means of a nation's interests. A liberal democratic state would emphasize the importance of preserving civil rights and the democratic political process. Marxist-Leninist states would strive to achieve a centrally planned economy which would promote relative income equality and universal health, education, and retirement benefits. Countries with a revolutionary ideology like communism or fundamentalist Islam often try to promote revolution elsewhere.

International System

Ideally, foreign policy is a grand plan to effectively overcome foreign challenges and create opportunities to advance national interests. But even in the most powerful states, policy-makers spend more time and energy reacting to rather than shaping international issues. Ultimately, a government's decisions on an international issue depend on the decisions of other states involved directly and indirectly in that issue. Policy is obviously shaped by a nation's power relative to that of other states involved in that international conflict. Depending on the issue, the global or regional geopolitical or geoeconomic power balance profoundly affects the options a government can pursue to serve its national interests.

Kenneth Waltz recently pointed out that the "international structure emerges from the interactions of states and then constrains them from taking certain actions while propelling them toward others."[26] There is thus a dynamic relationship between the actions of states and the system of which they are a part. The system's parameters are determined by the power balance and the values of the most powerful states. The system's parameters change through the countless actions of states, and the more powerful the state, the more it shapes the system. Yet, the system itself constrains the range of a state's policy options, and the less powerful the state the more the system constrains it. As John Ruggie argued, the international system "becomes a force that the units may not be able to control; it constrains their behavior and interposes itself between their intentions and the outcomes of their actions."[27]

Geography can also impose both policy opportunities and constraints. The most important issues for most countries are with their neighbors. Dealing with hostile neighbors becomes the central focus of a state's foreign policy. For example, Israel's foreign policy is largely shaped by the question of what to do about being a small country surrounded by hostile neighbors. Different Israeli governments have dealt with that reality by pursuing dramatically different policies of either confrontation, reconciliation, or some combination of the two. To explain these differences we must analyze the other levels of analysis.

Economic interdependence or outright dependence also constrains a nation's foreign policy. For example, because America's economy is so economically intertwined with Japan's, Washington would probably never seriously retaliate against Japan's neomercantilist policies for fear that both countries would be plunged into a deep depression. Developing countries which depend on world currency markets or the IMF for finance must often promise to reduce spending, devalue their currency, and free markets in return for loans.

Perfect freedom is impossible for states in an international system just as it is for individuals within a state. Those very constraints motivate many states to try to maximize their independence within an existing state system and shift the system's rules in their favor. According to Waltz, "states seek to control what they depend on or to lessen the extent of their dependency. This . . . explains quite a bit of the behavior of states: their imperial thrusts to widen the scope of their control and their autarchic strivings toward greater self-sufficiency."[28]

TYPES OF POLICIES

The more powerful a country, the more complex its international relations and the more extensive its range of policies. In his "World Event/Interaction Survey," McClelland analyzed 63 types of foreign policy behavior among the major states, and, among other things found three predominant behavior patterns—cooperative, routine, and conflictual, and that the five most active states were involved in 40 percent of all recorded behavior.[29]

Crisis Policy Making

A *crisis decision* or policy is one in which vital interests are at stake; there is the threat of violence, and a limited time in which to respond. The time constraints and high stakes limit those involved in decision making to a small group of advisors around the leader.

Usually neither side wants war or to give in to the other's demands. Participants in a crisis play the game of *chicken* in which they increase the pressure and stakes until the other side gives way. Sometimes they will carefully manage the crisis so that it is resolved short of war. At other times they mismanage the crisis, and war results.

Crisis management is very difficult. Given the time constraints, it is impossible to have all the information necessary to make a clear, rational choice among alternative policies. Thus decision makers make the best decision based on what information they can collect and process within what time the crisis allows. Unable to gain access to all the information they need and unable to make sense of what information they have received, crisis decision-makers often fall back on pre-existing stereotypes about their opponent's characteristics and behavior and the outcome of previous similar situations. They tend to believe the worst about their opponents and judge any action in that light. Henry Kissinger explained the psychology of crisis decision-making: "During fast-moving events those at the center of decision are overwhelmed by floods of reports compounded of conjecture, knowledge, hope, and worry. These must then be sieved through the [decision-makers'] preconceptions. Only rarely does a coherent picture emerge."[30]

Decision makers tend to fall back on "standard operating procedures" and *satisfice* or make the decision that seems to make the most sense at the time rather than examine alternative views of the situation.[31] The result is often a serious misjudgment or misperception about what is actually happening, and thus the crisis is escalated rather than defused.

The events leading to the outbreak of World War I provide a classic example of misperceptions leading to tragedy. World War I broke out largely because the participants were unable to successfully manage the crisis which preceded it. All the great powers had very rigid timetables for mobilizing their forces for war. Time was essential for all, particularly Germany, which faced the possibility of fighting a two-front war against France and Russia. When one country began its mobilization, all others had to begin theirs or face being overrun. Because mobilizations were based on highly intricate railroad schedules, any delay or cancellation would create mass havoc. The great powers were also locked into two rigid alliance systems. Thus, when Austria declared war on Serbia when the visiting Austrian Archduke Ferdinand was assassinated by anarchists in Serbian Sarajevo, Russia went to Serbia's defense, Germany to Austria's, and France and eventually Great Britain to Russia's. At no point did anyone attempt to determine whether the assassination of the Archduke was the work of Serbia (it was not), or even whether it was worth risking a European-wide war.[32]

Perhaps the most essential aspect of crisis management is allowing the opponent a face-saving way to back down, which often requires both sides to compromise. Kissinger writes that if:

> *crisis management requires cold and even brutal measures to show determination,*
> *it also imposes the need to show opponents a way out. Grandstanding is good for the*
> *ego but bad for foreign policy. Many wars have been started because no good line of*
> *retreat was left open. Superpowers have a special obligation not to humiliate each*
> *other.*[33]

During the Cuban missile crisis, Kennedy offered Khrushchev a face-saving opportunity by promising to withdraw American missiles from Turkey if Moscow withdrew theirs from Cuba, and further softened Khrushchev's defeat by describing the crisis' resolution as a "victory for peace" rather than an American victory. Rather than back Kruschev against the wall with humiliating terms, Kennedy allowed him a way out and in so doing probably avoided World War III.

Routine Policy Making

Noncrisis decisions and policies are reached after the issue has been debated by all relevant participants. Most policies are incremental and simply involve small policy adjustments to reflect new realities. For example, President Nixon's "Vietnamization" policy of gradually handing over the fighting to the South Vietnamese army did not represent a dramatic change from America's Indochina policy. Others are innovative and are characterized by a significant shift in policy. For example, President Nixon's decisions to establish relations with mainland China and take the United States off the gold standard were two highly innovative policies.

Intermestic Policies

As the world becomes ever more interdependent, policies become increasingly *intermestic* or involve both foreign and domestic issues. For example, the United States' 1993 military budget remained an enormous $274 billion despite the Cold War's end, not so much because there were clear and present military dangers abroad—there were none that justified that spending level or force structure—but because a rapid reduction in spending would exacerbate the recession at home and worsen George Bush's chances for reelection. During September 1992, George Bush promised to sell 150 F-15 fighter planes to Saudi Arabia and 50 F-16 fighters to Taiwan despite the complications both sales would cause American relations with Israel and China, respectively. The reasons for these sales were jobs and the President's reelection. During his 1992 campaign Governor Clinton promised that he would build two Seawolf submarines that the Pentagon had cancelled. The reason? Once again . . .

CONCLUSION

President Kennedy once said: "Domestic policy can only defeat us, foreign policy can kill us."[34] Certainly, the foreign policy stakes for a superpower in the nuclear age are high. Yet, despite the preponderant weight of the great powers in international relations, each country's foreign policy is vital to protecting and enhancing its own respective national interests. Virtually all countries share the goals of military security, economic development, political independence, and cultural preservation. Each state varies considerably, however, in how it defines these broad interests, and the means it uses to achieve them.

To try to understand foreign policy is to try to understand history. Why did things happen as they did? What alternatives existed, and why were they not followed? The answer varies from one policy and one government to the next. In every country, each policy is shaped by an often vastly different constellation of internal and external forces. The process by which national interests are defined is also largely the process by which they are promoted. As Waltz put it, the policies of countries "fluctuate with the changing currents of domestics, are prey to the vagaries of a shifting cast of political leaders, and are influenced by the outcome of bureaucratic struggles."[35] Invariably we come back to the level of analyis matrix to make sense of it all.

STUDY QUESTIONS

1. What is foreign policy?

2. What are national interests and why are they often so difficult to define?

3. When does ideology play an important role shaping foreign policy?

4. What are some models by which analysts attempt to understand how foreign policies are made? What are the flaws in those foreign policy models?

5. Does history make people or do people make history?

6. What are the five components of the level of analysis matrix?

7. In what ways can a leader's psychology and character affect foreign policy?

8. What are the psychological phenomena groupthink, mirror image, and cognitive dissonance, and how can they affect foreign policy?

9. How can a leader's immediate system of advisors, bureaucracy, political parties, interest groups, public opinion, and the mass media affect foreign policy?

10. How can a nation's history, culture, and power affect foreign policy?

11. How can the international system provide opportunities, constraints, and challenges for a nation's foreign policy?

12. What is "crisis decision making?" What are the ingredients of successful crisis management?

ENDNOTES

1. For some excellent recent overviews of foreign policy making and implementation, see: Margaret Hermann and Charles Hermann, "Who Makes Foreign Policy Decisions and How: An Empirical Inquiry," *International Studies Quarterly,* vol. 3,

December 1989, 316–388; Roger Hillsman, *The Politics of Policy Making in Defense and Foreign Affairs: Conceptual Models and Bureaucratic Politics* (Englewood Cliffs, N.J.: Prentice-Hall, 1990); Irving Janis, *Crucial Decisions: Leadership in Policymaking and Crisis Management* (New York: Free Press, 1989); Lloyd Jensen, *Explaining Foreign Policy* (Englewood Cliffs, N.J.: Prentice-Hall, 1982); Bahgat Korany, *How Foreign Policy Decisions Are Made in the Third World* (Boulder, Colo.: Westview Press, 1986); Jonathan Roberts, *Decision-Making During International Crises* (New York: St. Martin's Press, 1988).

2. Paul Kennedy, *Rise and Fall of the Great Powers* (New York: Random House, 1987).

3. Raymond Aron, *Peace and War: A Theory of International Relations* (New York: Doubleday, 1966), 91–92.

4. See Wolfram Hanrieder, ed., *Comparative Foreign Policy: Theoretical Essay* (New York: McKay, 1971); R.J. Rummel, *The Dimensions of Nations* (Beverly Hills, Calif.: Sage Publications, 1972); James Rosenau, ed., *Comparing Foreign Policies: Theories, Findings, and Methods* (Beverly Hills, Calif.: Sage Publications, 1974); Robert Wendzel, *International Relations: A Policy-Maker Focus* (New York: Wiley, 1980); James Caporaso et al., "The Comparative Study of Foreign Policy," *International Studies Notes,* vol. 13, no. 2, Spring 1987, 32–46.

5. The classic realist study is Hans Morganthau, *Politics Among Nations: The Struggle for Power and Peace,* 6th ed. (New York: Knopf, 1985).

6. Henry Kissinger, *The White House Years* (Boston: Little, Brown, 1979), 37.

7. Ted Sorensen, *Decision-Making in the White House* (New York: Columbia University Press, 1963), 19–20.

8. George Kennan, *American Diplomacy, 1900–1950* (Chicago: University of Chicago Press, 1951), 65–66.

9. Quoted from Carlton Hayes, *The Historical Evolution of Modern Nationalism* (New York: Macmillan, 1950), 40.

10. Quoted in Winston Churchill, *The Gathering Storm* (Boston: Houghton Mifflin, 1948), 315.

11. Cordell Hull, *The Memoirs of Cordell Hull* (New York: Macmillan, 1948), 1314–14315.

12. Graham Allison, *Essence of Decision* (Boston: Little, Brown, 1971); For a recent analysis of the crisis, see James G. Blight and David A. Welch, *On the Brink: Americans and Soviets Re-examine the Cuban Missile Crisis* (New York: Hill & Wang, 1989).

13. Among the more prominent works on the relationship between psychology, policy making, and politics, see: Ole Hosti, "The Belief System and National Image: A Case Study," *Journal of Conflict Resolution,* vol. 6, 1962, 244–252; Alexander and Juliette George, *Woodrow Wilson and Colonel House: A Personality Study* (New York: Day, 1956); Margaret Hermann, "Explaining Foreign Policy Behavior Using the Personality Characteristics of Policy Leaders," *International Studies Quarterly,* vol. 24, no. 1, 1980, 7–46; Joseph DeRivera, *The Psychological Dimensions of Foreign Policy* (Columbus, Ohio: Merrill, 1968); Robert Jervis, *Perception and Misper-*

ception in World Politics (Princeton N.J.: Princeton University Press, 1976); Pamela J. Conover and Stanley Feldman, "How People Organize the Political World: A Schematic Model," *American Journal of Political Science,* vol. February 1984, 95–126; Jon Hurwitz and Mark Peffley, "Public Images of the Soviet Union: The Impact of Foreign Policy Attitudes," *Journal of Politics,* vol. 52, February 1990, 3–28; James Kuklinski, Robert Luskin, and John Bolland, "Where is the Schema: Going Beyond the "S" Word in Political Psychology," *American Political Science Review,* vol. 85, December 1991, 1341–1355.

14. Kenneth Boulding, "National Images and International Systems," *Journal of Conflict Resolution,* vol. 3, June 1959, 120–131.

15. Doris Kearns, *Lyndon Johnson and the American Dream* (New York: Harper and Row, 1976), 264.

16. Alexander George, "The Operational Code," *International Studies Quarterly,* vol. 13., no. 2, 1969.

17. Ole Hosti, "The 'Operational Code' Approach to the Study of Political Leaders: John Foster Dulles' Philosophical and Instrumental Beliefs," *Canadian Journal of Political Science,* vol. 3, no. 1. March 1970, 123–157.

18. Charles Kegley and Eugene Wittkopf, *World Politics: Trend and Transformation* (New York: St. Martin's Press, 1992), 17.

19. Henry Kissinger, *The White House Years,* 1202.

20. Irving Janis, *Groupthink: Psychological Studies of Policy Decisions and Fiascoes* (Boston: Houghton Mifflin, 1982).

21. See Allison's examples and Morton Halperin, *Bureaucratic Politics and Foreign Policy* (Washington, D.C.: The Brookings Institute, 1974).

22. Morton Halperin, "Why Bureaucracies Play Games," *Foreign Policy,* vol. 2, Spring 1971, 83.

23. Glenn Hastedt, "Controlling Intelligence: Values and Perspectives of Administration," paper presented at the International Studies Association, Washington, D.C., April 1987.

24. Pat Choate, *Agents of Influence* (New York: Basic Books, 1991).

25. Thomas Risse-Kappen, "Public Opinion, Domestic Structure, and Security Policy in Liberal Democracies: France, Japan, West Germany, and the United States," paper presented at the International Studies Association, Washington, D.C., April 1990.

26. Kenneth Waltz, "Realist Thought and Neorealist Theory," in Robert Rothstein, ed., *The Evolution of Theory in International Relations* (Columbia: University of South Carolina Press, 1991), 21–38.

27. John Ruggie, "Continuity and Transformation in the World Polity: Toward a Neorealist Synthesis, " *World Politics,* vol. 35, January 1983, 261–285.

28. Kenneth Waltz, "Realist Thought and Neorealist Theory," in Robert Rothstein, ed. *The Evolution of Theory in International Relations* (Columbia: University of South Carolina Press, 1991), 110.

29. Charles McClelland and Gary Hoggard, "Conflict Patterns in the Interaction Among States," in James Rosenau, ed., *International Politics and Foreign Policy,* rev. ed. (New York: Free Press, 1969), 711–724; See also Arnold Wolfers, "The Pole of Power and the Pole of Indifference," in James Rosenau, ed. *International Politics and Foreign Policy,* rev. ed. (New York: Free Press, 1961); R.J. Rummel, "Dimensions of Conflict Within and Between States," *General Systems Yearbook,* vol. 8, 1963, 1–50; R.J. Rummel, Stephen Salmore and Donald Munton, "An Empirically Based Typology of Foreign Policy Behavior," in James Rosenau, *Comparing Foreign Policies: Theories, Findings, and Methods* (Beverly Hills, Calif.: Sage Publications, 1974.

30. Henry Kissinger, *The White House Years,* 627.

31. The term "satisfice" was popularized by Herbert Simon, *Models of Man* (New York: Wiley, 1957), 89.

32. See Marc Trachtenberg, "The Meaning of Mobilization in 1914," and Jack Levy, "Preference, Constraints, and Choices in July 1914," *International Security,* vol. 15, no. 3, Winter 1990–91, and vol. 16, no. 1, Summer 1991.

33. Henry Kissinger, *Years of Upheaval* (Boston: Little, Brown, 1982), 167.

34. Quoted in Arthur Schlesinger, *A Thousand Days: John F. Kennedy in the White House* (Greenwich, CT: Fawcett Publications, 1967), 395.

35. Kenneth Waltz, *Theory of International Politics* (Reading, Mass.: Addison-Wesley, 1979), 17.

Nonstate Forces and Actors in International Relations

International Law and Morality

Key Terms and Concepts

Arbitration
Comity
Conciliation
Condominium
Constitutive Theory
Corpus Juris Gentium
Court of Arbitration
Declarative Theory
Eclectic School
Good Offices
Immunity

International Court of
    Justice (ICJ)
Jurisdiction
Legal Person
Mediation
Naturalist School
Neorealist School
Pacta Sunt Servanda
Permanent Court of
    Arbitration (PCA)
Permanent Court of

International Justice
    (PCIJ)
Positivist School
Rebus Sic Stantibus
Recognition
Reservation
Sources of International Law
Sovereignty
Subjects of the Law
Terra Nullius
Ubi Societas Ibi Jus

One of the most striking characteristics of the modern world is the growing importance of law in governing human relations within and between states. Some people, however, question whether international law truly exists and, if so, whether it is relevant to international relations. Some argue that despite the plethora of legally binding treaties, customs, and principles, international law is more a moral and theoretical framework for international behavior rather than a legal one. Without a global legislature that creates laws, an international police force which can bring violators to trial, a comprehensive global court system, and a means of enforcing legal decisions, international law is meaningless. At best, the world is governed by frontier and often vigilante justice. International relations are shaped by a Darwinian survival of the fittest mentality in which the strong battle the strong and subject the weak.

Compliance with international law is purely voluntary. Although states may comply with most international laws most of the time, they do so because compliance serves national interests rather than international concepts of right and wrong. Whenever national interest and international law conflict, most states will serve the former. Israeli diplomat Abba Eban summed up this perspective by arguing that "international law is that which the wicked do not obey and the righteous do not enforce."

Although the above arguments may be true, it still does not mean that international law is nonexistent. Every legal system has people who comply with and those who break the law. Of the lawbreakers, some are caught and punished while others escape. In any legal system, individuals and groups choose to obey the law because it is in their interest to do so or because they fear the consequences of not doing so. National legal systems have often proved no more effective in preventing crime and sometimes a total breakdown of law than international law has. After all, civil wars are more common than international wars.

In reality, states are just as law-abiding in the global system as individuals and groups are in most national legal systems. As in national legal systems, international law may be vague or nonexistent in some disputes. Right and wrong may be blurred or ambiguous. Yet, international law does indeed exist.[1]

This chapter will analyze the role of law in international relations. It will examine the development of international law, its sources and subjects. It will also examine issues such as jurisdiction and immunity, sovereignty and recognition, the acquisition of territory, enforcement, and human rights.

DEVELOPMENT OF INTERNATIONAL LAW

Order, not anarchy, rules the world, and international law is a vital component of that order. International law has evolved with the global political economy and is inseparable from it. International law is nearly as old as international relations. Treaties were the first international laws, signed by ancient Egyptians, Assyrians, Hindus, and others. In time international law evolved beyond the legal obligations of treaty signers to the Roman Empire's *jus gentium,* or "law of nations."

Modern international law evolved with the modern state system. The Treaty of Westphalia in 1648, which ended the Thirty Years War, began the modern era of sovereign nation-states whose relations were increasingly governed by a steadily expanding body of international customs, treaties, and principles, known then as the "law of nations." Throughout the modern era the body of international law among nations, *corpus juris gentium,* expanded rapidly in response to the challenges the continual changes in the global political economy posed to international relations. There is a dynamic relationship between politics and law, in which laws emerge from attempts to resolve political issues and then in turn shape the context in which politics take place. Although international law primarily governs relations between states (public international law), it has expanded to include international organizations, multinational corporations, and individuals (private international law).

Although few people disputed international law's reality, there were fierce debates over its inherent nature and applicability. The first legal scholars argued that international law was rooted in natural law. Although three Spanish legal scholars—Francisco de Victoria (1486–1546), Alberico Gentili (1552–1608), and Francisco Suarez (1548–1617)—laid the groundwork, the Dutchman Hugo Grotius (1583–1645) is regarded as the father of international law and the *naturalist school.* Although Grotius agreed with the Spaniards that international law had a divine origin, in his "On the Law of War and Peace" (1625) he argued that international law would exist even without God. According to the naturalist school, there are some laws natural to all human beings despite the various cultures to which they belong. Human reason could break free of any culture's values and customs to discover the underlying natural laws. Samuel Pufendorf (1632–1694) went beyond Grotius to argue that the only true laws came from nature and denied the validity of any laws orginating from treaties or custom.

During the eighteenth century, increasing numbers of legal theorists began to argue that the origins of laws are human rather than divine or natural and involve consent and self-interest. The most prominent person of the *positivists school* was the Dutchman

Cornelis van Bynkershoek (1673–1743). The *eclectic school* attempted to bridge the gap between naturalists and positivists. The Swiss theorist Emerich von Vattel (1714–67) maintained that although states did indeed have natural rights and duties, they were only obliged to fulfill them if those laws were codified. According to Vattel, "the Law of Nations is the science of the rights which exist between Nations or States, and the obligations corresponding to those rights."[2]

The *neorealist school* of international law argues that power and policy shape the rules or laws of the international system. International law changes and develops with shifts in the power distribution and the proliferation of issues in an increasingly interdependent global economy. Just as the most powerful states make the system's laws to protect and promote their own rather than international interests, they use the same criteria when choosing to obey or to disregard international law.[3] In the late twentieth century, the neorealist school was reinforced by the statements of many Third World leaders who argued that international law is rooted in Western civilization's values and thus discriminated against non-Western peoples.

SOURCES OF INTERNATIONAL LAW

Although scholars and political leaders may bicker over the nature of international law, there is a near universal consensus on its *sources*. Article 38 of the Statute of the *International Court of Justice* (ICJ) requires the court to base its decisions on three primary sources of international law (treaties, customs, and general principles) and two secondary sources (judicial opinions and legal theorists).

Sometimes the sources of international law conflict on a given subject. Treaties generally override custom, yet they often form the basis for new customs. The more signatories to a treaty, the more easily it can sweep away existing customs. However, if countries continue to follow old practices rather than the proscriptions of a new treaty, then customs clearly are more important. Legal principles are considered more important than treaties. According to the 1969 Vienna Convention of Treaties, "a treaty is void if . . . it conflicts with a peremptory norm [principle] of general international law [*ius cogens*]." Judicial decisions and scholarship are generally subordinate to treaties, customs, and principles because judges and scholars use those sources as the basis for their own legal interpretations.

Treaties

Treaties are the most explicit sources of international law and are signed with the universal understanding that they are legally binding (*pacta sunt servanda*). The number of international treaties has soared over the modern era: between 1648 and 1919, the treaties filled 226 thick volumes; between 1920 and 1946, 205 volumes; and between 1946 and 1978, 1,115 volumes.[4] There is probably no aspect of international relations, no matter how obscure, that has not been regulated by treaty. There is even an international treaty—the 1969 Vienna Convention on the Law of Treaties—regulating the writing and signing of international treaties. The convention was the culmination of two decades of work begun in 1949 by the International Law Commission, which was set up by the United Nations as an advisory group to draft a treaty codifying several hundred years of customary law regarding treaties. The Law of Treaties came into force on January 27, 1980, when the thirty-fifth state ratified it.

The convention states that treaties "are an international agreement concluded by states in written form and governed by international law" that "is binding upon the parties to it and must be performed by them in good faith." Most treaties carefully explain the obligations of participants and the consequences if those obligations are violated. Not included are oral agreements between states, agreements between states and international organizations, and agreements between international organizations. Every sovereign state has the right to negotiate and sign treaties— or refuse to do so.

States may ratify a treaty with written *reservations* in which they unilaterally declare themselves not bound by certain aspects of that treaty. According to the Vienna Convention, states can sign or ratify a treaty with reservations as long as the treaty does not prohibit reservations or the reservations are not compatible with the treaty's purpose. The other parties then may or may not agree to those reservations. If the reservation is compatible with the treaty's purpose and obligations, the treaty is legally acceptable even if other signatories disagree. If the reservation is not compatible, the treaty must be renegotiated. Treaties are obviously weakened in proportion to the number and type of reservations imposed by signatories.

The Vienna Convention allows states to suspend or terminate a treaty if all parties agree to do so, one or more parties seriously violate a treaty, one or more parties cannot discharge their duties, a fundamental change in circumstances (*rebus sic stantibus*) occurs, the state's own diplomats were corrupted or coerced into agreements at odds with their instructions, the treaty was imposed by force, or the treaty conflicts with international law. Many treaties include provisions that terminate the signatories' obligations after a certain period or objectives have been fulfilled or that allow parties to withdraw from their obligations after giving notice, usually six months.

The Vienna Convention is not retroactive—any treaties that were negotiated by force before the convention went into effect remain valid. Under the Vienna Convention, if any party challenges a treaty's validity, the dispute must be taken to the International Court of Justice if the dispute has not been resolved among the signatories within one year of the official protest.

A treaty comes into force when all parties have ratified it or when provisions in the treaty allow it to come into force after a certain number (often two-thirds) of parties have ratified it. A treaty may also come into force by a certain date after it has been ratified to allow states to adjust to the new obligations or by any other arrangements the parties to the treaty deem appropriate. The more states that are party to a treaty, the more usual is the treaty's coming into force after a certain number of states ratify it. Treaties usually only apply to those states that have ratified it. However, fulfilling treaty obligations can imply tacit ratification. States can also become parties to a treaty by accession or by signing it after it has been negotiated by other states.

Customs

Customs may be the ultimate source of international law. Vattel defined customs as "certain maxims and customs consecrated by long use, and observed by nations in their mutual intercourse with each other as a kind of law."[5] Whereas treaties express explicit rules of international law, customs represent an implicit understanding. States practice certain customs that eventually are codified in treaties. However, customs must generally be practiced by most states before they are considered the basis of law. Although the General Assembly's recommendations are not legally binding in themselves, they often identify international customs that can be important legal sources. If states do not protest a particular custom, their consent to it is implied. Custom need not have been of long duration as long as it is, in the words of the International Court of Justice in the North Sea Continental Shelf case, "both extensive and virtually uniform."[6]

Are new states bound by existing customs? The Soviet legal theorist G.I. Tunkin argues that new states "are legally entitled not to recognize particular customary rules of general international law. However, entry into official relations with other countries without reservations means that the new state accepts a certain body of principles and rules of existing international law that form the basis of relations between states."[7]

A classic example of the use of custom in international law occurred in 1898, when the U.S. Supreme Court ruled in the Paquete Habana (1900) case that the Navy had illegally seized and sold at auction two Cuban fishing boats during the Spanish-American War. Although there was no explicit international treaty governing the situation, the Court reasoned that:

> by ancient usage among civilized nations, beginning centuries ago, and gradually ripening into a rule of international law, coast fishing vessels, pursuing their vocation of catching and bringing in fresh fish, have been recognized as exempt, with their cargoes and crews, from capture as prize of war.[8]

Principles

As sources of international law, principles are those considered so basic that they are found in most legal systems. Although specific laws vary considerably between countries, they may well be related by the same principles. Principles fill the theoretical gap between custom and treaty, particularly in new areas of international law. For example, in the nineteenth century the arbitration of international disputes became common. The trouble was that there were no existing customs or treaties regulating arbitration. The identification of general principles allowed diplomats to close that gap. Sovereignty and human rights are general principles of international law.

Many scholars argue that no greater principle guides international law than the "golden rule." Sir William Blackstone (1723–1780) wrote:

> The law of nations is a system of rules, deducible by human reason, and established by universal consent among the civilized inhabitants of the world .   .   . This general law is founded upon this principle, that different nations ought in time of peace to do one another all the good they can, and in time of war as little harm as possible, without prejudice to their real interests.

Court Decisions and Scholarly Opinions

The decisions of both international and national courts can also shape international law. The statutes governing the International Court of Justice do not legally obligate it to take legal precedence (*stare decisis*) into account when making decisions. In practice, however, the ICJ uses previous decisions in similar cases to help decide new cases. Judicial decision can also be signs of customary law. The U.S. Supreme Court has been particularly sensitive to international law in its decisions. Yet judicial decisions can create law where none previously existed.

Scholars originated the study of international law and have continued to shape its evolution throughout the modern era. They explore the vast and expanding body of international treaties, practices, and principles, and help codify and expand international law.

SUBJECTS OF INTERNATIONAL LAW

A *subject of the law,* or *legal person,* has legal rights and duties. Before the twentieth century, only states were legal persons in international law. Since then corporations, organizations, and individuals have also become subjects of international law. Yet even today, only states can be parties before the International Court of Justice. Because sovereign states, not governments, are the subjects of international law, each new government of a state assumes the same legal rights and responsibilites of the previous governments—even revolutionary regimes.

Whether or not individuals are proper subjects of international law has been highly controversial. When natural law perspective held sway, individuals were considered legal personalities. This view was rejected during the nineteenth century, when positivists argued that no international laws could affect individuals or corporations because they were bound by the national laws in which they resided. Behind this reasoning is the fear that accepting international personality for individuals would undermine national laws over citizens.

However, starting with the Nuremburg and Tokyo war crime trials, the notion of individual duties and rights has grown in importance, thus eroding the positivist contention that only states can be international law subjects. The Nuremburg Tribunal contended that "crimes against international law are committed by men, not by abstract entities, and only by punishing individuals who commit such crimes can the provisions of international law be enforced."[9]

JURISDICTION

When a dispute occurs, the parties must determine which country or international court has *jurisdiction. Comity* is a legal principle in which one state allows the intrusion of another state's laws into its territory. Extradition would be an example of comity.

There are times when jurisdiction over a crime can be shared and disputed by two or more countries. Under the territorial principle, a state has jurisdiction over crimes committed in its territory. The only exception would be if a crime occurs in two states (for example, a murder or robbery spree), in which case both states would have jurisdiction. The nationality principle allows states to prosecute their own citizens for crimes committed anywhere in the world. The protective principle permits a state to prosecute foreigners who commit crimes in another country if those crimes (for example, plots to overthrow the government, drug-running, spying) jeopardize the first state's national security. Finally, the universality principle allows states to prosecute foreigners who commit crimes elsewhere, even if they do not directly harm the prosecuting state's security, if the crimes threaten the international community as a whole. War crimes and aggression would be examples of the universality principle.

When criminals seek refuge in another country, they can be extradited back to the country in which they committed the crime. Without an extradition treaty, states are neither required to nor prevented from handing over criminals. Extradition treaties are usually bilateral and list the specific crimes (which must be considered crimes by both states) under which extradition would occur. If there is no extradition treaty between two states, one state may use its municipal law of deportation to get rid of criminals who committed crimes in the other state.

IMMUNITY

Sovereign states and their diplomats are generally immune from the jurisdiction of national laws. Sovereignty, by definition, means no state and its laws have power over another state. Thus when one state accuses another of having committed a crime, representatives of the accused state will only appear voluntarily in the other state's courts. *Immunity* is granted only to the actions and property of a state and not to those of its private firms, organizations, or individuals, unless the state has a proprietary interest in them.

Diplomatic immunity is one of the oldest, most developed, and universal areas of international law. The 1961 Vienna Convention on Diplomatic Relations codified centuries-old customs on diplomatic exchange and immunity. Article 29 states that "the person of a diplomatic agent shall be inviolable. He shall not be liable to any form of arrest or detention. The receiving State shall treat him with due respect and shall take all appropriate steps to prevent any attack on his person, freedom, or dignity."

Diplomats have several important functions. Their overall duty is to protect their country's national and private interests vis-á-vis the foreign country. This involves negotiating important issues; gathering information about and proposing policies for the foreign country; promoting a positive image of one's country and policies; and protecting the rights of national firms, organizations, and individuals operating in the foreign country.

Diplomatic relations between two or more states occur by mutual consent. The receiving state has the power to approve any members and the size of the foreign mission, and it can at any time declare foreign diplomats persona non grata (unacceptable) and expel them from the country. A state can unilaterally break its relations with others, which usually involves withdrawing its own embassy and expelling the other state's embassy from its own territory.

Diplomats and their families (unless they are nationals of the receiving state) are immune from all criminal and most civil prosecution, and from any arrest or detention.

The only civil law exceptions involve nonofficial commercial transactions. In cases where a diplomat commits a serious crime, the receiving state can always ask the other state to withold immunity, a request that is often granted to preserve good relations. The embassies, residences, archives, documents, communications, and property of diplomatic missions are also inviolable and can only be entered by permission. Embassies, however, are not extraterritorial and cannot harbor criminals who take refuge there or imprison people. The exception is when someone seeks political asylum. Embassies and diplomats are exempt from all taxes and can import any items for official or personal use duty free. The receiving state is obligated to protect foreign embassies and their personnel from attack.

All states with overseas embassies have a clear interest in supporting diplomatic immunity. Major violations of diplomatic immunity, such as when Iranians invaded the American embassy in Terehan in 1979 and held the diplomats hostage for 444 days, are extremely rare. The International Court of Justice ruled in that case that "there is no more fundamental prerequisite for the conduct of relations between States than the inviolability of diplomatic envoys and diplomats."[10]

Consulates and consuls differ from embassies and diplomats. Their primary duty is not diplomacy but such nonpolitical functions as issuing visas and passports and promoting their country's commercial interests. The 1986 Vienna Convention on Consular Relations grants consuls a more limited protection than diplomats, holding them liable for both criminal and civil offenses that were not official acts.

The United Nations also enjoys immunity from all legal processes. Its premises, archives, documents, and property are inviolable; and it is exempt from taxes and import duties. The Secretary-General and Assistant Secretaries-General enjoy complete diplomatic immunity, whereas staff members and foreign diplomats do not have diplomatic immunity.

SOVEREIGNTY

Political philosophers originally conceived *sovereignty* as the distribution of power and location of supreme power within a state. Jean Bodin, in his "The Republic" (1576), defined sovereignty as the supreme lawmaking and law enforcing authority in a territory. Eventually, it came to mean the recognition and relationship of states with one another. According to the 1933 Montevideo Convention on the Rights and Duties of States, a state is sovereign if it has a clearly defined territory, permanent population, government with ultimate power over that territory and people, and recognition of independence by other sovereign states.

Sovereign states are legal equals. Vattel made the classic natural law case for equality among sovereign states: "Since men are naturally equal, and a perfect equality prevails in their rights and obligations, as equally proceeding from nature, nations composed of men, and considered as so many free persons living together in the state of nature, are naturally equal, and inherit from nature the same obligations and rights. Power or weakness does not in this respect produce any difference. A dwarf is as much a man as a giant; a small republic is no less a sovereign state than the most powerful kingdom."[11]

A sovereign state is independent, but it is not above the law. A change in government does not affect the state's sovereignty or the state's obligations incurred by the previous governments. For example, the Soviet government that came to power after the November 1917 Revolution was still responsible for the foreign debts owed by the Russian government, although it denied that responsibility.

RECOGNITION

Governments are free to recognize or withold *recognition* of each other. Some states distinguish between recognizing the sovereignty of a state (de facto recognition) and having diplomatic relations with it (de jure recognition). Also, a government may not formally recognize another through the exchange of embassies yet carry on full economic, diplomatic, and other relations. Most governments recognize other governments when these governments have achieved control over their population and territory. Some governments, like the United States, have based recognition on whether or not they agree with another government's political ideology and practices. The United States did not formally recognize the communist government that took over China in 1949 as legitimate until 1978! Now most states, including the United States, recognize states rather than governments.

There are two perspectives on recognition. The *constitutive theory* argues that states can only be legitimate if they receive international recognition. The *declarative theory* argues that recognition has no legal effect; states either exist or they do not, and recognition simply acknowledges that fact. For example, the western states refused to recognize the German Democratic Republic (East Germany) because it was created by the Soviet Union in violation of treaties. By the 1970s, however, most of the western states abandoned their constitutive position for a declarative position and recognized East Germany as a state regardless of its origins.

The 1923 Tinoco Case illustrates both the international recognition and sovereign responsibilities issues. Frederico Tinoco was a dictator of Costa Rica who made concessions to British companies, some of which were payments in special banknotes. The government that came to power after Tinoco's overthrow repudiated his actions and promises. Britain sued Costa Rica. The arbitration court ruled that the Tinoco government clearly controlled Costa Rica, and the new Costa Rican government was responsible for the obligations of the old, even though the Tinoco regime was considered unconstitutional and was not recognized by several states, including Britain. Thus the declarative principle was weighed more important than the constitutive principle.

There is a body of international law that obligates states not to recognize territorial changes caused by aggression. After Japan took over Manchuria in 1931, Secretary of State Henry Stimson announced what became known as the "Stimson Doctrine," under which the United States would not recognize any changes brought by Japanese imperialism. In 1932 the League of Nations adopted the same principle when it resolved that "it is incumbent upon the members of the League of Nations not to recognize any situation, treaty or agreement which may be brought about by means contrary to the

Covenant of the League of Nations or to the Pact of Paris." The UN General Assembly passed a similar resolution in 1970 when it declared that "no territorial acquisition resulting from the threat or use of force shall be recognized as legal."

International law has a Janus face regarding whether or not states are free from external interference in their internal affairs. On the one hand, states are legally considered sovereign powers accountable to no higher authority, free to rule their inhabitants, and war against their neighbors as they see fit. Yet on the other hand, states can be condemned and sanctioned for their human rights abuses, are prohibited from launching aggressive wars, and have eroded their own sovereignty by signing countless international treaties and the United Nations Charter.

THE ACQUISITION OF TERRITORY

States can aquire territory by several means. One state can cede land to another. States can claim unoccupied territory (*terra nullius*). By controlling another country's territory without dispute, states can acquire "squatters' rights" to it. Nature can give territory through volcanoes or changes in river courses. Land disputes can be adjudicated by a third party that can decide to grant the land to one or more of the interested states. States can lease their territory to others, as China leased Hong Kong to Britain or Cuba leased Guantanamo Bay to the United States. States can also acquire rights over the resources of other states, such as water for irrigation or transportation. The 1888 Convention of Constantinople declared the Suez Canal open to ships of all nations. International authorities can redraw boundaries and award mandates. For example, the Versailles Treaty created Yugoslavia, Poland, Czechoslovakia, Hungary, and Austria, and mandated that the defeated powers give up some of their territory to the victorious allies as mandates. There have been times when two or more states jointly occupied a territory (*condominium*). For example, the New Hebrides Islands were a condominium of Britain and France before they received independence in 1980.

States traditionally could incorporate conquered territory into their own land if the incorporation was acknowledged by treaty and the international community. Today, given the United Nation and international law proscriptions against aggressive wars, land acquired by conquest is considered illegal, even if it is taken by the victim of aggression. For example, a large majority of states in the United Nations opposes any Israeli attempts to incorporate land it conquered in the 1967 War.

If conquest is no longer a valid means of acquiring territory, who is entitled to land that was conquered in the past? In 1961 India invaded the Portugese colony of Goa, even though Portugal had originally acquired the territory in the sixteenth century, its inhabitants wished to remain Portugese, and, following its independence in 1947, India itself had recognized Portugal's title. The Nehru government justified its takeover by claiming that the land was traditionally Indian. The United Nations did not protest the conquest. China used India's rationale as an excuse for invading part of northern India that had traditionally been Chinese but had been taken by the British in the nineteenth century. India shrilly protested China's action.

UPHOLDING THE LAW

Compliance with international law is largely voluntary. Yet, why do most states obey the law most of the time?

Self-interest is obviously an important reason for compliance. International laws are created to regulate behavior and thus provide a degree of security for all if they are obeyed. If a state regularly violates the law, other states will avoid relations with it or retaliate, thus hurting that state. States realize that whereas the law may work against them in one situation, it may work for them in other situations. When states break the law they create a precedent that can be used against them; others states can justify breaking that law in a different situation that may work against the original lawbreaker. This realization deters states.

Sanctions work best, when they work at all, if they are imposed by a large group of states on the international lawbreaker. In 1990 the United Nations imposed sanctions against Iraq for its invasion of Kuwait. All international trade with Iraq, except humanitarian and food shipments, was forbidden until Baghdad compensated Kuwait for the damage it caused during the invasion and surrendered all of its nuclear, chemical, and biological weapons. Despite years of enduring economic boycott and a devastating war sanctioned by the United Nations, Iraq remains defiant.

Reprisals against lawbreakers are legal as long as they are proportional to the original crime. For example, in 1986 the United States bombed Libya in reprisal for an earlier Libya terrorist attack that killed two members of the American armed forces. But 37 people were killed in the American bombing raid, sparking a controversy over whether the action was a legitimate reprisal or a crime.

Governments, like individuals, do not primarily obey the law because of fear of sanctions. States also obey the law because they have deeply internalized concepts of right and wrong, and they believe the law is just. International laws are often based on long-standing international customs. In other words, states have already followed a particular behavior long before it was codified into law. Akehurst argues that, paradoxically, the absence of an international legislature is one reason why most states comply with international law. States make law for themselves and thus are more apt to comply with it than if it were imposed by a higher authority.[12]

International laws provide clear rules of behavior that, when complied with, reduce international conflict. States recognize that they all lose if any state breaks the rules. Governments, however, sometimes weigh the short-term concrete advantages of breaking a law as greater than the long-term abstract advantages of obeying it. This is particularly common when the law is vague or ambiguous. Then, any behavior can be justified, and states will try to get away with what they can. International tensions, however, increase. One sign of international law's growing importance is the fact that states will often claim that they are obeying the law even as they are breaking it by pointing to possible loopholes in that law.

Most of the time states will settle their differences through negotiations, which are often decided by international law. There are several ways to negotiate conflicts that do not involve going to court but include a third neutral party. In international conflicts interested third parties can offer their *good offices* in which they provide a neutral location but refrain from moderating the actual negotiations, as when the United States hosted the Middle East Peace negotiations in 1992. Third parties can also offer *concili-ation,* whereby they provide advice to both sides of the conflict but do not offer a reso-lution. In addition, third parties can offer *mediation,* whereby they propose nonbinding solutions to the participants, as in the Camp David negotiations of 1977 when Presi-dent Carter mediated between Eygptian President Sadat and Israeli Prime Minister Begin. Finally, *arbitration* involves a neutral state or body giving a binding decision through a specially convened court for that particular conflict.

International arbitration of property disputes dates to the Jay Treaty of 1794 be-tween the United States and Britain, which set up the machinery to settle cases involv-ing national boundaries, seizures of ships at sea, and other expropriation of property. The Jay Treaty became the model for dozens of other bilateral and multilateral treaties on the subject. Between 1795 and 1914, more than 200 arbitration panels were insti-tuted among states. The 1874 Alabama case was an important step in international arbitration. The case centered on the question of whether Britain had violated interna-tional law of neutrality by allowing the Confederacy to build warships in Britain with which to attack Union shipping. A panel of five judges from the United States, Britain, Italy, Switzerland, and Brazil ruled that Britain had violated neutrality laws, and Britain was ordered to pay the United States $15,500,000 in damages. President Grant was so pleased by the decision and Britain's compliance that he predicted "an epoch when a court recognized by all nations will settle international differences instead of keeping large standing armies."[13]

In 1899, representatives at an international conference at The Hague signed the Convention for the Pacific Settlement of International Disputes in which they promised to submit conflicts to arbitration panels. The *Permanent Court of Arbitration* (PCA) was set up to hear and decide grievances. Between then and 1914 the PCA set-tled over 120 conflicts. The Court, however, had no powers to require disputants to ap-pear or to comply with its decisions. It has been rarely used since 1914, deciding only ten cases through today.

While the PCA has dwindled in importance, other, more specialized interna-tional arbitration courts are increasingly important forums in which conflicts can be resolved. In 1922 the International Chamber of Commerce (ICC) established a *Court of Arbitration* in Paris, which then has heard more than 5,000 cases and recently more than 250 a year. Parties in a dispute can elect to take their case to the Court of Arbi-tration. The cases are decided according to international law. The American Arbitra-tion Association is second only to the ICC in the number of international conflicts it has settled. The World Bank has its International Center for Settlement of Investment disputes.

In 1919, at the Versailles Peace Conference ending World War I, President Wilson lobbied the other delegates for the creation of a world court for the League of Nations. On February 15, 1922, the League of Nations established the *Permanent Court of Inter-national Justice* (PCIJ). Between 1921 and 1945 the court issued 31 judgments, 25 sub-stantive orders, and 27 advisory opinions, about 3 or 4 decisions annually. However, the World Court, like the League of Nations, did nothing to prevent World War II and sat for the last time on December 4, 1939.

Like President Wilson, President Roosevelt was determined to create a global as-sembly and court that would help preserve peace. Throughout World War II Roosevelt pressured U.S. allies to create a new set of institutions that would succeed where the

League and PCIJ had failed. In August and September 1944, the United States, Britain, and the Soviet Union agreed at Dumbarton Oaks to establish the International Court of Justice (ICJ). In March 1945 a committee of jurists made up of representatives from 44 countries met to draft the agreement for a new court, and submitted its proposal before the San Francisco Conference, which created the United Nations. The new court was formally established on April 18, 1946.

In form, function, and location, the ICJ is largely the continuation of the PCIJ. Located at The Hague, the ICJ hears cases and then rules. The Court has 15 judges, 5 of which are elected every 3 years to hold office for 9 years. The Security Council and General Assembly vote on the judges. International organizations, including the UN Security Council, General Assembly, and any other institutions, can ask the court for advisory opinions. Every signatory to the United Nations Charter agrees to comply with ICJ decisions. Between 1946 and 1988 the ICJ heard only 55 cases, rendered judgments on 30, and handed down 19 advisory opinions.[14] The ICJ or a party to a dispute can call on the UN Security Council to act against recalcitrant states. The Security Council can vote on the measures necessary to implement a court decision.

Although the court's decisions are binding, the jurisdiction of the court is not. Whereas 162 of the UN members have agreed to accept the court's jurisdiction, 155 have included reservations that allow them to determine the cases under which it would accept jurisdiction. For example, in 1984, the Reagan administration simply announced that it would not accept the ICJ's jurisdiction in a suit filed by Nicaragua that alleged the United States had mined its harbors, supplied rebels, and tried to overthrow the government.

There are two other important international courts: the European Court of Justice (ECJ) at Luxembourg and the European Court of Human Rights at Strasbourg. Unlike the ICJ, the ECJ has compulsory jurisdiction over member states that have broken the rules. The court has 13 judges—one from each member state and one rotated from different members. The judges are advised by six advocate generals. The court can hear cases brought by states, organizations, or private litigants—including firms, interest groups, and individuals—that involve a breach of European Community law. The court has the power to overturn decisions made by the Executive Commission and council. The ECJ case load is far greater than that of the ICJ.

There is disagreement over whether or not the ECJ is a true international court. Some argue that European Union law differs so significantly from international law that it is a different species. Furthermore, the Union is increasingly seen as a federal state and its laws municipal rather than international. Others argue that because members retain their sovereignty and can withdraw from the Union, the laws uniting them are by definition international and in most cases do not differ substantially from those international laws with a global dimension.

HUMAN RIGHTS

Which is more important: the sovereign rights of governments to do what they will within their country or the rights of all humans to be free of repression, ill treatment, and genocide? Sovereign rights are increasingly giving way to human rights.

In 1815, Britain launched perhaps the first human rights effort when it unsuccessfully attempted to forge an international treaty suppressing the slave trade. Throughout the nineteenth century and into the twentieth century, a number of multilateral treaties were signed that protected civilians in warfare. At the Versailles Conference there were agreements made to protect the rights of certain minorities in Eastern Europe, and the International Labor Organization was created to protect the rights of workers.

However, despite these efforts no systematic attempts to address human rights occurred until the United Nations was created in 1945. The Preamble of the United Nations Charter required signatories to "reaffirm faith in fundamental human rights, in the dignity and worth of the human person, in the equal rights of men and women and of nations large and small." Article 55 states that the United Nations will "promote . . . universal respect for, and observance of, human rights and fundamental freedoms for all without distinction as to race, sex, language or religion." Article 56 then requires that "all members pledge themselves to take joint and separate action in cooperation with the organization for the achievement of the purposes set forth in Article 55." Although the word *pledge* implies a legal responsibility, it leaves states the freedom to decide in what ways and degrees to implement the duty of respecting human rights. Thus, only states that regress in their fulfillment of human rights would be liable to criticism. The UN Commission on Human Rights was established in 1946 to monitor the progress of states in fulfilling their pledge. The Commission has only the power of publicizing human rights abuses in the hope that it will pressure states to curtail their violations.

On December 10, 1948, the General Assembly passed the Universal Declaration of Human Rights, with 48 votes in favor, none against, and 10 abstentions (the eight communist countries, South Africa, and Saudi Arabia). The Declaration proclaims itself "as a common standard of achievement for all peoples and all nations, to the end that every individual and every organ of society . . . shall strive by teaching and education to promote respect for these rights and freedoms and by progressive measures, national and international, to secure their universal and effective recognition and observance." More specifically, the Declaration listed dozens of civil, political, social, economic, and cultural rights. In 1966, after twelve years of negotiations, the United Nations offered two treaties for signature—the Convenant on Civil and Political Rights and the Convenant on Economic, Social, and Cultural Rights. Although both treaties came into force in 1976, the United States has yet to sign either one. The 1968 United Nations Conference on Human Rights asserted that "the Universal Declaration on Human Rights . . . constitutes an obligation for the members of the international community."

The efforts of the United Nations were paralleled in Europe on November 4, 1950, when representatives signed the European Convention for the Protection of Human Rights and Fundamental Freedoms. The Convention came into force on September 3, 1953, after the tenth state ratified the treaty. Unlike the UN Declaration on Human Rights, the European Convention is considered unambiguously legally binding. States are only allowed to circumvent the Convention in the case of war.

Two institutions serve the Convention. The European Commission on Human Rights investigates possible violations of human rights. Groups and individuals as well as states can petition the commission for a hearing. If the commission finds that a violation has occurred, it then offers to serve as an intermediary for a friendly settlement of the violation. If a settlement is not reached, the commission can refer the case to the European Court of Human Rights in Strasbourg for a binding legal decision. Expulsion from the organization is the ultimate penalty. If three months have elapsed since the investigation began, the commission can refer the case to the Committee of Ministers of the Council of Europe, which can decide by a two-thirds vote that there has been a violation. Individuals can only petition the commission, not the court.

Human rights in the western hemisphere are shaped by the 1948 Charter of the Organization of American States (OAS). In 1960, the OAS created the Inter-American Commission on Human Rights which investigates human rights violations. The 1967 Buenos Aires Protocol and 1969 American Convention on Human Rights strengthened the Inter-American Commission's powers and created the Inter-American Court, both modeled on Europe's human rights institutions. Only 18 of the 31 OAS members have ratified the Convention; the United States has refused to sign. Although the commission and court do render decisions, there is no means of enforcing their decisions.

Human rights extend to foreign nationals as well as citizens residing in a country. States cannot prosecute foreigners for crimes they have committed elsewhere although they can extradite them to the country in which the crime was committed. States, however, do not have to extradite their own citizens unless required by treaty. Foreigners cannot be drafted into the army unless they are permanent residents in that country. When a state expels an individual to another state, that state must receive the individual, unless he or she is willing to go to another state. International law allows each state to decide its own citizenship requirements.

The 1951 Geneva Convention declared that refugee status depends on "a well-founded fear of persecution for reasons of race, religion, nationality, membership in a particular social group, or political opinion." Recently, there has been an attempt to broaden the definition to include those displaced because of catastrophes.

States are not obligated to accept foreign nationals, although when they do, those individuals deserve full human rights. If a violation occurs, the government of that individual may sue for compensation on his or her behalf. States may agree to settle the dispute by arbitration or by court. If an injury is found, the compensation goes to the victim's government rather than to the victim. Of course, after winning compensation, the government can, and usually does, reward its citizen.

States are only liable for those crimes that its officials commit if they are following clear orders. States are never liable for actions of private citizens. Yet, states are liable when they encourage their citizens to attack foreigners, fail to provide enough protection for foreigners in case of an imminent attack, fail to punish crimes against foreigners, fail to provide foreigners with the legal ability to gain compensation for losses, benefit materially from the attack, or express approval of the attack.

Throughout the nineteenth and twentieth centuries, western governments argued that states were liable for harm to foreign nationals if they did not meet minimum international standards of human rights. Third World countries counter that they are only required to treat foreign nationals as they do their own citizens. Akehurst suggests that the sensible solution to this impasse is that "if the minimum international standard appears to give aliens a privileged position, the answer is for states to treat their own nationals better, not for them to treat aliens worse; indeed the whole human rights movement may be seen as an attempt to extend the minimum international standard from aliens to nationals. . . ."[15]

As in other areas of international law, the upholding of human rights depends largely on the actions of sovereign states. Two American political leaders recently presented two very different views of the importance of human rights in foreign policy. In 1978, on the thirty-ninth anniversary of the Universal Declaration of Human Rights, President Carter declared himself, "proud that our nation stands for more than military might or political might . . . Our pursuit of human rights is part of a broad effort to use our great power and our tremendous influence in the service of creating a better world in which human beings can live in peace, in freedom, and with their basic needs met. Human rights is the soul of our foreign policy."[16] Cyrus Vance, Secretary of State under President Carter, later argued that it was a "dangerous illusion" to believe that "pursuing values such as human rights . . . is incompatible with pursuing U.S. national interests . . . Our own freedom, and that of our allies, could never be secure in a world where freedom was threatened everywhere else."[17]

Secretary of State George Shultz gave a very different view in 1985 when he said that "we Americans have had to accept that our passionate commitment to moral principles could not be a substitute for sound foreign policy in a world of hard realities and complex choice . . . our moral impulse, noble as it might be, could lead either to futile and perhaps dangerous global crusades, on the one hand, or to escapism and isolationism, equally dangerous, on the other."[18]

The debate on human rights versus sovereignty and culture continues. During the June 1993 World Conference on Human Rights, the first held in 25 years, a coalition of countries including China, Cuba, Iran, and Syria argued that western countries were trying to impose their value of human rights on the rest of the world—a value that those western countries themselves did not uphold. Secretary of State Warren Christopher spoke for the majority when he argued that human rights were universal and transcended any contrary values of local tradition, religion, or culture. The conference eventually upheld the standards of the UN's 1948 Declaration of Human Rights and subsequent treaties and institutions protecting and enhancing those human rights.

CONCLUSION

International law is clearly riddled with seeming paradoxes, limitations, and contradictions. Power, not law, rules international relations. Although states are legally equal, they differ enormously in their respective power. Even if it might does not make right, it seems to determine when international law is used or neglected in regulating international behavior. Compliance with the existing law is voluntary. States choose whether or not to go before and heed the International Court of Justice and other arbitration courts, and law violators are the least likely to assent to legal rulings against them.

Yet, there are always limits to power. International relations are shaped by order, not anarchy, and international law is a major source of that order. True, states obey or break the law when they perceive it is in their interest to do so and, given the ambiguity of international law, can use it to justify virtually any action. But is this so different from how people act in any society? Lawbreakers exist in every legal system.

The United Nations Charter clearly represents shared community values, fulfilling the Roman precept that *ubi societas, ibi jus,* "where there is society, there is law." States signing the Charter agree to those values, whether they live up to them or not. International law should be considered important, if only because virtually all states think it is important and adjust their behavior accordingly. In the post-Cold War world, the United Nations Security Council is increasingly serving as a world court, police, and prosecutor.

National prosperity and security depend on a government's ability to promote its country's political economic interests in an increasingly interdependent world. Reputation is important, if only for reasons of self-interest. Virtually all states obey the law most of the time. Law-abiding states generally shun or retaliate against those that regularly violate international law, to the latter's detriment. Iraq is a classic example of what can happen to a state that aggressively violates international law.

The body of international law is expanding. One of the most remarkable milestones of the twentieth century is the outlawing of aggressive war. Most states are at peace most of the time, and international law of war has been an important factor behind that reality. However, international law involves more than questions of war and peace. Law regulates dozens of areas of international relations, such as trade, investments, debt, currency flows, travel, and embassies. International law and the institutions for enforcing it will continue to evolve into the twenty-first century.

STUDY QUESTIONS

1. Is international law really law?

2. What are the different schools of international law?

3. What were the major developments in international law's evolution from its origins through today?

4. What are the primary and secondary sources of international law?

5. Why and how are treaties a basis for international law?

6. Why and how are customs a basis for international law?

7. Why and how are principles a basis for international law?

8. Why and how are legal decisions and legal opinions a basis for international law?

9. What is the proper subject and jurisdiction of international law?

10. What is the extent of diplomatic immunity? How did the practice arise?

11. What is sovereignty and what is its significance for international law?

12. What is recognition? What are the constitutive and declarative schools concerning recognition?

13. Why do most states obey international law most of the time?

14. How is the International Court of Justice organized? What are its strengths and weaknesses?

15. Discuss the development of international law concerning human rights.

ENDNOTES

1. For some recent excellent studies of international law, see: Antonio Cassesse, *International Law in a Divided World* (New York: Oxford University Press, 1989); David Forsythe, *The Politics of International Law: U.S. Foreign Policy Reconsidered* (Boulder, Colo.: Lynne Reinner, 1990); Werner Levi, *Contemporary International Law: A Concise Introduction* (Boulder Colo.: Westview Press, 1990); Daniel Patrick Moynihan, *On the Law of Nations* (Cambridge, Mass.: Harvard University Press, 1990); Christopher Joyner, "The Reality and Relevance of International Law," in Charles W. Kegley and Eugene Wittkopf, eds., *The Global Agenda* (New York: McGraw-Hill, 1992), 202–215.

2. Quoted in Gerhard Von Glahn, *Law Among Nations* (New York, Macmillan, 1992), 32.

3. For an excellent overview of the neorealist perspective, see Eugene V. Rostow, *Law, Power, and the Pursuit of Peace* (Lincoln, Nebr.: University of Nebraska Press, 1968).

4. Irving Janis, *Crucial Decisions: Leadership in Policymaking and Crisis Management* (New York: Free Press, 1989), 11.

5. Quoted in Irving Janis, *Crucial Decisions: Leadership in Policymaking and Crisis Management*, 36.

6. 1969 ICJ Reports 4, 43.

7. Quoted in Michael Akehurst, *A Modern Introduction to International Law* (London: Allen & Unwin, 1987), 32.

8. Quoted in Irving Janis, *Crucial Decisions: Leadership in Policymaking and Crisis Management*, 38.

9. F.R.D, 69, 110 (1946).

10. 1979 ICJ Reports 7, 19.

11. Quoted in Irving Janis, *Crucial Decisions: Leadership in Policymaking and Crisis Management*, 51.

12. Michael Akehurst, *A Modern Introduction to International Law,* 8.

13. Quoted in Irving Janis, *Crucial Decisions: Leadership in Policymaking and Crisis Management,* 93.

14. LeRoy Bennett, *International Organizations: Principles and Issues* (Englewood Cliffs, N.J.: Prentice-Hall, 1988), 173–177.

15. Michael Akehurst, *A Modern Introduction to International Law,* 91.

16. Jimmy Carter, "December 6, 1978 Speech," Department of State Bulletin, January 1979, 2.

17. Cyrus Vance, "The Human Rights Imperative," *Foreign Policy,* vol. 63, 1986, 11.

18. George Shultz, "Morality and Realism in American Foreign Policy," Department of State Bulletin, December 1985, 247.

International Organizations

International organizations have profilerated throughout the modern world, particularly in the twentieth century as nation-states are increasingly bound by various interdependencies that demand new, systematic ways to manage new conflicts and interests and then go on to breed related ones in related fields. Over time, different international organizations merge to form stronger and more comprehensive ones. Organizations binding nations economically or socially eventually bind them politically, as people increasingly transfer their loyalties from the nation-state to the international state. These are the major assertions of *functionalist theory*. Its founder, David Mitrany, wrote in 1943 that functionalism proposed "not to squelch but to utilize national selfishness; it asks governments not to give up sovereignty which belongs to their peoples but to acquire benefits for their peoples which were hitherto unavailable, not to reduce their power to defend their citizens but to expand their competence to serve them."[1]

Although the United Nations and European Union were cited as the models for functionalism, it soon became evident that they were not living up to their ideals, as both entered periods of stagnation and stalemate during the 1960s and 1970s. While functionalists continued to maintain that these international organizations would evolve steadily in purpose and power, a new group of theorists following the *neofunctionalist theory* recognized that conflicts between a nation's sovereign instincts and international needs could limit or derail the development of international organizations.

The European Community provides the best illustration of neofunctionalist theory. Its development from a coal and steel organization through a common market and customs union by January 1, 1993, was slow and uncertain. Periods of community expansion and optimism were followed by stagnation and pessimism. The 1991 Maastricht Treaty would have achieved a common European currency and central bank by 1999 at the latest, but the treaty was not ratified by all its members and will be renegotiated. Yet, neofunctionalists argue that economic and eventually political union is inevitable—the question is when and how.

Although the European Community and the United Nations are the world's best known international organizations, there are thousands of others that evolved in similar ways. They differ greatly, however, according to their respective purposes, powers, and memberships. One distinction is between the more than 300 *intergovernmental organizations (IGOs),* such as the United Nations and European Community, and more than 4,646 *nongovernmental organizations, (NGOs)* such as Greenpeace, the Red Cross, and Amnesty International. There is a vast budget and personnel range among international organizations. Whereas the United Nations has a $15 billion annual budget and 50,000 employees, the average IGO has a $10 million budget and 200 employees. In contrast, the average NGO has a $1 million budget and 10 employees.[2]

There are four types of IGOs. General-membership and general-purpose organizations, such as the League of Nations and the United Nations, have global duties and many functions, including collective security, economic development, and human rights. General-membership and limited-purpose organizations such as the World Health Organization (WHO) and the General Agreement on Trade and Tariffs (GATT) focus on fulfilling one function, such as health or trade. Limited-membership and general-purpose organizations, such as the European Community (EC) and Arab League, are usually confined to states that share similar values and culture in the same region yet address a range of issues. Finally, limited-membership and limited-purpose organizations, such as the North Atlantic Treaty Organization (NATO) and Latin American Free Trade Association (LAFTA), are regional organizations dedicated to one specific function, such as defense or trade.

Despite the vast differences among international organizations, there are some similarities. Virtually all international organizations have a secretariat or full-time administrative staff in a permanent headquarters. The staff implements decisions, holds regular meetings for member representatives, a process to make binding decisions, and has an executive council. Although membership in all international organizations is voluntary, compliance with the IGO's treaty is mandatory.

International organizations are created by treaty, which means they are derived from and subsequently can be a source for international law. The International Court of Justice ruled that international organizations have international legal standing, which "is not the same thing as saying that it is a State, which it certainly is not, or that its legal personality and rights and duties are the same as those of a State . . . What it does mean is that it is a subject of international law and capable of possessing international rights and duties, and that it has capacity to maintain its rights by bringing international claims."[3] The extent of an international organization's legal standing, however, depends on the treaty creating it. Members have usually delegated some of their sovereign rights to the organization and thus any organization is only as strong as the powers granted to it.

Of all the international organizations, the most ambitious are those dedicated to collective security. National interests and security are closely linked. Until the late twentieth century, most states were trapped in a security dilemma, whereby if one state tried to make itself more secure from foreign attack by building up its military, it correspondingly made its neighbors less secure. They, in turn, built up their militaries to strengthen national security. The result was an arms race that often ended in war.

In a world knit ever more closely by nuclear, economic, and environmental interdependence, national interests and security requirements are increasingly indistinguishable. Virtually all states share a need for peaceful, prosperous relations with one another. Thus, security becomes collective, or grounded on the idea that "the basic requirement for peace is that states have the wit to cooperate in pursuit of national interests that coincide with those of other states rather than the will to compromise national interests that conflict with those of others."[4] In other words, states work with rather than against one another to achieve common interests and overcome common threats.

The central reason for the creation of the League of Nations and United Nations was *collective security*. But the hopes upon which those two organizations were founded eventually turned to disappointment, as they were unable to halt international aggression. Although most member-states shared those organizations' ideals, they differed sharply over how, where, and when those ideals should be implemented without eroding their own sovereignty.

This chapter will concentrate on analyzing both the potential and the problems of the United Nations' collective security efforts. Following that discussion, the chapter will survey some leading noneconomic IGOs and NGOs.[5] Full discussions of geoeconomic IGOs, such as the European Union, GATT, NAFTA, and OPEC, and NGOs, such as multinational corporations, will also be presented.

THE UNITED NATIONS AND COLLECTIVE SECURITY

Origins and Powers

During World War II, President Roosevelt became just as determined to create an international organization dedicated to maintaining the peace as President Wilson had become during World War I. When the United States and Britain signed the Atlantic Charter on August 14, 1941, they pledged themselves to, among other things, the creation of a United Nations. At the Moscow Conference of Foreign Ministers in October 1943, the American and British representatives convinced the Soviets and the Chinese to also support a future collective security organization. At the *Dumbarton Oaks Conference* in August 1944 and the Yalta Conference in February 1945, participants debated and began to forge a consensus on the United Nations' institutions and functions. Perhaps the most significant addition occurred in February 1945 at the Yalta Conference. Fearing the Soviet Union would continually be outvoted by the western powers, Stalin insisted on veto power for the permanent members, and Roosevelt and Churchill agreed. The finishing touches to the United Nations Charter were negotiated by representatives of 51 countries at the San Francisco Conference in April and May 1945, and the San Francisco Treaty was signed on June 26, 1945. The treaty was rapidly ratified by its signatories. On July 28, the Senate overwhelmingly voted 89 to 2 in favor of joining the United Nations.

The Charter's Preamble clearly states the United Nations' ideals: peace, human rights, international law, prosperity, and collective security. The central purpose of the United Nations is collective security. Article 2(3) maintains that all "members shall settle their international disputes by peaceful means in such a manner that international peace and security, and justice, are not endangered. Article 2(4) prohibits "the threat or use of force against the territorial integrity or political independence of another state."

The Charter attempts to balance the power of the United Nations and sovereign powers. Article 43 gives the United Nations an international legal personality by empowering it to make treaties with sovereign states. This was reinforced by the favorable International Court of Justice ruling in the 1948 Reparations for Injury case in which the United Nations asked for an opinion as to whether it had the legal personality to take a sovereign state to court and receive compensation for damages. Three articles of Chapter VII empower the Security Council to uphold the peace. Under Article 39 the Security Council is authorized to determine whether a breach of peace occurred; under Article 41 it can impose economic, transportation, and communications sanctions on the aggressors; and under Article 42, if sanctions under Article 41 fail, it can "take such action by air, sea, or land forces as may be necessary to maintain or restore international peace and security." National sovereignty is upheld by Article 2(7), which states: "Nothing contained in the present Charter shall authorize the United Nations to intervene in matters which are essentially within the domestic jurisdiction of any state or shall require the members to submit such matters to settlement under the present Charter; but this principle shall not prejudice the application of enforcement under Chapter VII."

Membership

In 1992 the United Nations had 179 members (20 of which joined that year), an increase from the 51 members who originally joined in 1945. The UN's membership will rise steadily throughout the 1990s and beyond, as more states achieve their independence. Membership is "open to all other peace-loving states which accept the obligations contained in the present Charter, and, in the judgment of the Organization, are able and willing to carry out these obligations." Some nongovernmental organizations, such as the PLO, enjoy nonvoting observer status. The Security Council and General Assembly vote on admission.

The United Nations can vote to suspend the membership of a state that violates the Charter. There are no provisions, however, for voluntary withdrawal from the United Nations, thus avoiding the situation of the League of Nations, in which aggressor states (such as Japan) quit the organization rather than subscribe to its obligations. In 1965 Indonesia announced its withdrawal in protest against the election of Malaysia (with which it had a territorial dispute) as a nonpermanent member of the Security Council. Indonesia later rejoined the United Nations without having to seek readmission.

For more than two decades following the Chinese revolution in 1949, there was a dispute in the United Nations over which government should represent China—the Communist Party, which controlled the mainland, or the Nationalist Party (Koumintang), which clung to Taiwan. The United States vetoed all attempts to unseat Taiwan until 1972, when the United Nations voted to expel Taiwan and seat the People's Republic of China. The American protests that the Beijing communist regime would not comply with the Charter were legally unsound. China's membership preceded the revolution, and the United Nations' members are states not governments.

Members pay dues based on a complicated ability-to-pay formula which takes into account GNP and population. In 1989 the United States paid 25 percent of the budget, the Soviet Union 11.6 percent, Japan 11.4 percent, West Germany 8 percent, France 6.3 percent, Britain 4.9 percent, Italy 4 percent, and Canada 3.1 percent—altogether, 71 percent of the budget. Seventy-nine countries pay the minimum of 0.01 percent, and nine countries pay 0.02 percent.

Institutions

The Security Council is the United Nations' executive branch and has the power to make decisions legally binding on the entire United Nations. It has 15 members, five of which—the United States, Russia, China, Britain, and France—are permanent and have veto power on nonprocedural issues, and the other 10 are elected for two-year terms by the General Assembly. In practice there is a quota system for the nonpermanent members—five come from Africa and Asia, two from Latin America, one from Eastern Europe, and two from the advanced industrial countries. The post of president of the Security Council is held for a month and rotated among the members.

A measure passes the Security Council with a majority vote of nine or more, unless of course it is vetoed by a permanent member. The pattern of vetoes changed significantly in the four decades from 1945 to 1989.[6] The United States did not cast a veto until 1970, the first of 20 during the 1970s, followed by 46 between 1980 and 1989, for a total of 66. In contrast, the Soviet Union cast 92 vetoes between 1945 and 1960, 13 in the 1960s, 9 in the 1970s, and only 4 between 1980 and 1989, for a total of 118. Of the other members, Britain cast 26, France 16, and China 3, of which 22 British, 12 French, and 2 Chinese vetoes were cast since 1971.[7]

There are two significant reasons for this shift in the balance of vetoes. During the first decade, Moscow often used its veto to block the admission of states with pro-western governments. In 1956 Washington and Moscow agreed not to block each other's allies from membership, so Soviet vetoes fell sharply after that time. The shift in vetoes also reflects changes in the General Assembly's composition. Up through the 1960s, most General Assembly members voted with the United States on most issues, and Moscow vetoed many resolutions that seemed to challenge its interests. The proliferation of newly independent states during the 1960s and 1970s, (many of them pro-Soviet, anti-Israel, and committed to a New International Economic Order involving a redistribution of global wealth), put the West on the defensive, leading Washington, London, and Paris to increasingly use their veto power.

All members of the United Nations have one vote in the General Assembly, which has the power to study, debate, and vote on any issue, as well as approve the annual budget. Decisions, however, are binding only if they achieve a two-thirds majority and are confined to addressing the administration of the United Nations. The General Assembly can issue declarations, or broad statements of principle, such as its 1948 Declaration on Human Rights, and resolutions, or policy recommendations, for specific issues. In addition, it can convene special sessions, which address a particular issue, such as disarmament or Namibia, conferences, which deal with broader issues such as women's rights or population; and conventions, which are treaties among UN members or between the UN and other states. Despite these limited powers, General

Assembly resolutions often represent global opinion and thus carry heavy political pressure. The resolutions may also identify international customs or principles that can be codified into law.

There has been a significant shift in the power balance within the General Assembly between 1945 and 1990. In 1945, 44 percent of the 51 members were from the Western bloc, 20 percent from Latin America, 16 percent from Asia and the Pacific, 12 percent from the Soviet bloc, and 8 percent from Africa. In 1990 only 14 percent of the UN membership was from the Western bloc, 33 percent from Africa, 26 percent from Asia and the Pacific, 21 percent from Latin America and 6 percent from the Soviet bloc.

The voting records of the United States and the Soviet Union in the General Assembly paralleled their veto record in the Security Council, in which at first the United States voted in favor of resolutions and the Soviet Union voted against them, until gradually the two nations reversed themselves. In 1986 Washington and Moscow voted "no" on 81 percent and 8 percent, respectively, of the resolutions.[8] In 1989 the United States voted with the majority on only 16.9 percent of all resolutions, with the European Community only 59.5 percent of the time, and with NATO 57.3 percent of the time. This is in contrast to the period between 1945 and 1950, when the United States voted with the majority 71 percent of the time.[9] Most American vetoes and negative votes involve resolutions that condemn Israeli aggression or human rights abuses.

The Secretariat is the United Nations' administration and includes 20,000 full-time employees, of which 6,000 are at the New York headquarters. It is headed by a Secretary-General, who is nominated by the Security Council and elected by the General Assembly for a five-year renewable term. The Secretary-General's role is to administer, rather than lead, the United Nations; its only power is to persuade. There have been six UN Secretary Generals, all from neutral or nonaligned states: Trygve Lie of Norway (1946-1952), Dag Hammarskjöld of Sweden (1953-1961), U Thant of Burma (1961-1971), Kurt Waldheim of Austria (1972-1982), Javier Perez de Cuellar of Peru (1983-1991), and Boutros Boutros-Ghali of Eygpt (1992-present).

No Secretary-General before or after Hammarskjöld has been as active in confronting international problems. Hammarskjöld saw crisis management as his primary role. In 1960 Hammarskjöld issued his policy of preventive diplomacy for those cases:

> *where the original conflict may be said either to be the result of, or to imply risks for, the creation of a power vacuum between the main blocs. Preventive action . . . must . . . aim at filling the vacuum so that it will not provoke action from any of the major parties . . . [t]he United Nations enters the picture on the basis of its noncommitment to any power bloc . . . to provide . . . a guarantee in relation to all parties against initiatives from others.*

Hammarskjöld died in a plane crash in 1961, and his successors have largely concerned themselves with administration rather than policy.

There are three other less prominent UN organizations. The 54-member Economic and Social Council (ECOSOC) oversees the dozens of UN agencies, organizes conferences, and dispenses funds. The International Court of Justice (ICJ) hears cases referred to it from any states or UN organs. Although the court's decisions are binding, its jurisdiction is not. The Trusteeship Council oversees those states that were given territories to manage for eventual independence. Only one of the original trusteeships—America's "strategic trusteeship" over several western Pacific island groups—has not received independence.

Collective Security

Although the Security Council has significant powers to enforce the peace, in most conflicts (if it agrees to do anything) it will simply issue a resolution calling on the parties to peacefully resolve their problems. The Security Council has only issued economic sanctions twice (against Rhodesia in 1967 and Iraq in 1990) and military sanctions twice (against North Korea in 1950 and Iraq in 1990).

Until 1990, the United Nations only acted against an international aggressor once. In July 1950 the Security Council voted first to condemn communist North Korea's invasion of South Korea and then to create a United Nations military force to defeat North Korea and restore peace to the peninsula. These votes in favor of intervention succeeded only because the Soviet Union was boycotting the Security Council for its refusal to seat the communist government as China's legitimate UN representative. Later the Soviets returned to the Security Council and vetoed several resolutions that would have imposed sanctions on China for intervening on North Korea's behalf.

In response to the Soviet vetoes, the United States lobbied the General Assembly to pass the Uniting for Peace Resolution, in which the assembly empowered itself to identify and sanction aggressors if a veto prevented the Security Council from acting. The General Assembly then used these powers in the 1956 Suez and Hungarian crises, the 1958 Middle East crisis, and the 1960 Congo crisis.

The United Nations response to Iraq's invasion of Kuwait on August 2, 1990, was its most intensive and successful yet. Between August and November the Security Council issued 12 resolutions that demanded that Iraq withdraw from Kuwait, held Iraq liable for all damages caused by its invasion and hostage-taking, imposed a near total economic and travel embargo against Iraq until it withdrew from Kuwait, and allowed countries to use force to uphold the embargo. On November 29, 1990, the Security Council passed (with 12 votes in favor, two opposed [Yemen and Cuba], and one abstention [China]) the demand that Iraq comply with all previous resolutions by January 15, 1991, or else the Security Council would use all necessary means to expel Iraq from Kuwait. President Hussein remained defiant, and on January 17 the American-led forces began a three week bombing campaign against Iraqi military targets, which culminated with a 100-hour ground war that defeated the Iraqi army and liberated Kuwait.

The Security Council action against Iraq would have been impossible during the Cold War. As President Bush said in his address to the General Assembly in October 1990, "this is a new and different world. Not since 1945 have we seen the real possibility of using the United Nations as it was designed, as a center for international collective security."

United Nations collective security and peace keeping efforts differ. Collective security actively attempts to deter or, if all else fails, defeat international aggressors. Peacekeeping originally attempted simply to keep belligerents apart, but more recently has broadened to include missions such as disarming rebels in Nicaragua; monitoring elections in Haiti, Nicaragua, and Namibia; providing humanitarian aid in Somalia and

Cyprus; monitoring the withdrawal of foreign troops in Afghanistan and Angola; and resettling refugees in Cambodia. UN peace keeping forces can be dispatched only after three conditions have been met: all parties in the conflict agree to accept UN forces, the Security Council and General Assembly agree to send them, and members agree to provide troops for the operation. The Charter does not explicitly empower the UN to dispatch peace keeping forces. The practice was inspired by Secretary-General Hammarskjöld's concept of preventive diplomacy.

Through 1993 the UN dispatched nine armed peace keeping forces and ten unarmed military-observer missions. Between 1956 and 1988, 15 UN peace keeping missions had employed more than a half-million people from 58 countries—733 people died in fulfilling their duty. In 1993 the budget for the eighteen existing peace keeping ventures deploying over 75,000 people reached $3 billion. UN troops are largely from nonaligned or smaller industrial states. Until the 1990s, the largest UN peace keeping force consisted of 20,000 people dispatched to the Congo (1961-1964). In November 1991, however, the Security Council approved the dispatch of the UN Transition Authority in Cambodia (UNTAC), which will use 22,000 troops and operate on a $1.9 billion budget to end the civil war, to resettle refugees, and to monitor elections in 1993. In November 1992 the United Nations approved the dispatch of what became 30,000 troops from 34 nations to Somalia to stop the civil war and famine that threatened to kill millions.

Most UN peace keeping forces have been dispatched to the Middle East. As early as 1948, the Security Council created the UN Truce Supervision Organization (UNTSO) to monitor the cease-fire between the Arab states and Israel, and in 1958 a UN Observer Group was set up in Lebanon. The first formal peace keeping venture was the creation of the UN Emergency Force (UNEF I) in 1956, which separated Eygptian and Israeli forces in the Sinai peninsula for the next decade. UNEF I was set up following the 1956 War, which broke out when Israel, Britain, and France attacked Egypt after President Nasser nationalized the Suez Canal. The 1967 War occurred after Nasser demanded that the UNEF I withdraw from the Sinai and threatened to attack Israel. UNEF II was established in the Sinai and the Golan Heights following the 1973 War, and it remains there today. In 1978 the UN Interim Force in Lebanon (UNIFIL) was created to separate Israeli and PLO forces in southern Lebanon, and it continues to patrol the region. UN missions have been active elsewhere in the Middle East. In 1988 the United Nations helped negotiate an end to the Iraq-Iran War, and it dispatched 350 troops to monitor the cease-fire. That same year, UN observer teams were sent to Kabul and Islamabad to observe the Soviet withdrawal from Afghanistan and the return of Afghan refugees. The UN peace keeping missions have been largely successful in managing conflicts that might well have broken into war.

Peacemaking involves the United Nations acting as an intermediary in negotiations over a conflict. Between 1945 and 1984, 137 of 319 international conflicts were referred to the United Nations for settlement. The United Nations succeeded in alleviating 53 percent and settling 25 percent of these conflicts.[10] Vetoes were issued in 220, or 35 percent, of the 642 Security Council resolutions between 1946 and 1990. During the late 1980s and into the 1990s, the United Nations has become increasingly active as the Cold War disappeared. United Nations' initiatives helped negotiate the Iraq-Iran War (1988), Soviet withdrawal from Afghanistan (1988), the Namibian civil war and

South African domination (1988), Cyprus division (1988), Nicaraguan election and civil war (1990), Cambodian civil war (1991), Iraqi invasion of Kuwait and nuclear and chemical proliferation (1990), Somalian civil war (1992), and civil war in the former Yugoslavia (1993). However, these operations all cost a large sum of money. In 1993 the Somalia operation alone cost $1.2 billion, but UN members were in arrears with their payment of only $1.5 billion to the total peace keeping budget. The biggest constraint on an expansion of UN peace keeping missions may be financial rather than political. Although most nations agree in principle to the UN peace keeping missions, few willingly pay their share.

Despite these successes, the United Nations has more often failed to keep the peace for several reasons. The Cold War was the most important obstacle to collective security. After 1945 the United States and the Soviet Union sponsored or participated in many international and internal conflicts, and thus would veto each other's attempts to secure United Nations intervention. Collective security depends on more than an international organization and ideals. The Security Council had to be united ideologically and politically before the United Nations could live up to its ideals. The collapse of communism and the Soviet empire made this unity possible.

A related reason for UN failures was the existence of the NATO and Warsaw Pact alliances, dedicated to defeating the other should war break out. Alliances and collective security are incompatible. Collective security can only work if states agree to resist aggression no matter who commits it. If a state's alliance commits aggression, that state would be more likely to fulfill its duties toward the alliance rather than its duties toward collective security. These problems diminished with the dissolution of the Warsaw Pact in 1991 and NATO's difficulty in justifying its continued existence in the post-Cold War era.

Another constraint on the UN is the difficulty in defining aggression itself. Although UN Charter Article 2 clearly prohibits the use of force, there are some exceptions. Under UN Charter Article 51, every sovereign state has "the inherent right of individual or collective self-defense if an armed attack occurs." States that attack other states try to justify their actions by citing self-defense. For example, was the United States the aggressor when it invaded Grenada in 1983 or Panama in 1990? Although many argued that those invasions were clear examples of aggression, the White House attempted to legally justify them by claiming that the United States was simply responding defensively to aggressive threats by the Grenadan and Panamanian governments.

Finally, the global power imbalance allows the most powerful states to act with impunity. Although most states may well have agreed that the Soviet Union was the aggressor in Hungary in 1956, Czechoslovakia in 1968, and Afghanistan in 1979, they did not attempt to sanction the Soviet Union for its actions because they lacked the political and military power to do so. On the other hand, the power balance between the United States and Soviet Union prevented them from acting decisively against each other. They have tolerated each other's aggression in their respective sphere of influence because they knew that to challenge those actions could have resulted in World War III.

Given these constraints, the United Nations successfully managed conflict when the issue (1) did not involve the superpowers or the East-West conflict; (2) was not opposed by Washington, Moscow, and the Security Council; (3) involved fighting and the fighting was in danger of spreading beyond the states involved; (4) involved a decolonization issue and small-sized and medium-sized states; and (5) was identified as a threat to peace by the Secretary-General, who actively lobbied the United Nations to overcome it.[11]

International Socioeconomic Issues

Although the United Nations may have sat on the sidelines of most international conflicts and poorly refereed others, it has attempted to address a range of other issues: decolonization, human rights, the environment, health, poverty, law of the sea, natural disasters, women's equality, trade, investments, agriculture, and food. One important UN contribution is simply gathering information about every country's socioeconomic conditions, which helps identity problems.

Most UN agencies assist global economic development and integration. The most important developmental organizations are the International Monetary Fund (IMF), which lends governments money to cover payments deficits and manage currency fluctuations, and the International Bank for Reconstruction and Development (IRBD, World Bank), which funds specific development projects. The World Health Organization (WHO) has made considerable progress in reducing or eradicating disease around the world. The Food and Agriculture Organization (FAO) sponsors research in food production and in application of better farming techniques, including the green revolution, to the Third World. The United Nations Educational, Scientific, and Cultural Organization (UNESCO) is involved in a range of activities, including gathering socioeconomic data; sponsoring scientific, cultural, and educational exchanges; and, more controversially, pushing a "New World Information Order," which would severely limit the news that could be reported about authoritarian governments. The International Labor Organization (ILO) monitors and tries to improve working conditions around the world. There are several communications and transportation organizations, including the Universal Postal Union (UPU), International Telecommunications Union (ITU), International Civil Aviation Organization (ICAO), International Maritime Organization (IMO), and World Meterological Organization (WMO). Increasing numbers of individuals and governments are understanding that genuine development conserves rather than destroys the environment. The UN Environmental Program (UNEP) has helped lead this shift in consciousness. Among its most important successes was the sponsorship of the UN Environmental Conference in Rio de Janeiro in June 1992, in which participants signed global warming and biodiversity treaties. The UN Development Program (UNDP) helps coordinate the efforts of the other agencies and has spent over $2 billion in various development projects around the world.

The United Nations provides the world's poorest and least-populated states with a forum in which to cite their grievances and proposals. The Third World has attempted to use the UN General Assembly as a law-making body. Although General Assembly resolutions are not binding, they can create new customs that eventually become the basis of treaties. The attempts of the Third World during the 1970s to create a New International Economic Order involved a vastly different legal view of property from the dominant western one. Many Third World states believe there is a double standard in the application of international law, in which the more powerful states can literally get away with murder and other violations, but the weaker states are forced to comply. Even if many governments believe their interests are not being met, the UN allows communication and debate of issues sometimes not possible elsewhere. For example, although the United States does not have diplomatic relations with the Palestinian Liberation Organization (PLO), it can meet with its representatives at the United Nations.

Evaluation

How effective has the United Nations been?

As John Kennedy once said, the United Nations "is our last hope in an age where the instruments of war have far outpaced the instruments of peace." Any evaluation of the United Nations' effectiveness must first address its major role—that of keeping the peace. It was hoped that the United Nations would succeed where the League failed in keeping the peace. Since 1945, there has been no world war and no use of nuclear weapons. What role, if any, the United Nations played in keeping the peace between the superpowers is impossible to say. The United Nations has played an important and often decisive role in hundreds of other conflicts, alleviating about half of all disputes brought before it and settling a quarter of them. Between 1945 and 1993, the United Nations dispatched twenty-two collective security and peace keeping forces, using troops or police from seventy-three countries. Clearly, if the United Nations never existed, international conflicts would most likely have been much more frequent and bloody.

Although the United Nations was founded on the collective-security ideal, it was structured to preserve sovereignty and national interests, particularly those of the great powers. By concentrating power in the Security Council, the architects hoped to avoid the inevitable indecision of scores of politically diverse members. Few if any states would consider threatening the peace if they faced the combined military forces of the five permanent members plus any other forces contributed by other members of the United Nations. It was not anticipated, however, that, as a result of the conflicting interests and ideologies of the five great powers, there was just as much chance of stalemate in the Security Council as in the General Assembly. In fact, granting veto power to each of the five permanent members not only virtually ensured deadlock, but also allowed them even more leeway to act as they wished in the international system. Although the five permanent members were empowered to uphold international law, they themselves could follow or break it as they wished. The power balance and spheres of influence, not the law, constrained their behavior.

Even when a consensus emerges, the United Nations is hampered by financial constraints. Virtually everyone favors peace; few willingly pay for it. As of August 31, 1992, UN members owed about $1.6 billion, of which $831.2 million was for regular dues and $735.2 million for peace keeping forces. Seventy-five percent of these debts were owed by 5 countries, of which the United States was the biggest debtor, with $733 million in outstanding dues. Russia followed with $420 million in outstanding debts, South Africa with $71 million, Japan with $54 million, and Ukraine with $46 million.[12] Of the $1.79 billion in the 1989 UN budget, the United States paid 25 percent, Japan 12.5 percent, and Russia 9.4 percent. Given the UN's limited resources and the vast array of problems it faces, the UN has been remarkably successful in many areas.

The United Nations has many critics, and during the 1980s the United States led the charge in demanding reforms of many inefficient, wasteful, and antiwestern practices. In 1983 the United States and Britain withdrew their membership and funding from the UN Educational, Scientific, and Cultural Organization (UNESCO), charging it with a persistent antiwestern bias and mismanagement of funds. In 1985 Congress passed a law threatening to cut American contributions by 20 percent unless the United Nations undertook reforms and gave Washington a say in budget matters equal to its 25 percent contribution. In 1987 Washington began cutting back its membership dues, until by 1993 it owed over $500 million. This pressure partially worked. The United Nations agreed to cut its staff by 15 percent, allowed all budgetary decisions to be approved unanimously, toned down some of the antiwestern rhetoric, and revamped UNESCO.

Many criticize the United Nations' one state-one vote system, which is based on the concept of the sovereign equality of states. There are some obvious flaws in this system. A two-thirds majority in the General Assembly can be assembled by states whose combined population is less than 8 percent of the world's total population. Some states argue that it is ridiculous that tiny states, such as Nauru (population 7,000), should have the same voting weight as China (population 1.2 billion), and they advocate that voting power should be proportional to a state's population. The smaller states are obviously opposed to that proposal. Some Americans argue that voting power in the United Nations should be based on one's financial contributions. The combined contributions of over 80 members make up less than 1 percent of the total budget. Because the United States contributes 25 percent of United Nation's budget, it should enjoy 25 percent of the votes. Virtually all other UN members object to basing voting on budget contributions.

The five permanent Security Council members are criticized for their monopoly of power. Some propose abolishing not just the veto power but the entire notion of permanent members. All Security Council members would be elected by the General Assembly. Other proposals would make Japan, Germany, Nigeria, India, and Brazil permanent members with veto power, which would only make stalemates more likely. To these proposals, some counter that although the veto has created deadlock on hundreds of issues, it has also preserved the Security Council—without veto power, any of the permanent members (particularly the Soviet Union) may well have walked out if a vote severely affected its national interests.

United Nations' politics have always mirrored global politics. The Cold War and North-South standoffs limited the United Nations' ability to deal decisively with international problems for much of its first 45 years. The Cold War is now over, and the emergence of newly industrializing countries has diluted the rancor between the world's rich and poor countries. Cooperation among the permanent Security Council members allows the United Nations to embark decisively on peace keeping and humanitarian missions that formerly would have been unlikely.

The United Nations will continue to expand its responsibilities and power. A consensus is building within the UN that sovereignty is no longer sacrosanct and can be set aside when a government violates human rights and self-determination. For example, in December 1992 alone the UN General Assembly voted overwhelmingly to rebuke Cuba, the Sudan, Serbia, Iraq, Iran, and Myanmar for widespread human rights abuses.

UN intervention is also justified when a government dissolves into anarchy and civil war, as in Cambodia, Somalia, and Bosnia. There is increasing support in favor of reviving the old UN trusteeship system in which unstable countries are administered until they become capable of self-rule. Many Third World countries, however, feel that UN calls for human rights, self-determination, and trusteeship are neocolonial attacks on their rights as sovereign states.

INTERGOVERNMENTAL ORGANIZATIONS (IGO)

The number and type of IGOs expanded steadily during the twentieth century—about 50 in 1914; 90 in 1935; and more than 300 today, with over 100,000 employees. Interdependence is the most important reason. New issues demand new international organizations to manage them. The failure of the nation-state system to keep the peace and the devastation of the two world wars stimulated the rapid expansions of international organizations to help resolve conflicts. After World War II, the emergence of low-cost jet travel and instantaneous communications further developed the global political economy and the organizations that manage it.

Several of these organizations have attempted to promote collective security. The Organization of American States (OAS), Organization for African Unity (OAU), Council for Europe, the Association of Southeast Asian Nations (ASEAN), and the Arab League are dedicated to regional collective security and development. However, they were no more successful than the United Nations in fulfilling their mission. Between 1945 and 1984, these organizations addressed 86 of 317 international conflicts, alleviated 56 percent of them, and settled 26 percent.[13]

Some regional organizations, however, have scored some notable successes in keeping the peace. In 1979 the Arab League negotiated the end of fighting between North Yemen and South Yemen and their unification into one country in May 1990. In 1988 the Organization for African Unity (OAU) negotiated a peace agreement between Chad and Libya, and in 1992 helped end a 15-year civil war in Angola. Throughout the 1980s and into the 1990s, the UN and ASEAN worked diligently to negotiate the withdrawal of Vietnamese troops from Cambodia and to end Cambodia's civil war.

Alliances differ from collective security. Everyone is encouraged to become a member of a global or regional collective security organization, but alliances are exclusive organizations that mobilize against an enemy country or alliance. The North Atlantic Treaty Organization (NATO) and Warsaw Pact (WTO) were the world's most powerful regional security organizations.

NONGOVERNMENTAL INTERNATIONAL ORGANIZATIONS (NGO)

There are more than 5,000 NGOs in the world, with more being created daily, and they include a vast range of political, economic, social, health, business, and religious interests. There is a difference between secular, religious, and national-liberation NGOs.

Secular NGOs

International economic interest groups are among the most powerful. The International Chamber of Commerce lobbies governments to ensure favorable business environments. The International Federation of Airline Pilots' Association (IFAP) boycotts flights to those countries that harbor skyjackers. In 1968 an IFAP boycott pressured Algeria to quickly end the detention of an El Al plane that had been skyjacked. The International Council of Scientific Unions (ICSU) is the world's foremost interest group, lobbying for greater scientific cooperation and openness. Private philanthropic groups, such as the Ford and Rockefeller foundations, have contributed to development projects around the world and act as international aid organizations.

International groups focusing on nuclear proliferation issues have been vocal in lobbying for their goals. The Committee for Nuclear Disarmament (CND) and Greenpeace played a significant role in mobilizing antinuclear support throughout the 1980s. In 1985 French government agents exploded a bomb on Greenpeace's ship, the *Rainbow Warrior,* which was about to monitor French nuclear testing in the Pacific. The *Rainbow Warrior* sank, and a Greenpeace volunteer was killed. When the agents were caught and their plot revealed, French atmospheric nuclear testing policies became thoroughly discredited, and Paris eventually agreed to conduct them underground.

Human rights and environmental organizations have become increasingly potent in pressing their interests. Amnesty International, Freedom House, America's Watch, Asia Watch, and other international organizations have been effective in alleviating human-rights abuses in many countries. The International Red Cross is committed to humanitarian relief in wars or natural disasters. International environmental organizations—such as Greenpeace, Friends of the Earth, and the Sierra Club—have become increasingly powerful in their ability to pressure countries to address local and international environmental crises.

International conflict and politics are inescapable, even for groups that are not ostensibly political. Even an organization like the International Olympic Committee is heavily involved in politics, if only because the members have so frequently disrupted the Olympics for political purposes. In 1980 the United States and many other states boycotted the Moscow Olympics because of the Soviet invasion of Afghanistan. In 1984 the Soviet bloc retaliated by boycotting the Los Angeles Olympics.

Religious NGOs

Religious groups can play an important role in certain international issues. The Catholic Church is perhaps the world's largest nongovernmental organization. Although the Vatican City consists of only a few acres, the Pope commands the loyalty of one out of eight humans and is the head of an international organization with a significant presence in most countries. The Catholic Church has not hesitated to involve itself in a nation's politics on issues it deems important. For example, the Church was instrumental in helping forge the popular revolution that toppled Poland's communist regime.

The Catholic Church, however is not as monolithic as it seems. There is great debate over theology and its application to the contemporary world. No issue has more greatly divided Catholicism than liberation theology. Liberation theology interprets

Christ's mission as one of expounding the need for socioeconomic justice by an over-throw of the existing system. During the 1970s, three works from Latin American theologians and political philosophers captured the ideas of liberation theology: *A Theology for Artisans for a New Humanity* by Argentinian José Miguez Bonino, *The Writings and Lectures on Liberation Theology* by Peruvian priest Gustavo Gutierrez and *Jesus Christ Liberator* by Brazilian Friar Boff.[14] Liberation theology has been influenced by Marxist notions of class struggle, and adherents argue that Jesus sympathized with society's outcasts and condemned the rich. Sandinista Culture Minister Father Cardeal succinctly captured the essence of liberation theology: "For me the four Gospels are equally communist. I'm a Marxist who believes in God, follows Christ, and is a revolutionary for the sake of His Kingdom."[15] In Latin America most of the lower-ranking priests are considered sympathetic to liberation theology, whereas in some countries, such as Brazil, at least half of the bishops are also advocates.

Liberation theology adherents reject the existing religious hierarchy, which they accuse of abandoning the religion's essential teaching; propping up corrupt, unjust regimes; and tolerating a decadent, exploitive society. Liberation theology adherents attempt to mobilize the masses of largely illiterate poor into a revolutionary struggle against the state. In 1986 the Vatican and Catholic liberation theology adherents achieved a consensus. According to the Vatican's "Instruction on Christian Freedom and Liberation," it is "perfectly legitimate that those who suffer oppression on the part of the wealthy or the politically powerful should take action."

Islamic fundamentalism like the kind that swept Iran in 1979 seeks to reverse the tide of modernity and restore society to a pure Islamic state based solely on the Koran's teachings.[16] The Islamic world is divided into two broad sects, the Sunni and the Shiite, and there are fundamentalist adherents within each sect. Under Islam, religion and government should be synonymous. The fundamentalist Muslim Brotherhood was founded in Cairo in 1928 and soon had cells throughout the Arab world. Through today, the Muslim Brotherhood has failed to achieve an Islamic revolution. Instead, its groups have been periodically crushed, and its adherents imprisoned throughout the Middle East. Yet they remain active and may be gaining strength. In 1979, fundamentalist Muslims took over the Holy Mosque in Mecca and demonstrated against what they called a heretical, corrupt, and hypocritical royal Saudi family. In 1981, fundamentalist Muslims succeeded in assassinating Egyptian President Anwar Sadat. Islamic fundamentalists set off a truck bomb that killed over 260 marines in Lebanon in 1983 and forced the Reagan administration into a humiliating retreat from the country. But the fundamentalists' only lasting success was the 1979 revolution in Shiite Iran that brought the Ayatollah Khomeini to power. More recently, in March 1993, fundamentalists exploded a powerful bomb in the World Trade Center in New York City, killing six people and wounding hundreds.

National Liberation NGOs

Many national-liberation movements are organized internationally but focus on political changes in one particular country. Many different political groups have been labeled national-liberation movements. Some are actually struggling to achieve the independence of their ethnic, religious, language, and/or racial group from a sovereign state—

such as the Basques of Spain, Québécois of Canada, Tamils of Sri Lanka, Catholic Irish in Northern Ireland, and the Palestinians in Israel. Other groups attempt to overthrow colonial rule and achieve independence, such as the Americans did from Britain, the Algerians from France, and the Arabs from Turkey. Finally, there are those groups that seek to overthrow existing governments and install themselves in power, such as the various former and existing communist movements around the world, the fundamentalist Muslim movements in the Middle East, and the African National Congress (ANC) in South Africa. The success or failure of any of these movements often depends on the ability to garner international political and military support.

CONCLUSION

Have the United Nations Charter and General Assembly resolutions been any more effective in restraining war since 1945 than the League of Nations and Kellogg-Briand Pact were before then? The growth of the UN and international organizations has paralleled the decline of interstate war. Is there a connection?

At best, the United Nations and most other international organizations reflect and supplement the global system and power balance. Although the United Nations has only implemented two collective security actions (Korea, 1950-1953 and the Persian Gulf, 1990-1993), it has successfully conducted scores of peace keeping and peacemaking efforts. Altogether the United Nations and regional collective security organizations addressed 223 of 317 international conflicts between 1945 and 1984, of which they alleviated about half of them and settled a quarter.[17]

International organizations are perhaps the most visible manifestation of interdependence. They serve many functions, the most important of which may well be to provide a forum in which states can debate issues and have a face-saving means for backing down in confrontations. Generally speaking, the more narrow an international organization's focus—mail, shipping, railroads, telecommunications—the more successful its performance.

Many believe that ever greater interdependence, the erosion of sovereignty, and the proliferation of international organizations may eventually lead to some type of world government in which nation-states abandon their sovereignty to a supreme authority. The amount of power a world government holds could vary from a relatively weak arrangement in a decentralized confederal system, to a more-centralized federal system, or highly-centralized unitary system. If a world government ever does emerge, international relations will have been fundamentally changed.

STUDY QUESTIONS

1. Discuss the functionalist and neofunctionalist theories of organization.

2. What is the legal status of international organizations established by treaty?

3. What is collective security and how have states attempted to achieve it throughout history?

4. What were the League of Nations' strengths and weaknesses, successes and failures?

5. What have been the United Nations' strengths and weaknesses, successes and failures?

6. What are the major UN institutions and what are their responsibilities?

7. Discuss the UN's collective security and peace keeping operations.

8. Discuss the ways in which secular and religious NGOs affect international relations.

ENDNOTES

1. David Mitrany, *A Working Peace* (Chicago: Quadrangle, 1966), 11.

2. See the *Yearbook of International Organizations* (Brussels, Union of International Organizations, 1990).

3. Irving Janis, *Crucial Decisions: Leadership in Policymaking and Crisis Management* (New York, The Free Press, 1989), 142.

4. Mitrany, *A Working Peace,* 11.

5. Some of the best recent books on international organizations include: LeRoy A. Bennett, *International Organizations: Principles and Issues,* 5th ed. (Englewood Cliffs, N.J.: Prentice-Hall, 1991); Inis Claude, *States and the Global System: Politics Law, and Organization* (New York: St. Martin's Press, 1988); Ernst Haas, *When Knowledge Is Power: Three Models of Change in International Organizations* (New York: Council on Foreign Relations, 1990); Terry Nardin and David R. Matel, eds., *Traditions of International Ethics* (Cambridge: Cambridge University Press, 1992); Paul Taylor and A.J.R. Grooms, eds., *International Institutions at Work* (New York: St. Martin's Press, 1988).

6. Sally Morphet, "The Significance and Relevance of the Security Council and its Resolutions and Vetoes," Paper presented to the International Studies Association, London, March 1989.

7. Recall that the Communist Beijing government replaced the nationalist Taipei government as China's representative in 1972.

8. Miguel Martin-Bosch, "How Nations Vote in the General Assembly of the United Nations," *International Organization,* 41, Autumn 1987, 713–718.

9. *New York Times,* October, 1990.

10. Ernst Haas, *Why We Still Need the United Nations: The Collective Management of International Conflict, 1945–1984* (Berkeley, Calif.: Institute of International Studies, 1986), 17.

11. For an excellent evaluation of collective security, see Inis Claude, *Swords Into Plowshares: The Problems and Progress of International Organizations* (New York: Random House, 1984).

12. Paul Lewis, "With U.S. the Biggest Debtor, President Finds U.N. Skeptical," *New York Times,* September 21, 1992.

13. Ernst Haas, *Why We Still Need the United Nations: The Collective Management of International Conflict, 1945–1984,* 17.

14. For an analysis of liberation theology, see Michael Novak, "The Case Against Liberation Theology," *The New York Times Magazine,* October 21, 1984; Alberto M. Piedra, "Some Observations on Liberation Theology," *World Affairs,* vol. 148, no. 3, Winter 1985-1986; Ken Medhurst, "Review Article: The Latin America," *Journal of Latin American Studies,* November 1985; Paul Sigmund, "Revolution, Counterrevolution, and the Catholic Church in Chile," *Annals of the American Academy of Political and Social Science,* vol. 483, January 1986.

15. Quoted in Novak, "The Case Against Liberation Theology," *New York Times Magazine,* October 21, 1984, 51.

16. See John Esposito, ed., *Voices of Resurgent Islam* (New York: Oxford University Press, 1983); Malise Ruthven, *Islam in the World* (New York: Oxford University Press, 1984); Cherly Benard and Zllmay Khalilzad, *The Government of God: Iran's Islamic Republic* (Irvington, N.Y.: Columbia University Press, 1984); David Menashri, *Iran: The Revolution and Beyond* (New York: Holmes and Meier, 1987/88).

17. Haas, *Why We Still Need the United Nations: The Collective Management of International Conflict, 1945–1984,* 17.

Geopolitical Conflict and Cooperation

Why Nations go to War or Stay at Peace

Key Terms and Concepts

Aspiration Gap
Balance of Power
Behavioralism
Bipolarity
Bipolycentric
Decoupling
Hegemonic Stability
 Theory
High Politics
Irredentism
Just War
Long Cycle Theory

Low Politics
Military Industrial
 Complexes
Mirror Images
Multipolarity
Mutually Assured
 Destruction
Neo-just War Theory
Organization for Economic
 Cooperation and
 Development (OECD)
Ostpolitik

Prisoner's Dilemma
Relative Deprivation
Scapegoat Theory
Security Community
Security Dilemma
Self-determination
Social Darwinism
Unipolarity

War is the central problem of international relations.[1] For as long as humans have existed, they have been murdering each other in increasingly well-organized, large-scale, and devastating ways. The human and material destruction of war in this century alone is incalculable. Why do nations go to war or stay at peace?

Every war has its own unique set of causes, which are invariably multiple, complex, and interrelated. Wars have been fought either exclusively or in some combination to gain or defend territory; security; wealth; national, religious, cultural, racial, and/or ideological identity and values; political dynasties; colonies; independence; allies or other friendly states; power balance; power imbalance; hegemony; freedom of the seas; foreign economic interests; endangered citizens; or national honor. Wars have also been fought to weaken or destroy rivals, retaliate against the aggressive actions of others, preempt an imminent or inevitable attack, avenge insults or past losses, fill power vacuums before someone else does, and/or maintain alliance credibility.[2] And these are merely some of the more prominent reasons for war.

To determine the reasons for any particular war, let alone the general phenomenon, one must tap into such fields as psychology, sociology, history, economics, political science, religion, biology, demography, ecology, game-theory, decision-making, and philosophy. As Quincy Wright puts it: "A war, in reality, results from a total situation involving ultimately almost everything that has happened to the human race up to the time the war begins."[3]

Given the vast range of reasons that states war against each other, is it possible to discern any underlying patterns to the causes of war and peace? There are some. War

185

essentially arises from conflict. Wars do not occur unless one or more sides in a conflict are convinced that their vital interests are threatened. States initiate war when they expect to win. Not surprisingly, most wars are fought by neighbors.[4] The wars of each historic period and geographic region have often had distinct patterns of causes. For example, throughout Europe's early modern era, the central reasons for war have changed dramatically: religion (1519–1648), dynastic rule (1648–1763), and revolution and nationalism (1776–1870).

Given the virtual universality of war, can we ever expect violent conflict between or within states to end? Many argue no, maintaining that wars are perfectly natural and are simply a violent means to resolve conflict: "War is a means for achieving an end, a weapon which can be used for good or bad purposes. Some of these purposes for which war has been used have been accepted for humanity as worthwhile ends; indeed, war performs functions which are essential in any society. It has been used to settle disputes, to uphold rights, to remedy wrongs . . . One may say . . . that no more stupid, brutal, wasteful, or unfair method could ever have been imagined for such purposes, but this does not alter the situation."[5] Traditionally, a state's ultimate sovereign power was the ability and right to wage war. Karl von Clausewitz considered war merely an extension of diplomacy by other means and rejected any limits to the violence of battle: "War is an act of force, and to the application of that force there is no limit."[6]

Others, however, argue that although wars grab the headlines, most states are at peace most of the time. From the mid-nineteenth century through today, states have signed a series of treaties limiting weapons and targets of war and in the twentieth century actually outlawed war itself. Although these international agreements have not appreciably reduced the number of wars being waged around the world, war increasingly is within rather than between states, and most states are obeying the restrictions on weapons and behavior. As the world becomes increasingly interdependent and politically democratic, international war will just as steadily diminish as its economic and political costs rise and benefits fall.

Even if this occurs, it remains to be seen whether war's increased moral and practical obsolescence will also reduce the range of reasons that states go to war. In his book *Man, the State, and War,* Kenneth Waltz points out that all theories of war find their source in the character and behavior of one of three areas: human nature, the nation-state, and the international system.[7] We will use that typology here.

WAR AND HUMAN NATURE

Nature and Nurture

Humans, along with many animals, are territorial. They struggle to acquire, maintain, and expand property and are one of the few animals that kill their own kind. But is violence innate (nature/hereditary), learned (nurtured/socialized), or some combination of both?

Many argue that human beings, and the groups to which they belong, are naturally aggressive. War, thus, is inevitable. Kenneth Waltz agreed: "Our miseries are ineluctably the product of our natures. The root of all evil is man, and thus he is himself the root of the specific evil, war."[8] Or as Albert Einstein put it in a letter to Sigmund Freud: "Man has within him a lust for hatred and destruction . . . It is a comparatively easy task to call this into play and raise it to the level of a collective psychosis."[9]

Konrad Lorenz studied aggression in various animal species, and considered humans killer apes, one of the few species that preys on itself. Although most species use aggression to hold or seize territory and protect themselves and their young, there is an internal check on aggression related to a species' innate ability to hurt others. A wolf, for example, will stop an attack on another wolf as soon as it shows signs of submission, whereas doves will continue to attack even when the other dove submits. Lorenz theorizes that because of the relatively limited means of humans to use their bodies to inflict pain on others, humans are more like doves than wolves in continuing to attack even when the other side submits. The innate checks on human aggression have not kept pace with the species' technological ability to destroy the world.[10]

Aggression comes from, and is essential to, evolution. Charles Darwin theorized that life evolved from a few simple species to millions of complex species through a survival-of-the-fittest struggle, as each species attempted to adapt to hostile environments. *Social Darwinism,* popularized by Herbert Spencer and others, argued that nations, like animal species, were engaged in a perpetual war of all against all, in which the stronger conquered the weaker. All humans, from the simplest hunter-gatherer groups of 100,000 years ago to the complex nation-states of today, have continually struggled to survive. Progress comes from competition, as the strong and more advanced vanquish the weak. Thus, imperialism is natural and even moral because it allows superior peoples to subdue and civilize the inferior ones. During the nineteenth century and the 1930s, governments used social Darwinism to justify their imperialism. As Hitler put it: "Nature knows no political boundaries. First she puts living creatures on this globe and watches the free play of forces. She then confers the master's right on her favorite child, the strongest."[11]

Others—behavioralists—argue that humans are shaped by their environment rather than by inner drives, and thus human aggression is learned rather than innate.[12] Some environments promote and others inhibit aggression. Wars are fought by governments, not individuals, and thus are political cultural inventions rather than biological necessities.[13] A Hitler or a Hussein can skillfully use ideology, religion, and/or nationalism to whip a population from passivity into aggression and to channel that collective emotion into imperialism. *Behavioralism* also distinguishes between sporadic acts of violence by individuals and small groups and war organized and conducted by states.

Humans have a need to identify with things greater than themselves. During the modern era, the nation has become the primary source of identity for many. Jack Levy explores the relationship between human psychology, nationalism, and war, which occurs when people:

> acquire an intense commitment to the power and prosperity of the state and this
> commitment is strengthened by national myths emphasizing the moral, physical,
> and political strength of the state and by an individual's feelings of powerlessness
> and their consequent tendency to seek their identity and fulfillment through the
> state, then assertive and nationalist policies are perceived as increasing state power

and are at the same time psychologically satisfying for the individual and, in this way, nationalism contributes to war.[14]

Psychological and sociological theories of war, particularly the innate-aggression school, have been criticized on several grounds. If humans are innately aggressive and that aggression leads to war, why then are people not at war all or most of the time? In reality, most states and humans are at peace most of the time. Whereas conflict among humans is inevitable, violence inherently is not. Studies of primitive societies find as many peaceful as violent ones.[15] Although humans are certainly capable of violence, they seldom commit it and instead resolve most conflicts peacefully. Most humans use rationality to check their aggressive drives. A human drive to cooperate with others may be more important than the drive to vanquish them. The aggression of states or individuals may well be deviant rather than natural behavior.[16] Although some peoples, such as the Germans and the Japanese, are commonly thought to be more aggressive than others, studies have failed to prove it.[17]

There is not necessarily a link between human and state aggression. Wars can occur even when the respective populations are disinterested or opposed; wars can be averted through skilled diplomacy even when the respective populations feverishly demand it.[18] Some argue that for every leader who dragged a reluctant populace to war, there is a reluctant leader who was pushed into war by an eager populace.[19] Yet one study of 25 wars found no case "precipitated by emotional tensions, sentimentality, crowd behavior, or other irrational motivations."[20]

Misperception and Escalation

The decision for war is not taken lightly, even among the most aggressive of governments and peoples. Few states and their peoples have ever wanted to risk destruction for political objectives. Yet most states have experienced war's horrors. Why the discrepancy?

Some argue that most wars happen because of states' mutual misperceptions about the others' intentions and power.[21] How do misperceptions occur? Misperceptions can involve a range of images, attitudes, and behaviors: a government's angelic self-image and diabolical image of the rival government; overconfidence in one's military power and disregard for the power of the other state; missed signals that show the other state's willingness to compromise; lack of understanding or empathy for the other state's interests. In conflicts, communications break down or are limited from the start. Governments and their peoples project their fears, ambitions, and capabilities on their rivals. Each side interprets the other's actions in the worst way and then counters them accordingly, resulting in spiraling tensions and saber rattling. Governments misperceive the military capabilities and intentions of each other. Once a decision for war is made, leaders convince themselves and their publics that they will enjoy a quick and easy victory.

The root of misperception is the human tendency to simplify information. There is only so much that any human or group of humans can comprehend. Instead of attempting to understand the world's complexities, decision makers and the public cling to and become trapped by a collection of simple prejudices and stereotypes. In a conflict, people see what they want to see and hear what they want to hear. *Mirror images* occur when each side "believes the other to be bent on aggression and conquest, to be capable of great brutality and evil-doing, to be something less than human . . . To hold this conception of the enemy becomes the moral duty of every citizen, and those who question it are denounced . . . The approaching war is seen as due entirely to the hostile intentions of the enemy."[22] Governments tend to believe their own propaganda about themselves and their rivals. In conflicts, and particularly in a crisis, governments tend to assume the worst about each other's intentions, power, and goals. Tragically, mirror images often become self-fulfilling prophecies, as even the most innocent of the rival's actions are interpreted in the worst possible way. The result is an existing gap between image and reality that worsens with a conflict. The more tense a situation, the more humans will stereotype themselves and their opponents, thus making mutual understanding and reconciliation increasingly difficult. This tendency is particularly heightened in an age of intercontinental missiles and supersonic bombers.

Political leaders often have several audiences: their domestic constituents, their foreign rivals, and the international community. Misunderstandings can arise when governments send different messages to different audiences. Even authoritarian governments can become the prisoners of public expectations. Once a government draws a line in the sand for a domestic audience, it often feels compelled to stick to it even if it secretly wishes to be more conciliatory toward its rivals. As conflicts escalate, states get trapped in a game of "chicken" with their rival, in which they charge each other, hoping the other will give way. The result is often war, because neither side wants to step aside and compromise.

Misperceptions themselves are not the cause of war. Real conflicts over vital issues must be present for either side to consider war as a means to resolve the conflicts. Often, the different sides in a dispute understand one another's intentions and capabilities quite clearly. Yet, war occurs anyway, because one or both sides made a rational decision that they could succeed by using force.

WAR AND THE NATION-STATE

Nationalism, Separatism, and Irredentism

Throughout the modern era, nationalism has increasingly been a major cause for war.[23] With the end of the cold war, nationalism has replaced ideology as the major cause of war. Nearly every one of the over 190 sovereign states has significant minority ethnic, religious, linguistic, and/or racial, populations that either currently or potentially demand independence or merger with a similar group in a neighboring country. Nationalism can spark a war for independence within a state (separatism) or a war by one state to "liberate" those of the same nationality in a neighboring state (irredentism).

The boundaries of modern nation-states were often drawn with complete disregard for the inhabitants. Frontiers grouped different nationalities and separated similar nationalities. Africa is the most glaring example. At the 1885 Berlin Conference, the imperial powers satisfied their conflicting claims to the continent by simply drawing lines through a map of Africa. Today Somalia is the only country with no significant minority group, although national unity did not prevent it from plunging into civil war in the early 1990s.

War often happens when a government refuses to accept a minority's demands and actively attempts to suppress the minority. Nationalism has destroyed all the great modern empires, from the Dutch independence struggle against Spain in the late sixteenth century, America's struggle against Britain in the late eighteenth century, and Latin America's struggle against Spain in the early nineteenth century, through the more than 100 nation-states that emerged from the breakup of the British, French, Dutch, American, Portugese, and Japanese empires after 1945, to the present wave of independence struggles in the former Soviet Union, Yugoslavia, Iraq, Israel, India, and dozens of other countries.

Irredentism has also been a major cause of war. In 1938 Hitler seized Czechoslovakia's Sudetenland province to "liberate" the three million ethnic Germans living there. The North Vietnamese fought the United States and South Vietnam (1954–1975) as much to unify the country as to impose communism on South Vietnam. However, economic as well as nationalist motivations can prompt a state's irredentist claims for neighboring territory. Hitler not only rejoined the Sudeten Germans to the nativeland, but took over two-thirds of Czechoslovakia's industrial capacity. Iraq's attempts to swallow Kuwait in August 1990 had as much to do with taking the latter's oil as joining two separate Arab populations.

The global system upholds two conflicting values—*self-determination* and stability. The world becomes increasingly unstable as more people demand autonomy or outright independence. These demands often result in war.

Wars for National Cohesion

Conflict is inseparable from life. When two or more groups conflict over an issue, the solidarity of each group is usually enhanced. Conflict between groups can be a safety valve that releases hostility over conflict within groups.

Sometimes a government may deliberately provoke a conflict with another state just to divert the population's attention from internal problems and divisions. According to the *scapegoat theory,* war with others "is sometimes the last chance for a state ridden with inner antagonisms to overcome these antagonisms, or else break up indefinitely."[24] For example, in 1861 Secretary of State William Seward encouraged President Lincoln to pick a fight with another state in order to unite the country and prevent civil war. The decision by Argentinia's government to invade the British Falkland Islands in 1982 may have been largely an attempt to distract the public's attention from economic stagnation and political oppression at home. One motive for President Hussein's decision to send his army into Kuwait may have been to sublimate the Sunni-Shiite and Arab-Kurdish strife within Iraq. Whereas victory might have helped repress these divisions, defeat only exacerbated them.

How common is this cause of war? Different studies reach different conclusions about how frequently scapegoating occurs. One study revealed that over half of all international wars between 1823 and 1937 were preceded by serious conflicts in one or more of the states.[25] Most other studies, however, found little correlation.[26] The resort to war to heal internal divisions relative to the number of countries torn by internal conflict is minute.[27]

The cement holding healthy societies together is shared values, traditions, behavior, and ambitions, not fear of government repression or foreign attack. From a practical point of view, if a nation is already divided, a government's decision to go to war would most likely weaken its cohesion and ability to fight.

War aside, do governments use foreign conflicts to heal internal conflicts and strengthen their own legitimacy? Sometimes. It depends on how serious the domestic problems are. For example, American presidents have been known to manufacture an international crisis in an election year (particularly when the economy is ailing) to distract people from their problems and rally them around both the flag and the president. Governments of countries with deep divisions are more likely to neglect foreign affairs.

Wars from National Incohesion

More commonly, civil wars lead to international wars. Civil wars occur when one group—class, religious, ethnic, regional—feels it is being exploited by the dominant group. A group's feeling of *relative deprivation* and the *aspiration gap* between what it receives and what it desires actually tends to worsen when things are improving as a "revolution of rising frustrations" replaces a "revolution of rising expectations."[28] A state torn by war offers an opportunity for other ambitious states to intervene on one side in return for certain advantages.

The Cold War led both Washington and Moscow (and to a lesser extent London, Beijing, and Paris) to intervene on behalf of the sympathetic side in civil wars. In fact, unable to fight each other directly because of *Mutually Assured Destruction,* the superpowers battled each other indirectly by supplying arms, training, and sometimes combat troops to opposing sides in Vietnam, Korea, Afghanistan, Angola, Nicaragua, Ethiopia, El Salvador, and China, to name the more prominent. Sometimes a power will justify intervening in another state to prevent its subversion by its rival, as Moscow did when it crushed democratic forces in East Germany (1953), Hungary (1956), Czechoslovakia (1968), and Poland (1980), and Washington did when it toppled unfriendly governments in the Dominican Republic (1965) and Grenada (1983).[29]

Democracy and War

In 1795, Immanuel Kant, in his essay "Perpetual Peace," argued that humans are naturally inclined to peace, democracies are more peaceful than dictatorships, and the number of wars will diminish as more countries become democratic.[30]

It is true that since 1812 democratic countries have never warred against each other.[31] Why? The rise of the democratic industrial state brought a shift from a *high politics* emphasis on military security issues to a *low politics* emphasis on welfare; geoeconomic interests have eclipsed geopolitical interests in importance for most democratic states. A common democratic ideology and economic interdependence prevent democratic states from going to war against one another. The implications of this are profound. Levy states that:

the absence of war between democracies comes as close as anything we have to an empirical law in international relations. It follows that as more states become democratic, the possibility of war decreases accordingly, and if all states were genuine democracies, war would cease to plague humankind, thus fulfilling Kant's dream of a perpetual peace.[32]

Encouraging as the propensity for peace among democratic states is, Levy points out that "democratic states have been involved proportionately in as many wars as non-democratic states."[33] For example, of the fifty wars examined between 1816 and 1865, liberal democratic states were involved in nineteen and started eleven.[34] Another study concluded that democracies are in fact less militaristic than authoritarian states.[35] According to Michael Doyle, the reason for continued armed conflict between democratic and authoritarian states is that "the very constitutional restraint, shared commercial interests, and international respect for individual rights that promote peace among liberal societies can exacerbate conflicts in relations between liberal and nonliberal societies."[36] However, as increasing numbers of states become democratic, we can expect to see the numbers of international wars decline.

Development and War

Many studies have shown that there is a close correlation between wealth and violence—the poor tend to war more than the rich.[37] Of 120 armed conflicts between 1955 and 1979, all but six involved Third World nations.[38] Wealthy states simply do not war against each other. Between 1945 and 1990, no war occurred between or took place within the now twenty-four members of the *Organization for Economic Cooperation and Development* (OECD), or the world's most developed nations. There were eight wars (defined as an armed conflict with more than 1,000 battle deaths) between OECD countries and less-developed countries (LDCs), and one with a communist country. Communist countries fought five wars, four of which were against other communist countries and one against an LDC. The LDCs were clearly the most war-prone. In addition to the war fought against a communist country and eight against OECD countries, the LDCs fought 19 wars against one another.[39]

The lack of wars between wealthy countries represents a major change in international relations. Traditionally, the wealthier a country the more it warred against wealthy and poorer countries alike. Throughout the modern era, Europe was the world's wealthiest and most war-torn region, accounting for 65 percent of all wars in the sixteenth and seventeenth centuries and 59 percent of all wars between 1816 and 1945, or one every one and a half years.[40]

The wealthier a country, the more it can financially afford to go to war. Yet, the greater the psychological and political constraints on doing so. There are more than 800 million people in the OECD; shared values and needs account for peace among its members. Most of the OECD states are liberal democracies, and all are increasingly interdependent. The benefits of international trade and investment far exceed any costs. Peace between these states is not simply the absence of war, it is also the complete lack of a perception among the leaders and public in each country that war could occur between them, and thus no preparations for war exist.

The economic development and interdependence among the OECD countries was accelerated by the challenge posed by their common enemy, the Soviet Union. These countries could contain the Soviet threat by creating a grand economic and military alliance. Yet none of the OECD countries ever fought the Soviet Union.

The world's wealthiest states have no desire to war against each other because the costs would be too great; the world's poorest states may have the desire to war against their neighbors, but lack the means. War may be largely a luxury of the middle income countries.

Economic Interest Groups and War

Self-interest shapes national interests; the more powerful the interest, the greater its ability to substitute its interest for the nation's. Some people argue that military industrial complexes are the most powerful interest groups in the United States, Russia, and other great powers. The military and the industries and politicians that benefit from and support the interest groups have a vested interest in high military spending and war itself. *Military industrial complexes* constantly try to justify and expand their existence. They do so by identifying genuine, exaggerated, or outright imagined enemies. Throughout the Cold War, the military industrial complexes of the United States and the Soviet Union fought any attempts to limit arms races, military intervention overseas, or the forceful resolution of conflicts.

The military industrial complex theory for war has little evidence, and military industrial complexes may not be as omnipotent as their critics maintain. Throughout the Cold War, military spending as a GNP percentage declined for both the Soviet Union and the United States. Other factors like nationalism, ideology, the power balance, and so forth are much more important in explaining the reasons why countries with large military industrial complexes have resorted to war.

Most wars have not been fought primarily for economic gain.[41] War has rarely conferred direct economic benefits upon those who fought it. In any national economy, war benefits only a few businesses but hurts most. Thus, most businesspeople prefer peace to war. In many wars, most profits went to those businesspeople from countries that sat on the fence and sold to both sides.

WAR AND THE INTERNATIONAL SYSTEM

The Power Balance, Imbalance, and War

Few concepts of international relations are cited more frequently and interpreted more widely than the *balance of power*. The most common use of the term asserts that international power can be distributed in several patterns or poles. *Unipolarity* occurs when one state has hegemonic, or predominant, military power, as the United States had between 1945 and 1949, when it held a monopoly on nuclear power, or as it had since the Soviet Union's collapse in 1991.

Bipolarity involves two states or alliances with a relative military power balance between them. In the late 1940s, the United States and the Soviet Union clustered weaker European states around themselves either through coercion or persuasion. From the 1950s until the late 1980s these two powers competed for allies throughout the Third World. As these two alliances solidified and after Moscow exploded an atomic bomb in 1949, breaking America's atomic monopoly, the global system became characterized as bipolar.

During the 1960s, the rigid alliances of NATO and the Warsaw Pact began to loosen, prompting analysts to label the new system *bipolycentric,* or bimultipolar.[42] The United States and Soviet Union remained the sole superpowers, but their ability to pressure their respective alliance members into compliance diminished, and some states, such as China and France, asserted their independence from their blocs. Relations were forged between members of the two blocs, such as West Germany's *ostpolitik* policy toward Eastern Europe and East Germany. Some of this *decoupling* from the alliances occurred because ICBMs lessened the need of the superpowers for forward bases to attack the other, and the NATO members in particular increasingly questioned Washington's resolve to retaliate with nuclear weapons in response to a Soviet attack on Western Europe. Britain, China, and France developed their own nuclear weapons. As the European Community and Japan economically caught up to the United States, they increasingly followed policies that promoted their own interests, even if it clashed with the Western alliance. China, meanwhile, challenged the Soviet Union for leadership of world communism. Under bipolycentrism, Washington and Moscow remained the sole superpowers, but other regions and countries became increasingly economically and militarily powerful and assertive.

If the United States and Russia continue to reduce their nuclear and conventional arsenals while the world becomes ever more interdependent, *multipolarity* may emerge in which there are a half dozen states with relatively equal military and economic power, including the United States, Japan, the European Community, China, and Russia. A neoclassical balance of power system could emerge, in which states compete and combine against one another as they did in an earlier era (1648–1792), doing so now for geoeconomic rather than geopolitical reasons. Or the power balance might be made up of regions rather than states, with a U.S.-led North American economic bloc; an expanded European Community, embracing Eastern Europe and Russia; and a Japan-led East and Southeast Asian bloc.

There are also other ways of defining the balance of power. Ernst Haas found seven.[43] Three involved the way power was distributed and the subsequent relations among states: any distribution of power, an equilibrium of power, and hegemony of power. Two concentrated on the notion of an equilibrium of power having two very different impacts on international relations and war: stability and peace, and instability and war. The two final uses of the term claim that either states will always attempt to strengthen their national security by countering the power of others and thus try to maintain an equilibrium in the international system (universal law of history), or (whether or not they do) they should (prescriptive).

The debate between A.F.K. Organski and Hans Morgenthau exemplifies the difficulty in achieving a consensus over just what the term means.[44] To Organski the balance of power simply means the constantly shifting distribution of power among individual states, whereas Morgenthau maintains that the balance of power refers to the power relations among shifting alliances of states rather than individual states.

A related argument centers on whether a balanced or imbalanced power system is more susceptible to war. There are those who argue that power imbalances rather than balances make war more likely. When one state has more power than others, it is more likely to go to war because it has a greater chance of winning.[45] Others argue that the more egalitarian the power distribution the greater the feeling among states that they can win a war against their rivals, and thus war is more likely:

> *an even distribution of political, economic, and military capabilities between contending groups of states is likely to increase the probability of war; peace is preserved best when there is an imbalance of national capabilities between disadvantaged and advantaged nations; the aggressor will come from a group of dissatisfied strong countries; and it is the weaker, rather than the stronger, power that is most likely to be the aggressor.[46]*

Both arguments are partially correct. A study of all wars between 1820 and 1965 found that there was no correlation between the power balance and war.[47] When power was distributed relatively equally, war was likely 50 percent of the time; when it was unequally distributed it was likely 46 percent of the time. Wars in the nineteenth century were different from those in the twentieth century. Wars in the former were more likely when there was an imbalance of power and wars in the latter were more likely when a relative power balance existed. Wars of rivalry are more likely when there is a power balance; wars of opportunity when there is a power imbalance.[48]

Those who maintain that a power balance increases the chance for war differ over whether a bipolar or a multipolar system is more unstable. Some argue that in a bipolar world each side focuses its attention on the other and counters every move the other makes. The increased tension and arms races inevitably make war more likely.[49] In contrast, the proliferation of issues and actors in a multipolar system tends to defuse tensions and thus the possibility of war. Destabilizing arms races are more likely in a bipolar than a multipolar system. Others argue just the opposite, and point out that the multipolar system of the early twentieth century led to two world wars, whereas the post-1945 bipolar system has remained at peace. Multipolar systems involving three powers, they argue, are much more unstable than a bipolar system, because of the tendency for two parties to ally against the third.[50]

Who is right? One study of all wars of the last five centuries found that wars were less likely in a multipolar system but that they were far more bloody, because they involved far more people.[51] Although no general wars like the wars during the Napoleonic era or the twentieth century's two world wars occurred during bipolar periods, wars were more likely. However, of all the systems throughout history, unipolar international systems have been relatively more peaceful than other power distributions. Roman and British hegemony were known respectively as *Pax Romana* and *Pax Britannica,* because other states lacked enough power to challenge them.

Whether the global system is predominantly multipolar or bipolar, war is more likely when that power distribution is changing. Power is more than tanks and missiles. The size and quality of the two sides' respective populations, industries, geographies, natural resources, technological levels, and, most importantly, political wills and national cohesions, all shape the power calculus. Karl Deutsch argues that whenever:

> there is a major change at any level—culture and values, political and social institutions, laws, or technology—the old adjustment and control mechanisms become strained and may break down. Any major psychological and cultural, or major social and political, or legal, or technological change in the world thus increases the risk of war, unless it is balanced by compensatory political, legal, cultural, and psychological adjustments.[52]

Many theorists believe that the most important shifts in regional or global power balances are technological and economic.[53] Organski and Kugler maintain that "war is caused by differences in the rates of growth among the great powers and . . . the differences in rates between the dominant nation and the challenger that permit the latter to overtake the former."[54] One side's introduction of a new weapons system can dramatically shift the power balance. For example, the English won the Hundred Years' War as much with the long bow as anything else. Although larger states are more aggressive than smaller states, the distribution of military technology can supply smaller or poorer states with an ability to wage war that they formerly did not have.[55]

Hegemonic Stability, Long-Cycles, and War

Some theorists see international relations shaped not by a balance of power but by a hierarchy of power. The powers struggle for power, and eventually one power emerges from a war to become a hegemon over the system, until eventually that power is vanquished by another. The concept of the rise and fall of hegemons, known as the *hegemonic stability theory,* is closely linked to the *long cycle theory* of history.[56] Shifts in economic and technological power and war are seen to recur in long cycles, generally of a century. The hegemonic wars of the modern era would include:

> (1) the Italian Wars (1494–1517), from which Portugal emerged as the world power; (2) the War of Dutch Independence (1585–1609), leading to the rise of the Netherlands as a world power; (3) the Wars of Louis XIV (1689–1715), which gave way to British leadership; (4) the French Revolutionary and Napoleonic Wars (1792–1815), which renewed the world-power role of Britain; and (5) the two World Wars of this century (1914–1939), marked the transition of the United States to world power.[57]

Goldstein nicely summarized the rise and fall of hegemons and other great powers:

> Countries rebuilding from war incorporate a new generation of technology, eventually allowing competition with the hegemonic country. For these reasons, each period of hegemony gradually erodes. Recurring wars, on several long wave upswings, eventually culminate in a new hegemonic war, bringing another restructuring of the core and a new period of hegemony.[58]

Most studies, however, do not find a war cycle for nations.[59] Jack Levy effectively demolishes the long cycle and hegemonic stability theories.[60] Even if these long cycles ever existed, hegemonic wars are increasingly unlikely as the world becomes ever more interdependent.

Arms Races

In an anarchic global system, states must rely on themselves for their own security. "If you want peace, prepare for war," has been the guide for political leaders throughout history. The power balance or peace through strength theory, however, can lead to arms races that destabilize international relations and make war more likely rather than less likely. Arms races occur when states become trapped in a *security dilemma*.[61] One state perceives a foreign military threat, so it builds up its forces. In seemingly alleviating its own security problem, it simultaneously threatens the security of the other state which responds by building up its own forces. The first state then reacts by further building up its forces, and the arms race spirals indefinitely. Arms races are easy to begin and very difficult to end, and they often result in war.

There may well be no hostile intent behind any participant in a given arms race, but each becomes a prisoner of its own fear and distrust for the other and the possibly dire results of not keeping up. Each side sees only the other's offensive capabilities and not its defensive intentions. Thus the race continues. This phenomena is known as the *prisoner's dilemma*.[62]

Arms races occur because of international rivalries and domestic politics. Which is more important? Choucri and North argue that:

> The primary importance of domestic factors . . . does not preclude the reality of arms competition. Two countries whose military establishments are expanding largely for domestic reasons . . . almost certainly will become acutely aware of each other's spending. Thereafter, although spending may continue to be powerfully affected by domestic factors, deliberate military spending may be over specific military features and may be a very small portion of total military spending.[63]

Do arms races tend to end in war? Scholars exploring the question have reached different conclusions.[64] One study of great-power arms races since 1815 found that most have ended in war.[65] Another study, which examined thirteen arms races in the nineteenth and twentieth centuries, found that only 5 ended in war.[66] And yet another study of arms races between 1816 and 1980 found that only 20 percent were followed by war.[67] One study found no example of an arms race being the primary cause of any war.[68]

Whom are we to believe? Arms races themselves may be difficult to define. Just because rival states annually increase their military budgets does not necessarily mean they are engaged in an arms race. Domestic politics and military industrial complexes may be more important in determining the amount and priorities of a nation's military budget than the international power balance. States may build up their arms yet not feel they are racing against others, and thus tensions remain low. The study that concluded that most arms races ended in war only analyzed those in which the participants increased their spending in direct response to that of their rivals. Clearly, some arms races do lead to war, whereas others are substitutes for war.

Arms races are symptoms rather than causes of war. Genuine arms races do not occur unless those countries already have deep conflicts. Arms races exacerbate existing conflicts; they do not create them. Although the mere possession of weapons is not enough to start a war, the more powerful a government's military forces, the more inclined it might be to use those weapons in a conflict. A state's military power is less important than what it intends to do with those forces. States with good relations do not engage in arms races. As Hans Morgenthau put it: "Men do not fight because they have arms. They have arms because they deem it necessary to fight."[69]

Regardless of whether arms races end in war or not, there is nothing positive about them. They consume enormous amounts of human, scientific, financial, and political resources that could be invested more profitably elsewhere. If a war does occur, it will probably be more destructive than if the arms race never preceded it. Although most people would agree that "guns don't kill, people do," the proliferation of guns certainly increases tensions that may result in war. It also makes war more likely, because in a crisis, leaders might feel more confident about militarily asserting their position.

Alliances

It is commonly believed that alliances, like arms races, can increase tension and make war more likely. A nation's power can obviously be augmented by alliance with other states, which in turn must be calculated into the overall power balance. An alliance is formed when its members anticipate the strong possibility of war.

Some consider alliances destabilizing because:

> *First alliances look menacing; hence it is likely that they will cause others to scramble for allies of their own, and therein raise tensions to a new, more dangerous level. Second, alliances are entangling; they can drag members into conflicts which do not affect their vital interests. Finally, alliances are sanguineous; their very existence means that even if a nation's armies are beaten and its leaders can see that resources are inadequate to sustain further combat, it would be encouraged to continue fighting by the hope of aid from its allies. In sum, whereas some theorists and statesmen advance the proposition that alliances sustain peace, others echo Sir John Frederick Maurices's lament that "f you prepare thoroughly for war you will get it."[70]*

Do allies make war more or less likely? In fact, alliances seem no more likely to cause a war than arms races. A study of 256 international conflicts between 1815 and 1965 concluded that wars were just as common whether or not an alliance was involved, although it did find that being in an alliance made smaller powers more likely to go to war.[71] Minor powers with great-power allies went to war in 42 percent of conflicts; without such allies they went to war only 17 percent of the time. An even more comprehensive study involving the last five centuries reached the same general conclusions.[72]

One study found that alliances decreased the chance for war throughout the nineteenth century, increased it in the twentieth century through 1945, and decreased it thereafter.[73] Another study, which spanned from 1495 to 1975, found that most alliances led to war within five years of their formation, except between 1815 and 1914, when no wars followed within five years of an alliance's formation.[74] Alliances, like increased arms, may not be a war's underlying cause but may aggravate existing tensions and thus make war more likely. In both studies, the most important effect was whether or not the alliance stabilized relations.

Interdependence, Security Communities, and War

The reasons why the world's wealthiest states do not war against one another may have less to do with their wealth than with the interdependence between them. The OECD countries have created, what Karl Deutsch would call a *security community,* or:

> *a group of people which has become "integrated." By integration we mean the attainment, within a territory, of a "sense of community" and of institutions and practices strong enough and widespread enough to assure . . . dependable expectations of "peaceful change" among its population. By sense of community we mean a belief . . . that common social problems must and can be resolved by processes of "peaceful change."[75]*

That is not to say that there is no conflict between or within the OECD countries. Economic disputes among the OECD are rife, yet they are handled diplomatically, with no thought of using military force. Violence within some OECD members is common—race riots in the United States, IRA bombings in Britain, Basque bombings in Spain, ethnic violence in Germany and France, and so on. The governments, however, successfully contain, if not solve, these conflicts, and there is little chance that they can affect international relations.

Although security communities are most common between ideological allies, they can also exist between countries that are ideological rivals. A security community evolved between the United States and the Soviet Union after 1945 as the crises, saber rattling, and brinkmanship of the 1950s were eventually transformed into the détente and restraint of the 1970s and 1980s. The superpowers continued to compete across the global geopolitical chessboard, but avoided any direct confrontation after the 1962 Cuban missile crisis. They bolstered this crisis-avoidance understanding with more than a dozen conventional and nuclear arms control treaties. With the collapse of the Soviet Union's communist regime and empire, Russia and the other newly independent countries are being slowly drawn into the interdependent global economy, a trend that will only strengthen the prevailing peace.[76]

Mutually Assured Destruction (MAD) was the basis of the American-Soviet security community. Gilpin writes that "it was not until after 1945 that the threat of an all out military conflict (including the use of nuclear and thermonuclear bombs) became catastrophic so that such wars as did occur took on a more limited character. The risks of trying to take new territory through military invasion mounted while the alternative of development through rational industrial and trade policies heralded new rewards for a peaceful strategy. This shift . . . has largely escaped notice in the study of international politics."[77]

The greater the world's economic, nuclear, and environmental interdependence, the lower the chance for war. According to Rosecrance,

> *a new "trading world" of international relations offers the possibility of escaping such a vicious cycle [war] and finding new patterns of cooperation among nation-states . . . the benefit of trade and cooperation today greatly exceeds that of military competition and territorial aggrandizement. States, as Japan has shown, can do better through a strategy of economic development based on trade than they are likely to do through military interventions in the affairs of other states . . . the new world that is unfolding contrasts very sharply with comparable periods of major historical transition. Unlike those earlier periods, no major new military threat is likely to replace the old one anytime soon.*[78]

International Morality and War

International law outlaws war, or at least aggressive war. Although some may scoff at the effectiveness of international law in deterring war, others argue that "statesmen nearly always perceive themselves as constrained by international principles and rules that prescribe and proscribe behavior," and that these "international norms are more important than countervailing power in constraining states."[79]

Until recently, the idea of outlawing war would have puzzled most philosophers and spiritual leaders, let alone political leaders. The notion of a *just war* emerged from early Christendom. Islam promotes the concept of "holy war" (jihad), in which it is just for Muslims to fight infidels. Although the debate over when going to war is justified can be traced to the ancient Greeks, it was St. Augustine (345–430) who most systematically addressed the subject. St. Augustine argued that just wars (*jus ad bellum*) "are usually defined as those which avenge injuries, when the nation or city against which war-like action is to be directed has neglected either to punish wrongs committed by its own citizens or to restore what has been unjustly taken by it. Further that kind of war is undoubtedly just which God himself ordains."[80] In other words, murder is not committed when done in self-defense or God's glory. Killing can be justified.

During the sixteenth century, three Spanish legal scholars—Vitoria, Ayala, and Suarez—attempted to synthesize ancient and medieval writings on warfare, in part to justify the Spanish conquest of the Western Hemisphere. Horrified by the slaughter of the Thirty Years' War, Hugo Grotius, the Dutch legal scholar, then built upon the efforts of the Spanish scholars. Grotius accepted war's inevitability, but argued that there should be treaty and ethical constraints governing its conduct. He distinguished between "the justice of a war" (*jus ad bellum*) in which a government must decide whether its decision to go to war is just, and "justice in a war" (*jus in bello*) in which governments accept restraints on the tactics used in warfare. His arguments influenced the Treaty of Westphalia of 1648, which inaugurated a period of restraint in warfare that lasted until the Napoleonic era.

Today, according to Inis Claude, international relations are governed by:

the neo-just war doctrine . . . [which] no longer seriously purports to accept the view that peace is unconditionally a higher view than justice. We have returned to the medieval view that it is permissible . . . to fight to promote justice, broadly conceived. Evil ought to be overturned, and good ought to be achieved, by force if necessary.[81]

The *neo-just war theory* includes six key components: (1) war can only be fought after all other means of resolving the issue have been exhausted; (2) only legitimate governments can decide to go to war; (3) wars should be fought for self-defense and not revenge; (4) there should be a good chance of winning; (5) the war should be fought to achieve conditions that would have been better than those that have occurred through nonresistance; and (6) war should be fought to resist aggression, not to change the enemy's government or society.[82] This conception of morality helped justify United Nations' intervention in Kuwait, Somalia, and Bosnia during the early 1990s and will prove to be an essential argument for similar interventions in the future.

These principles have been codified in a range of treaties throughout the twentieth century. Even self-defense is limited. Literally interpreted, the right to self-defense does not extend to launching a preemptive attack in response to the belligerent actions or words of another state, unless fighting has already broken out. According to various International Court of Justice rulings, there are three other restrictions on self-defense. Attacks on one's nationals abroad does not justify retaliation. Self-defense does not allow reprisals against the enemy territory. Any force used in self-defense must be necessary and proportional to the armed attack.

Although one state can sell arms to or station troops in another state, it is illegal for a state to do so without that other state's permission. In the case *Nicaragua* v. *U.S.A.* (1986), Nicaragua sued the United States for blockading its ports and aiding rebels who were fighting against the government. The United States argued that its actions were justified under the principle of collective self-defense—the Nicaraguans were sending arms to rebels fighting against the neighboring state of El Salvador. The International Court of Justice ruled that collective self-defense was valid only in the event of any actual attack, which never transpired. Thus it ruled against the United States and ordered it to compensate Nicaragua for its losses. The Reagan administration dismissed the Court's rulings, claiming that it did not have jurisdiction.

International law has been used to prosecute war criminals. Defendants at the Nuremburg and Tokyo war trials were charged with three crimes: (1) crimes against peace: namely, the planning, preparation, initiation, or waging of a war of aggression or a war in violation of international treaties, agreements, or assurances; or participation in a common plan or conspiracy for the accomplishment of any of the foregoing; (2) war crimes: namely, violations of the laws or customs of war. Such violations shall include, but not be limited to, murder, ill-treatment, or deportation for slave labor (or for any other purpose) of civilian population of or in an occupied territory; murder or ill-treatment of prisoners of war or persons on the seas; killing of hostages; plunder of public or private property; wanton destruction of cities, towns, or villages; or devastation not justified by military necessity; and (3) crimes against humanity: namely, murder, extermination, enslavement, deportation, and any other inhumane acts committed against any civilian population before or during the war; or persecutions committed on political, racial, or religious grounds in execution of or in connection with any crime within the jurisdiction of the Tribunal, whether or not in violation of the domestic law of the country where perpetuated.

How effective has international law been in deterring war? It is difficult to say with certainty. One sign of its increasing importance is the fact that most governments will rigorously claim that they are following it even as others maintain that they are violating it.

CONCLUSION

Although each war has its own unique set of causes, we can make some general observations. States are shaped by the international system of which they are a part. In a global system with no government, every state ultimately must fend for itself. At any given time in history, some countries are largely satisfied with the international status quo, whereas others wish to change it, sometimes by violent means. Wars occur because governments perceive them as being useful for resolving conflicts in their favor. "War," as Clauswitz pointed out, "is simply the continuation of politics by other means."

Yet, there are signs that war is becoming an increasingly unimportant part of international relations. The Cold War is over; the Soviet Empire and the Warsaw Pact have disappeared. Liberal democracy has replaced communism throughout eastern Europe and much of the former Soviet Union. The superpowers have made significant agreements over the downsizing of their respective forces. As countries become more wealthy and democratic, war's costs rise and benefits plummet. Throughout the twentieth century, international morality and law have evolved to the point where wars of aggression are outlawed and condemned. The national and international constraints on war are growing. Nations increasingly settle their differences peacefully. The percentage of conflicts that end in war have steadily diminished from about fifteen percent between 1815 and 1945 to only 3 percent since 1945.[83] Between 1919 and 1986, 68 of 97 international conflicts, or 70 percent, were settled peacefully, although there were 168 attempts to do so.[84]

Despite these favorable trends, it is unlikely that war will ever entirely disappear. Although international wars have diminished, civil wars continue to tear apart some states. People will continue to kill each other as long as they perceive a need to do so.

STUDY QUESTIONS

1. Are violence and war part of human nature?

2. What is social Darwinism? How has it affected attitudes toward war and peace?

3. What is behavioralism? How has it affected attitudes toward war and peace?

4. How can misperceptions affect conflict?

5. How has nationalism contributed to war?

6. What is the scapegoat theory of war, and how common is it?

7. How can a state's political and/or economic instability lead to war?

8. Why have liberal democratic countries never warred against each other? What implications does this have for international relations as more countries become liberal democracies?

9. What is the relationship between a state's level of economic development and its propensity for war?

10. What is the military industrial complex theory of war? How valid is that theory?

11. What is the relationship between the balance of power and the likelihood of war?

12. What are the different ways in which the term *balance of power* can be interpreted?

13. Evaluate the hegemonic stability and long cycle theories of war.

14. What is the security dilemma and prisoner's dilemma? How do they affect conflict, arms races, and war?

15. Do alliances make war more or less likely?

16. What are security communities? How do they affect conflict and war?

17. How has international morality changed concerning questions of war? How does international morality affect the propensity for war today?

18. How effective has international law been in regulating or preventing war?

ENDNOTES

1. Some material and ideas from this chapter were taken from William Nester, *American Power, The New World Order, and the Japanese Challenge* (New York: St. Martin's Press, 1993). For some recent prominent works on war and peace, see Robert Gilpin, *War and Change in World Politics* (Cambridge: Cambridge University Press, 1981); Michael Howard, *The Causes of War and Other Essays* (Cambridge: Harvard University Press, 1983); Robert J. Art and Kenneth Waltz, eds., *The Use of Force: International Politics and Foreign Policy* (Lanham, Md.: University Press of America, 1983); Melvin Small and J. David Singer, eds., *International War* (Homewood Ill.: Dorsey Press, 1985); John Stoessinger, *Why Nations Go to War* (New York: St. Martin's Press, 1985).

2. James E. Dougherty and Robert L. Pfaltzgraff, *Contending Theories of International Relations* (New York: Harper and Row, 1990), 337.

3. Quincy Wright, *A Study of War,* vol. 1 (Chicago: University of Chicago Press, 1942), 17.

4. Lewis F. Richardson, *Statistics of Deadly Quarrels* (Pittsburgh: Boxwood Press, 1960).

5. Clyde Eagleton, *International Government* (New York: Ronald Press, 1948), 393.

6. Karl von Clausewitz, *On War* (New York: Random House, 1943), 5.

7. Kenneth Waltz, *Man, the State, and War* (New York: Columbia University Press, 1959).

8. Ibid, 3.

9. James Strachey, ed., *The Standard Edition of the Complete Psychological Works of Sigmund Freud,* vol. 22 (London: Hogarth, 1964), 199.

10. Konrad Lorenz, *On Aggression* (New York: Harcourt Brace, 1966); See also Robert Ardrey, *The Territorial Imperative* (New York: Atheneum, 1966).

11. Adolf Hitler, *Mein Kampf* (Boston: Houghton Mifflin, 1943), 134.

12. B.F. Skinner, *Beyond Freedom and Dignity* (New York: Knopf, 1971).

13. Margaret Mead, "War Is Only an Invention," in Leon Bramson and George W. Goethals, eds., *War Studies from Psychological, Sociology, Anthropology* (New York: Basic Books, 1968), 269–274.

14. Jack Levy, "The Causes of War: A Review of Theories and Evidence," in Philip Tetlock et al., eds., *Behavior, Society, and Nuclear War* (New York: Oxford University Press, 1989), 271.

15. Clyde Kluckhohn, *Mirror for Man: A Survey of Human Behavior and Social Attitudes* (Greenwich, Conn.: Fawcett World Library, 1960).

16. For a study that indicates that chemical imbalances may be responsible for aggressive behavior, see Douglas Masden, "A Biochemical Property Relative to Human Power Seeking," *American Political Science Review,* June 1985, 448–457.

17. R.T. Green and G. Santori, "A Cross Cultural Study of Hostility and Aggression," *Journal of Peace Research,* vol. 1, 1969.

18. Otto Klineberg, *The Human Dimension in International Relations* (New York: Holt, Rinehart, and Winston, 1964); Albert Somit, "Humans, Chips, and Bonobos: The Biological Basis of Aggression, War, and Peacemaking," *Journal of Conflict Resolution,* vol. 34, September 1990, 553–583.

19. See Margaret G. Hermann and Thomas W. Milburn, *A Psychological Examination of Political Leaders* (New York: The Free Press, 1977).

20. Theodore Abel, "The Element of Decision in the Pattern of War," *American Sociological Review,* vol. 6, June 1941, 855.

21. For an in-depth analysis of the role of misperception and war, see John Stoessinger, *Why Nations Go to War;* See also Jack S. Levy, "Misperception and the Causes of War," *World Politics,* October 1983; Herbert Kelman, ed., *International Political Behavior* (New York: Holt, Rinehart, and Winston, 1965); Herman Kahn, *On Escalation* (New York: Praeger, 1965).

22. Arthur Gladstone, "The Conception of the Enemy," *Journal of Conflict Resolution,* vol. 3, 1959, 132.

23. R. Paul Shaw and Yuma Wong, "Ethnic Mobilization and the Seeds of Warfare: An Evolutionary Perspective," *International Studies Quarterly,* March 1987, 5–32.

24. Georg Simmel, *Conflict and the Web of Group-Affiliations* (New York: The Free Press, 1964), 93.

25. Geoffrey Blainy, *The Causes of War* (New York: The Free Press, 1988), 71–86.

26. Randolph Rummel, "Dimensions of Conflict Behavior Within and Between Nations," *General Systems Yearbook,* VIII, 1963; Raymond Tanter, "International War and Domestic Turmoil: Some Contemporary Evidence," in *Violence in America: Historical and Comparative Perspectives, A Report to the National Commission on the Causes and Prevention of Violence, June 1969* (New York: New American Library, 1969); Jonathan Wilkensfield, "Domestic and Foreign Conflict Behavior of Nations," in William D. Coplin and Charles W. Kegley, eds., *Analyzing International Relations: A Multimethod Introduction* (New York: Praeger, 1973), 96–112.

27. Jonathan Wilkenfield, "Domestic and Foreign Conflict Behavior of Nations," *Journal of Peace Research,* vol. 1, 1968, 55–59.

28. See Crane Brinton, *The Anatomy of Revolution* (New York: Vintage, 1965); Ted Gurr, *Why Men Rebel* (Princeton N.J.: Princeton University Press, 1970).

29. See Richard Little, *Intervention: External Involvement in Civil Wars* (Totowa, N.J.: Rowman and Littlefield, 1975); Peter Calvert, *Revolution and International Politics* (New York: St. Martin's Press, 1984); Joseph Whelan and Michael Dixon, *The Soviet Union in the Third World: Threat to World Peace* (New York: Pergamon-Brassey's, 1986).

30. Michael Doyle, "Kant, Liberty Legacies, and Foreign Affairs," *Philosophy and Foreign Affairs,* vol. 12, Summer 1987, 227–231.

31. Zeev Maoz and Nasrin Abdolali, "Regime Types and International Conflict, 1816–1976," *Journal of Conflict Resolution,* vol. 33, March 1989, 35.

32. Jack Levy, "Domestic Politics and War," *Journal of Interdisciplinary History,* vol. 18, no. 1, Spring 1988, 661–662.

33. Melvin Small and J. David Singer, "The War-Proneness of Democratic Regimes, 1816–1965," *Jerusalem Journal of International Relations,* vol. 1, Summer 1976, 50–69. See also, Steve Chan and Erich Weede, "Mirror, Mirror on the Wall . . . . Are the Freer Countries More Pacific," *Journal of Conflict Resolution,* vol. 28, December 1984; William Domke, *War and the Changing Global System* (New Haven, Conn.: Yale University Press, 1988).

34. R.J. Rummel, "Libertarianism and International Violence," *Journal of Conflict Resolution,* vol. l27, March 1983, 27–71; R.J. Rummel, "A Test of Libertarian Propositions on Violence," *Journal of Conflict Resolution,* vol. 29, September 1985, 419–455.

35. Levy, *Domestic Politics and War,* 661.

36. Michael Doyle, *"Kant, Liberal Legacies, and Foreign Affairs,"* 325.

37. The classic study was Quincy Wright, *A Study of War* (Chicago: University of Chicago Press, 1942).

38. Ruth Sivard, *World Military and Social Expenditures* (Leesburg, Va.: World Priorities, 1979), 3.

39. Melvin Small and J. David Singer, *Resort to Arms: International and Civil Wars, 1816–1990* (Beverly Hills, Calif.: Sage Publishers, 1991).

40. Quincy Wright, *A Study of War;* Melvin Small and J. David Singer, *Resort to Arms: International and Civil Wars, 1816–1990,* 58.

41. Lewis Richardson, *Statistics of Deadly Quarrels* (Pittsburgh: Boxwood, 1960).

42. See Richard Rosecrance, "Bipolarity, Multipolarity, and the Future," *Journal of Conflict Resolution,* vol. 10, 1966, 314–327.

43. Ernst Haas, "The Balance of Power: Prescription, Concept, and Propaganda," *World Politics,* vol. 5, July 1953, 442–477.

44. A.F.K. Organski, *World Politics* (New York: Knopf, 1967); Hans Morgenthau, *Politics Among Nations* (New York: Knopf, 1967).

45. See Michael Wallace, *War and Rank Among Nations* (Lexington, Mass.: D.C. Heath, 1973); Edward L. Morse, *Modernization and the Transformation of International Relations* (New York: The Free Press, 1976); A.F.K. Organski and Jacek Kugler, *The War Ledger* (Chicago: University of Chicago Press, 1980); Jack Levy, "Declining Power and the Preventive Motive for War," *World Politics,* October 1987, 82–107.

46. A.F.K. Organski and Jacek Kugler, *The War Ledger,* 61.

47. J. David Singer, Stuart Bremer, and John Stuckey, "Capability Distribution, Uncertainty, and Major Power War," in Bruce Russet, ed., *Peace, War, and Numbers* (Beverly Hills, Calif.: Sage Publications, 1972). For other attempts to measure the frequency of war, see Melvin Small and J. David Singer, *Resort to Arms: International and Civil Wars, 1816–1980;* See also Richard J. Stoll, "Bloc Concentration and Dispute Escalation Among the Major Powers, 1830–1965," *Social Science Quarterly,* vol. 65, March 1984, 48–59.

48. John A. Vasquez, "Capability, Types of War and Peace," *Western Political Quarterly,* vol. 39, June 1986.

49. Karl Deutsch and David Singer, "Multipolar Power Systems and International Stability," in James Rosenau, ed., *International Politics and Foreign Policy* (New York: The Free Press, 1969). See also Kenneth Waltz, "International Structure, National Force, and the Balance of World Power," in James Rosenau, ed., *International Politics and Foreign Policy.*

50. Kenneth Waltz, "International Structure, National Force, and the Balance of World Power," in James Rosenau, ed., *International Politics and Foreign Policy.*

51. Jack Levy, "The Polarity of the System and International Stability: An Empirical Analysis," in Alan Ned Sabrowsky, ed., *Polarity and War: The Changing Structure of International Conflict* (Boulder, Colo.: Westview Press, 1985), 59; See also Jack Levy, *War in the Modern Great Power System, 1495–1975* (Lexington, Ken.: University of Kentucky Press, 1983); Alan Ned Sabrosky, ed., *Polarity and War: The Changing Structure of International Relations;* Michael Haas, "International Subsystems: Stability and Polarity," *American Political Science Review,* vol. 64, March 1970; Bruce Bueno de Mesquita, "Systematic Polarization and the Occurrence of

War," *Journal of Conflict Resolution,* vol. 22, June 1978; William Thompson, "Cycles, Capabilities, and War: An Ecumenical View," in William Thompson, ed., *World System Analysis: Competing Perspectives* (Beverly Hills, Calif.: Sage Publications, 1983).

52. Karl Deutch, "Quincy Wright's Contribution to the Study of War: A Preface to the Second Edition," *Journal of Conflict Resolution,* vol. 14, December 1970, 474–475.

53. See: J.F.C. Fuller, *Armament and History: A Study of the Influence of Armament on History From the Dawn of Classical Warfare to the Second World War* (London: Eyre & Spottiswoode, 1945); William F. Ogburn, ed., *Technology and International Relations* (Chicago: University of Chicago Press, 1949); John U. Nef, *War and Human Progress* (Cambridge, Mass.: Harvard University Press, 1950); *Bernard Brodie and Fawn Brodie, From the Cross Bow to the H-Bomb* (New York: Dell, 1962).

54. Oganski and Kugler, *The War Ledger.*

55. Charles Gochman and Zeev Maoz, "Militarized Interstate Disputes, 1816–1976: Procedures, Patterns, and Insights," *Journal of Conflict Resolution,* vol. 28, December 1984, 585–616.

56. Some leading explorations of hegemonic stability theory include: George Modelski, *Exploring Long-Cycles* (Boulder, Colo.: Lynne Reinner, 1987); William Thompson, *On Global War: Historical-Structural Approaches to World Politics* (Columbia, S.C.: University of South Carolina Press, 1988); David Rapkin, ed., *World Leadership and Hegemony* (Boulder, Colo.: Lynne Reinner, 1990); For theories of wars occurring in generations, in which peace lasts only so long as the memory of the last war's horrors remains vivid, and a new leadership seeks to glorify itself through success in war, see Frank Denton and Warren Philips, "Some Patterns in the History of Violence," *Journal of Conflict Resolution,* vol. 1 no. 2, June 1968; See also Oswald Spengler, *The Decline of the West* (New York: Knopf, 1926); J.E. Moval, "The Distribution of Wars in Time," *Journal of the Royal Statistical Society,* vol. 122, 1949, 446–458.

57. Jack Levy, "Long Cycles, Hegemonic Transitions, and the Long Peace," in Charles Kegley, ed., *The Long Postwar Peace* (New York: HarperCollins, 1991), 156–155.

58. Joshua Goldstein, *Long Cycles: Prosperity and War in the Modern Age* (New Haven, Conn.: Yale University Press, 1988), 436–437.

59. Jack S. Levy and T. Clifton Morgan, "The War-Weariness Hypothesis: An Empirical Test," *American Journal of Political Science,* February 1986, 26–49.

60. Ibid.

61. The term "security dilemma" was introduced in John Herz, *Political Realism and Political Idealism* (Chicago: University of Chicago Press, 1951); The term "spiral model" in Robert Jervis, *Perception and Misperception in World Politics* (Princeton N.J.: Princeton University Press, 1976).

62. The psychology of the prisoner's dilemma is explored through game theory. See: Thomas Schelling, *The Strategy of Conflict* (Cambridge, Mass.: Harvard University

Press, 1960); Muzafer Sherif et al., *Intergroup Conflict and Cooperation: The Robber's Cave Experiment* (Normank, Okla.: University of Oklahoma Press, 1961); Robert Jervis, "Cooperation Under the Security Dilemma, *World Politics,* vol. 30, no. 2, January 1978, 167–214.

63. Nazli Choucri and Robert North, *Nations in Conflict* (San Francisco: Freeman, 1975), 218; See also Bruce Russet, "International Interactions and Processes: The Internal Versus External Debate Revisited," in Ada Finifter, ed., *Political Science: The State of the Discipline* (Washington, D.C.: American Political Science Association, 1983).

64. Lewis Richardson, *Arms and Insecurity* (Pittsburgh: Boxwood, 1960); Samuel Huntington, "Arms Races: Prerequisites and Results," in Robert J. Art and Kenneth Waltz, eds., *The Use of Force* (Boston: Little, Brown, 1971), 365–401; Bruce Bueno de Mesquita, *The War Trap* (New Haven, Conn.: Yale University Press, 1981); Stephen Majeski, "Expectations and Arms Races," *American Journal of Political Science,* May 1985, 217–245; Paul Diehl, "Arms Races and Escalation: A Closer Look," *Journal of Peace Research,* vol. 20, no. 3, 1983, 205–212; Paul Diehl, "Arms Races to War: Testing Some Empirical Linkages," *Sociological Quarterly,* vol. 26, no.3, 1985, 331–349; Paul Diehl, "Armaments Without War," *Journal of Peace Research,* vol. 22, no. 3, 1985, 249–259.

65. Michael Wallace, "Arms Races and Escalation: Some New Evidence," *Journal of Conflict Resolution,* vol. 23, no. 1, March, 1979, 3–16; See also Paul Diehl, "Arms Races and Escalation: A Closer Look," *Journal of Peace Research,* vol. 20, no. 3, 1983, 205–212.

66. Samuel Huntington, "Arms Races: Prerequisites and Results," in Robert Art and Kenneth Waltz, eds., *The Use of Force* (Boston: Little, Brown, 1971), 367.

67. Paul Diehl, "Arms Races to War: Testing Some Empirical Linkages," *Sociological Quarterly,* vol. 26, no.3, 1985, 342.

68. David Ziegler, *War, Peace, and International Politics* (Boston: Little, Brown, 1976), 206.

69. Hans Morganthau, *Politics Among Nations: The Struggle for Power and Peace,* 4th ed. (New York: Knopf, 1967), 392.

70. Charles Kegley and Greogry Raymond, "Alliances and the Preservation of the Postwar Peace," in Charles Kegley, ed., *The Long Postwar Peace* (New York: HarperCollins, 1991), 275.

71. Randolph Siverson and Michael Tennefoss, "Power, Alliance, and the Escalation of National Conflict, 1815–1965," *Amercian Political Science Review,* vol. 78, December 1984, 1062.

72. Jack Levy, "Alliance Formation and War Behavior," *Journal of Conflict Resolution,* vol. 25, December 1981, 581.

73. J. David Singer and Melvin Small, "Alliance Aggregation and the Onset of War, 1815–1945, in J. David Singer, ed., *Quantitative International Politics* (New York: The Free Press, 1968), 247–286.

74. Jack Levy, "Alliance Formation and War Behavior," *Journal of Conflict Resolution,* vol. 25, December 1981.

75. Karl Deutsch et al., *Political Community and the North Atlantic Area* (Princeton N.J.: Princeton University Press, 1957), 5.

76. See Jack Levy, "The Causes of War: A Review and Theories and Evidence," in Philip Tetlock et al., eds., *Behavior, Society, and Nuclear War,* vol. 1 (New York: Oxford University Press, 1983), 209–333.

77. Robert Gilpin, *War and Change in World Politics* (Cambridge: Cambridge University Press, 1981), See also John Mueller, *Retreat From Doomsday: The Obsolence of Major Power War* (New York: Basic Books, 1989).

78. Richard Rosecrance, "Bipolarity, Multipolarity, and the Future," *Journal of Conflict Resolution,* vol. 10, 1966, 160.

79. Terrence Hopkins and Immanuel Wallerstein, *World Systems Analysis: Theory and Methodology* (Beverly Hills, Calif.: Sage Publications, 1982), 28.

80. Quoted in Irving Janis, *Crucial Decisions: Leadership in Policymaking and Crisis Management* (New York: Free Press, 1989), 130.

81. Inis Claude, *States and the Global System: Politics, Law, and Organization* (New York: St. Martin's Press, 1988), 132.

82. See Louis Henkin, "The Use of Force: Law and U.S. Policy," in Stanely Hoffman, et al., eds., *Right v. Might: International Law and the Use of Force* (New York: Council on Foreign Relations, 1991), 37–69.

83. J. David Singer, "Peace in the Global System: Displacement, Interregnum, or Transformation," in Charles Kegley, ed., *The Long Postwar Peace,* 57.

84. Kalevi J. Holsti, *International Politics: A Framework for Analysis* (Englewood Cliffs, N.J.: Prentice-Hall, 1988), 420

The Cold War: Origins, Strategies, Aftermath

Key Terms and Concepts

Baruch Plan
Berlin Airlift
Berlin Wall
Brezhnev Doctrine
Brussels Pact
Carter Doctrine
Cold War
Cuban Missile Crisis
Détente
Dictatorship of the
    Proletariat
Domino Effect
Expansionists
Flexible Response
Four Policemen
Glasnost
Global Containment
Great Leap Forward
Helsinki Accord

Iron Curtain
Isolationists
Kuomintang (KMT)
Long Telegraph
Marshall Plan
Massive Retaliation
Missile Gap
More Bang for the Buck
Mr. X Article
My Way Doctrine
National Security Council
    (NSC)
North Atlantic Treaty
    Organization (NATO)
Nixon Doctrine
NSC 68
Peaceful Coexistence
Perestroika
Potsdam Conference

Reagan Doctrine
Roll Back
Strategic Arms Limitations
    Talks (SALT I & II)
Southeast Asian Treaty
    Organization (SEATO)
Second Front
Selective Containment
Slavophiles
Sphere of Influence
Sputnik
Trip Wire
Truman Doctrine
Vietnamization
Warsaw Treaty
    Organization
Westernizers
Yalta Conference

For nearly 50 years, the United States and Soviet Union were locked into a Cold War in which they used every means short of direct war between them to win their respective security and ideological interests in virtually all regions and countries around the world. By the early 1990s, the Cold War ended, as the Soviet empire and communism self-destructed.

The Cold War had two finales rich in symbolism. On November 9, 1989, the Berlin War crumbled amidst thousands of joyous sledgehammer blows and glasses of champagne. More than three years later, on May 6, 1992, Mikhail Gorbachev, the former Soviet president who permitted the subjected peoples of Eastern Europe and the Soviet Union to be free, gave a speech in Fulton, Missouri, the same place where on March 21, 1946, Winston Churchill had warned that an "iron curtain" had clanged shut across Europe, dividing a liberal democratic West from a totalitarian, aggressive East. Standing in the shadow of a huge bronze statue of Churchill, Gorbachev argued that the Cold War had been a vast unnecessary tragedy, that Moscow and Washington completely misunderstood each other's intentions and capabilities, and interpreted the other's actions in the worst possible way. The result was a spiraling arms race that eventually devastated both countries economically and a series of crises around the world in which the Soviet and American blocs more than once almost went to war.

Have we come full circle in the 46 years since Churchill's warning? Was the Cold War really born simply of a tragic misperception, as Gorbachev and others maintain, or were there genuine national and ideological interests at stake that made conflict between the United States and Soviet Union inevitable? Was the Cold War merely a long and tragic detour in the world's inevitable march toward international cooperation and the celebration of human rights? Why did the Cold War occur? How was it waged? Why did it end when it did and the way it did? This chapter will address these and related questions.

THE ORIGINS OF THE COLD WAR

The Cold War had many causes.[1] Essentially its origins lie in the expansionism of two great powers, the United States and the Soviet Union, which eventually confronted each other in Central Europe. Power rivalry, conflicting ideologies, and misperceptions were all essential to converting the World War II allies into Cold War enemies.

The Clash of Ideologies

The Cold War was at root a conflict between vastly different world views. Hans Morgenthau nicely summed up the role of ideology in the Cold War:

> *The claim to universality which inspires the moral code of one particular group is incompatible with the identical claim of another group, the world has room for only one, and the other must yield or be destroyed. Thus carrying their idols before them, the nationalistic masses of our time meet in the international arena, each group convinced that it executes the mandate of history, that it does for humanity what it seems to do for itself, and that it fulfills a sacred mission ordained by Providence, however, defined.[2]*

American foreign policy has been shaped by several powerful and sometimes conflicting values. From the first settlements in what became the United States, Americans have believed that their institutions and way of life were freer and presented more opportunities for individual advancement than those elsewhere. Thus, they were superior. From its very beginning, America was a shining city on a hill for all of humanity to emulate. President Reagan summed up this belief in 1987 when he said: "I have always believed that this anointed land was set apart in an uncommon way, that a divine plan placed this great continent between the oceans to be found by people from every corner of the world who had a special love of faith and freedom."

Although most Americans have held this belief, they have differed over how it should be applied to foreign policy. Many were *isolationists,* who agreed with President Washington that the United States should remain aloof from political entanglements with other countries. Others were *expansionists,* who argued that the United States had a moral responsibility as well as economic interest in spreading its concepts of democracy around the world.

In fact, these two visions have coexisted within American foreign policy from independence through today. The United States expanded across the continent to the Pacific and then beyond, defeating or negotiating with hundreds of Native American tribes, along with Spain, Mexico, France, Britain, Germany, France, China, Japan, and other countries. Like the other great powers, the United States designated certain regions as its sphere of influence in which others should not interfere. In 1823 President Monroe announced that the United States supported the independence struggles of Latin Americans against Spanish rule and thus would not tolerate any furthur European expansion in the region. America's perception of its foreign interests expanded with its industrial, territorial, and military power. In 1899 and 1900, the White House announced its commitment to an "open door" of free trade and would oppose any attempts of the other great powers to shut American merchants out of China or elsewhere. However, despite the continual assertion of American power, until World War I the United States avoided any European alliances or wars. After World War I, Washington returned to political isolation until 1941.

It has only been since World War II that the United States has consistently been involved in shaping the world according to American ideals of free trade and anticommunism. During World War II, President Roosevelt clearly articulated American foreign policy goals for the postwar world as based on universal economic and political freedom. To realize these goals, Washington led the creation of the United Nations and such international economic institutions as IMF, World Bank, and later GATT.

However, by 1947 the Truman administration had concluded that the Soviet Union threatened America's foreign policy goals. Containing the Soviet Union became essential to the successful expansion of the global political economy and achievement of American ideals. In believing their country to be the personification of "good," by definition anyone fundamentally opposed to the United States and American ideals must be "evil" in some profound way. Throughout the Cold War, Washington and the American public perceived the Soviet Union as an *evil empire,* bent on achieving global conquest and communism.

Like Washington, Moscow saw the world divided into two diametrically opposed and hostile camps, in which it was the champion of all socialist and progressive forces, and the United States supported all imperialist and antirevolutionary forces. Equally important was the incorporation into the Soviet world view of traditional Russian perceptions, values, and policies.

Russia's world view has been shaped by over 1,000 years of continual invasions by foreign powers. In the twentieth century alone, the Soviet Union lost more than 10 million people in World War I and in the Russian Civil War, and more than 20 million in World War II. Not surprisingly, Russians are naturally suspicious of foreigners. In order to survive, Moscow had to develop a highly authoritarian system to mobilize the population and to continually expand against its neighbors. In addition to simply surviving the onslaughts of others, Russians saw themselves as the champions of the Christian Orthodox Church and Slavic peoples. Thus, Russians were not merely survivors but a special people who championed a great religion and people that extended far immediate borders.

Moscow's foreign policy has thus largely involved deterring or defeating surrounding hostile states and expanding Russian territory toward defensible borders beyond the steppes. Like Washington, Moscow identified its own spheres of influence that were considered vital to Russian security, such as East Europe, the Black Sea and access to the Mediterranean Sea, and the Far East and access to the Pacific Ocean. Empires, however, can never be truly secure because each new conquest must be defended, which makes other states more fearful and resistant to that expansion.

Russia's geography and deeply ingrained xenophobia and exclusiveness has set it apart from the West. Russians have traditionally felt a sense of cultural, political, and economic inferiority in comparison to the West and have been torn over the proper relationship with it. Since Peter the Great first tried to westernize Russia in the late 1600s, Russia's elite has been split between *westernizers,* who see Western Europe and the United States as models for political and economic development, and *slavophiles,* who advocate continued Russian authoritarianism and isolation from the West and the assertion of leadership over all the Slavic peoples of East Europe.

Soviet foreign policy incorporates these traditional Russian features. The Russian view that warfare was the natural characteristic of international relations was reinforced by communism, with its conception of class and international warfare between capitalists and socialists. Lenin's idea of a *dictatorship of the proletariat* and the totalitarian system created by Stalin were built upon a millenium of authoritarian Czarist rule. Until Gorbachev's rule, Soviet foreign policy clearly rejected the West and attempted to assert direct control over East Europe and to spread communism worldwide.

Kennan captured the essence of Soviet strategy and its relationship with traditional Russian foreign policy:

> *The Kremlin is under no ideological compulsion to accomplish its purposes in a hurry. Like the Church, it is dealing in ideological concepts which are of long-term validity, and it can afford to be patient . . . The . . . teachings of Lenin himself require great caution and flexibility in the pursuit of Communist purposes. Again these precepts are fortified by the lessons of Russian history: of centuries of obscure battles between nomadic forces over the stretches of a vast unfortified plain. Here caution, circumspection, flexibility, and deception are the valuable qualities . . . Thus the Kremlin has no compunction about retreating in the face of superior forces . . . The main thing is there should always be pressure, increasing constant pressure, toward the desired goal.[3]*

The Clash of Misperceptions

Whether the Cold War was inevitable or not rests on whether each side could have overcome a worsening collection of negative images about the other. Washington's first attempt to "contain" Moscow occurred as early as the 1890s when it joined with Tokyo in supporting an "open door" of trade and investment opportunities in Manchuria, which Russia was attempting to colonize. From the very beginning of the conflict between these two rising powers, American leaders mistrusted and condemned the Russians. President Theodore Roosevelt described the Russians as "utterly insincere and treacherous; they have no conception of the truth . . . and no regard for others."[4]

President Woodrow Wilson's closest adviser, Edward House, lamented the choice of the lesser of two evils that he saw facing the United States on the eve of its entry into World War I: "If the Allies win, it means the domination of Russia on the continent of Europe; and if Germany wins, it means the unspeakable tyranny of militarism for generations to come."[5] Throughout the twentieth century, most presidents and foreign policymakers would echo and act on Roosevelt's stereotype and House's dilemma.

Moscow too tended to interpret every American action in the worst way. To Soviets, America's containment of communism began, not in 1947, but between 1918 and 1920, when Washington deployed 10,000 troops into Russia to aid the "White" non-communist forces in the civil war against the "Reds." Soviet historians have avoided the fact that the primary reason that American troops were sent to the Soviet Union was to offset the power of Japanese troops, which were already rampaging through Siberia, and to guard millions of tons of supplies sent to the Czarist regimes during World War I. Moscow has also avoided educating its public that after withdrawing its troops, Washington sent millions of dollars in humanitarian aid to the Soviet Union during the early 1920s to relieve that country's mass famine. Although Washington refused to open diplomatic relations with Moscow until 1933, bilateral trade continued until in the late 1920s and surpassed the prewar level.

Throughout World War II, Stalin believed that Washington and London refused to open a *second front* in northern Europe until mid-1944 and limited the supplies it sent to Moscow so that the Soviet Union and Germany would destroy each other. Although there is no evidence that this was official policy, many Americans supported that strategy, including then Senator Harry Truman, who said in June 1941 that: "If we see that Germany is winning we should help Russia and if Russia is winning we ought to help Germany and that way let them kill off as many as possible, although I don't want to see Hitler victorious under any circumstances."[6] Roosevelt and Churchill twice promised a second front but instead sent their forces to North Africa and Italy before finally landing in Normandy, France, in June 1944. The reason for the Mediterranean campaign, however, involved Prime Minister Churchill's tragically misguided strategic concepts rather than a conscious attempt to weaken the Soviet Union. Washington sent Moscow $11 billion of lend-lease military supplies during the war, accounting for nearly ten percent of Soviet supplies and equipment. This aid may very well have proved the difference between victory and defeat on the Russian front.

The Clash of Security Interests

The most important conflict between Moscow on one hand, and Washington and London on the other, however, centered on Eastern Europe's postwar fate. The August 1941 Atlantic Charter issued by Roosevelt and Churchill proclaimed that the war should be fought for democracy and free trade everywhere. Roosevelt sincerely believed in these ideals; Churchill was more willing to compromise them. In 1944 the Bretton Woods Conference attended by representatives of 44 countries agreed to create the International Monetary Fund (IMF) and International Bank for Reconstruction and Development (IBRD, World Bank) to supply the finance vital to reconstruct the global economy. It also began talks that would culminate with the General Agreement on Trade and Tariffs (GATT) in 1947, whose expanding membership agreed to free trade principles and policies. Washington hoped to include all of East Europe in the free-trade system, even if Moscow refused to open its own economy.

While creating the infrastructure of the global political economy, however, Roosevelt also agreed to allow Moscow a *sphere of influence* in East Europe after the war. The alternative, Roosevelt feared, might be a separate peace between Hitler and Stalin that would allow German forces to be transferred to the Western front. Roosevelt envisioned a postwar world ruled by both the United Nations and the *four policemen* (the United States, Britain, Soviet Union, and China), each of which would be responsible for maintaining order in their respective regions, or spheres of influence. In October 1944, Churchill flew to Moscow to cut a deal with Stalin in which Soviet control over Romania and Bulgaria would be exchanged for British control over Greece.

East Europe's fate was sealed by two conferences during 1945. At the February *Yalta Conference,* Roosevelt, Churchill, and Stalin formally agreed to a Declaration of Liberated Europe, which promised free elections and trade, while informally agreeing that the East European governments be "friendly" toward Moscow. They also agreed on the division of Germany and Berlin into three temporary occupation spheres, which would eventually be reunited following a peace treaty. After prolonged protests by provisional French President Charles de Gaulle, Washington and London agreed to allocate part of their spheres to create a French sphere. At the June *Potsdam Conference,* Truman, Stalin, and Churchill agreed that each power could take reparations from their respective spheres and, in addition, the Soviets could have 25 percent of the reparations from the three western zones.

However as the Soviet Union began undermining non-communist political parties and groups and imposing communist party rule throughout Eastern Europe, the Roosevelt administration and, after April 1945, Truman administration protested. The Soviets rigged elections in Poland, Romania, and Bulgaria to bring communist parties to power and overthrew democratic governments with military coup d'états in Hungary in 1947 and in Czechoslovakia in 1948. Having been devastated by the German invasion, the Soviets began the systematic looting of Germany and the rest of East Europe, shipping back entire industries. Meanwhile, communist parties in West Europe, particularly in France and Italy, acquired increased representation in local and national elections.

Washington's worries about Europe's fate soon expanded to East Asia. At the Yalta Conference, Roosevelt had elicited Stalin's promise to fight against Japan within three months of Germany's defeat. At the time, having the Soviets as an ally in Asia seemed essential to winning the war against Japan. Japan's armies fought to virtually the last man for tiny coral islands in the Pacific and its government was mobilizing every old man, woman, and child in the Japanese islands themselves for mass human wave attacks on the Allied invaders. An Allied invasion of Japan was expected to cost the lives of at least half a million Americans and tens of millions of Japanese. However, the successful explosion of an atomic bomb at Alamogordo, New Mexico, in June 1945 completely changed the power calculus. Japan now could be defeated without an invasion—Soviet troops were no longer needed.

As it had promised, however, Moscow did enter the war against Japan. On August 6, 1945, the United States dropped an atomic bomb on Hiroshima. On August 8 the Soviets invaded and quickly overran Manchuria and Korea. On August 9 an atomic bomb destroyed Nagasaki. Then on August 15 Tokyo announced it would surrender. In a matter of weeks, the Soviet Union had enormously expanded its influence throughout Northeast Asia.

Washington feared that Moscow's influence would soon engulf China and took steps to counter it. A civil war in China between a corrupt, oppressive Nationalist Party, or *Kuomintang* (KMT), regime under Chiang Kai-shek and the Chinese Communist Party (CCP) under Mao Zedong had raged since 1927 and continued throughout the war against Japan, from 1937 to 1945. When Japan surrendered, the communist forces controlled one-fifth of the population and landmass, and their influence expanded daily. Roosevelt and Truman had gotten Stalin to support Chiang's regime as the "fourth policeman" in return for Soviet-Chinese joint control over the railroads and economic infrastructure of Manchuria and northern China. This deal was legalized by a Treaty of Friendship and Alliance signed between Chiang and Stalin in 1945. As LaFeber put it, "Stalin preferred a chaotic, divided China that would not threaten Russia rather than a united China under either Chiang or Mao."[7] But despite the deal with Chiang and the desire to keep China divided, after overrunning Manchuria, the Soviets transferred captured Japanese arms and equipment to the communists. Meanwhile, Truman sent 100,000 American troops to China and allowed Japanese troops to maintain their arms in order to support Chiang's forces against the communists. In addition, Truman sent special envoy George Marshall to help negotiate peace between the KMT and CCP. The communists gained steadily despite America's efforts.

The Middle East was another disputed region. In 1941, Britain and the Soviet Union occupied Iran to prevent, among other things, the Shah from forming an alliance with Germany. The United States joined the occupation in 1942. Later that year the three powers signed an agreement pledging to withdraw their forces once the war had ended. By March 1946, the British and American troops had largely withdrawn. Soviet troops not only stayed in violation of the occupation agreement but also incited an Azerbaijani revolt in northern Iran. The Truman administration severely protested the Soviet actions. In March, Moscow agreed to leave after signing a treaty with Teheran that created a Soviet-Iranian oil company that would pump and ship oil to the Soviet Union. After the Soviet troops withdrew, the Iranian parliament rejected the treaty.

The eastern Mediterranean Sea became another contested region. During the war, Churchill and Roosevelt had agreed to allow Soviet control of the Dardanelles Straits linking the Black and Mediterranean seas. After the war, Moscow demanded that Ankara agree to joint control over the straits. Washington then reversed its policy, flatly rejecting any Soviet control over the Dardanelles, and sent a U.S. fleet to the eastern Mediterranean to emphasize its position. By autumn 1946 Moscow backed off. Meanwhile, a civil war raged in Greece between communist and non-communist factions. The British supported the non-communist faction, but had to solicit American aid in the struggle. In 1946 alone, Washington sent $260 million in aid to Greece. Although Soviet contact with the Greek communists was minimal, the White House increasingly saw the communist threat to takeover Greece as part of a global conspiracy directed by Moscow.

Fearing that Washington would use Moscow's dependence on American largess and the global economy to force it to retreat from Eastern Europe, in 1946 Stalin rejected a $1 billion American loan and membership in the IMF and World Bank. Stalin also rejected an American proposal (the *Baruch Plan*) to give up its monopoly over the atomic bomb to the United Nations in return for all other countries to agree not to research or possess such weapons. Compliance would be ensured through UN inspections and control over the raw materials that make atomic bombs.

Although the Soviet Union continued to probe for advantages in various regions and countries on its periphery, it posed no military threat. As early as November 1945, an American intelligence report argued that the Soviet military was severely stretched to fulfill existing commitments and had no significant offensive potential against West Europe and would be unlikely to become a threat for another 15 years.[8] Despite the growing international tension, the Soviet Union and United States continued their mass troop demobilizations. Between 1945 and 1947, the Soviet military declined from 12 million to 3 million troops and the American military from 10 million to 1.4 million troops. Although the Soviet army was twice the size of America's, it was mostly deployed to maintain its Eurasian empire, and, unlike the United States, it lacked an atomic bomb and a vast navy.

STRATEGIES OF CONTAINMENT

Selective Containment (1947–1950)

The Soviet and British declarations of the Cold War preceded America's by a year. On February 9, 1946, Stalin declared that the wartime alliance with the West was dead, and war between capitalism and communism was inevitable. Thus, the Soviet Union's people and resources had to be mobilized for that struggle. On March 5, 1946, Churchill declared during a speech in Fulton, Missouri, that an *iron curtain* had descended on Europe dividing the free West from the Communist East.

More than a year later, on March 12, 1947, President Truman declared a Cold War against the Soviet Union and maintained that the United States would do anything to contain Soviet expansion, a policy which became known as the *Truman Doctrine*. To that end, Truman asked Congress for $400 million in military and economic aid to support friendly governments in Greece, Turkey, and other governments threatened by communism. Then on June 5, 1947, Secretary of State George Marshall announced that the United States would have to extend enormous aid to help reconstruct Europe's economy in order for the United States and global economies to revive, a proposal which became known as the *Marshall Plan*. Between 1947 and 1952, the United States gave Europe $17 billion and Japan $2.2 billion in economic aid, which was essential for their economic revival. Although Congress did not approve the Marshall Plan until March 1948, in July 1947 it passed the *National Security Act*, which created the National Security Council, the Central Intelligence Agency, and the Defense Department.

How was the containment policy conceived? In early 1946, George Kennan, an American diplomat in Moscow, sent a policy paper, known as the *long telegraph*, to Washington, in which he carefully analyzed the Soviet threat. According to Kennan, Soviet expansion in East Europe was simply an extension of the traditional Russian drive to secure a buffer zone of natural frontiers and compliant states. The Soviet threat to the West was primarily ideological and political, not military. If the United States could help the world's industrial powers, West Europe and Japan, to reconstruct their economies and expand their middle class, the Soviet threat would fade. Communist movements elsewhere in the world were primarily motivated by nationalism; even if successful, they posed no threat to American security, because those governments could only survive through integration into a global economy. Within several generations, communism in the Soviet Union and elsewhere would collapse because of its inability to develop those nations' economies or to provide higher living standards for the people. Kennan elaborated this analysis and coined the word "containment" in his anonymous *Mr. X article* in the Spring 1947 issue of *Foreign Affairs*. Kennan advocated a *selective containment* policy targeted on those regions of the world—West Europe, Japan, and the Middle East—that were of vital geopolitical and geoeconomic importance to the United States. He advised ending American involvement in China and other poor countries in which some kind of revolution was inevitable and in which the United States had no real interests. In mid-1947 Kennan was made head of the State Department's Policy Planning Section.

Despite Kennan's selective containment strategy, America's global commitments expanded. Throughout the summer of 1947, representatives of the western-hemisphere countries met in Rio de Janeiro to negotiate a collective self-defense treaty, signed on September 2, 1947, in which an attack on one would be considered an attack on them all. In Southeast Asia, Washington abandoned Roosevelt's pledge to advocate decolonization and now began to supply limited aid to the Western powers attempting to reassert their control, such as the French in Vietnam, the Dutch in Indonesia, and the British in Malaya and Burma. After Washington granted independence to the Philippines in 1946, it extended considerable aid to the new government to help it suppress a communist insurgency. However, America's most-important efforts were in China, where the United States gave the KMT billions of dollars in military and economic aid, most of which was squandered.

The Soviets were also busy expanding their influence during this time. In 1947 Moscow announced the creation of the Communist Information Bureau (Cominform) through which it would ferment and coordinate communist revolution worldwide. As early as July 1947, Moscow began integrating the Soviet and East European economies, and in January 1949 it formalized these ties by creating the Council for Mutual Economic Assistance (COMECON), the Soviet equivalent of the Marshall Plan. On June 24, 1948, Moscow blocked the overland routes to the Allied sectors in Berlin in hopes that the West would eventually surrender their sectors. On June 28, the United States began the *Berlin airlift*, which lasted 324 days and delivered 13,000 tons of supplies a day to the beleaguered city. In April 1949, Moscow began lifting its blockade.

With a monopoly of atomic power, the Truman administration could always deter a Soviet attack on West Europe by threatening to bomb Soviet cities. However, once the Soviets developed atomic power, America's atomic power would be neutralized and its deterrent value diminished. Clearly, the United States had to develop conventional as well as atomic military power in order to maintain an effective deterrent against Soviet aggression. Washington encouraged the *Brussels Pact* of 1948, in which Britain, France, Belgium, the Netherlands, and Luxembourg agreed that an attack on one would be considered an attack on all. In 1949 the United States, Canada, Norway, Denmark, and Portugal joined the alliance, which was renamed the North Atlantic Treaty Organization (NATO), with the same "one for all and all for one" commitment. Congress quickly ratified the treaty and passed the *Mutual Defense Assistance Act,* which initially supplied its allies with $1.5 billion in military aid.

Despite NATO's creation, several other events occurred in 1949 and 1950 that dramatically changed the global power balance. In September 1949, the Soviet Union exploded its first atomic bomb. On October 10 the Chinese communists announced their victory in the civil war, while KMT troops and followers continued their retreat to Taiwan. On January 13, 1950, the Soviet delegation to the UN walked out after the Security Council refused its proposal to eject the KMT Chinese delegation and seat the CCP representatives. On January 14, the Chinese invaded the American consulate in Beijing. Then in February, news leaked out that in the previous month Moscow and Beijing signed a treaty pledging to join against any attack on either of them. The global balance of power seemed to have shifted decisively in Moscow's favor.

Global Containment (1950–1969)

In response to these changes, the *National Security Council* formulated a new version of the containment policy, known as *NSC-68,* and presented it to Truman in April 1950. The policy rejected Kennan's selective strategy for the premise that the Soviets had a grand plan for world conquest and their foreign policy was primarily motivated by Marxist-Leninism rather than geopolitics. Thus, if the United States did not hold the *anti-Communist* line everywhere, it would be challenged and eventually overrun everywhere. A loss of one country to communism would lead to a *domino effect,* as neighboring countries succumbed. Emboldened by these victories, the Soviet Union would become increasingly aggressive. Thus, no country was too small or too insignificant to be protected. Military rather than economic power was the key to containing the Soviet Union. Secretary of State Dean Acheson and adviser and (later Secretary of State) John Foster Dulles were global containment's architects.

The advocates of *global containment* seemed vindicated on June 24, 1950, when communist North Korea attacked South Korea. Why did the invasion happen? In 1945 Moscow and Washington had agreed to divide the peninsula at the 38th parallel, with Soviet troops occupying the country north of that line and American troops to the south. Both sides withdrew their troops by 1949, but only after imposing sympathetic governments on their respective halves. In the months preceding the North Korean invasion, Pyongyang's communist dictator Kim Il Sung and Seoul's non-communist dictator Syngman Rhee had both been threatening to unify the peninsula by invading the other. Between January and June 1950, Washington had sent mixed messages about its commitment to South Korea. At a press conference on January 12, Acheson seemed to leave out South Korea in a discussion of America's defense perimeter in East Asia, although he pointedly included South Korea in similar briefings throughout the next few months. Kim traveled to Moscow in early 1950 to receive Soviet approval for the invasion, although Stalin refused to commit Soviet forces.

The Truman White House assumed not only that Moscow supported the invasion, but that it also largely controlled the communist governments of China and North Korea. The North Korean attack was thus seen as part of an orchestrated communist offensive across East and Southeast Asia. In response, Truman ordered General Douglas MacArthur in Japan to supply South Korea's armies. In addition, he sent the U.S. Seventh Fleet between China and Taiwan to prevent a communist invasion of the latter and increased assistance to French forces in Vietnam and to the Philippine government. With the Soviets continuing to boycott the UN, the United States was able to get the Security Council to pass two resolutions on June 27, 1900, one branding the North Koreans as aggressors and demanding an immediate cease fire and withdrawal north of the 38th parallel, and another resolution calling on the UN members to jointly aid South Korea. On June 30, Truman sent American troops to bolster the South Korean perimeter around Pusan. Although military contingents from 16 countries joined the alliance, the United States led it and contributed 50 percent of its ground forces, 86 percent of its naval forces, and 93 percent of its air forces. In August 1950 General MacArthur launched a brilliant attack behind the North Korean lines at Inchon, routed the North Korean army, and in September pushed the remnants far north of the 38th parallel. Tragically, MacArthur disregarded intelligence reports that Chinese troops had infiltrated North Korea and were massing to attack. On November 26, a Chinese and North Korean counterattack caught MacArthur's forces by surprise and forced them back down the peninsula, where the lines solidified and were accepted by an armistice in 1953.

Washington worked hard to globalize its containment strategy. Over the next few years following the North Korean attack, the United States negotiated and signed a half dozen bilateral and multilateral treaties, including ones with Australia and New Zealand (1951), Japan (1952), and the Southeast Asian Treaty Organization (*SEATO,* 1954). The American defense budget increased from $13.5 billion in 1950 to $50 billion in 1951 and $60 billion in 1952, and the number of troops increased during those years by 50 percent, to 3.5 million. In 1955, the United States rearmed West Germany and made it part of NATO. Moscow responded to West Germany's rearmament and integration within NATO by organizing its Eastern European satellites into the *Warsaw Treaty Organization* (WTO), also known as the Warsaw Pact.

In 1952, Dwight Eisenhower was elected president, partly because of his platform, which rejected the containment policy as too passive. He promised instead to *roll back* communism. Eisenhower's Secretary of State, John Foster Dulles, rejected any possibility of negotiating with the Soviets, whom he considered unworthy of being trusted. Despite his own tough campaign rhetoric and his ideologically-minded Secretary of State, Eisenhower actually modified the global containment policies of his predecessor. He reduced the military budget to $31 billion by 1955, canceled plans for an American troop buildup in Europe to 50 divisions, reduced the American military from 1.5 million to 1 million people, and ordered an increase in America's nuclear forces, which he argued would give the United States *more bang for the buck.*

Washington would respond to any Soviet invasion of West Europe with a *massive retaliation* of nuclear weapons. For the massive retaliation deterrence strategy to be the most effective, an optimum number of American troops had to be stationed in Europe. The fewer American troops in Europe, the greater the chance of a Soviet conventional victory, and thus the greater certainty that Washington would massively retaliate with nuclear weapons. However, there had to be enough American troops to act as a *trip wire* for massive retaliation. The stakes of American lives had to be enough for Washington to retaliate to avoid losing but not enough to win a conventional war.

With the power balance settled in Europe between its increasingly prosperous Western half and harshly suppressed Eastern half, the superpowers turned their struggles toward gaining the hearts, minds, and pockets of governments of the often abysmally poor countries of Latin America, Africa, and Asia. The Eisenhower White House sponsored coups in Iran in 1953 and Guatemala in 1954 which brought pro-American governments to power. The United States also began massively aiding the South Vietnam government. The government was created at the Geneva Conference of 1954 in which the French granted independence to Vietnam. Vietnam was then "temporarily" divided into a communist north under Ho Chi Minh and non-communist south under Ngo Dinh Diem until national elections were held.

Ironically, while Washington's global containment and massive retaliation policies were being implemented, Moscow briefly became more conciliatory. Stalin died in February 1953. Until 1956 power in the Kremlin was shared by several leaders. Moscow announced in 1956 the policy of *peaceful coexistence* in which war between the communist and capitalist worlds was not inevitable and both systems could coexist peacefully. In 1955 the Soviets signed a peace treaty with Austria, which reunited the country in return for its neutrality. In 1956 Nikita Khrushchev emerged as the Soviet Union's undisputed ruler. At the Twentieth Communist Party Congress in February 1956, Khrushchev revealed details of Stalin's genocidal policies and proclaimed that the Soviet Union would adopt more humanistic policies. In April 1956 the Kremlin announced the dissolution of Cominform.

Despite these changes, it soon became apparent that there were limits to Soviet flexibility. In June 1956, demonstrations broke out in Hungary and Poland protesting communist rule and continued sporadically into the autumn of that year. In Poland, Wladyslaw Gomulka, a reformist communist, came to power and advocated sweeping political, economic, and social changes. When Khrushchev denounced Gomulka, he threatened to mobilize the Polish people against the Soviets. Khruschev backed down. Heartened by Gomulka's victory, a mass demonstration in Hungary forced Khruschev to allow the Stalinist Erno Gero to be replaced as president with reformist Imry Nagy and to withdraw Soviet troops from Hungary. While these events were occurring, on October 28 Israel launched a sneak attack on Egyptain forces in the Sinai Peninsula. By early November, in conjunction with British and French troops, Israel captured the Suez Canal, which had been nationalized by President Gamal Nasser in July. Washington protested the invasion and threatened to cut off financial ties with the belligerents until they withdrew. Moscow used the diversion of international attention over the war in the Middle East to reverse its own policy in Eastern Europe. In early November, Soviet troops crushed Nagy's reformist regime and imposed a puppet dictatorship ruled by Moscow.

Meanwhile, the Moscow-Beijing alliance crumbled steadily throughout the 1950s. A shared communist ideology poorly veiled the rivalry for power between the two countries that had lasted several hundred years. Mao proclaimed himself Stalin's successor after the Soviet leader died in 1953, and maintained that a Chinese-style peasant-based revolution was far more relevant to the Third World than a Soviet-style industrial-worker revolution. Beijing also rejected Moscow's peaceful coexistence approach toward the West and instead advocated a more confrontational policy. In 1958 Mao discarded the Soviet development model and launched his *Great Leap Forward,* in which he tried to distribute wealth and industry as widely as possible. The result was mass famine and economic collapse. Moscow responded by withdrawing its technicians and aid.

Although it would be another 13 years before Washington would take advantage of the Sino-Soviet rift by playing each side against the other, American policies were adapted to other new geopolitical realities. Washington's massive retaliation policy essentially gave the United States the option of either surrender or full-scale nuclear war in response to a Soviet attack on Western Europe. In August 1957 Moscow launched the world's first intercontinental ballistic missile (ICBM). In October, Moscow beat Washington into space when it launched its *Sputnik* satellite into orbit. Although the United States soon launched its own ICBMs and satellites, America's nuclear supremacy had seemed to disappear and with it Washington's massive retaliation policy. As the Soviet nuclear arsenal grew, massive retaliation would mean the devastation of both countries. Although massive retaliation and MAD might deter a Soviet attack, if one did occur an American administration might well run up the white flag rather than risk annihilation.

Once the Soviet Union began to acquire its own nuclear weapons, they became political rather than military weapons. World opinion has solidly rallied against any use of nuclear weapons, which may have been an important factor in restraining the White House from using such weapons to defeat North Korea or North Vietnam. Washington twice hinted vaguely about considering them as an option: once to bring about a settlement with the North Koreans and Chinese during the Korean War in 1953, and again to "deter" China from attacking the tiny Taiwan islands of Quemoy and Matsu in the late 1950s. And even then, there is no evidence that Washington's quiet nuclear saber rattling was an important factor in settling those conflicts. Once Moscow achieved nuclear parity, Washington never even hinted at the use of nuclear weapons in any conflict.

America's nuclear might and strategy clearly did not deter the Soviets from continuing to provoke crises. In November 1958 Khrushchev demanded that the Western powers withdraw their military forces from Berlin, make it a "free city," and negotiate with East Germany. Washington rejected Khrushchev's demands, and the second Berlin crisis continued until August 13, 1961, when the Soviets built a wall around the Western sectors. The *Berlin Wall* became the Cold War's most vivid symbol.

In 1960 John Kennedy won the White House in part by claiming there was a *missile gap* with the Soviets, which he was determined to overcome. In fact, the United States still maintained a healthy nuclear lead. The Kennedy administration, however, abandoned the massive retaliation deterrent strategy in favor of *flexible response,* in which there would be a gradual, controlled escalation of warfare from the conventional level through the tactical, regional, and intercontinental nuclear levels, if Soviet forces prevailed at lower levels.

Most Europeans, and particularly French President Charles de Gaulle, protested this change in strategy. Under massive retaliation, the United States and the Soviet Union would fire at each other over the heads of the Europeans; under flexible response they would first devastate Europe and then later, maybe, each other. Even if a nuclear war never occurred, flexible response would be more expensive for Americans and West Europeans alike, because it required a massive increase in conventional forces. In 1966 President de Gaulle withdrew his country from NATO's command structure, although not from the treaty itself, in which an attack on one member was considered an attack on all.

This new strategy was almost tested by the 1962 *Cuban missile crisis,* which was the closest the two superpowers came to starting World War III.[9] Without a Cuban revolution there would have been no Cuban missile crisis. From 1956 Fidel Castro organized and led a rebellion in Cuba that eventually overthrew the corrupt Batista regime on January 1, 1959. Although Castro had originally fought as a reformist, he soon publicly embraced communism and signed a friendship treaty with the Soviet Union in 1960. In April 1961 the United States launched an attack by an American-trained Cuban exile force against the Castro regime. The attack failed, and the men were killed or captured. In January 1962 Washington severed its last trade and diplomatic relations with Cuba. In early 1962 Khrushchev and Castro agreed that the Soviet Union would deploy intermediate range ballistic missiles with a 2,000 mile range in Cuba. On October 14, American satellites revealed the construction of missile silos in Cuba.

The Cuban missile crisis lasted for the next ten days, during which time the Kennedy administration debated and decided on a proper response, and then negotiated with Khrushchev for an agreement, which defused the crisis. In the first few days of the crisis, Kennedy's cabinet was split between those who advocated an air strike or blockade and those who favored a diplomatic approach. Kennedy finally decided on backing up his demand that Khrushchev remove the missiles with a naval blockade (which was officially described as a quarantine, since a blockade was considered an act of war) of Cuba and placing American forces on full alert. Khrushchev eventually agreed to withdraw the missiles in return for a public American pledge not to invade Cuba and a private pledge to remove American nuclear missiles from Turkey.

During the 1950s and into the 1960s, the world was bipolar only militarily, never economically. The bipolar balance was based on conventional and nuclear power. Despite the occasional crisis, the bipolar world was highly predictable and stable. According to Gaddis, "the two superpowers have so ordered their affairs that they have neither stumbled into another war nor allowed others to upset the international system in which they coexist."[10] Washington and Moscow carefully managed not only their respective systems, but also their bilateral relationship. Each side escalated its conventional and nuclear power, but never used these vast arsenals to destroy the international status quo. Even Moscow's probes of Western resolve, as in Berlin (1948–1949 and 1958–1962) and in Cuba (1962), were rare, and those crises were carefully managed by both sides, so they did not escalate into war. The geopolitical and ideological differences between the American and Soviet blocs were largely fought throughout the Third World, where the stakes and chances of a direct clash were relatively low. Although each side largely refrained from stirring up trouble on the other's side of the iron curtain, spheres of influence elsewhere in the world were fair game. When Washington began to aid a government, Moscow was certain to aid groups trying to overthrow that government, and vice versa.

Washington and Moscow used similar tactics throughout the Cold War, including spying, overthrowing unfriendly governments, helping repress rebellions against friendly states, and waging wars in Afghanistan and Vietnam. For example, in 1965 the Johnson administration sent 25,000 troops into the Dominican Republic to help its right-wing government suppress a rebellion by supporters of elected president Juan

Bosch, whom they had recently overthrown. Bosch had been the first freely elected president in 38 years and had promised sweeping reforms. Johnson ordered the invasion by arguing that the United States was helping defeat a communist revolution that was just using Bosch as a symbol. The Soviet Union and others condemned the American invasion as violating the UN Charter. In 1968 the Soviet Union launched Warsaw Pact forces into Czechoslovakia to put down a reformist socialist government under President Alexander Dubcek. Moscow justified the invasion by declaring that Dubcek was a tool of the Western imperialists whose victory in Czechoslovakia would lead to anti-communist revolutions elsewhere. Now it was Washington's turn to condemn the Soviet Union for its invasion.

The similarities between the two invasions are obvious; however, there were differences. The Dominican Republic had democratic elections shortly after the American invasion, and American forces were withdrawn. Czechoslovakia, however, remained under a dictatorship until 1990. In terms of their relative strategic importance, Czechoslovakia was a key member of the Warsaw Pact. The Dominican Republic is a poor Caribbean country with little strategic importance. A communist revolution in the Dominican Republic could have made it a second Cuba, but Havana itself has never posed any military threat to the United States (except for the missile crisis of 1962), and there was little likelihood that the Soviets would try to reimpose missiles in Cuba or elsewhere in the Western Hemisphere.

Although the United States had been aiding anti-communist forces in Vietnam since the late 1950s, Kennedy escalated America's number of advisers from 500 to 16,000 between 1961 and 1963. The communist insurgency continued despite America's increased involvement. President Johnson used an alleged attack by North Vietnamese torpedo boats in August 1964 to get Congress to pass the Tonkin Gulf Resolution, which essentially gave the president the freedom to pursue a war in Vietnam as he wished. By 1968 Johnson increased the number of American troops in South Vietnam to 550,000 and launched a massive bombing campaign across Indochina. But despite this huge military escalation, the American forces seemed incapable of decisively defeating the communists.

Détente and Selective Containment (1969–1979)

The bipolar stability and parity paved the way for a period of *détente* and selective containment from 1969 to 1979. Richard Nixon inaugurated this period after being elected president in 1968. Although a hard-line anti-communist, President Nixon was also a realist, who realized that as America's relative geopolitical and geoeconomic power declined, it was imperative to employ new policies to secure American interests. Nixon's *Vietnamization* policy of slowly withdrawing American troops and turning over the fighting to the South Vietnamese armies represented a broader realignment of American commitments throughout the Third World. Although the United States would aid besieged friendly governments, it would avoid committing American troops to the fighting, a policy known as the *Nixon Doctrine.*

At the same time, Nixon embarked on negotiations with North Vietnam, the Soviet Union, and, to the surprise of many, China to resolve outstanding issues. In February 1973, after years of grueling negotiations, Washington, Saigon, Hanoi, and the

South Vietnamese communists signed a peace treaty designed to preserve the existing status quo. But after the American forces left, the communists broke the agreement, conquered South Vietnam, and reunited the country under communism. Nixon had much greater success with the Soviet Union, negotiating the Strategic Arms Limitation Talks (*SALT* I) treaty, in which both sides agreed to limit their antiballistic missile (ABM) sites and ICBMs. In addition, he negotiated several trade agreements. Nixon tried to further strengthen détente with Moscow by establishing relations with communist China in 1971 and in 1972. By pursuing better relations with both the Soviet Union and China, Nixon drove the wedge between them deeper and encouraged them to further develop relations with the United States.

Détente continued through the Ford administration (1974–1976) and through most of the Carter years. In 1975 Washington, Moscow, and 33 other countries signed the *Helsinki Accord,* which accepted the existing European boundaries as permanent and required signatories to respect human rights. In 1977 Washington signed a treaty with Panama, in which it agreed to return the Panama Canal by the year 2000. That same year, Carter helped negotiate the Camp David Peace Accords between Israel and Eygpt. In July 1979 Washington and Moscow signed SALT II, which imposed new limits on ICBMs. In 1979 Washington and Beijing formally established full diplomatic relations and exchanged ambassadors.

Despite these triumphs, the United States faced growing geopolitical and geoeconomic challenges. Détente did not inhibit Moscow from aiding Marxist governments or guerrilla fighters in Ethiopia, Angola, Somalia, the Sudan, and Mozambique. In February 1979 America's ally, the Shah of Iran, was toppled by a fundamentalist Islamic revolution and the new government under Ayatollah Khomeini was fiercely anti-American. That same month, Iranians invaded the American embassy in Teheran and held the 54 diplomats there prisoner for the next 444 days. In July 1979 the communist Sandinista movement overthrew the Somoza dictatorship of Nicaragua, and the new government threatened a revolution without borders, which would replace other Central American governments with communist governments. To make matters worse, OPEC further doubled oil prices in 1979 and in 1980, worsening global inflation and stagnant economic growth. The global balance of power seemed to be tipping against the United States.

Global Containment (1979–1991)

The Soviet invasion of Afghanistan in December 1979 ended a decade of détente and began a decade of tension and confrontation. Washington swung back toward a global containment policy. The Carter administration cut agricultural and technology exports to the Soviet Union, boycotted the Olympic Games in Moscow, and withdrew SALT II from ratification procedures in the Senate. Carter also announced that the Persian Gulf was a region of vital American interests and that the United States would go to war if it were invaded by an outside power, a strategy that became known as the *Carter Doctrine.*

Promising to revive American power, Ronald Reagan defeated Jimmy Carter in the 1980 presidential race. Reagan expanded the global containment strategy reestablished by Carter, intervening in Central America, the Caribbean, southern Africa, the

Middle East, and Southeast Asia. The new administration's interventionist policies became known as the *Reagan Doctrine*. Defending the administration's policies, Secretary of State George Schultz captured the essence of global containment when he said:

> *Either we are willing to act on a vital issue close to our shores at a critical moment when the world is watching or we are not. Either we help Nicaraguans to gain their freedom, or we do not. In Europe, and in the Middle East, in Afghanistan, and in Cambodia, in South America, and in southern Africa, our friends and our enemies will draw their own conclusions about what we decide.[11]*

Shortly after taking power in March 1985, Mikhail Gorbachev inaugurated a second period of détente, in which Moscow and Washington negotiated and agreed on several key issues, including a treaty eliminating all intermediate nuclear forces from Europe. Despite these better relations, the Reagan and Bush administrations continued their trillion dollar military buildup and global containment policies.

REASONS FOR THE COLD WAR'S END

For 72 years (1917–1991), the Soviet Union's system remained intact. For at least 47 years (1947–1991), the United States and the Soviet Union were locked in a Cold War. Then in 1991 the Communist system collapsed, and the Cold War ended. Why?

There are two long-term reasons and one short-term reason.[12] George Kennan had been right all along. America's containment policies would eventually lead to the collapse of the Soviet Empire and communism. Containment and communism's fatal flaws were the two long-term reasons for the Cold War's end, Gorbachev was the short-term catalyst.

The Failure of Communism

Communism's destruction was inevitable. The economic policies of communist countries have emphasized the distribution rather than the creation of income and wealth. By dividing the pie more equitably rather than expanding the pie, the communists have merely succeeded in making more people poor. Pre-revolutionary middle and upper classes were eliminated and replaced with a new elite class, the communist party, that exploited what little wealth the system produced.

The massive and costly industrialization efforts of communist states contributed little to development or wealth. Central planning failed to create dynamic, profitable industries, infrastructure, or agriculture. Russia actually produces less grain today than before the revolution. Virtually none of the former Soviet Union's industries are competitive with foreign industries. What happened in every communist country was a tremendous misallocation or waste of human, natural, technological, and financial resources. Meanwhile, the democratic industrial nations soared further ahead economically.

Gorbachev's Reforms

Mikhail Gorbachev understood that central planning had failed to achieve prosperity or equality. By the late 1980s the Soviet Union could no longer afford to maintain its East European empire and its military buildup and to operate a centrally planned economy. Gorbachev chose to give up the empire and military buildup in a desperate attempt to concentrate all resources to reform and revive the Soviet economy. In February 1986 Gorbachev denounced the *Brezhnev Doctrine,* which justified a Soviet invasion of any communist country that was threatened by a democratic revolution. Instead, Gorbachev called for radical reform in the Soviet Union, which would be achieved by *glastnost,* or open information and discussion, *perestroika,* or institutional restructuring, and democracy. Political prisoners were released, Jews and others were allowed to freely emigrate, labor unions were given the right to bargain and strike, religions were allowed to worship freely, and the mass media were allowed to investigate and report freely. In March 1989 Gorbachev allowed competitive elections for the national People's Congress, and many reformist communists won seats from hard-liners. Later, Gorbachev announced that the communist party would no longer monopolize political power. In March 1990, Russia had democratic elections for the first time in 1,000 years of history. The people elected representatives to the Russian parliament, which in turn elected Boris Yeltsin as president.

The Collapse of Empire

Although Gorbachev had intended to reform the Soviet Union and the communist party, the political changes that he enacted proved so revolutionary that they eventually destroyed both the Soviet Empire and communism. Ironically, the domino effect of revolution that American policymakers feared so much throughout the Cold War only occurred in Eastern Europe. The democratic revolutions that swept East Europe in 1989 and 1990 were largely the result of peaceful mass demonstrations that convinced the communists to allow free elections. Only Romania experienced a violent revolution, in which the communist dictator Ceausescu and other members of his government were executed. Elections brought democratic parties to power in Poland, East Germany, Hungary, and Czechoslovakia, and reformist communist governments to power in Romania and Bulgaria. Gorbachev's policy of allowing each East European country, and eventually each Soviet republic, to choose its own system, even if it meant the end of communism, was popularly known as the *my way doctrine.*

The only significant resistance to political revolution was in the Soviet Union itself. On August 19, 1992, the day before Gorbachev would have signed a treaty allowing the Soviet republics to become independent, hard-line communist leaders attempted to overthrow him. For three days between August 19 and August 21, the conspirators held Gorbachev hostage at his Crimean home and attempted to besiege Russian President Yeltsin and his supporters inside the Russian Parliament. Over 50,000 Russians rallied around the Russian Parliament building, putting their bodies in front of the Soviet tanks and troops loyal to the communists. As increased numbers of Russian troops defected to Yeltsin, the coup leaders gave up and released Gorbachev, who returned to Moscow. The coup leaders were arrested and tried for treason.

The failed coup accelerated the destruction of communism and the Soviet Empire. During the coup, Latvia and Ukraine declared their independence, while statues of Lenin were toppled in Estonia and Lithuania. On August 24, Gorbachev resigned as head of the Communist party and recommended that its Central Committee be disbanded. On August 29, Yeltsin and Gorbachev appeared before the Russian parliament. Over Gorbachev's protests, Yeltsin dramatically issued a decree abolishing the Communist party in Russia. On September 2, the Soviet Congress of People's Deputies approved a plan to reduce the Kremlin's authority and allow a looser federation of the Soviet republics. On September 6, the Soviet Union recognized the independence of Latvia, Lithuania, and Estonia. On October 18, Gorbachev and the presidents of eight other Soviet republics agreed to join an economic union, Ukraine joined the union on November 4. Finally, on December 4 Russia, Ukraine, and Belarus declared the Soviet Union dead but agreed to form a commonwealth in its place. Communism and the Soviet Empire had all but vanished.

Containment and the Reagan Military Buildup

During the Republican national convention in August 1992, speaker after speaker claimed that it was the Reagan and Bush military buildup that won the Cold War, and these claims were continued throughout the 1992 elections. Did Reagan and Bush really win the Cold War?

The founder of the containment policy, George Kennan, dismissed the Republican victory claims in 1992 as "ridiculous," and went on to argue that: "Nobody—no country, no party, no person, 'won' the Cold War. It was a long and costly political rivalry, fueled on both sides by unreal and exaggerated estimates of the intentions and strength of the other party."[13] Kennan, of course, had predicted in the late 1940s that the collapse of the Soviet Empire and communism was inevitable, given the historic tendency of all empires to eventually collapse and the inability of communism to satisfy even the most basic needs of the people under its rule. America's containment policy undoubtedly accelerated communism's inevitable collapse, but the strategy was a bipartisan policy that was started by a democratic president and continued by Republican and Democratic presidents alike.

There is no evidence that the Reagan military buildup contributed to, let alone caused, the Soviet economy's collapse. Moscow did not increase military spending to keep up with the Reagan administration increases. The Soviet economy would have collapsed regardless of American policy. Soviet Marshal Nikolai Ogarkov admitted in 1983 that the Cold War had essentially ended with the West's victory, arguing that "we will never be able to catch up . . . in modern arms until we have an economic revolution. And the question is whether we can have an economic revolution without a political revolution."[14] In other words, communism had failed.

The Reagan buildup may have actually propped up rather than undermined the Soviet empire. Throughout the 1980s, Kremlin hard-liners pointed to the Reagan military buildup and interventions around the world to argue that Gorbachev's reforms were dangerous and should not be attempted.[15] Ironically, throughout the course of the revolutionary events of August and September 1991, President Bush's response was either passive or seemingly favorable to retaining the communist and Soviet status quo, and avoided any support of Yeltsin. In September Bush flew to Kiev to stand beside Gorbachev and actually implore the Ukrainians not to break away from the Soviet Union.

The Reagan and Bush policies reflected the flaws of the global containment strategy pursued by previous administrations. As Kennan pointed out:

> The extreme militarization of American discussion and policy, as promoted by hard-line-circles . . . consistently strengthened comparable hardliners in the Soviet Union. The more America's political leaders were seen in Moscow as committed to an ultimate military rather than political resolution of Soviet-American tensions, the greater was the tendency in Moscow to tighten the controls by both party and police, and the greater the breaking effect on all liberalizing tendencies in the regime. Thus the general effect of cold war extremism was to delay rather than hasten the great change that overtook the Soviet Union at the end of the 1980s.[16]

THE POST-COLD WAR RELATIONSHIP

Although the Cold War is over, many problems remain, including the reduction of nuclear and conventional forces and political and economic development in Russia and the other former Communist countries.

The Economic Crisis

The collapse of the Soviet Empire and communism should allow the United States and its allies an enormous peace dividend. Some of the savings will have to be extended to Russia and the other newly independent states to help them reconstruct their economies. Russia's economy in particular is in a state of crisis and near collapse.

In contrast to the revolutionary impact of Gorbachev's political reforms, his economic reforms failed to revive the fossilized Soviet economy. Although Gorbachev allowed for some limited privatization, fewer controls on foreign investment, and the leasing of land to farmers, the economy continued to stall. However, there are more than 1,700 military factories (employing six million people) in the former Soviet Union, and few of these factories have been converted to civilian production.

The other former Soviet republics are also experiencing difficulties converting from central planning into managed-market economies. Foreign investment and privatization has been limited. More than 90 percent of all trade of the former republics remains with Russia. Complicating matters is the presence of 25 million Russians and hundreds of thousands of Russian troops scattered across the 14 former republics.

Russia is in dire need of investment capital but has poorly invested the large foreign loans and grants it has already received. Through December 31, 1991, the Soviet Union accumulated $68 billion in foreign debts, of which $50 billion came from government lenders known as the Paris Club and $18 billion from commercial lenders known as the London Club. The Paris and London Clubs negotiate with Moscow over rescheduling Russia's debt and extending new loans.

In April 1992, President Bush and German Chancellor Kohl promised Russia another $24 billion, including $11 billion in bilateral aid, $2.5 billion in deferred debt repayments, $3.0 billion in new IMF loans, $1.5 billion in new World Bank loans, and $6.0 billion to stabilize the ruble. An additional $20 billion was allocated for the other former Soviet republics, including $7.0 billion in bilateral aid, $3.0 billion in deferred debt payments, $2.5 billion in new World Bank and IMF loans, and $7.5 billion from undecided sources. Unfortunately, red tape in both Moscow and the West continues to mean only half of the $24 billion was actually profitably invested in the Russian economy. In April 1992 the IMF and World Bank admitted all the former Soviet republics as full members with full borrowing privileges and obligations. However, any country that borrows from the IMF and World Bank must agree to stringent economic reforms, something to which Russia has been reluctant to agree. Despite these efforts, Russia's debts continued to mount. Moscow had already assumed 84 percent of the Soviet debt, and in 1992 Russia borrowed an additional $18 billion and deferred payment on a debt of $18 billion. By early 1993, Russia owed $86 billion.

On April 6, 1993, President Clinton met with President Yeltsin in Vancouver, Canada, and promised $1.6 billion in additional aid. The aid would include large amounts of medicine and food, money to dismantle nuclear weapons, to construct houses, to convert military industries into consumer industries, to bring 3,000 Russians to the United States to study, and to underwrite American investments and trade with Russia. At the Group of Seven meeting in Tokyo on April 15, the participants agreed to a $28 billion aid package to Russia, which included $13.1 billion in new IMF loans, of which $6 billion were to stabilize the Russian ruble; $15 billion from the World Bank to fund various Russian industries; and $300 million from the European Bank for Reconstruction and Development. During the meeting, President Clinton announced that he would more than double American aid to $4.5 billion. Clinton also convinced the Japanese to extend $1.8 billion to Russia, although over $1.5 billion of that was in loans tied to purchases of Japanese goods and services.

Although Russia desperately needs foreign capital, technology, and markets, its economic development depends on its own reform policies. To the surprise of many, in a referendum on April 25, 1993, Russians overwhelmingly supported Yeltsin and his reforms and condemned the largely communist legislature. Although the referendum clearly mandated Yeltsin and his policies, the political stalemate between him and the legislature continued.

The Political Crisis

Russia's political system plunged into yet another crisis on September 21, 1993, when President Yeltsin, fed up with the gridlock led by communist politicians, dissolved the parliament. Although some legislators quietly left, most legislators defiantly called for Yeltsin's overthrow and began arming themselves and the Parliament building (which is called the White House). On October 4, Yeltsin ordered Russian troops to capture the building and arrest those inside. They did so after a bloody shoot-out that left hundreds dead and wounded.

Having crushed the largely communist parliamentary opposition, Yeltsin then promised elections to be held December 12, 1993, to ratify a new constitution and elect a new parliament. Although two-thirds of voters accepted the proposed constitution, the new parliament remains divided between a coalition of reformist groups and a Nationalist/Communist alliance. Yeltsin will not be up for reelection until 1996, and the new constitution empowers him to dissolve parliament if it is too obstructionist. Despite Yeltsin's powers, his varying opponents will continue to struggle against his rule and reform policies.

Russia's liberal democratic revolution thus remains fragile. The communist system may be officially dead, but Communists, Nationalists, Czarists, and Separatists continue to hold or to struggle for power and to vow to reimpose an authoritarian state. No matter what their political orientation, bureaucrats continue to do what they do best—obstruct. Free-market capitalism remains alien to most people, and most people's living standards continue to decline. There is some fear that Russia itself could crumble. Only about 82 percent of the 150 million inhabitants are actually Russians. Russia is a federal republic of 130 recognized nationalities and ethnic groups, with 31 autonomous regions.

With communism's collapse, many former Soviet citizens are experiencing a deep ideological void, which liberal democratic values and behaviors will not soon, if ever, fill. Throughout their lives, Soviets were constantly socialized to believe in communism as a religion that contained eternal truths and in Marx and Lenin as gods. Now those gods and that religion have been all but destroyed. A fierce nationalism has filled the void for many former Soviets. One of communism's worst legacies was the destruction of entrepreneurial instincts in people. The saying, "the state pretends to pay us and we pretend to work" was mostly true. Communism was synonomous with shoddy workmanship, inefficiency, absenteeism, rudeness, drunkenness, and red tape. Communism politically, economically, and socially repressed and exploited people, while giving people a basic material and psychological security. Although there was clearly a class system dominated by the communist party (whose five percent of the population monopolized what meager wealth and privileges the system created), their consumption was not conspicuous, and most people could believe they were all equally poor. People still fear taking risks, competing, and trying new things, and they deeply resent it when others are successful enterprisers. Those few who have made money have often engaged in orgies of conspicuous consumption that seems to mock the poverty and hopelessness of everyone else. As long as most Russians fear political and economic freedoms, the new liberal democratic institutions, values, and behaviors will remain precarious.

CONCLUSION

The United States and most other countries pray that a democratic, free market, and peaceful Russia emerges from the ruins of the Soviet Empire and communism. Whatever form Russia's political and economic system eventually takes, it is unrealistic to believe it will be an American-style system.[17] Liberalism in Russia must take root in the soil of a millenium of centralized political and economic authoritarianism.

The United States is now the world's only genuine military superpower. While America's defense budget declined slightly from $294 billion in 1985 to $261 billion in 1992 in constant dollars, Russia's plunged from $241 billion to $39.6 billion. Although Moscow continues to maintain a vast conventional and nuclear force, it is oriented toward maintaining the cohesion of Russia itself in the face of economic depression and deep political divisions. Russia has even asked to join NATO. Like the United States,

Russia must further reduce its military establishment and invest any peace dividend into productive economic and social enterprises.

Tensions and conflicts between the United States and Russia will continue. But even if the Yeltsin government loses an election or is overthrown by a nationalistic communist regime, the new government will face the same crisis as the old one and will be even less able to handle it. A highly nationalistic, antagonistic Russia will not pose any threat to the United States. Moscow's policies will be focused on economically and territorially maintaining Russia itself and will have no power or inclination left for expansion. The Cold War is over forever.

STUDY QUESTIONS

1. Was the Cold War really born simply of a tragic misperception as Gorbachev and others maintain, or were there genuine national and ideological interests at stake that made conflict between the United States and Soviet Union inevitable? Explain.

2. Was the Cold War merely a long and tragic detour in the world's inevitable march toward international cooperation and the celebration of human rights? Explain.

3. Why did the Cold War occur? How was it waged? What were its major phases and incidents?

4. What are the strengths and weaknesses of the three major schools of thought regarding the Cold War's origins?

5. What conflicts in the Middle East, China, and Eastern Europe during the late 1940s helped escalate the Cold War?

6. Why and how was the Korean War a turning point in the Cold War?

7. What was George Kennan's analysis of the Soviet threat? What strategy did he propose to counter it?

8. What was the difference between the selective containment strategy and the global containment strategy? Why did American foreign policy alternate between them?

9. What caused the Sino-Soviet split?

10. Why did the United States intervene in Vietnam? What were the sweeping consequences of that intervention?

11. How did America's nuclear strategy shift over the decades?

12. Why did the Nixon administration inaugurate détente with the Soviet Union and China in the late 1960s? What were détente's major accomplishments? Why did it end in December 1979?

13. What were the Nixon, Carter, and Reagan Doctrines? How did they complement and contradict one another?

14. What were Gorbachev's reforms? Why did he make them? What did he hope to accomplish? Why did they lead to the collapse of communism and the Soviet Empire?

15. Why did the Cold War end when and as it did?

16. What significant problems between Russia, the former Soviet Republics, East Europe, and the West continue into the post-cold-war world?

ENDNOTES

1. For perhaps the best single volume on the Cold War, see Walter LaFeber, *America, Russia, and the Cold War, 1945–1990* (New York: McGraw-Hill, 1991). Much of the information and quotes from this section comes from LaFeber.

2. Hans Morganthau, *Politics Among Nations* (New York: Knopf, 1967), 249.

3. George Kennan, *American Diplomacy 1900–1950* (Chicago: University of Chicago Press, 1951), 118.

4. Quoted in William Harbaugh, *Power and Responsibility: The Life and Times of Theodore Roosevelt* (New York: Octagon Books, 1961), 277.

5. Quoted in Arthur Link, *Wilson: The Struggle for Neutrality, 1914–1915* (Princeton N.J.: Princeton University Press, 1960), 48.

6. Quoted in Walter Lafeber, *America, Russia, and the Cold War, 1945–1990*, 7.

7. Walter Lafeber, *America, Russia, and the Cold War, 1945–1990*, 31.

8. See Matthew Evangelista, "Stalin's Postwar Army Reappraised," *International Security,* vol. 7, Winter 1982–1983, 121–122.

9. The best account of the Cuban missile crisis is James Blight and David Welch, *On the Brink: Americans and Soviets Reexamine the Cuban Missile Crisis* (New York: Hill and Wang, 1989).

10. John Gaddis, "Great Illusions, the Long Peace, and Future of the International System," in Charles Kegley, ed., *The Long Postwar Peace* (New York: Harper-Collins, 1991), 34.

11. George Shultz, "Nicaragua: Will Democracy Prevail?" *Current Policy,* no. 97. Washington, D.C.: Department of State, Bureau of Public Affairs, Feburary 27, 1986.

12. For the best account, see Michael R. Beschloss and Strobe Talbott, *At the Highest Levels: The Inside Story of the End of the Cold War* (Boston: Little, Brown, 1993).

13. George Kennan, "The G.O.P. Won the Cold War? Ridiculous," *New York Times,* October 28, 1992.

14. Leslie Gelb, "GOP Can't Take All Credit for Winning the Cold War," *New York Times,* August 21, 1992.

15. Fred Chernoff, "Ending the Cold War: The Soviet Retreat and the U.S. Military Buildup," *International Affairs,* vol., 67, no. 1, 1991, 111–126; Strobe Talbott, "Rethinking the Red Menace," *Time,* January 1, 1990, 66–72.

16. Kennan, "The G.O.P. Won the Cold War? Ridiculous," *New York Times,* August 21, 1992.

17. George Kennan, "America and the Russian Future," *Foreign Affairs,* vol. 69, no.2, Spring 1990, 157–166.

The Nuclear Arms Race and Its Control

Key Terms and Concepts

Air-Launched Cruise Missiles (ALCM)
Alamogordo
Atomic Bomb
Baruch Plan
Basic Deterrence
Brilliant Pebbles
Brinkmanship
Compellence
Confidence Building Measures
Counterforce
Countervalue
Deterrence
Electromagnetic Pulse (EMG)
Equivalent Megatons (EMT)
Extended Deterrence
First Strike Capability
First Strike Weapon
Gradual and Reciprocated Initiatives in Tension-Reduction (GRITS)

Hard-Target Kill (HTK)
Hydrogen Bomb
Intercontinental Ballistic Missile (ICBM)
Intermediate Range Nuclear Force Treaty (INF)
International Atomic Energy Agency (IAEA)
Limited Test Ban Treaty
Manhattan Project
Minimum Deterrence
Mutually Assured Destruction (MAD)
Nuclear Autumn
Nuclear Ladder
Nuclear Nonproliferation Treaty (NPT)
Nuclear Utilization Theory (NUT)
Nuclear Winter
Overkill
Permissive Action Link (PAL)

Sea Launched Ballistic Missile (SLBM)
Second-Strike Capabilities
Second-Strike Weapon
Single Integrated Operational Plan (SIOP)
Small Mobile Intercontinental Ballistic Missile (SICBM)
Sputnik
Strategic Arms Reduction Talks (START)
Strategic Defense Initiative (SDI)
Submarines with Ballistic Missiles (SSBM)
Triad
Use 'em or Lose 'em
Window of Vulnerability

Humans have always been interdependent, but, until the modern era, usually only at a family or village level. Modernization makes all of humanity globally interdependent in many ways, not all of which are positive. The world today groans under the weight of over 50,000 nuclear weapons which pack the destructive power of 1 million atomic bombs such as the one dropped in Hiroshima, or 1,600 times the "firepower released in World War II, the Korean War, and the Vietnam War that killed 44,000,000 people."[1]

One kiloton equals 2,200 pounds of trinitrotoluene (TNT). The atomic bomb dropped on Hiroshima was equal to 20 kilotons, or 44,000 tons, of TNT. One megaton equals 2.2 million pounds of TNT. The destructive power of one B-52, or cruise missile, let alone an MX, is mind-boggling. One B-52 alone carries 25 megatons of nuclear explosives, or 12.5 times the destructive power of all bombs dropped during World War II![2] A cruise missile launched from a submarine can fly 1,500 miles and explode with 13 times the destructive power of the Hiroshima bomb. Intercontinental ballistic missiles (ICBMs) are the most destructive nuclear weapons of all. An MX ICBM launched from Nebraska can travel 8,000 miles at 15,000 miles per hour to explode with 300 times the destructive power of the Hiroshima bomb.[3]

A nuclear explosion includes three elements: initial blast; thermal, or heat; and radiation. A megaton bomb can destroy all brick buildings within four miles and burn human flesh up to nine miles from the place of impact. A 10-megaton bomb can destroy buildings up to nine miles and burn flesh up to twenty-four miles from the place of impact, and a 100-megaton bomb can destroy buildings up to eighteen miles and burn flesh up to seventy-five miles away. The explosion's intense heat creates a fire storm that sucks in and hurls out vast winds of oxygen that vaporize virtually everything in the vicinity.

Death also occurs from radiation, which a 10-megaton bomb could spew over 100,000 square miles. Human exposure to 100 to 200 roentgens of radiation would cause vomiting, nausea, and weakness, and, inevitably, cancer and genetic mutations. Exposure of over 200 roentgens can cause death for most people, either immediately after exposure or shortly thereafter. As Khrushchev said, after a nuclear war the survivors would envy the dead. The psychological effects would be devastating for those who escaped direct injury but understood that their society was destroyed and would never recover.[4]

Although there are six known nuclear powers and perhaps several others, the United States and Russia have by far the most nuclear weapons. The number of strategic (used against each other's homeland) nuclear weapons peaked in 1988, when the United States had 13,000 and the Soviet Union 11,000. The United States and the Soviet Union each had an additional 20,000 tactical (battlefield) warheads.

America's nuclear-war-fighting strategy is known as the *Single Integrated Operational Plan* (SIOP). It involves strikes on Soviet nuclear and conventional forces; industrial bases; and command, control, communication, and intelligence centers (*C3I*). Over 120 warheads are targeted on Moscow alone, a situation known as *overkill*. The National Security Council estimates that a full nuclear exchange would kill a minimum of 115 million Soviets and 140 million Americans.[5] Tens of millions more would die of starvation, radiation sickness, and disease. Diseases would spread as the transportation, communications, and energy systems failed; crops rotted in the fields; medical supplies ran out; and refrigeration failed.

In the worst case, a nuclear exchange of 5,000 megatons would throw so much ash into the atmosphere that most of the sun's rays would be blocked from the earth. Some predict that the result would be a *nuclear winter,* in which temperatures would plunge as much as 36 degrees Fahrenheit (20 degrees Celsius), in the northern hemisphere where 90 percent of the world's population lives, wiping out crops and causing mass starvation. The radiation would also destroy the earth's protective ozone layer, without which virtually all life would become extinct.[6] A different study concluded that a 5,000 megaton nuclear exchange would create a *nuclear autumn,* in which temperatures would fall

9 to 27 degrees Fahrenheit (5 to 15 degrees Celsius although the effects on human life might well be just as catastrophic as in a nuclear winter.[7]

The nuclear threat may be more insidious than an all-out nuclear war. Accidents have left at least 50 nuclear warheads and nine reactors strewn across the world's oceans. The Chernobyl meltdown rendered a huge area of Ukraine uninhabitable and spewed radiation that drifted worldwide. There may be at least a dozen other Chernobyl plants on the verge of meltdown. Twice as much radiation as from Chernobyl has been released as nuclear waste into Lake Karachai from the nearby Chelyabinsk nuclear warhead production plant, making the lake the most polluted spot on earth.[8] Without protective clothing, someone standing on its shores would die instantly.

Between 1945 and 1992, the six nuclear powers conducted 1,948 nuclear explosions at 35 sites, an average of one every 9 days.[9] From 1945 until the 1963 *Limited Test Ban Treaty*, 424 nuclear bombs were exploded in the atmosphere, an average of 23.6 a year. China and France refused to sign the treaty, which banned tests in the atmosphere, underwater, and in space. Between 1963 and 1991, France conducted 41 atmospheric tests and China 23, for a combined average of 2.4 tests a year. The fallout from every atmospheric nuclear test since 1945 has drifted around the world, and all human beings have a cocktail of radioactive elements in their bones.

What is the purpose of these vast nuclear forces, all the testing, tens of thousands of scientists and engineers, trillions of dollars and diversion of enormous human, financial, and technological resources from economic development?

Many people argue that, paradoxically, the vast nuclear arsenals of the superpowers preserve the peace. By the late 1950s, the United States and the Soviet Union had each accumulated enough weapons to annihilate the other, a situation known as *Mutually Assured Destruction* (MAD) and the essence of nuclear deterrence. Early in the nuclear age, Winston Churchill captured the paradoxes of deterrence: "it may be that we shall by a process of sublime irony have reached a stage where safety will be the sturdy child of terror and survival the twin brother of annihilation."[10]

Nuclear *deterrence* is essentially is making the other side believe that if it attacked it would lose far more than it gained. Deterrence has two essential elements: capability and credibility. Capability includes not just a large and survivable nuclear force, but also a C3I system that can survive a nuclear attack and a leadership with the political resolve to retaliate. A state with the military and political capability to defeat a foreign attack has only the power to win. To deter a foreign attack in the first place, it must clearly communicate its military capability and resolve to any potential enemies and establish its credibility by not failing to use that power when its interests are threatened. Only then does it have deterrent power. Psychology is as important to deterrence as hardware.

Nations possess nuclear weapons to deter other nuclear powers from attacking them.[11] Nuclear power is effective only in how convincingly its holders can threaten its use, and in how rationally and carefully national decision makers analyze the costs and benefits of their actions. Deterrence cannot be a bluff, because it just might be called. Deterrence has failed if nuclear power is actually used.

This chapter will explore the key concepts, developments, and paradoxes of the nuclear arms race and its control.

THE NUCLEAR ARMS RACE

Massive Retaliation

Amidst World War II, four nations—the United States, Germany, Japan, and the Soviet Union—struggled to create atomic bombs. Code named the *Manhattan Project,* America's $2 billion effort was the only one among the four which had the scientific, financial, and material resources vital for the bomb's creation. On July 16, 1945, at *Alamogordo,* New Mexico, American scientists exploded the world's first atomic bomb.

President Truman received word of the successful test while he was meeting with Prime Minister Churchill and Premier Stalin at Potsdam, Germany. The Allied leaders had gathered to discuss the strategy for defeating Japan and to determine the postwar world's fate. Truman realized that with the atomic bomb the war could be won quickly without the estimated loss of a half million American lives that would be necessary to invade and defeat Japan (as well as tens of millions of Japanese who were determined to fight to the death) and without the need for the Soviet armies that Stalin had promised would soon attack Japanese forces in China. Truman casually mentioned that the United States now had an atomic bomb to Stalin, who was not visibly moved by the news. The United States dropped an atomic bomb on the Japanese city of Hiroshima on August 6, 1945, Soviet forces attacked the Japanese army in China on August 8, an atomic bomb was dropped on Nagasaki on August 9, and Japan surrendered on August 15.

The nuclear age, which began with the atomic bombing of Hiroshima and Nagasaki, has passed through two phases and is entering a third. The first phase lasted from 1945 to 1957 and was characterized by American nuclear dominance, one that the United States almost gave up. Fearing the proliferation of nuclear power, in March 1946, the Truman administration asked the UN Security Council to approve a plan whereby all countries would surrender atomic power to the United Nations, which could authorize its use. The Soviet Union vetoed the *Baruch Plan,* because it included a provision that would take away a permanent Security Council member's right to veto decisions of the atomic authority. The Soviet Union also feared that the United States would still retain knowledge of how to manufacture such bombs.

Initially disappointed by the Soviet veto, the Truman administration soon reasoned that it did not matter if the use of nuclear power was now available as long as the United States controlled it. With a monopoly over atomic power, the United States could deter any attack on its vital interests and defeat any enemies it should war against. After America's wartime alliance with the Soviet Union broke down into Cold War in 1947, nuclear weapons became central to America's containment policy.

Although the Soviet Union exploded its first nuclear bomb in September 1949, the United States still enjoyed an overwhelming superiority in the number, quality, and delivery of nuclear weapons for the next decade. Moscow had nuclear bombs, but lacked the means of delivering them. Soviet bombers had only enough fuel for a one way trip to the United States, and America's air defense system of radar and interceptors would probably have wiped out such an attack before it reached the country. In contrast, American B-36 bombers based in West Europe, Japan, and Alaska could quickly reach most of the Soviet Union. Nuclear technology advanced steadily during this period.

The first bombs were fission bombs (*atomic bombs*), but they were rendered obsolete in 1952, when the United States tested its first fusion bomb (*hydrogen bomb,* or thermonuclear bomb). The Soviets exploded their own hydrogen bomb the following year.

American nuclear strategy during this period was based on *compellence,* or using the nuclear threat to force others to concede in diplomatic problems, and deterrence of a Soviet invasion of Western Europe, Japan, or the Middle East. The United States played the game of *brinkmanship,* in which it would go to the brink of war with the Soviet Union and other adversaries in order to force them to back down. If war broke out and Moscow attacked the West, then Washington would respond with the massive retaliation of all its nuclear arsenal against the Soviet Union. Because slow-flying bombers were the only means of delivering the nuclear payload, the targets would be relatively accessible Soviet cities and industries, a strategy known as *countervalue.*

Although this strategy was an integral part of American policy from 1947, it became explicit following the North Korean attack on South Korea in 1950. At that time, American Secretary of State John Foster Dulles announced that henceforth any communist attack on the West would be countered "in a manner and at a place of our own choosing," implying strongly that Washington would retaliate with nuclear weapons against the Soviet Union, even if it was not directly involved militarily in that communist aggression. The Eisenhower administration rattled its nuclear saber against North Korea and China during negotiations for an armistice for the Korean War in 1953 and to compel China to back off from its threat to attack Taiwan's islands in 1957.

American nuclear superiority clearly began to erode when in 1957 the Soviet Union was the first to launch an intercontinental ballistic missile (ICBM) and place its *Sputnik* satellite into orbit. Although the United States successfully launched both an ICBM and satellite shortly thereafter, the Soviet ability to target ICMBs across America appeared to be a significant shift in the nuclear-power balance. Psychologically, Americans perceived themselves to be vulnerable and in danger of losing their lead. The 1960 American presidential election was fought and won partially over the issue of a missile gap, which candidate John Kennedy claimed the United States suffered with the Soviet Union. In reality, the Soviet Union would not achieve genuine nuclear parity with the United States for another decade. Although the Soviets had many nuclear bombs, they remained behind in their ability to deliver them. It was estimated that a full nuclear exchange would have resulted in as many as 50 million Soviet deaths but "only" 5 to 10 million American deaths.

The Cuban Missile Crisis of 1962 occurred, in part, because of Moscow's desire to bridge its missile gap with the United States. Soviet Premier Nikita Khrushchev ordered short range nuclear missiles placed in Cuba to offset the advantage the Americans had from ringing the Soviet Union with nuclear missile bases in West Germany, Turkey, and Japan. In early October, U.S. spy planes reported that Soviet nuclear bases were being built and would soon become operational. President Kennedy and his closest advisers quickly agreed that they had to convince the Soviets to withdraw their missiles. The question was how. Bombing the sites was rejected, and the administration finally settled on a naval blockade (or quarantine, as they euphemistically called it, because a blockade was an act of war). The U.S. Navy was ordered to intercept any Soviet ships bound for Cuba, up to 800 miles from its shores. Meanwhile, Kennedy promised Khrushchev that he would complete the withdrawal of obsolete American nuclear missiles from Turkey, which had been ordered but never accomplished earlier that year. Confronted with the American blockade and the face-saving gesture of withdrawing weapons from Turkey, Khrushchev finally agreed to withdraw Soviet missiles from Cuba.

During the ten-day crisis, nuclear war seemed imminent. The Cuban Missile Crisis vividly presented the risks of Mutually Assured Destruction (MAD) to Americans and Soviets alike and to the rest of the world. Although Moscow became committed to achieving parity with the United States, both sides realized that they risked nuclear annihilation by playing the game of brinksmanship in crises. During the 1960s, Washington and Moscow avoided direct crises with each other and began a series of negotiations over nuclear arms control.

Flexible Response

With nuclear parity and the development of new weapons systems, Washington shifted its nuclear war strategy from massive retaliation to flexible response. Henceforth, if the Warsaw Pact attacked NATO, Washington would only use nuclear weapons if the Soviets appeared on the verge of winning a conventional war. But rather than launch ICBMs against Moscow, the United States would use tactical nuclear weapons against Warsaw Pact armies in central Europe. If the Soviets responded by using their own tactical nuclear weapons, the United States would escalate to regional nuclear weapons that could hit targets in Eastern Europe and the Western Soviet Union. If Moscow matched that escalation, only then would Washington launch ICBMs at targets across the Soviet Union. With the highly accurate and fast ICBMs, the United States now targeted Soviet missile silos and command and control centers rather than cities and industries, a strategy known as *counterforce*. Fearful that its brinksmanship and compellence games with the Soviet Union or another country could lead to nuclear war, Washington abandoned those strategies and concentrated on deterring a Soviet attack on the West and striking first at each level of nuclear escalation, should deterrence fail and a conventional war ensue.

The flexible response strategy had several flaws. Most basic was the question of whether the United States could control a step-by-step escalation up the *nuclear ladder*, from conventional to tactical to regional, and, finally, to strategic levels. A counterforce strategy depends on striking first. Obviously there is no point in targeting the other side's silos and waiting for them to fire first, because if you retaliate you will simply be destroying empty silos. If one side either explicitly or implicitly declares a first-strike strategy, then both must adhere to the logic of either *use 'em or lose 'em*, which in turn exacerbates tensions and the chance for nuclear war in a crisis. Not surprisingly, Moscow rejected Washington's flexible response strategy and maintained that it would massively retaliate against the United States itself, even if Washington exploded just one nuclear device on the battlefield of central Europe.

Although there was little question that Washington would retaliate if Moscow fired nuclear weapons at the United States, there was doubt whether the White House would be willing "to trade Chicago for Hamburg." In other words, the flexible response strategy dictated that if Moscow dropped a nuclear bomb on Hamburg, the United States would respond by destroying a comparable Soviet city, such as Minsk. This threat of American retaliation presumably would deter a Soviet nuclear attack on Western

Europe. But many Soviets and others thought Washington was bluffing in its determination to uphold its *extended deterrence* strategy for Europe, as opposed to its *basic deterrence* strategy of protecting solely the United States. If a Soviet attack on Hamburg was followed by an American attack on Minsk, Moscow would certainly retaliate by striking an American city like Chicago. Faced with this probability, the president might well abandon Europe to a Soviet takeover rather than risk America's nuclear devastation. After leaving the presidency, Jimmy Carter admitted that if faced with this dilemma, he would have backed down rather than escalated the nuclear war. Henry Kissinger also asserted that extended deterrence involves "strategic assurances that we can not possibly mean or if we do mean, we should not execute because if we should execute, we risk the destruction of civilization."[12] Thus nuclear deterrence can work both ways: an American attack on the Soviet Union can be deterred, as well as a Soviet attack on the United States.

There are first-strike and second-strike nuclear capabilities and weapons. A *first-strike capability* means that a country can strike first and destroy most of the enemy's nuclear force so that the enemy would not retaliate with its remaining forces because it would then suffer a nuclear attack on its cities. A country has a *second-strike capability* if it can absorb an enemy first strike and then retaliate and inflict "unacceptable damage" to the enemy, which Secretary of Defense McNamara defined in 1964 as the ability to destroy half of Soviet industry and a quarter of its population. As will be seen, the United States may well have a first strike capability and most certainly has a second-strike capability. Arguably, despite its vast array of nuclear weapons, the Soviet Union has neither.

Washington has a *triad* strategic force built upon *first-strike weapons* and *second-strike* weapons. First strike weapons include ICBMs, which are fast and accurate but, in their fixed silos, vulnerable to an enemy attack. Second-strike weapons include bombers that can either directly drop nuclear bombs or fire *air-launched cruise missiles (ALCMs)* and *submarines with ballistic missiles (SSBMs)* or *sea launched ballistic missiles (SLBMs)*. Nuclear bombs launched from bombers and submarines are slower and less accurate but also less vulnerable to a Soviet attack. Cruises missiles are the most versatile nuclear weapons, because they can be launched by submarines, surface ships, bombers, and land-based systems. First-strike weapons are best used in a counterforce strategy against the enemy's ICBM silos and headquarters, whereas second-strike weapons are better targeted against an enemy's cities and armies. There is some overlap between second-strike and first-strike weapons. An ICBM in a hardened missile silo could survive an enemy strike and retaliate. SLBMs are now as fast and accurate as ICBMs and thus have some first-strike capabilities.

Although by the late 1960s there was a rough parity in the number of warheads, there was and remains an asymmetry in the superpowers' types of nuclear weapons and delivery systems. By the 1990s about 80 percent of America's strategic nuclear weapons were in second-strike delivery systems—41 percent in sea-based, 40 percent air-based, and only 19 percent in land-based ICBMs. Thus, in a nuclear war Washington could launch a first strike with its ICMBs against Soviet missile silos and bomber bases, while using its attack submarines and helicopters to destroy Soviet nuclear submarines. Even though some Soviet nuclear forces would probably survive an American attack, Moscow would probably not retaliate, knowing that the United States would use its second-strike SLBMs and bombers against Soviet cities.

Although Moscow also had a triad system, its ICBM leg is overwhelmingly the largest, with 59 percent of the total strategic warheads, whereas air-based systems account for 10 percent and sea-based account for 31 percent. None of the Soviet triad legs is considered very sturdy. The Soviet bomber command is thought to be unable to successfully penetrate American air defenses, and its submarine fleet is vulnerable to American attack submarines and helicopters. The SS-18 ICBM is huge. It has ten 750-kiloton MIRVs (multiple independently targetable reentry vehicles), each of which packs 600 times the explosive power of the Hiroshima bomb. The SS-18 has the throw weight, or ability to launch, a 200 ton, ten story high missile and is twice the physical, throw weight, and explosive size of an American MX ICBM, but it is considered far less accurate. Whereas an MX has a circular error probability (CEP) of 265 feet after a 6,500 mile flight, the SS-18's CEP is only 1,000 feet, which means that half of those fired would probably fall within and half beyond 1,000 feet of the target, and most would fail to destroy a hardened silo. Moscow reduced the vulnerability of its land-based forces during the 1980s by deploying MIRVed SS-24s and single-warhead SS-25s ICBMs which are much smaller than the SS-18 and can be mounted and launched from tractor trailers and railroad cars.

Yet, Russia's nuclear forces remain much more vulnerable than Washington's. In a war, Moscow might feel compelled "to either use or lose" its entire system, particularly its most vulnerable ICBM force. However, Moscow has ruled out a first-strike, because it is deterred by America's vast second-strike capability. The Soviet Union claimed it would only use nuclear weapons if the United States employed its flexible response strategy of gradually moving up the nuclear ladder from tactical to regional to strategic. Once the United States exploded the first nuclear bomb, even if it was tactical, Moscow would respond with a massive retaliation or full-fledged nuclear war against the United States. Although Moscow hopes to deter an American flexible response strategy, it may encourage an American massive retaliation if war breaks out in Europe.

Several technical factors further deter an ICBM first strike by either side. One is the probability that missiles flying over the Arctic would be thrown off course by the magnetic North Pole. Also, even if the ICBMs are able to fly directly to their targets, the explosion of one bomb would throw out an immense *electromagnetic pulse* (EMG) that would knock all other incoming missiles off course and might well destroy them in flight. Building thousands of dummy silos while camouflaging the real ones can make accurate first-strike targeting nearly impossible. Electronic countermeasures can jam the sensitive guidance systems of the incoming missiles and throw them off course. Finally, both sides have already hardened their missile silos to survive an impact of 2,000 pounds of explosives per square inch.

Calculations of the nuclear balance and appropriate strategies were complicated by the development of multiple warheads or MIRVs, during the 1970s and the Reagan administration's *strategic defense initiative* (SDI), or Star Wars, during the 1980s. Of America's strategic nuclear force, a Minuteman III carries three MIRVs, a D-5 Trident submarine SLBM carrier eight MIRVs, and a MX (Peace keeper) missile carries ten MIRVs. The Soviets have a similar MIRV system. MIRVs simultaneously weakened American and strengthened Soviet deterrence. The more Moscow MIRVed its ICBMs and SLBMs, the greater the chance that enough nuclear forces would survive an American first strike to retaliate against American cities. Knowing this, Washington would hesitate before launching a first strike, even at the tactical level. Thus, America's vast nuclear arsenal might not deter a conventional Soviet attack on the West.

America's submarine fleet is particularly formidable. One submarine equipped with 20 MIRVed D-5 Trident SLBMs could devastate more than 200 targets across Russia. The D-5 SLBM can be used as both first-strike and second-strike weapons. It is as accurate as an ICBM and far less vulnerable to an enemy attack. Yet, it does have its drawbacks. A Trident submarine's wake, even deep underwater, can be detected by satellites and its engine noises picked up by listening devices. In wartime, communications between the commander in chief and the submarine fleet would be tenuous at best, which is why submarine commanders are given the discretion, or *permissive action link* (PAL), to fire their SLBMs without a direct command under certain circumstances.

Although the number of nuclear warheads increased steadily until the late 1980s, their destructive power has been decreasing since the 1960s. In 1988 America's total warhead destructive power was only 25 percent of its 1960 level. Moscow's destructive power has also declined, although not as dramatically. Increased accuracy has negated the need for immense payloads. Now that both American and Russian missiles theoretically can strike within 100 yards of their target, they no longer need to be equipped with enough megatons of explosives to devastate everything within twenty or so miles. Another reason is the development of conventional weapons that have as much destructive power as small nuclear bombs but without the radioactive fallout, thus rendering the latter obsolete.

From MAD to NUT

In 1980 Ronald Reagan won the presidency, in part because of his claim that there was a nuclear *window of vulnerability* with the Soviet Union and his promise to revive American military power that would include regaining nuclear superiority over the Soviet Union and the ability to win a nuclear war. Despite Reagan's claims, there was no more a window of vulnerability in 1980 than there was a missile gap in 1960. Although the Soviets had a greater first-strike capability in ICBM missiles and warheads, or more *equivalent megatons* (EMT) of explosives, this advantage was more than offset by the greater accuracy or *hard-target kill* (HTK) capability of American ICBMs and its second strike superiority in SLBMs, bombers, and cruise missiles. By placing its ICBMs in superhardened sites, America's land-based missiles were relatively protected, which helped deter a Soviet first strike upon them. Also, only 20 percent of America's nuclear bombs were atop land-based ICBMs, whereas ICBMs made up 70 percent of the total Soviet nuclear forces. The Soviet Union thus was much more vulnerable to a first strike.

The idea of winning a nuclear war, known as the *nuclear utilization theory* (NUT), was diametrically opposed to MAD, whose premise was that there would be only losers in a nuclear exchange. Those who advocated NUT claimed that increasing America's ability to win a war strengthened deterrence and thus lessened the actual chance of war. MAD advocates countered by arguing that the opposite would occur, that in a crisis the White House would be more inclined to pull the nuclear trigger than retreat from the brink. Henry Kissinger dismissed NUT by pointing out: "What in the name of God is strategic superiority.   .   .   . What can you do with it?"

In 1983 President Reagan announced his goal of creating a space-based antimissile system, which he claimed would shield the United States from a Soviet attack and make "nuclear weapons impotent and obsolete." A Reagan administration television commercial promoting SDI had a little girl's voice describing a child's drawing of the world, in which Soviet missiles were being exploded high in space while Americans with smiling faces survived below.

The initial SDI scheme would have involved at least three different ballistic missile defense (BMD) layers of satellites, placed between the Soviet Union and the United States and a fourth stationed on ground in the United States. The first defense layer would be parked in space directly above the Soviet ICBM silos to destroy as many as possible in their relatively slow-moving, easily tracked "boost phase," before the MIRVs are released in space. Another layer would counter the busing phase, in which the cone releases the MIRVs along with such decoys as metal flakes and infrared aerosols to reflect laser beams. A third layer would counter the mid-course phase, in which the MIRVs disperse toward their separate targets and their speeds reach the highest levels. The ground-based fourth layer would target those remaining missiles in their terminal phase, when they had reentered the atmosphere. Each layer would fire a barrage of lasers or particle beams at the incoming ICBMs.

Reagan's scheme was attacked from several directions. SDI was seen by many experts and Moscow as the most destabilizing system yet devised. The Soviets argued that SDI would give the United States an overwhelming first-strike advantage. In a crisis Washington could launch an overwhelming first strike against Soviet ICBMs, SLBMs, bombers, and command and control centers, and then use SDI to destroy any remaining missiles that Moscow launched in retaliation. SDI could be used for offensive as well as defense purposes, destroying Soviet satellites and even radar and communications facilities on the ground. Moscow threatened to counter SDI by building thousands more ICBMs in superhardened bunkers that could withstand an American first strike and overwhelm the SDI system. Or the Soviets could avoid the expense of building more missiles by simply putting hundreds of decoys in their existing ICBMs. Then the SDI satellites would be overwhelmed by having to fire at hundreds of targets, only a fraction of which were actual nuclear warheads. A final Soviet option was to deploy antisatellite (ASAT) weapons, park them in space beside SDI, and detonate them before launching a first strike. It would have cost the Soviet Union far less to neutralize or overwhelm SDI than it would have cost the United States to build it. The closer the United States got to deploying SDI, the more incentive the Soviets would have to strike first. Moscow also stepped up its own SDI research.

In addition to this argument, American critics pointed out that SDI would cost at least $500 billion and possibly $1 trillion, consuming scarce resources that were desparately needed for investment elsewhere in the economy. SDI would violate both the 1968 Weapons in Outer Space and 1972 Antiballistic Missile Treaty. Most scientists, including the U.S. Office of Technology Assessment, argued that the technological obstacles to SDI were insurmountable; SDI would require the ability of a bullet to hit another bullet traveling as fast as 30,000 miles per hour. Furthermore, there was no means of testing it if it should become operational, and it would have to work perfectly the first time. It would take only 30 minutes for an ICBM fired from Siberia to run the SDI gauntlet and obliterate New York. Also, an operational system could be easily destroyed by Soviet ASAT weapons or overwhelmed by decoys. Even if it worked, the space shield against an ICBM attack would not protect the United States against an attack by SLBMs, cruise missiles, or bombers. Finally, America's allies complained that the scheme would protect the United States, while they would remain vulnerable to an attack. Thus SDI would spark an endless nuclear arms race that would deepen tensions, economically weaken both sides, increase the chance for war, and finally, fail to protect the United States from a devastating nuclear attack.[13]

By 1993 the "modest downpayment on the future" that Reagan had promised for SDI, had cost American taxpayers more than $40 billion and some of the country's best scientists, technicians, and laboratories, while the program remained largely in the theoretical stage. Reagan's original $500 billion scheme for protecting population centers had been rejected as unfeasible and the goals were shifted to protecting ICBM sites. SDI advocates shifted from the layered defense system to a *brilliant pebbles* scheme involving thousands of small nonnuclear satellites in orbit that would ram incoming missiles. Opponents argued that this less ambitious and expensive SDI scheme would fail just as grossly as the layered defense in destroying incoming missiles.

In early 1993 there were several revelations that even the modest achievements claimed by the Pentagon for SDI were untrue. In March, SDI official Eldric Saucier confirmed the critics worst fears about Star Wars when he accused the program of "systematic illegality, gross mismanagement and waste, abuse of power and the substitution of political science for the scientific method." He admitted that the SDI leaders faked the "successful" tests and grossly underestimated costs, even though they knew that the project would never be successful no matter how much was spent. SDI's purpose came to be one that would "keep the research and development money flowing" regardless of how SDI adversely affected America's well-being. MIT physicist Theodore Postol also stated that SDI claims have "proven to be false and made without technical or scientific merit." Another SDI scientist, Elliot Kennel, admitted that by 1987 those on the project realized that despite their efforts to achieve "Reagan's vision of an impenetrable space shield," they had failed. On May 13, 1993, the Clinton administration announced that it had ended the SDI program and instead asked Congress for $3.8 billion in research funds for a ground-based antimissile system.

Other weapons systems were debated during this time, although none was as controversial as SDI. The less vulnerable one's nuclear force, the greater its deterrent value. During the late 1970s and into the 1980s, Washington debated whether to mount MX ICBMs on tracks and move each one among as many as twenty different silos. The plan would have cost more than $150 billion and a chunk of the American West as large as Connecticut in which to base it. Although many in Congress and across America's political spectrum wanted to cancel the MX program altogether as wasteful and unnecessary, the Reagan administration ruled that it would drop the mobile-basing scheme and simply replace the older but highly accurate Minutemen ICBMs in their hardened silos with the newer MXs and use the MX as a bargaining chip in negotiations with Moscow.

Eventually it was hoped to replace the MX with a small mobile ICBM (*SICBM*), or midgetman, which would not require the mobile MX's vast and expensive tracking system. In fact, SICBMs could be placed in trucks and wheeled around the nation's interstates making it impossible for the Soviets to ever know where they were. The SICBM did have some drawbacks. Each missile had only one warhead, so it was necessary to deploy ten times as many to give the same punch as one MX. The Midgetman's small size, accuracy, explosive power, and mobility were politically costly. In 1990 the Bush administration dropped the Midgetman plan as too expensive and disquieting for a public that finds the interstate highway system dangerous enough without it being used to hide ICBMs.

NUCLEAR ARMS CONTROL

Nuclear Proliferation Control

Vertical proliferation occurs when one country diversifies its type and increases its number of nuclear weapons, such as has occurred between the United States and Soviet Union. Horizontal proliferation occurs when new countries acquire nuclear weapons. Regardless of who owns them, the possession of nuclear weapons has clear benefits and costs. Nuclear weapons can bring a country more prestige, allies, power over others, independence, and security from attack. They can also suck up scarce resources and undermine economic development, spark one's adversaries to get or increase their own nuclear weapons, and make the owner a nuclear target in the event of war.

Until the Soviet Union's breakup, there were six official nuclear powers—the United States, which exploded its first atomic weapon in 1945; the Soviet Union in 1949; Britain in 1952; France in 1960; China in 1964; and India in 1974. In 1991 the Soviet Union had 27,300 nuclear weapons, the United States 19,000, China 415, Britain 200, France 525, and India from 0–20. In addition to Russia, three other countries with nuclear weapons emerged with the Soviet Union's breakup—Ukraine with 1,650 nuclear weapons, Kazakhstan with 1,400, and Belarus with 72. On May 23, 1992, those three countries signed a treaty with Moscow and Washington, in which they agreed to either destroy or surrender their nuclear weapons to Russia.

In addition to these official nuclear powers, there is evidence that Israel and South Africa have long cooperated on the development of nuclear weapons and may have tested such a weapon in 1977. Israel is said to have an arsenal of between 100 to 200 nuclear weapons, and South Africa is thought to have 10 to 20. In March 1993 South Africa announced that it had first started to develop nuclear weapons in 1974 and eventually deployed six, but had destroyed them in 1989. Other countries, such as North Korea, Taiwan, Argentina, Libya, South Korea, Iran, Pakistan, Algeria, and Iraq have attempted to create nuclear weapons.[14]

Although it would take decades for Washington and Moscow to agree to cap their own nuclear arms race, by the 1960s they had reached a firm consensus that they wanted to limit the proliferation of nuclear weapons among other states. Neither side wanted to see unstable countries lead by messianic and irrational leaders armed with nuclear weapons. Even worse than the fear that someone like Libya's President Qadhafi, Iraq's President Hussein, or North Korea's Kim Il Sung, would have access to the nuclear trigger, was the fear that terrorist groups could acquire nuclear weapons.[15]

Not everyone agrees that nuclear proliferation is necessarily bad. Some argue that "the spread of nuclear weapons is something that we have worried too much about and tried too hard to stop .   .   . the measured spread of nuclear weapons is more to be welcomed than feared."[16] The argument is: if nuclear deterrence can work for the superpowers, why not for everyone else, including the Third World?

Washington and Moscow sponsored and guided the negotiations for the *Nuclear Nonproliferation Treaty* (NPT), which was signed in 1968. Signatories to this treaty pledged: "not to receive the transfer from any transferor whatsoever of nuclear weapons or other nuclear explosive devices directly, or indirectly; not to manufacture or otherwise acquire nuclear weapons or other nuclear explosive devices; and not to seek or receive any assistance in the manufacture of nuclear weapons or other nuclear explosive devices." The *International Atomic Energy Agency* (IAEA) is empowered to regulate the treaty by inspecting nuclear energy and other facilities to ensure they are not being used to create nuclear weapons. To date, all of the known nuclear powers have signed it, and none of the thirty non-signatories have publicly violated the treaty. By 1993, 153 countries had signed the NPT. Unfortunately, some of holdouts include those most capable of producing nuclear weapons: Argentina, Brazil, India, Israel, Pakistan, Chile, and South Africa.

In addition to the NPT, the 1959 Antarctic Treaty, the 1967 Outer Space Treaty, the 1967 Treaty for the Prohibition of Nuclear Weapons in Latin America, the 1971 Seabed Arms Control Treaty, and the 1985 South Pacific Nuclear Weapons Treaty limited nuclear weapons in those regions. Washington attempted to strengthen NPT by founding the Nuclear Suppliers' Group in 1975, which regulated the export of nuclear technology and materials. This was followed in 1978 by the passage of the Nuclear Nonproliferation Act, which authorizes the White House to retaliate against any nuclear transfers that violate the NPT or Nuclear Suppliers' Group.

Although the NPT has clearly slowed proliferation, it has not stopped it. As Iraq's nuclear weapons program of the 1980s proved, there are ways in which states that are determined to develop nuclear weapons can bypass the NPT. There are more than 850 nuclear power plants in more than 60 countries. Running a nuclear plant and dealing with its plutonium by-product provides some of the essential expertise and raw materials necessary to build a nuclear bomb. The rest can be obtained from illegal imports of technicians, parts, and plans from advanced nuclear powers. With the Soviet Union's breakup and recent nuclear treaties reducing the Commonwealth of Independent State's nuclear weapons and facilities, it is feared that thousands of unemployed nuclear experts may sell their services abroad.

On March 12, 1993, North Korea gave the required three month notice that it was withdrawing from the NPT. Pyongyang signed the NPT in 1985, but did not begin to allow the required inspections until May 1992, and then refused to permit the IAEA to inspect suspected nuclear weapons laboratories. North Korea's action reversed several years of reduced tensions on the Korean peninsula and in northeast Asia. If North Korea does deploy nuclear weapons, South Korea and perhaps even Japan will feel compelled to follow suit, making the region even more volatile. Washington's threats to use the Security Council to force North Korea to comply with the NPT were blocked by China's veto threat. The crisis was partially defused in June 1993 when North Korea agreed to remain in the treaty, although it continued to deny the IAEA entrance to suspected nuclear bomb-making facilities. The stand-off and North Korea's nuclear development continues.

Between the Superpowers

Throughout the Cold War, most leaders have clearly recognized the horrors of nuclear war. As President Kennedy put it in 1961: "Today, every inhabitant of this planet must contemplate the day when this planet may no longer be habitable. Every man, women, and child lives under a nuclear sword of Damocles, hanging by the slenderest of threads, capable of being cut at any moment by accident or miscalculation or madness . . . The mere existence of modern weapons—ten million times more powerful than any that the world has ever seen, and only minutes away from any target on earth—is a source of horror, and discord and distrust . . . in a spiraling arms race, a nation's security may well be shrinking even as its arms increase." A year later Soviet Premier Nikita Khrushchev declared that after a nuclear war "the survivors would envy the dead."

By the 1960s nuclear parity and MAD gave Washington and Moscow strong incentives to negotiate some limits to the nuclear arms race. The object was not to eliminate nuclear weapons but to achieve a stable nuclear balance. Ideally, nuclear deterrence would be based solely on each side enjoying a limited number of invulnerable second-strike weapons. The worst case would be if both sides had only first-strike weapons, the equivalent of each holding a revolver to the head of the other. In any crisis the impulse would be to either fire first or die.

There have been several treaties affecting nuclear testing. The most important was the multilateral 1963 Nuclear Test Ban Treaty, which prohibited atmospheric, underwater, and outer space, but not underground testing. The bilateral 1974 Threshold Nuclear Test Ban treaty prohibited underground tests of bombs with explosive yields greater than 150 kilotons, and the 1976 Peaceful Nuclear Explosions Treaty outlawed explosions greater than 150 kilotons for peaceful purposes like mining or excavation. The 1990 Underground Testing Verification Treaty specified the means for verifying compliance with the 1974 and 1976 treaties.

During the 1970s, Washington and Moscow signed two Strategic Arms Limitation Treaties (SALT), which attempted to cap the expansion of destabilizing first-strike weapons while securing second-strike forces. Negotiations for the 1972 SALT I Treaty began in 1969. SALT I included two elements. First, the superpowers agreed to restrict any antiballistic missiles systems to one protecting their respective capitals and one elsewhere. Second, the treaty restricted the growth in number of ICBM and SLBM launchers for five years while allowing their modernization. The Soviets were allowed to have 1,408 ICBMs and 950 SLBMs and the Americans 1,000 ICBMs and 710 SLBMs. The negotiators reasoned that the Soviet advantage in the numbers was offset by the American lead in bombers (450 U.S. to 150 U.S.S.R) and greater number of MIRVed ICBMs.

The 1979 SALT II Treaty was more comprehensive. The superpowers agreed to limit the combined number of ICBM launchers, SLBM launchers, heavy bombers, and ASBMs (air-to-surface ballistic missiles with ranges of more than 600 kilometers) to 2,250 launchers and 1,320 MIRVs, of which no more than 820 could be land-based on each side.

Although SALT I was ratified by both sides, Carter withdrew SALT II from the ratification process begun in the U.S. Senate following the Soviet invasion of

Table 11.1

Tactical Nuclear Weapons: Where They Stand Now

Delivery vehicle	Number deployed	Warheads per vehicle	Total stock of warheads	Number deployed	Warheads per vehicle	Total stock of warheads
LAND-BASED	**UNITED STATES**			**SOVIET UNION**		
Aircraft	1,300	1 to 3	1,800	2,560	1 to 3	3,100
	F-4's, F-16's, and F-111's, F-15's starting in 1992			*Tu-95, Tu-26, Tu-22 and Tu-16 bombers; various tactical aircraft*		
Missiles	100	1	1,282	1,331	1	3,130
	Lances			*SS-1 Scud B's; FROG-3's, -5's and -7's, and SS-21 Scarabs*		
Artillery	4,700	1	1,540	7,000	1	2,000
	155mm and 203mm guns			*152mm, 203mm and 240mm guns*		
Air defense missiles	None			3,600	n.a.	n.a.
				SA-10 and SA-5 antiaircraft missiles; antiballistic missile system at Moscow		
Land mines	None			n.a.	n.a.	n.a.
SEA-BASED	**UNITED STATES**			**SOVIET UNION**		
Attack aircraft	850	1 or 2	1,350	400	1 to 3	1,010
	A-6's, A-7's, and F/A-18's			*Tu-26's, Tu-22's, Tu-16's, Su-24's, Su-20's*		
Anti-submarine aircraft	500	1	850	330	1	350
	P-3's, S-3's, SH-3D helicopters			*Be-12's, Il-38's, Tu-142's, helicopters*		
Missiles	325	1	325	1,571	1	995
	Tomahawk cruise missiles			*Various ballistic and cruise missiles*		
Torpedoes	None			520	1	520
				Type 65's and ET-80's		
Air defense missiles	None			47	1	200
				SA-N-1's and SA-N-3's		

January 1991 figures. Many are estimates. Some weapons have both nuclear and non-nuclear roles.

n.a. = Not available.

Source: Stockholm Institute World Armaments and Disarmament Yearbook 1991

Afghanistan in December 1979. Both sides followed SALT II's tenets, despite the failure to ratify it. In order to gain even initial Senate approval for SALT II, Carter had to promise to develop the MX ICBM, which further fueled the arms race. SALT II, however, did prevent the scheduled deployment of 8,500 additional weapons by 1985—2,500 additional ICBMs for the Soviet Union and 5,100 for the United States. Through the mid-1980s, there was an impasse on the nuclear arms talks.

It was not until after Mikhail Gorbachev took power in the Soviet Union in 1985 that this impasse on nuclear weapons, conventional forces, and several other important issues was broken. The 1987 *Intermediate Range Nuclear Force Treaty* (INF) was a turning point in arms control. For the first time, the superpowers were actually required to destroy certain weapons rather than just limit their expansion. The superpowers agreed to eliminate all missiles in Europe having ranges between 300 and 3,400 miles, which required: "the United States to destroy 859 missiles: 429 medium range Pershing 2S and ground launched cruise missiles deployed in Europe, 260 medium range missiles not employed, and 170 Pershing 1A shorter range missiles stockpiled in the United States. The Soviet Union is required to destroy 1,752 missiles: 470 medium range SS-20 and SS-4 missiles deployed, 356 medium range missiles not deployed, 387 deployed shorter range missiles and 539 of those weapons in storage."[17] Also ground-breaking were the verification procedures which allowed each side to conduct on-site inspections of the other.

The *Strategic Arms Reduction Talks* (START) had begun as early as 1982. The Reagan administration called for cutting the number of warheads from 7,500 to 5,000, of which no more than half could be on ICBMs. After nine years of sporadic negotiations, the START I treaty was finally signed on July 31, 1991, in which both sides agreed to reduce their land, sea, and air-based ICBM's to 1,600 and their warheads to 6,000. Because the treaty allows both sides to increase and modernize other types of warheads, Soviet missiles will be reduced overall from 10,841 to 8,040 and American warheads from 12,081 to 10,395. The treaty allowed for twelve types of on-site inspections of both missile sites and production facilities.

START was followed by a series of unilateral announcements, in which both sides reduced their nuclear forces. In September 1991, President George Bush announced that he would cancel the 24-hour alert for long-range bombers, remove nuclear weapons from many navy ships, halt the planned deployment of MX ICBMs on railway cars, and called for even greater bilateral cuts in nuclear weapons. President Boris Yeltsin announced in January 1992 that Russia no longer considered the United States its enemy and would no longer target American cities. Four days later, Bush responded by announcing that the United States would cease production of the B-2 bomber, the Midgetman mobile nuclear missile, advanced cruise missiles, and Trident SLBM warheads. Hours later, Yeltsin countered by calling for cuts of up to 2,500 warheads for each superpower and the elimination of all strategic nuclear weapons by 2,000, and announced he would cut Russian military spending to one-seventh of the previous year's budget and would decrease the Russian army by half. At this point the momentum of arms reductions broke down as Bush refused to reduce SLBMs, in which the United States had an advantage, below one-third of the then current level and called for the elimination of ICBM MIRVs, in which the Russians were superior. But at the June 1992 Washington summit, Bush and Yeltsin agreed to reduce their combined warheads from 16,000 to 6,527 by 2003, of which they would be allowed roughly 3,250 each, and eventually eliminate all of their land-based MIRVs. This agreement eliminated "the most threatening Russian missiles while allowing the United States to retain its most advanced missiles." Although by eliminating the most destabilizing weapons, the United States clearly got the best deal, Russia and all of humanity benefit.[18]

Although START I was to have lasted 15 years, a START II agreement was signed in January 1993, which incorporated many of the unilateral announcements and additional bilateral agreements. Under START II, by 2003 the United States and Russia would cut their nuclear forces to 3,500 and 2,997, respectively. Moscow and Washington agreed to eliminate all MIRVed ICBMs. Each side would retain about 500 single-warhead ICBMs. The United States would keep 1,728 SLBMs and 1,272 cruise missiles, and Russia would keep 1,744 SLBMs and 752 cruise missiles. Whereas the previous nuclear treaties were balanced, START II overwhelmingly favored the United States. Russia had to eliminate the backbone of its ICBM forces, while the United States retained its superior SLBM and cruise missile forces.

The arms race appears to have been finally stopped and reversed. Until the late 1980s, the arms control agreements only stopped weapons systems that had become obsolete or were simply developed as bargaining chips. Yet there are still important areas of disagreement. Russia, the nonaligned movement, and many other countries have repeatedly called for a comprehensive test ban (CTB) treaty. The Bush administration and foreign allies rejected a CTB, arguing that nuclear testing is vital for ensuring the safety, effectiveness, and thus deterrent value of nuclear weapons. Others counter that actually exploding nuclear weapons is no longer necessary, now that computers can evaluate their ability. In 1993 President Clinton declared a testing moratorium contingent on the reciprocation of the other nuclear powers.

LESSONS OF THE NUCLEAR ARMS RACE

Compellence and Deterrence

Was the nuclear arms race necessary? Could deterrence, assuming that either side ever had any intention of attacking the other, have been purchased at a much lower cost in financial, technological, and human resources? Did the nuclear arms race make the superpowers and the world more or less secure? Was a Third World War prevented because of or despite the nuclear arms race?

The United States did use nuclear weapons to compel other states to change their behavior. By one authoritative account, America's nuclear strategy may have prevented at least ten crises from escalating into war. In his book, *Nuclear Blackmail and Nuclear Balance,* Richard Betts carefully examined four crises in which Washington's nuclear forces either probably prevented war or protected American interests—Cuba (1962), Berlin (1948), Korea (1953), and Taiwan (1955), and were of uncertain value in the another six crises—Berlin (1958–1961), Middle East (1973), Suez Canal (1956), Lebannon (1958), Taiwan (1958), and the Persian Gulf (1980).[19] But Washington's power to compel others diminished steadily as the Soviet Union achieved parity.

And what about nuclear deterrence? Although deterrence is supposed to prevent an attack, we can never truly know whether deterrence has actually worked. It could be that the other side never intended an attack in the first place regardless of how much or how little military power its opponent held. Nuclear deterrence, like power, is more about psychology than weapons. It also involved paradoxes—Moscow and Washington safeguarded peace by preparing for war, expanded their number and type of weapons while negotiating arms-control treaties.

If deterrence worked at all, it did so because the forces of both sides were relatively invulnerable to an enemy first strike, and thus retained enough power to wipe out the other. The Americans and Soviets have protected their second-strike capabilities by several means. One is through sheer numbers—simply producing so many ICBMs, SLBMs, and bombers that enough would survive even the luckiest first strike to devastate the enemy. Dispersing those weapons as widely as possible increases their invulnerability, as does protecting ICBMs in hardened sites, keeping SLBMs underwater and bombers in the air, and both constantly on the move and hidden. Two other policies might strengthen one's second-strike capability at the expense of creating more tension and the chance of war between the superpowers. Antiballistic missile systems (ABM) like SDI, although forbidden by the 1972 ABM Treaty, might further protect nuclear weapons but could be used in conjunction with that side's first strike against the enemy. Likewise, a launch-on-warning system, in which American missiles automatically fire if there is an attack on the United States, increases the odds that America's missile force will survive, but would devastate the other side even if the initial attack was caused by an accident or an unstable person.

Nuclear weapons have become useless for actually fighting wars or for even preventing a war with a nonnuclear country. When the United States dropped atomic bombs on Hiroshima and Nagasaki, no one understood the grevious harm that radiation posed humanity. As an understanding of their vast and continual destructiveness grew, more governments and people became convinced that nuclear weapons should never be used. The nuclear standoff and international morality have deterred the other nuclear powers from using their weapons even against nonnuclear countries. The Americans in Vietnam (1964–1972), the Soviets in Afghanistan (1979–1989), the Chinese against Vietnam (1979), and the British against Argentina (1982) never even threatened to use, let alone used, nuclear weapons to win those wars.

Nuclear weapons may well diminish rather than enhance a nation's power. Clearly, nuclear weapons provide the bearer with prestige. Yet the scientific, financial, and psychological costs of developing and deploying nuclear weapons are enormous. Those same resources invested properly elsewhere in a state's economy could produce far larger amounts of wealth and power. Nuclear weapons are largely very elaborate, costly, and destructive ornaments. They can be brandished but their use might well result in national suicide.

The Chances of Nuclear War

Nuclear war is the world's worst nightmare. How possible is it?

Even during the height of the Cold War, the chance of nuclear war was remote. The Cuban missile crisis was the closest the world came to a nuclear war, although the superpowers also neared the brink of war during the Berlin crises of 1948–1949 and 1959–1961. There is no evidence, however, that either power at any time considered launching a massive first strike on the other in these or other crises. Because a conventional war never occurred, neither side ever employed either a massive retaliation or flexible response strategy. In any event, the second-strike capabilities of both sides would have probably deterred a first strike.

Nuclear war, however, could have been sparked by other causes. An accidental launch caused by a computer error, a false warning of an enemy attack, the unauthorized firing by unstable people in a submarine or silo, or the attack by a third country on one of the superpowers could have caused the victim to retaliate or the other to launch a preemptive attack in anticipation of just such a retaliation. During an 18 month period between January 1979 and June 1980, America's nuclear forces received 3,703 warnings of an incoming missile attack, of which 147 were deemed serious enough to cause an alert and evaluation. There have been at least 32 accidents involving American nuclear weapons, although none were detonated.[20]

The superpowers, however, have taken significant steps, known as fail-safe systems, to minimize these chances of war. As important as the nuclear weapons in the field, is the "command, control, communication, and intelligence" (C3I) system. Both powers have continually upgraded their C3I to avoid human and technical error. They have also strengthened the national command authority (NCA), or hierarchy from the president on down, which has the power to authorize an attack if the leadership above is killed. Nuclear weapons can only be launched by two individuals simultaneously turning the keys to their activation. The two-key system reduces the possibility of an unstable person making an unauthorized launch.

In addition, Washington and Moscow signed several treaties strengthening their ability to communicate in a crisis. These include the 1963, 1971, and 1985 hot-line agreements, which established and strengthened direct communications between the White House and Kremlin; the nuclear accidents agreement of 1971, which reduced the chance for an accident leading to nuclear war; the 1972 high-seas agreement, which helped prevent any accident or unauthorized firing between the American and Soviet ships or submarines from escalating; the 1973 nuclear war prevention agreement, which strengthened crisis-management abilities and communication channels between them; and the 1987 Crisis Reduction Treaty, which established crisis control centers in each capital. The provisions of the 1968 Nuclear Nonproliferation Treaty have reduced the chances of nuclear weapons getting into the hands of terrorist states or groups.

Reasons for the Nuclear Arms Race

Why did the nuclear arms race last more than four decades? There were many obstacles to slowing, let alone reversing, the nuclear arms race. Each side held a mirror image of the other as aggressive, deceitful, and dedicated to achieving superiority. Neither side trusted each other and neither one was willing, until recently, to include the verification procedures in a nuclear agreement that could have strengthened that trust.

There were good reasons for some of that distrust. Profound ideological differences and the aggressive actions and statements of both sides were the most important reasons for the arms race. Moscow's assertion that it was leading a global Communist revolution; its subjugation of East Europe; invasions of Czechoslovakia, Hungary, and Afghanistan; and involvement in dozens of other countries were certainly aggressive by any measure and ultimately a threat to American security. Washington's assertion of a containment policy starting in 1947; its nuclear arms buildup; creation of NATO; military intervention in Korea, Vietnam, Grenada, and Panama; and indirect manipulation of politics in scores of other countries certainly seemed threatening to the Soviet Union.

But domestic politics were also important in fueling the nuclear arms race. As the budget, personnel, institutions, and responsibilities of each side's military industrial complex expanded, it acquired increasing political power to demand and receive even more resources. All those involved in military policies and industries—bureaucrats, politicians, contractors, labor unions, scientists—had a vested interest in continually gaining more money and responsibilities. Once a weapons program was begun, it proved almost impossible to kill. Many weapons began as "bargaining chips" but, often for political rather than strategic reasons, soon became "vital" to national security. On average it took a decade to build a new weapons system from the first blueprints and models, through the testing, to the finished product. Canceling a project would put people out of work and threaten the reelection of the congresspeople from those districts. Politics often resulted in weapons systems being built even if they were obsolete or unworkable. For example, the Carter administration canceled the B-1 bomber, arguing that it was a waste of money that could be better spent elsewhere, because existing B-52s armed with cruise missiles could do the job just as effectively. The Reagan administration revived the B-1 project, which eventually cost American taxpayers $40 billion, and accelerated the B-2 Stealth bomber, which has cost about $35 billion so far. Although the first B-52s became operational in 1954 and the type is now 40 years old, it remains a superior bomber to the newer B-1 and B-2 bombers that appeared during the 1980s and 1990s. There have been eight different B-52 versions, each a large improvement over the previous. The B-1 bomber fleet has been grounded indefinitely because of technical problems, and the B-2 bomber is experiencing similar difficulties. The Reagan administration claimed that it would enhance American security by completing the B-1 and B-2 bombers. Critics argue that American security was actually undermined because those bombers consumed vast amounts of scarce financial, human, political, and scientific resources that could have been much more profitably employed elsewhere. Moscow, meanwhile, felt compelled to counter the B-1 and B-2 with its own new weapons systems, and the nuclear arms race accelerated.

Then the arms talks themselves often bogged down over several issues. Verification was one of the biggest obstacles to nuclear arms control. Each side was afraid that the other would cheat, yet each side resisted opening up its own military industrial complex to a comprehensive inspection system that would minimize the chance to cheat. Even with verification agreements, the process becomes ever more difficult in an age of cruise missiles, which are highly mobile, only 20 feet long, relatively inexpensive, able to carry both nuclear and conventional warheads, and have a range of thousands of miles. The 1987 INF treaty was the first to allow on-site inspections, and subsequent treaties have included that provision.

Until recently, the superpowers disagreed on how to calculate the nuclear balance. Moscow insisted that British, French, and Chinese nuclear missiles be included with those of the United States in negotiating any limitations or actual reductions. Washington said that only the superpower missile forces should be negotiated. During the 1980s, they agreed to concentrate on their own forces.

Paradoxically, arms control talks seemed to quicken the arms race, as each side tried to develop duplicate and sometimes triplicate weapons systems that it then used as bargaining chips at the negotiating table. As a result, each side scrambled to build ever more advanced systems that would either match or surpass the others side.

Breaking the Impasses for Arms Control

How can these walls of distrust be dismantled? Charles Osgood advocates a policy he calls *Gradual and Reciprocated Initiatives in Tension-Reduction* (GRITS), in which one side makes a concession, such as not building or even scrapping a weapons system, and then encourages the other side to reciprocate. If this occurs, the first side then makes another more significant concession, which ideally will be reciprocated by the other side. If the other side continues to build up its forces, the first side should only match and never exceed the other's increases. Thus, an arms buildup can be replaced by an arms build down. President Gorbachev initiated such a GRIT with President Bush in 1991, and it was continued by President Yeltsin after the Soviet Union collapsed. The nuclear arms buildup has been replaced with its build down.

Nuclear arms negotiations over relatively limited restrictions on slowing or capping increases in weapon numbers and types, let alone decreases, took years and sometimes decades. The limited steps of unilateral disarmament over the last few years have been much more effective and faster than negotiations in producing deep, balanced, and reciprocal cuts in numbers and weapons systems. However, unilateral steps were not always reciprocated. Between August 1985 and February 1987, Gorbachev unilaterally stopped all Soviet nuclear tests and asked Reagan to reciprocate. Reagan refused and Gorbachev eventually resumed testing.

There are several other ways in which small *confidence-building measures* could have been taken, which could have stimulated more meaningful cuts later. Over the decades, many have advocated a freeze on testing or building new weapons for a certain time period, to be resumed if the other side did not reciprocate. A more sweeping measure would be for the United States or Russia to announce that it would agree to reduce its overall military budget to one percent of GNP within five years if the other great powers would reciprocate.

Denuclearizing regions is also seen as a good way to build confidence and achieve more significant cuts or eliminations elsewhere. Washington and Moscow negotiated agreements banning the introduction of nuclear weapons into Antarctica, space, and the moon. Although neither side may have ever had any reason to employ nuclear weapons in those realms, the successful negotiation of those agreements gave both sides the momentum to confront more contentious issues. While the United States initially opposed the nuclear-free zone treaties of Latin America in 1967 and the South Pacific in 1985, those zones did reinforce arms control efforts elsewhere.

The Value of Nuclear Weapons

As the atomic bombing of Hiroshima and Nagasaki proved, atomic bombs can win wars and save lives in the long run. If that is true, then why have Washington, Moscow, and the other nuclear powers not used nuclear weapons in their respective wars?

Over the past 50 years, the military value of nuclear weapons declined as their numbers, destructive power, and possessors increased. The Reagan administration initially embraced the nuclear utilization theory (NUT) that the United States could successfully wage and win a nuclear war and should build up its nuclear forces and Star Wars to do so. The supporters of the theory argued that by trying to protect your population and nuclear weapons from attack, you enhance deterrence. They maintain that theoretically a nuclear war can be won quickly by targeting the other side's leadership and its command, control, communications, and intelligence. Thus, in a crisis the supporters of the theory would favor a "launch under attack" (LUA) to ensure the ability to retaliate or even a "launch on warning" (LOW) of an imminent attack to preempt it.

Most people (including eventually the Reagan administration), however, agree that nuclear war could only result in mutually assured destruction (MAD) and thus can never be won and should never be fought. Those who believe a nuclear war can be won and then prepare to do so, simply make a nuclear holocaust more likely. The risks of sparking a nuclear war far exceed any benefits. In a full nuclear exchange between the United States, more than 200 million American and Russians would die immediately, or shortly thereafter. The resulting nuclear winter, ozone-layer depletion, radioactive fall out, collapse of the global and regional economies, and worldwide failure of crops, would kill billions of people in the following months, until the human race itself might well become extinct. A LUA or LOW strategy exacerbates the "use 'em or lose 'em" mentality that makes nuclear war more likely. Furthermore, what if the warning of an impending attack is wrong. Instead, the supporters of MAD advocate a "launch upon impact" (LUI) strategy in which the United States would retaliate only if Russian missiles actually began exploding across the country. The MADs reason that the United States second-strike force of SLBMs, cruise missiles, and bombers would survive largely intact and thus deter the Russians from even considering a first strike.

In fact, America's nuclear war fighting plan (SIOP) contains elements of NUT and MAD. Supporters of NUT applaud the flexible response strategy, which involves fighting a nuclear war through first strikes at each nuclear level. America's nuclear forces, however, are heavily weighted in favor of second-strike weapons, which supporters of MAD favor, because they are the essence of deterrence. In an all-out war, the Pentagon has targeted not only Russia's nuclear forces but also 65 percent of its industrial power and 35 percent of its population. SIOP thus contains both counterforce and countervalue targets.

Most analysts agree that at some point acquiring more nuclear weapons no longer enhances that country's military or political power. With the ability to destroy the world twenty or so times over (or "to make the rubble bounce," as Churchill put it), the military value of nuclear weapons was no doubt exceeded long ago. Although nuclear weapons can be used to compel or deter others, because they are so destructive, nuclear weapons are only valuable when they are used to threaten others. If nuclear weapons are actually used as weapons, they have failed to serve their purpose. It is much more difficult to determine when building more nuclear weapons no longer increases that country's deterrent or political power.

Eventually, the nuclear powers will reduce their weapons to a *minimum deterrence,* which maintains strategic parity. What is the minimal level of nuclear forces that would maintain deterrence yet reduce the chances for accidental war or a nuclear winter? Could minimum deterrence rest on, say, one American and one Russian nuclear submarine cruising a vast range of deep ocean into which the other sides' ships and submarines are not allowed? As we have seen, one submarine with MIRVed SLBMs can destroy more than 200 targets. Most analysts would answer "no" and would argue that a stable deterrence requires far more second-strike weapons with anywhere from 200 to 1,000 warheads.

Would the world be better off without nuclear weapons? Ideally, yes of course. But nuclear power is available and increasing numbers of governments are able to use it. Whether nuclear power deters war and promotes stability or encourages war and promotes instability depends upon who controls it. Complete nuclear disarmament would involve all states agreeing not only to give up all nuclear-weapons technology but also to submit to extensive inspection of their facilities and budgets. Knowledge, however, cannot be dismantled. A nuclear disarmament treaty would put hundreds of thousands of scientists and technicians out of work. A global fear would be that even with a disarmament treaty and inspection regime, somehow, somewhere, a terrorist group or government is feverishly attempting to put together a nuclear bomb. It seems humanity must exist under the nuclear shadow for the foreseeable future.

Ultimately, there is no guarantee that deterrence, controls, or rationality will continue to work. Luck may well have been the most important factor in so far sparing the world from nuclear warfare. As long as there are nuclear weapons on earth, there is a chance they will be used either from cold, rational choice, frenzied fear, or unforeseen accident.

STUDY QUESTIONS

1. What are the effects of 1-megaton, 10-megaton, and 100-megaton nuclear explosions on a city?

2. What is nuclear winter and nuclear autumn?

3. How many nuclear weapons have been tested to date? What have been the human effects of nuclear testing?

4. What is deterrence? What role do capability and credibility play in effective deterrence?

5. Analyze the phases of America's nuclear war fighting strategy from 1945 through today.

6. Analyze the different force structures of the United States and Soviet Union. What were the strengths and weaknesses of each?

7. What are the arguments for and against MAD and NUT?

8. What was the Strategic Defense Initiative? Why did Reagan propose it? Why was it eventually abandoned as unworkable?

9. What attempts were taken to prevent nuclear proliferation? What countries other than the United States and Russia have or might have nuclear weapons? How large are those nuclear arsenals?

10. Was the nuclear arms race necessary? Could deterrence, assuming that either side ever had any intention of attacking the other, have been purchased at a much lower cost in financial, technological, and human resources? Explain.

11. Did the nuclear arms race make the superpowers and the world more or less secure? Was a Third World War prevented because of or despite the nuclear arms race? Explain.

12. Is nuclear war still possible? If so, under what scenarios? What are some ways to make nuclear war less possible?

13. Why did the nuclear arms race last more than four decades? What are some ways in which an arms race might be halted and reversed? Did the superpowers use any of those methods?

14. What value do nuclear weapons have? Could the world ever be nuclear-free?

ENDNOTES

1. Ruth Leger Sivar, *World Military and Social Expenditures* (Washington, D.C.: World Priorities, 1991), 16.

2. John Spanier, *Games Nations Play* (New York: Holt Rinehart, and Winston, 1984), 157.

3. Ruth Leger Sivar, *World Military and Social Expenditures*, 13.

4. John Spanier, *Games Nations Play*, 157–159.

5. Harold Brown, *Thinking About National Security: Defense and Foreign Policy in a Dangerous World* (Boulder, Colo.: Westview Press, 1983), 5.

6. See U.S. Congress, *The Effects of Nuclear War* (Washington, D.C.: U. S. Government Printing Office, 1979); Arthur Katz, *Life After Nuclear War* (Cambridge, Mass.: Ballinger, 1982); Carl Sagan, "Nuclear War and Climactic Catastrophe: Some Policy Implications," *Foreign Affairs,* Winter 1983/84, 256–292.

7. Stanley Thompson and Stephen Schneider, "Nuclear Winter Reappraised," *Foreign Affairs,* vol. 64, Summer 1986, 981–1005.

8. *New York Times,* August 16, 1990, A3.

9. *The Defense Monitor,* vol. 21, no. 3, 1992, 3.

10. James Simpson, *Simpson's Contemporary Quotations* (Boston: Houghton Mifflin, 1988), 2. For an interesting argument that nuclear deterrence has not been the reason for peace between the superpowers, see John Vasquez, "The Deterrence Myth:

Nuclear Weapons and the Prevention of Nuclear War," in Charles Kegley, *The Long Postwar Peace* (New York: HarperCollins, 1991), 205–223.

11. For the leading recent studies, see Robert Jervis, Richard Lebow, and Janice Gross, *Psychology and Deterrence* (Baltimore: Johns Hopkins Press, 1985); Graham Allison, Albert Carnesale, and Joseph Nye, *Hawks, Doves, and Owls: An Agenda for Avoiding Nuclear War* (New York: Norton, 1985); Richard Betts, *Nuclear Blackmail and the Nuclear Balance* (Washington, D.C.: The Brookings Institute, 1987); Richard Smoke, *National Security and the Nuclear Dilemma: An Introduction to the American Experience* (New York: Random House, 1987); Regina Karp, ed., *Security with Nuclear Weapons? Different Perceptions of National Security* (New York: Oxford University Press, 1991); Charles Kegley and Eugene Wittkopf, eds., *The Nuclear Reader: Strategy, Weapons, War* (New York: St. Martin's Press, 1991); David Tarr, *Nuclear Deterrence and International Security: Alternative Nuclear Regimes* (New York: Longman, 1991).

12. Henry Kissinger, *The White House Years* (Boston: Little, Brown, 1979), 238.

13. See James Schlesinger, "Rhetoric and Fantasies in the Star Wars Debate," *International Security,* vol. 10, no. 1, 1985, 3-12; Harold Brown, "Is SDI Technically Feasible?" *Foreign Affairs,* vol. 64, no. 3, 435-454; Philip Boffey et al., *Claiming the Heavens: The New York Times Complete Guide to the Star Wars Debate* (New York: New York Times Books, 1988); Sanford Lakoff and Herbert York, *A Shield in Space: Technology, Politics, and the Strategic Defense Initiative* (Berkeley, University of California Press, 1989).

14. Eric Schmitt, "Despite Euphoria on Arms Control, Deterrence Remains a Potent Force," *New York Times,* July 30, 1991; David Sanger, "West Knew of North Korean Nuclear Development," *New York Times,* March 13, 1993. See also Stephen Meyer, *Nuclear Proliferation: Models of Behavior, Choice and Decision* (Chicago, University of Chicago Press, 1984); Leonard Spector, *Nuclear Ambitions: The Spread of Nuclear Weapons 1989-1990* (Boulder, Colo.: Westview Press, 1990).

15. See Alva Myrdal, *The Game of Disarmament: How the United States and Russia Run the Arms Race* (New York: Pantheon, 1976).

16. Kenneth Waltz, "The Spread of Nuclear Weapons: More May be Better," *Adelphi Papers,* no. 171, London: International Institute of Strategic Studies, 1982, 29–30.

17. Marshall Shulman, "The Superpowers: Dance of the Dinosaurs," *Foreign Affairs,* vol. 66, no. 3 Winter 1987–1988, 512.

18. Thomas Friedman, "Reducing the Russian Arms Threat," *New York Times,* June 17, 1989, A7.

19. Ibid.

20. Arthur Cox, *Russian Roulette: The Superpower Game* (New York: Time Books, 1982). See also Robert Alexrood, *The Evolution of Cooperation* (New York: Basic Books, 1984); S. Plous, "Perceptual Illusions and Military Realities: The Nuclear Arms Race," *Journal of Conflict Resolution,* vol. 29, no. 3, September 1985, 363–388; Joshua Goldstein and John Freeman, *Three-Way Street: Strategic Reciprocity in World Politics* (Chicago: University of Chicago Press, 1990); Charles Osgood, *An Alternative to War or Surrender* (Urbana, Ill.: University of Illinois Press, 1963).

The Changing Nature of War and International Relations

Key Terms and Concepts

Brinksmanship

Conference on Security and Cooperation in Europe (CSCE)

Conventional Armed Forces in Europe Treaty (CFE)

Conventional Arms Transfer Talk (CATT)

Hague Conferences

Irish Republican Army (IRA)

Low-Intensity Conflict (LIC)

Mid-Intensity Conflict (MIC)

Missile Technology Control Regime (MTCR)

Mutual and Balanced Force Reduction (MBFR)

Organization of American States (OAS)

Terrorism

If you want peace, prepare for war
(Si vis pacem, para bellum).

> *The adversaries of the world are not in conflict because they are armed. They are armed because they are in conflict and have not yet learned peaceful ways to resolve their conflicting national interests.* (Richard Nixon)

Throughout the 5,500 years of recorded history there have been more than 14,500 wars in which over 3.5 billion people have died. Wars occur an average of 94 of every 100 years.[1] Increasingly costly in lives and destruction, the wars of this century alone have killed more than 100 million people and destroyed trillions of dollars of property. Globally, one of every twenty dollars is spent on the military. In an increasingly interdependent world, the fallout from a distant conventional war is not obvious or measureable, but nonetheless exists in terms of refugees, destruction, foregone socioeconomic development, further arms races and tensions, and so on.

War has traditionally been the engine of history, bearing with it the rise and fall of great powers and power constellations. As James Shotwell points out: "War . . . has been the instrument by which most of the great facts of political national history have been established and maintained. It has played a dominant role in nearly all political crises; it has been used to achieve liberty, to secure democracy, and to attempt to make it secure against the menace of its use by other hands. The map of the world today has been largely determined on the battlefield . . . (E)ven in peace, the war system has to a large degree determined not only international relationships but the character and history of the nations themselves."[2] Or, as Frederick the Great put it more succinctly: "Diplomacy without armaments is like music without instruments."[3]

War, many argue, is natural and inevitable. Wherever there are people, there are conflicts, and many people will be prepared to assert their interests violently in those conflicts. As Hans Morgenthau put it: "Men do not fight because they have arms. They have arms because they deem it necessary to fight. Take away their arms and they will fight each other with their bare fists . . . The elimination of certain types of weapons altogether would have a bearing upon the technology of warfare . . . It is hard to see how it could influence the frequency of war."[4] Thus, if you want peace you must prepare for war. Others argue that if you prepare for war you will probably get it. This chapter will analyze war's major characteristics.

THE CHANGING NATURE OF WAR

Wars can occur between sovereign states (interstate war), between sovereign states and a nonsovereign people struggling for independence (imperial, or colonial war), and between groups within a sovereign state (civil war). But are all armed conflicts wars? The Correlates of War (COW) project at the University of Michigan, which has been studying war since 1963, uses the arbitrary threshold of 1,000 or more combat deaths to designate a war. Between 1816 and 1988, there were 181 international wars in which battle deaths exceeded 1,000.[5] By this standard, the American invasions of Grenada in 1983 and Panama were not wars. A broader definition of war obviously increases the number. By defining war as any time two or more states use armed forces violently beyond their borders, there were 269 wars involving 591 states between 1945 and 1988, of which the great powers started one-fourth of them.[6]

During the industrial era, wars have diminished as a percentage of the average number of states in the system: 1816–1848, 33 wars and 28 states; 1849–1881, 43 wars and 39 states; 1882–1914, 38 wars and 40 states; 1915–1944, 38 wars and 40 states; 1945–1988, 43 wars and 117 states. Only 20 of those 172 years were peaceful. Traditionally, aggression paid. Between 1495 and 1985, the initiators won 58.1 percent of the time, or 51.5 percent between 1495 and 1799 and 69.2 percent between 1800 and 1985. However, this upward trend was reversed in the 1980s when only 18 percent of initiators won their wars![7] Peace through strength, however, may not be a foolproof means of security. More than half or five of the nine wars involving great powers between 1815 and 1965 involved militarily weaker countries attacking stronger ones that were further building their military power.[8]

Revolutionary technological changes in weapons, communications, and transportation have greatly expanded war's destructiveness and often geographic extent. The invention of the railroad, rifle, airplane, tank, jet, and nuclear power each stimulated vast changes in how wars are fought. Mass nationalism, ideologies, communications, and transportation allows governments the ability to mobilize virtually everyone for war either as a soldier, producer, or supporter. Most countries have highly professional militaries that are prepared to fight on short notice.

Throughout the modern era, wars between the great powers have diminished in number but grown in the amount of troops and countries engaged, death, destruction, and the geographical area.[9] Seventy-five percent of all great-power wars between 1495 and 1980 occurred before 1735. Before 1800 only about 3 of 1,000 people (0.3 percent) in a country directly participated in its wars. By World War I, 1 of 7 citizens (14 percent) were direct participants in their nation's wars.[10] Only 20 percent of all countries during the past 500 years have never experienced war. Wars have become increasingly destructive. Since 1500 the world has experienced "589 wars and lost 141,901,000 . . . . So far, in the 90 years of this century, there have been four times as many war deaths as in the 400 years preceding."[11] More than eleven million people have died in wars since 1960, and the carnage mounts daily.[12] About 90 percent of those who died from war in 1990 were civilians.

There have been some clear and dramatic changes since 1945 in where wars occur, who fights them, and how they are fought. With 29 wars between 1600 and 1945, Europe had been the most war-prone region of the world up through World War II. Until the recent civil war in former Yugoslavia, there have been no international or civil wars there since then. Before 1945 the advanced industrial nations were the most belligerent both against themselves and against less-developed states; since then, no industrial states have fought one another, and they have fought only five wars in the Third World. John Gaddis described the lack of war between the great powers since 1945 as the long peace.[13] There have been other periods of relatively long peace between the great powers, such as after the Congress of Vienna (1815–1848) and the Franco-Prussian War (1871–1914). But the long peace since 1945 is different in many ways. Since 1945 most international and all civil wars have occurred within the Third World. The nature of war has also changed dramatically. Until 1945, 80 percent of wars were conventional international wars; since then 80 percent have been unconventional or low-intensity guerrilla civil wars.[14]

Why have these changes occurred? For the advanced industrial nations, the costs of war far exceed the possible benefits. As economic interdependence deepens, national and international interests increasingly mesh and war's potential destruction rises to exorbitant heights for winners and losers alike. War has become inconceivable between prosperous, democratic industrial countries. Not only have the great powers never fought since 1945, there have been no wars among the 48 richest countries.[15] Skills in managing crises so that they do not escalate into war is another reason for the long peace. Although on several occassions the superpowers went to the brink of war with each other (Berlin 1948–1949, 1961–1962; Cuba 1962), they succeeded in managing those crises. Europe was the one region where the superpowers stared eyeball to eyeball. Once Europe's two halves had been stabilized politically and economically, the superpowers largely respected the status quo. The superpowers then focused their animosities on winning the hearts, minds, and pocketbooks of the Third World, where the stakes for both were relatively low. Whether or not mutually assured destruction (MAD) of nuclear weapons was the most important constraint on war between the superpowers is debatable.[16] Superpower miltary strategies emphasize deterring rather than winning wars with each other.

UNITED STATES MILITARY POLICY

Of the two superpowers and all of the great powers, no country has been more involved in armed conflicts since 1945 than the United States. Between 1946 and 1984, the United States either directly or indirectly threatened to use force 286 times, or an average of seven times a year.[17] Although this number seems immense, Washington actually used force on relatively few occasions. Between 1945 and 1973, Washington militarily intervened only 4 times—Korea (1951–1953), Lebannon (1958), Dominican Republic (1965), and Vietnam (1961–1972)—out of the 149 situations in which American interests were threatened but Washington did not intervene.[18] These situations include 31 cases in which a communist government threatened to come to power in a country of strategic interest; 13 cases in which communists countries threatened other countries; 35 threats by communist governments to strategic regions; 8 situations of conflict on the frontiers of communist states; 9 conflicts within communist states; and 53 situations in which American military intervention might have propped up friendly regimes.

A variety of reasons may explain the nonuse of military force in these situations. In some cases, political constraints within the United States or elsewhere may have inhibited American intervention at any level, whereas in other cases Washington may have found diplomatic, economic, and/or covert means, or the use of proxy forces more effective. But regardless, America's four military interventions, only two of which involved fighting, must be put in the perspective of almost 150 situations in which the White House rejected a military option. Another study identified 215 incidents between 1945 and 1975 in which Washington used the threat of force or proxy military forces to protect American interests.[19] Half of the cases involve the movement of naval forces, and another large category includes movement of ground or air forces. Washington's threats were not very successful—about one out of five resulted in a favorable outcome for the United States. Overall, Washington was more successful in situations in which Moscow was not involved.

For nearly five decades, much of Washington's military planning and resources have centered on fighting a massive World War II style battle in central Europe against a Warsaw Pact invasion. With the Cold War over, the Pentagon and other advocates have tried to find missions to justify continued enormous military spending, forces, and facilities.[20] The shift in strategy is toward fighting *mid-intensity conflicts* (MICs), such as the Persian Gulf War against Iraq. The emphasis will be on mobility, a rapid buildup, close coordination between the services, and the use of overwhelming force to defeat the enemy as quickly and decisively as possible, while keeping American and Allied losses to a minimum. Ideally, the mere presence of a large American military, periodic reassertions of American resolve to counter aggression, and the memory of how easily Iraq's forces were defeated would deter any challenges.

MILITARY SPENDING, POWER, AND SECURITY

Military power can be a double-edged sword. Under some circumstances it may actually undermine rather than enhance a nation's security. When states become trapped in arms races that consume an ever greater amount of resources, war can become more likely rather than less likely and thus render the state more vulnerable rather than less vulnerable to destruction. And even when soldiers and weapons are never used, they become an enormous financial, human, economic, and technological drain on that country.

Since 1930, military spending has exceeded world population and economic growth.[21] Rosecrance dramatically reveals the ever-rising costs of defense: "in constant dollar terms, tanks went from less than $50,000 per unit in 1918 to more than $2,000,000 in 1980. Fighter planes that cost less than $100,000 in 1944 rose to at least $10,000,000 per copy forty years later."[22] During the 1980s alone, the United States alone spent $3 trillion on defense, or $45,000 for each household. In 1989 the world's total military budget surpassed $1.035 trillion or 4.9 percent of global GNP. Of that amount, the developed countries spent $867 billion or 83 percent of the total and 4.3 percent of their respective GNP. The less-developed countries spent $168 billion or 17 percent of total spending, and 5 percent of their GNP.[23] From one-quarter to one-third of the world's total research and development spending and 750,000 of some of the world's finest scientists and engineers are involved in building better weapons.[24] Many of these were American. From 1945 through today, the United States has annually spent an average of 30 percent of its total public and private research and development budget on defense compared to 7 percent for Germany and 4 percent for Japan.[25]

Many weapons are exported. Between 1960 and 1991, annual international arms sales increased from $2.4 billion to $45 billion.[26] Of the two top sellers during the 1980s, Washington supplied arms to 59 countries and Moscow to 42 countries.[27] In 1988, 116 countries, of which 84 were Third World countries, imported military weapons. During the 1980s alone, 540 warships and submarines, 3,100 combat aircraft, 20,000 cannon, 37,000 surface-to-air missiles, and 11,000 tanks and self-propelled guns changed hands.[28] About 75 percent of all weapons sales go to the Third World.[29]

The Third World annually spends twice as much on defense as it receives in foreign aid. Sixty percent of the all the world's soldiers are in the Third World, and that amount doubled from 8.4 to 16.4 million between 1960 and 1988. Most of the weapons acquired by the Third World are imported. Between 1985 and 1989, the Soviet Union was the largest arms exporter to the Third World, with 43.8 percent of the total, followed by the United States with 20.2 percent, France with 11.6 percent, China with 6.3 percent, Britain with 5.3 percent, the Third World itself with 3.5 percent, West Germany with 1.8 percent, Italy with 1.6 percent, and other countries with 5.8 percent. Within the Third World, the Middle East imported 41.1 percent of these arms, followed by South Asia with 23.9 percent, the Far East with 15.9 percent, Sub-Saharan Africa with 7.1 percent, South Africa with 5.5 percent, North Africa with 4.4 percent, and Central America with 2.0 percent.[30]

Increasing military budgets and arms exports occur for many reasons. Until recently cold-war politics were the most important reason. Washington and Moscow filled the arsenals of their immediate allies (in NATO and the Warsaw Pact, respectively), and that of scores of more ephemeral, potential, and actual "allies" and "friends" throughout the Third World. When one superpower began to aid a side in a regional or national conflict, the other superpower would inevitably feel compelled to begin aiding the other side to maintain the balance of power. The United States still targets many of its sales of weapons to friendly countries in the Middle East in order to maintain the balance of power against its foes. The other great powers—Britain, France, and China—also became big arms dealers during the Cold War.

Figure 12.1
Arms Transfers Among Countries, 1967 and 1989

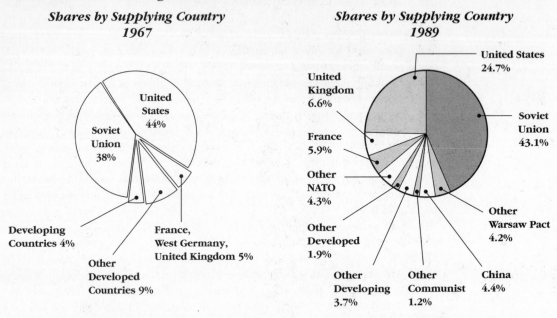

Shares by Supplying Country
1967

Shares by Supplying Country
1989

Shares by Recipient Region

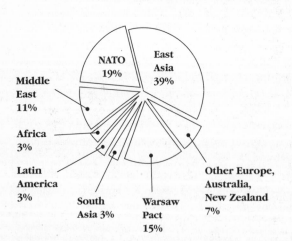

Shares by Recipient Region

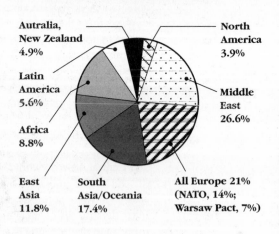

Sources: 1967 adapted from U.S. Arms Control and Disarmament Agency, *World Military Expenditures and Arms Transfers 1967–1976* (Washington, D.C.: U.S. Government Printing Office, 1978), pp. 115–156; 1989 from U.S. Arms Control and Disarmament Agency, *World Military Expenditures and Arms Transfers 1990* (Washington, D.C.: U.S. Government Printing Office, 1990), pp. 10, 15.

Figure 12.2
World Military Expenditures, 1979–1989

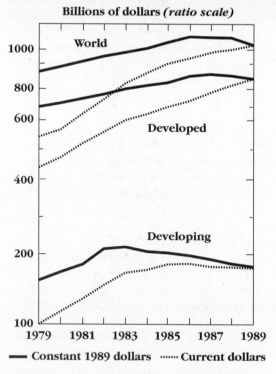

Billions of dollars *(ratio scale)*

World

Developed

Developing

━━ **Constant 1989 dollars** ┈┈ **Current dollars**

Source: U.S. Arms Control and Disarmament Agency, *World Military Expenditures and Arms Transfers 1990* (Washington, D.C.: U.S. Government Printing Office, 1992). p. 1.

Figure 12.3
Percentage of World Arms Imports, 1990

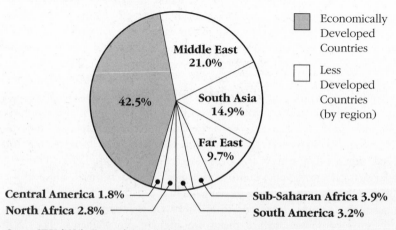

Economically Developed Countries

Less Developed Countries (by region)

Middle East 21.0%

South Asia 14.9%

Far East 9.7%

42.5%

Central America 1.8% — Sub-Saharan Africa 3.9%
North Africa 2.8% — South America 3.2%

Source: SIPRI (1991). Figures do not equal 100 percent due to rounding.

Ironically, the political gains of arms sales for the sellers may be illusory. For example, Moscow sold enormous amounts of equipment and sent advisers to Eygpt during the late 1950s through the early 1970s. In 1972, President Sadat ordered all of the Soviet advisers to leave, and by the late 1970s Egypt was receiving most of its military imports from the United States. The superpowers and other great powers have frequently found themselves arming both sides of a conflict, which meant greater sales in the short run but a greater chance of political setbacks over the long run. During the 1980s the Reagan and Bush administrations sold billions of dollars of military equipment to Iraq, only to see much of it used against the United States in the takeover of Kuwait and the Persian Gulf War (1990–1991).

Until recently, fishing for allies was more important than making money from these sales. With the end of the Cold War, profits have become the primary reason in most cases. Weapons exports are big business and a particularly excellent source of hard currency for the Soviet Union, China, and less-developed weapons manufacturers, whose governments often own them. Since the Soviet Union's breakup, Russia, Ukraine, Georgia, and other former republics have been indiscriminately selling off even their most-advanced and secret weapons systems for hard currency. Russia and the other former Soviet republics have been criticized for selling to countries like Iran, North Korea, Serbia, Syria, and others that threaten to upset regional power balances. About 80 percent of these sales go to China, Iran, Syria, and India, and Russia is trying to add Taiwan and Malaysia, among other states, to its customer list. Another fear is that former Soviet scientists are finding employment in those countries, thus contributing to the proliferation of chemical, biological, and even nuclear weapons.

Over-all, arms exports from Russia and other members of the Commonwealth of Independent States (CIS) have dropped considerably. As recently as 1988, the Soviet Union sold $15 billion to overseas buyers, well above America's $12 billion in foreign sales. Since then, while American sales have remained stagnant, Soviet sales have plunged to about $4 billion in 1991.[31] There are several reasons for the plummet in sales. Of $146 billion owed the former Soviet Union for weapons, 40 percent is considered uncollectable, so Russia and the other CIS members demand hard currency rather than IOUs for their hardware. UN arms embargoes on Libya, Iraq, Bosnia, Croatia, and Serbia cost the CIS $7 billion in lost sales in 1992 alone. CIS arms sales are further inhibited by the inferior quality of many Soviet weapons systems and the lack of credit, spare parts, and service. Sales will likely diminish further.

The international arms trade is dominated by the United States. In 1988, nine of the world's top ten private arms manufacturers were American and the other was British. Those nine American producers sold $65.7 billion in arms overseas and employed 440,000 people in the United States. The top ten producers generate 36 percent of the top one hundred producers' arms sales. Of the world's top one hundred defense contractors, forty-eight are American, twelve are British, ten are French, and nine are German. The competition for arms sales is growing. Increased numbers of countries (60 in 1990) have begun selling arms.[32] The great powers now account for 50 percent to 75 percent of annual sales, while some Third World countries, such as Brazil, South Africa, Israel, China, and India, are capturing more niches in the market.

The scramble for arms producers to sell overseas is intensifying as countries, particularly the superpowers, reduce their own military procurements. The 1990

Conventional Armed Forces in Europe Treaty (CFE) required signatories to sharply cut back their numbers of tanks, artillery, armored personnel carriers, and other equipment. Many of these weapons will be exported rather than destroyed. Arms producers are just as caught up in the logic of scale economies as any other producer. The more they sell, the lower the price of their components and the lower the final price, and so on. The dropping demand of the 1990s will undoubtedly bankrupt many producers.[33]

There are several other reasons for global arms sales. As engineers keep devising better ways of killing, they render existing weapons obsolete and thus create the need for their replacement. Thus arms races are fueled as much by new technology as geopolitics and the drive for profits. Of course, there could not be sellers without buyers. The wealthier a country, the more arms it can afford to import. Many arms sales have gone to the Middle East, which increased its imports from 11 percent of the total arms shipped in 1967 to 26 percent shipped in 1989.[34] It was not just the Arab-Israeli, Arab-Iran, and intra-Arab rivalries that stimulated this vast influx. OPEC's quadrupling of prices in 1973 and further doubling of prices in 1979 gave the oil-rich Middle East states the opportunity to finance their military ambition and in so doing set off an ever-spiraling regional arms race.

Yet, there would not be any arms exports if governments did not have real or imagined internal and international enemies that they hope to deter or defeat with more numerous and advanced weapons. Although many Third World governments import arms to counter perceived international threats, most use them against their own population. Sometimes a government will buy advanced weapons simply for the prestige associated with owning them rather than for their military utility.

Military power is supposed to make countries more secure rather than less secure; it is valuable only when it actually deters or defeats real enemies. The larger and better-equipped a country's military, the more likely that the government might use it to resolve a conflict. More than 25 million people have died in wars in the Third World since 1945, and the international arms trade was a major contributor both to the large number of wars and deaths.[35]

The indirect costs of militarization are just as enormous. Even if arms are never used, spending ever more money on the military can actually undermine rather than enhance security. As President Eisenhower put it, the "problem in defense spending is to figure out how far you should go without destroying from within what you are trying to defend from without . . . Every gun that is made, every warship launched, every rocket fired signifies, in the final sense, a theft from those who hunger and are not fed, those who are cold and are not clothed. This world in arms is not spending money alone. It is spending the sweat of its laborers, the genius of its scientists, the hopes of its children." Or as Eisenhower's chairman of the Council of Economic Advisers, Arthur Burns, put it: "The real cost of the defense sector consists . . . not only of the civilian goods and services that are currently foregone on its account; it includes also an element of growth that could have been achieved through larger investment in human or business capital."[36]

Studies have shown that generally the higher a country's military budget as a percentage of GNP, the lower its manufacturing productivity growth: "intercountry comparisons suggest that high military expenditures have curtailed productivity growth . . . heavy defense spending seems to have a particularly important impact

Table 12.1
Arms Control Treaties

Treaty	Provisions	Date Signed	Number of Signatories
Geneva Protocol	Bans using of gas or bacteriological weapons	1925	125
Antarctic Treaty	Internationalizes and demilitarizes the continent	1959	39
Limited Test Ban	Bans nuclear tests in the atmosphere, outer space, or under water	1963	119
Outer Space Treaty	Internationalizes and demilitarizes space, the moon, and other celestial bodies	1967	93
Latin American Nuclear Free Zone	Bans nuclear weapons in the region	1967	23
Non-Proliferation Treaty (NPT)	Prohibits selling, giving, or receiving nuclear weapons, nuclear materials, or nuclear technology for weapons	1968	141
Seabed Arms Control	Bans placing nuclear weapons in or under the seabed	1971	83
Biological Weapons Convention	Bans the production and possession of biological weapons	1972	112
Strategic Arms Limitation Talks Treaty (SALT I)	Limited the number and types of U.S. and USSR strategic weapons (expired 1977)	1972	2
ABM Treaty	U.S.-USSR pact limits antiballistic missile sites (two each) and bars further ABM deployment	1972	2
Threshold Test Ban	Limits U.S. and USSR underground tests to 150 kt	1974	2
Environmental Modification	Bans environmental modification as a form of warfare	1977	55
SALT II	Limited the number and types of USSR and U.S. strategic weapons	1979	2
South Pacific Nuclear-Free Zone	Prohibits the manufacture or acquisition of nuclear weapons in the region	1985	11
Intermediate-range Nuclear Forces (INF)	Eliminates all U.S. and Soviet missiles with ranges between 500 km and 5,500 km	1987	2
Conventional Forces in Europe Treaty (CFE)	Reduces conventional forces in Europe. Nonbinding protocol in 1992 covers troops	1990/ 1992	20 27
Strategic Arms Reduction Talks Treaty (START I)	Reduces strategic nuclear forces between the United States and the USSR/Belarus, Kazakhstan, Russia, and Ukraine	1991/ 1992	2 5
START II	Reduces U.S. and Russian strategic nuclear forces	1993	2
Chemical Weapons Convention	Bans the possession of chemical weapons after 2005	1993	130

SALT II was never ratified. As of January 1993 START I has been ratified by the United States and Russia, but not by all the other FSRs with nuclear weapons. START II has not been ratified by either the United States or Russia.

Data sources: SIPRI 1991; Sivard (1991); Kegley, Wittkopf, *International Relations,* 1994; various news sources.

on dampening capital formation and investment, which in turn reduces economic growth in the long run."[37] One study compared the impact on employment of one billion dollars. A billion dollars worth of guided missiles created only 21,392 workers, the lowest of six different employment categories. That same amount of money would create 21,783 railroad equipment workers, 26,145 solar-energy and energy-conservation workers, 26,459 public-utility construction workers, 27,583 housing workers, and 31,078 mass-transit workers.[38] Overall, a billion dollars spent on contruction creates 100,070 jobs or 1.3 times more than the 75,710 defense jobs created by those same dollars. And those construction jobs are largely productive—things are built that increase a nation's efficiency and wealth. Much of the money spent on the military is nonproductive—millions of able-bodied men and women sit in barracks around the world rather than use their brains and muscle to develop their countries. Militaries undermine rather than enhance development. Because they consume rather than produce, the impact of their spending is inflationary.

Of the so-called superpowers, the Soviet Union collapsed largely because of the enormous resources it had poured into the military over decades to the neglect of everything else. America's economic growth, productivity, savings and investments ratio, literacy, and per capita income are among the lowest of the democratic industrial countries, while infant mortality, life expectancy, low birth-weight babies, and per-capita spending for education and health are among the highest. Both the United States and Russia are trying to wean their economies from dependence on high military spending into more economically and socially productive pursuits, but the conversion is extremely painful and disruptive.

For several decades the United States has been locked into a vicious cycle of low productivity, growth, investment, literacy, and student test scores and high rates of unemployment, inflation, crime, drug abuse, poverty, and malnutrition. There is no telling how much these problems could have been alleviated if, for example, the $35 billion spent on the B-1 bomber or $40 billion on Star Wars would have been invested in infrastructure, education, or research and development, let alone if the defense budget remained at the same level during the 1980s rather than increasing threefold. There is enormous duplication and sometimes triplication of conventional and nuclear weapons systems, which exist solely to reinforce the abstract notion of deterrence. Unfortunately, America's buildup was continually matched by a Soviet buildup, and both sides became deeply mired in a security dilemma.

Military spending is even more damaging to the Third World. Countries of the Third World are trapped in a vicious cycle, whereby poverty and stagnant growth lead to political instability that prompts governments to spend scarce resources on military equipment. This further inhibits development, causing greater instability, more military spending, and so on. For every dollar the Third World spends on defense, it loses 25 cents of economic investments and 20 cents of agricultural output. Thus, as military spending rises, economic growth declines.[39] By one estimate, the Third World loses 187 million human-years of income for its total annual military spending; the industrial countries lose 56 million human-years annually. There are eight times more soldiers than doctors in the Third World, and 30 times more money is spent on the military than on education.[40]

Global military spending peaked in the late 1980s. The end of the Cold War and the winding down of regional conflicts in Cambodia, Angola, Ethiopia, Afghanistan, and elsewhere has resulted in a decline in total military spending among the developed and developing countries alike.

MILITARY ALLIANCES, POWER, AND SECURITY

The greater a nation's military spending, the greater the sacrifices made in foregone investments and opportunities in more economically and socially productive pursuits. Alliances would seem to be a way to share defense burdens. But that is not always the case. Whether alliances help or hurt their members varies considerably from one alliance to the next. There can be weakness as well as strength in numbers.

There are many kinds of alliances. States balance or counter threats, not power. What is important is not how powerful another state or group of states is, but whether it is threatening. Some alliances are between countries of a similar ideology facing a common ideological threat, such as the American-led North Altantic Treaty Organization (NATO), which has successfully helped contain the Soviet Union for more than four decades. Most alliances are based on the principle that "the enemy of my enemy is my friend." They are "marriages of convenience" between countries of quite different ideologies facing the same threat, such as when the democratic powers of the United States, Britain, and France teamed up with the communist Soviet Union to defeat the fascist powers Germany, Japan, and Italy. Since its creation in 1948, Israel has maintained its security in part by playing off the various intra-Arab, Sunni-Shi'ite Muslim, and Arab-Iranian rivalries through secret diplomacy in which it would favor one side against the other. India formed an alliance with the Soviet Union and Pakistan with China to strengthen themselves against each other.

How do governments decide whether or not to join an alliance? An imminent or actual attack is an obvious reason. However, when these conditions are not present William Riker theorizes that alliance "participants create coalitions just as large as they believe will ensure winning and no larger."[41] The reason is that although the larger the coalition, the greater the chance for victory, the share of the spoils diminishes accordingly. This may have been true of coalitions before the mid-twentieth century, when the victors often took territory and wealth from the losers. The benefits of contemporary alliances are more intangible than in the past—security, community, and prestige rather than the spoils of war.

When faced with a threat, it sometimes pays to not join an alliance if it is clear the alliance will defeat or deter that threat. France dropped out of NATO's command structure in 1964, thus regaining its independence and shedding its duties while continuing to shelter under that alliance's conventional and nuclear umbrella. The United States sat on the sidelines of both world wars until it was directly attacked. It can be argued, however, that the United States would have gained more by joining an alliance with Britain and France in the late 1930s. An alliance possibly could have lead to a negotiated settlement or bolstered allied forces in France, which would have made a German victory there in 1940 much less likely and perhaps deterred an attack altogether. The human and material costs of waiting may have been greater for the United States in the long run. The trouble with this scenario is that, given America's deep isolationist sentiment before Pearl Harbor, it would have been politically impossible for President Roosevelt to have formally entered an alliance with Britain and France unless the United States was directly attacked.

The benefits of being in an alliance seem obvious. A nation's security tends to strengthen with its alliances' troops, weapons, geographical expanse, coordination, and will. Alliances can deter aggression. States with smaller populations, economies, and militaries can particularly benefit by joining an alliance. A study of alliances between 1815 and 1965 found that, if attacked, a state with allies received help 76 percent of the time; without allies only 17 percent of the time.[42]

The balance of power theory holds that weakness invites aggression, whereas there is strength and a greater chance for peace in numbers. In a world of sovereign states, each struggles to enhance its interests, often at the expense of others. When one state grows too powerful and aggressive, other states tend to ally to offset that power and potential threat. Being in an alliance, however, does not guarantee victory. The key to victory in war from 1816 to 1976 was who initiated rather than whether or not there was an alliance.[43]

At times an alliance's costs exceed its benefits. For very sound reasons, George Washington in his farewell address warned his fellow Americans against entanglements in foreign alliances: "it must be unwise . . . to implicate ourselves by artificial ties in the ordinary vicissitudes of her [Europe's] politics, or the ordinary combinations and collisions of her friendships or enmities."[44] Or, as Jefferson put it even more succinctly: "Commerce with all nations, alliance with none, should be our motto."[45]

George Kennan eloquently explored the reason for the caution with which most states approach alliances:

> The relations among nations, in this imperfect world, constitute a fluid substance, always in motion, changing subtly from day to day in ways that are difficult to detect from the myopia of the passing moment, and even difficult to discern from the perspective of the future one. The situation at one particular time is never quite the same as the situation of five years later—indeed it is sometimes very significantly different, even though the stages by which this change came about are seldom visible at the given moment. This is why wise and experienced statesmen usually shy away from commitments likely to constitute limitations on a government's behavior at unknown dates in the future in the face of unpredictable situations.[46]

Great powers sometimes force minor powers into alliances in order to more easily dominate and extract benefits from them. For example, most would agree that the Soviet Union created the Warsaw Pact simply to justify subjugating and exploiting East Europe.[47] Far less convincingly, some have made the same claim for the American creation of NATO and the *Organization of American States* (OAS).

If change is constant, the longer an alliance exists, the more likely it is oriented toward past rather than present challenges and opportunities. Alliances themselves can prevent positive change by freezing rivalries and conflicts. Although alliances provide states with a greater potential military resources, they take away their members' diplomatic flexibility. Alliance building is a type of arms race, with a similar escalation of perceived threats and tensions. One alliance's creation is likely to spark the creation of an opposing alliance, thus possibly worsening the threat that the first alliance was originally created to deter. If war breaks out, the destruction and death can become as widespread as the alliance itself.

With the 1991 collapse of the Soviet Union, communism, and the Warsaw Pact, NATO is trying to justify its continued existence. NATO's 1991 Rome Summit issued "The Alliance's New Strategic Concept," which formed a North Atlantic Cooperation Council (NACC) to "build genuine partnership among the North Atlantic Alliance and the countries of Central and Eastern Europe." Russia and many of the former Soviet republics and Eastern European countries are trying to join NATO. There is a growing consensus within NATO that it should evolve from a strictly military alliance into a broader security community that addresses economic, humanitarian, democratic, and environmental concerns.

Napoleon once said, "I'd rather fight than join a coalition." The difficulty in coordinating the strategy and tactics of an alliance at war are vast and often unmanageable. The more states in an alliance, the weaker the influence of any one state on the alliance's policies and the greater the difficulty in reaching decisions. Napoleon and many other leaders have found that the advantages of fighting alone with a unified and decisive command outweigh the added troops and resources that alliances can provide.

Historically, alliances have been ephemeral, arising and dissolving with perceived threats. Most governments recognize that in a constantly changing world they have no permanent friends or enemies, just national interests that must be preserved. Today's friend can be tomorrow's enemy. One of four wars between 1815 and 1965 were fought between allies![48]

THE PERSIAN GULF WAR (1990–1991)

On August 2, 1990, Iraqi military forces invaded and conquered Kuwait. President Saddam Hussein repeatedly asserted his intention to make Kuwait Iraq's nineteenth province. Within days of the invasion, the Bush administration had decided to force Iraq from Kuwait. The question was how. Over the next six months the Bush administration forged and led a coalition of armed forces, which began a massive air assault on Iraq on January 17, 1991, and a ground attack on February 23 that destroyed Iraq's forces in Kuwait and liberated that country. The coalition bill for fighting the war was $61 billion dollars; the regional cost of destruction, reconstruction, capital flight, and foregone trade, investment, and employment was a mind-boggling $676 billion! The cost in lives was enormous, including hundreds of coalition members, thousands of Kuwaiti citizens, and hundreds of thousands of Iraqi soldiers and civilians. Why did Iraq invade Kuwait? Why did the United States lead the coalition against Iraq? Could both Hussein's invasion of Kuwait and the war against him have been avoided?

The Persian Gulf War provides a good case study of how the international community may handle future wars of aggression, the difficulties of coalition building, the importance and weaknesses of high technology weapons, the successes and failures of American policies toward Persian Gulf geopolitical struggles, and economic and environmental costs of war.

Prelude

During the 1980s, the Reagan and Bush administrations backed Iraq in its war against Iran.[49] In 1982 the Reagan White House removed Iraq from the list of states that sponsor terrorism, allowing the United States to resume trade with that country. In 1984 the Reagan administration abandoned its official neutrality and tilted toward Iraq. For the next six years, until Iraq invaded Kuwait, the United States supplied Iraq with several billion dollars worth of military weapons, equipment, technology, intelligence, and food, while overlooking its support for international terrorist groups and gross abuse of human rights. Throughout the 1980s, the White House did not have a uniform policy toward states that promoted terrorism. Although Libya, Iran, and Iraq supported terrorism, the White House cut its trade and diplomatic relations with Libya, ransomed hostages from Iran, and built up Iraq. Congressional voices demanded the United States sever its relations with Iraq, pointing out that the Hussein regime used chemical weapons against its own Kurdish population and harbored Palestinian terrorists. The White House rejected these reports, claimed that the Hussein regime was liberalizing, and rebuked Congress for attempting to "micromanage" foreign policy. The White House placed Iraq on its list of countries that support terrorism only after it invaded Kuwait. Between 1985 and 1990, the White House approved 771 licenses to export $1.5 billion in advanced equipment and technology to Iraq, much of it with direct military applications, and an additional $5 billion in agricultural credits.[50] The Reagan and Bush administrations thought that they could moderate Iraq's behavior by appeasing President Hussein with technology, weapons, and trade. Instead, by building up President Hussein's military, Reagan and Bush strengthened a Frankenstein that eventually turned against the United States.

Would Iraq have invaded Kuwait if the White House had not built it up militarily and not been seemingly indifferent to Kuwait's fate? In the half year leading up to Iraq's invasion, Baghdad's actions revealed that the Reagan and Bush appeasement policy had failed. Intelligence sources had long known that Iraq was trying to build nuclear weapons and estimated that Baghdad could successfully detonate a nuclear weapon within five years. Iraq test launched its first SCUD, missiles with a range of 400 miles, in December 1989. In February it demanded that the United States withdraw its forces from the Persian Gulf. In March, U.S. intelligence revealed that Iraqi SCUDs were located near the border with Jordan and thus in range of Israel. In April, Hussein threatened to "burn half of Israel" with chemical weapons, if Israel launched any attack on Iraq. Throughout these months, Bush was more puzzled than worried about Hussein's actions, and was quoted by one senior adviser as saying: "Gee we're trying to be reasonable, yet this guy says and does these crazy things."[51] Yet, Bush never considered any alternative to his appeasement policy. In the first half of 1990, the White House approved $500 million in agricultural credits and asked Congress for another $500 million.

In the weeks leading up to the Iraqi invasion, the White House sent Hussein a series of messages that seemed to tolerate an Iraqi invasion of Kuwait. Although some in Congress called for economic sanctions against Iraq for its threats against Kuwait, the White House rejected those calls. On July 28, 1990, Bush sent a personal message to Hussein saying he wanted peace in the region and better relations with Iraq. There was no mention of Iraq's threats against Kuwait, whether the United States would object to an Iraqi invasion, or what it would do if an invasion actually occurred. When asked whether Hussein would fulfill his threat to invade Kuwait, Jordan's King Hussein and Saudi Arabia's King Fahd replied that it was all a bluff.

U.S. Decision and Buildup

Within hours of the invasion, Kuwaiti Prime Minister and Crown Prince Sheik Saad al-Abdullah al-Sabah called the White House and pleaded for help against the Iraqi invasion. The Bush administration denied the request, concluding that Kuwait was already lost and, anyway, the United States did not have enough American military forces in the Persian Gulf to help Kuwait. The White House concentrated on what to do if Iraq invaded Saudi Arabia and the effects of higher oil prices on the global economy. Bush, however, did denounce the invasion as "naked aggression" and ordered the freezing of all Iraqi and Kuwaiti assets in the United States. The UN Security Council voted to condemn the invasion and demanded Iraq's total and unconditional withdrawal.

For several days following the invasion, the White House was split between those who wanted to accept it as a fait accompli and those few who argued for resistance. The turning point in the White House policy occurred after Bush met with British Prime Minister Margaret Thatcher, who urged him to resist Iraq's aggression. On August 5, 1990, Bush declared that the Iraqi invasion "will not stand," implying that his administration was committed to using any means to bring about an Iraqi withdrawal.

After Bush's decision, the White House began forging the international coalition that would eventually drive Iraq from Kuwait. On August 6, the Security Council voted to impose a trade and financial embargo on Iraq and on occupied Kuwait. On August 7, American forces began landing in Saudi Arabia to help deter a possible Iraqi invasion. The following day, Bush vowed to protect Saudi Arabia. On August 10, the Arab League voted to send troops to Saudi Arabia. On August 12, the American Navy began blocking all Iraqi trade except some food shipments.

Hussein escalated the crisis on August 19 when he declared he would use foreign civilians interned in Iraq as "human shields" in military and industrial sites. On August 25, the UN Security Council voted 13 to 0, with two abstentions, to give the United States and other nations the right to enforce the previously declared embargo. On August 29, OPEC voted to allow its members to pump all the oil they desired in order to alleviate the shortage caused by the boycott of Iraqi and Kuwaiti oil. On August 30, Bush announced that he would pass the hat to his allies to help defray the costs of the Persian Gulf buildup and possible war.

But the possible costs of war mounted. As Iraqi forces in Kuwait were reinforced, the United States had to increase its own forces to give it an edge in any future fighting. On October 30, 1990, Bush approved a timetable for launching an air war against Iraq by mid-January and a ground war by mid-February. Meanwhile, throughout October and November, Secretary of State James Baker shuttled around the world to convince the Security Council members and Arab states to support the U.S. plan for evicting Iraq from Kuwait. Buying the support of some key countries was costly. For example, the White House agreed to forgive Egypt's $7.1 billion military debt to the United States. In late November, the Bush administration announced that new intelligence revealed that Hussein could detonate a nuclear bomb within a half year.[52] The Security Council voted on November 29 to allow the use of force if Iraqi forces did not withdraw from Kuwait by January 15, 1992. Having won UN approval, Bush now put pressure on Congress to support possible war with Iraq. Congress finally granted approval in late December.

There were attempts to negotiate the peaceful resolution of the conflict. Between August and January, American and Iraqi diplomats met numerous times to address the Iraqi invasion and related issues, but all the meetings ended in deadlock. In the week leading up to the air war, the Soviet Union and France also failed in their independent attempts to negotiate the withdrawal of Iraqi troops.

Battle and Aftermath

The air campaign began on January 17, 1991. For six weeks coalition air forces and cruise missiles systematically destroyed Iraqi forces in Kuwait and Iraq's entire logistical, communications, and command infrastructure. Each air attack was preceded by electronic countermeasures (ECM), which either destroyed or neutralized the Iraqi radar. Coalition losses were minimal.

Despite these successes, the White House feared that the Israelis would retaliate against Iraqi missile attacks and then the Arab states would withdraw from the coalition. However, when asked about that possibility, the Arab leaders replied that they would tolerate any Israeli retaliation against Iraq as long as it was "proportionate." The United States sent Patriot antimissile batteries to Israel to help defend against the Iraqi SCUD attacks.

The ground war began on February 23, 1991, and lasted 100 hours. The coalition commander, American General Schwarzkopf, conducted a brilliantly conceived and executed strategy in which coalition forces quickly outflanked and encircled Iraqi forces in Kuwait and southern Iraq. With Coalition forces prepared to completely destroy his army, Hussein indicated that he would accede to the UN resolutions. The peace terms imposed on Iraq were tough. The UN International Atomic Energy Agency (IAEA) was allowed to systematically inspect Iraq's suspected chemical, biological, and nuclear facilities and supervise their destruction.

Bush's handling of the crisis from Iraq's invasion on August 2, 1990, to his order to end the fighting on February 26, 1991, was masterly. Over half a year, Bush overcame formidable international diplomatic and domestic political obstacles to forge a coalition that eventually decisively destroyed Iraq's army in Kuwait and liberated that country. Eventually, 37 states contributed troops to the coalition, although American troops composed 70 percent of the total ground, air, and naval forces.

Yet, American policy before the Iraqi invasion and Bush's order to stop fighting can be criticized. The Reagan and Bush administrations helped build up the Iraqi army that the United States and its allies eventually had to destroy. The Bush administration's indecisive and ambiguous response to Iraq's buildup on Kuwait's borders and threats to invade may have given Hussein the green light to do so. Then in mid-February 1991, with coalition forces poised to decisively destroy the Iraqi army and march to the gates of Baghdad itself, an action that would have probably resulted in Hussein's overthrow, Bush ended the fighting. By 1994, the man Bush described as "worse than Hitler" remained firmly in power. Meanwhile, Bush's popularity rose to 89 percent immediately following the war. However, it steadily diminished over the next year and a half, until Bush lost the November 1992 election.

America's high-tech weapons gave a much more mixed performance than the film footage released to the mass media by the Pentagon indicated. Although the Pentagon claimed that its Patriots destroyed 70 percent of the SCUDs fired at Saudi Arabia and 40 percent against those fired at Israel, an independent MIT report concluded that the Patriot destroyed at most only one SCUD and probably none. In contrast, 85 percent of the Navy's Tomahawk cruise missiles hit their targets.

Overall, the United States accomplished some important objectives in the Persian Gulf War. Iraq's military was forced to withdraw from Kuwait and the UN's IAEA demolished virtually all of Iraq's nuclear and chemical weapons and facilities. As part of his concessions to the Arabs for their participation in the coalition, Bush pressured Israel to join a series of negotiations with Syria, Jordan, and the Palestinians to resolve their deep and bitter conflict. These efforts led to the August 1993 treaty between Israel and the PLO granting Palestinian autonomy in the Gaza Strip and Jericho. Peace treaties between Israel and the other Arab states seem imminent.

These successes were extremely costly. Hussein remains firmly in power. And although Iraq's offensive military capability may have been temporarily destroyed, the military power balance in the Persian Gulf has shifted to Iran. The war cost the region $676 billion in destruction and war-fighting costs. The figure does not include the region's environmental devastation and foregone economic opportunities. The region's average seven percent economic growth rate turned into a seven percent economic contraction during the year surrounding the war. An additional $51 billion was lost in capital flight and canceled foreign investments. Iraq may have lost at least $256 billion in oil revenues and infrastructre destruction. Countries outside the Persian Gulf, such as Egypt, Yemen, the Philippines, Bangladesh, Pakistan, and India, also lost an important source of income and employment when their citizens, who worked in the region, were sent home.[53]

NONCONVENTIONAL ARMED CONFLICTS

Civil War and Low-Intensity Warfare

Most wars are civil wars that occur within one country rather than betweeen two or more countries. More than 85 percent of all wars between 1945 and 1976 were civil wars. Most of these were extremely destructive—10 of the 12 bloodiest wars of the last 200 years were civil wars.[54] Of those relatively few international wars since 1945, most occurred when a great power got involved in a civil war. There were 161 civil wars with more than 1,000 deaths between 1816 and 1988. Civil wars mostly occur in poor countries. Of the 60 civil wars that have occurred since 1945, all but one were in newly independent countries; 14 became internationalized. The possibility of civil war, of course, increases with the number of states.[55]

Civil wars can involve mostly conventional warfare, such as the American Civil War. Most civil wars, however, are guerrilla or *low-intensity conflicts.* Arguably the most successful guerrilla leader in history, Mao Zedong argued that victory depended on five elements: a sympathetic population, a strong military force, a tightly organized party, favorable terrain, and an ample and secure source of supply.[56] Although guerrilla warfare can successfully defeat the government on the battlefield, a revolutionary struggle can only overthrow the government with conventional warfare. At some turning point in the revolutionary struggle, the guerrilla war of hit and run becomes a conventional war of position.

Civil wars can become international wars when the government and/or antigovernment forces receive outside help. Throughout the Cold War, civil wars almost inevitably became international wars as Washington, Moscow, and sometimes other states lined up behind the side that seemed to best represent their interests—even if that interest involved simply bleeding the material, human, and psychological resources of the other side. For example, during the 1980s, Washington sponsored guerrilla forces against pro-Soviet regimes in Afghanistan, Ethiopia, Angola, and Nicaragua. Ideally, Washington wanted the pro-Soviet regimes toppled and Soviet advisers and troops removed. But usually the United States was content with forcing the Soviets to commit even more resources to maintain their position. Over the years, Moscow played the same game against the United States in Vietnam, El Salvador, Cuba, and the Korean peninsula, to name a few.

Terrorism

On February 27, 1993, a bomb exploded in one of the World Trade Center towers in New York, killing seven, wounding nearly 1,000, and forcing the buildings' closure for over a month, until it was repaired. Although many groups claimed responsibility for the bombing, investigators arrested, charged, and eventually convicted a half dozen fundamentalist Muslims.

The World Trade Center bombing was a classic case of *terrorism*. The U.S. State Department defines terrorism as: "the use or threatened use of violence for political purposes to create a state of fear that will aid in extorting, coercing, intimidating, or otherwise causing individuals and groups to alter their behavior." To this can be added the requirements that terrorism "is ruthless and does not conform to humanitarian norms, and that publicity is an essential factor in terrorist strategy.[57] V.I. Lenin put it more succinctly: "The purpose of terrorism is to inspire terror."

Terror is a group's use of violence against noncombatants in a struggle to achieve its goals. There is a difference in motivation, if not tactics, between criminal and political terrorists. Whereas criminals use terror to extort money or other forms of wealth from their victims, political groups use terror to change or discredit entire political systems. Political terrorism is a type of low-intensity warfare; it is the tactic of the weak against the strong and is usually only one of several means that the group employs to overthrow a government or promote change. A well-publicized terrorist act causing relatively limited deaths and damage can set off a chain reaction that grievously harms the targeted country or cause. For example, the number of American tourists going to Europe decreased by half in 1986 following terrorist attacks and American reprisals, costing Europe hundreds of millions in lost potential revenue. Violence against governmental institutions and personnel is not considered terrorism; violence against civilians is. It is not terror when the Irish Republican Army (IRA) assassinates a police officer; it is when the IRA explodes a bomb in Harrod's department store. International terrorism occurs when two or more countries are the supporter, target, or refuge of a terrorist group.

Who commits terrorism? Terrorism can be one tactic of many used by a large political organization struggling for independence; the sole means of a tiny, close knit group to assert its views, whatever they may be; or the acts of an individual. Whereas many terrorists operate against states, others are employed by states to terrorize their own or foreign citizens. Terrorism has increasingly become a policy of some states. The United States, the Soviet Union, Israel, Libya, Syria, Iraq, and Iran, to name a few, have all supplied, trained, and/or led groups that launched terrorist attacks against other states. Authoritarian governments frequently use terror to intimidate their own citizens into compliance.

Terrorism may be more widespread than is commonly perceived. It can be argued that those:

> who are described as terrorists, and who reject that title for themselves, make the uncomfortable point that national armed forces, fully supported by democratic opinion, have in fact employed violence and terror on a far larger scale than what liberation movements have as yet been able to attain. The 'freedom fighters' see themselves as fighting a just war. Why should they not be entitled to kill, burn, and destroy as national armies, navies and air forces do, and why should the label 'terrorist' be applied to them and not to the national militaries.'[58]

Whether a group is composed of "freedom fighters" or "terrorists" depends largely on the viewer's perspective.

The oldest continuous terrorist organization is the *Irish Republican Army* (IRA), whose efforts to liberate Ireland from British rule date to the eighteenth century as the "Irish Volunteers" first employed terror. They organized a massive revolt against British rule in 1916, which was brutally repressed by the British army. The struggle continued. In 1919 the Irish Volunteers renamed themselves the Irish Republican Army. In 1922 Britain finally granted independence to those counties that were predominantly Catholic, while retaining the 6 counties of Northern Ireland, or Ulster, that are 60 percent Protestant under British rule. The IRA split between those who were content with free Ireland and those who wanted to liberate all of Ireland. In Northern Ireland the Protestants discriminated against the Catholics in housing and jobs. Today there are 950,000 Protestants and 650,000 Catholics in Northern Ireland.

The IRA has continued to struggle for the end of British rule over Northern Ireland. Between 1971 and 1992 alone, more than 3,023 people have died in the fighting, 900 of which were security troops killed by the IRA and 300 were members of the IRA. Most of the casualties were civilians. An estimated 300 to 400 IRA guerrillas have tied down more than 30,000 British troops and police. The IRA subsists on about $10 million a year, and even pays its guerrillas a weekly salary of about $200.[59]

International terrorism is relatively easy to commit given the widespread availability of arms and explosives, international air travel, and mass communications. Although bombings are the most common terrorist tactic, accounting for 413 of 855 international terrorist acts in 1988, there were many others, including arson (239), armed attacks (129), kidnapping (32), assault (16), sabotage (8), barricades without hostages (5), extortion (4), nonair hijackings (3), barricades with hostages (2), skyjackings (2), thefts (1), and other means (1). Of the 185 terrorist tactics directed against the United States that year, 140 were bombings, 22 were armed attacks, 14 were arson, 5 were kidnapping, and 1 case each was extortion, skyjacking, theft, and nonair hijacking. Of those targeted by international terrorists, the most common was the "other" category with 516 victims, followed by 256 businesspeople, 96 diplomats, 92 government officials, and 50 military personnel. Of those terrorist acts against Americans, 96 were against businesspeople, 42 against diplomats, 23 against "other," 21 against military personnel, and 12 against government officials. In 1990, there were 533 terrorist attacks in 73 countries.[60]

Bombing is the most popular terrorist tactic because it is the safest to pull off; a bomb can be planted well ahead of its explosion, allowing the terrorist ample time for a getaway. A bomb also can be planted virtually anywhere and go off without warning. The explosion of one small bomb can thus terrorize entire populations. In 1983 the Reagan administration sent marines into Beirut with troops of European allies in an attempt to restore order. A truck bomb blew up an American barracks, killing 241 marines. Shortly thereafter Reagan ordered the pullout of all American forces from Beirut. Kidnapping can also be an effective tactic. President Carter's inability to free the 52 American diplomats seized by Iran was the most important reason for his reelection loss. In the mid-1980s, the Reagan administration violated its own pledge not to negotiate with terrorists when it traded arms to Iran in exchange for the release of American hostages held by pro-Iranian Islamic fundamentalist groups in Lebanon.

Because terrorists are weak, their only possible victories are political. There are several ways by which governments can contain terrorism's political victories.[61] Governments should not overreact by imposing draconian measures that end up alienating the population and magnifying the terrorist group's importance and appeal. Nor should governments allow themselves to be paralyzed and thus appear weak and ineffectual, or be intimidated into granting concessions. Governments should be particularly careful not to alienate the political moderates. Once the terrorist group captures the sympathy of political moderates, it is close to victory. Repressing moderates who are sympathetic to terrorists only drives them closer together. Isolating and retaliating against the states that sponsor terrorism can also inhibit it.[62]

THE CONTROL OF CONVENTIONAL ARMS AND WAR

History records relatively limited attempts by states to negotiate arms control. Scholars and treaties among ancient civilizations in China, India, and the Middle East created often elaborate restrictions against certain tactics of killing. For example, the fourth century B.C. Indian Book of Manu, among other things, forbade using concealed, barbed, poisoned, or fire-tipped weapons and killing those without weapons.

Throughout the modern era, as war has become more destructive, its restrictions have increased. The earliest of these restrictions attempted to protect nonbelligerents. At the Concert of Europe in 1815, participants signed a treaty guaranteeing Switzerland's neutrality for perpetuity. In 1817, the United States and Britain signed a treaty demilitarizing the Great Lakes. In 1839, a treaty guaranteed Belgium's neutrality. In 1856, Great Britain, France, Austria, Prussia, Russia, Sardinia, and Turkey signed the Declaration of Paris, which protected neutral shipping during war. In 1864 a dozen European states signed the Geneva Red Cross Convention protecting hospitals and medical personnel.

During the late nineteenth century, there was a growing consensus that states should limit the weapons and practices of war itself. During the American Civil War, the Union army issued a manual instructing officers how to deal with such aspects of war as prisoners, civilians, private property, and so on. Many European countries subsequently issued their own manuals. The first international agreement restricting war occurred with the 1868 Declaration of St. Petersburg, signed by 17 nations, which outlawed the use of certain explosives and weapons.

Many of today's restrictions on warfare derive from the 1899 and 1907 *Hague Conferences* which produced a score of treaties including: Pacific Settlement of International Disputes (1899); Laws and Customs of War on Land (1899); Adaptation to Maritime Warfare of the Principles of the Geneva Convention (1899); Prohibiting Launching of Projectiles and Explosives from Balloons (1899); Prohibiting Use of Expanding Bullets (1899); Prohibiting Use of Gases (1899); Exemption of Hospital Ships From Taxation in Times of War (1904); Pacific Settlement of International Disputes (1907); Limitation of Employment of Force for Recovery of Contract Debts (1907); Opening of Hostilities (1907); Laws and Customs of War on Land (1907); Rights and Duties of Neutral Powers and Persons in War on Land (1907); Status of Enemy Merchant Ships at the Outbreak of Hostilities (1907); Conversion of Merchant Ships into Warships (1907); Laying of Automatic Submarine Contact Mines (1907); Bombardment by Naval Forces in Time of War (1907); Adaptation to Maritime Warfare of Principles of the Geneva Convention (1907); Restrictions with Respect to Right of Capture in Naval War (1907); Rights and Duties of Neutral Powers in Naval War (1907); Prohibiting Discharge of Projectiles and Explosives from Balloons (1907).

A third Hague Conference was scheduled for 1915, but no one showed up because of World War I. In January 1918, President Wilson announced his Fourteen Points, or goals, for a peace settlement for World War I that he hoped would be "the war to end all wars." Some of Wilson's ideas were incorporated into the 1919 Versailles Peace Conference, the most important of which was the creation of a League of Nations dedicated to collective security in which members pledged to peacefully resolve conflicts and unite against aggressors. Signatories of the 1928 Kellogg-Briand Pact agreed to renounce aggressive war.

The League of Nations and the Kellogg-Briand Pact were reinforced by some significant arms control agreements during the 1920s. The 1919 St. Germain Convention, the 1925 Geneva Convention, and the 1929 Geneva Convention all restricted certain types of weapons, arms exports, and war practices. The Washington (1921–1922) and London (1930) Naval Treaties among the great naval powers imposed a strict ratio of warship tonnage among them. There were no limits, however, on the amount of firepower that those ships could deploy, and the tonnage limitations helped stimulate a technology arms race.

All of these treaties were no more successful in preventing World War II than the two Hague conventions were in preventing World War I. Like President Wilson, President Roosevelt was determined to create a lasting peace. He helped found the United

Nations in 1945 as a new and improved version of the League of Nations that shared the goal of achieving collective security. Since then there have been several important multilateral treaties that have attempted to further restrict war and weapons. The 1949 Geneva Convention, 1977 Geneva Conference, and 1980 United Nations Conference systematized existing laws governing the conduct of war.

The restrictions on war include: (1) no attacking of unarmed enemies; (2) no firing on undefended localities without military significance; (3) no use of forbidden arms or munitions; (4) no improper use of immune buildings (for example, embassies) for military purposes; (5) no pillaging; (6) no killing or wounding those who have surrendered or are disabled; (7) no poisoning wells or streams; (8) no ill-treating of war prisoners; (9) no assassinating and hiring assassins; (10) no compelling the inhabitants of an occupied territory to supply information about the enemy; (11) no air bombardments of civilian populations; (12) no assaults on enemy ships that have surrendered by striking their colors; and (13) no destroying civilian cultural objects or places of worship.

There have been some recent attempts to limit the proliferation of conventional weapons. Between 1973 and 1991, the *Mutual and Balanced Force Reduction* (MBFR) talks were conducted between NATO and the Warsaw Pact. During the late 1970s, Washington and Moscow conducted the *Conventional Arms Transfer Talks* (CATT), but they were suspended in 1979 and later resumed in 1987. The *Conference on Security and Cooperation in Europe* (CSCE) has been meeting since 1973 to discuss broader security issues, including the Confidence Security-Building Measures (CSBM) sought to reduce tensions by improving communications between East and West. CSCE's 35 members include all NATO, Warsaw Pact, and neutral European countries. None of these negotiations made progress until recently.

Soviet President Gorbachev dramatically broke the impasse on conventional arms talks and related issues in December 1988, when he announced in a speech before the UN General Assembly that he was ordering the Soviet military to cut 500,000 personnel by 1991, of which 146,330 came from Soviet forces deployed in East Europe. He also announced that he would withdraw large amounts of military hardware from Europe to the eastern side of the Ural Mountains, which eventually totaled 15,000 tanks, 9,000 artillery pieces, and 900 aircraft. A multilateral agreement on even more significant cuts followed relatively quickly. The Conventional Force Reductions in Europe (CFE) talks started in March 1989 and were concluded in November 1990, when 23 countries signed an agreement leading to cutbacks in conventional forces. The treaty limited American and Soviet troops in Central Europe to 195,000, tanks to 20,000, other armored vehicles to 20,000, artillery to 20,000, and helicopters and aircraft to 8,500. In February 1990, amidst the talks, Moscow and Washington agreed to reduce their respective forces in Europe to 195,000 each. In November 1990, the CSCE established a permanent secretariat and Conflict Prevention Center, which has tried to help manage the enormous changes caused by the collapse of communism and the Soviet Empire.

While the superpowers have made considerable progress in reducing conventional forces arrayed against each other, military power continues to expand across the Third World. Some Third World countries are either developing or acquiring space launch vehicle (SPV) technology, which gives them the ability to hit targets thousands of miles away. In May 1989, India launched its Agni missile which can deliver a one-ton payload as far east as Hong Kong and as far west as Teheran. Israel has its Jericho II, Argentina its Condor II, Brazil its SS-1000, and Iraq its Tammuz 1 missiles, all with ranges of 500 to nearly 1,000 miles. During the Persian Gulf War, Iraq fired scores of SCUD missiles at Israel and Coalition forces in Saudi Arabia.

The United States and its allies have long been concerned with this proliferation of missile technology to the Third World. In 1987, the United States, Germany, Britain, Japan, France, Italy, Canada, and Spain negotiated the *Missile Technology Control Regime* (MTCR) in which they agreed to limit exports of ballistic missiles, their parts, or production facilities. The most successful effort to stop Third World proliferation was the cease-fire agreement imposed on Iraq following the Persian Gulf War. UN inspectors have searched most military and scientific facilities across Iraq to find and destroy chemical, nuclear, and long-range conventional weapons. Iraq's humiliating defeat and inspection may serve as a powerful deterrent on other ambitious Third World states.

Proliferation is also a problem for chemical and biological weapons. Chemical weapons were widely used during World War I, resulting in over 100,000 deaths and 1 million casualties.[63] Both sides used chemical weapons during the Iraq-Iran War (1980–1988). It was feared that Iraq would use chemical weapons during the Persian Gulf War (1990–1991), but it refrained. As many as 20 Third World states are considered "likely" or "possible" either to develop or already possess chemical weapons, while an additional four are considered likely developers of biological weapons.[64]

There are some treaties addressing biological and chemical weapons. The 1972 Biological and Toxin Weapons Convention prohibits the development, production, and stockpiling of biological weapons, and it followed a 1925 Geneva Convention treaty banning the use, but not possession, of biological and chemical weapons. Although the United States, Britain, and Japan developed biological weapons, they have since been voluntarily destroyed. In 1990 Washington and Moscow signed the Chemical Weapons Destruction Agreement in which they pledged to stop the production and reduce their numbers of chemical weapons.

CONCLUSION

Throughout history, war or the threat of war has been an intricate and often dominant part of international relations. As warfare changes so, too, do international relations, and new technology underlies the changes in both. New weapons—gunpowder, the tank, submarines, atomic bombs—can dramatically shift the nature of warfare and, in turn, the balance of power. Can that link among war, technology, and international relations ever be broken?[65]

Throughout history, people have devised more effective means of destroying lives, property, and environments. For the first several thousand years of history, bows and catapults were the most powerful delivery systems. During the fourteenth century in Europe, gunpowder was first used for crude muskets and cannon, and improved versions of these weapons systems shaped warfare for the next 500 years. Then, during World War I, the introduction of warplanes and dirigibles allowed the first massive air bombardments. The first missiles were developed and used by the Germans during World War II, when their V-2 rockets could deliver a one ton bomb several hundred miles away. These first rockets were inaccurate, however, and were mostly targeted on large cities. More importantly, the United States exploded its first atomic bomb in 1945 and first nuclear bomb in 1952, and the Soviet Union and other countries soon followed with their own bombs. During the late 1940s, jet warplanes came on line, and in the late 1950s, the first International Continental Ballistic Missiles (ICBMs) were deployed.

Some of the more recent developments have been just as dazzling. Television viewers during the Persian Gulf War safely witnessed the performance of a vast array of high tech weapons, including sea-launched conventional cruise missiles that flew hundreds of miles and then precisely downed the air shafts of bunkers it was programmed to hit. Conventional weapons are becoming increasingly powerful: "a bomber can drop 50 or more bombs of 500-1,000 pounds each . . . a single cluster bomb detonates into several hundred bomblets. Fuel air explosives disperse fuel into the air and then detonate the fuel cloud. Both in lethality and in area covered, so-called conventional weapons today approach small nuclear weapons in destructive power."[66] These new conventional weapons pack the destruction of nuclear weapons without the radioactive fall-out and thus might make them obsolete.

There have been two conflict systems since 1945. Conflicts among the world's most advanced countries and between them and the Soviet bloc have been managed peacefully. Conflicts among the less developed countries and between the great powers and the Third World have often resulted in war. The Cold War entangled every region and country. Superpower rivalry exacerbated regional conflicts. Although the Cold War may be over, many of those regional and national conflicts are just as virulent. Almost all wars since 1945 have occurred in the Third World. With the breakup of the Soviet Union and Yugoslavia and scores of separatist movements around the world, the number of Third World countries is increasing rather than diminishing.

Meanwhile, weapons exports and proliferation continue. With the Cold War over, the primary motive in most cases is to enjoy the income such sales provide. But as the superpowers and the great powers cut back their arsenals, the competition among arms dealers grows more intense elsewhere. The United States and Russia in particular are dependent on arms sales for a large percentage of their respective exports and wealth. Although global spending for arms may continue to diminish, the Third World will consume an increasing share of the total. War, however, will increasingly be within, rather than between, states.

STUDY QUESTIONS

1. How has the nature of warfare—its weapons, strategies, tactics, scale, and so on—changed throughout history? What accounts for those changes?

2. What have been the effects of high military spending on a nation's economic development?

3. How has global military spending changed over time? What accounts for the increases? How has it been affected since the end of the Cold War?

4. What have been the effects of high military spending on a nation's economic development?

5. What is the relationship between military alliances, power, and security?

6. What steps led Iraq to invade Kuwait in August 1990? What steps led the United States to adopt a policy of expelling Iraq from Kuwait by any means possible? Analyze the American efforts from August 1990 to January 1991 to build up and lead an alliance to victory against Iraq.

7. What is a crisis? In what ways can international crises be managed?

8. What is the nature of low-intensity warfare?

9. What is the nature of terrorism? How can it be combated?

10. What conventional arms and war restrictions have been negotiated throughout history?

ENDNOTES

1. Francis Beer, *Peace Against War: The Ecology of International Violence* (San Francisco: Freeman, 1988).

2. James Shotwell, *War as an Instrument of National Policy* (New York: Harcourt Brace, 1929), 15.

3. Quoted in Geoffrey Blainey, *The Causes of War* (New York: The Free Press, 108).

4. Hans Morganthau, *Politics Among Nations* (New York: Knopf, 1967), 392.

5. Charles Kegley and Eugene Wittkopf, *World Politics: Trend and Transformation* (New York: St. Martin's Press, 1993), 437–438.

6. Herbert Tillema, *International Armed Conflict Since 1945: A Bibliographic Handbook of Wars and Military Interventions* (Boulder, Colo.: Westview Press, 1991).

7. Ruth Leger Sivard, *World Military and Social Expenditures 1991* (Washington, D.C.: World Priorities, 1991), 20.

8. David Singer and Melvin Small, "Foreign Policy Indicators: Predictors of War in History," *Policy Sciences,* vol. 5, September 1974, 271–296.

9. Jack Levy, "Historical Trends in Great Power War, 1495-1975," *International Studies Quarterly,* vol. 25, June 1982, 298; Jack Levy and T. Clifton Morgan, "The Frequency and Seriousness of War: An Inverse Relationship?" *Journal of Conflict Resolution,* vol. 28, December 1984, 731–749.

10. John Rouke, *International Relations* (Guilford, Conn.: Duskhin, 1994), 264.

11. Ruth Leger Sivard, *World Military and Social Expenditures* 1991, 20.

12. John Gaddis, *The Long Peace: Inquiries Into the History of the Cold War* (New York: Oxford University Press, 1987).

13. Ibid.

14. Bruce Russett and Richard Starr, *World Politics: A Menu for Choice* (New York: Freeman, 1990), 171.

15. John Mueller, *Retreat from Doomsday: The Obsolescence of Major War* (New York: Basic Books, 1989), 5.

16. For an outstanding collection of arguments, see Charles Kegley, ed., *The Long Postwar Peace: Contending Explanations and Projections* (New York: HarperCollins, 1991).

17. Philip Zelikow, "The United States and the Use of Force: A Historical Summary, in George K. Osburn et al., eds., *Democracy, Strategy, and Vietnam* (Lexington, Mass.: Lexington Book, 1987), 31–84. For studies of evaluating the United States use of force, see: Alexander George, David Hall, and William Simons, *The Limits of Coercive Diplomacy* (Boston: Little, Brown, 1971); Barry Blechman and Stephen Kaplan, "U.S. Military Forces as a Political Instrument," *Political Science Quarterly*, vol. 94, 193–210.

18. Herbert K. Tillema, *Appeal to Force: American Military Intervention in the Era of Containment* (New York: Crowell, 1973), Chapter 5.

19. Barry Blechman and Stephen Kaplan, *Force Without War: U.S. Armed Forces as a Political Instrument* (Washington, D.C.: The Brookings Institute, 1978), Chapter 4.

20. See Graham Allison and Gregory F. Treverton, eds., *Rethinking America's Security: Beyond Cold War to the New World Order* (New York: Norton, 1992); Murray Weidenbaum, *Small Wars, Big Defense, Paying for the Military After the Cold War* (New York: Oxford University Press, 1992).

21. Daniel Papp, "Soviet Unconventional Conflict Policies and Strategies in the Third World," *Conflict Quarterly*, vol. 8, no. 4, Fall, 1988, 50–55.

22. Richard Rosecrance, *The Rise of the Trading State: Commerce and Conquest in the Modern World* (New York: Basic Books, 1986), 157.

23. U.S. Arms Control and Disarmament Agency, *World Military Expenditures and Arms Transfers 1990* (Washington, D.C.: U.S. Government Printing Office, 1992).

24. Mark Thee, "Military Technology, Arms Control, and Human Development," *Bulletin of Peace Proposals*, vol. 18, 1–11; See also, Lester Kurtz, *The Nuclear Cage: A Sociology of the Arms Race* (Englewood Cliffs, N.J.: Prentice-Hall, 1988).

25. John Rothgeb, *Defining Power: Influence and Force in the Contemporary International System* (New York: St. Martin's Press, 1993), 155.

26. Steven Pealstein, "A Wholesale Change in the Arms Bazaar," *Washington Post National Weekly Edition*, April 15–21, 1990, 8.

27. Michael Klare, "Wars in the 1990's: Growing Firepower in the Third World," *Bulletin of the Atomic Scientists*, vol. 46, May 1990, 12.

28. Michael Klare, "Who's Arming Who? The Arms Trade in the 1990's," *Technology Review*, vol. 93, May–June, 1990, 44.

29. *The Defense Monitor*, vol. 20, no. 4, 1991, 6.

30. SIPRI Yearbook 1990: *World Armaments and Disarmament* (New York: Oxford University Press, 1990).

31. Steven Erlanger, "Moscow Insists It Must Sell the Instruments of War to Pay the Costs of Peace," *New York Times*, February 3, 1993, A6.

32. Ruth Leger Sivard, *World Military and Social Expenditures 1991,* 11.

33. See Andrew Pierre, *The Global Politics of Arms Sales* (Princeton, N.J.: Princeton University Press, 1982).

34. ADCA, 1992, 9.

35. Ruth Leger Sivard, *World Military and Social Expenditures 1991,* 23.

36. Arthur Burns, "The Defense Sector and the American Economy," in Seymour Melman, ed., *The War Economy of the United States* (New York: St. Martin's Press, 1971), 115.

37. Steve Chan, "The Impact of Defense Spending on Economic Performance," *Orbis,* vol. 29, Summer 1985, 407–412. See also PaulCraig and John Jungerman, *Nuclear Arms Race: Technology and Society* (New York: McGraw-Hill, 1986).

38. David Gold et al., *Misguided Expenditure, and Analysis of the Proposed MX Missile Systems* (New York: Council on Economic Priorities, 1981).

39. Michael Klare, "The Arms Trade: Changing Patterns in the 1980's," *Third World Quarterly,* vol. 9, October 1987, 1279–1280.

40. Ruth Leger Sivard, *World Military and Social Expenditures 1991,* 11.

41. William Riker, *The Theory of Political Coalitions* (New Haven, Conn.: Yale University Press, 1962), 32–33; See also Stephen Walt, The Original of Alliance (Ithaca N.Y.: Cornell University Press, 1987).

42. Randolph Siverson and Michael Tennefoss, "Power, Alliance, and the Escalation of National Conflict, 1815–1965," *American Political Science Review,* vol. 78, December 1984, 1063.

43. Bruce Bueno de Mesquita, *The War Trap* (New Haven, Conn.: Yale University Press, 1981).

44. Quoted in Robert Tucker and David Hendrickson, "Thomas Jefferson and American Foreign Policy," *Foreign Affairs,* vol. 69, no. 2, Spring 1990, 138.

45. Ibid, 147.

46. George Kennan, *The Fateful Alliance: France, Russia, and the Coming of the First World War* (New York: Pantheon, 1984), 238.

47. See Richard Starr, "The Warsaw Treaty Organization," in Francis Beer, ed., *Alliances* (New York: Holt, Rinehart, and Winston, 1970).

48. Bruce Russett and Harvey Starr, *World Politics: The Menu for Choice* (New York: Freeman, 1992), 89.

49. For an excellent overview of Reagan and Bush policies toward Iraq, see Alan Friedman, "The President Was Very, Very Mad," *New York Times,* November 7, 1993, 15a, which is adapted from his book, *The Spider's Web: The Secret History of How the White House Illegally Armed Iraq.* See also Elaine Sciolino and Michael Wines, "Bush's Greatest Glory Fades as Questions on Iraq Persist," *New York Times,* June 27, 1992.

50. Elaine Sciolino, "Bush Ordered Iraqis Plied with Aid," *New York Times,* May 28, 1992.

51. Elaine Sciolino and Michael Wines, "Bush's Greatest Glory Fades as Questions on Iraq Persist," *New York Times,* June 27, 1992.

52. Thomas Friedman and Patrick Tyler, "From the First, U.S. Resolve to Fight," *New York Times,* March 3, 1991.

53. For an account analyzing the effectiveness of America's high-tech weapons, see Eric Schmitt, "Missile's War Record Revised," *New York Times,* April 7, 1991. For an account analyzing the war's economic costs to the region and beyond, see Youssef Ibrahim, "Gulf War Is Said to Have Cost the Region $676 Billion in 1990–1991," *New York Times,* April 22, 1993.

54. Ted Gurr, *Why Men Rebel* (Princeton, N.J.: Princeton University Press, 1970), 14.

55. David Singer, *Policy Indicators,* 66–72; See also Loren Thomson, ed., *Low Intensity Conflict: The Pattern of Warfare in the Modern World* (Lexington, Mass.: Lexington, 1989).

56. Mao Zedong, *Selected Works* (Peking: Foreign Language Press, 1967), vol. 1, 63.

57. Walter Laquer, "Reflections on Terrorism," *Foreign Affairs,* vol. 65, Fall 1986, 87.

58. Conor Cruise O'Brien, "Liberty and Terrorism," *International Security,* vol. 2, Fall, 1977, 557.

59. James Clarity, "For All the Bombs, the IRA is no Closer to its Goals," *New York Times,* December 13, 1992.

60. U.S. Department of State, *Patterns of Global Terrorism, 1990* (Washington, D.C.: U.S. State Department, 1991), 37.

61. Michael Roskin and Nicholas Berry, *IR: An Introduction to International Relations* (Englewood Cliffs, N.J.: Prentice-Hall, 1990), 330.

62. Uri Ra'anan et al., eds., *The Hydra of Carnage: International Linkages of Terrorism* (Lexington, Mass.: Lexington Books, 1985); Charles Kegley, ed., *International Terrorism: Characteristics, Causes, Controls* (New York: St. Martin's Press, 1990).

63. Steve Fetter, "Ballistic Missiles and Weapons of Mass Destruction: What is the Threat? What Should Be Done?" *International Security,* vol. 16, Summer, 1991, 15.

64. Ibid, 16.

65. For some recent perspectives, see Geoffrey Blainy, *The Causes of War* (New York: The Free Press, 1988); Patrick Brogan, *The Fighting Never Stopped: A Comprehensive Guide to World Conflict Since 1945* (New York: Vintage Books, 1990); Betty Gilad, *The Psychological Dimensions of War* (Newbury Park, Calif.: Sage Publications, 1990); Stuart Bremer and Barry Hughes, *Disarmament and Development: A Design for the Future* (Englewood Cliffs, N.J.: Prentice-Hall, 1990); Randolph Siverson and Harvey Starr, *The Diffusion of War* (Ann Arbor, Mich.: University of Michigan, 1991).

66. Ruth Leger Sivard, *World Military and Expenditures 1991,* 13.

Geoeconomic Conflict and Cooperation Among the Democratic Industrial Countries

Geoeconomic Strategies for a Global Political Economy: Regulatory, Developmental, and Social Capitalism

Key Terms and Concepts

Cartel
Comparative Advantage
  Currency Policy
Fiscal Policy
Free Market
Industrial Policy
Invisible Hand
Macroeconomic Policy

Market Imperfections
Mercantilism
Monetary Policy
Monopoly
Neomercantilism
Oligopoly
Plaza Accord
Regulatory System

Social Market System
Strategic Industry
Supply-side Policy
Trickle down

The "free world" is based on liberal political and economic values. Ideally, a liberal democratic country has a written constitution in which all people are subject to the law, sovereignty rests in the people, and all the people enjoy a full range of human and civil rights. In addition a political system exists in which the people's needs and desires are served by representatives and/or referendums. As Lincoln put it, democracy is "of, by, and for the people." The major economic value of economic freedom that involves the ideals of free markets, private property, and minimum government interference.

There is, inevitably, a wide gap between liberal political economic ideals and reality, and great variations in the institutions and practices of countries espousing those ideals. Although the ranks of democratic countries are expanding, their number accounts for only about one quarter of all the world's nation-states. Among the liberal democratic countries, there are many different political systems that range from the relatively decentralized federal systems of Switzerland, the United States, Canada, and Germany to the relatively more centralized parliamentary systems of Britain, Japan, and Italy. And, of course, there are many countries whose governments claim to be democratic but are not.

The same condition is true for a country's economic orientation. Most democratic industrial countries claim to have liberal economies. Yet there are enormous variations in the degree of government interference among the so-called *free market* countries. All governments intervene in the economy—the difference is the ways and degrees of intervention.

Among the free market economies there are three significantly different orientations. Of the world's economies, none have freer systems than the United States and Hong Kong, whose governments have a *regulatory* orientation. In pursuing the free market ideal, the government regulates business to ensure that no domestic firms achieve *monopoly* or *oligopoly* power, and maintains minimal import barriers and export

291

incentives. These governments generally put economic freedom first, even if it means continual trade and payments deficits, relatively low economic growth, and inequitable income distribution.

Then there are states like France or Japan which have both liberal political systems and heavily state-guided market systems. These states follow a *neomercantilist* or *developmental market* strategy in which the nation's economic security is equated with a relatively high growth rate and equitable income distribution; continual trade and payments surpluses; and diversified sources of foreign raw materials, energy, and markets. To these ends, the government targets important industries and technologies for development with export incentives, subsidies, *cartels,* protection from competitive imports, and so on.

Finally, there are the *social market* economies, exemplified by the Scandanavian countries, in which policies emphasize the equitable distribution of existing wealth rather than the creation of new wealth. In this type of system government spending as a percentage of GNP is relatively high, the state provides citizens with cradle to grave benefits, the most important industries are often publicly owned, and markets are heavily regulated.

Although every country has an economic orientation and policies, this chapter will concentrate on exploring the different economic orientations and policies of the advanced liberal industrial countries. It will first examine the different political-economic ideologies that can guide the governments of liberal democratic states, discussing their strengths and weaknesses. It will then explore the range of possible *macroeconomic,* industrial, and trade policies that states can follow. Only after understanding these basic principles and policies can we understand the international issues of the chapter.

POLITICAL ECONOMIC IDEOLOGIES

Ideology and policy are often closely related. Ideologies are value systems that help shape a country's actions or policies. Sometimes states pursue policies that seemingly violate their values. At other times there is a close accord between ideals and action. It is important to understand why countries vary in their ability or willingness to live up to their values and ideals.

Regulatory Market Ideology

Notions of economic and political freedom developed together. In 1776, the United States declared its liberty from Great Britain. That same year, Adam Smith's classic study of free trade, *The Wealth of Nations,* was published.[1] In his study Smith argued that everyone benefits from free trade because competition forces everyone to specialize in producing what they produce best and then trading that good for anything else they desire. The forces of supply and demand are the "magic of the marketplace," or *invisible hand,* in which consumer and societal needs and desires are met.

Markets should be free not just within a state but among states as well. Every nation, like every individual, has certain natural productive strengths and weaknesses known as *comparative advantage*. Smith argued that "what is prudence in the conduct of every private family can scarcely be folly in that of a great kingdom. If a foreign country can supply us with a commodity cheaper than we ourselves can make it, better buy it of them with some part of our own industry."[2] According to economist Paul Samuelson, "free trade promotes a mutually profitable division of labor, greatly enhances the potential real national product of all nations, and makes possible higher standards of living all over the globe."[3]

Like political liberals, economic liberals maintain that the less government the better. Government, according to Adam Smith, should have:

> only three duties . . . first, the duty of protecting the society from the violence and invasion of other independent societies; secondly, the duty of protecting, as far as possible, every member of the society from the injustice or oppression of every other member, or the duty of establishing an exact administration of justice; and thirdly, the duty of erecting and maintaining certain public works and certain public institutions, which can never be for the interest of any individual, or small number of individuals.[4]

Liberal economic theory has been severely criticized.[5] The central criticism is that free trade is based on ideal assumptions which do not exist in the real world. Markets are distorted by governments, cartels, and other forces everywhere, including in the United States. Robert Kuttner points out that liberal economic theory "to most of the world . . . seems utopian and the practice hypocritical. America seems to practice a chaotic ad hoc mercantilism—weapons procurement, farm price supports, textile quotas, and various 'voluntary' restraints extracted from trading partners—while it stridently preaches free trade."[6] In reality, the trade of all states is more or less managed rather than free.

Freer trade is an advantage to a leading industrial country but can impede the growth of a developing country trying to catch up with more advanced nations. After studying Britain's economy, the nineteenth century German political economists, Friedrich List, advised Germany against free trade, arguing that:

> . . . free competition between two nations which are highly civilized can only be mutually beneficial in case both of them are in a nearly equal position of industrial development, and that any nation which owing to misfortunes is behind others in industry, commerce, navigation . . . must first of all strengthen her own individual powers, in order to fit herself to enter into free competition with more advanced nations.[7]

John Spanier expands the argument:

> the free market may well be a superior mechanism for allocating goods when those competing and exchanging goods are of approximately equal power. When one nation is clearly more advanced economically however, free trade benefits it more because it is able to penetrate the markets of weaker countries. The laws of the free market are not neutral. Power is the 'invisible hand' determining the distribution

of wealth. Among nations that are equal in economic power, economic relations
may well breed interdependence, as in the EEC and relations between them and
the United States. But between the economically strong and the economically weak,
the inevitable result is the dependence of the latter.[8]

And as Scott and Lodge point out, it:

is not surprising that the leading advocates of free trade have been those who were
strong at the time, first the United Kingdom, then the United States . . . Free
trade, like free competition, has political as well as economic content: taken literally
it is a system that enhances the power of the powerful and makes it all the more
difficult for the poor to catch up.[9]

Liberals claim that economics and politics can and should be separated. But this is
an impossible task in the real world in which economics and politics are so closely
meshed that they are inseparable. All economic conflicts are political, and all political
conflicts have some economic dimension. The difficult question is determining just
how they influence each other. Where struggles over wealth end and struggles over
power begin is a chicken and egg problem.

According to liberalism all industries are of equal value—a billion dollars worth of
potato chips is just as important as a billions dollars worth of computer chips. Critics
argue that equating potato and computer chips is ludicrous. The potato chip industry's
technological, job, or wealth "multiplier," or ripple effects on the economy, are as limited as the computer industry's multiplier effects are enormous.

Liberal economists assume that with less government interference in the economy
economic development will be greater and more rapid. This simply is not true. Completely free markets are not necessarily the best means of creating wealth and allocating
resources. Perhaps no other country in the world, with the possible exception of the tiny
British colony of Hong Kong, has a more deeply entrenched free market mentality and
economy as does the United States. Yet America's growth, productivity rate, and its
middle class as a percentage of the total population, are much lower than other democratic industrial states whose governments are more active in directing the economy.
Many observers fear that America's free trade policies are allowing the economy to be
"hollowed out" as foreign competition undercuts American businesses while American
multinational corporations transfer their operations overseas to enjoy access to markets,
resources, and cheaper labor. They point out that the United States has suffered chronic
trade deficits since the early 1970s.

Developmental or Neomercantilist Market Ideology

As an ideology, *mercantilism*—maximizing the nation's exports through state-licensed
monopolies and subsidies, and minimizing imports through high trade barriers—is
much older than liberalism.[10] States have always intervened in the economy whether it
was for generating tax receipts, promoting certain industries or classes, or realizing
God's will. During the early modern era, states targeted important or *strategic industries*
for development with subsidies, import barriers, and export incentives in order to

develop their economies and achieve national security. Economic and military security were closely linked and many of the strategic industries targeted for development produced military weapons and equipment. Much of the revenue gathered by the state was used to build up the nation's military forces and either defend or expand the realm against other states.

Mercantilism, according to Jacob Viner, has four main propositions:

1) wealth is an absolutely essential means to power, whether for security or for aggression; 2) power is essential or valuable as a means to the acquisition or retention of wealth; 3) wealth and power are each proper ultimate ends of national policy; 4) there is a long-run harmony between these ends, although in particular circumstances it may be necessary for a time to make economic sacrifices in the interest of military security and therefore also of long-run prosperity.[11]

Neomercantilism is the contemporary version of mercantilism; it is a developmental and national security strategy for liberal democratic countries in an interdependent world. Rather than spend scarce resources on the military sector, neomercantalist states concentrate on promoting high technology consumer- and equipment-industries that most efficiently create wealth and expand the middle class.

In many ways, neomercantilism is a reaction against liberal idealism. Liberal economists construct an ideal world and then attempt to shape the real world accordingly. In contrast, neomercantilists attempt to understand the way global political economy really operates and act accordingly. While liberalism's goal is free markets, neomercantilism's is the creation, distribution, and securing of wealth. Thus, neomercantilists first determine which industries can create the most wealth and then map a strategy whereby those industries can be developed. In addition, neomercantilists see international trade as largely a zero-sum competition in which one side's gain is another's loss. Thus, neomercantilist governments use any means they can to tip the international trade playing field in favor of its own firms.

Free markets exist only in theory, not in the real world. All markets are distorted and often outright managed by domestic and foreign governmental policies. Since the benefits of international trade are not evenly distributed among participants, there are net winners and losers in any transaction, both over the short- and long-term. For example, when foreign firms "dump" their goods in a market, consumers benefit while the domestic producers of those goods lose market share and profits and are sometimes forced into bankruptcy. Thus, over the short-term, domestic consumers and foreign producers win and domestic producers lose. Over the long-term, consumers lose too because the economy suffers as wealth flows to foreign rather than domestic producers. As the nation's tax, employment, and wealth base erodes relative to foreign competitors, consumers inevitably have less money with which to buy goods and services. To make things worse, after they have driven their competitors into bankruptcy, the foreign firms usually raise prices to recoup earlier losses sustained from dumping.

There are winners and losers in international investment flows as well. Liberals claim foreign investments are mutually beneficial. The Reagan administration summed up this outlook on foreign investments in the United States in a 1983 statement: "We believe that there are only winners, no losers, and all participants gain from it."[12]

Realists argue that it depends.[13] The country, for example, may enjoy a net gain if foreigners buy money-losing firms or real estate, such as country clubs and skyscrapers. The foreign investor often must pour money, managerial expertise, and technology into the asset before it can turn a profit. And after being bought out, the original owners will invest their money elsewhere, ideally in more productive domestic industries. But a country may well suffer a net long-term loss if foreign firms buy money-making high technology firms, banks, factories, mines, or farms which generate much of a country's wealth. Greenfield sites or new foreign investments in an office, factory, or resturant can also represent either a net gain or loss for the recipient country. The bottom line is whether either a buy out or greenfield site investment brings more money, technology, skills, and dynamism into a country than it takes out.

International trade and investment battles are becoming fiercer as increasing numbers of governments understand how serious the stakes are and try to intervene to tip the geoeconomic power balance in their favor. Given a relatively equal power distribution and development level, neomercantilist countries will grow faster, export more, and import less than liberal countries. The larger and more advanced the neomercantilist country's economy, the greater the adverse effects on development elsewhere. Governments which do not systematically attempt to assist the creation and distribution of wealth through rational macroeconomic, industrial, and trade policies according to a long-term plan, increasingly find their nation's economy shaped and distorted by foreign governments which do.

Many analysts argue that America's liberal economic ideals are increasingly at a disadvantage in an ever more neomercantilist world. Blake and Walters point out that "liberal economists who dominate American economic scholarship are ill-equipped to evaluate systematically the political forces shaping, and political implications of, their prescriptions for 'rational' economic policies in an era of highly politicized global economic relations."[14]

The Clinton administration seems to understand these American and international economic realities. Increasingly throughout the 1990s, the United States will emulate the neomercantilist macroeconmoic, industrial, and trade policies of its competitors. International trade and investment flows may become increasingly managed as governments struggle to negotiate the best deal for their nation's firms.

Social Market Ideology

While both liberalism and neomercantilism are concerned with the creation of wealth, social democracy is more concerned with equitably distributing existing wealth. Markets are distrusted as arenas in which the rich and powerful feed off the poor and weak. The freer the markets, the greater the gap between rich and poor. A powerful state must be constructed to prevent the exploitation and continued subjugation of the latter by the former.

In the late nineteenth century under Chancellor Otto von Bismarck, Germany was the first country to begin establishing welfare, health, and social security institutions. Other industrial states slowly began developing their own systems. It was the Great Depression of the 1930s which convinced the United States and a few other laggards of the state's interest in regulating the economy.[15]

There are very good political as well as economic reasons for a greater state role in the economy:

Modern governments have become increasingly insensitive to demands for a wide variety of welfare services and have taken on the responsibility for mass social and economic welfare. The improvement through state intervention of the material . . . . well-being of its citizens has become one of the central functions of state activity. The satisfaction of rising claims by citizens has become a major source of the state's legitimization and of a government's continuance in office.[16]

Social democracy has been criticized on several grounds. By focusing on dividing rather than expanding the pie, living standards stagnate over the long run. By heavily regulating and taxing markets, social democrats reduce incentives for entrepreneurs to create new wealth.

Sweden is the ultimate social market state, with cradle to grave health, education, and welfare benefits for all citizens.[17] These benefits have been expensive and the price may have become exorbitant. Between 1970 and 1990, Sweden's welfare programs grew from 44 percent to 70 percent of its GNP. In 1990, Swedish taxes as a percentage of GNP were 56.9 percent compared to America's 29.9 percent. Like other democratic industrial states, Sweden has experienced an economic slowdown and rising socioeconomic problems. Unemployment rose from 1.4 percent in 1989 to 6.2 percent in 1993. Between 1992 and 1994, the annual budget deficit as a percentage of GNP rose from 5.6 percent to 11.1 percent.

In 1991, a coalition of moderate-conservative parties took over the government after a half century of nearly uninterrupted social-democratic rule. The reform government has tried to pare back Sweden's welfare state. Payments to workers injured on the job have been reduced and the age to receive partial pensions has been raised from 60 to 62, and full pensions from 65 to 66. Compensation for women who choose to stay home with their children has been reduced from 90 percent to 80 percent of their regular pay. The Swedish krona has been devalued to boost exports and the government has employed private companies to perform some tasks traditionally done by the state. In 1992, the government cut $9 billion from the budget. Increasing numbers of countries will emulate Sweden's welfare state cutbacks into the 1990's and beyond.

POLITICAL ECONOMIC POLICIES

Governments everywhere intervene actively in the economy to make up for myriad *market imperfections,* although they do so in greatly varying degrees and areas. Economic policy can be divided into three broad areas—macroeconomic, industrial, and trade—each of which is thoroughly integrated with the others. Macroeconomic policies are those government actions or inactions directed at affecting the entire economy. In contrast, industrial policies are focused on particular industries, technologies, or firms. Trade policies, as the name implies, are chiefly concerned with the country's trade balance and composition of exports and imports.

Macroeconomic Policies

Governments can shape the national economy through several means: (1) *fiscal* or government budget policy; (2), *monetary* or money-supply and interest-rate policy; (3) *supply side* or tax policy; and (4) *currency policy*. Each of these policies is designed to either stimulate a depressed economy or deflate an inflationary economy, a practice known as "fine tuning" business cycles. Ideally, all four macroeconomic policies are used so that they complement the government's goals. In practice, this coordination is extremely difficult to achieve; a government may follow a stimulatory fiscal policy and deflationary monetary policy, and so on.

Fiscal policy or government budget policy is usually the most influential of the four. In every country, the government is the largest single buyer of goods and services. When governments increase spending they stimulate the economy, and when they cut back spending they deflate it. Fiscal policy is also an important source of industrial policies because the budget allocates or denies money to specific industries.

Monetary policy primarily involves the money supply and interest rates. When an economy is depressed, a country's central bank (the Federal Reserve in the United States), will lower the interest (discount) rate it charges banks when they borrow money from it. Banks take advantage of the lower rate and increase their borrowing, and, in turn, offer lower interest rates (prime) for the money they lend to credit-worthy businesses. Lower interest rates stimulate increased economic activity—households borrow money to buy a car or boat, factories to invest in new equipment, and entrepreneurs to start new businesses. When an economy becomes overheated or inflationary, central banks may raise interest rates to take more money, and thus demand, out of the economy, and thereby reduce inflation.

Raising or lowering taxes is yet another way to affect the economy. Cutting taxes (supply side policy) puts more money in the pockets of businesses and households. If the extra money is used to buy something, it creates a demand and thus supply. If it is saved, it makes more money available to businesses or households to borrow and spend. As a result, the economy is stimulated. Raising taxes has the opposite effect. Like fiscal policy, tax policy can be an important industrial policy tool as well since most countries' tax codes favor some industries, classes, firms, or individuals more than others. Social democratic countries have relatively progressive tax codes in which the richer a household, the larger the percentage of their income is taken in taxes. Other countries may cut taxes for the rich in the hopes that they will use at least some of the extra income to invest in businesses which create wealth and jobs, a policy known as *trickle down*. At best, even in the most economically advanced countries with strong entrepreneurial straditions, trickle down policies simply make the rich richer while having little effect on economic growth. It fails completely in countries lacking an entrepreneurial tradition.

All governments recognize the importance of currency rates in macroeconomic policy. Liberal economists believe that a nation's currency reflects national strength, or as former Treasury Secretary Don Regan put it: "A strong dollar means a strong America." Thus, liberal and social democratic governments prefer an overvalued currency which gives consumers more buying power and higher living standards, at least in the short-run. Neomercantilists take the opposite view, that an undervalued currency can be an important source of national wealth and power as it encourages exports and discourages imports.

How does a currency's value affect consumer prices and national wealth? Let's say you are shopping for a family car and you find that both a Ford and Volkswagen offer you all the features you desire. And let's say the Ford costs $10,000 in the United States and the Volkswagen 10,000 deutschemarks in Germany. If one dollar equals one deutschemark and the transportation and insurance costs of importing the Volkswagen are not included in the final price, then it would cost $10,000 when it is sold in the United States. You might well buy either car since their cost is the same. The same would be true for a German consumer since the Ford would cost 10,000 deutschemarks.

But what if one dollar equals two deutschemarks? Then the American consumer has twice as much buying power for German goods, and the German consumer half as much buying power for American goods. You would definitely buy the Volkswagen because it would be priced $5,000 in the United States. Your German counterpart would also buy the Volkswagen because the Ford's price would double to 20,000 deutschemarks. You and other American consumers would gain a tremendous savings in the short-term while Ford, other American industries, and the entire economy suffer a loss to their German counterparts. Over the long-term, your initial savings may well disappear as America's economic growth slows, jobs are lost or pay less, lower government revenue may be made up in higher taxes, and so on—unless, of course, you happen to be employed by or own a company that imports German products. The German consumer neither gains nor loses directly, but because Germany's economy will grow faster the German consumer will enjoy more wealth over the long-term.

What determines the value of a nation's currency? Many factors shape a currency's value, but the most important factor is the relative demand and supply of that currency. A government can manipulate a currency's supply in various ways. Japan provides a good case study of how governments undervalue their currencies. After currencies began to float in 1973, the Bank of Japan bought dollars on international currency markets which increased the dollar's demand and thus its value. Meanwhile Tokyo limited the amount of Japanese trade that was denominated in yen, thus restricting the appeal of, and demand for yen by international currency traders. Tokyo also encouraged Japanese firms to invest overseas while restricting foreign investments in Japan. Japanese firms invariably convert their yen into dollars when investing overseas, thus increasing international demand for dollars. Since foreign investments in Japan are limited, demand for yen is weak and thus undervalued. While Tokyo pursues policies that undervalue the yen, Washington usually follows policies that overvalue the dollar. High interest rates and open financial markets attract foreign investors to the United States, which means more demand and thus a higher value for the dollar.

Direct government intervention in international currency markets is increasingly ineffective since the amount of private trading outnumbers international trading by over 30 to 1. Governments can, however, affect the psychology of markets and thus the relative value of currencies. In September 1985, the *Plaza Accord* among the United States, Japan, Germany, France, and Britain (Group of Five) attempted to devalue the dollar by intervening in international currency markets. The amount they invested was actually quite small, but the fact that they were working together to devalue the dollar created a bandwagon effect. Other governments and private traders dumped dollars before the price dropped, thus weakening demand for dollars and accelerating its fall. Within two years, a dollar dropped from 265 yen to 125 yen.

Industrial Policies

Alexander Hamilton recognized long ago that "not only the wealth but the independence and security of a country appear to be materially connected to the prosperity of manufactures," and he advocated government policies that would nurture American industries that included subsidies and import protection.[18] Hamilton was clearly a man ahead of his time, particularly in the United States. Today, Hamilton's policies would be described as neomercantilist policies designed to boost the economy's strategic manufacturing, technological, and financial sectors.

Every government either directly or indirectly picks economic winners and losers. This process is called industrial policy and involves any government initiatives "that will improve growth, productivity, and competitiveness," including "increasing the economy's supply potential (that is, increasing resources, and labor supply and capital stock), developing technology, fostering industrial development, and improving mobility and structural adaptation," or "a complex set of trade, financial, and fiscal policies, conducted within a political environment, with outcomes at variance from market solutions."[19] In some countries like France or Japan, the government creates five year plans to develop strategic industries and technologies. In other countries like the United States, industrial winners and losers are determined by the relative political power balance they enjoy in Washington rather than their intrinsic value to the economy.

Like any policy, industrial policies can either succeed, fail, or have mixed results. A systematic comparison of the five leading industrial countries revealed that Japan was the only country whose industrial policies were consistently successful. Between 1967 and 1981, Japan gained market share in thirteen of the twenty industries targeted for development, remained the same in three, and lost out in four. The four losers were all chemical industries which did fine until their "created" comparative advantage was undercut by the quadrupling of oil prices in 1973. In comparison, the four other key industrial countries—the United States, France, Germany, and Britain—stagnated or lost ground.[20]

Trade Policies

There will always be a global trade equilibrium or a balance between the value of all exports and all imports. The trade surpluses of some countries must be offset by the trade deficits of all the other countries. A nation's international trade account includes the export and import of all material products. An international "payments account" includes the export and import of the value of manufactured goods, services (banking, insurance, shipping), direct foreign investments, portfolio investments (stocks, bonds, etc.), tourism, and government expenditures (foreign aid, military bases, embassies, etc.).

As we have seen, neomercantilists argue that a state must maximize exports and minimize imports in order to boost national wealth and power, while liberal economists are either indifferent or argue that a trade deficit is a sign of strength. Despite these philosophical differences, all governments manipulate trade. Neomercantilist states manipulate trade with an overall strategic plan, while liberal states do so largely through a political process.

Governments can use a variety of policies to affect the national trade and payments balances. Tariffs and quotas are the most obvious trade barriers. Tariffs are a tax on imports which raises the prices for foreign goods and thus weakens the demand for them. Quotas allow only a certain amount of a product into a country. Tariffs are a more effective means of promoting national wealth than quotas since they simultaneously boost government and domestic industry revenues and deplete foreign industry profits. Quotas, on the other hand, do not provide any government revenues, and tend to encourage both foreign and domestic firms to raise prices at the expense of consumers.

As the eighth GATT round of negotiations gradually reduces tariff and quota trade barriers, nontariff barriers have taken their place. Vountary Export Restraints (VERs) or Orderly Marketing Agreements (OMAs) are unofficial quotas which are often negotiated by governments when one country's exports capture enormous market share in another country. About ten percent of all global trade is currently subject to VERs and OMAs. These measures grew rapidly during the 1980s, as Japan's trade and payments surpluses soared and those of the United States and European Union plunged. Of the roughly 100 VERs or OMAs existing in the mid-1980s, the United States accounted for about half and the European Union for about one-third.[21] The poorer and weaker the country, the more easily an industrial country can force it to accept a VER. About 40 percent of all Third World exports to advanced industrial countries are restrained by nontariff barriers.[22] The Multifiber Agreement involving forty countries and strict quotas on textile trade is the world's largest VER.

Red tape can also be an effective nontariff barrier. For example, in October 1982, Paris reacted to a VCR dumping campaign by Japanese consumer electronics producers by decreeing that henceforth all imports of that product had to pass through Poitiers, a small inland city in western France that symobolically was the site where Arab invaders were defeated in A.D. 732. The tiny customs office in Poitiers simply lacked the resources to clear the hundreds of thousands of VCRs piling up there. Japan's exporters filed a complaint with the European Community Executive Committee which later ruled that France had violated Brussels' free trade rules. The European Community, however, later negotiated a VER with Japan while Japanese corporations, which had set up shop in Europe, agreed to buy more local components. As a result of these initiatives, Europe's VCR industry was saved from sure extinction and wealth was circulated within the Community that would otherwise have flowed to Japan.

There are significant pros and cons to a neomercantilist trade policy. Economists estimate that 22,000 more people are unemployed for every $1 billion of a nation's trade deficit. In 1987, the United States suffered a trade deficit of $178 billion, which meant that 3.916 million more people were unemployed and economic growth much lower than would have been the case with a trade equilibrium. Paul Krugman has calculated the costs of a trade war between the United States, the European Union, and Japan in which 100 percent tariff barriers are raised and import levels cut in half. Although liberals would predict a calamity, the actual result would only be an average 2.5 percent decrease in income for these countries, a rate equal to a one percent increase in the unemployment rate. The reason for this mild result would be that imports would eventually be replaced with domestically produced alternatives that would contribute to that country's economic growth.[23] Yet protectionism can be expensive, by one estimate American trade barriers "were costing American consumers $80 billion a year—equal to more than $1,200 per family."[24]

The net effects of protection can either enhance or impede that nation's development. It all depends on whether or not government policies use that protection to promote strategic industries, technologies, and exports. If they do, as in Japan and Newly Industrializing Countries (NICs)—like South Korea, Taiwan, and Singapore—the economy strengthens. If they do not, as in most countries, the economy stagnates as consumers suffer from higher prices and scarce resources are diverted to inefficient, declining economic sectors.

CONCLUSION

It is said that "except for the distinction between despotic and libertarian governments, the greatest difference between one government and another is the extent to which market replaces government and government replaces market."[25] Every economy thus is mixed; governments and markets interact in both the most state controlled and laissez-faire of systems, albeit in vastly different ways and degrees. If capital is the material, financial, and human means of production, then every system is capitalist.

Most states recognize economic development as a national interest. Traditionally, this meant that a government should maximize its economic self-sufficiency and promote agriculture, mining, and other industries. In those days a trade surplus and the accumulation of gold were the primary measure of a nation's economic security. Today, the creation, distribution, and securing of national wealth in the modern, interdependent world economy is more complex, and states differ greatly in the means by which they accomplish this.

All of the theories and policies we have examined have involved a debate over the state's proper role in a nation's development. Of all these perspectives, "regulatory" and "social" market orientations provide the most extreme positions. Regulators maintain that "government is not the solution, it is the problem." Thus the state's role should be the minimal measures necessary to help markets become as free as possible. Social market adherents would scoff at such notions as the "magic of the marketplace" and "the less government the better." In their view more, not less, government is needed to overcome entrenched poverty, inequality, and a host of other socioeconomic ills. In a truly just democratic system, the state should provide citizens with cradle to the grave protection.

Neomercantilists reject both the regulatory and social market visions as completely unrealistic. To say that the state should do everything or nothing, they argue, is absurd. Instead, the state's role should be to maximize the creation and distribution of wealth, by whatever means possible. The means by which a state aids development will inevitably vary considerably from one country to the next, given their vastly different needs, resources, cultures, political systems, and aspirations. The means may also vary just as greatly within a country as it develops, and its needs, resources, and aspirations change.

America's laissez-faire traditions are the exception in a world in which states have traditionally guided economies, often heavy-handedly. Both neomercantilist and welfare state adherents would argue that "classical laissez-faire liberalism may be a wasteful, experimental approach to economic problem-solving in a technocratic global economy with resource scarcity and payoffs for tightly structured teamwork."[26]

Why do states have the economic orientations that they do? Among the industrial countries, there is a clear distinction in the state's role between early and late industrializers. Britain and the United States were early industrializers, and the state played a secondary role in each country's development. One reason was that in those days industrial competition between and within countries was limited and thus, there was less political pressure by industrialists on the state for protection and guidance. A liberal political and commercial culture in both countries was perhaps equally important. In relatively late industrializing countries, like Japan and Germany, the state took a much more active role in guiding development through protectionism and investing in strategic industries. The strong statist tradition of both Japan and Germany was also an important reason. More recently, the newly industrializing countries (NICs) of East Asia—South Korea, Taiwan, Singapore, Thailand, and Malaysia—have all pursued variations of Japan's development strategy.

Which strategy is the best means for maximizing economic development and national security? Robert Gilpin distinguishes between economic idealism and reality when he confesses that although "my values are those of liberalism, the world in which we live is one best described by the ideas of economic nationalism, and occasionally by those of Marxism as well."[27]

STUDY QUESTIONS

1. What are the major characteristics of regulatory, developmental, and social market systems? What are their major positive and negative aspects?

2. What are the major tools of macroeconomic policies?

3. What are the major tools of industrial policies?

4. What are the major tools of trade policies?

5. Why do states have the economic orientations that they do?

ENDNOTES

1. For the classic liberal economic works, see *Adam Smith, An Inquiry into the Nature and Causes of the Wealth of Nations,* Edwin Cannan, ed., (New York: Modern Library, 1937); James Mill, *Elements of Political Economy,* 2nd rev. ed. (London: Henry G. Bohn, 1844); John Stuart Mill, *Principles of Political Economy,* 7th ed. of 1871, J.W. Ashley, ed. (London, Longmans, Green & Co., 1909).

   For more recent liberal theorists, see some contemporary, prominent, free trade theorists including Milton Friedman, Robert Eisner, Herbert Stein, Robert Barro, Robert McKinnon, Robert Mundell, Jude Wanniski, and Jagdish Bhagwati.

2. Quoted in Peter Kenen, *The International Economy* (Englewood Cliffs, N.J.: Prentice-Hall, 1985), 6.

3. Paul Samuelson, *Economics,* 11th ed. (New York: McGraw Hill, 1980), 651.

4. Adam Smith, *Wealth of Nations,* 314.

5. For critiques of liberalism, see such leading economic realist theorists as Kenneth Waltz, *Man, the State, and War. A Theoretical Analysis* (New York: Columbia University Press, 1954); Edward Hallett Carr, *The Twenty Year's Crisis, 1919–1939: An Introduction to the Study of International Relations* (New York: St. Martin's Press, 1962); Charles Kindleberger, *Power and Money: The Economics of International Politics and the Politics of International Economics* (New York: Basic Books, 1970); David Calleo and Benjamin M. Rowland, *America and the World Political Economy* (Bloomington, Ind.: Indiana University Press, 1973): Klaus Knorr, *Power and Wealth: The Political Economy of International Power* (New York: Basic Books, 1973); Peter Katzenstein, *Between Power and Plenty* (Madison, Wis.: University of Wisconsin, 1978); Robert Gilpin, *War and Change in World Politics* (Cambridge: Cambridge University Press, 1981); Robert Gilpin, *The Political Economy of International Relations* (Princeton N.J.: Princeton University Press, 1987); William Nester, *American Power, The New World Order, and the Japanese Challenge* (New York: St. Martin's Press, 1993).

6. Robert Kuttner, *End of Laissez-Faire* (New York: Knopf, 1991), 141.

7. Friedrich List quoted in John Spanier, *Games Nations Play: Analyzing International Politics* (New York: Holt, Rinehart and Winston, 1984), 354.

8. Ibid, 355.

9. George Lodge, *Comparative Business-Government Relations* (Englewood Cliffs, N.J.: Prentice-Hall, 1990), 94.

10. For some classic works on mercantilism, see: Eli F. Hecksher, *Mercantilism,* 2 vol., Mendel Shapiro, trans. (London: Allen & Unwin, 1936); Jacob Viner, "Power Versus Plenty as Objectives of Foreign Policy in the Seventeenth and Eighteenth Centuries," *World Politics,* vol. 1, October 1948, 1–29.

    For some more recent works, see: Helmut Schoek, ed., *Central Planning and Mercantilism* (Princeton, N.J.: Van Nostrand, 1964); R.J. Barry Jones, *Conflict and Control in the World Economy: Contemporary Economic Realism and New Mercantilism* (Atlantic Highlands, N.J.: A. Hilger, 1982); Robert Gilpin, *The Political Economy of International Relations* (Princeton N.J.: Princeton University Press, 1987).

11. Jacob Viner, *Power Versus Plenty as Objectives of Foreign Policy in the Seventeenth and Eighteenth Centuries,* 286.

12. Quoted in Robert Kuttner, *End of Laissez-Faire,* 173.

13. Martin and Susan Tolchin, *Selling Our Security: The Erosion of America's Assets* (New York: Knopf, 1992).

14. David Blake and Robert Walters, *The Politics of Global Economic Relations* (Englewood Cliffs, N.J.: Prentice-Hall, 1987), 67. For an interesting discussion of different theoretical perspectives on American foreign and economic policymaking and policies, see Chapter 8.

15. See Charles Kindleberger, *The World in Depression, 1929–1939* (Berkeley, Calif.: University of California Press, 1988).

16. Wolfram Hanrieder, "Dissolving International Politics: Reflections on the Nation-state," *American Political Science Review,* vol. 72, no. 4, December 1978, 1278.

17. The following information has been taken from Richard Stevenson "Swedes Facing Rigors of Welfare Cuts," *New York Times,* March 14, 1993.

18. Quoted in Eugene V. Rostow, *Law, Power, and the Pursuit of Peace* (Lincoln, Nebr.: University of Nebraska Press, 1968), 189. For the classic American argument for a rational national industrial policy, see Alexander Hamilton, "Report on the Subject of Manufactures," in Arthur Harrison Cole, ed., *Industrial and Commercial Correspondence of Alexander Hamilton Anticipating His Report on Manufactures* (New York: A.M. Kelley, 1968).

19. Hugh Patrick and Larry Meissner, eds., *Japan's High Technology Industries: Lessons and Limitations of Industrial Policy* (Seattle: University of Washington Press, 1986), xiii; Chalmers Johnson, ed., *The Industrial Policy Debate* (San Francisco: ICS Press, 1984), 3.

20. George Lodge, *Comparative Business-Government Relations,* 94. 80–95.

21. Clemens Boonekamp, "Voluntary Export Restraints," *Finance and Development,* vol. 23, December 1987, 3.

22. *World Development Report, 1991,* 104–105.

23. Paul Krugman, *The Age of Diminished Expectations* (Cambridge, Mass.: MIT Press, 1990), 105. See also Michael Mastaduno, David Lake, and G. John Ikenberry, "Toward a Realist Theory of State Action," *International Studies Quarterly,* vol. 33, December 1989, 457–475; Michael Mastaduno, "Do Relative Gains Matter? America's Response to Japanese Industrial Policy," *Internal Security,* vol. 16, Summer 1991, 73–113. Duncan Snidal, "International Cooperation Among Relative Gains Maximizers," *International Studies Quarterly,* vol. 35, December 1991, 387–402.

24. James Bovard, "Fair Trade Is Unfair," *Newsweek,* December 9, 1991, 13.

25. Charles Linblom, *Politics and Markets: The World's Political-Economic Systems* (New York: Basic Books, 1977), ix.

26. Robert Isaak, *International Political Economy: Managing World Economic Change* (Englewood Cliffs, N.J.: Prentice-Hall, 1991), 15.

27. Robert Gilpin, *The Political Economy of International Relations* (Princeton N.J.: Princeton University Press, 1987), 25.

The Politics of Interdependence Among the Democratic Industrial Countries

Key Terms and Concepts

Dollar Gap
Dollar Glut
European Coal and Steel
  Community (ECSC)
European Currency Units
  (ECU)
Fair Trade
Group of Five
Group of Seven
Hegemon
Hegemonic Stability Theory

Interdependence
International Bank for
  Reconstruction and
  Development (IBRD)
International Monetary
  Fund (IMF)
International Trade
  Organization (ITO)
Keiretsu
Mercantilism

Most Favored Nation
  (MFN)
Multinational Corporation
  (MNC)
North American Free Trade
  Agreement (NAFTA)
Omnibus Trade Act
Plaza Accord
Smithsonian Agreement
Smoot-Hawley
Special Drawing Rights

With modernization, all the world's countries and individuals, to varying degrees, are drawn ever more closely into an ever more complex economic, political, technological, ethical, communications, transportation, and cultural web.[1] The wealthier a country or individual, the greater its *interdependence* with others. While accounting for only 20 percent of the world's population, the wealthy countries account for 80 percent of global GNP and 55 percent of its trade. About three-quarters of the advanced industrial states' trade and investments are with each other. The advanced countries are not wealthy compared to the other countries, but that wealth is relatively equitably distributed so that at least 70 percent of each advanced country's population is in the middle socioeconomic class. Interdependence is perhaps most evident in the world's trade. An American middle-class home may include a German car whose engine was assembled in Mexico, a Japanese stereo system whose components were made in Malaysia, clothing made in China, shoes from Italy, a shingle roof made from Canadian timber, and so on.

Interdepedence can have its drawbacks. The greater the interdependence, the greater the vulnerability of nations and individuals to events taking place around the globe. A recession in the European Union or a stock market crash in Japan can mean less demand for American goods, and thus an economic slow-down for the nation and unemployment for many individuals. Likewise, foreign competition can bankrupt domestic firms and throw people out of work. Interdependence and economic conflict among nations increase in lock-step, as governments charge that their national firms and economies are disadvantaged by the governmental and corporate practices of other nations.

Yet, even as interdependence increases international conflict, it softens it. The greater the interdependence between two countries, and the more symmetrical their levels of development, economic size, and types of trade, investment, financial, cultural, and travel ties, the less likely that they would consider severing their economic relations, let alone go to war, over a clash of interests. They simply need each other too much.

Hegemonic stability theory attempts to analyze the relations among the advanced industrial countries.[2] Adherents argue that the global economy needs a leader or *hegemon* that can manage or stabilize relations and supply the system with capital, markets, technology, and military security. Britain performed this hegemonic role in the nineteenth century and the United States since 1944. A hegemon is not just the world's most powerful state; it is a state dedicated to creating and developing a global free trade system. It does so first by opening its own markets to foreign goods and services and then encouraging others to do the same. Hegemons can also strengthen the global economy by leading the creation of regimes, or "principles, norms, and decision-making procedures around which actor expectations converge."[3] For example, the United States led the creation of three regimes which have formed the superstructure of the global economy—the IMF, World Bank, and GATT. Without hegemonic leadership, protectionist forces could deflate the global economy, leaving everyone worse off. The inability of Britain and unwillingness of the United States to lead the global economy during the 1920s led to depression and economic nationalism in the 1930s.

The same forces which allow a nation to rise into the global political economy's hegemon inevitably undermine that power. Britain in the early twentieth century and the United States in the late twentieth century became exhausted from the economic and military costs of maintaining the system, and thus declined in relative economic power as other states surged in manufacturing, technological, and financial dynamism. Both Britain and the United States had difficulties getting their allies to "burden share." A major reason for a hegemon's exhaustion is the problem of "free riders" or countries which enjoy the benefits of the open global system while limiting access to their own markets and contributing miserly aid or defense to help maintain the system. The United States was a free rider during Britain's hegemony just as Japan has gotten a free ride on America's hegemony.

Henry Kissinger once wrote that the "biggest challenge to statesmen is to resolve the discordance between the international economy and the political system based on the nation-state . . . . The world needs new arrangements."[4] This chapter will analyze the geoeconomic conflict and cooperation between the advanced industrial nations in an increasingly interdependent world, and their attempts to resolve the conundrum that Kissinger identified. It will first recount the major steps in the global economy's evolution, with an emphasis on those developments from the 1930s through today. It will compare the political economic orientations and strategies of the three major democratic industrial powers, the United States, the European Union, and Japan. Finally, it will analyze some of the major geoeconomic disputes among the geoeconomic superpowers.

EVOLUTION OF THE GLOBAL ECONOMY

The first strands of what would become a global political economy were knit in the mid-fifteenth century when Portugese caravels attempted to sail to the earth's far ends. From these first voyages until the mid-nineteenth century, global geoeconomic and geopolitical relations were shaped by mercantilism and imperialism. During those four hundred years, powerful nation-states emerged, one by one, from the political-economic feudalism that had characterized Europe for the previous millenium. They derived their power from achieving a virtuous cycle of political and economic forces. The creation of professional armies, navies, and bureaucracies enabled these states to conquer and rule first outlying provinces and adjacent territories of other princes, and then lands overseas. But these institutions and conquests would not have been possible without the money to finance them, which was obtained from nurturing domestic industries, gathering taxes more efficiently, and economically exploiting new conquests.

Essential to the creation of wealth was the policy of *mercantilism*—maximizing the nation's exports through state-licensed monopolies and subsidies, and minimizing imports through high trade barriers. The idea was to gain a continual trade surplus and thus a steady influx of gold into the coffers of the state and domestic businesses. Overseas colonies enlarged the state's raw material and market resource base, enabling entrepreneurs to enjoy large-scale production and profits. The goal was for autarky or self-sufficiency. The result was not a unified global political economy, but one in which a half-dozen imperial systems existed alongside each other with minimal trade among them.

There was also sometimes a dicrepancy between a state's power globally and within Europe. Some of the most powerful states in the global political economy—Spain, Portugal, Holland—were secondary powers in Europe. Three of the most powerful states in the European system—Austria, Prussia, and Russia, along with some smaller princedoms in Central Europe and Italy—had no significant role in the global economy.

This fragmented global political economy began to slowly unite during the nineteenth century when the world's great industrial and sea power, Great Britain, first began to use its hegemony to champion economic liberalism. Liberal political economic theorists like Adam Smith, David Ricardo, and John Stuart Mill had been advocating liberalism for several generations, and their voices were joined by the new class of merchant and industrial leaders. By the 1830s, the new industrial interests had displaced the old agrarian interests in Parliament, and began dismantling Britain's import barriers and encouraging foreign powers to do the same. Although Britain's barriers fell rapidly, it was much more difficult to convince the other Europeans to follow suit. The other great and minor powers only slowly and partially abandoned the mercantilist policies which had enabled them to industrialize, export, and garner wealth from others.

Britain had more success in using gunboat diplomacy to force non-European states like Turkey, China, Thailand, and Argentina to open their markets to British goods. More often than not, the result of this forced "free" trade was the destruction of domestic industries in those states as cheap, mass-produced British textiles and other goods swamped their markets. Although nominally independent, these states became increasingly poorer and dependent on British goods and protection.

Other foreign lands suffered even worse fates. Technological advances, like the steamship, telegraph, fast-firing rifles and cannon, and medicines which treated tropical diseases, enabled most of the European powers, Japan, and the United States to acquire overseas empires. By the early twentieth century, most of Africa and Asia had succumbed to Western imperialism. Despite the rapid rise of a half-dozen imperial rivals, Britain remained the world's leading global power, or hegemon, supplying finance, products, technologies, and diplomacy to an increasingly interdependent global political economy. British hegemony, however, was destroyed in the trenches of World War I, and from then until World War II no nation or nations attempted to manage the global political economy and carry the free trade banner.

Although by the early twentieth century, the United States was clearly the world's greatest industrial power, Washington refused to assume the role of hegemon.[5] At the Versailles Peace Conference ending World War I, President Wilson attempted to create a League of Nations designed to settle international disputes, but the Senate later rejected the treaty that would have made the United States a member. Even more isolationist was Congress' 1930 *Smoot-Hawley* law that raised tariffs 50 percent. The law was designed to help America's industries by deterring cheaper imports. But other countries also raised their tariffs and devalued their currencies, and the result was a world trade war in which everyone was worse off.[6]

Washington's policies toward the global economy shifted with the 1933 inauguration of the Roosevelt administration which based its policies on the classic liberal belief that the greater the free trade and interdependence among states, the lower the likelihood of war. Writing amidst the trade and military wars of the 1930s, Secretary of State Cordell Hull clearly articulated this view:

> *unhampered trade dovetailed with peace; high tariffs, trade barriers, and unfair economic competition, with war . . . if we could get a freer flow of trade—freer in the sense of fewer discriminations and obstructions—so that one country would not be deadly jealous of another and the living standards of all countries might rise, thereby eliminating the economic disatisfaction that breeds war, we might have a reasonable chance of lasting peace.[7]*

Congress went along with this new approach. In 1934, it passed the *Reciprocal Trade Act* which authorized the president to negotiate trade treaties with other countries. But the Roosevelt administration's domestic and foreign economic initiatives were no panacea and the United States remained mired in depression. America's economy was locked in a vicious economic cycle—there was not enough consumer buying power to demand more goods and not enough finance available to producers to supply more goods.

World War II was the catalyst which broke this vicious economic cycle in which the United States and global economy was trapped. Government expenditures for the war effort stimulated production, new jobs, and wealth. The United States was converted from an economic depression to an economy with rapid growth and full employment. During World War II, the United States asserted leadership over both the military effort against the Axis countries and the attempts to create a liberal global political economy.

Washington's most important initiative occurred in July 1944 when it invited representatives of 44 countries to meet at Bretton Woods, New Hampshire to create a new global economy. The diplomats signed agreements designed to end the trade barriers and competitive currency devaluations which had devastated the global political economy throughout the 1930s and contributed to the rise of fascism and imperialism in Japan, Germany, and Italy. Henceforth, there would be a fixed currency system in which each currency would be tied to the dollar which in turn would be tied to gold at a value of $35 an ounce. At that time the United States owned 70 percent of the world's official gold reserves. Currency rates were allowed to fluctuate no more than one percent, plus or minus, from the parity, or fixed rate. Countries which earned dollars from trade could, if they wished, redeem them with gold. This fixed gold system would eliminate the problem of competitive currency devaluations.

But the architects of the system recognized that a fixed currency system was not enough. Every advanced industrial country except the United States had been devastated by war and had to be reconstructed before world trade could revive. To assist reconstruction, the Bretton Woods participants agreed to create an *International Bank for Reconstruction and Development* (IBRD, or World Bank) which would extend low-interest loans to countries. In addition, the *International Monetary Fund* (IMF) was created to lend money to countries suffering trade deficits. The money would be invested in infrastructure and industries which would allow greater competitiveness and exports, thus eventually eliminating the trade deficit. The IMF worked like a bank. Countries could join the IMF by depositing money. Then, when that country needed money it could borrow up to 125 percent of its deposit for up to 18 months. In special cases a five year loan was available. The original membership contributions to the IMF were $8.8 billion.

Negotiations began in 1946 for the creation of an *International Trade Organization* (ITO) which would help create and maintain a global free trade system. In 1947, the Havanna Charter was signed creating the ITO. The Truman administration, however, refused to submit the treaty to the Senate for ratification, fearing that the combination of protectionists who felt the treaty went too far, and liberals who felt it did not go far enough, made its passage unlikely.

In the ITO's place, the United States and other countries used the General Agreement on Trade and Tariffs (GATT), which had been created in 1947 by 23 countries, as a forum in which participants would negotiate tariff and other trade barrier cuts. The GATT is based on the *most favored nation* (MFN) principle in which if one nation gives an advantage to another nation it must give that same advantage to all other members. This multilateralism was deemed superior to the older bilateral method of conducting trade agreements.

Yet, despite these new international organizations, the global political economy did not revive. The industrial countries had been too devastated economically, politically, and psychologically by the war, and their economies remained stagnant. They were dependent on the United States for vital energy, food, machinery, medicine, vehicles, and hundreds of other products, but had no money to pay for them. The result was a *dollar gap*.

The Cold War between the United States and Soviet Union proved the catalyst for overcoming the dollar gap. In 1947, the Truman administration announced its containment policy whereby Soviet and communist advances would be checked by rebuilding Europe and Japan through massive aid, and by helping any government threatened by a communist rebellion. From 1947 through 1952, the United States government poured $17 billion worth of grants into sixteen Western European countries and $2.2 billion into Japan, and expended billions of dollars more by deploying its troops in those lands. Meanwhile, Washington tolerated European and Japanese protectionism which allowed industries in those countries to resume the production, and exports of goods and the creation of wealth. With access to massive American aid and markets, Japan and the Western European countries rapidly reconstructed and developed their economies. Despite, or perhaps because of, the Cold War, the global economy grew quickly throughout the 1950s and 1960s.

By the late 1950s, the dollar gap had become a *dollar glut.* The United States continued to send far more dollars into the global economy than it took back, thus suffering continous balance of payments deficits. By 1959, the European and Japanese holdings of U.S. dollars was $19.4 billion, slightly less than the U.S. gold reserves of $19.5 billion. New gold could not be produced fast enough to keep up with the expansion of dollars. The following year, the amount of dollars in foreign hands exceeded U.S. gold reserves, a problem known as the "dollar overhang," and this deficit has deepened each year since then.

The result was a deepening crisis of confidence in the dollar's ability to support the global economy. If the Europeans and Japanese decided to buy American gold with their dollars, both the U.S. gold reserve and the foundation for the fixed currency system would be wiped out. Starting in 1960, there were minor runs by speculators on America's gold reserves but no government challenged the system since its collapse would hurt everyone. As long as the gold/dollar ratio remained constant and dollars could be redeemed in gold, countries were not hurt by holding dollars. In fact, most states preferred to hold dollars rather than gold because dollars earned interest and were "liquid," or easily used for transactions. And no state wanted to set off a run on America's gold reserves that would destroy the Bretton Woods system.

Foreign states, however, did complain that the United States could continually run deficits without taking the type of strict deflationary policies—cutting back government expenditures, devaluing the currency, and so on—that any other country would have to follow if it persistently had a payments deficit. More important for some countries was the fact that America's payments deficit was largely the result of its vast overseas military and aid commitments. By holding rather than converting American dollars into gold those governments were financially supporting American foreign policy, including its war in Vietnam, its web of overseas bases, and its support for a range of brutal dictators such as Samoza of Nicaragua, Thieu of South Vietnam, Rhee of South Korea, to name a few.

French President Charles de Gaulle did not feel constrained by these restrictions and throughout the 1960s demanded U.S. gold for dollars. De Gaulle's challenge to the Bretton Woods system was part of his systematic attempt to rebuild French prestige and power while simultaneously undermining that of the United States. He condemned America's war in Vietnam, tested an atomic bomb in 1964, rapidly built up a French "force de frappe" (nuclear strike force), and withdrew France from NATO in 1966.

The "Group of Ten," composed of the leading industrial nations—the United States, Britain, France, Germany, Japan, Italy, Canada, Sweden, Swizerland, the Netherlands, and Belgium—met throughout the 1960s to manage the dollar crisis by intervening in currency markets to maintain prices. The "dollar overhang" problem could have been addressed by increasing the gold's value to dollars, but this would have simultaneously devalued the dollars that were being held. Instead, in 1968, they created a two tier system in which gold prices could fluctuate in a free market and would remain fixed in a government system. In 1969, the Group of Ten created *Special Drawing*

Rights (SDRs), an artificial currency that could be used instead of the dollar to settle international accounts. Yet, only $6 billion of SDRs were created that year while over $100 billion in currency circulated throughout the global system.

Meanwhile, the United States tried to improve its balance of payments by trying to stimulate exports and inhibit American foreign investments. But any gains were wiped out by the tens of billions of dollars sent overseas to finance the Vietnam War. President Johnson's refusal to raise taxes to pay for both his Great Society set of welfare programs and the Vietnam War caused high inflation which further eroded America's competitiveness. Another severe problem was the dollar's increased overvaluation throughout the 1960s, thus exacerbating America's growing payments deficits and, starting in 1971, trade deficits. The dollar became overvalued as European and Japanese growth in GNP and productivity exceeded those of the United States. The fixed exchange rates were not adjusted to reflect the steadily diminishing competitiveness of America's economy, thus making it even more difficult for American producers to compete abroad or at home.

In 1971, the United States suffered its first trade deficit since 1893, running up $2 billion in merchandise and $10.6 billion in payments deficits. Meanwhile its gold reserves shrank to $10 billion and foreign holdings of dollars rose to over $80 billion. On August 15, 1971, President Nixon dealt with these interrelated problems by announcing two international policies—henceforth the dollar would no longer be converted into gold and there would be a temporary ten percent surcharge added to existing U.S. tariffs. In December 1971, the leading industrial nations signed the *Smithsonian Agreement* in which the dollar was devalued 10 percent against the existing price of gold, other currencies would be revalued against the dollar, and currencies could now float within a 2.5 percent margin of the fixed rate.

This new system unraveled quickly. In June 1972, Britain and Ireland broke off from the fixed rate system and allowed their currencies to float on international markets. Other countries followed suit. America's trade and payments deficits continued to mount and were unaffected by another 10 percent dollar devaluation in February 1973. By March 1973, the fixed rate system was abandoned and a "free-floating system" was adopted in which currency values were set by market forces rather than by government intervention.

As if these currency and payments problems were not enough, in November 1973, the Organization of Petroleum Exporting Nations (OPEC) imposed strict production quotas, while the Organization of Arab Petroleum Exporting Countries (OAPEC) temporarily refused to supply oil to the United States and the Netherlands since they had supported Israel in the Yom Kippur War in October. The result was that global oil prices quadrupled from $2.75 a barrel to $12 a barrel over the next several months, thus plunging the global economy into a severe recession and imposing low growth and high inflation for another decade. In 1974, OPEC's current account surplus rose from $1 billion to $70 billion, and in 1980, after oil prices doubled again from about $18 to $34 a barrel, the surplus rose to $114 billion. These high oil prices were the underlying cause for the Third World's growing debt burden which reached crisis proportions in the 1980s.

The United States and other leading industrial nations dealt with these new challenges through several means. Starting in 1975, the leaders of the world's most powerful industrial nations, the *Group of Seven*—the United States, Japan, Britain, France, Germany, Italy, and Canada—began meeting annually to coordinate broad macroeconomic policies and to deal with any crises. International organizations also attempted to deal with the global slowdown. In January 1976, the IMF amended its charter to allow SDRs to replace gold as the world economy's principal reserve asset. During the Tokyo Round of GATT (1973–79), Washington achieved some success in negotiating the reduction of nontariff as well as tariff barriers. Along with reduced tariffs, the Tokyo Round succeeded in creating a Code on Subsidies and Countervailing Duties and a Code on Government Procurement, the first comprehensive attempts to deal with some nontariff barriers. Each code included rules, surveillance, and methods to settle disputes. Yet, these codes are vaguely written and relatively easily evaded.

These efforts nibbled around the problem's edges, but did not address the global economy's central problem, which was the rise in oil from $2.75 to $34 a barrel between 1973 and 1980, and the corresponding stagflation. Market, rather than government action, alleviated the high energy price problem. The high oil prices encouraged consumers to conserve energy and to seek more efficient uses of energy. Meanwhile, those countries that had unexploited oil reserves found they could afford to invest in petroleum production. Finally, OPEC members began to cheat on their quotas in an effort to garner even more revenue. The result was an oil glut by the mid-1980s that brought prices down to around $20 a barrel, which in "real prices" (adjusted for inflation) were actually cheaper than before 1973.

These gains for the global economy provided little relief for the United States which by the mid-1980s was facing an ever deepening payments and trade deficit crisis. This crisis was largely the fault of misguided American policies. The Reagan administration had hoped that by following a supply-side policy of massive cuts the economy would grow and the government would later regain earlier revenue losses as larger business and household incomes generated more taxes. But the Reagan White House also increased the federal budget, largely by nearly tripling defense spending. The annual budget deficit rose from an average $50 billion during the Carter administration to an average $200 billion during the Reagan years. In 1980, the federal debt was $970 billion; in 1988, it was $3 trillion!

Meanwhile, the Federal Reserve raised interest rates to cut inflation and encourage both domestic and foreign investors to lend money to the United States government to help pay for the growing budget deficit. Foreigners invested hundreds of billions of dollars in the United States, buying government bonds, playing financial markets, taking over U.S. companies, and starting new subsidiaries. When they invested in the United States, the foreigners exchanged their currency for dollars. As the foreign demand for a stable supply of dollars rose, the dollar's value soared. The result for the United States was an increasingly severe trade deficit and slower American economic growth.

The global economic power balance shifted dramatically. In 1985, the United States was transformed from being the world's greatest creditor country into the worst debtor nation. By that time the amount of foreign money invested in the United States exceeded the American money flowing overseas by $112 billion. By 1987, America's global trade deficit peaked at $171 billion and its deficit with Japan at $59 billion. That same year, Japan enjoyed a trade surplus of $96.5 billion and Germany one of $70 billion. Japan inherited America's role as the global creditor nation, amassing $241 billion in net external credit in 1987.

The United States was trapped in a vicious economic cycle composed of high interest rates, an overvalued dollar, and deep trade and payments deficits. In addition the nation faced low economic growth, low government revenues, high government deficits and long-term debt, and high interest rates. During its first five years, the Reagan administration seemed indifferent to the worsening crisis, arguing that the "magic of the marketplace" would take care of everything. Treasury Secretary Don Regan further talked up the dollar's value, claiming that "a strong dollar represents a strong America."

In 1985, President Reagan reshuffled some of his advisers, making free market purist Don Regan his Chief of Staff and economic realist Jim Baker his Treasury Secretary. Baker immediately sought to devalue the dollar. At the September 1985 secret meeting the *Group of Five*—the United States, Japan, Germany, France, and Britain—it was agreed that there should be a joint effort to devalue the dollar as a way to restore equilibrium to the global system. Although the other states, particularly Japan, enjoyed an enormous transfer of wealth to their own economies as a result of the Reagan administration's policies, they realized that the United States could not continue to run huge budget, trade, and payments deficits indefinitely. The foreign debts had to be serviced, and the larger those debts, the less money the United States had available to invest in its own economy. The result would be a steady American decline, that ultimately would drag down the rest of the global economy as well. By agreeing to intervene in global currency markets by selling dollars and buying up other leading currencies, the Group of Five succeeded in devaluing the dollar, which fell dramatically against the Japanese yen, from about 265 yen in 1985 to 125 yen in 1987. Satisfied with the devaluation, the Group of Seven met in February 1987 at the Louvre in Paris and announced that the dollar had fallen far enough.

This realignment clearly was not enough to address the deep problems within the United States and, by extension, problems of the global economy. Over the short-term, America's trade and payments deficits continued to mount because of the J-curve effect in which the deficit increases as the cost of imported goods already ordered rises. In October 1987, rumors that Japanese investors were going to stop buying U.S. treasury bonds sent the New York Stock Market into a free fall in which it lost 15 percent of its value. In December 1987, the Group of Seven met again and agreed on further measures to stabilize exchange rates and stock markets.

Since then, into the 1990s, the dollar's value has remained stable while the global economy has grown steadily. Despite all of America's economic problems, the dollar remains the most important reserve currency. While the dollar is used to pay for about 65 percent of all international trade, deutschemarks account for about 12 percent, yen 8 percent, and SDRs 5 percent. The global economy annually expands about two to three percentage points while global trade rises even faster, about 5 to 7 percent a year. About three-quarters of all trade and investment flows between the democratic industrial countries rather than among them and the less developed countries.

THE ECONOMIC SUPERPOWERS

The United States continues to lead the global economy while the dollar underwrites most international trade. Yet there is a widening gap between America's leadership of the global economy and its geoeconomic power. There is a relative power balance among the three geoeconomic superpowers, the 12 nation European Union with 24 percent of global GNP, the United States with 22 percent, and Japan with 18 percent. Although the United States continues to be the world's largest economy, it also continues to suffer from relatively low economic growth, and severe trade and payments deficits. In contrast, Japan has a growth rate twice that of America's, runs immense trade and payments surpluses, and has surpassed the United States by most financial, technological, and manufacturing indicators. The European Union's economic bulk is clearly the largest, but its members continue to squabble over unification and they lack economic dynamism and innovative advances compared with the United States and Japan. This section will explore the different development paths that each of the three took to become an economic superpower.

The United States

The powers and responsibilities of nation-states often change over time to adapt to new political, economic, and social challenges. The United States began in 1776 as a weak confederation of thirteen sovereign states. In 1787, it adopted a federal system in which the national government had limited abilities and inclination to nurture economic development. Yet today the national government consumes over a quarter of the nation's GNP, and regulates directly or indirectly virtually all economic sectors.

The turning point from the government's largely passive to active role in managing the economy occured in the early 1930s. America's stock market crash and subsequent Great Depression discredited classical economic theory that asserted that markets should be self-regulating rather than government-regulated. Unbridled speculation had created and then popped a huge speculative stock bubble. The resulting depression was deepened by President Hoover's classic, liberal economic hands off response. While the economy was sinking further into depression, President Hoover actually called for federal spending cuts to balance the budget.

After Franklin Roosevelt became president in 1933, the government increasingly assumed more responsibility for managing the economy. In his first 100 days in office, Roosevelt pushed 15 bills through Congress which, by a variety of means, stimulated the economy through greater government spending and programs. This action represented the first time the United States had systematically attempted to smooth out an economic boom and bust cycle. During World War II, the government shifted its policy from stimulating specific sectors of the economy to direct management of the economy for the war and targeted strategic industries for development.

From World War II through today, the government has continued to target specific economic sectors for development through its industrial policies. But instead of the rational, far-sighted policies of the war years, Washington picks industrial winners and losers largely through a political process in which the most established industries pour money into enough political coffers and, in turn, are then rewarded with a range of government subsidies, protections, and other advantages. The power of the agriculture and textile lobbies, for example, have enabled those industries to receive vast government largess and import protection. Other industries have received favorable treatment by being part of the military industrial complex. America's semiconductor, computer, aerospace, and microelectronics industries, to name some of the more prominent, were all shaped by Washington's military industrial and technology policies.

Just as it initiated the process of industrial policies, the Roosevelt administration forged a consensus on the importance of international trade for American prosperity, and the president's role in regulating it. The Constitution grants the power of regulating trade to Congress. Since 1934, however, Congress has periodically allocated powers to the president to negotiate trade agreements. The greatest increase in presidential trade power occured with the passage of the 1988 *Omnibus Trade Act* which made it much easier for the president to retaliate against foreign dumping and other unfair practices that can harm America's economy. All of the American presidents from Roosevelt to Clinton have recommitted the United States to the ideal, if not practice, of free trade. Like any country, the United States has industrial and trade policies designed to give its industries advantages over their foreign rivals. The difference is that most officials and politicians deny it and continue to champion liberal economic theory as the basis for America's economy.

America's traditional free trade liberalism has been criticized. Many argue that Washington's piecemeal and politically shaped industrial, technology, and trade policies are hurting the United States in an increasingly competitive, interdependent global economy. The Tolchins write that "none of America's major trading partners subscribe to the U.S. vision of free trade. None regard technology with the cavalier notion that ownership doesn't matter—unless they are the owners. Instead, each nurtures technologies it deems vital to its economic competitiveness in the 21st century."[8]

The United States has attempted to increase its economic growth and bargaining power with other countries by forging a free trade association with its neighbors. In 1988, the United States and Canada signed a free trade agreement whereby they agreed to eliminate tariffs and nontariff barriers toward most of each other's exports. In 1991, the United States, Mexico, and Canada began negotiations to create a *North American Free Trade Association* (NAFTA) which would unify 363 million consumers and $6.5 trillion in economic activities. A treaty was signed in May 1992, but many members of Congress vowed to vote against it for fear that the United States would lose jobs to Mexico. During the 1992 presidential campaign, democratic candidate Bill Clinton supported President Bush's treaty in principle but vowed to overcome its defects by negotiating labor and environmental side-agreements. In his first year as president, Clinton negotiated his promised agreements with Mexico and after a major push during the autumn to rally congressional support, succeeded in gaining NAFTA's ratification by November 20, 1993.

The United States had far more to gain from NAFTA than Mexico, whose trade and investment barriers were three or more times higher than those north of the border. The United States has already gained from the closer ties. In 1986, the United States had a $5.7 billion trade deficit with Mexico. Then, a 1987 trade agreement with Mexico nearly doubled bilateral trade and nearly tripled American exports from $15 billion to $41 billion in exports in 1992. America's trade surplus of $5.4 billion has translated into 350,000 net new jobs in the United States. In 1992, 8.5 percent of total American exports went to Mexico, making that country America's third largest trading partner after Canada and Japan. The Economic Policy Institute, a Washington think tank, predicts that over the next decade NAFTA will create 325,000 new jobs for the United States in export industries. The institute also projects that 150,000 jobs will be lost in the agricultural, textile, and other labor-intensive industries. Thus, overall the United

States will enjoy not only more but better paying jobs since export related jobs pay 17 percent more than non-export jobs.[9]

Corporations set up branches overseas for many reasons including access to restricted markets, raw materials, and technology. Corporations also seek lower operating costs including cheap labor and weaker environmental standards, and/or access to government investment incentives. At the same time, red tape, poor infrastructure, political instability, corruption, and unskilled workers work to discourage overseas investments. For those American corporations that set up branches in Mexico, most will do so to take advantage of the $1.80 an hour average wage there in contrast to the $14.77 an hour average wage for American workers. Since only 1 percent of production costs are related to environmental regulations, few firms are expected to relocate to Mexico only because of its lax environmental protection. Jobs lost in the United States to Mexico would have disappeared even without NAFTA since American corporations would have had to have responded to the growing foreign competition by either investing overseas in cheap labor countries or declaring bankruptcy.

Recently, the United States appeared to be moving toward an even greater management of its economic development and trade relations. By the late 1980s, the notion of fair trade rather than free trade largely shaped American perceptions and policies. The 1992 election was clearly a choice between President Bush's laissez-faire, Governor Clinton's "plan," and Ross Perot's "bitter medicine" approaches to the economy. Clinton rejected the old dichotomy between free trade and protectionism, and said his policies would be based on a "third way" which would restore America's competitiveness. He won largely because a majority of Americans agreed that strong measures had to be taken, and a plurality of the voters thought Clinton's plan was the best of the three. Until then, periodic attempts by Democractic presidential candidates to raise industrial policy issues had been defeated by Republican charges that such policies violated American free trade ideals. Whether President Clinton's attempts to implement systematic and rational industrial, technology, and trade policies are any more successful than the old political approach in developing America's economy remains to be seen.

Japan

No country has developed more successfully since 1945 than Japan, which has surpassed the United States by most measurements. While America's economy remains larger, Japan's has grown faster and will surpass the United States's economy within twelve years if current growth rates hold. With half the population of the United States, Japan will then have a per capita income twice that of the United States. Between 1950 and 1973, Japan's economy grew at an average annual rate of 10 percent, four times America's 2.5 percent rate. From 1974 through today, Japan's economy has grown an average annual rate of 4.5 percent, more than twice America's 2.2 percent rate. Japan's economy grew from 3 percent of global GNP in 1950 to 18 percent in 1991, while America's share shrank from 35 percent to 22 percent during the same period. Japan has replaced the United States as the world's trade power—it ran its first postwar surplus in 1965. By 1992, the surplus reached $132 billion. In 1985, Japan became the world's greatest net creditor country while the United States plummeted into being the world's worst debtor. A recent Commerce Department report revealed that Japan was ahead in ten of twelve technologies considered essential for an advanced economy in the twenty-first century, and neck-and-neck with the United States in the other two technologies.[10]

Japan has achieved this remarkable development by following rational policies designed to create, distribute, and secure wealth, and by establishing the institutions to implement those policies.[11] The Ministry of Finance (MOF) and Ministry of International Trade and Industry (MITI) shared the creation and implementation of most policies designed to systematically target and develop strategic industries and technologies within the context of five year indicative plans. Other ministries, such as Construction, Transportation, Posts Telecommunications, Education, and Justice have their own industries that they carefully nurture. Each industry, in turn, is organized into an industrial association and cooperates in both writing and implementing government policies through cartels, the diffusion of technology, import barriers, and export promotion.

Obtaining foreign technology has been a vital component in Japan's rise as an economic superpower. The 1949 Foreign Exchange Control Law and 1950 Foreign Investment Law gave Tokyo enormous powers to restrict foreign trade and investments. Unable to import to or invest in Japan because of government restrictions, foreign firms often simply licensed their advanced technology to their nascent Japanese rivals as the only way to make money in Japan. Between 1950 and 1980, the Japanese spent about $10 billion buying or licensing over 30,000 foreign technologies. The total cost for the foreign companies to research and develop these technologies was anywhere from $500 billion to $1 trillion![12] Japanese firms used this technology to modernize their factories and mass-produce inexpensive products which were then sold around the world, often at below production costs in order to capture a large-market share and to drive their rivals out of business.

During the 1980s, Japan caught up to the United States and Europe. Tokyo then embarked on a "leapfrog" or "technology-substitution" strategy whereby it hoped to jump far ahead of its competitors, industrially and technologically. To do so, it has targeted a series of advanced technologies that have yet to be mastered, like fifth and sixth generation computers, superconductors, virtual reality, and micromachines. Tokyo organizes consortia of private corporations to work together to develop these technologies and the hundreds of products they spawn.

The importance of Japan's industrial policies has diminished as its economy has grown more complex and powerful. While MITI and other ministries continue to target industries and technologies for development, their ability to force recalcitrant firms to cooperate with their rivals has diminished as corporate financial power has grown. Today, the Japanese govenment has dismantled most of the more blatant trade and investment barriers, and its tariff rates are now lower than those of either the United States or European Community. Japan's markets, however, remain guarded by arrays of nontariff trade barriers.

As important as Japan's rational industrial, technological, and trade policies, were macroeconomic policies which maintained a high savings/investment ratio and an undervalued yen. Although the household savings rate in Japan has fallen from about 34 percent of income in 1950 to 13 percent of income in 1993, the current savings rate is over four times higher than that of the United States. Tokyo traditionally encourages high savings by limiting such government benefits as welfare, education, and security, and by keeping consumer prices high and credit limited. Consumers thus have to save a large percentage of their incomes not only to educate their children and survive on after retirement, but also—without access to credit—to pay for an automobile or home. Tokyo further limited the investment opportunities for savers by providing mostly bank or post office savings accounts which paid very low interest rates. Tokyo then channeled these vast savings—the Postal Savings Bank assets alone in 1990 were $1.3 trillion or 31 percent of all of Japan's banking assets and four times larger than the world's largest commercial bank—into cheap loans for strategic industries, which in turn invested the money into the most advanced production techniques technologies.

Also vital to Japan's development was an undervalued yen. Originally set at 360 yen to a dollar in 1949, the yen became increasingly undervalued as Japan's economy expanded during the next 22 years. The yen remained undervalued even after President Nixon forced the yen's revaluation to 308 to a dollar in December 1971, and the yen like other currencies, began to float in 1973. The Japanese government used a variety of means to maintain an undervalued yen. The Bank of Japan intervened in global currency markets to buy dollars and sell yen. The Finance Ministry continued to restrict foreign investments in Japan while allowing increased Japanese overseas investments. The Ministry also restricted the use of yen in trade in an attempt to limit demand for yen which would raise its value.

The dynamic core of Japan's economy are its six major industrial groups—*keiretsu*—whose combined economic activity accounts for 25 percent of the GNP. Each keiretsu has a range of interrelated manufacturing firms in steel, petrochemicals, microelectronics, automobiles, mining and metal forging, shipbuilding, and aerospace. These firms are largely financed by the keiretsu bank, trading firm, and insurance company. Each corporation within the keiretsu either wholly or partially owns scores of smaller subcontracting and distribution firms. About 70 percent of each keiretsu's stock is directly owned by other keiretsu members or affiliates. During the 1980s, Washington and Brussels complained that the keiretsu discriminated against foreign firms and violated antitrust laws. Tokyo has dismissed these complaints as unfounded and refused to break up the keiretsu.

Japan's institutions and policies were not created and implemented in a void. They would never have succeeded if the United States had not imposed revolutionary political and economic changes during its occupation of Japan after World War II. First, the United States pumped in $2.2 billion of humanitarian and development aid over seven years, and then contributed tens of billions of dollars more through the procurement policies of its military forces based in Japan and the region. The United States scrapped Japan's totalitarian political system and replaced it with a democratic constitution which guaranteed the full spectrum of human rights. The Americans also pushed through land, labor, and industrial reforms which coopted the major reforms advocated by the socialist and communist parties, thus allowing the conservatives to gain political power that they have held for all but nine months since 1945. In addition, the American authorities forced the government to adhere to strict macroeconomic policies and set the yen at a rate whereby all of Japan's major industries could export successfully. The Americans created MITI and helped launch the industrial and technology policies which fueled Japan's economic development. While America's defense burden averaged

6–7 percent of GNP, the United States allowed the Japanese to keep their defense spending at around 1 percent of GNP, which meant that the Japanese had five percentage points of GNP more to invest in far more productive consumer industries. The United States also overcame the resistance of the Europeans to integrating Japan into the regional and global systems. Finally, for several decades, the United States opened its own markets wide to Japanese goods while tolerating firmly closed Japanese trade and investment markets.

Successful development depends on the integration of traditional and modern values and institutions. Although Japan's contemporary political and economic system is superficially modern, it is built upon traditional values and institutions. The Japanese have achieved a societal-wide consensus over where and how they want their country to develop. No country has been more successful in creating, distributing, and securing the sources of wealth than Japan.

The European Union

The more economically, politically, and socially entangled states become with each other, the more inconceivable the use of force to solve differences. Federalism is a theory which recognizes the political and economic benefits of integration, and advocates uniting peoples, policies, and markets through a web of institutions.

The European Union (EU) provides the most successful example of intergration.[13] Federalists had advocated European unity throughout the early to mid-twentieth century, arguing that Europe's perennial problem of war could only be solved by dissolving the endlessly squabbling sovereign nations into one grand European state. This drive for European unity became increasingly powerful after World War II as Europeans feared the ultimate revival of German economic and military power. Rather than isolate Germany, the federalists proposed integrating Germany within Europe's larger economy. With the Cold War, Washington joined the integrationists, seeing an economically united Europe as the best bulwark against possible Soviet expansion.

There was perhaps no more fervent federalist than former French Foreign Minister Jean Monet who argued:

> There will be no peace in Europe if countries build up their strength on the basis of national sovereignty.   .   .   . The countries of Europe are too limited to assure their people the prosperity that modern times afford.   .   .   . Larger markets are needed. Prosperity and social development are inconceivable unless the countries of Europe unite into a federation or a European entity which in turn creates a common economic union.[14]

Europe's integration has been preceded by a series of stages. While Monet advocated political and then economic union, the opposite has occurred. In May 1950, France and West Germany announced that they were uniting their coal and steel industries in order to create economies of scale and alleviate tension between them. The following year in April 1951, six states—France, Italy, West Germany, the Netherlands, Belgium, and Luxembourg—signed the Paris Treaty which created the *European Coal and Steel Community* (ECSC). In 1957, the six states signed the Rome Treaty, which created the *European Economic Community* (EEC) whose members pledged to gradually reduce their trade barriers toward each other and create common external tariff and nontariff barriers. They also signed a treaty in which they agreed to standardize and work jointly to develop their nuclear energy industry. In 1967, the EEC and Euroatom were merged into the *European Community* (EC). The EC's membership expanded along with its economic integration: Britain, Ireland, and Denmark in 1971, Greece in 1981, and Spain and Portugal in 1985. In 1986, the twelve signed the Single European Act in which they pledged to remove all remaining trade barriers by December 31, 1992 and rename their association the European Union.

Creating a customs union was only the first step to economic union. The Union could never be truly unified without a central bank and currency. The first significant step taken toward this goal occurred in December 1978 when the members created the European Monetary System (EMS) in which the currencies would be tied to each other with 2.5 percent fluctuation margins, the system would float against other currencies, and the system would be anchored by the creation of *European Currency Units* (ECU), the European equivilent of IMF SDRs. The German central bank and the deutschemark have played a role similar to what the United States Federal Reserve and dollar do for the global economy.

The second stage toward financial union was taken in 1991 with the signing of the Maastricht Treaty, in which the members promised to merge their national banks and currencies into one European central bank and currency by 1997 at the earliest and 1999 at the latest. Europeans were evenly divided over whether or not they supported this measure. Throughout the summer and fall of 1992, one by one, each member voted on the Maastricht treaty, either through parliament or referendum. In June, Denmark voted down the treaty in a referendum with 51 percent against. In September, in France the treaty barely passed ratification with a referendum in which 51 percent voted "yes." Although eleven of the twelve EC members eventually voted for the treaty, the ratification had to be unanimous in order for the treaty to take effect. Throughout 1993, the members renegotiated the treaty to make it universally acceptable. By autumn 1993, all the EC members had ratified the treaty allowing financial union by 1999.

The European Union is governed by a Commission, whose members are appointed by the member states, and which is located in Brussels. But the Commission receives broad directives from the decisions of the Council of government heads which meet annually to address issues. Unlike the Commission, the European Parliament is popularly elected. It is located in Strasbourg and its powers are those of persuasion rather than law-making. The European Court of Justice serves as the Union's supreme court and is located in Luxembourg. The Union's bureaucracy has grown steadily in pace with its expanded responsibilities. In 1960, the Commission had 1,000 civil servants and there were 167 lobby groups registered in Brussels. In 1988, there were 15,000 civil servants and 435 official lobby groups.

European Union policies largely reflect those of its member states. None of the European states have ever entirely abandoned the mercantilist outlook and policies of the early modern era. Europeans have always intervened far more in their respective economies than the Americans. The West European countries are to greatly varying degrees welfare states in which the government heavily subsidizes its citizens' health, education, income, and employment, as well as strategic industrial sectors.

Figure 14.1
European Union Membership and Organization, 1993

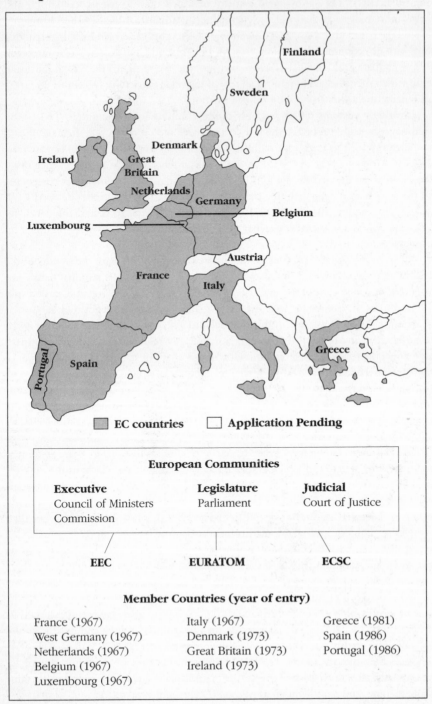

Yet, unlike Japan, Brussels has no overall five year development plans that target virtually every economic sector for government protection and nurturing. European industrial policy is actually a collection of policies for specific industries and technologies. The Union's most important and controversial initiative is its Common Agricultural Policy (CAP) that subsidizes agriculture under which the Community's 12 million farmers receive about $45 billion in various direct and indirect subsidies. CAP consumes 65 percent of Brussels' $70 billion budget. Environmental policy is an increasing concern. The Union has issued strict standards on water and air pollution, energy use, and waste disposal.

Brussels also supports an increasing range of other industries and technologies to make Europe more competitive. For example, Brussels' Airbus policy has been very successful. After receiving over $26 billion since its inception in the 1970s, the Airbus has risen steadily in global market share until it captured 29 percent in 1992, leapfrogging McDonald Douglas and threatening Boeing's lead. During the 1980s, Brussels launched a range of high technology policies including the European Strategic Program for Research and Development (ESPRIT) and Research and Development in Advanced Communications Technology (RACE). Brussels has also helped raise $180 billion for the development of a Union-wide high speed train network known by its French initials, T.G.V. (*Train à Grande Vitesse*). The Union's role is to coordinate each member's contributions so that they adhere to the same construction, speed, and safety standards.

Brussels' macroeconomic policies also have been successful. It imposes strict fiscal and monetary discipline on its members whose budget deficits are not allowed to exceed 3 percent of GNP or inflation more than 1.5 percent above the average of the three lowest members' inflation rates. Although the ECU is not yet a legal currency, it is used to settle government and international accounts. About 25 percent of the Commission's bills are paid in ECUs, and, after the dollar, the ECU is the most common currency used to underwrite the primary international bond market. There are ECU bank loans, checks, and credit cards. Accepting the ECU for payment is voluntary. It is currently worth about $1.25.

There is no question that these integration, trade, industrial, technology, and macroeconomic policies have been successful. Between 1960 and 1986, intra-Community trade rose from 34.4 percent to 56.8 percent of its total trade, while the Union's percentage of world trade rose from 24.5 percent to 38.8 percent. Europeans are far more wealthy and economically dynamic than if their respective countries had decided not to integrate. Yet, despite these successes, there is a great debate among those who want to broaden the Community by adding more members, those who want to deepen it by working toward a genuine federalism, and those nationalists who want to leave the community altogether.

Europeans leaders are rethinking the concept of "subsidiarity" that appeared in the Maastricht Treaty. The concept is Europe's equivalent of American federalism, in which any powers not constitutionally given to the national government revert to state and local government. But about half of the European public and many of its leaders oppose the federal United States of Europe that subsidiarity implies. The close votes over ratification of the Maastricht Treaty reveal that there is great fear among many that they are giving away their national sovereignty and identity for rule by Eurocrats and perhaps domination by a unified Germany. By June 1993, all the members had ratified a modified version of the Maastricht treaty in which some countries like Denmark and Britain opted out of some of the requirements.

Broadening the membership has its pitfalls as well. Austria, Sweden, the Czech Republic, and Finland are the most likely new members to join the Union in the 1990's. Any widening would have to be accompanied by a restructuring of the European Parliament so that it does not become too unwieldy. And unless Europe adopts a common language and culture, a European identity is unlikely to supercede the existing national identities.

CONFLICTS OF INTERDEPENDENCE

GATT Weaknesses and the Uruguay Round

Since its inception, GATT has helped expand international trade. After eight negotiation rounds, tariffs have been reduced to an average 2.5 percent for Japan, 3.4 percent for the United States, and 4.3 percent for the European Community. The Tokyo (1973–1979) and Uruguay (1986–1992) rounds achieved significant results in addressing nontariff barriers, intellectual property protection, and trade in services and agriculture. GATT's membership has expanded from 23 to 116, with dozens of other states impatiently awaiting membership.

Yet, despite these successes, increasing numbers of officials and analysts are questioning whether GATT is capable of managing the world's increasingly bitter trade conflicts. GATT has some major weaknesses. Although members can bring disputes before GATT panels, which can issue judgments, there is no authority which can back up a decision. While GATT's Charter enshrines the MFN principle, it also allows for countries to continue existing imperial preference systems, to create regional free trade associations, to discriminate in favor of less developed countries, and to temporarily impose higher trade barriers to offset persistent trade deficits.

GATT clearly allows states to retaliate against foreign industries which have dumped or sold their products at below production cost to drive their rivals out of business and capture market share. Under GATT, states can also match another state's export subsidies by raising tariffs. The trouble is that GATT does not allow states to retaliate directly against the country whose firms have engaged in dumping. Import barriers must be erected against all countries, even those which are fair traders, or none. Faced with this dilemma in which the only way they can protect themselves is to hurt everyone, most states seek alternative means of dealing with dumping by negotiating voluntary restraint agreements (VRAs), such as Voluntary Export Restraints (VERs) or Orderly Marketing Agreements (OMAs) with states whose corporations have engaged in widespread dumping and captured enormous market share. GATT also fails to address the more insidious and effective nontariff trade barriers, such as government red tape, business cartels, import licensing, export subsidies, and undervalued currencies that some countries—most notably Japan—use to systematically minimize the penetration of competitive imports.

Since GATT was instituted in 1947, there have been eight negotiation rounds in which members attempted to make deeper cuts in tariffs and other trade barriers. The last round of negotiations, the Uruguay Round, has been the most contentious. From 1986 through 1992, GATT's 108 members represented at the Uruguay Round addressed several broad issues, including safeguards such as VRAs, the settling of disputes, and such products as textiles, tropical products, agriculture, services, and intellectual protection. Washington had pushed for negotiations in the last two areas because they were increasingly important to America's economic vitality. In 1986, when the talks began, American service exports were $148.4 billion or 39.8 percent of total exports.[15] Liberal economists argued that a successful GATT round would annually increase overall global economic activity by $100 billion as each country specialized in producing what it produces best and imports everything else.[16]

Despite these high stakes, the successful conclusion of the Uruguay Round was held up by a trade dispute between the United States and European Union over agriculture. It is ironic that among the advanced industrial countries no industry is more protected than agriculture. Farmers comprise a small and diminishing percentage of population in all three economic superpowers—in the United States about 2 percent; in the European Union about 5 percent; and in Japan, about 7 percent. But the political power of farmers far exceeds their numbers. Although sparsely populated, farm districts are numerous and farmers are well organized. Over the decades the farm lobby in each of these nations has been able to wring increased benefits from the system. The governments of the United States, the European Union and its members, and Japan, all promote agriculture through a range of subsidies, import barriers, price supports, and infrastructure. The degree and type of protection offered, however, varies considerably among the nations.

Some countries have a greater natural advantage in agriculture than others. During the Uruguay Round a coalition of fourteen countries with a comparative advantage, including the United States, Canada, Australia, Argentina, and Hungary, made agriculture a key issue. Washington led the charge in addressing this issue by demanding that all countries completely dismantle their agricultural protection policies, and cited the European Union for its huge agricultural subsidies.

Brussels' farm subsidies are larger than those of the United States and are the most important reason for the increasingly larger share that European farmers take in the global agricultural market. The Union's share of the global grain market rose from 16 percent in 1982 to 21 percent in 1992, while America's share has fallen from 46 percent to 31 percent during the same period. At the same time, the Union's overall share of agricultural trade rose from 14 percent to 18 percent while America's fell from 23 percent to 19 percent.[17]

Although Washington had initially demanded complete elimination of farm supports, by late October 1992 its position had been modified considerably. Now Washington demanded merely a 24 percent reduction in the Union's export subsidies over seven years. Brussels countered by offering an 18 percent reduction over six years or 21 percent over seven years. But Brussels asserted that it would have to be coupled to new taxes on imports of American corn gluten and the cancellation of the so-called Andriessen Understanding, under which it promised not to subsidize meat exports to Japan and other East Asian countries. In addition, Brussels asked Washington not to challenge as illegal the direct payments it was now making to farmers in place of price supports.

In early November the dispute narrowed to the Union's subsidies for soybean and rapeseed products. Washington contended that the United States could sell another $1 billion worth of soybean products in Europe if the Union rapeseed subsidies and barriers were dismantled, an action that would benefit America's 400,000 soybean farmers. Throughout October and early November, Washington made eleven proposals to resolve the issues and Brussels rejected them all. The last American proposal was for Brussels to cut its future production to 8.9 million metric tons from an estimated harvest of 13 million tons in 1992. Brussels agreed to reduce its acreage to 1986 levels, which it claims will reduce the harvest to 10 million tons. The Americans countered that under Brussels' proposal the real figure would be over 10.5 million tons. They also complained that Brussels was not offering any real concession, that it would simply take away with one hand any advantages it offered with the other. U.S. Trade Representative Carla Hills threatened to impose the punitive tariffs on $1 billion in Union exports, the amount that American producers are estimated to lose from European barriers and subsidies. Washington also repeatedly pointed to the decisions of two GATT panels (1989, 1992) which ruled that European oilseed subsidies were unfair and violated GATT trade rules. Brussels argued that these decisions have no standing unless the GATT has approved them. Brussels, however, has vetoed their approval. GATT's credibility itself was at stake in the conflict. Hills argued that the U.S. action should be seen not as retaliation, but as a legitimate procedure that upholds GATT. The U.S. position was strongly backed by other soybean exporters, including Argentina, Australia, Chile, Brazil, Uruguay, New Zealand, and Canada.

The impasse was partly the result of French politics. President François Mitterand faced legislative elections in the spring of 1993. His popularity was extremely low and the farm sector in particular was rebellious. Any concessions would mean the loss of seats for his Socialist Party. Meanwhile Commission President Jacques Delors was said to want Mitterand's job as president, and thus took a protectionist line. Another reason for the stalemate was Brussels' hopes that if Clinton were elected president in November he might be more conciliatory.

On November 5, the Bush administration declared it would impose 200 percent import taxes on $300 million of European imports within 30 days if no progress was made in the trade talks. The White House singled out white wine and truffles as the target for some of the sanctions, since they were luxury goods which would not hurt America's economy and were mostly French goods that would hurt the prime European protectionist. Washington was prepared to escalate the trade war. Trade Representative Carla Hills also released a list of $1.7 billion worth of manufactured goods that would also receive tariff increases if the Europeans retaliated.

Each side blamed the other for the trade war. Although Brussels responded by threatening to retaliate, officials and prime ministers negotiated behind the scenes to avert a war. In late November 1992, a compromise was struck between Washington and Brussels in which there would be a 21 percent reduction in the international tonnage of subsidized grain exports. However, Brussels and France squabbled over the decision until June 8, 1993 when Paris finally agreed in return for promises of higher ECU subsidies for affected French farmers.

With this impasse resolved, the GATT continued to negotiate a range of other issues. Between June and December 15, 1993, diplomats squabbled over such issues as American attempts to retain its legal ability to retaliate against foreign dumping, subsidies, European protection for its aerospace industry, and French subsidies to industry at the expense of America's film industry. Last minute compromises allowed the Uruguay Round to be completed with a package of trade, investment, financial, intellectual protection, and technology agreements that when implemented could spur global economic growth by an estimated $280 billion annually.

Multinational Corporations

Multinational corporations (MNCs) have been around a long time. In the late Middle Ages, firms like the Fuggers based in Augsburg, Germany conducted trade, extended credit, and nurtured industries across Europe. Most of the ships which sailed to the earth's far ends during the early modern era were privately owned by corporations that received a charter from the crown to explore, conquer, and govern distant realms. The British East India Company and the Hudson Bay Company in particular enjoyed a monopoly over vast territories. From the eighteenth through the twentieth century, scores of other MNCs emerged to conduct business and investments around the world.[18]

Today, probably no greater force has contributed more to international interdependence than MNCs. The world is girded together by tens of thousands of MNCs, whose ranks swell daily. Although most of these MNCs are from advanced industrial states, increasing numbers come from newly industrializing countries. This proliferation of MNCs was stimulated by the telecommunications, computer, and transportation revolutions since 1945 in which global communications and financial transactions take place instantaneously.

An MNC is defined as a firm with a foreign office which conducts business. MNCs are involved in every imaginable type of business—extraction (mining, logging, oil-production); agriculture; manufacturing of both finished and semi-finished goods; finance (banking, investing); and services (insurance, tourism, wholesale and retail sales, advertising, management, transportation, and public utilities). Some multinational corporations actually have overseas businesses in all of these categories. An MNC's control over its foreign subsidiary ranges from whole to partial ownership. Many MNCs will form joint business ventures with other MNCs or local entrepreneurs to spread the investment risks. Others MNCs prefer to maintain a wholly owned subsidiary because they have total control over its operations. When an MNC buys up an existing factory, office, or business, or builds a new one, it is directly investing in that country. When an MNC buys stocks, bonds, or other financial assets, it is making a portfolio investment.

Although MNC activities have risen steadily since 1945, there was a huge jump in MNC direct foreign investments between 1984 and 1989 when they rose an average 29 percent, three times faster than trade increases. In 1989, the global stock of direct foreign investments was $1.5 trillion. The United States, European Community, and Japan accounted for 81 percent of the total compared with their 47 percent of global trade. Direct foreign investments among the three superpowers accounted for 39 percent of the global total. As of 1988, European firms had directly invested $193.9 billion in the United States and only $1.7 billion in Japan; American firms had $131.1 billion in the Union and only $17.9 billion in Japan; Japanese firms had $53.4 billion in the United States and $12.5 billion in the Union.[19]

Periodically, host countries have expressed concern over the influx of direct foreign investments. In the 1960s, many Europeans feared that a mounting wave of American investments was jeopardizing the European Union's political economic independence.[20] During the 1980s, the overpriced dollar and higher trade barriers attracted a huge wave of foreign investment into the United States, prompting some Americans to fear that their sovereignty was threatened. The Tolchins' book *Buying into America* and Pat Choate's *Agents of Influence* made powerful cases that this foreign investment was hindering rather than helping America's economic development.[21] The Tolchins revealed how foreign corporations succeed in lobbying California and other states to repeal their unitary taxes which taxed both foreign and domestic firms on their global rather than local sales to limit their ability to engage in transfer pricing. Choate pointed out that Japan's government and businesses were annually spending at least $400 million at the federal, state, and local level to influence policies in their favor, an amount greater than the sum of lobbying money spent by America's leading business federations. While the practices of some foreign corporations that invested in the United States were criticized, American corporations were blasted for exporting jobs, wealth, and tax revenue by investing overseas. Once the United States largely exported products; today it builds them overseas and often exports them back to the United States. Classical economists dismissed these criticisms as groundless, arguing that free trade and investment markets are always good, and if other countries do not reciprocate America's relative openness they are only hurting themselves.

Each of the superpowers has different policies toward foreign investments. The European Union has dealt with the problem of transfer pricing and worsened trade and payments problems by setting domestic content laws for some products. For example, an automobile built in Europe must contain at least 45 percent parts made within the Union to be considered European. In 1988, Brussels allowed France to block the importation of 300,000 Japanese television sets which were assembled in Europe but failed to meet domestic content standards.

Washington has been far less restrictive of foreign investments than Brussels. Citing free trade, the Reagan and Bush administrations blocked Congressional efforts to push through domestic content laws simlar to those of Brussels. However, the United States does have considerable power to limit the activities of foreign firms in the United States. The 1976 International Investment and Trade in Services Act and 1977 International Emergency Economic Powers Act enable the president to block or force the divestiture of any foreign acquisition of an American firm that is considered vital for America's national security. Presidents have rarely used these laws. Fearing that disclosure would inhibit foreign investment in the United States, the Reagan administration blocked the Bryant amendment to the 1988 Omnibus Trade Bill which would have required foreign firms to disclose the details of their operations.

In 1987, a controversy arose when Japan's Fujitsu corporation tried to buy the American firm, Fairchild Semiconductor. Many in and out of Washington argued that the sale should be blocked because it would reinforce Japan's semiconductor industry at the expense of America's, despite the fact that Fairchild was already owned by a French firm, Schulumberger. While the Japanese cried racism, opponents of the sale countered that there was investment reciprocity between the United States and France, and France's microelectronics industry is far behind America's. In contrast, Japanese firms can invest freely in the United States and buy out virtually any American firm they desire, while American and other foreign firms are restricted from investing in Japan and prevented from hostile takeovers of Japanese firms. In addition, Japan's semiconductor firms had dumped their products for years in the United States and captured a huge market share, while American and other foreign firms still faced heavy Japanese trade barriers and thus had only a minuscule market share. Although the Reagan administration did not block the sale, Fujitsu eventually dropped its bid.

In the 1992 presidential campaign, Governor Clinton promised to eliminate the transfer pricing of foreign corporations in the United States that allows many of them to pay no taxes at all. In 1988, foreign firms with American subsidiaries enjoyed $825.6 billion in business but paid a minuscule $5.8 billion in taxes. Through closing loopholes and investigations, Clinton hopes to raise $45 billion, of which $7 billion would go to state coffers. Indirectly American firms will profit too since they have been hurt by the foreign corporations' ability to evade taxes. The Bush administration opposed Clinton's plan because it claimed it would deter foreign investments in the United States.[22] Since taking office, Clinton has not yet made good on his promise.

Of the three economic superpowers, none restricts foreign investments more systematically than Japan. Until recently, the Japanese government severely restricted the amount and type of foreign investments in Japan. The government screened all foreign investments and allowed entry only if the MNC's products did not compete with those of Japanese firms targeted by the government for development, and even then they were limited to a 49 percent share of the investment with Japanese investors holding the other 51 percent. Profits from most foreign investments could not be repatriated until 1967. The screening process did not end and 100 percent foreign ownership was not allowed until passage of the 1980 Foreign Exchange and Foreign Trade Control Law. The Law still allows the government the right to impede any foreign investments that violate national security. Despite these legal changes, Japan continues to screen foreign investments and inhibits those which are competitive with Japanese industry. Tokyo has specific industry laws which empower it to impede competitive foreign investments. Foreign MNCs face numerous unofficial obstacles to investing in Japan including government red tape designed deliberately to impede foreigners, restrictions on advertising, buying or renting land, and business cartels which will not sell to or buy from foreigners.

There is conflicting evidence over the positive and negative effects of foreign investments. MNCs may clearly affect the trade balance. For example, the automobile VER that Washington negotiated with Tokyo in 1981 was partially an attempt to encourage Japan's manufacturers to invest directly in the United States to help alleviate Japan's growing trade deficit. Japan's automakers did open factories in the United States during the 1980s, but these investments actually worsened the trade deficit since most of the components were shipped from Japan.

Most studies indicate that American foreign investments actually help America's trade and payments accounts. Were it not for American MNCs and their foreign subsidiaries, America's trade deficit would be much worse. American corporations selling to their foreign subsidiaries accounted for about 35 percent of all American exports.[23] It is argued that the exports from the United States would have often been lost whether the American MNC invested abroad or not as other foreign firms simply filled the gap. If American MNCs invest abroad, they continue to hold on to those markets.

Other studies show that welcoming foreign investments can help one's economy. An extensive Canadian study in 1968 concluded that "the host country typically benefits and often substantially from foreign direct investment."[24] The report did note, however, that there was a tendency for foreign MNCs to buy goods and services from its subsidiaries rather than from local businesses. The European Community Caborn Report of 1981 found "favorable impacts on productivity, growth rates and overall level of employment, on the dissemination of new products and processes and also of managerial know-how."[25] Other benefits included better payment and trade accounts, greater research and development, and technology advances. A study of the impact of foreign investments in the United States likewise found a largely positive impact.[26]

There are winners and losers in any economic transaction, but overall foreign investments among advanced industrial countries are probably a net gain for all. Yet, while the fears of foreign investments may be exaggerated, there may be good reasons for states to regulate the type, amount, and practices of some foreign investments.

Japan

At his first press conference on March 23, 1993, President Clinton declared that:

> *If you look at the history of America's trade relationships . . . the one that never seems to change very much is the one with Japan. That is, we're sometimes in a position of trade deficit, but we're often in a position of trade surplus with the European Community. . . . We once had huge trade deficits with Taiwan and South Korea, but they've changed now quite a bit; they move up and down. . . . But the persistence of the surplus the Japanese enjoy with the United States and with the rest of the developed world can lead one to the conclusion that the possibility of obtaining real, even access to the Japanese market is somewhat remote.*

In other words, all of America's bilateral trade relations seem to be governed by market forces except that with Japan.

Statistics support Clinton's assertion. Between 1987 and 1992 as the dollar's devaluation took effect, an American trade deficit of $24.3 billion with the European Community was converted into a trade surplus of $16.7 billion surplus! During the same period, America's trade deficit with Japan dipped slightly from $59.3 billion to $52.7 billion, despite the fact that the American dollar declined in value far more sharply against the Japanese yen than the European currencies.

In 1992, Japan enjoyed a trade surplus of $132 billion, of which $52 billion was with the United States and $31 billion with the European Union. That same year, while the total direct investments of Japanese corporations had reached $93 billion in the United States and $55 billion in the European Union, total American and European direct investments in Japan were only $9.5 billion and $3.2 billion, respectively. Both Washington, Brussels, and the various European capitals have continually condemned Japan's immense and intractable trade and investments surpluses, but to no avail.

Japan has been a serious geoeconomic issue since its economy began to revive in the late 1940s. For four years between 1951 and 1955, the Europeans opposed Washington's attempts to sponsor Japan's membership in GATT. The Europeans argued that Japan would continue its neomercantilism despite its promises to abandon it to join

GATT. In 1955, Washington finally succeeded in gaining Tokyo GATT membership, but most of the other members used GATT Article 35, the "safeguard clause," which allowed them to continue discriminating against Japanese imports. The EC and Japan negotiated away these barriers throughout the 1960s. In retaliation against Japanese neomercantilism, Europeans continued to keep out specific Japanese goods, although the type and amount varied from one country to the next. For example, Italy restricted Japanese automobiles to a 1 percent share, France to 3 percent, and Britain to 11 percent, while the other Community members had few or no restrictions. Brussels retaliated promptly against most Japanese products which quickly captured large market shares through dumping. By 1992, VRAs restricted 40 percent of Japanese exports to the Union.

Washington itself clashed frequently with Tokyo over waves of Japanese dumping of various products in the United States that hurt or bankrupted many American firms. The first negotiations began in 1955 over Japanese "dollar blouses" that were gaining market share from American producers. Conflicts and negotiations continued over various types of Japanese textiles throughout the 1960s, culminating with a 1969 agreement limiting Japanese imports to certain levels. In the late 1960s and into the 1970s, Japanese television and steel producers captured increased market share, and the remaining beleaguered American producers pressured the White House to intervene. The government's response to the television industry was "too little too late," and today there is only one American television producer, Zenith, remaining of the 24 during the mid-1960s. The White House was more prompt in responding to Japanese and European steel imports. In 1968, Washington negotiated VRAs with Japanese and European steel producers to limit their share of America's market. In 1978, the Carter administration responded to a new surge of Japanese steel dumping by imposing the "trigger price mechanism" in which any steel entering the United States below a certain average Japanese production cost would automatically trigger a dumping investigation.

During the 1980s, the Reagan administration conducted two sets of negotiations. One tried to stem the influx of Japanese imports which threatened to destroy America's automobile, semiconductor, motorcycle, and other industries. Another negotiation attempted to reduce Japanese trade barriers and gain greater market share for such American products and services as baseball bats, beef, oranges, semiconductors, portable phones, satellites, lawyers, telecommunications equipment, and banks, to name a few.

Perhaps the most important of these conflicts was over automobiles. Washington negotiated a VER with Tokyo which restricted Japanese exports to 1.68 million annually from 1981 to 1984, and from 1.85 million from 1984 through the present. These restrictions may well have prevented the total collapse of America's automobile industry, but they cost consumers over $5 billion in higher sticker prices as both American and Japanese producers raised prices in the restricted markets. Each American job saved cost $160,000.[27] Between 1980 and 1985, the American automobile industry lost over $6 billion and 200,000 jobs, while Japan's share of America's market rose to 21 percent. By the late 1980s, Detroit was making a profit again but Japan's producers made even higher profits and soon got around the restrictions by building automobile plants in the United States. Between 1991 and 1992, America's Big Three Automakers lost over $6.5 billion and Japan's market share from exports and transplants rose to 30 percent.

Despite these losses, American automakers have made enormous cost reduction and quality gains over the past decade, surpassing their Japanese rivals by many measurements. In 1981, the average American car cost $1,500 to $2,500 more to produce than the average Japanese car. In 1993 the cost for Ford to produce a small car was $5,415 and Chrysler $5,841, while the lowest cost Japanese producer was Toyota at $6,216. General Motors at $7,205 was by far the highest cost producer among both American and Japanese firms. While American labor costs still exceeded those of Japan, Ford and Chrysler have brought their parts, materials, and other production costs far below their Japanese competitors. American labor costs are driven up by health and pension costs. The American producers are also penalized by the fact that they only used 62 percent of capacity in 1991 while the Japanese used 95 percent, a difference which cost the Americans $800 to $1,500 more per car.[28] Overall, America still suffers a nearly $45 billion automobile trade deficit with Japan despite the comparative advantage of Ford and Chrysler.

Another major trade battle of the 1980s was over computer chips. The Japanese are leading the microelectronics revolution, mastering such interrelated fields as semiconductors, telecommunications, fiber optics, virtual reality, and industrial ceramics. Industries are composed of "foodchains," which include equipment makers, components, and finished products. Semiconductors are to the microelectronics industry as steel is to automobiles and shipbuilding.

Japan's semiconductor makers captured enormous market share during the early 1980s because of the overvalued dollar and undervalued yen, and the strategy of massive dumping designed to drive their American and other foreign rivals into bankruptcy. This advantage was further strengthened by the ability of Japanese firms to raise money at 4 percent interest rates in Japan's managed financial market system while American producers paid 12 percent in America's open capital markets. By being able to spend twice what the Americans were spending on reseach and development, the Japanese were able to offer a cheaper, better quality product.

In 1986, after years of pleading from American chipmakers, the Reagan White House agreed to negotiate a VER with Japan. An agreement was finally struck in which floor prices were set for Japanese chipmakers and United States chipmakers were promised a 20 percent market share in Japan by 1991. The White House followed up this agreement by attempting a Japanese-style industrial policy in 1987, in which the White House allocated $100 million to help create Sematech, a semiconductor research consortium in a belated attempt to emulate and catch up to the Japanese.

Although the bilateral agreement and Sematech helped save the American semiconductor industry, neither has fulfilled expectations. America's market share in Japan has risen from 8.5 percent to 17.5 percent, which represented $1 billion in additional sales. But the current share is short of Tokyo's promised 20 percent share. Meanwhile Sematech has failed to achieve any major techological or product breakthroughs. Throughout the 1980s, America's global market share tumbled from 59 percent in 1980 to 39 percent in 1991 after bottoming out at 37 percent in 1988, while Japan's market share rose from 32 percent to 49 percent after peaking at 51 percent in 1988. In 1991, $20.9 billion worth of semiconductors were sold in Japan, $15.4 billion in the United States, $10.1 billion in Europe, and $8.2 billion elsewhere.[29] American chipmakers have retreated upmarket to more sophisticated microprocessors while the Japanese dominate the memory chip market. Many believe that the Japanese producers will eventually master microprocessors as they have memory chips.

The Reagan and Bush administrations' efforts to open Japan's markets had a mixed success. After years of tough and sometimes bitter negotiations Tokyo agreed to liberalize its orange and beef markets, but remained adamantly opposed to any concessions on rice. One measure of the farm lobby's political clout is that Washington chose to spend enormous diplomatic resources on agriculture, which comprises a small percentage of total bilateral trade, when so many other American industries and technologies are struggling against Japanese exports and are allowed only a limited share of Japan's markets.

While negotiations were conducted over specific products, Washington also tried to address the problem of systematic Japanese import and investment barriers. Between 1988 and 1991, Washington and Tokyo conducted the Structural Impediments Initiative (SII), in which the Americans cited examples of Japanese trade barriers such as the industrial groups (keiretsu) that tend to buy from each other, distribution cartels, highly subsidized agriculture, lack of patent protection, and artificially high savings rates, and so on, while the Japanese pointed out examples of American practices which inhibit economic growth, such as low savings and investment, the large budget deficit, crumbling infrastructure, and crime. Unfortunately the talks went nowhere as neither side implemented any of the other's suggested changes.

Tokyo has recently turned the tables on the United States and European Union, labeled them "protectionists," and demanded that they remove their barriers. On June 8, 1992, Tokyo released a report labeling the United States as being the most unfair trader among the advanced industrial countries.[30] The report cited Washington's tendency to impose unilateral and often protectionist decisions in bilateral trade disputes, to unfairly use dumping laws to restrict to imports, to impose voluntary export restraints on others, and to widely use "buy American" laws. Tokyo claimed that Brussels was only slightly less protectionist than the United States. Japan is increasingly turning to GATT to help settle trade conflicts. As long as the imbalances between trade practices and results exist there will be continued bitter conflicts.

Trade Blocs

The global economy is increasingly defined by three trade blocs comprising the European Union, North American, and Asia Pacific countries. A 1991 World Bank study compared these three blocs.[31] The North American bloc or NAFTA includes the United States, Canada, and Mexico with a $6.203.1 trillion GNP, 363.6 million population, and $17,060 per capita income. The European Union has twelve members—Germany, France, Britain, Italy, Spain, the Netherlands, Belgium, Denmark, Ireland, Portugal, Greece, and Luxembourg—with a $5.517.4 trillion GNP, 342.5 million population, and $16,107 per capita income. The Union's total GNP, population, and per capita income would be much higher if the seven nation European Free Trade Association (EFTA), Finland, and Switzerland were included. Although there is no formal Asia Pacific trade alliance, an informal Japan-centered bloc has been evolving for several decades. The combined assets of Japan, Hong Kong, Malaysia, South Korea, Singapore, and Thailand alone amount to a $3.592.8 trillion GNP, 248.3 million population, and $14,467 per capita income. The Asia Pacific bloc would be the largest in GNP and population and much lower in per capita income if China, Taiwan, Indonesia, Brunei, and the Philippines were included.

A trade bloc's strength can be measured in several ways. One is a trade bloc's degree of intraregional trade as a percentage of total trade. By that measurement, the European Union is the most cohesive of the trade blocs with its 59 percent intraregional trade compared to 27 percent for NAFTA, and 24 percent for the Asia Pacific.[32] All of the blocs clearly depend far more on other countries than on their members for their trade.

Another measure of strength is whether or not a trade bloc is running a trade surplus with the others. By this measure the European Union is the weakest of the three. In 1991, it ran $38.390 billion and $24.406 billion trade deficits with Japan and the United States, respectively. While the United States enjoyed a huge surplus with Europe, it also suffered a $46.863 billion deficit with Japan. The figures for the United States and Japan, of course, do not take into account the effects of other bloc members.

Yet another way of determining a bloc's strength is to measure its relative trade dependence in relation to the others. Despite its lower relative economic size, if other countries are added to the Community and Asia Pacific blocs, NAFTA will remain the most important of the three because the other two blocs depend on America's huge affluent market as a target for exports. The United States and NAFTA can use the threat of closed markets to counter any European or Asia Pacific protectionism. The Asia Pacific bloc is particularly vulnerable. Although most of the countries run trade deficits with Japan they enjoy trade surpluses with the United States. Thus any threat of closed NAFTA markets can wring concessions from the Asia Pacific bloc.

Some fear that these regional economic blocs will eventually declare an all out trade war on each other. This fear is unfounded. Autarky, or the severing of one's economic relations with other countries, is increasingly difficult in an increasingly interdependent world. Although it is true that most of the European Union's foreign trade occurs between the twelve members, that intra-Union trade does not mean that Europe's continued prosperity is any less dependent upon the global system. The same can be said of the America's fifty states; more than 80 percent of all trade occurs within the United States and less than 20 percent with foreign countries. Yet, America's foreign trade is accounting for an increasingly important slice of the economy, up from about 10 percent in 1960.

President Clinton has skillfully played the trade bloc game to enhance American geoeconomic interests. First, he succeeded in getting NAFTA's ratification which most members of Congress were solidly against. In late November 1993, he won by stressing that NAFTA would lead to more and better American jobs rather than less, but he also warned that if the United States did not form closer ties with Mexico, Japan might, to America's detriment. "If we turn our back on free trade with our closest neighbor," the president declared, "how credible will we be in the eyes of the Europeans or Japanese in asking them to accept lower trade barriers. . . ?" He also argued that the United States could use NAFTA's geoeconomic power to pry open closed markets in Japan, the European Union, and other countries and regions. Clinton then proceeded to do just that. Fresh from his congressional victory, the president flew to Seattle for a summit meeting of the four-year-old 15 member Asian Pacific Economic Cooperation (APEC) forum on November 19 and 20. America's trade with the Pacific basin is 50 percent greater than its trade with the Atlantic basin. But while the United States enjoys a trade surplus with Europe, it suffers a trade deficit with Asia. During the summit, Clinton pressed for and succeeded in gaining APEC's approval to convert the forum into a huge free trade association by the late 1990s. With the APEC and NAFTA victories under his belt, Clinton then trained his geoeconomic guns on France which was holding up a GATT accord. By December 15, 1993—the date the president's congressional authorization for trade negotiating powers ran out—last minute compromises by all sides allowed the Uruguay Round to be successfully completed which will stimulate a stalled global economy.

Clinton's deft and farsighted diplomacy on NAFTA, APEC, and GATT will characterize global geoeconomic relations into the twenty-first century. While trade squabbles will continue, there will be no return to the "beggar-thy-neighbor" currency devaluations and high trade barriers of the 1930s. International trade and investments will continue to expand. Geoeconomic relations, however, will be increasingly managed between countries and blocs to prevent anyone from garnering too many benefits by following predatory industrial, technology, investment, and trade policies. In an increasingly interdependent global economy, most governments will become more neomercantilist as their nations' dependence on international trade steadily deepens. Trade conflicts will involve specific cases of dumping, subsidies, market share, or investments and broader negotiations over national industrial and trade policies. Yet, more geoeconomic management will mean more rather than less global trade and prosperity.

CONCLUSION

Since 1945, the global economy has been enormously resilient, continuing to expand despite the occasional oil price hikes and periodic recessions and stock market crashes of its more prominent member states. Global GNP has expanded over 20 times and trade over 25 times in volume since 1950, and it continues to increase at average annual rates of 5 and 7 percent, respectively. In 1990, over $3 trillion in goods and services were traded internationally, around 15 percent of total global GNP. The three great geoeconomic powers—the European Union, United States, and Japan—account for over two-thirds of world GNP and half of its trade.

The benefits of world economic growth and trade, however, have not been evenly distributed among the participants. Some countries have grown faster than others and thus, there have been huge shifts in the geoeconomic power balance. Although over-all interdependence undoubtedly increases prosperity, there are clearly winners and losers. Jobs, wealth, revenues, firms, and entire industries can be lost as well as gained from the international flow of trade, investments, and finance. Economists estimate that a nation loses 25,000 jobs for every billion dollars it suffers in trade deficit. So America's trade deficit of over $84.340 billion in 1992 meant that 2.1 million more Americans were unemployed than would have been the case if there were a trade balance. The $52 billion deficit America suffered with Japan translated into 1.350 million net lost American jobs. Some have argued that the United States is "deindustrializing" or being "hollowed out" by the effects of American multinationals investing abroad and foreign multinational corporations and governments engaging in unfair trade and investment practices against the United States.

The United States has declined relative to the rise of Japan and the European Union. Between 1888 and 1971, the United States continuously ran trade surpluses, which showed that America's industrial base was dynamic, diversified, and globally competitive. Since 1971 the United States has continually run trade deficits, which rose steadily to $15 billion in 1981, then, because of the Reagan White House's policies, skyrocketed to $152 billion in 1987, declined to $62 billion in 1991, and then rose to $84 billion in 1992. Meanwhile, Japan's GNP will surpass that of the United States within a dozen years if each country's respective growth rates hold—Japan's economy continues to grow twice as fast as America's. If Japan's GNP equals that of the United States, but with half the population, Japan's per capita income will be twice that of Americans. The European Union's growth rate is comparable to that of the United States. But with 80 million more consumers than the United States and other countries waiting to join, the Union's GNP is larger even while its per capita income is lower.

Both the United States and the European Union suffer trade deficits with Japan, and have become increasingly protectionist, restricting about 45 percent and 60 percent of manufactured imports, respectively. Meanwhile, Japan, largely because of foreign pressure, has become much more open. During the 1980s, the Reagan and Bush administrations tried to convince Japan and the Union "to be more like us," all the while imposing greater import restrictions. The Clinton administration is more protectionist in rhetoric as well as policy. Fair rather than free trade is the battle cry for the 1990s and beyond. Trade battles among all three economic superpowers will become more frequent and bitter.

Despite these challenges and relative decline, the United States will continue to be the center of world trade and two vast regional systems spanning the northern Pacific and Atlantic basins. The economic power balance between the United States, the European Union, and Japan will continue.

STUDY QUESTIONS

1. What are the advantages and disadvantages of interdependence?

2. What were the major stages in the evolution of the global political economy?

3. What is mercantilism, and what are its strengths and weaknesses?

4. What is economic liberalism, and what are its strengths and weaknesses?

5. What is neomercantilism, and what are its strengths and weaknesses?

6. What steps did the United States take in the twentieth century to first push the global economy into depression and then reconstruct the global economy and lead it into prosperity?

7. What institutions were created in the 1940s that became the superstructure of the global economy? What are their functions?

8. How did the fixed currency system work? What pressures built upon it during the 1960s? Why did President Nixon abandon the fixed system in 1971? How has the new floating currency system worked?

9. What problems did the American and global economy suffer throughout the 1970s and 1980s through today?

10. What was the 1985 Plaza Accord supposed to accomplish? How successful was it in achieving its goals?

11. What are the advantages and disadvantages of NAFTA for each of its members?

12. What have been the major characteristics and government policies shaping America's economic development?

13. What have been the major characteristics and government policies shaping Japan's economic development?

14. What have been the major characteristics and government policies shaping the European Union's development?

15. What are the GATT's strengths and weaknesses? How have the GATT rounds varied in the focus of negotiations?

16. What are the pros and cons of allowing unrestricted foreign investment in one's country?

17. What conflicts and different policies have the three economic superpowers had over multinational corporations and foreign investments?

18. Why have Japan's economic policies and trade surpluses been so severely criticized by the European Union and the United States? What have been the major trade conflicts among these economic superpowers and how have they been managed?

19. Analyze the power balance among the three economic blocs—the EU, NAFTA, and East and Southeast Asia. Will the conflicts among the three continue to be managed or will relations break down into trade war?

ENDNOTES

1. For the classic work on complex interdependence, see Robert O. Keohane and Joseph S. Nye, *Power and Interdependence: World Politics in Transition,* 2nd ed. (Glenview, Ill.: Scot Foresman/Little, Brown, 1989).

2. The founder of this perspective was Charles Kindleberger, *The World in Depression, 1929–1939* (Berkeley, Calif.: University of California Press, 1973). See also: Robert Keohane, *After Hegemony: Cooperation and Discord in the World Political System* (Princeton, N.J.: Princeton University Press, 1984).

3. Stephen Krasner, "Structural Causes and Regime Consequences: Regimes as Intervening Variables," *International Organization,* vol. 36, Spring 1982, p. 185.

4. Henry Kissinger, *The Washington Post,* November 24, 1984.

5. For excellent accounts of American leadership of the global political economy, see Charles Kindleberger, *The World in Depression, 1929–1939;* David P. Calleo and Benjamin Rowland, *America and the World Political Economy* (Bloomington, Ind.: Indiana University Press, 1973); Joan Spero, *The Politics of International Economic Relations* (New York: St Martin's Press, 1990).

6. For an excellent argument that Smoot-Hawley simply exacerbated an existing global depression, see Susan Strange, "Protectionism and World Politics," in Kendall Stiles and Tsuneo Akaha, eds., *International Political Economy* (New York: HarperCollins, 1991), 133–156.

7. Quoted in Richard N. Gardner, *Sterling-Dollar Diplomacy in Current Perspectives: The Origins and Prospects of our International Economic Order,* expanded ed. (New York: Columbia University Press, 1980), 9.

8. Martin and Susan Tolchin, *Selling Our Security: The Erosion of America's Assets* (New York: Knopf, 1992), 132.

9. Keith Bradsher, "An Ideological Divide," *New York Times,* October 7, 1992.

10. See Selig Harrison and Clyde Prestowitz, "Pacific Agenda: Defense or Economics?" *Foreign Policy,* no. 79, Summer 1990, 56–57.

11. Among the more prominent studies of Japan's development, see Ira Magaziner and Thomas Hout, *Japanese Industrial Policy* (Berkeley, Calif.: Institute of International Studies, University of California, 1980); John Zysman, *Governments, Markets, and Growth* (Ithaca, N.Y.: Corneal University Press, 1983); Ed Lincoln, *Japan's Industrial Policies* (Washington, D.C.: Japan Economic Institute of America, 1984); William Nester, *The Foundations of Japanese Power: Continuities, Changes, Challenges* (Armonk, N.Y.: M.E. Sharpe, 1990); William Nester, *Japanese Industrial Targeting: The Neomercantilist Path to Economic Superpower* (New York: St. Martin's Press, 1991).

12. See Chalmers Johnson, John Zysman, Laura Tyson, *Politics and Productivity: The Real Story of Why Japan's Economy Works* (Cambridge, Mass.: Ballinger, 1989), Chapter 1.

13. See Ernst Haas, *The Uniting of Europe* (Stanford, Calif.: Stanford University Press, 1957). For recent studies, see Edward Nevin, *The Economics of Europe* (London: Macmillan, 1990); William Nester, *The European Community and the Japanese Challenge* (London: Macmillan, 1993).

14. Quoted in Willem Molle, *The Economics of European Integration* (Aldershot, England: Dartmouth, 1990), 476.

    Unless otherwise indicated, all trade statistics come from the *International Money Fund, Direction of Trade,* various issues, Washington, D.C.

15. United Nations, *International Financial Statistics Yearbook,* 1987, 701.

16. *New York Times,* October 21, 1992.

17. *New York Times,* July 8, 1992.

18. For example, see Mira Wilkins, *The Emergence of Multinational Enterprise: American Business Abroad From the Colonial Era to 1914* (Cambridge, Mass.: Harvard University Press, 1970).

19. *The Economist,* August 24, 1991.

20. See Jean-Jacques Servan-Schreiber, *The American Challenge* (New York: Atheneum, 1968).

21. Martin and Susan Tolchin, *Buying into America: How Foreign Money Is Changing the Face of Our Nation* (New York: Times Books, 1988); Pat Choate, *Agents of Influence* (New York: Knopf, 1990).

22. John Cushman, "Clinton Seeks Taxes on Hidden Profits," *New York Times,* October 23, 1992.

23. David Blake and Robert Walters, *The Politics of Global Economic Relations* (Englewood Cliffs, N.J.: Prentice-Hall, 1987), 118–119.

24. *Task Force, Foreign Ownership and the Structure of Canadian Industry* (Ottawa: Privy Council Office, 1968), 37.

25. European Communities, *Report on Enterprises and Governments in Economic Activity,* Doc. 1-169/81, May 15, 1981, 5.

26. Richard Cooper, *The Economics of Interdependence: Economic Policy in the Atlantic Community* (New York: McGraw-Hill, 1968).

27. Robert Crandall, "Import Quotas and the Automobile Industry: The Costs of Protection," *The Brookings Review,* Summer 1984, 16.

28. *New York Times,* June 18, 1992.

29. *New York Times,* April 9, 1992.

30. *New York Times,* June 8, 1992.

31. *World Bank Atlas 1991* (Washington, D.C.: the World Bank, 1992), 6–9.

32. United Nations, *World Economic Survey 1991* (New York: United Nations), 6.

Geoeconomic Conflict and Cooperation Between the First and Third Worlds

Political Development, Underdevelopment, and International Relations

Key Terms and Concepts

Bi-party System	Kleptocracy	Revolution
Catch-all Party	Legitimacy	Revolution of Rising
Charismatic Leader	Mobilization	Expectations
Corruption	Multi-party System	Revolution of Rising
Coup d'État	One-party System	Frustrations
Development	Patron-client Groups	Structural Corruption
Economic Development	Political Development	

Modernization's most central concept is *development,* which is, essentially how a society adapts to the challenges of a rapidly changing world while fulfilling its goals and ideals. A country develops economically when it achieves self-sustaining economic growth that brings a higher living standard and quality of life to an ever-greater percentage of the population. It develops politically when its government expands and changes its institutions and policies to meet society's growing needs and desires. There is clearly a virtuous relationship between economic and political development. Political philosophers since Aristotle have observed that democratic political systems are middle class societies. Today, almost all of the world's wealthiest states are liberal democracies. In contrast, although there are exceptions like India or Costa Rica, authoritarian governments rule most poor countries. A nation's political economic development is further shaped by the policies its government pursues in an increasingly interdependent world.[1]

This chapter will analyze the prerequisites for successful *political development* and its relationship with *economic development* within the Third World. First it will address the controversy over just what the Third World is, then it will discuss some of the major arguments of those who advocate external and internal explanations for development. An exploration will then follow of political instability, coups, and revolutions in some countries. A country's relative development successes or failures depend, to varying extents, on that country's foreign relations and dependence on the global political economy. Each section will examine the relationship between a nation's political development and international relations.

WHAT IS THE THIRD WORLD?

There are many names for the world's poorer countries: the Third World, the South (since many of them are in the Southern Hemisphere), the less developed countries (LDCs), and developing countries. This group of countries is contrasted with the First World, the North, the more developed countries, the developed countries, and the industrialized countries. Those who use First and Third worlds also include a Second World of socialist countries which are industrializing. With communism's collapse in Eastern Europe and the Soviet Union, this category has fallen into disuse.

None of these categories adequately capture the range of levels of development among these countries. The terms "developed" and "developing" countries are particularly inadequate. If development is synonymous with progress, then most rich and many poor countries are "developing" as measured by achieving higher living standards and quality of life. If measureable progress is truly unending then we cannot say any country is "developed" per se. Likewise the terms "North" and "South" are inadequate since many poor countries are found in the Northern Hemisphere and rich countries in the Southern Hemisphere. Although the terms "more" and "less" developed countries capture the relative differences in development, they lack precision in explaining exactly when a country is one or the other.

For convenience's sake, if nothing else, most people use the term *Third World* to designate the world's relatively poorer countries. The word *Third World* (or Tiers Monde) was coined by French intellectuals in the 1950s as a means of distinguishing between the "First World," or American bloc, and the "Second World," or Soviet bloc. It has been heavily criticized since, in part, because it might denote "third rate" in social or ethnic as well as economic terms. Another problem is that it groups too many very different countries together. Although Third World countries are said to share poverty and victimization by Western imperialism, even these two characteristics are inadequate. Not every poor country was a former colony. Iran, Turkey, Thailand, Ethiopia, Afghanistan, Liberia, Tibet, Yemen, China, and Japan were never directly colonized while most of Latin America received its independence from Spain in the 1820s. Also, the degree of poverty varies so greatly from one country to the next that the category appears meaningless. For example, the difference in political economic development between the Third World countries Bangledesh and South Korea seems as great as that between South Korea and the United States.

Yet another criticism is that the term implies shared political as well as economic orientations. The over 130 countries grouped in the Third World include flourishing liberal-democratic and high-authoritarian states, free-market, mixed-market and centrally planned economies, and pro-Western, non-aligned, and pro-Soviet (at least until recently) governments. The Third World includes countries, such as China and India, both armed with nuclear weapons and huge armies, and with 1.2 billion and 880 million people respectively, and micro-states like Nauru with 9,000 and Vanuatu with 23,000 people. Shiva Naipaul, the noted Trinadad novelist, complained that the "Third World is a form of bloodless universality that robs individuals and societies of their particularity. To blandly subsume, say, Ethiopia, India, and Brazil under the banner of Third Worldhood is as absurd and as denigrating as the old assertion that all Chinese look alike."[2]

Table 15.1
Quality of Life Indicators for Select Countries, 1988, 1990

Income Category[1]	Per-capita GNP 1988 ($)	Physical Quality of Life Index (PQLI) 1990	Life Expectancy at Birth (years)	Infant Mortality (per 1,000 births)	Literacy (%)
Low-income	319	68	63	66	60
Guinea-Bissau	190	36	44	140	37
China	330	81	71	27	73
India	340	60	60	88	48
Sri Lanka	420	90	72	24	88
Lower-middle-income	941	76	64	53	75
Philippines	630	83	65	40	90
Yemen, Arab Rep.	640	48	53	107	39
Zimbabwe	650	70	61	55	67
Cuba	1,170	96	76	13	94
Upper-middle-income	2,299	83	69	39	81
Poland	1,860	94	72	17	98
Brazil	2,160	79	66	57	81
Gabon	2,970	58	54	94	61
Korea, Rep.	3,600	92	71	21	96
High-income	14,421	97	75	12	97
Kuwait	13,400	87	74	15	73
United States	19,840	98	76	8	99
Japan	21,020	101	79	5	99
Switzerland	27,500	100	78	7	99

Source: Adapted from *U.S. Foreign Policy and Developing Countries: Discourse and Data 1991* (Washington, D.C.: Overseas Development Council, 1991), pp. 37–41 Kegley, Wittkopf, *International Relations,* 1994.

[1]Income categories are based on the following criteria: *low-income,* a per-capita income of less than $515; *lower-middle-income,* $515–$1,304; *upper-middle-income,* $1,305–$14,529; *high-income,* $14,530 or above.

Some argue that the term can have more meaning if we limit the category of Third World countries to those which have achieved relatively high degrees of economic, social, and infrastructure development, and have the potential to develop into First World states.[3] Countries like Argentina, Chile, China, South Korea, South Africa, Costa Rica, Saudi Arabia, Brazil, and the former socialist countries in the Soviet Union and Eastern Europe, would be among those designated as Third World countries. The Fourth World would include such countries as Zambia, Malaysia, and Indonesia, which remain poor, but because of their human and/or natural resources and development policies have the potential and will to develop further. The Fifth World would include those with little real potential or will to develop, such as Niger, Chad, and Bangladesh, to name a few. This distinction between Third, Fourth, and Fifth Worlds is certainly an analytical improvment.

The World Bank designation of countries is the most precise. It divides states into three broad classes according to their per capita income. In 1989, Low-income countries had a per capita income of $580 or less, 2.948 billion people, an average 4.1 percent annual economic growth (1980-89), and a $330 average per capita income. Middle-income countries had per capita incomes of between $580 and $6,000, 1.105 billion people, an average 0.5 percent annual growth rate, and average $2,040 per capita income. High-income countries had per capita incomes of over $6,000, 831 million people, 2.3 percent average annual economic growth, and average $18,330 per capita income.

The World Bank also distinguishes three other categories of states. The ten "oil exporting countries" had energy exports which accounted for at least half their GNP, 553 million people whose countries averaged a negative 2.5 percent annual growth. The 20 "severely indebted middle-income countries" included such countries as Brazil, Mexico, Argentina, Poland, Egypt, Morocco, and the Philippines and a total population of 554 million, an average negative 0.3 percent economic growth, and $1,720 per capita income. The 24 Organization of Economic Cooperation and Development (OECD) countries had a $19,090 per capita income, 2.4 percent average growth rate, and total population of 773 million. This book will use all of these possible terms for differentiating among countries.

THIRD AND FIRST WORLD PERSPECTIVES

Dependency theorists maintain that all countries are caught up in a vast global system in which the rich industrial or "core," countries exploit the poor "periphery" and "semi-periphery" countries.[4] Third World countries cannot develop because the core countries will not allow them to do so. The poor are dependent on the industrial countries for markets for their goods, finance, technology, managerial expertise, and weapons. The core countries use that Third World dependence to prevent them from developing. Thus, colonialism has simply been replaced by a more subtle but no less effective form of exploitation called "neocolonialism." Newly independent states are still dependent on their former masters, and other industrial countries for technology, finance, markets, and products. The plantations and mines first created by the imperial powers often remain in foreign hands, and regardless, continue to be economic enclaves or islands within the former colony. Little if any wealth from this production trickles down to the native population. Those countries which use much of their arable land to plant one or a few cash crops for export often end up importing most of their food. The result is the "development of underdevelopment" in which multinational corporations (MNCs) serve the same function in administering these countries as the old colonial governments did. The MNCs also form political economic alliances with the elite of the Third World country in exploiting the population.

Other observers argue that reality is far more complex than dependency theory allows. They point to vast differences between countries within the so-called the Third World. But they also argue that despite these differences, the Third World is developing and the First World is becoming as dependent upon its markets, products, and resources as vice versa.

Table 15.2

The Distribution of World Population and Gross National Product per Capita, by Selected Countries and Country Groups

Country or Group	Per-capita GNP 1988 ($)	Population, 1990 (millions)
Country Data		
Switzerland	27,500	6.7
Japan	21,020	123.6
United States	19,840	251.4
France	16,090	56.4
United Arab Emirates	15,770	1.6
Soviet Union	4,550	291.0
Yugoslavia	2,520	23.8
Brazil	2,160	150.4
Thailand	1,000	55.7
Zimbabwe	650	9.7
China	330	1,120.0
Burundi	240	5.6
Mozambique	100	15.7
Groups averages[1]		
First World	13,749	32.6
Third World	1,871	31.7
Least developed countries (LDCs)	343	11.4
Oil-exporting countries	4,976	24.5
Organization of Petroleum Exporting Countries (OPEC)	5,075	35.6
Newly industrialized countries	5,014	47.8
Asian newly industrialized countries	7,165	17.9

Source: Based on data drawn from *Human Development Report 1991* (New York: Oxford University Press, 1991), pp. 122–123, 174. Data for Taiwan drawn from *Handbook of Economic Statistics, 1991* (Washington, D.C.: Central Intelligence Agency, 1991), p. 35, and *1988 World Population Data Sheet* (Washington, D.C.: Population Reference Bureau, 1988); Kegley, Wittkopf, *International Relations,* 1994.

[1]Group averages are based on available data for Taiwan and the 161 independent and dependent territories commonly used by United Nations agencies for statistical purposes. Kiribati and Tuvalu, dependent territories among the forty-one entities classified as LDCs, are omitted from the calculations; data for Andorra, Faroes Islands, Liechtenstein, Monaco, and San Marino, European entities that are part of the First World, are also excluded. Data for most remaining dependent territories, all of which belong to the Third World, are not available.

A U.S. State Department publication pointed out that: By the mid-1980s, the World Bank expects economic growth in the more advanced LDCs to have a significant, positive impact on the growth rates of the developed countries. The collective demand of the LDCs is already influential in sustaining the production of goods and services in the U.S. and other industrialized countries during periods of economic recession and in accelerating their recovery from recession.[6]

Yet, despite this growing interdependence, and contrary to the claims of dependency theories, the advanced industrial countries do not gain most or even much of their wealth from the Third World. In 1987, only 21 percent of all advanced industrial country exports were with the Third World, while only 22 percent of their total imports were from the Third World. Likewise, about 75 percent of foreign investments are within the advanced industrial countries rather than between them and the poor countries. Joan Spero points out that in 1987, 76 percent of total American direct foreign investment was in other industrial states and only 24 percent in the Third World.[7] The share of American direct foreign investments in the First World has risen since 1961 when they accounted for 61 percent of the total while 35 percent were in the Third World. Altogether in 1987, American firms earned only 30 percent of their total profits from Third World countries, which consisted of only 2.2 percent of all U.S. business earnings, and an infinitesimal part of American GNP. The rate of return on investments was an average 20.3 percent in the developed and only 13.7 percent in the Third World countries. Clearly, the advanced industrial states rely largely on relations with each other for the bulk of their prosperity.

Who is right? Clearly, there are profound truths to both First and Third World perspectives. There is no doubt that the First World generates most of its wealth within itself rather than from the Third World, and in relative terms the Third World's importance to First World development is diminishing. Still, both the First and Third Worlds need each other, although the Third World needs the First World much more than vice versa. The global economy provides every country goods, services, technology, finance, managerial expertise, and ideas that it otherwise would not have. Those Third World countries that have grown the fastest have been the ones most heavily involved in world trade. Yet the rules and power distribution within the global economy may well mean a very uneven playing field between First and Third World countries.

CONSTRAINTS ON SUCCESSFUL DEVELOPMENT

Daily the headlines blare news of coups, mass poverty, or famine in far away countries. Less often, one can read stories of some nations which have experienced economic growth, rising health standards, or democratic elections. Why do some states succeed and others fail to develop?

Monte Palmer, a leading authority on *development,* identifies five ingredients for successful development: 1) Leadership: the values and skills of the dominant elite; 2) System: the regime's institutional capacity to control and mobilize its human and material resources; 3) Resources: the availability of human and material resources; 4) Ideology:

the values, attitudes, behaviors, and other cultural attributes of the masses; and 5) International Relations: the regional and global environment in which the state must operate.[8] This section will examine the roles that leadership, institutions, mobilization, legitimacy, corruption, and ideology can play in a country's political development within a global system.

Leadership

Leadership is the ability of a government to mobilize a population and promote the policies which better people's lives. Max Weber identified three types of legitimate leadership—rational or constitutional, traditional, and charismatic.[9] Development theorists argue that rational or constitutional style governments have the best chance of achieving economic development. *Charismatic leaders,* on the other hand, lack the institutions that constitutional or traditional governments have for maintaining political stability and mobilizing the population. Thus charismatic leaders have particular problems in achieving economic development.

Most struggles for independence have been led by charismatic leaders who succeeded by getting most of the population to identify with their successes, dynamism, and dreams. Charismatic leaders appeal to the dominant segments of the population and can provide unity when there might otherwise be factionalism. They become symbols of the state and thus rise above criticism. They also serve as role models and sources of pride and national unity for most people. The net effect is to give the new regime stability while it attempts to fulfill its promises. Often vague about the specific policies they will follow once in office, charismatic leaders capture people's hearts rather than minds.

Charismatic leaders have an enormous psychological grip over most of the population. They claim to and seem to personify the nation. Most people want to believe in a messiah who will make everything right, and charismatic leaders fulfill that need. The more fervent followers of China's Mao Zedong and Indonesia's Sukarno have actually deified them. The power of charisma is nicely illustrated by Cuba's president, Fidel Castro. Why has Castro remained in power since 1959 despite the failure of his economic policies and collapse of communism elsewhere? His magnetic charisma may be the most important reason. He still electrifies the Cuban people when most other leaders would have been overthrown long before. By continuing to mobilize the population against a non-existent American threat, he distracts them from protesting his failures.

Charismatic leaders often devise their own ideologies—Maoism, Nasserism, Nkrumahism, Sukarnoism—to give meaning to their policies and goals.[10] Many of these ideologies share similarities. They identify a past golden age which was destroyed by Western imperialism. The leader promises to revive the nation's past glories by forging a modern, just society built upon workers and peasants. Although the population must be mobilized to devote itself to building a future ideal society, liberal democracy is deemed unsuitable for the nation's needs. Instead, the charismatic leader imposes a social or guided democracy in which he listens carefully to the masses and fulfills their wishes. Likewise, the economy would be guided rather than free. Although the country has cast off colonialism's shackles, the leader and people must remain vigilant against foreign powers. Western imperialism remains a threat that must be constantly thwarted.

These ideas are nicely captured by the Charter of the United Arab Republic:

> *This socialist solution is the only path where all elements participating in the*
> *process of production can meet, according to scientific rules, capable of supplying*
> *society with all the energies enabling it to rebuild its life on the basis of a carefully*
> *studied and comprehensive plan. Efficient socialist planning is the sole method*
> *which guarantees the use of all national resources, be they material, natural, or*
> *human, in a practical, scientific, and humane way aimed at realizing the common*
> *good of the masses, and ensuring a life of prosperity for them.*[11]

While charismatic leaders do provide their countries a source of unity and pride, there are dangers as well. Charismatic leaders are particularly notorious for generating a *revolution of rising expectations* that soon becomes a *revolution of rising frustrations* when promises remain unfulfilled. All the power that charisma brings often goes to a leader's head and he embarks on programs that squander scarce human, natural, and material resources on wasteful monuments to himself and the country rather than investing those resourses in development. When a population is loyal to a person rather than to a constitution and its institutions, the regime crumbles easily when the leader is deposed or discredited. Charismatic leaders are often loath to designate successors and there is often a bitter power struggle when one dies or is driven into exile.

Political Institutions and Systems

Leaders, whether they are charismatic or not, must operate within some type of political system.[12] The most charimatic of leaders will accomplish nothing without a government which can impose order and implement policies. Governments rule through political, media, social, and economic institutions. Order is essential. As Samuel Huntington put it:

> *The primary problem is not liberty but the creation of a legitimate public order.*
> *Men may, of course, have order without liberty, but they can not have liberty*
> *without order. Authority has to exist before it can be limited, and it is authority*
> *that is in scarce supply in those modernizing countries where government is at the*
> *mercy of alienated intellectuals, rambunctious colonels, and rioting students.*[13]

The more efficient and comprehensive the institutions, the more easily a government can rule a population. But institutions and order are not enough. Governments must be able to devise and implement policies that develop the economy and improve most people's lives. Until recently, communist countries have experienced stability largely because of the communist party's ability to create a national organization that controlled every neighborhood, village, and workplace. But communism never succeeded in significantly raising people's living standards. Although most observers were surprised by the democratic revolutions in 1989 through 1991, which swept away one communist regime after another, the collapse of the communist bloc was inevitable given its developmental failures.

The most important political institutions for any country are the bureaucracy, the political parties, the interest groups, and the police and military. The bureaucracy gathers information and revenues and formulates and implements policies. Political parties link the government with the people; they act to mobilize the population and determine the people's needs and dissatisfactions. Interest groups lobby the political parties, bureaucrats, and politicians for privileges or redress of grievances. Finally, the police and military maintain order and collect political information (the role of the military and police in politics will be discussed in the next section). Political instability often results if one or more of these institutions or forces are corrupt, inefficient, and/or disloyal.

The ideal bureaucracy is an apolitical set of institutions whose role is to gather information, present policy options to the leadership, and then implement the subsequent choices. The bureaucracy is divided into ministries or departments, each of which deals with a specific area of responsibility—welfare, education, defense, industrial development, and so on. Bureaucrats or officials are highly educated and trained experts who conscientiously fulfill their respective ministry's responsibilities. They have been selected and are promoted on the basis of their skills.

Unfortunately, few national bureaucracies match this ideal. A bureaucracy is often largely a huge drain on scarce financial, human, and material resources, and impedes rather than promotes development. In many countries, particularly less developed ones, the bureaucracy is simply a jobs program for those loyal to the government. Officials lack training, education, and commitment to their ministry's mission, and are often corrupt, inefficient, and wasteful.

Political parties mobilize segments of the population, provide a power base for elected officials, gather information on popular views and frustrations, socialize the population into certain attitudes and opinions, define issues, and criticize opposing parties. Throughout the world there is a wide spectrum of political parties of the political systems in which they operate. Some parties have an extremely narrow scope, and only attempt to represent a particular religion, ethnic group, or class. *Catch-all parties*, as the name implies, strive to include as much of the population as possible under their banner. Many less developed countries are essentially one-party states that may tolerate opposition parties but a single party dominates most reins of political, economic, and social power. In Mexico the Party of Revolutionary Institutions (PRI) has ruled since 1927. India's Congress Party has ruled for all but two years since the nation's independence in 1947. Genuine *multi-party* or *bi-party systems*, in which parties change power, have succeeded in some less developed countries like Costa Rica and Jamaica.

In every political system there is a danger that political parties will lose touch with their primary purpose—serving as a conduit of needs, ideas, support, and accountability between the government and the people. Since they already dominate the system and are not accountable to the public through competitive elections, political parties in *one-party systems* are particularly apt to disregard the need to address society's ills. Yet there is no guarantee that a multi-party system will better address a country's problems than a one-party system. Many political parties in both multi-party and one-party systems are simply personal political machines which are created by politicians to win elections and maintain power.

Every social grouping, whether it be religious, ethnic, regional, professional, gender, sexual, generational, racial, urban, or rural, has distinct interests or needs which ideally government can better serve. Sometimes these interests are organized and they systematically lobby the government for help. There are four types of economic interest groups: 1) Business Interest Groups, which pressure government for more protection from competition and subsidies, less or no taxes, and often fewer or no restrictions on safety, pollution, or quality; 2) Industrial or Farm Labor Interest Groups, which support higher wages, health, safety, and job security standards for employees; 3) Consumer Interest Groups, which seek lower prices, and safer and better quality products; and; 4) Environmental Interest Groups, which advocate restricting business' destruction of the natural and human environment through their pollution, logging, mining, and construction.

Governments ideally find a balance between giving too much or too little to the interest groups which make demands upon it. This is best accomplished when there is a power balance among a profusion of contending interest groups. Few if any political systems achieve this ideal. Of the four types of economic interest groups, it is business interests which are the most powerful in most non-socialist countries. Business groups gain the upper hand by their greater financial and organizational resources and thus overwhelm the often vocal but poorly financed and organized demands of labor, consumer, and environmental interests.

Mobilization and Legitimacy

Mobilizing the people's energies, loyalties, and efforts is essential for political stability and economic development. The population must be convinced to not only support but to make sacrifices for governmental policies and national identity. Under the right circumstances, the state can mobilize virtually anyone no matter whether their outlook is primarily traditional, modern, or transitional. Governments mobilize the loyalties of people through the mass media, political parties, and local patron-client systems.

Although mass rallies and constant socialization through the mass media are important, a government's success in mobilizing its population ultimately depends on its ability to tap into local patron-client relationships. Patrons are usually local strongmen with wealth and political power who dispense favors—jobs, loans, housing, help in forming a business, protection of businesses, entrance to college, potential spouses, advice and information—to those in the community in return for their political loyalty and a portion of their income. Local patrons, in turn, become the clients for national leaders and parties in which each does favors for the other. *Patron-client groups* tend to diminish in power as a country modernizes and its citizens find alternate ways to achieve their interests.

People are loyal to those individuals, governments, and institutions that they believe are legally, morally, and culturally legitimate. An individual, government, or institution loses its *legitimacy* and loyalty if it is corrupt, inefficient, brutal, or grossly violates cultural norms. The ease with which the legitimacy of a political system's leaders, institutions, and values are questioned, however, varies with a society's modernization level. Traditional peoples generally do not question the legitimacy of their culture's political, economic, and social institutions, and the actions or inaction of those who control them. They do not expect much so they do not demand much. Although modern individuals believe they can make a difference and thus question their society's leadership and policies, by definition a modern society provides most of its members with enough benefits and opportunities so that there is no need to question the culture's basic values and institutions. Modern individuals are loyal by choice, and they choose to remain loyal because most of their material and psychological needs are met. Traditional individuals are loyal because they cannot imagine being anything else. The most intense questioning of a political system's legitimacy comes from people within countries that are in a transitional stage between tradition and modernity. In transitional societies, political system are often unable to satisfy most people's needs, expectations, and demands.

Like the Wizard of Oz, governments and other institutions hide behind elaborate curtains and manipulate "sound and light" shows designed to instill awe and devotion in their subjects. Presidents, claiming to personify the nation, are housed in massive buildings, presented with trumpets and motorcades, and surrounded by the symbols of office.

In any political system, a government's greatest power is the power to persuade. The more democratic the country, the more a government must attempt to persuade a population to follow its policies. The more authoritarian a government, the greater the tendency to coerce a population into compliance with its policies. Coercive power, however, often proves ultimately self-defeating. Mass alienation deepens even if most people sullenly perform their duties. There are always at least a handful of radicals agitating for the government's overthrow. Too much economic deprivation or political brutality can swell the anti-government forces' support and lead to civil war.

Corruption

Corruption is the illegal use of public or private resources for personal gain. Every society has a different threshold for the tolerable amount and type of corruption. If officials exceed that threshold there will be a backlash, and they may end up in jail. A society's corruption threshold varies over time and is related to the evolution from an agrarian into an advanced industrial nation. Agrarian societies and their sources of wealth are relatively simple. Corruption and the toleration threshold increase with industrialization as enormous amounts of wealth are created. Some governments are outright *kleptocracies* that seem to do little more than transfer enormous amounts of national wealth into private estates, businesses, or bank accounts. The Duvaliers of Haiti, the Marcos' of the Philippines, the Somozas of Nicaragua, and the Mobutus of Zaire were among the most notorious pillagers of their countries' public and private wealth.

Structural corruption characterizes many countries in which everyone from the president down to the lowest official requires a "gift" in return for favors. In many countries, there is no concept of civil service in which officials are devoted solely to national goals. Instead, one's primary loyalty is to one's kinship group. Those who attain powerful political or economic positions are expected to aid others from their clan. This is particularly a problem in nation-states with little or no national consciousness.

Rather than being civil servants, all too many bureaucrats abuse their power for private rather than national gain. Although they usually have security, salaries are low. Officials supplement their meager paychecks by demanding "tips" from the public just to perform simple functions. The size of the "bite" (mordida) depends on the official's rank and the supplicant's needs. A multinational corporation requesting, for example, a building permit might have to hand over thousands of dollars to top officials.

This official corruption is often reinforced by the culture.[14] In many cultures an office job is considered to have high status while a business, construction, or factory job has lower status. Thus the most talented and best educated individuals may strive for a bureaucratic career which may offer little responsibility or pay but is high in status.

With no responsibilities or accountability, absenteeism is rife. A survey of Turkish officials found that 76 percent of 362 surveyed preferred "maximum security/low salary."[15] Of course, it is expected that they will supplement their salaries with "tips." A 1982 Egyptian newspaper editorial pointed out that: "No sooner is an official promoted to the post of manager than he ceases to accomplish any constructive work. His primary concern is to receive the compliments indiscriminately leveled at him from every quarter, and to smile with condescending magnanimity at the servile flattery lavished at him by his former colleagues."[16]

Another problem is the refusal of many officials to take responsibility for a problem. Bureaucrats avoid any innovation or experimentation and simply follow "standard operating procedures" even if they do not work at all. Fearing that they will be blamed if anything goes wrong, many officials simply direct a public appeal to another bureau. Supplicants wander through a seemingly endless maze of officials with none willing to address their particular problem. Thus: "Trial and error and free discussion might only prove that superiors are not infallible . . . Confronted by a basic sense of insecurity, everyone must fall back on the safest course of action; everyone must adhere strictly to form, to procedure, and to ritual."[17]

Can this corruption ever be rooted out? A 1976 survey of Thai corruption mirrors the bureaucracies of many less developed countries, with 80 percent of public officials and 86 percent of citizens identifying the "teamwork corruption" embedded in the system, and 65 percent of public officials and 71 percent of the citizens were pessimistic about uprooting corruption.[18] The reasons for this entrenched, structural corruption included:

(1) endless desires of human beings; (2) opportunities and loopholes in laws and regulations; (3) deeprooted habits arising out of being accustomed to resorting to corruption; (4) lack of control by superiors; (5) learning from others' experiences; (6) excessive authority; (7) economic necessities; (8) need for convenience; (9) demise of morality; and (10) patron-client relationships.[19]

In such a work environment, even the most idealistic of individuals who really wants to accomplish the ministry's responsibilities will soon settle down into the bureaucracy's routine. What else can one do when everyone else has their hands in the till and enriches themselves and their families while disregarding their responsibilities.

Corruption may not be all bad. Bribery or the "user pays system," generally does accomplish specific tasks while the bureaucracy provides some welfare to the extended families of the officials.[20] There is no doubt, however, that corruption is an enormous drag on a country's political and economic development.

POLITICAL INSTABILITY: COUPS, REFORM, AND REVOLUTION

A political system is stable when the population views its basic institutions and processes as legitimate, decision makers have enough authority to make and implement national policies, and the transfer of power from one leader to the next is smooth and widely accepted. Poor, authoritarian countries and wealthy, liberal democracies are usually stable. In the most poverty-stricken authoritarian states, the masses of poor do not challenge the government usually because they are ignorant of alternatives or fatalistic about improving their lot. Most citizens in liberal democracies accept the system as legitimate because their lives are secure and comfortable and the government seems largely responsive to the demands made upon it.

Societies in transition from traditionalism into modernity are the most politically, economically, and socially unstable. Political economic development has failed when armed bands take to the hills and streets. Why do states dissolve into civil war?[21]

Unrealistic goals and the means to achieve them are the most common reason for a nation's failure to develop. Even seemingly modest plans are unrealistic if a nation lacks the institutions necessary to implement them. Many countries lack enough experts with the technical and administrative knowledge necessary to implement even the simplest development projects. Even if the experts are in place, a country may still lack the material and technological resources with which to build a project, or the communications, marketing, or transportation infrastructure that can service it. Money is a perennial problem. Most Third World countries do not have a banking system which can gather and lend enough capital for the nation's developmental demands. Governments often end up importing everything needed for a project—experts, institutions, technology, finance, construction materials—and thus deepen rather than alleviate their foreign debt and dependence.

Likewise, political institutions fail if they are not rooted in the country's culture. Virtually every Latin American country has experienced swings between authoritarianism and democracy, with little economic development resulting from either system. As they won their independence from Spain in the 1820s, the newly independent Latin American countries created liberal democratic constitutions modeled on that of the United States. However, the cultures and institutions of these new countries, unlike in the United States, were rooted in authoritarianism and feudalism rather than democracy and free enterprise. The newly created democratic political systems were unable to manage the growing problems posed by independence and internal rivalries, and in one country after another military coups took over the government. In the late nineteenth and early twentieth centuries, many of these countries reverted to democratic rule as a growing middle class clamored for representation. Democracy in Argentina, Chile, and Uruguay seemed to become particularly well-rooted. Yet, in 1973, military coups toppled the democratic governments of Chile and Uruguay. These Latin American democracies failed for many of the same reasons Germany's democracy failed in the early 1930s. The governments were unable to deal with worsening economic problems, such as hyperinflation, capital flight, stagnant growth, and mass poverty.

Governments must have the means to achieve their development ends. Many countries have dissolved into chaos and civil war because the government promised more than it could provide. The result was a "revolution of rising expectations" which soon because a "revolution of rising frustrations." A transitional society "teaches people to become consumers long before it teaches them to become producers; it teaches them to place demands upon the government long before it imbues them with the responsibilities of citizenship."[22] If only a minority of people in even the most modern societies are entrepreneurs, then the possibility of an entrepreneur class emerging from a traditional society is remote.

Violence usually occurs amid sharp socioeconomic inequality, between rich and poor, between cities and countryside, or between regions. Economic problems are often exacerbated by a rapidly increasing population. If the population increases faster than the economy grows, then, overall, people are becoming poorer. Most of the new wealth is flowing into the bank accounts of those who are already rich.

Ethnic rather than class conflict seems to be the primary cause for the civil wars tearing apart some countries, such as Malawi and Azerbaijan. Elsewhere, religion is seen as the stimulus for violence in Ireland, the former Yugoslavia, Israel, and Lebanon. Yet beneath both ethnic and religious violence, economic inequalities are invariably present. In each of these countries one ethnic or religious group is better off than the others, a condition which in some cases has lasted hundreds of years.

In many countries, a lack of political and socioeconomic mobility frustrates the rise of those who aspire to more. Economic development often creates new socioeconomic classes. Industrialization, for example, creates a class of factory workers which may make political demands that are not satisfied. The creation of new wealth, if it remains concentrated in the hands of a few, can disrupt a society. For example, the discovery of oil in Libya in the 1950s caused a small segment of the population to become very rich while the rest of society suffered from inflation and poverty. As a result, King Indrus was overthrown in 1969.

Sometimes governments are too traditional, and their policies and attitudes fail to keep up with the modernity that is sweeping the country. By resisting change rather than attempting to channel it into constructive directions, most traditional regimes are eventually swept away by modernity. New sources of wealth and classes emerge to surpass and challenge the traditional rulers. The regime may respond with a crackdown that may succeed in quelling dissenters in the short-run but that further undermines the government's legitimacy over the long run.

Sometimes a government's policies and attitudes are too modern for the population. The Shah's "White Revolution," for example, attempted systematically to transform Iran from a traditional into a modern state. Increasing segments of the population rejected the Shah's attempts to destroy traditional society. The Shah invested in symbols of modernity—dams, steel mills, petrochemical plants—while neglecting such things as education, welfare, and small businesses. Rapid economic growth was inflationary, which made the poor poorer and increasingly disgruntled as they compared themselves to the smaller groups of rich and middle class and their conspicuous consumption. The result was the 1979 revolution that swept the Shah from power and imposed an Islamic regime.

Military Coups

Prolonged political instability often leads to a military *coup d'état* in which one government is violently overthrown and a new one imposed.[23] The successful coup is well-planned, includes elite or strategically placed units, targets the leading government leaders and mass media outlets, is executed quickly and decisively, and can justify its takeover. Usually a coup involves only a small segment of the military. Most commanders and their troops stay in their barracks until they see which way the coup is going. Fighting rarely lasts long. Escalation into civil war is uncommon. Most people's lives are unaffected. Anywhere from one-third to one-half of all coups are crushed by troops loyal to the existing government. Some governments have attempted to guard against coups by creating a para-military or national guard force to offset the regular military.

Coups breed coups. Once a country has an established tradition of military intervention, it is hard to change it.

Robert Clark identifies eleven conditions which make coups likely: 1) the government's prestige sharply declines; 2) there are deep schisms among political leaders; 3) there is little chance of foreign intervention to help the government; 4) there have recently been coups in neighboring countries; 5) the nation is split by deep and growing social, economic, ethnic, religious, and/or political antagonisms; 6) there is a growing economic crisis, and a worsening gap between rich and the masses of poor; 7) government and bureaucratic corruption and inefficiency are entrenched and growing; 8) there is a rigid class structure in which military service is the only means of social mobility; 9) the military increasingly believes it is the only institution with the power, legitimacy, and ideas to reform the country; 10) foreign business interests, diplomats, and/or military advisors encourage a coup; 11) the military has recently been defeated in war and blames the civilian government for the defeat.[24]

In some countries the military is the most modern institution and the only one capable of pushing through commands. Most militaries in less developed countries are primarily used to maintain internal rather than external security. Thus the military already intervenes in politics at the government's behest. Most military forces believe they personify the nation and contrast their national role with the corruption or inefficiency of politics.

The socioeconomic composition of the officer class is an important factor in coups. In many militaries there is a class division between the high-ranking officers which have come from the traditional elite and the lower- and middle-ranking officers who have risen from more humble backgrounds. The lower-ranking officers are often appalled by the corruption they see in the military as well as politics and are frustrated by the lack of advancement opportunities and discrimination.

An officer's military education and experience also help to determine whether or not he will participate in a coup. Some officers receive training in the United States, and most of them are socialized to support pro-American rulers and oppose anti-American rulers. The more military aid the United States gives a country, the more likely that country's military will overthrow its government. In contrast, some officers may have participated in an independence struggle during which they became fiercely anti-Western.[25]

The ability of a military coup government to maintain power varies considerably. A study identified 60 countries which had experienced military governments from 1946 through 1984 and found the percentage of that time varied from 100 percent for Taiwan to a few days for Gambia.[26] Most military governments are sooner or later overthrown by another military faction. In some cases, however, a military government will either directly hand power over to civilian leaders or call elections that result in a return to civilian rule.

There are advantages and disadvantages for military rule.[27] The military is often development oriented and inclined to favor policies that develop the economy. With its command system it is able to make decisions relatively easily and has the ability to back up its decisions with force. It also appears to represent the entire nation compared to the politicians who represent special interests, so military rule can have a certain amount of legitimacy. Yet despite all these positive features, the development record of military regimes may actually be worse than the civilian regimes they replaced. Most military officers have no conception of how a modern economy works. With their hands in the treasury, many succumb to the same temptations of their civilian counterparts.

Reforms

The same conditions that prompt a military coup can also stimulate a mass reform movement that "attempts to change limited aspects of a society but does not aim at drastically alternating or replacing major social, economic, or political institutions."[28] America's political development has been pulled by a series of mass reform movements. The antislavery movement of the 1850s, the civil rights and antiwar movements of the 1960s, and the women's, environmental, gay, anti-pornography, prayer-in-public-schools, and pro- and anti-abortion movements of the 1970s and 1980s were all organized, mass attempts to reform through accepted political means that which their adherents believed were defective parts of the existing system rather than to overthrow and transform the entire society through violence.

There is a clear connection between economic and political development. The demands for political representation expand with a country's middle class. As people achieve material security, many of them demand more intangible benefits from the state, such as human rights, a multi-party system, or a cleaner environment. Members of the middle class—businessmen, housewives, the retired—may join students and unions in protesting government corruption or repression. Faced with these mass protests, most governments eventually promise reforms.

In South Korea and Taiwan, for example, rapid growth and the emergence of a large middle class stimulated mass pressure for political reforms. Authoritarian governments in Taiwan and South Korea succeeded in rapidly developing their once poverty-stricken peoples into increasingly wealthy middle class ones. In the late 1980s, South Korea's government experienced increasing mass pressure to democratize, and in 1987 it did so, allowing a free presidential election that year, and free parliamentarian elections the following year. Today South Korea has a multi-party, liberal democratic political system. Political change has been slower in Taiwan. Although Taiwan's government remains authoritarian, the ruling party, the Koumintang (KMT) is slowly relaxing its controls over the opposition parties and the population. In a decade, Taiwan may have also evolved into a multi-party, liberal democracy in which human rights are guaranteed.

During the mid-1980s, the Philippines also experienced a successful democratic reform movement in which the government was forced to abide by its constitution. During its colonial period (1899–1946), the United States nurtured democracy and free markets in the Philippines. For nearly three decades after its independence, the Philippines grew steadily, although unevenly. The rich got much richer and the middle class expanded, but more than 70 percent of the population remained mired in poverty. Then, in 1972, President Marcos declared martial law to deal with growing political and economic crises. The military successfully defeated a separatist movement among Muslims in the southern Philippines and contained a growing communist insurgency. But rather than use the power to develop the Philippines, Marcos and his cronies looted the country and worsened economic conditions. In the mid-1980s, Corazon Aquino, the wife of a former political rival of Marcos who was murdered by Marcos' henchmen, helped lead a mass democracy movement against Marcos. The United States pressured Marcos to resign and leave the country. Mrs. Aquino became the president, and since 1986 the Philippines has enjoyed democratic rule.

Since people power helped overthrow the Marcos dictatorship in the Philippines in 1986, similar democratic movements have succeeded in South Korea, Taiwan, Bangledesh, Mongolia, and Thailand, while others in China and Burma have been crushed. Most of these reform movements have been stimulated by profound economic changes, often for the better, that enable many people to demand greater representation in government.

Revolution

A *revolution* sometimes occurs when coups or mass reform movements fail to alleviate harsh and worsening political and socioeconomic conditions. A revolutionary movement "is a social movement in which participants are organized to alter drastically or replace totally existing social, economic, or political institutions."[29] Revolutionaries:

> picture a vastly improved pattern of human relationships in a future realization, then impart their vision to the masses, hoping to motivate them to revolutionary action. The revolutionary describes a more perfect social situation—more freedom; more equality; more consciousness of community; more peace, justice, and human dignity; more of the transcendentals that appeal to human beings everywhere.[30]

Or, as Hannah Arendt eloquently puts it, revolutionaries are fueled by a "pathos of novelty" in which "the notion that the course of history suddenly begins anew, that an entirely new story, a story never known or told before, is about to unfold."[31]

Revolutions can differ greatly in their goals. Until recently, left wing or socialist revolutions, which aimed at achieving equality through a massive redistribution of wealth and state ownership of property, were the most common. Yet there are conservative or right wing revolutions as well that aim at restoring a society's traditional institutions, values, classes, hierarchy, and behaviors which modernization has lost or eroded. Iran's Islamic revolution is a classic conservative revolution that has attempted to transform the country into a strict fundamentalist theocracy. In contrast to the left and right wing revolutions that espouse a totalitarian system, are liberal democratic revolutions that espouse political, economic, and social freedom.

Revolutionary conditions may exist for decades before a revolutionary movement emerges. When revolutions do occur we must ask why—given the history of repression, exploitation, brutality, and corruption that preceded it—did it not take place earlier? Several vital conditions precede every revolution.[32]

Mass poverty itself is not enough. The most impoverished nations are often the least revolutionary. When most people are illiterate, teeter on starvation's brink, and spend virtually all waking hours searching for food, fuel, or shelter, they do not have the time or energy to question let alone challenge the prevailing order.

What is necessary is a widespread view that the vast gap between a few rich and many poor is unjust. This mass awareness of unjustness emerges in changing rather than stagnant societies. Revolutionary conditions proliferate in rapidly modernizing societies rather than traditional societies. Modernization promises prosperity, social mobility, and new opportunities. Increasing numbers of people must be motivated by the possibility of achieving a better life. Revolutionary conditions flourish when modernization's fruits appear to be enjoyed only by the few. There must be a vast, obvious, and growing gap between a small minority of political, social, and economic "haves" and the masses of "have nots." As Tedd Gurr puts it: "the necessary precondition for violent civil conflict is deprivation, defined as the actors' perceptions of discrepancy between their value expectations and their environment's apparent value capabilities."[33] While some people are enriching themselves, conditions must be perceived as getting worse for most. Shantytowns ring wealthy neighborhoods, armies of unemployed wander the cities, crime rises, population growth spirals. Much of the population glimpses but fails to grasp a better life. Thus a revolution of rising expectations becomes a revolution of rising frustrations.

But even this is not enough. Revolutions cannot happen unless society's traditional values, institutions, behaviors, expectations, and leaders are largely discredited. The movement from countryside to city, from field to factory or schoolroom, from candle to electricity, can as severely disturb as enhance an individual's life. Rapid modernization can completely disorient people, destroying old communities and beliefs while failing to provide new ones. Modernization swamps society's existing institutions and leaders. Society's institutions are increasingly incapable of serving their functions, are deadlocked and impotent, and eventually collapse. Inefficiency and corruption are often closely tied. Officials abuse their positions for private gain rather than public service, and that corruption pervades the entire system rather than being confined to a few nefarious individuals. The demands for changes increase. Although a successful revolution may be centered in one particular class or group, it must appeal to most classes and groups. Unions, farm cooperatives, student organizations, churches and other groups demand sweeping changes. The society is polarized between radically different extremes with no compromise possible. The political, social, economic, and religious elite becomes demoralized, split, and indecisive, while continuing to reject the membership of the radical elite in its ranks. Increasing numbers of the old elite defect to the radical elite. The military and police both increase their repression and are incapable of containing the protests. Increasing numbers of officers, soldiers, and police either sympathize with or openly join the radical cause. When the old order fails to accommodate the needs and demands of the new, its legitimacy becomes thoroughly destroyed.

Despite all these preconditions, not everyone joins a revolutionary movement let alone leads one. Most people usually avoid taking sides and just try to stay out of the line of fire. Peasants are particularly traditional and apathetic and unwilling to challenge the status quo.

A revolution needs leaders, an ideology for change, and an organization. Increasing numbers of prominent intellectuals must not only criticize the old order but also advocate a new order. New myths must replace old myths. The masses can be won over with simple slogans, but the revolutionary leaders themselves must have an ideology or analytical framework for understanding the world, for exposing the defects of the old order, and for proposing revolutionary changes that will inaugurate a new ideal order.[34] Revolutions are ultimately organized and won or lost by small, cohesive, highly motivated conspiratorial elites that can mobilize masses of loyal followers willing to risk their lives for ideals.

Revolutions are usually preceded by a crisis that thoroughly discredits the existing system. Defeat in war, natural disasters, invasion, the massacre of opponents, economic crises, withdrawal of foreign aid, or a foreign embargo can all spark a mass insurrection that joins hands with existing guerrilla movements. The 1917 Russian revolution, for example, would not have occurred without Russia's military defeat by the Japanese and the massacre of hundreds of protesters before the Czar's Winter Palace in 1905, and the deaths of millions and the severe deprivation for virtually all Russians in World War I.

While revolutionary movements often involve a broad coalition of groups, they are usually centered around one particular class, region, or group, or start in rural or urban areas. Marxist-Leninists based their entire philosophy and struggle on blue collar workers known as the proletariat. Mao, in contrast, realized that the proletariat was only a tiny percentage of China's vast population. Instead, Mao based his revolution on the peasants which comprised 85 percent of the population. Sometimes the most disaffected members of a society are its middle class. The American revolution was largely a middle class revolution.

Revolutions are often sparked as much against foreign influences as against domestic power holders. The Cuban, Vietnamese, and Chinese revolutionaries, for example, tapped deeply into the mass resentment against the respective American, French, and Japanese interference in their countries' internal affairs. Many revolutions are meshed with independence struggles. The United States simultaneously achieved independence from Britain and a democratic revolution; Ho Chi Minh led an independence movement against France and a communist revolution; and from 1989 to 1991, Eastern European revolutionaries overthrew both communist and Russian rule.

Revolutions, in turn, often have profound international consequences. The American and French revolutions stimulated revolutionary movements elsewhere. The Latin American independence and revolutionary struggles of the 1820s were inspired by America's similar struggles 50 years earlier. The French revolutionary ideals of liberty, equality, fraternity, and nationalism were spread by Napoleon's troops across Europe. Those ideals provoked revolutions in Europe throughout the early nineteenth century. The impact of revolution is even more powerful today in an age of instant mass, global communications. People can turn on their radio or television and learn of foreign revolutionary conditions, ideals, and strategies.

A revolution's success or failure often depends on the reaction of other countries. Could America's revolution have succeeded without massive French aid? Throughout Eastern Europe and the Third World, the United States, Soviet Union, and sometimes China backed different revolutionary or counter-revolutionary groups with arms, money, propaganda, advisers, and even troops. Revolutions are sometimes imposed by foreign forces. After 1945, the Soviet Red Army replaced the existing governments of Eastern Europe with communists dictatorships. Revolutions are also at times squashed by foreign forces. The Soviet Union destroyed democratic revolutionary forces in Hungary in 1956, Czechoslovakia in 1968, and Poland in 1981. The United States successfully helped quell communist revolutionary movements in Guatemaula, El Salvador, Nicaragua, and the Philippines but failed in Cuba, Vietnam, Cambodia, and Laos. In 1989, a majority of Nicaraguans voted for the liberal democrat Violetta Chamorro rather than the Marxist-Leninist Sandinista party, in part, following a decade of America's covert attempts to undermine the Sandinistas rule.

CONCLUSION

The potential power inherent in a nation's human and natural resources is only as good as its political economic system which offers individuals and groups the opportunity to exploit and mobilize those resources. Some political economic systems are clearly better able to realize some aspects of a nation's potential power than others. For example, communist systems are more adept at mobilizing raw human and natural resources than other states, but they have failed miserably at creating wealth. Other types of authoritarian regimes can also make relatively quick decisions and mobilize a nation's population, but have a mixed development record.

There is a chicken and egg relationship between political and economic development. Political instability leads to economic stagnation and vice versa. Countries experience riots, coups, and insurgencies for many reasons. Often the government has created a revolution of rising expectations based on unrealizable goals which eventually becomes a revolution of rising frustrations. The political leadership fails to socialize and mobilize a population behind it and is instead perceived to be excessively corrupt, brutal, and/or inefficient. There is a widening gap between a few rich and growing numbers of poor and a shrinking middle class.

Within the Third World, there is no relationship between a country's political system and economic level. Both authoritarian and liberal democracies alike have either successfully promoted or bungled economic development. China maintains a communist dictatorship and crushed a mass democracy movement in June 1989. Yet since China's government launched a mixed market system and land reforms in 1978, the economy has grown about 10 percent annually. During the 1980s, while some democratic countries like Jamaica, Costa Rica, and Venezuela experienced stagnant growth, others like Botswana, Malaysia, and Thailand experienced rapid growth. Liberal democracies can be very poor—although India's democratic political system has been evolving for over a century, India has a per capita income of $600.

In the 1980s and into the 1990s, increasing numbers of Third World countries adopted liberal democratic political systems based on universal adult suffrage, competitive elections, and civil rights. Liberal democratic economies are largely privately owned, although the government's economic role varies starkly from South Korea's carefully state-managed markets to Hong Kong's more loosely regulated markets.

Meanwhile, political instability and violence has lessened. The ratio of successful coups to elections in the Third World has shifted remarkably, from 1974 when there were five coups and two elections or 1980 when there were eight coups and 10 elections, to the late 1980s when democratic revolutions broke out in Eastern Europe, East Asia, Latin America, and elsewhere. In 1989, there were three coups and 18 elections and in 1990, there was only one coup and 17 elections.[35]

Whether liberal democracy will take firm root in the Third World is questionable. Liberal democracy has the best chance of success if it promotes economic development and will probably fail if it does not. The greater a society's creation and distribution of wealth, the fewer the popular demands on government, which allows it to concentrate on pursuing policies that enhance wealth's creation and distribution. Democratic values and behavior will expand with the middle class. Yet, as we have seen, political systems fail to achieve socioeconomic development for many reasons. Misguided policies and inefficient and/or corrupt institutions can impede rather than promote economic development, and thus ultimately undermine political stability.

STUDY QUESTIONS

1. What is economic development? What is political development? What is the relationship between the two?

2. What factors are essential for political development?

3. What causes a *revolution of rising expectations* and why does it often lead to a *revolution of rising frustrations* and political instability?

4. What is a charismatic leader? How can a charismatic leader both aid and hinder development?

5. Among less developed countries, how can bureaucracies, political parties, interest groups, and patron-client groups hinder and aid development?

6. Define mobilization and legitimacy. What is the relationship between the two and their significance for development?

7. What is corruption? Why is corruption a severe problem in many less developed countries? How does a country's relative corruption level change with development?

8. Why are some political systems stable and others unstable?

9. What are military coups and when are they most likely to occur?

10. What are some countries which experienced successful reform movements and why were they successful?

11. What are revolutions and when are they most likely to occur? What makes for a successful revolution?

ENDNOTES

1. See Max Weber, *The Theory of Social and Economic Organization* (New York: Oxford University Press, 1947); W. Chai and C. Clark, *Political Stability and Economic Growth: Case Studies of Hong Kong, Singapore, and the R.O.C* (Lantham, Md.: University Press of America for the University of Virginia Press, 1987); C.L. Taylor, "Indicators of Political Development," *Journal of Developing Studies,* vol. 8, no. 3, April 1975; P.W. Preston, *Making Sense of Development* (London: Routledge and Kegan Paul, 1987); Myron Weiner and Samuel P. Huntington, *Understanding Political Development* (Boston: Little, Brown, 1987); Stephen Chilton, *Defining Political Development* (Boulder, Colo.: Lynne Reinner, 1988).

2. Quoted in Charles Lane, "Let's Abolish the Third World," *Newsweek,* April 27, 1992, 43.

3. World Bank, *World Development Report 1991* (New York: Oxford University Press, 1991).

4. For two classic dependency studies focusing on Latin America, see Paul Prebisch, *The Economic Development of Latin America and Its Principal Proble.*

5. For a sweeping exploration of this perspective, see Jagdish Bhagwati, *Essays in Development Economics: Wealth and Poverty,* vol. 1, and *Dependence and Interdependence,* vol. 2 (Cambridge, Mass.: MIT Press, 1985).

6. United States Department of State, *Gist,* August 1978.

7. Joan Spero, *International Political Economy,* (New York: St. Martin's Press, 1990), 152.

8. Monte Palmer, *Political Development in Changing Societies* (Lexington, Mass.: Heath Lexington, 1971), 20.

9. Max Weber, *The Theory of Social and Economic Organization* (New York: Free Press, 1947).

10. Monte Palmer, *Political Development in Changing Societies,* 180–181.

11. United Arab Republic, *Draft of the Charter* (Cairo: Information Department, 1962), 45.

12. See Gregor McLenna, David Held, and Stuart Hall, *Idea of the Modern State* (London: Open University Press, 1984).

13. Samuel Huntington, *Political Order in Changing Societies* (New Haven, Conn.: Yale University Press, 1968), 78.

14. For the relationship between culture and development, see Ralph Braibanti and Joseph J. Spengler, eds., *Tradition, Values, and Socio-Economic Development* (Durham, N.C.: Duke University, 1961).

15. A. T. J. Mathews, "Emergent Turkish Administrators," in Jerry Hopper and Richard Levin, eds., *The Turkish Administrator: A Cultural Survey* (Ankara, Turkey: U.S. Aid, 1967), 229.

16. Quoted in Monte Palmer, *Political Development in Changing Societies,* 271.

17. Lucian Pye, *Politics, Personality, and Nation-Building* (New Haven, Conn.: Yale University Press, 1962).

18. Jon S. T. Quah, "Bureaucratic Corruption in the ASEAN Countries: A Comparative Analysis of their Anti-Corruption Strategies," *Journal of Southeast Asian Studies,* vol. 13, March 1982, 164.

19. Ibid.

20. See, for example, Michael Johnston, "The Political Consequences of Corruption: A Reassessment," *Comparative Politics,* July 1986.

21. For a succinct and comprehensive explanation, see Harry Eckstein, "On the Etiology of Internal Wars," *History and Theory,* vol. 4, Fall 1965.

22. Monte Palmer, *Political Development in Changing Societies* (Lexington, Mass.: Heath Lexington, 1971), 136.

23. See Eric Norlinger, *Soldiers in Politics* (Englewood Cliffs, N.J.: Prentice-Hall, 1977), 20, Robert Wesson, ed., *New Military Politics in Latin America* (New York:

Praeger, 1982); William Foltz and Henry S. Bienen, eds., *Arms and the African: Military Influences on Africa's International Relations* (New Haven, Conn.: Yale University Press, 1985); Miles D. Wolpin, *Militarization, Internal Repression, and Social Welfare in the Third World* (New York: St. Martin's Press, 1986).

24. Robert Clark, *Power and Policy in the Third World* (New York: Wiley, 1982), 111.

25. E. N. Muller and M. A. Seligson, "Inequality and Insurgency," *American Political Science Review,* vol. 81, no. 2, June 1987; E. N. Muller, "Dependent Economic Development, Aid, and Dependence on the United States and Democratic Breakdown in the Third World," *International Studies Quarterly,* vol. 29, no. 4, December 1985, 21–39.

26. Talikder Maniruzzaman, *Military Withdrawal From Politics: A Comparative Study* (Cambridge, Mass.: Ballinger, 1987), 221–222.

27. See Nicole Bell, "Military Expenditure and Socio-Economic Development," *International Social Science Journal,* vol. 95, no. 1, 1983; Bruce Arlinghaus, *Military Development in Africa: The Political and Economic Risks of Arms Transfers* (Boulder, Colo.: Westview Press, 1984); Steve Chan, "The Impact of Defense Spending on Economic Performance: A Survey of Evidence and Problems," *Orbis,* vol. 29, no. 2, Summer 1985; Basudeb Biswas and Rati Ram, "Military Expenditures and Economic Growth in Less Developed Countries," *Economic Development and Change,* vol. 34, no. 2, January 1986; Saadet Deger, "Economic Development and Defense Expenditure," *Economic Development and Cultural Change,* vol. 35, no. 1, October 1986.

28. James DeFonzo, *Revolution and Revolutionary Movements* (Boulder, Colo.: Westview Press, 1991), 8.

29. Ibid.

30. James Dougherty and Robert Pfaltzgraff, *Contending Theories of International Relations* (New York: Harper & Row, 1990), 321.

31. Hanna Arendt, *On Revolution* (New York: Viking, 1965), 3.

32. See Crane Brinton, *Anatomy of Revolution* (New York: Norton, 1938).

33. Ted Gurr, "Psychological Factors in Civil Violence," *World Politics,* vol. 20, January 1968, 252–253.

34. See Rollo May, *Power and Innocence: A Search for the Sources of Violence* (New York: Norton, 1972); Bruce Mazlish, *The Revolutionary Ascetic: Evolution of a Revolutionary Type* (New York: Basic Books, 1976).

35. Rosemarie Phillips and Stuart K. Tucker, *U.S. Foreign Policy and Developing Countries, Discourses and Data 1991* (Washington, D.C.: Overseas Development Council, 1991), 16.

Economic Development, Underdevelopment, and International Relations

Key Terms and Concepts

Agricultural Revolution
Economic Development
Export Substitution
Import Substitution
Newly Industralized
    Countries (NIC)

In an interdependent world, perhaps no national interest is more important than suc-cessful *economic development.*[1] A nation's potential power and international status in-creases with its wealth. Although all nations aspire to develop, there remains a vast gap between the world's wealthiest and poorest countries, and by some measures that gap is widening. The Third World itself is just as divided between those few newly industrial-izing countries (NICs) that are struggling to join the rich countries' ranks and the many countries that remain mired in poverty and political instability.

Why do some countries develop while others remain stuck in mass poverty? This chapter will examine the possible constraints on development among Third World countries. It will conclude by analyzing the successful development strategies of the *newly industralized countries* (NICs)—Taiwan and South Korea, and the relevance of those countries' experiences to other Third World countries.

DEVELOPMENT AND UNDERDEVELOPMENT CONDITIONS

Clearly, no country is an island in the modern world. All are linked together in an in-creasingly dense web of economic, social, cultural, political, and ethical ties, that vary considerably from one country to the next. Despite interdependence, successful devel-opment ultimately rests on a government's ability to maximize its economic strengths to overcome its economic obstacles. Yet no government can successfully develop an econ-omy by relying solely on domestic strengths. States successfully develop by integrating foreign capital, technology, markets, and managerial skills into their country's nascent economic enterprises and infrastructure. Government must also overcome traditions which impede development. This section will explore the different obstacles and oppor-tunities that Third World countries face.

The Colonial Legacy

Over five centuries, the Western powers and Japan colonized virtually every region on earth. It is not easy to weigh imperialism's relative costs and benefits. Colonialism's impact varied from one imperial power and colony to the next. Each imperial country had its own administrative philosophy and style. Some colonies were administered for several centuries, others for several decades. Some were extensively developed, others largely left as they were found.

Western imperialism did grant some long-term benefits. There is a tendency for many inhabitants of countries which experienced Western imperialism to lament a lost pre-colonial "golden age." That golden age almost never existed. In many lands, Western rule toppled more oppressive regimes, imposed order on regions of incessant warfare, and abolished such local customs as human sacrifice and mutilation. The Chinese Imperial Customs Service, for example, generated far more revenue for China under the efficient British administration than the previous corrupt Chinese one. Notions of human rights, sexual equality, political representation, and constraints on government, were the profound, if originally unintended, gifts to all non-Western cultures. People today live far longer, healthier, more leisurely, and wealthier lives than they did when the first Western gunboats or troops appeared on their respective frontiers.

Many people argue, however, that the costs have far outweighed the benefits. In many places, Western imperialism's short-term impact on traditional cultures was devastating. There were an estimated 25 million people in Mexico and Central America when Cortez arrived in 1521. Within fifty years European diseases, for which the natives had no immunity, had reduced the population to 2 million! Everywhere, colonialism destroyed not just native political elites but traditional cultures as well. Western imperialism simultaneously discredited and transformed traditional cultures, so that every culture around the world, to varying extents, is now a hybrid of traditional and Western values. The cross was more important than the sword in forcing these changes. Western missionaries pressured the natives to reject old gods and embrace Christianity. This conversion was frequently incomplete. Today, many peoples find themselves neither fully of the old or new faith, but somewhere in between.

Some imperial leaders were well aware of the revolutionary impact of their culture on traditional cultures. As Lord Lytton, the Viceroy of India, put it in his speech before his Legislative Council in Calcutta in 1878:

> the problem undertaken by the British rulers of India .   .   . is the application of
> the most refined principles of European society, to a vast Oriental population, in
> whose history, habits, and traditions they have had no previous existence. Such
> phrases as religious toleration, Liberty of the Press, Personal freedom of the subject
> .   .   . are here in India .   .   . the mysterious formulas of a foreign .   .   .
> administration .   .   . to the greater number of those for whose benefit it is
> maintained .   .   . there is no disguising .   .   . that .   .   . we have placed,
> and must permanently maintain ourselves at the head of a gradual but gigantic
> revolution—the greatest and most momentous social, moral,   .   .   .
> religious,   .   .   . and political revolution which .   .   . the world has ever
> seen.[2]

Colonialism created a small, well-educated, Westernized elite that it used to help administer and exploit the territory. This elite usually led the independence movement and ruled the newly independent country. Often, however, the elite remains more culturally western than native, and thus has trouble relating to the population's attitudes and problems. Their ranks and minds often remain as closed to their nation's population as those of the Western imperialists who preceded them.

Both the elite and masses of people from less developed countries often have an inferiority complex toward the more developed western countries. Defeat, subjugation, and the imposition of second class status by an imperial power, often combined with the failure of that country to develop following independence, has forced people to feel somehow beneath as well as behind the West. People with inferiority complexes sometimes try to compensate by being overly assertive or critical of those to whom they feel inferior, or toward their own society. Von Laue describes among non-Western peoples a perennial:

> search of roots, and certitude; inwardly split, part backward, part Western, camouflaging their imitation of the West by gestures of rejection; forever aspiring to build lofty halfway houses that bridged the disparate cultural universes, often in all embracing designs, never admitting the fissures and cracks in their lives and opinions; and always covering up their unease with a compensating presumption of moral superiority based on the recognition that the promptings of heart and soul are superior to the dictates of reason.[3]

Leaders of Third World countries are aware of this identity crisis, and its potential negative impact on development. Mohatma Gandhi was one of the first to recognize and to try to overcome an increasingly entrenched Westernization within India's traditional culture, arguing that "if India copies England, it is my firm conviction that she will be ruined."[4] Gandhi tried to base the independence struggle on select traditional Indian concepts.

Most of the 190 nation-states existing today are the artificial creations of imperialism, and most of them are multinational. When the Western powers carved up Africa, for example, they arbitrarily drew lines across the map and divided up the continent among themselves without regard to the mosaic of existing nations, which were often divided up among two or more states. Thus every country in Africa today is multinational except Somalia, and in most of these countries the different nations coexist uneasily and in many countries their antagonisms have deteriorated into violence and civil war. In most multinational states, the colonial language is the only lingua franca. It was deemed better to use a foreign language than allow one of the native languages to become dominant. Nonetheless, often only a small percentage of the population speaks the foreign language, thus isolating the government all the more from its people.

Virtually every seemingly positive contribution of imperialism has its negative side. Although the colonists improved living conditions by introducing higher standards of health care, hygiene, nutrition, and education, they set off a population explosion as the death rate fell dramatically while the birth rate remained largely unchanged. The result is that in many countries the population exceeds the territory's ecological carrying capacity, setting off rapid environmental degradation, crop and livestock loss, and mass starvation. Many survivors flee to the cities and thus overwhelm existing job opportunities and social services.

Imperialism completely disrupted the native economy. Traditionally, most villages were self-sufficient. Land often was held communally and the people usually grew enough to survive, although droughts, monsoons, and other natural disasters sometimes lead to famine. There was little trading between villages. An imperial power introduced the notions of private property by brute force. It confiscated communal village cropland and converted it into huge, privately owned plantations. In Latin America, the land was divided up into latifundias or huge estates which were owned by the conquistadors and their families. Elsewhere, huge companies acquired the land. The plantations converted land that had grown food for the local people into the mass production of products like cotton, sisal, coconut oil, coffee, tea, hemp, tobacco, pepper, sugar, jute, and other largely non-food crops for export. Thus, the typical colonial economy was divided into commercial and light industrial city, large plantation and mining, and subsistence-level agrarian sectors. While the cities, plantations, and mines were linked to the global economy with modern transportation and communication, most peasants remained isolated and backward. Often the agrarian sector was too inefficient to produce enough food for the cities and plantations, so the colony ended up importing food. For most countries little has changed since independence, at least not for the better. Most of these countries continue to rely on one or two cash crops or minerals that sometimes are subject to wide price fluctuations in international markets.

In most colonies, little if anything was done to prepare the country for independence. When the colonizers left, they often took with them most of the skills, capital, and equipment necessary to run the modern sectors. Most Third World bureaucracies were inherited from colonialism. Colonial bureaucracies had two main tasks—to extract wealth from the territory and to control the population. Few imperial powers allowed natives to climb high in the civil service. At independence, the bureaucracy—particularly the higher echelons—was gutted by the withdrawal of the foreign specialists. For example, when the Belgians retreated from the Congo (Zaire) in 1961, they left only 20 natives with a college education and 3 high-ranking civil servants to run a country with 14 million people divided among over 200 tribes.[5]

What then is imperialism's impact on Third World development? After reminding us that the concept of development itself is Western, Von Laue maintains that the blame for development failures must be shared by all:

> Westerners must accept the blame for the hardships and tragedies in the developing countries. The anti-imperialist radicals are right. Before the Western impact, traditional societies existed in reasonable harmony within the intellectual, spiritual, and material resources at their command, in precarious balance with their environment. It was the Western impact which forced them, against their will, into a complex world beyond their comprehension and resources, destroying in the bargain the former bonds of community. The anti-imperialists in turn should recognize the inevitability of inter-cultural contact in a shrinking world; let them also appreciate the goodwill and opportunities that came with the West. In any case, there is no chance of returning to the pre-colonial era, nor comfort in the nostalgic yearning, sometimes heard, for the good old days of colonialism. Both sides have no choice but to look forward.[6]

Post-Independence Socioeconomic Stagnation

Most Third World countries, whether they achieved their independence during the 1820s like most Latin American countries or since 1945 like most African and Asian countries, have failed to develop economically. These countries share characteristics.

The most obvious similarity is the reality that in Third World countries a majority of the population is not only poor, but often lives a hand-to-mouth existence in which they are malnourished, illiterate, unemployed, homeless, and wracked by health problems. Although most Third World countries are experiencing some economic growth, their populations are growing at an even faster rate. Thus, overall most people are becoming poorer. Most of these people are landless peasants who must hand over what little crops they produce to wealthy landlords. Others live in overcrowded disease- and rat-infested shantytowns lacking sewage, running water, and most importantly, well-paying jobs.

Most Third World countries are locked into a vicious political and economic cycle that prevents them from developing—political instability and violence disrupts business and impedes economic development which in turn spawns more political instability and violence.

Economic growth is stimulated by the wealthy and middle class, not the poor.[7] While the poor number anywhere from 50 to 90 percent of the population, the middle class accounts for only 25 to 40 percent and the wealthy about 5 percent. The more poverty stricken a country, the lower the chance it can achieve sustained development. Because most people are poor, their ability to buy things is extremely limited. Thus a Third World economy has a very small market confined to the middle and upper class. Market size is important because the more a business sells the more profit it makes, which it can in turn reinvest to increase productivity and thus its competitive power.

Domestic businesses trying to compete with multinational corporations are like unarmed Davids fighting Goliaths—they have little chance of success. Entrepreneurs often lack technology, equipment, managerial skills, and access to foreign markets that are vital to creating a prosperous business. They often must license or buy these things from multinational corporations, sometimes the very ones they are competing against. Gaining access to foreign technology, equipment, managerial skills, and markets costs money. Without access to large domestic or foreign markets, businesses cannot expand and are often squeezed out by super-competitive multinational corporations which sell or invest in their country.

Money is in short supply in Third World countries. One result of political instability and economic stagnation is that the rich send their money to safe havens overseas rather than invest it at home. Thus, with limited domestic financial reserves and high interest rates to attract what little savings exist, states must borrow heavily from foreign sources. For example, in 1986, if there were no capital flight, Argentina's foreign debt would have been $1 billion instead of $50 billion, Mexico's debt $12 billion rather than $97 billion, and Venezuela's debt zero instead of $30 billion.[8]

Domestic banks lack financial clout and investment skills. Thus entrepreneurs often cannot find enough money at home to finance their businesses. In order to start a business, they must either borrow from an international bank or form a joint venture with a multinational corporation. Either way they end up sending much of their earnings overseas to pay interest on their debt or share profits from their joint venture.

Perhaps the most crippling problem that many less developed countries face is a lack of private entrepreneurial spirit. Many Third World governments attempt to make up for the lack of private business drive by building huge heavy industries from the ground up. The trouble with this strategy is that the state—its political leadership and bureaucracy—lacks the skills vital to create and manage a modern economy and industry.[9] More often than not the newly independent government has used the bureaucracy as a "spoils system" to reward their political followers rather than filling those positions with lower-ranking officials who had at least some inkling of the ministry's responsibilities. Thus, most post-independent bureaucracies bear no resemblance to the ideal bureaucracy of an apolitical institution designed to address specific national problems. Instead, most Third World bureaucracies have simply become a source of wealth and security for its appointees and the political leadership. A particular problem with coup-prone countries is that each new regime packs the bureaucracy with its own followers and devises its own often grandiose development projects and priorities while abandoning those of the previous government.

As if this were not bad enough, the independence governments and their successors often had a set of national goals for which the existing bureaucracy was ill-equipped to administer. Third World governments often embarked on highly ambitious crash industrialization and welfare programs, and new ministries were created to implement these programs. *Import substitution* policies in which the government attempts to create industries from scratch are very expensive. Lacking significant indigenous financial resources, governments embarking on ambitious industrial development programs had to borrow the money from global bankers. The result was that countries like Brazil, Mexico, Argentina, South Korea, Venezuela, and Chile, which followed import substitution, became the world's heaviest debtors. The state-created industries in particular are rarely successful and act like black holes in a nation's economy, sucking in huge amounts of financial, natural, and human resources and contributing little if anything to development. Sometimes the state-owned industries sell their products for less than the sum of their raw materials, let alone labor costs. Bela Belassa, a classical economist, argues that "the export performances of a number of developing countries were adversely affected by their own policies: the bias against exports in countries pursuing import substitution policies led to a loss in their world shares in primary exports and forestalled the emergence of manufactured exports."[10] The result of import substitution policies, more often than not, is chaos, waste, inefficiency, disillusionment, and political instability.

Unlike most countries that have followed them, Brazil's import substitution policies have been largely successful in developing a range of advanced industries, such as automobiles, steel, aircraft, weapons, and petrochemicals, that generate enormous wealth within the country that otherwise would have flowed overseas to foreign producers. Brazil's development of an aircraft industry from nothing was a typical success story. Until the mid-1970s, Brazil imported all of its light passenger planes. The United States supplied virtually all of these planes, and most of them were bought from Piper Aircraft—408 in 1974 alone. The Brazilian government targeted light industry as a strategic industry, and created and implemented a plan for its development. First it negotiated a joint-production agreement with Piper Aircraft Corporation, using the threat of buying its planes from other corporations as the means of forcing an agreement. Then it imposed a 50 percent tariff on all imported planes, including those from Piper. By 1976, Piper Aviaco produced 75 percent of all light planes purchased in Brazil and began exporting them to Latin American and African countries, while the U.S. export share fell from 100 percent to 1 percent![11] Today, it exports planes to countries all around the world.

Some countries embarked on industrialization programs without worrying about the effects on the income distribution. Brazil and Mexico, for example, targeted and succeeded in developing strategic industries like automobiles, steel, and petrochemicals. They did so, however, by heavily borrowing the essential ingredients of finance, technology, managerial skills, and so on from overseas banks and corporations. They also relied on an import-substitution strategy in which their industrial products sell in large protected, domestic markets but have had mixed and limited success in global markets. Most of those profits that did not go to foreign corporations or financial institutions mostly made rich Brazilians and Mexicans richer. Very little wealth or jobs trickled down to the populace. Recognizing the failure of state-owned industries to make a profit or be internationally competitive, many Third World countries have recently tried to privatize their industries. For example, between 1982 and 1990, Mexico sold off 875 of 1,155 existing government-owned corporations, which attracted more than $10 billion back to the country that had previously been expatriated.[12]

Brazil and Mexico are exceptions. Most Third World countries have developed little if any industry which can compete with that of the wealthier countries. Some countries like Nigeria or India have tried to build huge steel or petrochemical plants, but the finished product is often more expensive than similar American, Japanese, or German products. Even more simple labor-intensive industries like textiles have trouble competing with the multinational corporations. Indonesia, for example, once had a flourishing textile industry but opened its markets to foreign investment in the 1970s. Japanese multinational textile corporations took advantage of this opening, set up automated factories, and within a decade succeeded in wiping out Indonesia's less-efficient, labor-intensive businesses. As a result, hundreds of thousands of Indonesians lost their jobs while most profits are sent back to Tokyo rather than reinvested in Indonesia. Japan rather than Indonesia develops.

What wealth a Third World economy generates often comes from the sale of one or two agricultural or mineral products like cotton, rice, iron ore, or bauxite. The companies which own these plantations or mines are often foreign, and thus once again profits flow overseas rather than remain in that country. Price levels for these products are often erratic. Gluts in international markets cause prices and profits to drop for that Third World producer. For example, American-owned United Fruit Company owns most of the banana production in Guatemala, Costa Rica, El Salvador, and Honduras, giving it enormous political as well as economic power in those countries. In 1954, President Arbenz of Guatemaula attempted to nationalize United Fruit's unused land holdings. United Fruit complained to Washington. The Eisenhower administrative used the CIA to sponsor a coup which overthrew Arbenz and installed a new government which continued to allow United Fruit a free hand in Guatemala.

Although many Third World countries have rich troves of a natural resource or two, this is no development guarantee. Zaire, Uganda, Burma, Peru, and Bolivia, to name a few, are rich in natural resources yet their people are even poorer, more malnourished and illiterate, and plagued by violence today than they were at independence. Some oil rich countries like Nigeria, Indonesia, and Mexico also have huge populations to support. The only resource-rich countries which have achieved any significant development are those with large oil reserves and small populations like Kuwait, the United Arab Emirates, and Saudi Arabia. The governments of these countries have distributed enough of the oil revenues to satisfy most people's basic needs and forestall any pressures for political change, whether it be into a liberal democracy, Marxist, or radical Islamic state.

There is a popular image that Third World countries are rich in natural resources. In fact, almost all Third World countries must import most of their vital staples such as energy (oil, natural gas) and food (wheat, rice). When OPEC quadrupled its oil prices in 1973 and further doubled them in 1979, the poorest countries were the worst hit. Without oil their economies would collapse completely so they had to use what little money they had to pay the higher prices. Eventually, most Third World countries went deep into debt to international bankers to cover their oil bills. Less money than ever went into development projects, and those countries became poorer. Yet even resource rich countries will suffer the same fate if they fail to use their resource earnings to diversify their economy. Eventually their oil wells or mines will run out, thus eliminating the major source of their wealth.

Modern, prosperous economies are built on advanced, complex transportation and communications systems—highways, ports, telecommunications, and railroads. This infrastructure is often severely deficient in Third World countries. Telephones do not work, mail is not delivered, roads are narrow, unpaved, and full of potholes, and food rots for lack of refrigeration or storage.

Equally important to development are skilled, literate workers and technicians who build, repair, and invent products. Many people lack even the most basic reading, writing, and arithmetic skills. And those who finish high school or college may not have received the technical training necessary to keep an economy running, let alone develop it. The lack of health or birth control education ensures that most people will remain assailed by preventable diseases while the population continues to soar, continually exacerbating all other development problems.

Von Laue points out that Third World countries cannot master Western industries and technology until they internalize Western values:

> cultures evolved in different natural settings are essentially incompatible with each other, like languages. External manifestations like weapons, machines, written constitutions, or political values can be transferred, but not the aptitudes and social habits responsible for their sucessful operation. Unless these already exist in some form in the receiving country—as in Japan—their acculturation cannot be forced by the will of a leader or a decision of government. The transfer of cultural achievement demands no less than a permanent revolution of reculturation, the recreation of the original setting in a new and uncongenial environment, a feat never yet accomplished.[13]

In several ways, the Cold War may have impeded development. Certainly the American and Soviet backed coups, guerrilla movements, and enormous military aid grossly distorted some countries' development. Latin American intellectuals argue that the Cold War distorted the choices available to Third World nations, and particularly for those who followed Marxist-Leninism. The crumbling of communism through

Eastern Europe and the Soviet Union completed the discrediting of statism that had been popular among many Latin American intellectuals and governments throughout the postwar era. Mexican poet Octavio Paz asserts that "It is as though the Cold War had been a mask that blinded us to the reality of the world," an argument picked up by another Mexican writer, Carlos Fuentes who argued that the "fact that we can see the problems in their proper perspective rather than through a mask of anti-communism or pro-communism is the beginning of the resolution of those problems on their real terms."[14] Sergio Bitar, a former minister in President Allende's socialist government of Chile, admits that communism's fall "has forced us to look much more at concrete proposals rather than theoretical ideas, to understand that we need to be more competitive and productive, and to put democracy at the center of all progressive thinking."[15]

The United States has been obsessed with destroying communist movements in Latin America through the twentieth century. During the early 20th century, the United States periodically sent the marines into Central America and the Caribbean to protect American economic assets and shore up friendly governments. Direct intervention subsided with President Franklin Roosevelt's Good Neighbor policy, but the United States continued to aid its regional allies to promote political and economic stability.

Castro's 1959 Cuban revolution became the catalyst for a revival of direct American intervention. Washington feared that the Cuban revolution would set off a domino effect of communist revolutions throughout the western hemisphere. From President Kennedy's Alliance for Progress in 1961 to President Reagan's Caribbean Basin Initiative the United States has attempted to counter communism's appeal by building up Latin America's economic vitality. Meanwhile, Washington intervened covertly to topple unfriendly governments in Guatemala, Chile, the Dominican Republic, and Nicaragua, while supporting friendly governments elsewhere.

The Cold War's end has had its negative aspects. After the El Salvadoran government settled with the communist rebels and the communist Sandinistas were swept from power in Nicaragua, the White House no longer felt the need to pour as much aid into the region; American aid to Latin America dropped 27 percent from 1990 to 1991. The region still is not free of political violence and instability. Colombia, Guatemala, and Peru are all torn by communist insurgencies. The military sits impatiently in the wings of virtually every Latin America country, ready to take over if the civilian politicians blunder badly.

African development also was distorted by the Cold War as the United States, Soviet Union, and lesser powers extended hundreds of billions of dollars in economic and military aid to various governments and movements. African dictators became adept at playing the foreigners against each other to obtain greater aid. The superpowers, in turn, converted civil wars in Angola, Ethiopia, and Somalia into Cold War battlegrounds. Today, socialism and statism are becoming as discredited in Africa as they are elsewhere. As in other Third World countries, foreign aid has dropped considerably with the Cold War's end.

Yet another important development obstacle is time. Third World countries which have achieved independence since 1945 are attempting to do in a generation or two what the United States, Britain, and France achieved over several hundred years. Unfortunately few politicians have the patience or vision to invest in long-range development projects. Political leaders worried about the next election or coup are particularly tempted to promote policies—tax cuts, unimpeded consumer imports, high defense spending, subsidized food, fuel, or housing, or generous welfare—that pay off key interest groups but might actually impede national development. Governments without a long-term development strategy often find themselves merely reacting hastily to one worsening economic crisis after another until they are swept away by ballots or tanks.

THE NEWLY INDUSTRIALIZING COUNTRIES

Only a handful of previously poverty-stricken, economically stagnant countries have broken free from the Third World and have embarked on successful political economic development. Although the specific policies and circumstances of the newly industrializing countries (NICs)—South Korea, Taiwan, Malaysia, Singapore, Thailand, and Chile—differ greatly, they share an emphasis on export-led development. This section will concentrate on analyzing the development success of South Korea and Taiwan, while relating general development lessons.

Development Prerequisites and Unique Factors

South Korea and Taiwan are the two most successful NICs. Both were Japanese colonies. During its rule over Taiwan (1895–1945) and South Korea (1910–45), Japan developed a certain degree of human, transportation, and communications infrastructure as well as mines, plantations, and light industry. South Korea received its independence in 1948 and Taiwan became the sanctuary for Chinese Nationalist forces which had been defeated by the communists in mainland China. Had it not been for American military intervention in 1950, both South Korea and Taiwan would have been overrun by victorious communist armies. In June 1950, communist North Korea invaded South Korea and quickly conquered most of the country except for a small perimeter around the port of Pusan in the southeast. President Truman chose to save both noncommunist regimes. He sent the U.S. 7th Fleet between mainland China and Taiwan, thus preventing a communist invasion, and got the United Nations to send an American led and largely staffed army to push the communists out of South Korea. Washington then poured billions of dollars of economic and military aid into both countries while opening American markets for South Korean and Taiwanese products. The United States also exerted pressure on both Seoul and Taipei to launch sweeping land reform programs. Thus, Japanese colonialism and American Cold War imperatives gave both Taiwan and South Korea all the essential developmental prerequisites.

Agricultural Revolution

An industrial revolution must be preceded by an *agricultural revolution* that in turn depends on successful land reform. South Korea and Taiwan both experienced massive land reform programs in which land tenancy was reduced from over 50 percent to less than 10 percent. In the process disgruntled peasants were transformed into conservative affluent farmers. How was this achieved? The government broke up the huge plantations and distributed the land to the peasants along with easy access to markets, cheap credit, fuel, fertilizer, and other technological inputs that were essential for the new land-owners to prosper. But in both countries, land reform would never have been implemented had not the United States exerted enormous pressure on those governments to do so, and then held out the promise of providing massive financial aid and open American markets if they succeeded.

In addition to land reform, an agricultural revolution involves developing through four stages. Using the example of rice production, in the first stage, farming is conducted by traditional methods of animal or human plowing, uses rainfall for water, and yields a metric ton per hectare. During the second stage, land is improved with irrigation, drainage, and organic fertilizer, and yields two metric tons per hectare. In the third stage, the farmer introduces improved types of seed, fertilizers, pesticides, storage, and transportation, and the harvest rises to four metric tons per hectare. In the final stage, the farmer can utilize the fruits of credit banks, cooperatives, laboratories, and weather services, and the crop rises to six metric tons per hectare.[16]

Few Third World countries have successfully completed an agricultural revolution. In the 1960s and 1970s, some tried a massive investment in the "Green Revolution" which involved the introduction of new high yield strains of rice, wheat, and other grains. The trouble was that many of these seeds required large infusions of fertilizer and water in order to flourish, which raised the costs. Without credit, few peasants could afford to invest in the "revolution." Most Third World farms still rely on traditional means of sowing, fertilizing, and reaping. Much of the crop rots on the way to market for lack of storage or refrigeration. Harvests steadily diminish as the topsoil erodes or degrades from poor planting techniques. The production and wealth gap between wealthy landowners and poor peasants steadily widens. In contrast, agriculture in the industrial democracies has reached the fourth development stage and heavily uses hybrid seeds, fertilizer, irrigation, herbicides, and insecticides. Thus, food production in most Third World countries lags far behind that in the advanced industrial countries. South Korea and Taiwan, in contrast, have largely succeeded in reaching the fourth agricultural development stage.

Import, Export, and Technology Substitution

The newly industrializing countries (NICs) have excelled at creating and distributing wealth largely by targeting a set of "strategic industries" for development—those industries that create the most wealth, best jobs, most advanced technology, and a range of related industries. Not all industries were developed at once. The government would first target such labor-intensive strategic industries as textiles and consumer electronics. After acquiring expertise, technology, markets, and capital from these industries, the government would then gradually add other, more sophisticated capital- and technology-intensive industries to the economy, such as steel, automobiles, ships, semiconductors, and computers. These strategic industries and the entire economy are nurtured through two distinct stages. During the first stage—import substitution—the government faces the problem of creating the targeted industries, while in the second stage—*export substitution*—it must nurture those newly created industries into global champions.

Since other countries already have developed the targeted industries, the first stage is obviously the toughest. The government must attract foreign technology, equipment, and capital while preventing foreign control. To this end the state uses a combination of high trade barriers to force consumers to buy domestic products, an overvalued currency to lower the price for buying essential foreign technology, machinery, and equipment, and low investment barriers to encourage foreign corporations to establish factories in the country.

The export substitution phase begins after the new industries have become established and have saturated domestic markets. The goal now is to create even greater economies of scale by selling in global markets. To do so, the currency is devalued so that the country's products have a comparative price advantage over those from other countries. Trade barriers might be slightly reduced to force domestic industries to become more productive in order to compete. By following this two-stage strategy, the government can nurture a range of strategic industries into global champions.

Successful industrialization depends on acquiring and adapting advanced technology. Although many countries have tried licensing foreign technology, only a few have succeeded in building that technology into viable products. A country must already have advanced laboratories and a well-educated corps of technicians in order for a technology-buying strategy to succeed. The nation must also be able to gradually wean itself from dependence on foreign technology by creating its own. Many cultures lack the tradition of experimentation and innovation necessary to develop simpler technology into more advanced technology.[17]

Culture and Development

Some argue that development ultimately rests on a society's values, and point to a "Protestant" or "Confucian" work ethic as being essential to Western and East Asian development, respectively. Historically "Confucian capitalism" was an oxymoron. Although Confucianism formed a basis of Chinese, Korean, Japanese, and Vietnamese culture and society throughout their histories, it may well have impeded rather than enhanced development. As important as values is an elite consensus over the means and ends of development. The "Confucian capitalists" did not begin to develop from feudal into modern societies until their leaders achieved a consensus to do so. Japan and the other East Asian "miracles" only began to develop after their political and economic leaders agreed to concentrate single-mindedly on rapid economic growth.

While there is no question that modernization is impossible without modern values, they can certainly exist independently of Protestantism or Confucianism. The revival of trade and the first nascent industries emerged in Catholic northern Italy long before the Protestant Reformation. Traditional Confucianism actually relegated merchants to society's lowest rung because they made money from exchanging rather than producing things.

Evaluation

Modernization theorists uphold South Korea and Taiwan as development models. Dependency theorists discount the development of South Korea and Taiwan by claiming that those countries were geopolitically and geoeconomically vital to Washington's containment of communism, and were thus allowed to develop as non-communist models. To that end, Washington pumped up both countries with billions in aid and allowed them access to American markets.

Dependency theorists neglect to point out that Washington also targeted dozens of other countries as vital to its containment strategies, such as Vietnam, Pakistan, Egypt, Panama, and the Philippines, and poured billions into those countries, and allowed their products preferential access to United States markets, yet those countries failed to develop successfully like Taiwan and South Korea. It was up to the governments of those countries to create and implement successful developmental policies. Both Taiwan and South Korea made the most of American aid and open markets. They modeled their industrialization strategy on that of Japan, and targeted a series of industries for export-led development.

Clearly, the development successes of Taiwan and South Korea give considerable weight to those who argue that development ultimately depends on a government's policies which make the best of internal human and natural resources in a global economy. It is unlikely, however, that many countries can successfully industrialize by rigidly following the strategies of South Korea and Taiwan.[18] Those countries were aided by a range of other development factors that most countries do not enjoy. South Korea and Taiwan began their export substitution phases in the early 1960s, a decade before global trade and development was damaged by OPEC's quadrupling of oil prices. World trade has slowed and the advanced industrial nations are becoming more protectionist.

CONCLUSION

Third World representatives tend to blame their developmental problems on the rich industrialized nations. Reality is much more complicated. Even a Marxist once admitted that: "the misery of being exploited by capitalists is nothing compared to the misery of not being exploited at all."[19] The only thing worse for a Third World nation's development than being dependent is not being dependent at all. Those countries like Burma, Albania, or China until 1978, that tried self-reliance policies failed miserably in increasing their wealth.

In contrast, those countries which have grown the fastest and often the most equitably have been the most involved in international trade. No country can industrialize and modernize on its own. Successful industrialization depends not just on factories and heavy machinery, but involves the development of a complex national transportation, communications, financial, technological, market, and entrepreneurial infrastructure. The components and knowledge for creating modern industry comes from those who have already achieved it.

Governments make choices. There is clearly a virtuous development cycle. Sensible policies bring economic development which builds that government's political legitimacy which in turn helps create a stable environment in which more economic development can occur. Sensible policies are determined by the constraints and opportunities offered by national history, culture, natural and human resource endowments, and socioeconomic conditions.

Although each country has its own distinct development, they can be grouped into one of five patterns: 1) states which achieved both rapid economic growth and a more equitable income distribution; 2) states which achieved economic growth but maintained a relatively inequitable income distribution; 3) states which achieved a more equitable income distribution but no significant growth; 4) states which have had little growth or income distribution; and 5) states whose growth and income distribution has stalled or worsened.[20]

Whatever development path a government chooses, it is often extremely difficult to measure just what positive or negative changes have resulted. The most obvious means is to look at economic growth rates, per capita income, income distribution, literacy, infant mortality, and so on. These statistics must be weighed against the government's stated goals and ideals. We can then compare the performance with that of countries with similar socioeconomic, geographic, natural and human resource, historic, and cultural conditions—Peru and Ecuador or Kenya and Tanzania, for example. Then we can compare a nation's current economic performances with those of the past.

The trouble with this approach is that statistics can be very misleading. Even the most advanced countries with small armies of statisticians evaluating a range of socioeconomic conditions will only give a more or less accurate impression of that country's reality. The less well-run a country, the more inefficient and corrupt its bureaucracy, and the more questionable the socioeconomic statistics it submits to the World Bank or other international development agencies are. Frankly, the books are often altered to give as favorable a view of the country as possible. Another problem is that much of the poor population uses barter rather than money for trading, while, to avoid paying taxes, many businesses rarely report all of their income. As a result, many people may be better off than official statistics indicate.

Per capita income, purchasing power parity, and income distribution measure a nation's living standards or material wealth. The Physical Quality of Life Index (PQLI) attempts to determine a country's quality of life by using life expectancy, infant mortality, and literacy rates. By this measure some very materially poor peoples have a relatively high quality of life, such as Sri Lanka with a $420 per capita income in 1991 but PQLI index of 90 on a 100 scale, China with a $330 per capita income and 84 PQLI, or the Philippines with a $630 per capita income and 83 PQLI. Much more common, however, were nations with both abysmally low per capita incomes and PQLIs, such as Guinea-Bissau with $190 and 36, Yemen with $640 and 48, or India with $340 and 60.[21]

The socioeconomic gap among people within a single Third World country is often as great as between that country and the world's wealthiest countries. Virtually all Third World countries have two societies, one relatively small but modern, urban, industrial, and literate, and the other trapping most of the population in tradition, poverty, subsistence farming, and illiteracy. When a country's population grows faster than its wealth, it becomes poorer overall. Trickle down economic theory appears to work no better in poor countries than in rich countries.

A United Nations Development Program (UNDP) showed how the concept of development is changing:

Human development is moving to center stage in the 1990s. For too long, the question has been how much is a nation producing? Now the question must be: how are its people faring? The real objective of development is to increase people's choices. Income is one aspect of these choices—and an extremely important one— but it is not the sum-total of human existence. Health, education, a good physical environment and freedom—to name a few other componets of well-being— may be just as important.[22] The report concluded that "there seems to be a high correlation between human development and human freedom.[23]

There is clearly a relationship between economic development and democracy.

STUDY QUESTIONS

1. What is modernization theory? What are the strengths and weaknesses of modernization theory?

2. What is dependency theory? What are the strengths and weaknesses of dependency theory?

3. What are the prerequisites for successful industrial development?

4. What was Western imperialism's legacy to the Third World? How has that legacy affected those countries' economic and political development?

5. What accounts for the continuing stagnant or declining economic and political life of many Third World countries?

6. What accounts for the successful development of such "newly industrializing countries" (NICs) as South Korea, Taiwan, Singapore, and so on?

ENDNOTES

1. The literature on economic development is vast. Some of the leading works are Gove Hamidge, ed., *Dynamics of Development* (New York: Praeger, 1964): Albert O. Hirschman, *The Strategy of Economic Development* (New Haven, Conn.: Yale University Press, 1958); Gerald Meier, *Leading Issues in Development Economics* (New York: Oxford University Press, 1964); Theodore Morgan, George W. Betz, and N.K. Choudhry, eds., *Readings on Economic Development* (Belmont, Calif.: Wadsworth, 1963); Ian Livingston, ed., *Approaches to Development Studies* (Brookfield, Vt.: Gower, 1982); Kenneth Nobe and Rajan Sampath, eds., *Issues in Third World Development* (Boulder, Colo.: Westview Press, 1984); Andrew Webster, *Introduction to the Sociology of Development* (London: Macmillan, 1984); Charles K. Wilber, ed., *The Political Economy of Development and Underdevelopment* (New York: Random House, 1984); J.P. Cole, *Development and Underdevelopment* (New York: Methuen, 1987); For two excellent recent analyses of development, see Jan Black, *Development in Theory and Practice* (Boulder, Colo.: Westview Press, 1991); Leslie Sklair, *Sociology of the Global System* (Baltimore: Johns Hopkins Press, 1991).

2. Betty Balfour, ed., *The History of Lord Lytton's Indian Administration, 1876–1880* (London: Macmillan, 1899), 510–512.

3. Theodore Von Laue, *The World Revolution of Westernization* (New York: Oxford University Press, 1987), 31.

4. Theodore de Bary, ed., *Sources of Indian Civilization* (New York: Columbia University Press, 1958), 803.

5. Tamar Golan, *Educating the Bureaucracy in a New Polity* (New York: Teacher's College Press, 1968), 223.

6. Theodore Von Laue, *The World Revolution of Westernization,* 315–316.

7. See Dale L. Johnson, ed., *Middle Classes in Dependent Countries* (Beverly Hills, Calif.: Sage Publications, 1984); Allan Findlay and Anne Findlay, *Population and Development in the Third World* (New York: Methuen, 1987).

8. "Has Capital Flight Made U.S. a Debtor of Latin America," *Businessweek,* April 21, 1986; Donald R. Lessard and John Williamson, *Capital Flight:*

9. For the leading literature on the relationship between bureaucracy and development, see Joseph La Palomabara, ed., *Bureaucracy and Political Development* (Princeton, N.J.: Princeton University Press, 1963); A.L. Adu, *The Civil Service in the New African States* (New York: Praeger, 1965); R. Braibanti, ed., *Asian Bureaucratic System Emergent From the British Imperial Tradition* (Durham, N.C.: Duke University Press, 1966); Ferrel Heady, *Public Administration: A Comparative Perspective* (New York: Marcel Dekker, 1984); Jamil E. Jreisat and Zaki R. Ghosheh, *Administration and Development in the Arab World: An Annotated Bibliography* (New York: Garland, 1986); Oskar Gans, ed., *Appropriate Techniques for Development Training* (Ft. Lauderdale, Fla.: Beeiterbach, 1966); B. Bola-Ntotele, "Introduction to a Study of the Efficiency of Administrative Systems in Sub-Saharan Africa" *International Review of Administrative Sciences,* vol. 52, no. 2, June 1986; Daniel Landau, "Government and Economic Growth in the Less Developed Countries: An Empirical Study for 1960–1980," *Economic Development and Cultural Change,* vol. 35, no. 1, October 1986; Bean Forbes, *The Socialist Third World: Urban Development and Territorial Planning* (New York: Basil Blackwell, 1987); Jerald Hage and Kurt Finsterbusch, *Organizational Change as a Development Strategy: Models and Tactics for Improving Third World Organizations* (Boulder, Colo.: Lynne Reinner, 1987); Gregory J. Kasza, "Bureaucratic Politics in Radical Military Regimes," *American Political Science Review,* vol. 81, no. 3, September 1987; Monte Palmer et al., "Bureaucratic Rigidity and Economic Development in the Middle East: A Study of Egypt, Saudi Arabia and the Sudan," *International Review of Administrative Sciences,* vol. 53, no. 2, June 1987.

10. Bela Belassa, "The 'New Protectionism' and the International Economy," *Journal of World Trade Laws,* vol. 12, no. 5, 1975, 15.

11. David Blake and Robert Walters, *The Politics of Global Economic Relations,* 162.

12. Bruce Russet and Kenneth Star, *International Political Economy* (Cambridge, Mass.: Harvard University Press, 1990), 435.

13. Theodore Von Laue, *The World Revolution of Westernization,* 314.

14. Tim Golden, "Sweeping Political Changes Leave Latin Poor Still Poor," *New York Times,* May 30, 1992.

15. Quoted in Golden, Ibid.

16. W. David Hopper, "The Development of Agriculture in Developing Countries," *Scientific American,* vol. 235, no. 3, 197, 197–205.

17. Carol Dahlman, *Local Development and Exports of Technology: The Comparative Advantage of Argentina, Brazil, India, the Republic of Korea, and Mexico* (Washington, D.C.: World Bank, 1984).

18. Robin Broad and John Cavanagh, "No More NICs," *Foreign Policy,* vol. 72, Fall 1988, 81–103.

19. Joan Robinson, *The Modern World System,* 2 vols. (San Diego: Academic Press, 1974), 1980.

20. Monte Palmer, *Political Development in Changing Societies* (Lexington, Mass.: Heath Lexington, 1971), 326.

21. See *U.S. Foreign Policy and Developing Countries: Discourse and Data 1991* (Washington, D.C.: Overseas Development Council, 1991), 37–41.

22. United Nations Development Program, *Human Development Report, 1991,* 13.

23. Ibid, 37.

The Politics of Dependence Between the First and Third Worlds

Key Terms and Concepts

Core
Dependence
Dependency Theory
Economic Liberalism
General Agreement on
Tariffs and Trade
(GATT)
General System of
Preference (GSP)
Group of Seventy-seven
Import Substitution
Industrial Policy
Interdependence

International Bank for
Reconstruction and
Development (IBRD)
International Monetary
Fund (IMF)
Modernization
Multi-Fiber Agreement
(MFA)
Multinational Corporation
Neocolonialism
New International
Economic Order
(NIEO)

Official Development
Assistance (ODA)
Organization for Oil
Exporting Countries
(OPEC)
Periphery
Semi-periphery
Stagflation
UN Commission on Trade
and Development
(UNCTAD)

One of the modern world's paradoxes is that it offers so many life-enhancing economic, social, and political opportunities yet so much of humanity can only dream of attaining them. A 1988 World Bank report revealed a Third World in crisis: Since 1980, matters have turned from bad to worse: economic growth rates have slowed, real wages have dropped, and growth in employment has faltered in most developing countries. . . . "In some the prolonged economic slump is already more severe than it was during the Great Depression in the industrial countries. The tide of poverty and misery in those countries is rising, not receding. . . . Without significant changes in policies, the present world economic uncertainty may soon be followed by a worldwide recession. . . . This is a fragile situation—one that could rapidly deteriorate."[1]

Third World socioeconomic and political crises have yet to drag the global economy into an intractable depression. But, as the report makes clear, the advanced industrial and Third World countries are deeply dependent on each other, although in vastly different ways. The world's rich and poor countries are divided by more than wealth. While relations between advanced industrial states are characterized as "interdependent" in which there is a relative power balance, there is a power imbalance between rich and poor countries in which the latter are "dependent" on the former.

The world's poor countries are becoming relatively poorer as the vast income gap grows wider between them and the wealthiest countries. In the global economy there is a rich class of about 15 percent of the total number of countries, a middle class of about

35 percent of all countries, and a low income class which includes more than half of all countries. The Third World holds 80 percent of the world's population but only 20 percent of its wealth. In 1992, the average person living in one of the 24 richest countries lived on $17,000 annually and lived 76 years while the average person in the Third World survived on $650 annually and lived 55 years. The world's income distribution among countries mirrors that of many developing countries in which there is a tiny wealthy class, a small middle class, and masses of poor.

How do we explain the vast gulf between the world's few rich countries and its many poor countries? There are no easy answers. Most Third World countries are trapped in a vicious cycle of political and economic underdevelopment while others have broken free of this development trap and are rapidly developing. Why have a few succeeded and most others failed? Why cannot all poor countries be equally successful? And what role does the global economy and relations between advanced industrial and Third World countries play in development or underdevelopment?

There are bitter divisions over these questions of dependence and relative development, and whether internal or external factors are more important.[2] Some argue that a country's relative success or failure is largely explained by internal factors, such as government policies, the political economic system, national culture, and human, natural, and technological resources. The leaders of the advanced industrial countries and organizations like the *International Monetary Fund* (IMF) assert that the poor have only themselves to blame. "Follow our successful policies and you too will succeed," they maintain.

Several schools of thought and many representatives of the world's poorer countries point the finger of blame toward the wealthy nation. They argue that external factors, such as colonial experience, foreign aid, multinational corporations, and international markets make the difference. The industrial countries, they argue, have used their political, economic, and military power to create a global economy in which they exploit the natural resources and cheap labor of the poor countries, and have an interest in keeping the poor poor.

This chapter will analyze this debate by examining important issues dividing the world's wealthier and poorer countries including trade discrimination, foreign aid, multinational corporations, the debt crisis, and the New International Economic Order (NIEO).

TRADE DISCRIMINATION

From the negotiations leading up to the Havana Charter and *GATT* of 1947 through today, less developed countries have attempted to gain favorable trade concessions from the advanced industrial countries. The Third World countries argue that GATT's free trade and most favored nation principles actually harm rather than help their development. If Third World countries remove their trade barriers, their few industries will be bankrupted by the much cheaper products of the advanced industrial countries. The result would be economic stagnation rather than development as the Third World countries would have to continue to rely on exporting commodities in which they have a natural comparative price advantage. Thus, the less developed countries have requested infant industry protection, the elimination of trade barriers within the industrial countries, and stable prices for Third World commodity exports.

Many of these demands were actually incorporated in the Havana Charter which would have created an International Trade Organization (ITO). This was the major reason why American industries lobbied against the Havana Charter, and the Truman administration decided against submitting it to the Senate for ratification. As a result, GATT has become the world's trade organization even though it was intended as an interim organization which would eventually yield to the ITO. GATT is much more strictly based on liberal economic ideals than the ITO, and less developed countries have lobbied ever since its inception for relief from many of its tenets. Another problem with GATT is that most negotiations have involved eliminating barriers to manufactured goods rather than commodities. Thus, Third World countries still find that their commodity exports are inhibited by relatively much higher tariff barriers.

A continuing Third World complaint is that the commodity goods they export are losing their value relative to the consumer goods, equipment, and other finished goods that they import.[3] The average value of non-oil primary commodities imported as a percentage of the value of manufactured goods exported by developed countries has declined from 130 to 70 between 1957 and 1990.[4] In other words, the industrial countries received almost twice as many primary goods for their manufactured exports in 1990 as they did in 1957, while Third World countries were receiving less than half the value for their commodity exports as they were 33 years before. Commodity prices have not only declined steadily in relative value over the last three decades, but have fluctuated sharply over the short term as they were traded on markets by investors. Both the long-term drop and short-term fluctuations in commodity prices can devastate those countries which depend on one crop for most of their export earnings. About 85 percent of Cuba's export earnings come from sugar, 60 percent of Ghana's from cocoa, 50 percent of Bolivia's from tin, 60 percent of Sri Lanka's from tea, 65 percent of Honduras' from bananas, and 50 percent of Zaire's from copper, to name a few of the more highly dependent economies.

There are several reasons for the decline in the relative value of commodities. The prices for some commodities have dropped because industrial countries have found substitutes. For example, fiber optics have replaced copper wires in telecommunications. The 20 percent drop in demand for copper between 1973 and 1986 has deeply hurt such producers as Chile. Consumers are increasingly substituting saccharine and aspartame for sugar, thus hurting sugarcane producing countries. Nylon has replaced cotton or wool in textiles, thus depressing prices in cotton and sheep producing countries.

Meanwhile, trade unions in the industrial countries have kept up wages and benefits; trade unions either do not exist in the Third World or are ineffective. Because wages constitute an important part of a good's final price, prices of goods from industrial countries are more apt to rise than those of less developed countries. Productivity gains in the First World which bring down prices are often offset by labor demands which raise costs, and thus the good's price remains relatively stable. Increased productivity in the Third World in the absence of labor unions may simply mean cheaper prices.

Many industrial countries are also major commodity producers. The United States, Canada, Australia, and New Zealand produce grains, livestock, and minerals. Because of their higher labor costs, these goods are often more highly priced than those from the less developed countries. Thus these industrial countries have erected high trade barriers to protect their own less competitive commodity producers.

However, most industrial country tariffs on commodity imports are lower than those on finished goods, a phenomenon known as "cascading tariffs." These higher tariffs on finished goods are often accompanied by other trade barriers including strict labeling, health, and inspection standards. The result is to restrict Third World exports to commodities rather than allow them to expand into semi-finished or manufactured goods.

GATT itself has sometimes blatantly discriminated against the Third World. In 1962, GATT negotiated the Long-Term Arrangement Regarding Trade in Cotton Textiles (LTA) which allowed members to impose quotas and market share limits on cotton textile imports. The advanced industrial countries then negotiated bilateral agreements under the LTA. In 1974, under GATT auspices, the *Multi-Fiber Agreement* (MFA) was signed by industrial and less developed countries which created a multilateral quota system for the global trade of artificial fiber and wool textiles and materials. Two decades later, the Multi-Fiber Agreement still upholds a global quota system for textiles. In 1990, over 60 percent of Third World yarn and fabrics and 80 percent of clothing exports were restricted under the MFA. The World Bank estimated that a free global textile market would increase textile and clothing manufacturing in the Third World by 35 percent and create $11.3 billion in additional wealth for those countries.[5]

Not only do Third World countries get less money for their commodity exports but they complain that when the industrial countries catch an economic cold (recession), the poor countries get pneumonia (depression). There is a direct relationship between the growth rates of industrial countries and that of developing countries.[6] One reason for this is that as their own economies slow down, the United States and the European Community raise import barriers, while Japan continues to maintain longstanding high barriers against competitive imports.

The Third World political economic fate is particularly tied to the United States which usually absorbs about 70 percent of Third World exports, and almost 90 percent of Latin America's. In order to protect American jobs, Washington has often raised trade barriers against many Third World products. For example, over two decades through 1988, American barriers against agricultural imports rose from about 30 percent to 90 percent of the total.[7] Between 1975 and 1985, the American imposition of "voluntary export restraints" (VERs) on imports, many of which came from developing countries, rose from 10 percent to 25 percent of total imports. When the United States raises import barriers, the exports of Third World countries suffer greatly. Inevitably almost everyone is hurt by protectionism. Recession in the Third World means less demand for American and other First World products. With 40 percent of American exports going to the developing world, the United States then loses potential economic growth.

Perhaps the most negative effect the United States has on developing countries is America's own foreign debt, which is now greater than that of the entire Third World. There is only a finite amount of global finance—the more the United States borrows the less there is available for the Third World. Commercial bankers would much prefer to lend to the still credit-worthy United States than to a poor country whose existing debt is huge and has often been rescheduled. And America's huge demand for international finance raises world interest rates, which means yet more Third World income is transferred to global bankers.

THE NEW INTERNATIONAL ECONOMIC ORDER

In the early 1960s, Third World countries collectively began to overcome these problems. In 1963, the *Group of Seventy-Seven* Third World countries in the United Nations issued its "Joint Declaration of the Developing Countries" which argued that:

> *The existing principles and pattern of world trade still mainly favor the advanced parts of the world. Instead of helping the developing countries to promote the development and diversification of their economies, the present tendencies in world trade frustrate their efforts to attain more rapid growth. These trends must be reversed.*[8]

They called for an international conference to address these trade and investment concerns.

In 1964, the United Nations created the *UN Commission on Trade and Development* (UNCTAD) and named Raul Prebisch, the father of *Dependency Theory*, as its first Secretary-General. Prebisch tried to make UNCTAD an alternative to GATT, the IMF, and the World Bank.[9] These efforts eventually succeeded in several ways. UNCTAD pressured GATT to address many Third World issues. In 1965, GATT issued a Part IV to its charter which called for the elimination of trade barriers to products from less developed countries, allowed commodity price agreements, and permitted Third World countries to opt out of the reciprocity principle. The only trouble with Part IV was that adherence to it by GATT members was voluntary.

In 1968, after several years of negotiation, most of the advanced industrial countries agreed in principle to a *General System of Preferences* (GSP) in which they would reduce their trade barriers to Third World products. But it was not until 1971 that GATT approved the GSP by waiving its most favored nation reciprocity principle. The GSP did not formally emerge until 1975 when nineteen advanced industrial countries agreed to unilaterally eliminate tariffs for a decade on a range of manufactured and semifinished goods for 140 poor countries. The agreement lasted for ten years and was renewed in 1985. In the recent GSP agreement, the United States has eliminated tariffs on $13 billion worth of imports from developing countries.

Although the GSP has helped promote some Third World exports, its value has been more symbolic than economic. The advanced industrial countries found ways around these concessions. Generally, they only remove barriers to Third World products that do not compete with their own. For example, the United States excludes textiles, shoes, import-sensitive steel, import-sensitive electronics, and import-sensitive glass from the GSP and refuses to extend it to any OPEC country or any product that captured more than a 50 percent share of America's market.

During the 1970s, the Group of Seventy-Seven movement reached its peak of activism. In 1974, in the UN General Assembly it proposed the creation of a *New*

International Economic Order (NIEO) that would run on different principles than the "Liberal International Economic Order" developed by the United States. Among the NIEO goals were: 1) the creation of buffer stocks to prevent fluctuations in commodity prices; 2) multilateral long-term contracts for commodity prices which would guarantee prices; 3) massive debt write-offs; 4) the elimination of trade barriers in industrial countries to Third World exports; 5) the liberalization and extension of GSP privileges to semi finished and finished goods; 6) the increase in the Third World share of global industrial production to 25 percent by the year 2000; 7) an increase in foreign aid from donors at least equal to 0.70 percent of their GNP; 8) increased technology transfers and the set-up of research and development institutes within the Third World; 9) the stabilization of exchange rates, movement away from the dollar as the international currency, and increased use of SDRs issued by the IMF; and 10) the regulation of multinational corporation investments and profits.[10] In December 1974, the Group of Seventy-Seven also got the General Assembly to pass a "Charter of Economic Rights and Duties of States," which included: 1) sovereignty for all states which means the right to use any wealth and resources in whatever way it wants; 2) the right to nationalize all foreign property in return for appropriate compensation; 3) the right of states to create commodity cartels and the duty of other states to adhere to the cartel's prices and other arrangements.

In 1976, UNCTAD inaugurated the Integrated Program for Commodities (IPC) to help control fluctuations in prices and the average price level for commodities. IPC has attempted to negotiate such agreements for 18 commodities that comprise 75 percent of the Third World's commodity exports. Prices can be further managed by stockpiling some commodities and selling off some of the stock when the price rises too rapidly and buying more when the price falls. IPC identified ten of these buffer stocks: rubber, sugar, tea, tin, cocoa, coffee, copper, cotton and cotton yarns, hard fibers, and jute and jute products. By 1980, UNCTAD had granted IPC a $400 million fund to finance these buffer stocks, and allocated another $350 million to help diversify Third World economies particularly dependent on sales of one or a few commodities. States join the IPC by making a financial contribution to the buffer stock finance pool.

The IPC has had limited success in achieving its ambitious goals. By the early 1990s, there were only five international commodity agreements (ICAs)—cocoa, tin, sugar, rubber, coffee, and tropical lumber. Only rubber and tropical lumber were IPC agreements. The industrial nations were leery of the IPC and other ICAs, fearing that they would spawn OPEC type cartels that would raise prices. These agreements are further undercut by the fact that some industrial nations like the United States, Canada, Australia, and South Africa are also important commodity exporters. The Third World contributes only 32 percent of the world's non-oil commodity exports and 45 percent of its known non-energy minerals.

Among the advanced industrial states, the European Community has been the most accommodating to Third World demands. Since 1975, Brussels has signed four agreements (known as Lome Conventions) with 66 developing countries. The most important of these agreements was STABEX, which acts like an IPC or club in which states join by making a contribution to a common fund. STABEX covers 48 commodities and extends grants or loans to any member whose commodity earnings fall below a certain percentage of their exports to the European Community for three previous consecutive years.

UNCTAD was also influential in the GATT Tokyo Round of negotiations from 1973 through 1979. The GATT approved the various agreements that UNCTAD has negotiated with the industrial countries. However, GATT also passed a graduation clause in which countries that achieved a certain level of development would no longer be eligible for preferential treatment.

UNCTAD continued to be active during the 1980s and 1990s and its ranks swelled to over 130 members. But its power decreased despite its growing membership. As we have seen there is no monolithic Third World whose countries' interests are identical. The range of development levels within the Third World has expanded enormously. As countries develop their interests change. Third World solidarity was always more of a slogan rather than a reality, but never more so than today. And when some Third World countries do attempt to work together on an issue, the industrialized countries will invariably play them off against each other through offers of aid, investments, or lower trade barriers. Stockpiling, conservation, alternative products, and multiple suppliers doomed any attempt by countries to stabilize commodity prices. Finally, the collapse of communism has removed both a state-development model and source of support for UNCTAD's more radical members.

Faced with these realities, UNCTAD has quietly set aside its NIEO goals and focused on working with GATT on specific issues. During GATT's Uruguay Round (1986–93), the less developed countries were put on the defensive by industrial country demands that they grant intellectual property protection and reduce their trade barriers. Meanwhile, four industrial and nine Third World agricultural exporting countries, known as the Cairn Group after the Australian city in which they first met, have joined to pressure the European Community to abandon its agricultural trade barriers and export subsidies.

Throughout the Uruguay Round, there has been a clear division between the First and Third Worlds over technology. The advanced industrial nations believe that the inventors have the right to withhold or to license their technology as they see fit. They point out that if intellectual property is not protected and compensated, there will be no incentive for inventors to create new technology. Computer software, for example, is easily copied, thus costing the creators lost royalties and giving them little incentive to create new software. Third World countries argue that technology should be used by all without restriction or compensation. They argue that intellectual property protection simply perpetuates the political economic supremacy of the advanced industrial countries and the subjection of the poor. Although the World Intellectual Property Organization (WIPO) was set up to address the problems of intellectual piracy, it has been unable to stem such thefts. The Uruguay Round does not appear to have been any more successful in addressing the technology issue.

THE ORGANIZATION FOR PETROLEUM EXPORTING COUNTRIES

Until the early 1970s, no economic sector seemed a more blatant example of Third World dependence than oil.[11] Seven oil corporations known as the "Seven Sisters" (the American firms Exxon, Chevron, Gulf, Mobil, and Texaco, British Petroleum, and

Dutch Royal Shell) controlled virtually all the world's noncommunist oil wells, transportation, refineries, and markets. They had operated as a global cartel since the 1920s when they first began to divide markets, fix prices, drive independents out of business, and impose lucrative extraction agreements on governments. Their wealth grew even greater after 1945 when oil replaced coal as the most important energy resource. In 1952, the seven major oil firms produced 90 percent of the oil outside North America and the communist countries, a percentage which dropped to 75 percent by 1968.[12]

The first challenge to the Seven Sisters occured in 1953 when the Iranian government attempted to nationalize the holdings of the British Petroleum subsidiary—Anglo-Iranian Oil—that monopolized Iran's oil industry. Britain responded with an economic embargo and threats to invade Iran unless compensation was made. The United States succeeded in overthrowing Iran's government, imposing the Shah, and cutting a deal with the new government whereby American oil firms would replace British Petroleum.

During the mid-1950s, several Persian Gulf governments succeeded in negotiating a fifty-fifty split on extraction profits, resulting in a significant increase in revenue. For example, Saudi Arabia's profits rose from $0.17 to $0.80 a barrel between 1956 and 1957 when a barrel of oil cost about $1.80.[13] In 1960, representatives of Iran, Iraq, Kuwait, Saudi Arabia, and Venezuela, the world's five leading oil producers other than the United States and Soviet Union, met to discuss the possibility of acting jointly to offset recent price decreases pushed through by the Seven Sisters. Although they did nothing to offset the price decreases, they did form the *Organization for Petroleum Exporting Countries* (OPEC), whose ranks increased to thirteen by the early 1970s. Despite these developments, the Seven Sisters continued to dominate the global oil market from well-head to gas station.

Although OPEC remained quiescent during the 1960s, the vulnerability of the industrial world to a potential oil cut-off grew steadily. In 1973, OPEC accounted for 85 percent of global oil exports, and the Middle Eastern countries represented about 75 percent of that. Middle Eastern and North African oil accounted for 75 percent of Japan's total oil imports, 60 percent of Western Europe's, and 15 percent of America's.[14]

OPEC's 1970s activism was stimulated by Colonel Muammar al-Qadhafi, who took over Libya in a 1969 coup. In 1970, Qadhafi threatened the nationalization of foreign oil holdings if they did not grant Libya higher taxes and boost prices. The oil firms gave in to Qadhafi's demands. In December 1970, OPEC also demanded tax and price increases. In February 1971, faced with this collective demand, the oil firms signed a five year oil price and tax increase agreement with OPEC in which oil would rise from $1.80 to $2.29 a barrel. OPEC soon called for a renegotiation of the agreement when it became clear that the dollar's devaluation in December 1971 had cut their revenues. The price was subsequently raised to $2.48 a barrel. In December 1972, OPEC called for an ownership share of the oil subsidiaries in their countries starting at 25 percent and eventually rising to 51 percent by 1982. The oil firms complied with these demands. Despite these agreements, the dollar's floating and devaluation in the spring of 1973 had diminished OPEC's revenues and they called for even greater price increases from the oil firms.

Two days before these negotiations were to commence, the Arab states attacked Israel on October 6 in what became known as the Yom Kippur War. Although initially caught by surprise, Israel counterattacked and, with massive American military and intelligence aid, managed to defeat the Arab armies. On October 16, the Organization of Arab Petroleum Exporting Countries (OAPEC), an OPEC subgroup, increased the price of oil to $5.12 a barrel, and on December 23 raised it further to $11.65, effectively quadrupling oil prices within a month. OAPEC also imposed a temporary boycott on oil sales to the United States, the Netherlands, and Portugal for helping Israel during the war.

The United States responded to this crisis by attempting to organize a buyers cartel called the International Energy Agency (IEA) which would attempt to offset OPEC's power by members stockpiling at least a 90 days oil supply, sharing supplies, developing alternative fuels, and acting together diplomatically. France, however, refused to join. The IEA was largely ineffective in countering OPEC.

OPEC's oil price hikes succeeded for three central reasons. First, there was no easy energy alternative to oil. Second, the Europeans and Japanese were dependent on OPEC for most of their oil needs. Third, the oil sources were dispersed so widely and could be so easily sabotaged that it would have been impossible for the United States and its allies to take over the oil fields.

OPEC maintained prices by assigning production quotas for its members. With the world's largest proven oil reserves, Saudi Arabia served as OPEC's price leader. When global oil supplies were tight, Saudi Arabia increased production and when supplies were abundant it cut back production. OPEC was divided within by countries—Iran, Iraq, Venezuela, and Nigeria—that had smaller reserves, larger populations, and more ambitious development strategies and thus wanted ever higher oil prices, and by moderates—Saudi Arabia, Kuwait, and the United Arab Emirates—that were content with existing increases.

Between 1974 and January 1979, oil prices drifted up to $14.34 a barrel, then more than doubled in 1980 to $33 a barrel. There were several reasons for this second dramatic price increase. Throughout 1978, Iran was torn apart by a revolution in which the pro-Western Shah was overthrown and the Islamic fundamentalist Ayatollah Khomeini was brought to power in January 1979. Iranian oil shipments had been cut during the last months of 1978, exacerbating existing global supply shortages. In December 1978, OPEC agreed to a 10 percent price hike, and to a further price hike in July 1979. In December 1979, the Soviet Union invaded Afghanistan, prompting fears among some that this was the first step in the Soviet conquest of the Persian Gulf. In September 1980, Iraq attacked Iran, limiting oil shipments from both countries as each side attacked the other's oil facilities. Throughout these two years, oil prices on the spot market, or the free market, beyond OPEC's control rose higher and faster than the OPEC prices. By December 1980, OPEC's official price reached $33 a barrel and spot market prices topped $41 a barrel.

The result of the oil price hikes between 1973 and 1980 was a startling shift in global geoeconomic power. OPEC revenues rose from $15 billion in 1972 to peak at $300 billion in 1980. Meanwhile, American oil imports soared from $4.8 billion to $80 billion during the same period, and other industrial nations posted similar increases in their oil bills. The result was a decade of *stagflation*—high unemployment, high interest rates, high inflation, and low economic growth.

OPEC's success inspired developing countries to attempt to force concessions from the industrial democratic countries in other areas. The Group of Seventy-Seven unsuccessfully pushed its NIEO agenda during 1974 and 1975. Also during that time, many feared that other commodity producers would follow in OPEC's footsteps by creating cartels and raising prices. These fears were unfounded. Although several commodity producers did attempt to create cartels, none became another OPEC. Stockpiles, diverse and abundant sources, and alternatives undermined efforts to create bauxite, copper, phosphates, bananas, cocoa, tea, and natural rubber cartels.

OPEC's overwhelming success in raising oil prices during the 1970s turned to failure during the mid-1980s when international oil prices dropped to half their highest level. Prices collapsed for several reasons. As prices rose throughout the 1970s, non-OPEC members, like Britain, Norway, Mexico, Malaysia, and China, began exploiting existing sources and discovering new ones that would have otherwise been too expensive. Between 1973 and 1983, OPEC's share of the global oil market dropped from 63 percent to 33 percent.[15] Hard pressed for additional revenues, OPEC members themselves cheated and sold more oil than their quotas allowed and flooded the spot market with it. Meanwhile, almost all countries, but particularly the oil-guzzling industrial countries, embarked on severe conservation policies to make their energy use more efficient. They also created huge oil reserves that could supply their respective needs for up to 90 to 120 days. The combination of increased supply and decreased demand led to a global oil glut and subsequent oil price drop in 1986 from $30 to $15 a barrel. The glut continued despite the Persian Gulf War which temporarily eliminated Kuwaiti and Iraqi oil production from global markets. By November 1992, OPEC's daily production of 25.15 million barrels was the highest since 1980, which helped push oil prices down from $21 a barrel to $19.60 a barrel. Today the price for a barrel of oil is actually cheaper in constant dollars (adjusted for inflation) than before 1973.

There are currently twelve OPEC members—Algeria, Gabon, Indonesia, Iran, Iraq, Kuwait, Libya, Nigeria, Qatar, Saudi Arabia, the United Arab Emirates, and Venezuela—Ecuador left OPEC in September 1992. These countries vary considerably in wealth, population, and territory, from states like Kuwait and the United Arab Emirates with small populations and lands and large per capita incomes, to countries like Nigeria and Indonesia with huge territories and populations but mass poverty.

Throughout the 1990s, OPEC's cartel power will probably not revive. The oil glut will continue as supplies steadily rise while demand remains slack from extensive conservation and efficiency efforts. Although OPEC currently produces only about 35 percent of global oil production, 65 percent of the world's proven oil reserves are within the Persian Gulf countries. Over the long-term, OPEC's power, and particularly that of its Persian Gulf members, may well reemerge as finite oil reserves eventually dwindle. Whether the global economy will have found and shifted to non-oil energy sources by that time remains to be seen.

FOREIGN AID

Foreign aid continues to be the most important source of international development funds and expertise for most Third World countries.[16] In 1990, foreign aid represented

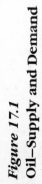

Figure 17.1
Oil—Supply and Demand

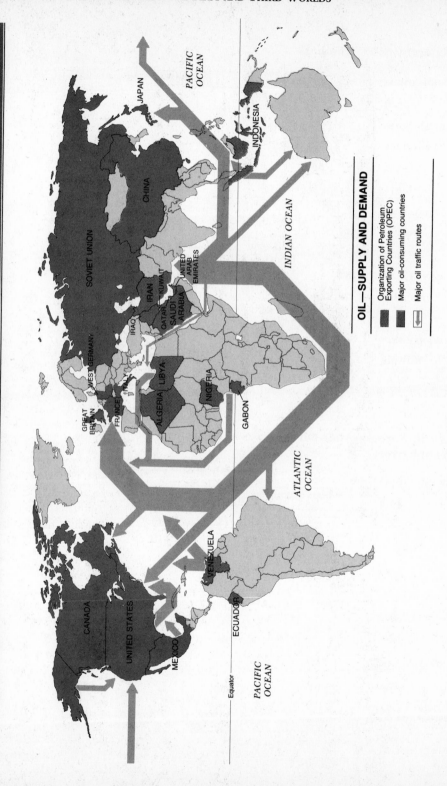

Source: Wallbank/Taylor, *Civilization: Past and Present*, New York: HarperCollins, 1992, p. 962.

Figure 17.2
Oil Production by OPEC Members

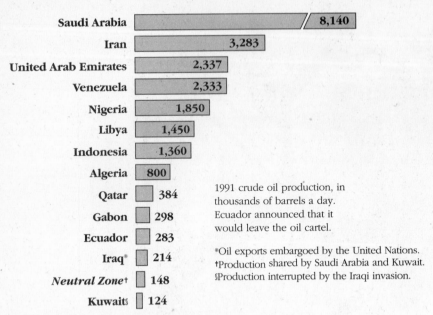

Saudi Arabia	8,140
Iran	3,283
United Arab Emirates	2,337
Venezuela	2,333
Nigeria	1,850
Libya	1,450
Indonesia	1,360
Algeria	800
Qatar	384
Gabon	298
Ecuador	283
Iraq*	214
Neutral Zone†	148
Kuwait§	124

1991 crude oil production, in
thousands of barrels a day.
Ecuador announced that it
would leave the oil cartel.

*Oil exports embargoed by the United Nations.
†Production shared by Saudi Arabia and Kuwait.
§Production interrupted by the Iraqi invasion.

Source: The Petroleum Finance Company

Figure 17.3
Countries with Largest Crude Oil Reserves as of Jan. 1, 1990, in billions of barrels

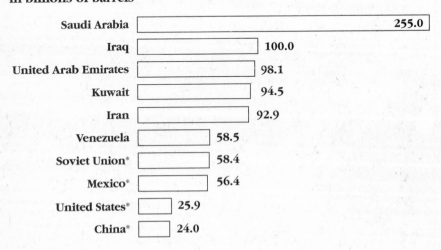

Saudi Arabia	255.0
Iraq	100.0
United Arab Emirates	98.1
Kuwait	94.5
Iran	92.9
Venezuela	58.5
Soviet Union*	58.4
Mexico*	56.4
United States*	25.9
China*	24.0

Source: Oil and Gas Journal, Dec. 25, 1989.   *Non-OPEC countries

almost one-third of the Third World's sources of international finance. This aid is from both bilateral (country to country) and multilateral (international organization to country) sources. There are several types of aid. Emergency aid is generally for crises like famines and includes supplies of food, medicine, and clothing. Development aid is generally targeted to specific projects, whether it be a village well or huge dam. Although military aid is not considered *official development assistance* (ODA), advocates argue that development of a nation's military forces can contribute to both political stability and economic development. Opponents argue that the opposite effect is more common.

Bilateral Aid

After 1945, the United States was the most important aid donor and continues to provide the most aid in volume if not as a GNP percentage. Between 1945 and 1990, the United States dispensed more than $212 billion in official development aid, and throughout the 1980s into the 1990s has annually dispensed about $9 billion to the Third World. Today, although the United States still gives the most aid, as a percentage of GNP it is the lowest among the OECD countries.

America's aid program started out vast and generous. For a decade after 1945, Washington's aid policy concentrated on reconstruction of the industrial countries rather than on development of the world's poor countries. The United States gave $17 billion to 16 European countries and $2.2 billion to Japan between 1945 and 1952. But from the mid-1950s, for several reasons, the Third World became the recipient of massive aid. One reason was that the reconstruction of Europe and Japan was finished. Those countries had been restored to rapid economic growth and relative prosperity, and they were now able to begin their own foreign aid programs. During the 1950s and into the 1960s, an increased number of colonies achieved independence and were in desperate need of economic assistance. Finally, in 1956 Soviet Premier Nikita Khrushchev announced that his country would compete with the Western powers for the loyalty of developing countries.

To counter Soviet advances and to deal with the development problems of a rapidly enlarging Third World, the United States and its allies significantly increased their foreign aid programs. For two decades after the mid-1950s, global foreign aid increased steadily. After OPEC's quadrupling of oil prices in 1973, many of the wealthier Arab states also began large aid programs, although those were mostly targeted on poorer Arab or Muslim states.

Washington clearly linked American economic and political security with that of the less developed countries, and its aid program was seen as a vital means of achieving that security. A Senate committee nicely summarized the ends and means of the U.S. foreign aid program:

> *A comprehensive and sustained program of American economic assistance aimed at helping the free underdeveloped countries to create the conditions for self-sustaining growth [that] can, in the short run, materially reduce the danger of conflict triggered by minor powers, and can, say, in two or three decades, result in an overwhelming preponderance of societies with a successful record of solving their problems without resorting to coercion or violence. The establishment of such a*

*preponderance of stable, effective, and democratic societies gives the best promise of
a favorable settlement of the Cold War and of a peaceful, progressive world
environment.[17]*

But by the mid-1970s, most of the advanced industrial countries, particularly the
United States, began to experience donor fatigue. Classical economic assumptions
guided America's aid program. It was thought that a lack of money was the most important development constraint for poor countries. Thus, large American grants to a
country would theoretically set off a virtuous savings/investment cycle. Unfortunately,
development proved far more complex than liberal economic theory allowed. In all too
many poor countries, there seemed to be little development to show for all the aid. Instead, the result of most aid programs was widespread waste, corruption, and inefficiency. And as for the United States, often the recipient country politically bit the hand
which fed it by refusing to go along with Washington on UN votes, military bases, or
economic policies. For these reasons, plus the global economic slowdown, from the late
1970s, the amount of aid from the United States and many other industrial countries
leveled off. Then during the 1980s, OPEC aid declined in absolute and relative terms as
oil-prices plunged.

Few countries give aid for purely altruistic purposes. The United States, the former
Soviet Union, and some other aid donors have often used aid to influence the recipient's
policies.[18] Aid with this motivation does not always succeed in advancing the donor's
national interests. For example, the massive economic and military aid that Moscow extended Egypt did not prevent President Sadat from kicking out all Soviet advisers and
reducing bilateral diplomatic ties in 1972. Nor did the tens of billions of dollars the
United States gave South Vietnam, along with a massive U.S. military involvement,
prevent Saigon from falling to communism in 1975.

Despite such failures, America's aid program has, largely for political reasons,
shifted in type and targeted countries. In 1973, 78 percent of American aid was for economic development and 22 percent for direct geopolitical purposes. By 1985, the Reagan administration nearly reversed these priorities, with 67 percent of American aid
geopolitical and 33 percent economic.[19] American law also prohibits aid to countries
which have nationalized American assets without adequate compensation.

Several major aid donors have concentrated their aid on a relatively few recipients.
Since the 1977 Camp David Accords signed between President Sadat and Prime Minister Begin, about 40 percent of American aid goes to Israel and Egypt. President Carter
used the promise of massive aid to both countries as a lure for a peace agreement. In
1992, $5.1 billion, or 36 percent of America's $13.9 billion aid budget, still went to Israel and Egypt, while only $650 million went to Russia in 1991 and 1992. The Reagan
administration concentrated its aid even more narrowly by emphasizing "front-line"
states in regional conflicts like Turkey, Pakistan, and the Central American countries, as
well as Israel and Egypt. France gives much of its aid to itself—about 40 percent of its
aid goes to four of its overseas departments and territories. About 85 percent of OPEC's
aid goes to Arab or Muslim countries. Until the Soviet Union's breakup, about 80 percent of Moscow's aid went to Vietnam, Cuba, and Mongolia. Now, of course, the former Soviet republics are themselves the recipients of massive foreign aid.

Most donors tie at least some aid to the recipient's purchase of the donor country's
goods and services. Japan has been considered to have the most blatantly tied program.

Tokyo has been tying its aid since it sent abroad its first reparations during the 1950s. As Japan's economic power grew, increasing numbers of other donors followed suit. America's 480 agricultural aid programs give recipients loans to buy American grain, and is thus largely a subsidy to producers.

Multilateral Aid

Recipients generally favor multilateral over bilateral aid. Direct donor-to-recipient bilateral aid tends to be tied and restricted; multilateral aid is usually targeted on specific projects but at least the recipient has slightly more discretion over how it is spent. There are a variety of multilateral aid organizations, including regional development banks, various United Nations programs, the European Community, OPEC, private philanthropic institutions, and OECD's Development Assistance Agency (DAC).

The IBRD or World Bank and IMF are the world's two most important multilateral lending agencies. Their aid programs complement each other. The World Bank funds specific development projects while the IMF extends short-term development loans to countries suffering from international payments deficits. Both institutions are headquartered in Washington D.C. in buildings next to each other. Although the World Bank is often criticized for investing in wasteful large-scale projects that are inappropriate for the recipient country, the IMF's lending policies have been particularly criticized.

The IMF is like an international lending club. States become members by agreeing to follow IMF policy guidelines and contributing money to the IMF pool that was about $100 billion in 1990. Members vote on IMF policy, with their votes weighted according to their financial contributions. When members are suffering payments deficits they can borrow up to 125 percent of their original contribution, but only if they agree to strictly follow the IMF policy prescription. Although the IMF was founded in 1944, it did not become an important international lender until the 1970s, when the Third World debt grew rapidly.

Most Third World countries take IMF loans only as a last resort. Debtors are highly critical of the IMF prescription which includes massive cutbacks in government spending, restrictive fiscal and monetary policies, currency devaluations, high interest rates, and the removal of trade and investment barriers. Government cutbacks in price supports for food, fuel, and other necessities hurt the poor the most. A currency devaluation inflates prices for those with enough money to afford foreign consumer goods and for industries that depend on foreign equipment and technology. Finally, the removal of trade and investment barriers often leads to an influx of foreign goods and services which bankrupt domestic businesses which cannot compete. The result is that the economy is pushed into a deep and sometimes intractable recession. "IMF riots" are common in which those worst hurt economically rampage in the streets. Thus, debtors complain bitterly that the result of following IMF policies is not economic development but economic chaos and a political crisis that often leads to a coup or even revolution.

Despite these often grim results, Third World nations accept IMF loans for one clear reason—poor nations find it almost impossible to borrow money from international banks without an IMF loan. An IMF loan signals to private international bankers that the recipient is considered creditworthy, and they may also loan money to that country. If a country defaults, no one will lend to them. Given the alternatives, the IMF seems the lesser of two evils.

Third World countries have no power to change IMF policies. Although they make up 75 percent of IMF's membership, their relatively low contributions mean that they only account for about 35 percent of the votes. The United States alone accounts for about 20 percent of the votes, while the other leading industrial states make up another 45 percent.

Evaluation

Since its inception, the Group of Seventy-Seven has called on the wealthier nations to annually transfer at least 0.7 percent of their GNP, as well as give more grants, softer loan interest rates and longer repayment schedules, and to eliminate tying aid to purchases of the donor's goods and services. Only the Scandanavian countries and the Netherlands have complied with those requests. The two wealthiest countries, the United States and Japan, are actually among the stingiest in terms of aid as a percentage of GNP and the terms to which it is extended.

Does foreign aid help a nation's development? Over time, aid donors and recipients have learned to use resources more effectively. During the 1970s, the World Bank shifted some of its funding from the development of large industrial and infrastructure projects to basic human needs, and many other countries' aid programs followed suit.[20] Humanitarian aid has generally been the most successful in nurturing development. While many industrial projects have failed to make money, such basic needs as health, sanitation, and education have improved or at least have not deteriorated as rapidly as would have been the case without such humanitarian aid.

Yet, some studies indicate that even aid which is relatively well-administered may only add 0.6 percent to 1.5 percent to a nation's annual growth.[21] "Donor fatigue" has afflicted virtually all aid donors. For many donor countries, the hundreds of millions of dollars in aid they have sent abroad seems to have neither sparked genuine development nor gratitude among the recipients. Although foreign aid will remain important to many Third World countries, it is clearly no development panacea.

DEBT CRISIS

During the 1980s, the global economy seemed threatened by the Third World's inability to service its rapidly growing debt. It was feared that the default of the world's largest debtors would bankrupt overextended international banks which in turn would drag down the global economy into a deep and intractable depression.

It is said that if you owe someone a thousand dollars you are in debt to him, but if you owe him a million dollars he is in debt to you. That notion mirrors the Third World debt problem. When a huge debtor like Mexico or Brazil threatens to default, the global bankers have no choice but to respond. The most common means of managing a crisis is to reschedule that country's debt repayment, which usually involves reducing the country's interest rates while extending its payments out over more years.

Sometimes bankers or other investors will actually buy back part of the debt at a reduced rate. And finally, they have simply written off large chunks of debt for those countries which have threatened to default. Throughout the debt crisis, global bankers have been like firefighters, rushing from one country to the next rescheduling one debt payment after another.

The debt crisis was caused by several interrelated problems. The most important underlying reason was OPEC's quadrupling of oil prices in 1973 and further doubling in 1979. By the early 1980s, a barrel of oil sold for $35, more than 15 times its price a decade earlier. The result was a huge shift in money to OPEC, with its earnings increasing from $1 billion in 1973 to $70 billion in 1974![22] Most of the OPEC states lacked a banking system sophisticated enough to manage this ocean of money or domestic development projects vast enough in which to invest it. Instead, they deposited much of the money in Western banks. But even the sophisticated international banks had trouble finding creditworthy borrowers in a stagnant global economy and became increasingly desperate to find borrowers who would pay an interest rate higher than what the banks were giving to their oil-rich depositors.

Eventually, many of these "petrodollars" were recycled to the Third World. Although OPEC had wielded its "oil weapon" to hurt the industrial democracies and exact revenge for decades of exploitation by the huge oil corporations, it was the poor, struggling Third World which was damaged the worst. The bill for the oil-importing Third World increased by $250 billion annually between 1974 and 1979, and then doubled to $500 billion. Thus money earned by Third World countries from exports was used to pay for oil imports rather than being invested in domestic industries and infrastructure. As investments fell, so did economic growth and exports. When export earnings fell short of skyrocketing oil bills, the impoverished countries borrowed increasing amounts from international bankers to pay for the difference. To make matters worse, global interest rates rose to 21 percent in the early 1980s, reflecting the greater demand for funds and the need to keep ahead of the hyperinflation set off by soaring oil prices. Poor countries sank ever deeper in the quicksand of debt with no way out. Economic development, which seemed promising for many Third World countries during the 1960s and early 1970s, stalled and often reversed. As the Third World fell deeper into debt and recession, the hard-pressed private bankers cut back their new loans to those countries, thus exacerbating the situation. The Third World's total debt rose from about $100 billion in 1973 to $831 billion in 1982 and $1.3 trillion in 1988.

The Third World leaders themselves must bear much of the responsibility for the debt crisis. Much of the borrowed money was squandered, some ended up in Swiss bank accounts, other money was poured in grandiose construction projects. Little was invested in production or infrastructure that would stimulate rather than impede national development. There were some exceptions. Modeling its development on that of Japan, South Korea invested most of its loans in strategic industries, such as steel, automobiles, shipbuilding, consumer electronics, and semiconductors, with great success.

Oil prices dropped to half their former price during the mid-1980s as new non-OPEC production in the North Sea, China, Mexico and elsewhere began, and virtually every country attempted to invest in energy saving equipment. Although this equipment relieved the pressure on non-oil producing nations, now it was the turn of oil-rich but heavily populated countries like Mexico, Venezuela, Nigeria, and Indonesia to borrow heavily to maintain the huge development projects they had embarked upon during the late 1970s.

Third World debt had been soaring for almost a decade when a crisis erupted in 1982. In July, the Mexican government announced that it would suspend the interest payments on its national debt. Mexico's foreign debt in 1982 was $85 billion, one-tenth of the total Third World debt of $831 billion.[23] Mexico defaulted for several reasons. By 1982, Mexico had borrowed $85 billion to invest in a range of development projects and serviced its debt primarily through its oil export earnings. But in 1982, oil prices began to drop while interest rates soared.

The fear was that if Mexico were allowed to default, other huge debtors would follow. Most of this debt was owed to commercial banks and a series of defaults would devastate the global financial and trading system. In 1982, five countries alone—Brazil, Mexico, Argentina, Venezuela, and Chile—had a total of $260 billion in debt, and all of them were having trouble servicing their debts. American bankers were particularly vulnerable to any default since they owned 40 percent of Latin America's total debt.

The IMF led the global bankers in managing the debt crisis. The IMF, and those banks which had lent the most to the debtor country, would organize an advisory committee to negotiate directly with that government and other smaller lending banks. The government, in turn, represented all of the country's debtors. By working together, the IMF, World Bank, industrial country governments, and commercial lenders formed a "lender's cartel" which worked with each country on a case-by-case basis, thus preventing the emergence of a debtor's cartel.

Within two days of Mexico's announcement, Washington directly lent its southern neighbor $2 billion in credits to service its immediate payments, and pressured a group of banks to reschedule payments that would save Mexico an additional $1 billion. Then the IMF and Mexico began to negotiate a more comprehensive settlement. In November 1982, in return for $3.84 billion in IMF loans and $5 billion in commercial loans, Mexico agreed to an intensive austerity program in which it devalued its currency, reduced government spending, and cut back its subsidy programs. For the first time the IMF made its loan conditional on the recipient negotiating a large commercial loan.

The fear that other debtors would follow suit was justified. In December 1982, Brazil asserted its own inability to meet interest payments and its intention to reschedule payments on its $91 billion debt. Other debtor countries soon defaulted. By the end of 1983, twenty-five countries with over $200 billion in outstanding debts had convinced their lenders to reschedule their loans. Once again, prompt action prevented these crises from destroying the global economy. By following the IMF prescription, most of these countries made progress in addressing their economic problems. Within a year, Mexico and Brazil had converted a payments deficit into a payments surplus and were able to continue servicing their debts.

The lender's cartel worst fear, the emergence of a debtor's cartel, almost became a reality in 1984 and 1985. In early 1984, Argentina's government announced that it would reject the IMF austerity plan and continued to threaten to defer interest payments on its debt. Argentina then proposed at the September 1984 ministerial meeting of the Latin American Economic System (SEAL) that the debtor nations devote no more than 25 percent of their export earnings to service their debts. Most members of this Cartegena Group, named after the city in which they met, rejected the proposal.

Brazil and Mexico then pressured Argentina to eventually settle with the IMF. In 1985, Peru became the only Latin American country to actually limit its payments to only 10 percent of export earnings. As a result, the global bankers refused to extend new loans to Peru and thus deterred other debtors from following Peru's lead.

The means by which global bankers managed the continuing crisis shifted throughout the 1980s. At first debt rescheduling lasted only one year so countries continued having to reschedule their debts. But in 1984, Mexico again became a trendsetter by agreeing to two repayments schemes—an initial four years program which the international lenders would extend a further 14 years if Mexico kept up with its payments. This arrangement became the model for dozens of other reschedulings.

In September 1985, U.S. Treasury Secretary Jim Baker announced a plan before the World Bank and IMF that targeted the 15 most indebted countries for comprehensive debt rescheduling. In return for the recipients agreeing to the IMF austerity program, commercial bankers would extend to them a further $20 billion and the World Bank $3 billion in credits. The Baker Plan took awhile to take off because many of the countries did not make sweeping enough reforms and commercial bankers refused to pour more money into those credit-poor countries. Although the commercial bank and World Bank targets were reached by 1988, the IMF cut back new lending, and overall, the debtor countries gave back more money to the global lenders than they received.

Thus the debt crisis continued. Many Third World countries remained trapped in a vicious economic cycle as they sent more money abroad in interest payments than they received in loans, aid, or export earnings. The more money governments diverted to pay interest on their debt, the less money they had to invest in export industries that could earn the country money. Unable to keep up with their interest payments, governments borrowed yet more money and sank further into debt and poverty. Economic stagnation often led to political instability—food riots, coups, communist insurgencies—which further gutted the economy. Those with money often sent it to safe overseas havens rather than investing it in the local economy. Third World capital flight alone is estimated to exceed its loans.[24] Between 1982 and 1988, the net outflow from the Third World was $140 billion! The 1988 outflow of $43 billion was higher than that year's total official development aid (ODA). Third World debt peaked at $1.3 trillion in 1990, a figure about half of those countries' combined GNPs and 125 percent of the total value of their exports.

Third World debt, of course, varied considerably from one region and country to the next. Africa's foreign debt represented 232 percent of its export value and 54 percent of its GNP, while debt servicing took 26 percent of all export value.[25] In 1988, the top five debtors were Brazil with $120 billion, which serviced its debt with 26.7 percent of the value of its exports, Mexico with $107 billion and 30.1 percent, Argentina with $60 billion and 45.3 percent, Venezuela with $35 billion and 22.4 percent, and Nigeria with $31 billion and 10 percent. Twelve of the twenty leading debtors were from Latin America. During the 1980s, per capita income declined by as much as 25 percent for Africans and 10 percent for Latin Americans, while the number of humans living in "absolutely poor" conditions rose from 650 to 730 million.[26]

The Baker Plan was unable to deal with these growing problems and there was pressure on the global bankers, particularly in the United States, to come up with a less stringent plan which would include widespread write-offs of debt for the poorest

Table 17.1
Debt of 15 Third World Countries, 1970 – 1990
($ billions)

Country	1970	1982	1990
Argentina	$ 8.47	$ 45.4	$ 61.1
Bolivia	.50	3.7	4.3
Brazil	6.84	85.3	116.2
Chile	2.58	18.0	19.1
Colombia	1.64	10.6	17.2
Equador	.26	7.5	12.1
Ivory Coast	.27	8.0	18.0
Mexico	5.97	87.6	96.8
Morocco	.75	11.3	23.5
Nigeria	.57	14.3	36.1
Peru	2.67	12.2	21.1
Philippines	1.56	29.5	30.5
Turkey	3.34	15.7	49.1
Venezuela	.97	37.2	33.3
Yugoslavia	2.06	20.0	20.7
Total	$ 38.05	$406.3	$559.1

Data source: World Bank (1992).

countries. In March 1989, U.S. Treasury Secretary Nicholas Brady announced a plan in which new commercial loans would be extended, more liberal means of repayment would be allowed, and in some cases there would be limited debt write-offs. The overall goal was to reduce the entire Third World debt burden by 20 percent over three years.

Mexico was once again used as a model. Commercial bankers were given a choice of three options of dealing with $54 billion of Mexico's total $69 billion debt. Two options involved buying back Mexico's debt for bonds that would either be valued at 35 percent less than the debt's face value or at the same price with a lower interest rate. The third option involved bankers extending new four year loans to Mexico at a level equal to 25 percent of the bank's exposure. These loans would be guaranteed by the IMF, World Bank, Japan, and Mexico. The first two options meant that bankers would actually write off part of Mexico's debt to them. The third option allowed Mexico to receive fresh financing while protecting the lenders against default. This Brady Plan has since been used for dozens of other debtors.

By the early 1990s, the debt crisis had passed. The Third World debt was still about $1.2 trillion in 1992, but the number of defaults had lessened considerably since the Brady Plan was adopted. A small but growing percentage of debt was retired by debt-for-equity and debt-for-nature swaps in which investors would buy debt from a Third World country in return for stock in a corporation or the government's agreement to protect an area of nature from development.

But although the crisis has passed, the debt's effects on development have been profound. While the per capita incomes of countries without debt-servicing problems rose 60 percent between 1978 and 1991, those countries that could not keep up their payments now have per capita incomes below those of 1978.[27] While foreign sources of finance are essential to Third World development, if that money is not invested wisely it may do more harm than good.

MULTINATIONAL CORPORATIONS

Liberal and dependency theorists differ totally on the role of foreign multinational corporations (MNCs) in a nation's political economic development.[28] Liberals believe that foreign investments represent a net gain for the recipient and are often the key to development. Poor countries lack money, technology, managerial skills, and access to foreign markets, and MNCs can provide all of those assets. Dependency theorists see MNCs as neocolonial powers which promise those assets in return for entry. Once entrenched, they suck out as much wealth as possible and corrupt the political process to keep that country poor and docile.

Reality, as always, is much more complex than these theories would suggest. It is impossible to generalize about foreign investments in the Third World. The relative positive and negative effects vary from one country, sector, corporation, and era to the next. For every example of a foreign investment behaving according to liberal theory, another can be found that mirrors the dependency perspective.

Potential Costs

The operations of multinational corporations in Third World countries have been criticized on many grounds. Perhaps the underlying criticism is the sheer power of most MNCs. Of the 100 largest economic entities in the world, about half are countries and the other half corporations. Many multinationals are much wealthier than many of the countries in which they invest. They thus have enormous bargaining and corrupting power to ensure they extract the best entry and operating terms from poor, weak foreign governments. MNCs offer things that poor countries desperately need, and can always play off one poor state against the others. Both before and after they have set up shop, the MNCs can always threaten to go elsewhere if the government does not surrender to its demands. By competing against each other to bribe officials for investment permits and other facilities, MNCs frequently exacerbate existing corruption. Those officials involved may gain wealth, but by allowing the MNCs often unlimited and subsidized investments, the country's development suffers and wealth flows abroad.

Although any state has the sovereign right to nationalize any businesses, foreign or domestic, international law requires that a government compensate foreign investors if it does so. If a government nationalizes an MNC's holdings without compensation, other MNCs may be afraid to invest there. Thus, that country's development will suffer the loss of potential jobs, wealth, managerial expertise, market access, and technology created by those potential foreign investments. Meanwhile, the victim will lobby its

Table 17.2

**Countries and Corporations Ranked According to Size of
Annual Product, 1989 (Countries) and 1990 (MNCs)**

Rank	Economic Entity	Dollars (millions)
1	United States	5,445,825
2	Japan	3,140,948
3	Soviet Union	2,600,000
4	Germany (Federal Republic)	1,411,346
5	France	1,099,750
6	Italy	970,619
7	United Kingdom	923,959
8	Canada	542,774
9	Spain	429,404
10	China	415,884
11	Brazil	402,788
12	India	294,816
13	Australia	290,522
14	Netherlands	258,804
15	Korea, Republic of	231,132
16	Switzerland	219,337
17	Mexico	214,500
18	Sweden	202,498
19	Belgium	154,688
20	Austria	147,016
21	Finland	129,823
22	GENERAL MOTORS (U.S.)	125,126
23	Denmark	113,515
24	ROYAL DUTCH/SHELL GROUP (Britain, Netherlands)	107,204
25	EXXON (U.S.)	105,885
26	Indonesia	101,151
27	FORD MOTOR (U.S.)	98,275
28	Norway	98,079
29	Turkey	91,742
30	South Africa	90,410
31	Saudi Arabia[1]	86,898
32	Thailand	79,044
33	Argentina	76,491
34	Yugoslavia	72,860
35	INTERNATIONAL BUSINESS MACHINES (U.S.)	69,018

Table 17.2 (Continued)

Countries and Corporations Ranked According to Size of Annual Product, 1989 (Countries) and 1990 (MNCs)

Rank	Economic Entity	Dollars (millions)
36	Hong Kong	66,666
37	TOYOTA MOTOR (Japan)	64,516
38	Poland	64,480
39	IRI (Italy)	61,433
40	Greece	60,245
41	BRITISH PETROLEUM (Britain)	59,541
42	MOBIL (U.S.)	58,770
43	GENERAL ELECTRIC (U.S.)	58,414
44	DAIMLER-BENZ (Germany)	54,259
45	Algeria	51,585
46	Israel	50,866
47	Portugal	50,692
48	HITACHI (Japan)	50,686
49	Venezuela	50,574
50	Czechoslovakia	49,225
51	FIAT (Italy)	47,752
52	SAMSUNG (South Korea)	45,042
53	PHILIP MORRIS (U.S.)	44,323
54	Philippines	43,954
55	VOLKSWAGEN (Germany)	43,710
56	MATSUSHITA ELECTRIC INDUSTRIAL (Japan)	43,516
57	New Zealand	43,185
58	Pakistan	42,649
59	ENI (Italy)	41,762
60	Malaysia	41,524
61	TEXACO (U.S.)	41,235
62	Colombia	40,805
63	NISSAN MOTOR (Japan)	40,217
64	UNILEVER (Britain, Netherlands)	39,972
65	E.I. DU PONT DE NEMOURS (U.S.)	39,839
66	CHEVRON (U.S.)	39,262
67	SIEMENS (Germany)	39,228
68	Romania	38,025
69	Singapore	33,512
70	Ireland	33,467

Table 17.2 *(Continued)*

Countries and Corporations Ranked According to Size of Annual Product, 1989 (Countries) and 1990 (MNCs)

Rank	Economic Entity	Dollars (millions)
71	NESTLÉ (Switzerland)	33,359
72	Kuwait[1]	33,089
73	ELF AQUITAINE (France)	32,939
74	United Arab Emirates	31,613
75	Egypt, Arab Republic	31,381
76	Nigeria	31,285
77	CHRYSLER (U.S.)	30,868
78	PHILIPS' GLOEILAMPENFABRIEKEN (Netherlands)	30,866
79	TOSHIBA (Japan)	30,182
80	RENAULT (France)	30,050
81	Hungary	30,047
82	PEUGEOT (France)	29,380
83	BASF (Germany)	29,184
84	AMOCO (U.S.)	28,277
85	HOECHST (Germany)	27,750
86	ASEA BROWN BOVERI (Switzerland)	27,705
87	BOEING (U.S.)	27,595
88	HONDA MOTOR (Japan)	27,070
89	ALCATEL ALSTHOM (France)	26,456
90	BAYER (Germany)	26,059
91	Chile	25,504
92	Peru	25,149
93	NEC (Japan)	24,391
94	PROCTER AND GAMBLE (U.S.)	24,376
95	Morocco	23,788
96	TOTAL (France)	23,590
97	PETRÓLEÓS DE VENEZUELA (Venezuela)	23,469
98	IMPERIAL CHEMICAL INDUSTRIES (Britain)	23,348
99	Bangladesh	22,579
100	DAEWOO (South Korea)	22,260

[1]Data are for 1989

Source: Gross national product data are from *World Bank Atlas 1991* (Washington, D.C., 1991), pp. 6–9. Gross national product data for Czechoslovakia, Romania, and the Soviet Union are from *Handbook of Economic Statistics, 1991* (Washington, D.C.: Central Intelligence Agency, 1991), p. 34. Sales of industrial firms are from *Fortune*, July 29, 1991, p. 245 John Rouke, *International Relations,* 1994.

home government to pressure the Third World government that has nationalized its holdings for compensation. They cite as examples the machinations of United Fruit Company in Guatemaula and ITT in Chile, and eventually the American backed coups which ensued in both countries when the host governments nationalized their investments. Washington is legally armed with the 1964 Hickenlooper and 1974 Gonzalez amendments which respectively empower the president to sever aid and GSP privileges with any country nationalizing American investments. The U.S. Overseas Private Investment Corporation insures businesses against loses in many though not all countries. Thus with every American foreign investment, Third World governments potentially face not only the power of that particular investor, but its home government and other MNCs.

Even when a government imposes limits on how much profit can be repatriated, the MNCs get around the limit through "transfer pricing"—the charging of enormous amounts on the equipment and components imported to their investment from other subsidiaries. The MNC does not really pay more since it is paying itself. It is simply a method to transfer profits out of the country and avoid paying taxes. As a result, the subsidiary sends home money that otherwise might have been spent on much cheaper components from indigenous businesses. By manipulating their accounts to make it look like their subsidiaries are losing money, the MNC often ends up paying little or no taxes to the host government.

Many foreign investments are seen as enclaves in which little if any wealth trickles down to the rest of the economy. Instead the investment acts like a sponge which soaks up local capital and expatriates it. For example, American investments in Latin America between 1958 to 1968 acquired 80 percent of their finance locally from loans or earnings.[29] In this way, MNCs minimize their own exposure and maximize that of their host government and local investors so that they will do all they can in support.

The MNCs often dominate the host economy's most advanced sectors, thus controlling any significant indigenous development. Once in a country, the MNC often gobbles up, Pac Man-style, other local businesses. Few local businesses can compete against an MNC, and many are bankrupted or bought out by the new investors. Productivity is usually much higher in the MNC than similar local businesses. Thus unemployment rises because local firms are often much more labor-intensive than the MNC. The foreign investors can offer more money and benefits, and better facilities to indigenous workers and thus often mop up a country's most talented workers. The MNCs create new socioeconomic classes that widen existing gaps between the "haves" and "have nots." They demand foreign luxury goods that further drain wealth from the economy and disrupt the culture. Meanwhile, there are no significant technology transfers. The technology that is invested is either obsolete or so advanced that it is inappropriate for that country. The result is often a net drain on a country's wealth and the "development of underdevelopment."

Thus, the impact of multinational firms is "seen not as external but as intrinsic to the system, with manifold and sometimes hidden or subtle political, financial, economic, technical, and cultural effects inside the underdeveloped country. These contribute significantly to shaping the nature and operation of the economy, society, and polity, a kind of 'fifth column' as it were."[30]

Potential Benefits

Despite these potential costs, most governments actively solicit investments from foreign corporations. Although Marxist dogma asserts that MNCs are neocolonial forces that enslave poor countries, even the communist governments of China, Vietnam, North Korea, and the former Yugoslavia and Soviet Union set aside their dogma and enacted policies to attract foreign investment. Few countries would attempt to attract foreign investors if the costs exceeded the benefits.

Over time, most Third World governments have become more adept at bargaining so that they maximize the gains and minimize the costs of foreign investment. Bureaucracies are slowly being filled with experts in international law, accounting, taxes, business, and other skills necessary to negotiate head to head with MNC representatives and then to carefully regulate established foreign investments. Third World power increases further after the MNC has set up shop. New regulations can be enacted and the MNC usually goes along because the compliance costs are lower than the disinvestment costs. Laws can be enacted that limit the amount of profits, royalties, and other income an MNC can repatriate, and the amount of goods an MNC can import. Domestic content and mandated export laws further encourage MNCs to buy components locally and export the finished products. Brazil, for example, has 99 percent local content requirements for its automobile industry. Other laws are even more restrictive. For example, some governments have laws whereby MNCs can only set up joint ventures in which a majority of shares are held by indigenous investors. There are "sunset laws" whereby an increased number of shares are turned over to indigenous investors until after several decades the entire operation has been nationalized. Indonesia, for example, has sunset laws of 30 years for most foreign investments. Most Latin American governments follow the Calvo Doctrine which asserts the host country's right to determine what is adequate compensation for nationalized investments.[31]

A government's success in enforcing or even enacting these laws depends on its relative power, and that power depends on how badly MNCs want access to that nation's markets and resources. Countries like Brazil, Indonesia, Mexico, and Nigeria, with their huge populations and rich resources obviously have much more bargaining power than small states with limited markets and resources. The bargaining power of virtually all Third World countries has grown as the global economy has become more competitive. Governments can play one MNC against the others, a practice that was much more difficult in the 1950s and 1960s when there were fewer MNCs and most were American.

An increasingly popular means of attracting and managing foreign investments is to designate an "export processing zone" (EPZ) in which firms can only produce for export. Host governments provide infrastructure and freedom to investors from tariffs on imported components. In return, the government and country enjoys a controlled laboratory in which to learn production, managerial, financial, and marketing skills.

There have been international attempts by both Third World and advanced industrial country groups to regulate MNC operations. At the first GATT round in Geneva in 1947, the United States attempted to enact provisions that would safeguard foreign investments against nationalization unless compensation was given. Representatives of Latin America and other developing countries succeeded in tabling the American proposal and instead pushed through provisions which allowed host governments to restrict

MNC operations. Passage of this proposal prompted American business interests to lobby against pending Senate ratification of the Havana Charter that would have created the International Trade Organization (ITO).

During the 1970s, there were several attempts to regulate foreign investments. The 1974 United Nations "Charter of Economic Rights and Duties of States" declares the sovereign right of nationalization but says only that compensation should be appropriate, thus giving governments wide latitude in determining it. That same year, the United Nations followed up the Charter by creating a Center on Transnational Corporations that collects data on international investment flows, and, in 1975, a Commission on Transnational Corporations in which issues are debated. But neither of these two organizations has adequately addressed the question of how to determine compensation for nationalized assets. In 1980, UNCTAD formulated a code that regulated MNC business practices including transfer pricing and cartels. There was a wave of nationalizations during the 1970s, most of which were in extraction investments. But the practice has declined since then as host governments have acquired more skill at indirectly managing foreign investments.

In 1977, Congress addressed a different foreign investment issue by passing the Foreign Corrupt Practices Act, which made it illegal for American firms to use bribes to obtain foreign business. Shortly thereafter, with considerable American pressure, the Organization for Economic Cooperation and Development (OECD) issued its "Guidelines on International Investment and Multinational Enterprise," but the provisions are nonbinding and vague. Except for the U.S. Foreign Corrupt Practices Act, neither the UN or OECD measures are legally binding.

During the 1980s, foreign investments in South Africa were heavily criticized by some people who argued that they strengthened the apartheid system. Leon Sullivan, a former GM board member proposed what became known as the "Sullivan principles" as voluntary guidelines for American firms doing business in South Africa. These rules include the desegregation of the workplace and equal treatment for black, colored, and white South Africans. In 1986, Congress passed the Comprehensive Anti-Apartheid Act which prevented U.S. firms from investing further in South Africa or extending loans to the government. Other countries including the European Community, Canada, and the British Commonwealth imposed similar restrictions on their firms' business with South Africa. Hundreds of foreign firms closed down their South African businesses as a result of these restrictions. The sanctions may have helped convince South Africa's government to begin to dismantle the apartheid system.

Some go so far as to argue that MNCs can evolve into truly global organizations that transcend national concerns. This global vision was perhaps best expressed by an IBM president in 1970 who argued that:

> *For business purposes the boundaries that separate one nation from another are no more real than the equator. They are merely convenient demarcations of ethnic, linguistic, and cultural entities. They do not define business requirements or consumer trends. Once management understands and accepts this world economy, its view of the marketplace—and its planning—necessarily expand. The world outside the home country is no longer viewed as a series of disconnected customers and prospects for its products, but as an extention of a single market.[32]*

World Bank President A. Clausen went even further, arguing that "the idea that this kind of business enterprise can be a strong force toward world peace is not so far-fetched. Beyond the human values involved, the multinational firm has a direct, measurable, and potent interest in helping prevent wars and other serious upheavals that cut off its resources, interrupt its communications, and kills its employees and customers."[33]

Evaluation

The issue of direct foreign MNC investments in the Third World must be put in perspective. First, as we have seen, about 75 percent of MNC direct foreign investments are within the First World. Of those in the Third World, many are concentrated in a few countries. In 1990, five countries—Singapore, Brazil, Mexico, China, and Hong Kong—accounted for more than half of all accumulated investments in the Third World. Although mining corporations have invested wherever there are viable sources of minerals and oil, manufacturing investments tend to be limited to those countries with favorable infrastructure, markets, and policies. Thus, although direct foreign investment may be a minuscule portion of Third World GNP, the investments are often a prominent portion of the recipient's GNP and are concentrated in the economy's most advanced sectors. Because they are highly capital- and technology-intensive, extractive investments particularly tend to take over that entire sector. Until the early 1970s, the Western oil corporations controled virtually all oil in the Middle East, while huge multinationals dominated the copper industries of Zambia and Chile and the bauxite mines of Jamaica. MNCs from each of the three superpowers had their own cluster of poorer countries in which they invested. The Europeans invested heavily in Eastern Europe, the Soviet Union, and Brazil; the Americans throughout Latin America, the Philippines, and Saudi Arabia; the Japanese in East and Southeast Asia.[34]

Furthermore, when most people think of MNCs they imagine the IBMs, Toyotas, and Philips of the advanced industrial countries. In fact many MNCs are based in Third World countries like India, South Korea, Venezuela, and Nigeria, to name a few. In the mid-1980s, there were over 10,000 Third World MNCs with over 90,000 foreign subsidiaries.[35] Most of these Third World MNCs, however, are much smaller than those from the advanced industrial countries. Many of these Third World MNCs invest in other poor countries.

MNCs invest overseas for many reasons—access to cheap labor, closed markets, raw material, energy resources, farm land, technology, or lax regulations. A corporation that provides a good or service to another corporation may well set up shop overseas when its client does. The bottom line is that foreign investments should make money.

Firms are sometimes pulled overseas by the actions of foreign governments that attempt to attract foreign investment by raising trade barriers while offering investment subsidies to foreign firms. These government subsidies can include free or cheap land, tax holidays, grants, loans, and infrastructure. MNCs can increase the amount of incentives they receive by playing one government against the others.

Firms are sometimes pushed overseas by their own governments. For example, starting in the late 1960s, Tokyo offered incentives to heavily polluting Japanese industries to move overseas in order to "houseclean" Japan. The United States tax code has encouraged many American corporations to move their operations overseas by deferring taxes on their income until they bring it home. As a result, most MNCs simply reinvest it elsewhere overseas. American firms can also deduct any taxes paid to overseas governments from the taxes they owe the United States. President Reagan's Caribbean Initiative, starting in 1985, offered tax credits and other benefits to U.S. corporations which invested in the region. The White House encourages this migration to help develop those countries; the trouble is that it means more unemployment, lower tax receipts, and greater socioeconomic problems in the United States.

Most MNCs reflect the culture, values, and sometimes even policies of the countries in which they are headquartered. For example, although it has not always been successful, the White House has not hesitated to pressure American corporations to follow government policy when the situation demands. It has imposed an economic embargo on American sales to Cuba since 1961. In 1968, the White House forbade the sale of factory equipment from a Belgian subsidiary of an American company to Cuba even though the Belgian firm had struck the deal before it was acquired by the American firm. Although Washington tried, it failed to rally American petroleum corporations around the flag when OPEC quadrupled oil prices in 1973. The American firms instead went along with OPEC, fearing that to do otherwise might result in all of their foreign assets being nationalized. In 1982, the Reagan adminstration ordered American firms to stop selling equipment that would be used for a gas pipeline from the Soviet Union to Europe. The result was that European firms got the business that the White House denied to American firms. And sometimes U.S. government policies follow the pressure of American MNCs. The White House helped topple the governments of Guatemala in 1954 and Chile in 1973 when the American corporations United Fruit and ITT complained that their respective investments in those countries were nationalized without adequate compensations.[36] But these dramatic examples are the exception rather than the rule and may well disappear in the post Cold War era.

There is conflicting evidence over an MNC's effect on the recipient's international trade and payments accounts, with some studies showing a net gain and others a net loss. Traditionally, the foreign investments of MNCs in Third World countries were twice as profitable as those in other advanced industrial countries. The balance changed during the 1980s. Now the reverse is true. Yet foreign investments, if managed properly, can be a net gain for the host country.

The relationship between MNCs and host countries varies widely from one country and time to the next. Some Third World countries are increasingly able to play one MNC against others that want entry, and thus extract more profit from the investment. Other Third World countries remain largely impotent in the face of MNC power and must accept the dictated terms.

FUTURE NORTH-SOUTH RELATIONS AND DEVELOPMENT

The Third World was the primary battleground during the Cold War as Washington, Moscow, and, for a time, Beijing competed to gain the loyalty of different governments. In doing so, they and the other advanced industrial countries lavished considerable aid, trade, and investment benefits throughout the Third World. Now that the Cold War is over, will the attention and resources previously extended toward the Third World dwindle? About 75 percent of international trade and investments already occur among the most advanced industrial countries, and this percentage is expected to rise. President Clinton has promised to "put America first," and the leaders of other advanced industrial nations are following suit by pushing their own respective interests. How will this affect Third World development?

Geopolitically, the entire Third World no longer commands the interest that it once did when both Washington and Moscow believed that every country, no matter how poor, small, or distant, was vital in the global power balance. Other than the Persian Gulf, no region has vital geopolitical importance. No longer the object of Cold War rivalries and the accompanying burden of high military spending, military coups, insurrections, and ideological stridency, most Third World countries can now focus their efforts on political and economic development.

Any development successes within the Third World, however, will come from immersion within rather than isolation from the global political economy. Third World attempts to gain more trade and investment concessions from the advanced industrial countries through its UNCTAD and NIEO agenda have largely failed. There were eight UNCTAD conferences between 1962 and 1992, and at best the participants succeeded in getting NIEO issues on the agenda and articulating the concerns of most less developed nations. The commodity bargaining power that the Third World enjoyed during the 1970s dissipated during the 1980s and 1990s. Meanwhile, the so-called Third World is becoming increasingly diversified as newly industrializing countries (NICs) break free of it, thus further undermining its political solidarity. More and more governments have converted to the belief that expanding market power rather than state power is the key to successful development. Increasingly the Group of Seventy-Seven is willing to accommodate itself to rather than transform the global political economy.

The Group of Seventy-Seven is being eclipsed by the emergence of a dozen regional free trade associations throughout the Third World. For example, in January 1992, a summit of the six members of the Association for Southeast Asian Nations (ASEAN) agreed to form a free trade association over the next fifteen years. In June 1992, the presidents of Argentina, Brazil, Uruguay, and Paraguay met and agreed to create a free trade zone by 1995, a union that would combine 190 million people and $450 billion in GNP. The leaders also agreed to harmonize their tax and investment policies to bring down inflation and attract more foreign investment. In November 1992, the Caribbean Economic Community (CARICOM) agreed to reduce its common external tariff (CET) from 45 percent to 35 percent by January 1, 1993, and eventually to 20 percent in 1998.

Overall, the development and trade performance of the Third World has been mixed. The Third World annually grew an average 6.1 percent between 1960 and 1980 and 3.8 percent between 1980 and 1986. Growth rates, however, varied considerably from one country to the next. East Asia's Newly Industrializing Countries (NICs) grew at a phenomenal rate while the economic conditions in some countries stagnated or even worsened. In 1986, the average per capita income for industrialized countries was $12,960 and less developed states $610.[37]

The Third World steadily accounts for a lower percentage of global trade. From 1950 through today, the total Third World share of world exports fell from about 31 percent in 1950 to about 15 percent today, while Latin America's share fell from about

12 percent to 5 percent. These statistics may not be as bad as they seem. In Latin America's case, exports have risen steadily but not as quickly as in other areas of the world, hence the decline as a percentage of the global total. The Third World is becoming increasingly dependent on the global trade system. Between 1970 and 1990, the ratio of exports to gross domestic product within the Third World rose from 11 percent to 25 percent.

However, the importance of the less developed countries to the industrial countries is diminishing. About 60 percent of the industrialized countries' trade and 75 percent of its foreign investments are with each other. To make matters worse, the industrialized countries often block competitive Third World exports, which further reduces the export earnings of Third World countries. In 1986, the advanced countries imposed non-tariff barriers on 21 percent of all Third World imports and only 16 percent of imports from other industrial countries.[38] The more interdependent the global economy, the more a depression or price-drop elsewhere can disrupt an already troubled society. Countries dependent on one crop or mineral for much of their earnings can be devastated when the global demand and thus price for that commodity drops precipitously.

Yet some countries in the Third World have experienced considerable industrialization, and as a group the percentage of commodities to total exports has dropped from 80 percent in 1960 to 45 percent in 1990, while manufactured exports have risen from 20 percent to 54 percent. The East Asian NICs, however, accounted for over 65 percent of all Third World manufactured exports, while Mexico, Brazil, and Argentina exported another 15 percent share. Despite this industrialization, in 1992 the Third World accounted for only about 11 percent of global manufacturing. Industrialization can bring penalties as well as prosperity. In 1989, the United States removed South Korea, Singapore, Hong Kong, and Taiwan from those countries to which it granted the GSP.

Third World trade problems were exacerbated by the debt crisis of the 1980s. Third World countries diverted an increasing percentage of their export earnings and savings to servicing their respective debts, thus undercutting their economic growth and worsening the debt. The global financial system itself was at risk. The fear was that the default of two or more of the biggest debtors would destroy the global financial system and plunge the world into a deep, intractable depression, possibly setting off a chain reaction of economic collapse and communist revolutions around the world. By the 1980s, the global debt crisis had diminished. Bankers agreed to write off a large part of Third World debt, oil prices were halved, and the global economy began to expand again, thus giving borrowers the export revenues with which to service their debts. Despite these improvements, throughout the 1980s into the 1990s, banks have steadily reduced the percentage of their total loans to developing countries.

Poor as well as rich countries can benefit from international trade and investments. It is a government's responsibility to ensure that its country maximizes the potential gains and minimizes the potential costs of international trade and investment in an increasingly interdependent global political economy. Most Third World regions and countries have geoeconomic importance—whether it be for its markets, resources, or industries—and thus will remain important to multinational corporations and the countries in which they are headquartered. Foreign aid will continue, and while its total volume may stagnate or even diminish for some countries, the content will increasingly be economic rather than military assistance.

In terms of political leverage, the global environmental crisis presents the Third World with the opportunities for extracting wealth and technology from the more advanced states that the Cold War once did. At the Rio de Janeiro environmental conference in June 1992, the Third World countries argued that any costs associated with dealing with the greenhouse effect and ozone layer should be born by the rich countries. The Third World would continue to industrialize, and if the rich countries were concerned about pollution then they would be forced to transfer the technology and wealth necessary to cut air and water emissions.

STUDY QUESTIONS

1. How do we explain the vast gulf between the world's few rich countries and its many poor countries? Why have a few Third World countries successfully developed and most others failed? Why cannot all poor countries be equally successful?

2. What role do the global economy and relations between advanced industrial and Third World countries play in development or underdevelopment?

3. What are the terms used to designate the world's relatively poorer and richer countries? In what ways are these terms inadequate?

4. What are the major complaints that Third World countries have in regards to their terms of trade with the industrialized countries?

5. What were the major demands of the Group of Seventy-Seven for the New International Economic Order? How many of these demands have been realized?

6. What accounts for OPEC's rise and fall, and for its successes and failures?

7. What are the controversies surrounding foreign aid?

8. What led to the world debt crisis? How was the crisis managed?

9. What are the potential costs and benefits for Third World countries of allowing foreign investments by MNCs?

10. The same question haunts the issues of personal development, the relative prosperity of different ethnic, religious, and racial groups in the United States and elsewhere. Does one's material status depend more on individual or cultural endowments or does the answer lie elsewhere? Is it nature or nurture?

ENDNOTES

1. World Bank, *World Development Report* (New York: Oxford University Press, 1988).

2. For some excellent recent studies, see Richard Feinberg and Delia Boylan, *Modular Multilateralism: North South Economic Relations in the 1990s* (Washington, D.C.: Overseas Development Council, 1991); Ivan Head, *On a Hinge of History: The Mutual Vulnerability of South and North* (Toronto: University of Toronto

Press, 1991); G.K. Helleiner, *The New Global Economy and the Developing Countries* (Brookfield, Vt.: Edward Elgar, 1990); Edward Weisband, ed., *Poverty Amidst Plenty* (Boulder, Colo.: Westview Press, 1989).

3. Dennis Pirages, *The New Context for International Relations: Global Ecopolitics* (North Scituate, Mass.: Duxbury Press, 1978), 170.

4. International Monetary Fund, *World Economic Outlook, 1991* (Washington, D.C.: World Bank, 1991).

5. World Bank, *World Development Report, 1991* (New York: Oxford University Press, 1991), 35.

6. See William Cline, *Systemic Risk and Policy Response* (New York: Washington, D.C.: Institute for International Economics, 1984).

7. Morris Miller, *Resolving the Global Debt Crisis* (New York: United Nations Development Program, Policy Division, 1989), 33.

8. United Nations General Assembly, 18th Session, *Official Records: Eighteenth Session,* Supplement no. 7, (A 5507), 24.

9. See Paul Prebisch, *Towards a New Trade Policy for Development, report by the Secretary General of the United Nations conference on Trade and Development,* E/CONF 46/3 (New York: United Nations, 1964).

10. David Blake and Robert Walters, *The Politics of Global Economic Relations* (Englewood Cliffs, N.J.: Prentice-Hall, 1987), 194.

11. For the definitive study on oil, see Daniel Yergin, *The Prize: The Epic Quest for Oil, Money, and Power* (New York: Simon & Schuster, 1991).

12. Mira Wilkins, *The Maturing of Multinational Enterprise: American Business Abroad from 1914 to 1970* (Cambridge, Mass.: Harvard University Press, 1974), 386–387.

13. Morris Adelman, *The World Petroleum Market* (Baltimore: Johns Hopkins Press, 1972), 207.

14. Joan Spero, *The Politics of International Economic Relations* (New York: St Martin's Press, 1990), 265.

15. Ibid, 277.

16. For two somewhat different views, see John Lewis, and Valeriana Kallab, eds., *Development Strategies Reconsidered* (New Brunswick, N.J.: Transaction Books, 1986); Peter Bauer, *Equality, the Third World, and Economic Illusion* (Cambridge, Mass.: Harvard University Press, 1981).

17. Joan Spero, *The Politics of International Economic Relations,* 161.

18. Joan M. Nelson, *Aid, Influence, and Foreign Policy* (New York: Macmillan, 1968).

19. Organization for Economic Cooperation and Development, *Development Cooperation: 1987 Review* (Paris: OECD, 1987), 327; For an excellent critique of Reagan administration aid policies, see John Sewell and Christine Contee, "U.S. Foreign Aid in the 1980's: Reordering Priorities," in Kendall Stiles and Tsuneo Akaha, eds., *International Political Economy* (New York: HarperCollins, 1991), 308–347.

20. See Richard Feinberg and Valeriana Kallab, eds., *Between Two Worlds: The World Bank's Next Decade* (New Brunswick, N.J.: Transaction Books, 1986).

21. Robert Cassen, *Does Aid Work?: Report to an Intergovernmental Task Force* (Oxford: Clarendon Press, 1986), 24–25.

22. Frank Miller, *Resolving Global Debt Crisis* (New York: St. Martin's Press, 1989), 50.

23. World Bank, *World Debt Tables* (Washington, D.C.: 1988).

24. Frank Miller, *Resolving Global Debt Crisis*, 42.

25. Ibid, 24.

26. Frank Miller, *Resolving Global Debt Crisis*, 52.

27. Charles Kegley and Eugene Wittkopf, *World Politics Trend and Transformation* (New York: St. Martin's Press, 1992), 293.

28. For arguments for the positive effect of MNCs, see Raymond Vernon, *Restrictive Business Practices* (New York: United Nations, 1972); Herbert May, *The Contributions of U.S. Private Investment to Latin America's Growth* (New York: The Council for Latin America, 1970); John Dunning, "Multinational Enterprises and Nation States," in A. Kapoor and Phillip D. Grub, eds., *The Multinational Enterprise in Transition* (Princeton, N.J.: Darwin Press, 1974); For arguments of the negative effect, see Richard Barnet and Ronald Muller, *Global Reach* (New York: Simon & Schuster, 1974), and the dependency theorists.

29. Ronald Muller, "Poverty is the Product," *Foreign Affairs*, vol. 13, Winter 1973–1974, 85–90; See also Sidney Robbins and Robert Stobaugh, *Money in the Multinational Enterprise: A Study of Financial Policy* (New York: Basic Books, 1972, 63–71.

30. Oswaldo Sunkel, "Big Business and 'Dependencia,'" *Foreign Affairs*, vol. 50, April 1972, 523; See also Volker Bornschier and Christopher Chase-Dunn, *Transnational Corporations and Underdevelopment* (New York: Praeger, 1985).

31. Paul Sigmund, *Multinationals in Latin America: The Politics of Nationalization* (Madison, Wis.: University of Wisconsin, 1980).

32. Richard Barnett and Ronald Muller, *Global Reach: The Rise of Multinational Corporations* (New York: Simon & Schuster, 1974), 14–15.

33. A. W. Clausen, "The Internationalized Corporation: An Executive's View," *The Annals, The American Academy of Political and Social Science*, vol. 403, 1972, 21.

34. "Foreign Investment and the Triad," *The Economist*, August 24, 1991.

35. David Blake and Robert Walters, *The Politics of Global Economic Relations* (Englewood Cliffs, N.J.: Prentice-Hall, 1987), 94.

36. See Raymond Vernon, *Sovereignty at Bay* (New York: Basic Books, 1971); Richard Barnet and Ronald Muller, *Global Reach: The Rise of Multinational Corporations*.

37. World Bank, *World Development Report, 1988*, 225, 223.

38. United Nations Development Program, *World Development Report, 1991*, 105.

Fate of the Earth

The Global Environmental Crisis

Key Terms and Concepts

Albedo
Carbon Dioxide
Chlorofluorocarbons
  (CFCs)
Deforestation
Desertification
Evapotranspiration
Global Warming Treaty
Green Revolution

Greenhouse Effect
Halon
Malthus
Methane
Montreal Protocol
Nitrous Oxide
Ozone Layer Depletion
Photosynthesis
Population Explosion

Rio de Janeiro
Stockholm
Sustained Yield
Tragedy of the Commons
United Nations
  Environmental Program
  (UNEP)
United Nations Population
  Fund (UNPF)

We master nature by obeying her.
(Francis Bacon)

*The substance of man cannot be measured by the Gross National Product. Perhaps it
cannot be measured at all, except for certain symptoms of loss.*
(E.M. Schumacher)

*What does it mean to redefine one's relationship to the sky? What will it do to our children's
outlook on life if we have to teach them to be afraid to look up?*
(Albert Gore)

In 1970, the ecologist Garret Hardin wrote, *The Tragedy of the Commons,* in which
he describes a New England town common upon which everyone can graze their sheep
but no one is accountable for its upkeep.[1] Without limitations on its use, the commons
is eventually overgrazed and destroyed. As people observe the common's degradation,
their impulse is to graze their livestock there as much as possible before its eventual dis-
appearance, thus accelerating that destruction. Those who grazed livestock there gained
in the short run; everyone in the village lost over the long-term.

Humanity faces the same "tragedy of the commons" with the earth. Within fifty
years, the world's current population of 5.4 billion will more than double to 11.5 billion. Like people today, future generations will demand an ever higher living standard
and quality of life. If the present global income distribution remains constant, the demand for goods, services, energy, recreation, and quality of life will double with the
population. In fact, people's material demands are growing even faster than the population, which means most people are getting wealthier.

The trouble is that the earth is rapidly reaching a crisis point where it can no longer sustain the material demands made upon it. The earth is being steadily degraded by several interrelated and accelerating environmental catastrophes— the *population explosion,* the *greenhouse effect, ozone layer depletion, deforestation, desertification,* air and water pollution, species extinction, and a worsening food shortage. Since the industrial revolution began two centuries ago, an ever growing amount of gases and chemicals have poured into and been trapped in the atmosphere. This buildup traps increasing amounts of heat that ordinarily would dissipate into the universe. The worsening greenhouse effect could result in the earth heating another four degrees over the next 50 years, leading to catastrophic climatic changes. Meanwhile, a variety of chemicals eat away at the ozone layer in the atmosphere which prevents many of the sun's ultraviolet rays from reaching the earth. As the ozone layer deteriorates, the increased ultraviolet radiation will destroy plants and microscopic animals on up the food chain, ultimately threatening human food sources. Around the world, rapidly growing populations have converted once bountiful regions into desert. Environmental refugees fleeing the world's most degraded lands increase demands on steadily diminishing productive lands elsewhere, thus quickening their degradation. The number of people and percentage of the world's population afflicted by famine, drought, floods, poverty, malnutrition, and joblessness will increase. Within fifty years, while billions more humans will lack even such basics as water, food, fuel, or shelter—as in Garret's overgrazed commons—every human will be hurt directly or indirectly by the earth's worsening degradation. Lester Brown clearly states the crisis' essence: "the global economy is literally destroying the natural systems that support it."[2]

Over the past two decades, environmental concerns have crept up the international agenda of priorities. The first comprehensive attempt to identify and deal with the range of environmental crises was the 1972 Stockholm Conference on the Human Environment and the creation of the United Nations Environmental Program (UNEP). Unfortunately, nothing much came from this initiative as most countries concentrated on geopolitical or geoeconomic issues for the next decade. Then during the mid-1980s, environmental concerns once again became a priority. Soviet President Gorbachev initiated a period of detente which alleviated Cold War tensions and allowed governments to pay more attention to other concerns. In 1986, the Chernobyl nuclear plant in the Soviet Union exploded, causing a massive release of radioactivity which devastated the region and drifted over Europe. In 1987, the United Nations published "Our Common Future," which systematically analyzed the environmental threats to humankind. Also in 1987, scientists discovered a hole in the ozone layer over Antarctica which encouraged 43 nations to sign the Montreal Protocol in which they agreed to reduce their production and use of chlorofluorocarbons which destroy the ozone layer. In 1988, to the surprise of many, highly conservative Prime Minister Margaret Thatcher declared herself a "green" and urged sweeping international efforts to deal with the world's worsening environmental catastrophes. In 1989, green parties won 15 percent of the vote in European Community parliamentary elections. In July 1989, the Group of Seven meeting of the leaders of the United States, Japan, Germany, France, Italy, Britain, and Canada announced that environmental threats to the world were as important as economic ones. By the late 1980s, more than 140 countries had national environmental agencies, up from 25 countries in 1972. In 1992, the Earth Summit at Rio de Janeiro brought together 7,000 representatives of 178 nations and 8,000 journalists. Two treaties were signed, one addressing the greenhouse effect and the other biodiversity.

These international efforts to manage the world's environmental crises are encouraging, but will they and subsequent agreements be enough to reverse the earth's rapid degradation? This chapter will explore those interrelated environmental crises and the international efforts to overcome them.

OVERPOPULATION

All the world's environmental problems inevitably result from too many people demanding too much of the planet. In "An Essay on the Principle of Population" (1798), Thomas Malthus predicted that in the future the world's population would grow exponentially while its food grew arithmetically. The result would ultimately be mass famine and death.

Malthus was certainly right about population. Between the time of Jesus and Malthus, the world's population increased from roughly 200 million people to 1 billion. Until then, population had grown very slowly, probably no more than 0.2 percent annually. Then, during the eighteenth and nineteenth centuries, the world's population boomed with the interrelated agricultural, industrial, technological, and medical revolutions that started in Europe and were spread globally through imperialism. Advances in health, hygiene, and food production and distribution cut infant mortality and malnutrition and allowed people to live longer. Population grew at an increasingly faster rate, as much as 2 to 3 percent annually in the poorest countries. By 1900, the world's population was 1.6 billion; by 1950 it had risen to 2.5 billion; by 1970 it was 3.6 billion; and by 1992 it was 5.4 billion! In 1900, there were 16 cities with one million or more people; in 1990, there were 276.[3]

In April 1992, the *UN Population Fund* (UNPF) published a study which projected that the world's population would annually increase by 97 million until 2000 then drop to 90 million for 25 years and finally diminish to 60 million until by 2050, the world's population reached 11.6 billion. That estimate may be very optimistic since it assumes significant decreases in the birth rate from 3.8 to 3.3 children per mother by the year 2000.

Almost 97 percent of that population increase is in the Third World. In 1950, Third World countries had twice the population of advanced industrial countries; in 1990, they had three times as many people; and by 2020 they are expected to have four and a half times more mouths to feed. One of five people is from China, while almost 45 percent of the world's population is Asian. Although most industrialized countries will achieve zero-population growth, America's population is expected to grow from 250 million to 383 million between 1990 and 2050. Although some of that growth will come from the birth rate, America's growing population also will swell from political, economic, and environmental refugees from around the world.[4]

A nation's birth rate is shaped by many factors. In traditional cultures, large families are a source of social prestige and economic security. A man is highly regarded if he fathers many children, in some cultures even with two or more mothers. Another reason

Figure 18.1
The Population Explosion

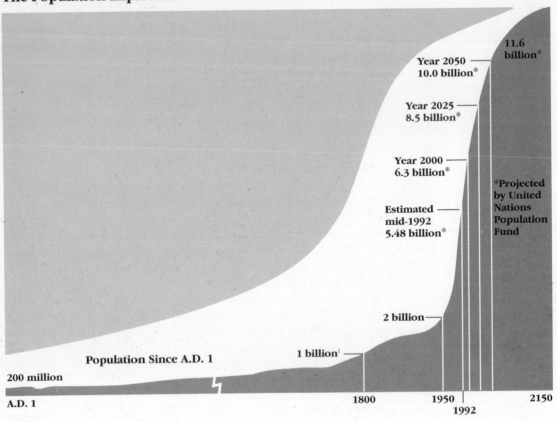

Nancy Sterngold/The New York Times; Illustration by Patricia J. Wynne

¹Nations Population Fund

is the lack of education about, and access to, contraception. Outside of China, only 30 percent of people in the Third World have access to contraception. The wealthier and more educated a population, the lower its birth rate. Population increases tend to slow only after a country reaches a per capita income of $1,000. The world's wealthiest nations have actually experienced stagnant or declining birth rates, and those populations have increased only through immigration.

While the percentage of people living in absolute poverty decreased from 52 percent in 1970 to 44 percent in 1985, the number increased from 944 million to 1.1 billion.[5] Birth rates have dropped globally over the last two decades. Between 1970 and 1990, the number of births per woman dropped from an average 6.4 to 6.1 in Africa, from 5.5 to 3.6 in Latin America and the Caribbean, from 5.9 to 4.6 in Asia and the Pacific, and from 2.6 to 1.6 in the advanced industrial nations.[6]

Throughout the modern era, new technologies have enabled an increased percentage of the world's population to lead better lives, allowing some to argue that overpopulation was a myth. During the 1980s the economist Julian Simon, asserted that the

Figure 18.2
**Population Age Pyramids for Developed and Developing
Countries, 1985 and 2025**

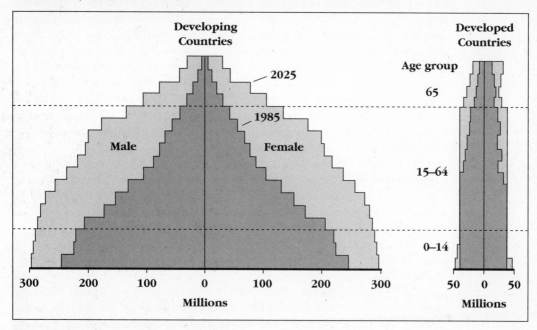

Source: Thomas W. Merrick, "World Population in Transition." *Population Bulletin,* vol. 41, no. 2 (Washington, D.C.: Population Reference Bureau, Inc. January 1988 reprint), pp. 4–19.

more people on the planet the better since there would be more minds to think up new technologies to improve living standards and a larger market in which firms can achieve scales economies.[7]

Most analysts dismiss optimists like Simon and warn that the world's rapidly increasing population will eventually devastate the planet, bringing misery to all. They argue that a massive, systematic international effort must be undertaken simply to slow the world's population increase to a doubling rather than tripling by 2020. Family planning education and access to contraception must become universal; research must be intensified on finding safe, cheap, easily administered contraception; and sustained development must be achieved. All of this costs money and requires organization, time, and political will.

Although the UNPF attempts to encourage family planning and contraception, its efforts have been undercut by some governments for religious or ideological reasons. In 1984 at the International Conference on Population in Mexico City, the Reagan administration anounced that henceforth it would withdraw American financial and political support from international population control programs, including the United Nations Population Fund and the International Planned Parenthood Federation. At the 1992 Rio de Janeiro Earth Summit, the population issue was forced off the agenda by the Bush administration, Vatican, and Saudi Arabia.

Family planning remains a national rather than international policy, with some states trying to curb population growth while most others are either unable to unwilling to do so. No country has taken more sweeping population control measures than China whose government promotes one-child families as the ideal. To that end, the government gives extra benefits for 14 years to a couple that has one child, takes those benefits away with the second child, and imposes a tax on the third child. Birth control clinics and family planning information are widely disseminated. These one-child incentives are reinforced by local officials who pressure women pregnant with a second child to have an abortion.

China's policies have been successful. Between 1960 and 1985, the birth rate dropped from 6.0 to 2.4 children per couple, a 60 percent drop. During the same period, Mexico's dropped from 7.2 to 3.8 or 47 percent; Brazil's from 6.2 to 3.4 or 45 percent; Indonesia's from 5.6 to 3.5 or 38 percent; and India's from 6.2 to 4.3 or 31 percent. Then, from 1988 to 1992, the average number of children born per woman in China dropped from 2.4 to 1.9, a level comparable to that of the advanced industrial democracies.[8] Yet many have criticized China's policy for the pressure exerted on women to abort any additional children, as well as the unintended effect of leading to the infanticide of female babies who are not valued as much as male babies.

Tragically, natural forces such as famine and disease may succeed where governments have failed in curbing population. As the earth's arable land diminishes and population increases, food is becoming scarcer and often nonexistent for many. The result is mass famine in which millions die. Disease, too, can devastate populations. For example, in some countries and regions, AIDS may drastically reduce birth rates. The African countries worst hit by the AIDS epidemic may see their births rates fall below zero by the year 2000.[9]

GREENHOUSE EFFECT

We take our life on earth for granted. Few understand how fragile our existence and all forms of life actually are. Only 0.03 percent of the earth's atmosphere is carbon dioxide; most of the rest is nitrogen. While seemingly minuscule, that carbon dioxide is essential. If there were no carbon dioxide in the atmosphere the earth would be 34 degrees centigrade colder and ice covered. Life exists on earth because the amount of carbon dioxide in the atmosphere traps just enough heat. Other planets are not so lucky. Mars has too little carbon dioxide so the planet is lifeless and frozen; Venus has too much so the planet's surface is so hot that lead melts.

Human beings have severely disrupted the earth's atmosphere to the point where it may eventually no longer sustain any life. On June 23, 1988, Dr. James Hansen, director of NASA's Goddard Institute for Space Studies, announced before a Senate committee that: "Global warming has begun."[10] The United Nations Intergovernmental Panel on Climate Change began investigating the possibility in 1988; in 1990, they announced the same conclusions that the earth was clearly heating up and the greenhouse effect was to blame. These studies proved a theory that has been around for almost a century. The greenhouse effect was predicated as early as 1896 by the Swedish chemist

Svante Arrhenius who argued that the burning of fossil fuels would eventually lead to the earth's warming. A 1957 study by the Scripps Institute of Oceanography estimated that half of all carbon dioxide released was being trapped in the atmosphere.

The greenhouse effect can be measured several ways. One is through examining ice cores drawn from the polar caps. In the mid-1980s, French and Russian scientists examined a 2000 meter core taken from Antartica which contained 160,000 years of accumulated ice and tiny air bubbles. By analyzing the chemical composition of each layer, they determined the amount of carbon dioxide in the atmosphere from today back to 160,000 years ago. The results from that ice core sample accord perfectly with measurements taken from a laboratory in Hawaii which has been analyzing carbon dioxide in the atmosphere since 1958.

During the last ice age 18,000 years ago, carbon dioxide concentrations in the atmosphere were 195 parts per million, a rate that increased slowly to 280 parts per million by the late 1770s. The industrial revolution was fueled by increased amounts of coal and later oil, the leading source of carbon dioxide in the atmosphere. In just three decades between 1958 to 1988, the amount of carbon dioxide in the atmosphere increased from 315 to 349 parts per million, the highest concentration in 160,000 years! Today, carbon dioxide has reached 352 parts per million, is increasing at a rate of 1.2 parts per million annually, and, if nothing is done, is expected to double within the next century.

There is a clear connection between greenhouse gas emissions and temperature increases. In the late nineteenth century, scientists began making the first systematic readings of global temperatures. In the 1890s, average global temperatures were about 58.2 degrees Fahrenheit; by the 1980s, they had risen to an average 59.4 degrees, or over one full degree. Six of the hottest years on record have occurred since 1980. Temperatures affect and are affected by "patterns of cloud cover, precipitation, winds, ocean currents, and glaciation."[11] Not only have average temperatures been hotter over the last decade, but global climates have been far more erratic than usual. Droughts, floods, hurricanes, and wild regional swings in temperature have been severe and will worsen.

The greenhouse effect is rapidly accelerating. The result will be a disaster for many, and economic and physical discomfort for all. The greenhouse effect could cause the average earth temperature to rise from three to eight degrees Fahrenheit by the year 2030, which would be the warmest the earth has been for over 2 million years! Humans will definitely feel the heat. For example, it is estimated that Washington D.C.s annual number of days with temperatures above 90 degrees will rise from thirty-six to eighty-seven, and days above 100 degrees from one to twelve. Regional climates would be severely affected with temperate regions moving north and leaving desert behind. Global precipitation rates would rise overall, but desertification would begin or be hastened in many regions. If the frozen tundra begins to melt, it will release huge amounts of methane that will further accelerate the greenhouse effect and make it unstoppable. Some argue that a global warming of six degrees will melt some of the polar ice caps which in turn could cause ocean levels to rise as much as three feet. Low lying regions around the world would be inundated with seawater. The greenhouse crisis could displace hundreds of millions of environmental refugees and their livelihoods. They would flee flooded coastal or drought-stricken areas for less affected regions which would then be devastated as their carrying capacity is overwhelmed.

Figure 18.3
Atmospheric Concentration of Carbon Dioxide, 1750–1988

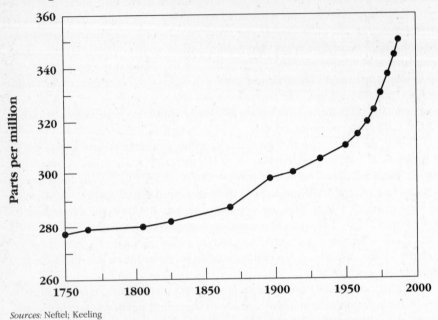

Sources: Neftel; Keeling

Figure 18.4
Global Average Temperatures, 1880–1988

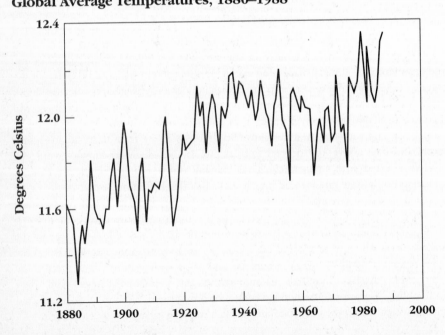

Despite these dire predictions, some argue that the greenhouse effect will help rather than harm most of humanity.[12] Not everyone on the planet would lose out from global warming—at least not for the first decades after the effects became severe. Northern Europe, Russia, and Canada would become warmer, their farm production would grow and heating bills would drop. As for fears of the ice caps melting, warmer temperatures will cause more snow in the polar ice caps that would actually increase the glaciers, and create more clouds worldwide that would reflect more heat from the sun back into space.

Who is right, the pessimists or optimists? In itself, the greenhouse effect might not be a catastrophe. But the greenhouse effect is only one link in a chain of interrelated environmental crises, such as overpopulation, deforestation, desertification, and a diminishing ozone layer that are unlikely to be significantly slowed, let alone solved. Even with a concerted international effort, the greenhouse effect will be extremely difficult to slow and impossible to stop.

Figure 18.5
Heat Trapping

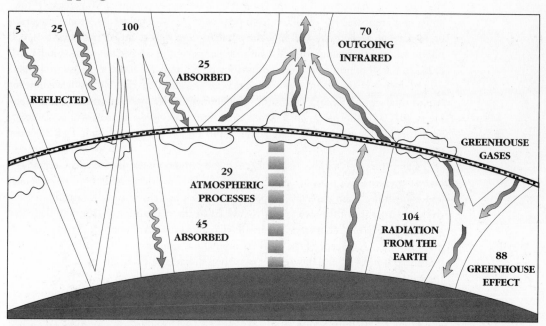

HEAT TRAPPING in the atmosphere dominates the earth's energy balance. Some 30 percent of incoming solar energy is reflected (*left*), either from clouds and particles in the atmosphere or from the earth's surface; the remaining 70 percent is absorbed. The absorbed energy is reemitted at infrared wavelengths by the atmosphere (which is also heated by updrafts and cloud formation) and by the surface. Because most of the surface radiation is trapped by clouds and greenhouse gases and returned to the earth, the surface is currently about 33 degrees Celsius warmer than it would be without the trapping.

Source: N/A

There are four main greenhouse gases—*carbon dioxide, chlorofluorocarbons* (CFCs), *methane,* and *nitrous oxide,* each of which has both natural and human sources. The burning of fossil fuels accounts for about 45 percent of the greenhouse gases. When fossil fuels such as coal, oil, wood, and natural gas are burned, the carbon combines with oxygen to make carbon dioxide. Today, about 20 percent of the carbon dioxide emissions in the atmosphere is the result of the destruction of the tropical rain forest. When those trees are cut down they no longer absorb carbon dioxide; when they are burned they release the stored carbon dioxide into the atmosphere. CFC's and *halons*—the same chemicals which deplete the ozone layer—also contribute to as much as 15 to 20 percent of the greenhouse effect by preventing infrared radiation from escaping into space. Methane and nitrous oxide account for the rest. About half of the carbon dioxide emissions are naturally absorbed by the world's oceans and forests through *photosynthesis.* The oceans are particularly effective at absorbing heat. The trouble is that the increased amounts of greenhouse gases spewed into the atmosphere are overwhelming nature's ability to absorb them.

The relationship between the populations and carbon dioxide emissions of the rich and poor countries has shifted over time. In 1950, there were 825 million people from rich countries that emitted 6.3 tons of carbon dioxide per person or 90 percent of total emissions, compared to 1.5 billion from poor countries that emitted 0.4 tons per person or 10 percent of the total. In 1985, the population of rich countries had risen to 1.170 billion whose inhabitants emitted 13.0 tons per person or 84 percent of the total, compared to 3.680 billion from poor countries who emitted 1.0 ton per person or 16 percent of the total. But by the year 2020, the poor and rich countries will both account for half of total carbon dioxide emissions. The poor countries' population will almost double to 6.720 billion of which 2.0 tons of carbon dioxide per person will be emitted, while the rich countries will have about 1.340 billion people and emit 10.0 tons per person.[13]

The three largest industrial countries—the United States, Japan, and Germany—had 4.7 percent, 2.3 percent, and 1.5 percent, of the world's population, respectively, and contributed 22.3 percent, 4.8 percent, and 2.9 percent of carbon dioxide, respectively, or a total of 30.1 percent of the world's carbon dioxide. In contrast, the three largest Third World countries—China, India, and Indonesia—had 21.0 percent, 16.0 percent, and 3.6 percent of the world's population, respectively, and contributed 10.9 percent, 3.0 percent, and 0.6 percent of carbon dioxide, respectively, or 15.5 percent of the world's carbon dioxide.[14]

There have been a series of international attempts to deal with the greenhouse effect. In 1979, 34 nations signed the United Nations Convention on Long-range Transboundary Air Pollution that dealt with atmospheric pollution. The 1987 Montreal Treaty on CFCs helped alleviate a percentage of the greenhouse gases. In 1987, the Intergovernmental Panel on Climate Change (IPCC) was set up to work closely with the World Meterological Organization (WMO) and *United Nations Environmental Program* (UNEP) to monitor and propose policies addressing the greenhouse effect. The 1988 World Conference on Changing Atmosphere in Toronto called on nations to reduce their fossil fuel use by 20 percent by the year 2005. Although only a few nations attended the Toronto Conference, it succeeded in putting the greenhouse crisis on the global agenda. In September 1989, the United Nations issued its "Climate Change:

Table 18.1
Major Greenhouse Gases

Gas	Atmospheric Concentration (ppm)	Annual Increase (percent)	Life Span (years)	Relative Greenhouse Efficiency ($CO_2 = 1$)	Current Greenhouse Contribution (percent)	Principle Sources of Gas
Carbon Dioxide (Fossil Fuels) (Biological)	351.3	.4	x^1	1	57 (44) (13)	Coal, Oil, Natural Gas, Deforestation
Chlorofluoro-carbons	.000225	5	75–111	15,000	25	Foams, Aerosols, Refrigerants, Solvents
Methane	1.675	1	11	25	12	Wetlands, Rice, Fossil Fuels, Livestock
Nitrous Oxide	.31	.2	150	230	6	Fossil Fuels, Fertilizers, Deforestation

[1]Carbon dioxide is a stable molecule with a 2–4 year average residence time in the atmosphere.

Sources: Worldwatch Institute, based on various sources including, U.S. Environmental Protection Agency, *Policy Options for Stabilizing Global Climate Change* (Washington, D.C.: U.S. Environmental Protection Agency, 1989, draft); V. Ramanathan et al., "Trace Gas Trends and Their Potential Role in Climate Change," *Journal of Geophysical Research,* June 20, 1985; James Hansen et al., "Greenhouse Effect of Chlorofluorocarbons and Other Trace Gases," *Journal of Geophysical Research,* in press.

Meeting the Challenge" which included a plan for addressing the greenhouse effect. In 1990, the United Nations General Assembly resolved to negotiate and sign a *Global Warming Treaty* at the 1992 UN Conference on Environment and Development in Rio de Janeiro.

The 1992 Global Warming Treaty called for industrial countries to reduce their greenhouse emissions and extend financial and technological aid to poor countries so they can eventually comply with the treaty. The Bush White House originally opposed the treaty, arguing that any emission reductions should be voluntary rather than man-dated, and the United States would probably reach the targets anyway so there was no need to sign. It only agreed to sign the treaty if the timetable were removed in which each signatory agreed to reduce its greenhouse emissions to 1990 levels by the year 2000. The other countries reluctantly agreed, and the treaty was signed by over 153

Table 18.2

Twenty-five Countries with the Highest Greenhouse Gas Net Emissions, 1987

		Carbon Dioxide Heating Equivalents, 000 metric tonnes of carbon *Greenhouse Gases*				
Country	Greenhouse Index Rank	Carbon Dioxide	Methane	CFCs (a)	Total	Percent of Total
United States	1	540,000	130,000	350,000	1,000,000	17.6
USSR	2	450,000	60,000	180,000	690,000	12.0
Brazil	3	560,000	28,000	16,000	610,000	10.5
China	4	260,000	90,000	32,000	380,000	6.6
India	5	130,000	98,000	700	230,000	3.9
Japan	6	110,000	12,000	100,000	220,000	3.9
Germany, Fed. Rep.	7	79,000	8,000	75,000	160,000	2.8
United Kingdom	8	69,000	14,000	71,000	150,000	2.7
Indonesia	9	110,000	19,000	9,500	140,000	2.4
France	10	41,000	13,000	69,000	120,000	2.1
Italy	11	45,000	5,800	71,000	120,000	2.1
Canada	12	48,000	33,000	36,000	120,000	2.0
Mexico	13	49,000	20,000	9,100	78,000	1.4
Myanmar	14	68,000	9,000	0	77,000	1.3
Poland	15	56,000	7,400	13,000	76,000	1.3
Spain	16	21,000	4,200	48,000	73,000	1.3
Colombia	17	60,000	4,100	5,200	69,000	1.2
Thailand	18	48,000	16,000	3,500	67,000	1.2
Australia	19	28,000	14,000	21,000	63,000	1.1
German Dem. Rep.	20	39,000	2,100	20,000	62,000	1.1
Nigeria	21	32,000	3,100	18,000	53,000	0.9
South Africa	22	34,000	7,800	5,800	47,000	0.8
Côte d'Ivoire	23	44,000	550	2,000	47,000	0.8
Netherlands	24	16,000	8,800	18,000	43,000	0.7
Saudi Arabia	25	20,000	15,000	6,600	42,000	0.7

Source: World Resources 1990–91, p. 15

countries. In April 1993, President Clinton declared that the United States would meet the original greenhouse treaty's goals of reducing emissions by the year 2000 below the 1990 level and unveiled a systematic program to achieve that goal.

Greater energy efficiency and substitutes for fossil fuels are the key to reducing carbon dioxide emissions. Traditionally, the creation of wealth and increased energy use marched hand-in-hand. Between the 1920s and early 1970s, energy use increased 0.9

percent for every 1.0 percent increase in GNP. OPEC's quadrupling of oil prices in 1973 and further doubling in 1979 forced most governments, businesses, and consumers to use energy more efficiently. As a result, global energy efficiency has doubled over the past two decades, which means that not only is the earth cleaner than it might have been, but there has been more money available to be invested elsewhere.

Further energy efficiency gains are possible. A recent study estimated that the United States would have to invest $2.7 trillion to reduce carbon dioxide 70 percent over the next 40 years. That investment, however, would generate $5 trillion in energy savings, for a net saving of $2.3 trillion. America's economy would grow faster with than without that investment.[15]

One major problem is that with oil prices at an historic low, there is no price incentive to increase efficiency. And while the advanced industrial nations have achieved significant efficiency gains, poorer nations, many with huge populations, are rapidly industrializing.

All the international and national measures taken may be too little too late. If energy efficiency annually increases by only 1 percent, atmospheric carbon dioxide will increase from 349 parts per million in 1988 to 600 parts per million in 2075. A two percent annual efficiency increase would hold down the concentrations to 463 parts per million by 2075.

OZONE LAYER DEPLETION

Until the 1980s, most people had either never heard of ozone or associated it with the ground ozone pollution.[16] Human life exists, in part, because the earth is cocooned in an ozone layer which absorbs most of the harmful solar ultraviolet radiation. Sunlight causes chemical reactions which continually destroy and recreate ozone. Until recently there was a natural balance in the ozone layer.

Human-made chemicals are now destroying that balance and rapidly eating away the ozone layer. The culprits are chemicals which contain chlorine and bromine, the worst of which are CFCs and halons. Each of these molecules can destroy as many as 100,000 ozone molecules. CFCs are used in air conditioners, aerosol sprays, seat cushions, computer chip cleaners, and foam insulation. Halons are used in fire extinguishers.

The damage to the ozone layer is already severe and it worsens daily. Between 1969 and 1986, the ozone layer thinned by about 4 to 6 percent in the mid-latitudes which has allowed 8 to 12 percent more ultraviolet radiation to reach the earth. The result is that New York now receives as much radiation as Caracas, Venezuela. During the late winter, the ozone depletes by as much as 40 percent over the United States, Canada, Europe, Russia, and Japan. Over the next 40 years, the ozone layer could thin by 5 to 20 percent. Even if all CFC and halon production ceased, those existing in the atmosphere will destroy ozone for another 100 years.

The ozone depletion will affect life on earth in various ways. Humans will suffer increased skin cancer, cataracts, and depressed immune systems. If the ozone layer declines 10 percent over all, there will be a 25 percent increase in nonmelanoma skin cancers. Even more troubling is the effect on some plants. To varying degress, all crops are sensitive to increased doses of ultraviolet rays. Crop yields will fall as ultraviolet exposure increases. Perhaps the worst effect will be on ocean life. High doses of ultraviolet rays kill the phytoplankton (one-celled animals) and krill (tiny shrimp-like creatures) that form the basis of the ocean food chain. If they die, all species higher up the chain could be eliminated as well. The world's climates will change as the ozone layer diminishes. When the stratospheric ozone absorbs ultraviolet rays, heat is generated, which in turn creates winds, the source of weather patterns.

No link in the chain of interrelated environmental crises has been more effectively addressed than the ozone layer destruction. Like the greenhouse effect, some scientists predicted an ozone layer depletion before it was scientifically proven. The first warning came in 1973 when two University of Michigan professors, Richard Stolarski and Ralph Cicerone explored the chlorine chemical effects of NASA rocket blasts on the atmosphere. The following year two professors at the University of California at Irvine, Mario Molina and Sherwood Rowland, found that, unlike most other gases, chlorofluorocarbons (CFCs) stayed in the atmosphere and destroyed it for decades.

A general scientific understanding of the CFC danger led to a public and eventually a political consensus in the United States and elsewhere. By the late 1970s, millions of Americans refused to buy aerosol spray cans and other CFC products. In 1977, the American government responded to public opinion by passing a law banning CFC's from 90 percent of aerosol sprays; Canada, Sweden, Demark, Finland, and Norway followed suit. These countries, known as the "Toronto Group," pressured other countries and international organizations to cut back their own CFC emissions. In 1980, the uropean Community froze production of two of the worst CFC chemicals, and cut back production 30 percent from its 1976 levels.

In the 1980s, the United Nations Environmental Program (UNEP) forged an international consensus on the need to take more comprehensive measures. In 1985, the world learned of the ozone layer over Antarctica thinning by as much as 50 percent during the winter. This scientific proof was an important impetus behind the efforts of twenty-four countries to negotiate and sign the Vienna Convention later that year on the Protection of the Ozone Layer which was the first international attempt to identify, if not systematically deal with, the problem. The Convention called for more far-reaching measures to be undertaken by 1987. In September 1986, the Alliance for Responsible CFC Policy, a coalition of over 500 American firms and consumer groups, called for sweeping international action, and the American government helped pressure other countries. International negotiations began in December 1986 and concluded in September 1987 with the signing of the *Montreal Protocol on Substances that Deplete the Ozone Layer.* The signatories agreed to freeze production by 1989, freeze halon production by 1992, and cut CFC emissions by 50 percent by 1998-99, and other countries eventually signed the treaty. In 1988, several international and NASA studies revealed that CFC emissions had doubled between 1975 and 1985 despite the national and international steps taken, making it apparent that the Montreal Protocol did not go far enough to address the problem. In March 1989, the Save the Ozone Conference called by Prime Minister Margaret Thatcher attracted 123 countries. In 1990, 93 nations signed the London Protocol in which they agreed to halt almost all CFC and other ozone destroying chemical production by the year 2000. The wealthier countries created a $240 million fund to help the poorer countries convert to CFC-free technologies.

There has been considerable progress toward reaching the goals of the London Protocol. The advanced industrial countries have granted various subsidies for firms researching CFC substitutes and taxes on CFC production. As a result, corporations have created substitutes for CFC's, including some based on citrus fruits. The trouble with current substitutes is that they cost more energy to run and require the replacement of existing machinery. Air conditioners and refrigerators are the largest CFC users in the United States. As much as 34 percent of CFC emissions come from leakage, 48 percent from recharging and repairs, and 18 percent from accidents, disposal, and manufacturing. CFC in air conditioners and refrigerators are increasingly better sealed and recyled rather than released into the atmosphere. Unfortunately, there are not yet any substitutes for halons. Yet, halon releases could be cut by two-thirds by curbing extinguisher discharge testing.

While virtually all countries agree on the danger of the ozone layer depletion, there were strong divisions between rich and poor countries over who should bear the costs of compliance with the treaties. About 25 percent of the world's population account for 85 percent of CFC use. The poor countries argue that either they should be allowed to use cheaper CFC for refrigeration, and air conditioning, or the rich countries should pay the tab for substitute chemicals and equipment. China, India, Brazil, Indonesia, and Iran—all with huge populations and ambitious industrialization programs—have refused to sign the various ozone treaties. The rich and poor countries remain at an impasse over the issue of transferring the CFC substitute technology.

Overall, the ozone-layer treaties are an outstanding example of the international identification of a problem and efforts to overcome it, even before scientific evidence established beyond a doubt the reality of the ozone crisis. Public opinion and interest groups, responding to widely publicized scientific studies, proved a decisive factor in pressuring the governments of the United States and Europe to act. National efforts led to international efforts which became increasingly comprehensive in addressing the problem. The earlier agreements gave industry the time and incentive to develop substitutes before an outright ban took place. Signatories can retaliate against any countries that refuse to abide by the treaty. The success of the ozone layer treaty can stimulate success in dealing with other international issues.

POLLUTION

Not all air and water pollution contribute to the ozone and greenhouse crises, yet all do inflict upon nations enormous health, productivity, foregone opportunities, and aesthetic costs. Over one billion people or one-fifth of humanity live in air considered unfit to breathe. In the United States alone, over 150 million, or about two-thirds of the population, live in areas where the air is considered unhealthy by the Environmental Protection Agency. In Athens the number of deaths rises six-fold on heavy pollution days; air pollution annually costs 120,000 American lives and $40 billion in health care and lost productivity; in Hungary, one of 17 deaths is attributable to air pollution; in Bombay breathing the air equals smoking ten cigarettes a day; in Mexico City, the pollution exceeds world health standards 300 days a year, and seven of ten newborn babies have lead levels which indicate brain damage.[17]

In high enough doses, air-borne chemicals can impair the body, the mind, and the food upon which we subsist. Sulfer dioxide can cause or worsen coughs, colds, asthma, bronchitis, and emphysema. Particulate matter can carry toxic metals into one's lungs. Ozone, formed when sunlight causes hydrocarbons and nitrogen oxide chemicals to react, can damage lungs. Nitrogen dioxide can cause lung problems, including bronchitis, pneumonia, and influenza. Carbon monoxide interferes with the blood's ability to absorb oxygen, which ultimately can cause death. Lead harms the brain, kidneys, circulatory, reproductive, and nervous systems. The damage to crops can also be severe. For every one percentage point increase in ultraviolet rays, soybean yields are reduced by the same amount. Ground-level ozone alone is estimated to reduce America's corn, wheat, soybean, and peanut yields by 5 percent. By cutting ozone pollution in half, crop yields would be increased annually by $5 billion.

Few regions of the world suffer worse pollution problems than Eastern Europe and the Soviet Union.[18] Together Eastern Europe and the Soviet Union account for 25 percent of the carbon dioxide and 17 percent of the CFC emissions that cause the greenhouse and ozone depletion effects. The region's centrally planned economies are grossly energy inefficient and indifferent to even basic environmental concerns. They rely for much of their energy on high sulfur brown coal or lignite. The result is that much of Eastern Europe and the former Soviet Union has become an environmental wasteland littered with toxic chemical and nuclear dumps, and beset by acid rain and noxious air and water pollution.

The region lacks the money, expertise, organization, and political will to confront its environmental catastrophe. All the countries are deeply in debt to international bankers and organizations. Governments hesitate to shut down even the worst polluting factories because there is no alternate employment for the tens of thousands of workers. It is estimated that the clean-up costs for East Germany alone will range from $249 billion to $308 billion over the next decade.

Air and water pollution in the United States, European Community, and Japan has lessened considerably because of sweeping laws passed in those countries during the 1970s and 1980s. For example, America's 1970 and 1990 Clean Air Acts and have had a significant effect on pollution. Between 1970 and 1987, the United States cut sulfur oxide emissions by 28 percent and particulates by 62 percent.

Environmentalism and business can compliment rather than conflict with each other. Those countries which master green technologies the fastest will become the most prosperous and powerful. The annual global market for environmentally sound products is already $200 billion and will increase steadily. In the United States alone, environmental protection is a huge and ever-growing industry which generates $98 billion annually and employs three million people. New technologies such as scrubbers, clean-burning coal, nitrous oxide controls, energy conservation, and catalytic converters, to name a few, have cut pollution and increased productivity. Alternative fuels such as ethanol, methanol, natural gas, and hydrogen cause much less pollution than coal and oil. Likewise, mass transportation, bicycles, and walking reduce pollution.

Environmentalism pays in greater productivity, health, profits, and lower taxes and insurance premiums. For example, the 3M Corporation's systematic waste reduction and recycling program has saved the company over $300 million over 15 years. That same program has saved America's tax and insurance payers enormous amounts since it annually prevents the generation of 100,000 tons of air pollution, 275,000 tons of solid wastes and sludges, and 1.5 billion gallons of wastewater.[19]

There are many steps which governments can take to reduce pollution. Taxing emissions forces producers to pay pollution's full costs, thus providing an incentive for businesses to invest in equipment and production techniques that minimize pollution. Another means of reducing pollution is through emissions trading. Industries are assigned a pollution level. If they excede it they can buy "pollution rights" from firms which have reduced pollution below that level.

Recycling can dramatically reduce the fossil fuels emissions that are the greenhouse effect's major cause. For example, steel produced from scap cuts air pollution by 85 percent, water pollution by 76 percent, and eliminates mining wastes completely; recycled paper cuts air and water pollution by 74 percent and 35 percent, respectively, and eliminates clear-cutting forests. Energy savings are also great: recycled aluminium costs only five percent of that produced from bauxite ore; steel from scrap only 35 percent that of steel from iron ore; recycled glass 65 percent that of glass from natural materials; newsprint from recycled paper 40 to 75 percent that from wood pulp.[20]

Other measures can help reduce pollution. Public opinion can have a powerful effect on polluters, and most firms do all they can to cover up their pollution. "Right to know" laws would require businesses to release data on their pollution, giving citizens an opportunity to boycott or protest those firms until they clean up their mess.

Although it has already taken some important steps, the United States could do much more to clean up its carbon dioxide and other pollution. Washington has lagged well behind its competitors in implementing policies that encourage the technological and product breakthroughs essential to remaining economically competitive and environmentally sound. America's government spending programs remain largely shaped by politics rather than an understanding of the economic and environmental challenges the country faces. In 1992, while Washington spent $540 million in subsidizing environmental technology, it gave $35 billion to farmers. American gasoline prices, for example, are three to four times cheaper than those of other advanced industrial countries. A $.50 federal tax on gasoline and other carbon emissions sources in the United States would simultaneously force people to use mass transportation, increase efficiency, and reduce America's trade and budget deficits, and dependence on foreign oil sources. Some of these carbon taxes could be invested in solar, wind, geothermal, and nuclear energy sources that do not contribute to the greenhouse effect.

Significant international measures were taken to deal with various forms of pollution even before the 1992 greenhouse emissions treaty. In 1979, the Geneva Convention on Long-Range Transboundary Air Pollution was signed by ten industrial countries in which they agreed to cut back air pollution. In 1984, 21 governments signed the Helsinki Protocol in which they pledged to reduce sulfur emissions by 30 percent, which was followed up by the 1988 Sofia Convention whereby signatories agreed to a further 30 percent cut in sulfur emissions and a reduction in nitrogen oxides.

Regional international agreements have complemented the more global treaties. European countries have cooperated extensively to deal with regional environmental issues. The European Community has attempted to create environmental standards to which all members must adhere. The EC's 1988 Directive on the Limitation of Emissions of Certain Pollutants created a country-by-country plan for pollution reduction in which the richest countries were required to reduce their emissions between 60 to 70 percent by 2003 while the poorer countries like Portugal, Greece, and Ireland were temporarily allowed to increase emissions. Other regional agreements involved a set of EC members or the EC and other countries. The 1976 Bonn Convention for the Protection of the Rhine Against Pollution by Chlorides, the 1974 Helsinki Convention for the Protection of the Baltic, 1974 Paris Convention for the Protection of the North Sea, and 1976 Barcelona Convention for the Protection of the Mediterranean addressed important pollution issues.

Although the United States, Canada, and Mexico have enacted important environmental legislation, there has been little coordination among them. Regional environmental concerns were not addressed until the 1992 North American Free Trade Association (NAFTA).

Although some countries and regions have made considerable progress in reducing some forms of pollution, it remains a severe problem virtually everywhere and imposes enormous losses in wealth, productivity, health, and life quality.

DEFORESTATION

Only 20 percent of the world's surface is land. Temperate and tropical forests together cover two-fifths, 13 and 7 percent, respectively, of that land.[21] The world's forests are essential for protecting and enhancing human life. Temperate and tropical forests act as the earth's lungs, annually absorbing vast amounts of carbon dioxide that would otherwise drift up into the atmosphere and contribute to the greenhouse effect. Forests are more than trees; they are vast, complex, and fragile ecosystems in which tree species live along with thousands of shrubs, flowers, mosses, and animals. Once destroyed ecologically diverse temperate forests are almost impossible to regrow and tropical forests are lost forever.

The surival of the world and its tropical forests are intricately linked. There are anywhere between three million and 30 million animal and plant species on earth, most of these in tropical forests. In one ten acre stretch of Borneo rain forest there were over 700 tree species! Tropical forests are treasure stores of medicines and other products. One of four drugs currently sold is derived from tropical forests. Over 70 percent of the 3,000 plants currently known to fight cancer are tropical. In the Amazon basin, Indians use over 1,300 plants for medicinal purposes. Gathering the fruits and plants of tropical forests creates much more wealth for many more people than does clear-cutting it and converting it to pasture or single-crop farms. One study in Peru found that the net annual value of harvesting forest fruits and latex was 13 times greater than clear-cutting. Finally, tropical forest reserves can bring in tourists and thus income.

The world's forests are rapidly diminishing. One-third of the world's forests have already been destroyed, and every year 20 to 25 million more hectares, an area the size of Belgium, is lost to chainsaws and fire. By 2020, at their current rate of destruction, between 80 percent and 95 percent of all tropical forests will have disappeared, and by 2050 all tropical forests will have been destroyed.

Deforestation adversely affects both the global and regional climates as it:

reduces transpiration of water vapor into the atmosphere, changes the albedo (reflectivity) of the earth's surface, removes an important 'sink' for ozone, and, through burning, contributes to the greenhouse effect through the release of carbon dioxide and other greenhouse gases into the atmosphere. At the same time, the essential services provided by intact forest ecosystems—such as watershed protection and regulation, the storage of carbon in plant tissues, or the breakdown of pollutants—are being degraded or destroyed.[22]

Deforestation's most serious impact is on the greenhouse effect. The cutting down and often outright burning of forests accounts for about one-third of all carbon dioxide emissions. In 1987, eleven countries—Brazil, Indonesia, Colombia, Ivory Coast, Thailand, Laos, Nigeria, Vietnam, Philippines, Burma, and India—were responsible for 82 percent of the net carbon release from deforestation.

Anywhere from 15 to 50,000 species annually become extinct, a daily rate of 50 to 150, most of them in tropical forests. At the current rate of deforestation, 25 percent of the species currently inhabiting the earth will be extinct by 2020. There has not been such a mass species extinction since the dinosaurs died off 65 million years ago. Destroying millions of species whose benefits to humankind remain unknown has been compared to "eating our seedcorn." Many of the indigenous peoples are dying with their forests, and with them the medicinal secrets of thousands of plants and animals.

About 95 percent of all tropical forest soils are infertile and extremely fragile. Most of the vegetation's nutrients come from their own ability to take nitrogen from the atmosphere. Thus clear-cutting rapidly erodes the land, making it unsuitable for agriculture or even livestock within a few years. It also silts streams and rivers which destroys fishing industries. For example, clear-cutting the South Fork of the Salmon River earned logging corporations $14 million but cost the fishing industry $100 million. Finally, clear-cutting destroys a region's tourist industry—few tourists would want to visit stump-filled and degraded landscapes.

Forests are being destroyed for several reasons. Perhaps the most important is that clear-cutting a forest is a quick and easy source of money for those involved. The huge logging corporations make most of the money; host governments skim off surprisingly little revenue—often far less than the money they invested in infrastructure and administration to destroy the forests. The United States government, for example, is notorious for selling permits to clear-cut national forests for a fraction of what logging firms would pay for access to private lands. Debt-burdened Third World countries are particularly apt to clear-cut forests for short-term gains even if it means future economic and environmental devastation for that region. As forests diminish, the value of their wood rises, and thus the incentive to clear-cut them even faster.

Huge livestock corporations clear-cut or burn forest and convert it to pasture land. Most of the beef production goes not to hungry people in that country but to hamburger chains in the advanced industrial countries. For example, while beef production in Central America increased threefold between 1955 and 1980, beef consumption in the region actually fell. But most of those ranches would be bankrupt if they did not receive huge government subsidies. Another reason for deforestation is the maldistribution of farm lands. In Latin America, for example, 7 percent of the population owns 93 percent of the land while 70 percent of the population has little or no land. Thus many peasants drift into the tropical forests to slash and burn a patch for farming. The problem with both ranching and subsistence farming is that tropical soils are very fragile and easily washed away within a few years, forcing the rancher or peasant to move on and clear yet another swath of forest.

The bottom line of deforestation, like all other environmental problems, is over-population. The populations of countries like India, Brazil, Nigeria, and Indonesia have more than doubled over the past 30 years, and the resulting increased demand for goods, services, jobs, and land eats away at tropical forests. Many governments actually subsidize the migration of the poor to the forests to relieve the pressure on existing cities and farmlands. Indonesia, for example, spends $10,000 for each family it relocates in the tropical forests.

About 2 billion of the world's population use wood as their primary energy source. In Africa alone, 76 percent of all energy comes from wood. Virtually everywhere, people are stripping wood from the land faster than it can be replenished. Once the local wood supply is depleted, people use dried human and animal dung for fuel rather than for fer-tilizer, and in so doing degrade existing farm land. Eventually the land is exhausted and the people migrate elsewhere where they repeat the same vicious cycle of land degrada-tion. Simply building roads into tropical forests not only encourages developers to move in but destroys vast amounts of trees.

The Japanese have been particularly notorious for clear-cutting the world's tropi-cal forests and account for one-third of world timber imports. Japanese are very waste-ful of the tropical woods they import. A 1989 World Wildlife Fund study singled Japan out as the world's most voracious user of tropical woods.[23] Japan uses nonre-newable but cheaper tropical woods largely for plywoods and chopsticks even though it could use renewable but more expensive temperate woods for the same purposes. Much of the imported woods are wasted. For example, every year Japanese throw away 20 billion wooden chopsticks which if piled together would make a mountain as high as Mt. Fuji!

While deforestation leads to economic gains for loggers, ranchers, subsistence farm-ers, and foreign consumers, the nation's real assets just as steadily diminish—by as much as 4 to 6 percent annually for major tropical timber exporting countries. Special interests benefit from deforestation in the short run; everyone suffers enormous direct and indirect costs over the long run.

A number of national measures can be taken to slow the destruction of the world's forests, particularly the priceless tropical forests. Land reform is an essential step. Peas-ants migrate to tropical forests and systematically destroy them because they lack land and basic needs elsewhere. Land must be redistributed from the huge plantations, which often leave vast amounts fallow, to the poor landless peasants. Land distribution, how-ever, will not work unless it is accompanied by the extension of credit, technology, fer-tilizer, and education to the new peasant proprietors so that they can productively work their land. Allowing indigenous people the right to the land they have lived on for mil-lenia would protect both them and the forests. Over the long-term, family planning and free universal access to contraceptives can alleviate some of the population pressure on forest lands.

International debt relief including more debt-for-nature swaps can protect forest tracts while reducing the pressures on poor governments to clear-cut other forests to help service their debts. Fourteen countries account for about half of the Third World's foreign debt and two-thirds of tropical deforestation. Targeting these countries for debt-reduction combined with sustained development and conservation policies could remove the incentive for clear-cutting forests for short-term gains.

Economic policy in most countries is divided among a range of ministries and agencies whose interests and actions often conflict. The result is enormous mismanagement, misallocation of resources, slower economic growth, and worsening environmental problems. In order to be effective, development and land use planning must be coordinated under an umbrella of goals and means which incorporate notions of long-term sustained and quality growth rather than short-term special interest payoffs or market solutions.

Environmental impact studies should precede any development schemes that will destroy forests. Short-term gains for a few must always be weighed against the long-term loses, not just for that nation but for all of humanity. An important step in this direction would be to change the system of computing national wealth so that it includes the depreciation of national natural assets. If clear-cutting forests were counted as a net economic loss rather than gain, governments would do more to preserve rather than destroy them. Unfortunately, it is difficult to compute the value of a forest's positive effect on alleviating the greenhouse effect, watershed protection, and so on.

New forestry techniques seek to manage existing forests rather than convert them to tree farms. Clear-cutting is abolished. Instead, small clumps of trees are cut selectively leaving most of the forest intact. Trees are cut down only at the rate at which they are replanted, a practice known as *sustained yield*. In the tropics, only 0.1 percent of all the forests can be logged at sustained yield. Tropical forestry involves managing the sustained yield of logging and the gathering of medicinal plants, rubber, fruits, nuts, and selective tree cutting.

In the United States, as in most timber producing countries, the government subsidizes the logging industry. If loggers had to pay market costs for the trees they cut on public lands, the treasury would gain and the higher prices for wood products would decrease demand and stimulate greater conservation and use of substitutes. While more logs were harvested during the 1980s, the number of people employed by the timber industry fell steadily. Meanwhile, one of four logs was exported, and most of them went to Japan. If the United States and Canada forbade the export of raw logs, the foreign demand for wood products would cause employment to rise in both countries as refined wood products were made at home rather than overseas.

International efforts to address deforestation have been limited. In 1985, the UN Food and Agricultural Organization (FAO) submitted the Tropical Forestry Action Plan (TFAP) to offer assistance to governments to preserve their tropical forests. In 1987, the International Tropical Timber Organization (ITTO) was set up by 48 national governments to encourage sustainable timber harvests.

The most sweeping measure addressing deforestation was the Bush administration proposal at the 1992 Earth Summit which called for a ban on the cutting of tropical forests and pledged $150 million to aid forestry programs. The tropical forest countries protested the proposal, arguing that they had just as much right to log their forests as oil producing countries had to pump oil. They also asked where the income foregone from logging would come from and suggested the advanced industrial nations could pay them not to log if they were so concerned about the issue. Finally, they demanded that the proposed treaty cover temperate as well as tropical forests. The Bush administration did not effectively counter these charges and the proposal lost its remaining credibility when aerial photos were circulated showing the devastation of America's forests from clear-cutting. The treaty was rejected and a nonbinding statement declared which simply recommends that countries assess their deforestation and attempt to arrest it.

While the tropical forest treaty was rejected at the Earth Summit, a Biodiversity Treaty was signed by 153 countries in which they agreed to preserve plant and animal species by creating and implementing their own management plans. The wealthier countries pledged to help the poorer countries accomplish their biodiversity preservation plans. The Bush administration refused to sign, arguing that the treaty was too vague in detailing how foreign aid would be used and that it would not agree to transfering technology to the Third World without compensation.

DESERTIFICATION

We take water and food for granted. We think nothing of turning on the tap and filling our glass, taking long, hot showers, or washing our cars. We also think nothing of going to huge supermarkets in which there are tens of thousands of cheaply priced foods. These activities may someday be luxuries if the world's population continues to increase, fresh water sources just as steadily dry up, and once productive land is transformed into desert.

Only 20 percent of the earth's surface is land. More than two-thirds of the land's surface is already desert or mountain. Since 1945, over 3 billion acres of land, an area the size of India and China combined, or 11 percent of the world's arable land, has lost all or most of its productivity.[24] Every year, roughly 15 million acres of productive land, an area the size of West Virginia, becomes desert; an additional 50 million acres becomes too degraded to support grazing or crops. As Lester Brown puts it, "an estimated 24 billion tons of topsoil washes or blows off the land annually—roughly the amount of Australia's wheatland. Each year, the world's farmers must try to feed 88 million more people with 24 billion fewer tons of topsoil."[25] A 1993 UN study revealed that desertification threatens about 8 billion acres upon which 1.2 billion of the world's 5.5 billion people currently live a largely subsistence existence by raising crops and livestock. When their soils blow away and water holes run dry, where will all those people go and how will they live? By the year 2030, if current erosion rates continue, the world may have to feed two or three times more people with 960 billion fewer tons of topsoil (more than twice the amount on U.S. farmlands) and total cropland will have fallen by one-third.[26]

Until recently, global food production kept up with the amount of new mouths to feed. The global food problem involved distribution rather than production. When droughts and famines occurred around the world, foreign nations which cared tried to redistribute food to the afflicted.[27] However, during the late 1980s and into the 1990s, the world's population began to surpass the amount of food available to feed it.

Global per capita grain consumption fell 2 percent between 1986 and 1990. In 1988, America's grain production fell for the first time in history. Desertification of Africa's Sahel has caused a 28 percent drop in that region's grain production since the

1960s. The result is mass famine and death. Over 100 million Africans are thought to be malnourished. As global food supplies dwindle, prices rise adding yet another source of debt to many struggling Third World countries.

Soil is one of our most precious natural resources. Trees, brushes, and grasses hold soil in place and absorb water. An inch of soil may take anywhere from 200 to 1,000 years to form. An exposed inch or more of soil can be swept away in one violent storm. In increasing numbers of regions, land is overcultivated, deforested, overgrazed, and/or overirrigated. Over-use erodes the soil; continued over-use converts once productive land into desert. In America's corn and wheat regions, the yield falls by three to six bushels per acre or as much as 6 percent for every inch of topsoil lost. Soil nutrients are further depleted in poor countries which have suffered deforestation. Without wood, the only fuel hundreds of millions of people around the world have to burn is human and animal waste, which would normally be used to fertilize fields. Erosion not only diminishes a land's crop or grazing productivity. When soil has been stripped away to bedrock, water runs off quickly rather than percolating down through the earth to replenish aquifers. The run off collects in huge floods downstream. Between 1960 and 1984, India's flood-prone regions almost tripled from 47 million to 124 million acres.

Fresh water comes from one ultimate source—the sky—which feeds streams, lakes, rivers, fields, reservoirs, and underground aquifers. Fresh water is disappearing for many interrelated reasons. The demand for water increases with a population's numbers and affluence, and at some point inevitably overwhelms that region's existing surface and aquifer supplies.

Most desertified regions can never be restored. The soil has been washed and blown away or has become salinated. Surface and aquifer waters have dried or have become polluted. The remaining people eke out meager existences, and there are no financial, technological, or political resources to limit, let alone reverse, the land's steady degradation.

Deforestation and desertification change regional climates. Vegetation and rainfall decrease and increase together, a process known as *evapotranspiration*. Abundant vegetation absorbs moisture and then releases it back into the air which causes clouds and more precipitation. As vegetation is destroyed, less water is absorbed and thus less is released back into the atmosphere. A related phenomenon is *albedo* in which more solar radiation is reflected back into the atmosphere as vegetation decreases, which in turn causes dryer air to sink and rainfall to decline further.

Perhaps nowhere has desertification been more tragic than in the African Sahel, a vast belt of savanna lands south of the Sahara Desert. Over the past several decades, the human population has steadily exceeded the Sahel's carrying capacity. The land's grasses have been overgrazed, its trees chopped down for fuel, its soil blown or washed away, and its water drunk dry. The result has been the steady advance of the Sahara Desert toward the south and the equally steady march of environmental refugees to lands and cities beyond. Those lands in turn deteriorate as the population swells under the weight of a high birth rate and millions of refugees. This environmental domino effect will become increasingly severe as the population increases and available lands diminish. A fraction of Africa's soil loss represents a gain for others. Winds carry African soils all the way across the Atlantic Ocean to South America and the Caribbean.[28] Most soil, however, ends up in rivers and oceans.

The Sahel is only one of at least a dozen regions around the world that are becoming desert. The Nile River valley, the north China plains, the Indian subcontinent, the Jordan River valley, and Central Asia are the most prominent regions experiencing rapid desertification. Conflicts over remaining water sources will increase steadily and could be a major cause for future wars. For example, the Arab-Israeli stand-off is further complicated by the reliance of Israel, Lebanon, Jordan, and Syria on the Jordan River. Israel currently takes 95 percent of the Jordan River's waters. Israel's population has increased sixfold since it achieved independence in 1948. Although Israeli farmers have mastered drip agriculture which maximizes water efficiency, the increased demands of farmers, factories, and households is rapidly outstripping all available surface and aquifer water sources. Seawater has seeped into and polluted some aquifers as they are drawn down, compounding the shortages. By 2000, Israel's water supply could fall as low as 30 percent below demand. Meanwhile, neighboring states are growing just as rapidly in population and will clamour for a greater share of the Jordan River and other regional water sources for themselves. The result could be wars for water.[29]

Egypt is another country highly vulnerable to desertification. In 1993, almost 60 million people were crammed along the tiny ribbon of vegetation and concrete bordering the Nile River, and the population is increasing by one million people every nine months. Further up the Nile, Sudan, Kenya, and Ethiopia have embarked on development projects that could divert considerable water from Egyptian homes, farms, and factories downstream. To supply households, the Egyptian government may have to cut back water to cotton and sugar cane farmers, which would worsen Egypt's trade deficit and ability to service its $44 billion foreign debt.

Desertification also is afflicting the Indian subcontinent. The once vast forest which protected the watersheds of the Ganges, Indus, and Brahmaputra river systems has been decimated, thus, leading to enormous flooding downstream during the monsoon season and droughts at other times. As the populations of India, Pakistan, and Bangladesh continue to rise, the tropical forests are clear-cut, surface and aquifer water sources are polluted or dry up, and once fertile soils erode into barren desert.

China's 1.2 billion people account for one-fifth of the world's total population but have access to only 8 percent of the world's fresh water. Today, in northern China, over 300 cities suffer varying degrees of water shortages that will worsen as surface and aquifer sources dry up or become fouled. Between 1950 and 1992, the water table below Beijing annually dropped three to six feet for a total drop from 16 feet to 160 feet below the surface; meanwhile Beijing's two reservoirs have frequently dried up.

For several decades, the former Soviet Central Asian republics served as the Soviet Union's fruit, vegetable, cotton, and rice basket. But massive irrigation and industrialization projects have converted once rich grasslands and huge freshwater lakes into deserts. The Aral Sea region has been the most devastated. The diversion of water from the Aral caused it to rapidly recede and salinate, thus destroying a once rich fishery and ruining much of the surrounding farmland.

The first serious international attempt to identify this problem and propose possible solutions was a 1977 United Nations conference in Nairobi which produced the "Plan of Action to Combat Desertification." Although the Plan presented 28 recommendations, the United Nations and those countries most in need lacked the funds, organization, and political will to implement them. The International Fund for Agricultural Development (IFAD) has set up hundreds of pilot programs to teach peasants more efficient farming methods that conserve rather than exhaust the soil and their own livelihoods, but its efforts remain limited and underfunded. The United Nations Environmental Program estimated that it would take at least $4.5 billion annually for two decades to arrest desertification. This may be an optimistic assessment.

Governments can take many relatively simple measures to conserve water and soil. Contour and terraced plowing combined with leaving strips of vegetation, along and within the plowed lands, can minimize soil erosion and increase water infiltration into the crops and aquifers. Replanting trees and other vegetation and spreading mulch can slow the erosion of existing soils and begin the centuries long process of soil creation. Leguminous trees are particularly good at absorbing nitrogen in the air and fertilizing the soil. The most important target for replanting should be the watersheds where most surface water originates.

Huge water subsidies to farmers are a major reason for the overuse of water and subsequent desertification. If farmers had to pay market rates for water, they would try to conserve it as much as possible. But when they pay water rates as little as 10 percent of what households pay, they are encouraged to waste as much of it as possible.

Globally, the amount of irrigated lands increased from 232 million acres in 1950 to 615 million in 1980, a rate faster than population growth. Since then, however, the amount of new irrigated lands has fallen behind population growth. Irrigated lands are generally three times more productive than rain-fed land. Yet this higher productivity can be costly. Improper irrigation techniques can both deplete underground water tables and waterlog and salinate soils. Ironically, while irrigation drains aquifers, the water table may actually rise directly under the irrigated lands. The result is sometimes a waterlogged soil in which crops rot from the roots up, a phenomenon known as a wet desert. Drip irrigation is much more water conserving than simply flooding a field. Long hoses are stretched along each crop row and a hole drips water at the root of each plant. The only problem is that it is initially much more expensive.

The *Green Revolution* of the 1960s was supposed to be the solution to predictions of growing food shortages and famine. New strains of high yield seeds would dramatically increase farm productivity. The trouble was that these seeds required huge amounts of water and fertilizer to flourish. This was particularly costly for Third World countries which had to import the fertilizer or divert even more water to farming from other needs. Between 1950 and 1990, world artificial fertilizer use increased from 14 million to 145 million tons. Without fertilizer, world crop yields would plummet by 40 percent. National debts and degraded lands increased along with crop yeilds. A second Green Revolution would be based on new strains of seeds that can survive in poor soil with little water and repel insects and disease.

Yet, in the long-term, these measures will slow rather than halt desertification. As in all other environmental crises, desertification occurs when a human population exceeds a region's carrying capacity. As long as populations steadily increase, desertification will continue to engulf one region after another around the world, loosening floods of environmental refugees which soon overwhelm yet another region's carrying capacity. If the world is currently failing to feed all of its 5.4 billion people, how can it ever feed two or possibly three times that amount?

THE DYING OCEANS

Anyone who has ever stood on a beach and gazed out to sea or flown or sailed over it cannot help but feel awe at the ocean's immensity.[30] However, the oceans are not indestructable. The demand on the oceans' resources and the amount of pollution dumped into them increases with the world's population.

Fish are a vital food source. About 25 percent of the world's population or over 1.4 billion people rely on fish as their major source of animal protein. Some species are important for more than being part of food chains. For example, oysters filter pollution. The oyster population of Chesapeake Bay was once so abundant that it could clean the entire bay in three days; today it takes the remaining oysters one year.

Between 1950 and 1987, the world fish catch quadrupled from 21 million tons to 84.5 million tons and is fast approaching the maximum sustainable yeild of 100 million tons. Some species have already been devastated by overfishing, which of course puts more pressure on surviving fish species. Of the world's 280 commercial fish species, only 25 are lightly or moderately exploited while 42 have already been overexploited or depleted. In 1990, the world fish catch declined for the first time in two decades.

The world's fish species are not only rapidly diminishing because of demand, but also because of destructive fishing methods. Drift-net fishing by over 700 Japanese, South Korean, and Taiwanese ships has devastated many fish species. Drift nets are up to 40 miles long and act as huge vacuums which sweep up and kill everything in their way. In 1988, the salmon harvest off Alaska's coast dropped to 12 million from the usual 40 million fish, a population crash attributed to drift-net fishing.

Pollution also destroys fish populations or makes them unfit to eat. Human waste released into water can increase nitrogen levels and the algae which feed on nitrogen. When algae blooms, it sucks the oxygen, and thus fish life, out of the surrounding waters. Many seas and lakes have "died" at least partly from nitrogen-algae blooms, such as the Adriatic and Baltic seas, Lake Erie, and various coastal zones along the United States. The immediate short-term economic losses are in lost fishing and tourist revenue; the long-term losses involve increased fishing pressure on other regions which may lead to the depletion of those sources.

Other pollutants are also harmful. Heavy metals are released in the oceans by mining, industry, ship discharges, incineration, pesticide runoffs, and other pollution sources. The ocean food chain rests on the tiny zooplankton and phytoplankton which live in the 1/100th inch thick microlayer of the ocean's surface. Heavy metals and chemicals such as mercury, lead, copper, PCB, DTT, cadmium, and zinc concentrate in the microlayer at rates 10 to 10,000 times greater than elsewhere in the ocean. These heavy metals enter the ocean food chain and ultimately human beings, with harmful effects on each link. They have devastated some local animals such as seals in the North and Baltic seas, beluga whales in the St. Lawrence Seaway, and made it advisable for humans not to eat tuna, swordfish, and other deep-sea fishes more than once a week. Sometimes these chemicals directly harm humans. Between 1953 and 1968, 649 people died from eating mercury contaminated fish from Minamata Bay in Japan. Every year, about 21 million barrels of oil enter the sea from land run off and 600,000 barrels are accidentally spilled into the ocean. These oil spills devastate local sea life. Plastic bags can kill animals, such as turtles and seals, that mistake them for jellyfish. Over 30,000 fur seals die annually from injesting plastic bags.

Coral reefs, sea grass ranges, and mangroves are the nurseries for much ocean life, and have been called the tropical forests of the oceans. Coral reefs alone are home to over one million species and 2,000 kinds of fish. Hundreds of millions of people are directly employed harvesting these species and many more people supplement their diets with seafood from the reefs. Pollution has destroyed hundreds of reefs, underwater grasslands, and mangroves around the world. It is estimated that 100,000 jobs and $80 million in income disappears annually from reef destruction alone, while millions more suffer malnutrition.

The worst threat to the world's oceans is the ozone depletion. The amount of ultraviolet rays striking the earth will increase between 5 to 20 percent over the next half century. Ultraviolet radiation slows photosynthesis and inhibits phytoplankton growth and mutates its genes. The 15 percent ozone depletion over Antarctica resulted in a 15 to 20 percent decrease in surface phytoplankton. As the ozone thins over the earth the phytoplankton will correspondingly die off, which would in turn devastate the entire ocean food chain. This phytoplankton die off would also exacerbate the greenhouse effect. Until now, the oceans have slowed the greenhouse effect by absorbing about 45 percent of the carbon dioxide produced, with phytoplankton being the major absorbent. There is absolutely no guarantee that the dying phytoplankton ranks would eventually be filled by radiation resistant species.

Several international agreements have helped manage ocean fish and natural resources. More than 90 percent of all fish can be found within 200 miles from shore. During the 1970s, increasing numbers of countries declared exclusive economic zones (EEZs) of 200 miles from their coastline. Those states then attempted to regulate fishing within their EEZs. This practice was legally codified with the 1982 Law of the Sea Treaty. To date over 70 countries have declared EEZs. The Law of the Sea calls the oceans beyond the EEZ's the "common heritage" of humankind and includes tenets which regulate and distribute the profits of ocean mining, as well as address navigation rights and pollution control. The United States has refused to sign the treaty and has encouraged others to do likewise. The Treaty needs about 20 more ratifications before it comes into force. The trouble is that enforcement of licensing and quotas within the EEZs is difficult. Even the United States with its huge Coast Guard and Navy cannot prevent poaching within its oceans.

Another important treaty was the 1972 London Dumping Convention which bans the dumping of hazardous radioactive, chemical, and heavy metal wastes into the oceans. Since 1972 the treaty has been amended to ban the incineration of trash at sea by 1994 and the discharge of plastic bags and oil by ships.

Even when international treaties are ratified, countries can simply ignore them. For example, in 1982, the International Whaling Commission declared a global moratorium on whaling beginning in 1986. Japan, Norway, and Iceland continued to defy the moratorium, pointing to a loophole which allows each country annually to kill up to 2,000 whales for "scientific" purposes.

Japan has also continued to use drift-net fishing despite concerted international demands that it desist. Japanese fishermen account for about half of the Pacific Ocean tuna catch and Japan refused to sign any multilateral treaty restricting its catch or fishing techniques. In September 1989, Japan announced that it would cut its number of fishing boats in the Pacific Ocean using drift nets by two-thirds to 26, the same number that fished there in 1986 before the number shot up to over 60 in 1988. Tokyo's action followed years of international criticism, two months after 15 countries called on Japan to stop its drift-net fishing, and pressure by groups in the United States on the government to invoke a 1987 law which would cut imports from countries which used drift nets. Tokyo all along insisted that there was no scientific proof that drift nets were as destructive as claimed.

In November 1989, both the United Nations and the annual meeting of the International Fisheries Conference called for a moratorium on the use of drift nets by 1992, citing scientific studies that proved their use annually killed over 80,000 marine mammals such as whales, dolphins, seals, and a million sea birds.[31] Salmon fisheries were devasted by drift-net fishing. In contrast to the huge nets used by the Japanese, American and Canadian fishermen are limited by law to nets no bigger than 900 feet. American fishermen suffered a huge drop in their salmon catch from 17,000 tons in the early 1980s to 2,500 in 1989.

On March 20, 1991, Washington threatened Tokyo with a cut off on $53 million in imports because Japan's continued hunting the endangered hawksbill turtle. Trade of products made from the hawksbill turtle has been illegal since 1975 when more than 100 countries signed the Convention on International Trade in Endangered Species. Washington pointed to its own 1967 law which allows it to retaliate against any country which continues to hunt an endangered species. In 1974 and 1988, the United States threatened to use its law to pressure Japan to stop whaling, but has never actually done so.

In May 1992, ten countries—the United States, France, Mexico, Costa Rica, Nicargua, Panama, Spain, Japan, Venezuela, and Vanuatu—which account for virtually all tuna fishing in the Pacific Ocean, signed a treaty protecting dolphins. This recent agreement follows a 1986 agreement in which dolphin deaths dropped 80 percent up through 1992. It is hoped the present agreement will further reduce dolphin deaths from the current 25,000 level to around 5,000. The public outcry and boycott of fish from countries which killed dolphins was the most important reason for the treaty.

CONCLUSION

A statement concluding the 1990 American Assembly Conference on "Preserving the Global Environment" captured the threat the environmental crises pose to us all:

> *Three indivisibly linked global environmental trends together constitute an increasingly grave challenge to the habitability of the earth. They are human population growth; tropical deforestation and the rapid loss of biological diversity; and global atmospheric change, including stratrospheric ozone loss and greenhouse warming. These trends threaten nations' economic potential, therefore their internal political security, their citizens' health (because of increased ultraviolet*

radiation), and, in the case of global warming, possibly their very existance. No more basic threat to national security exists. Thus, together with economic interdependence, global environmental threats are shifting traditional national security concerns to a focus on collective global security . . . The certainty that all nations share a common destiny demands that they work together as partners.[32]

The statement goes on to argue that government agreements are not enough to address these issues—billions of people and millions of businesses around the world must shift their values and behavior from an environmentally destructive to constructive orientation.

International cooperation is imperative for addressing the world's environmental crises. Yet, although important international steps have already been taken to address some problems, they are dwarfed by the world's interrelated environmental crises. Between the first Earth Summit at Stockholm in 1972 and the second at Rio de Janeiro in 1992, the world lost 500 million acres of trees, an area one-third the size of the United States, and 500 million tons of topsoil, which would equal the arable land of India and France combined.[33]

Can the world achieve sustainable development in which living standards and life quality for an increased percentage of the world's population continue to improve while the environment's degradation is halted? Or will the world's population and development pressures continue to degrade the global environment until living standards and life quality deteriorate steadily for an increasing percentage of future generations?

The cost of simply slowing the vicious cycle of global environmental crises will be exorbitant. Nations will have to find the political will to devote as much money and effort to cleaning up the earth as they have in destroying it. By one estimate, the advanced industrial and Third World countries will have to annually expend $125 billion and $500 billion, respectively.[34] The largest international environmental program is the $1.3 billion annual budget of the Global Environmental Facility, which is jointly run by the UNEP, the World Bank, and the UN Development Program.

Political inertia remains the biggest obstacle to dealing with these problems. It is much easier to do nothing than to undertake the vast financial and administrative efforts needed to address those crises. This "tyranny of the immediate" causes politicians to serve entrenched interest groups rather than the general welfare of present and future generations. Governments, businesses, and people fiddle today while generations to come will literally burn.

Another problem is how economic growth and environmental destruction are measured. Perceptions precede policy. In order to act on an issue one must first perceive it. Our perceptions are shaped by existing methods of analyzing phenomena. Many people point out that many of those methods distort our understanding of the real world. Environmentalists argue that economists treat pollution as a free indulgence for business without weighing in the often far greater costs of pollution for society and eventually the world as a whole. Measurements of a nation's economic size do not account for such losses as clear-cut forests, polluted streams, and eroded soils. Forests, for example, are valued for their "stumpage" or amount of cut logs and not for their value in protecting watersheds, promoting tourism, filtering pollution, or producing medicines, fruits, nuts, fish, game, and biodiversity. The difficulty is in assigning values to these foregone environmentally sound economic opportunities.

Most countries outright subsidize environmental exploitation and degradation. The United States sells its water, trees, and grazing land at below market costs to farmers, loggers, and ranchers. If these businesses had to pay the full costs of exploiting these resources, including their depreciation, they would carefully nurture rather than waste these assets. The exploitation of natural resources should reflect its true cost.

Yet there has been some progress. There has been a significant shift in consciousness about the relationship between economic growth and a clean environment. Traditionally, both economists and environmentalists assumed that there was a trade-off between growth and the environment. Increasingly, economists and environmentalists recognize that such practices as reducing waste, conserving forests, recycling, increasing energy efficiency, and promoting mass transportation, actually stimulate economic growth. Similarly, environmental degradation—pollution, deforestation, desertification, the greenhouse effect—hurt the economy and increase poverty, unemployment, and health problems.

What more can be done? Some have proposed a GATT-style multilateral organization that addressed a range of global environmental issues through continuous organizations and clear principles and goals. United Nations Secretary General Boutros Boutros-Gali opened the 1992 Earth Summit by calling for all nations to embark on the development of a "new collective security."

STUDY QUESTIONS

1. What is the "tragedy of the commons"? How is it a metaphor for the fate of the earth?

2. What accounts for the world's population explosion? What will be its most likely consequences? What measures have been taken to slow population growth? Are these enough?

3. What evidence is there that a greenhouse effect is taking place? What will be its most likely consequences? What efforts have been made to slow the greenhouse effect? Are these enough?

4. What accounts for the ozone layer depletion? What will be its most likely consequences? What efforts have been made to slow the ozone depletion? Are these enough?

5. What are various forms of pollution and how do they affect the quality of life and economic development? What efforts have been made internationally and in the United States to slow air and water pollution? Are these enough?

6. What accounts for deforestation? What will be deforestation's most likely consequences? What efforts have been made to slow deforestation? Are these enough?

7. What accounts for desertification? Which regions have been the worst hit? Which others are being rapidly turned into desert? What will be desertification's most

likely consequence? What efforts have been made to slow desertification? Are these enough?

8. What accounts for the world's dying oceans? What will be the most likely effect if oceans continue to deteriorate? What efforts have been made to slow the deterioration of the oceans? Are these enough?

9. How are all the world's environmental problems interrelated? Are you relatively optimistic or pessimistic about humanity's ability to overcome these problems? Why?

ENDNOTES

1. Garret Hardin, "The Tragedy of the Commons," *Science*, vol. 162, December 1970, 1243–1248.

2. Lester Brown, ed., *The World Watch Reader: On Global Environmental Issues* (New York: Norton, 1991), 13.

3. Unless otherwise indicated, all population statistics come from Nathan Keyfitz, "Population Growth Can Prevent the Development that Would Slow Population Growth," in Jessica Matthews, *Preserving the Global Environment: The Challenge of Shared Leadership* (New York: Norton, 1992).

4. Paul Lewis, "Curb on Population Growth Needed Urgently, U.N. Says," *New York Times,* April 30, 1992.

5. Ibid.

6. Jane Perlez, "In Rwanda, Births Increase and the Problems Do Too," *New York Times,* May 31, 1992, 1, 11.

7. Julian Simon, *Population Matters: People, Resources, Environment, and Immigration* (New Brunswick, N.J.: Transaction Press, 1990).

8. Jodi Jacobson, "China's Baby Budget," in Lester Brown, ed., *The World Watch Reader: On Global Environmental Issues* (New York: Norton, 1991); Nicholas Kristoff, "China's Crackdown on Births: A Stunning and Harsh Success," *New York Times,* April 25, 1993.

9. Jane Perlez, "Briton Sees AIDS Halting African Population Rise," *New York Times,* June 22, 1992, 7A.

10. Quoted in Christopher Flavin, "The Heat Is On," in Lester Brown, ed., *The World Watch Reader: On Global Environmental Issues.* Unless otherwise indicated, all statistics come from Christopher Flavin or George Rahjens, "Energy and Climate Change," in Jessica Matthews, *Preserving the Global Environment,* 154–186.

11. George Rahjens, "Energy and Climate Change," in Jessica Matthews, *Preserving the Global Environment,* 157.

12. Ibid.

13. Peter Passell, "Economists Start to Fret Again About Population," *New York Times,* December 18, 1990, 1C.

14. Sylvia Nasar, "Cooling the Globe Would Be Nice . . . ," *New York Times,* May 31, 1992, 6.

15. William Stevens, "New Studies Predict Profits in Heading Off Warming," *New York Times,* March 17, 1992, 1C.

16. Unless otherwise indicated all statistics come from Richard Benedick, "Protecting the Ozone Layer: New Dimensions in Diplomacy," in Jessica Matthews, *Preserving the Global Environment,* 112–153, and Cynthia Shea, "Mending the Earth's Shield," in Lester Brown, ed., *The World Watch Reader: On Global Environmental Issues.*

17. Unless otherwise indicated, all statistics come from Hilary French, "You Are What You Breathe," in Lester Brown, ed., *The World Watch Reader: On Global Environmental Issues.*

18. Statistics on this region have been taken from Hilary French, "Eastern Europe's Clean Break with the Past," in Lester Brown, ed., *The World Watch Reader: On Global Environmental Issues.*

19. Hilary French, "Eastern Europe's Clean Break with the Past," in Lester Brown, ed., *The World Watch Reader: On Global Environmental Issues.*

20. Lester Brown, ed., *The World Watch Reader: On Global Environmental Issues,* 308–309.

21. Unless otherwise indicated, all statistics come from Alan Durning, "Cradles of Life" and John Ryan, "Sustainable Forestry," in Lester Brown, ed., *The World Watch Reader: On Global Environmental Issues;* and Kenton Miller, et al., "Deforestation and Species Loss," in Jessica Matthews, *Preserving the Global Environment,* 78–111.

22. Kenton Miller et al., Deforestation and Species Loss," in Jessica Matthews, *Preserving the Global Environment,* 79–80.

23. "Hard Luck for Hardwoods," *The Economist,* April 22, 1989, 63.

24. Twig Mowatt, "Soil Degradation Study, "The *New York Times,* March 31, 1992. Unless otherwise indicated, all statistics will come from Sandra Postel, "Restoring Degraded Land," in Lester Brown, ed., *The World Watch Reader: On Global Environmental Issues,* 25.

25. Marlise Simons, "Winds Sweep African Soil to Feed Lands Far Away," *New York Times,* October 29, 1992, 1, 15.

26. Lester Brown, ed., *The World Watch Reader: On Global Environmental Issues,* 148.

27. David Pitt, "Nations Mobilize to Limit Deserts," *New York Times,* December 10, 1993; Lester Brown, ed., *The World Watch Reader: On Global Environmental Issues,* 311.

28. Sandra Postel, "Emerging Water Scarcities," in Lester Brown, ed., *The World Watch Reader: On Global Environmental Issues.*

29. Unless otherwise indicated, all statistics come from Lester Brown, "Feeding Six Billion," in Lester Brown, ed., *The World Watch Reader: On Global Environmental Issues.*

30. For an excellent account of the causes and effects of ocean pollution, see Nicholas Lassen, "The Ocean Blues," in Lester Brown, ed., *The World Watch Reader: On Global Environmental Issues.* Unless otherwise indicated, the statistics from this section come from his chapter.

31. Timothy Egan, "New Evidence of Ecological Damage Brings a Call to Ban Drift Net Fishing," *New York Times,* November 1989, 24A.

32. Quoted in Jessica Matthews, *Preserving the Global Environment,* 325–326.

33. Philip Elmer-Dewitt, "Rich Vs. Poor," *Time,* June 1, 1992, 42.

34. Ibid, 43.

The Global Political Economy into the Twenty-first Century: Perils and Prospects

Key Terms and Concepts

Faust
Kantism
Leninism
New World Order
Wilsonism

Two centuries ago, in 1795, Immanuel Kant predicted in his "Essay on Perpetual Peace" that the global political economy would eventually evolve into a system in which conflicts are resolved by peaceful cooperation rather than war.[1] Kant foresaw three developments which would lead to a "perpetual peace": 1) the conversion of authoritarian states into liberal democracies (republicanism); 2) the evolution of international law and organization into an authoritative system which binds all sovereign states (federalism); and 3) economic development and interdependence (hospitality).

Kant's vision is fast becoming a reality. Geoeconomic conflict is replacing geopolitics as the dominant force in international relations. As the modern world becomes increasingly tightly bound by a web of economic, nuclear, moral, and environmental relations, conflicts are increasingly over economic and human welfare rather than territory and ideology. Instead of a world whose relations are characterized by violence and anarchy, there is instead an increasingly orderly world in which the nature and effectiveness of power varies according to what the issue is, how other issues and priorities are related to it, and how skillfully the participants bargain.

State goals remain the same: states strive for strategic and economic security. But the means to achieve those ends have greatly changed. Richard Rosecrance neatly summarizes the differences between a geopolitical and geoeconomic outlook:

> in a power world states act as coherent units, force is a usable instrument of policy and there is a hierarchy of international issues dominated by questions of military security. Interdependence refers to a world in which states can no longer fully regulate policy, there are multiple channels of access between societies, no hierarchy of issues, and force is generally unusable. The difference between these two systems concerns the means that are used to advance state interests.[2]

This chapter will discuss the changes and continuities in the global political economy and international relations now and into the twenty-first century.

GEOPOLITICAL CONFLICT AND COOPERATION

The Cold War and Aftermath

In many ways, the twentieth century's central struggle has been between two diametrically opposed internationalist visions: Wilsonism and Leninism. *Wilsonism* espoused political, economic, and national freedom, and international cooperation to resolve conflicts. *Leninism* advocated class struggle, revolution, war, and totalitarian state power. That struggle symbolically ended with the Berlin Wall's destruction on November 9, 1989.

Complicating this ideological struggle for the hearts, minds, and pocketbooks of the world's people was the military superpower of the United States and Soviet Union, that championed Wilsonism and Leninism, respectively. The world entered a new era, the nuclear era, in July 1945 with the explosion of an atomic bomb in New Mexico. By 1949, the Soviet Union too had obtained an atomic bomb, and the nuclear race to acquire ever more and numerous destructive weapons has continued until recently. The nuclear arms race eventually led to the stockpiling of tens of thousands of nuclear weapons, bringing all of humanity under the nuclear shadow of potential global destruction.

Recent agreements between the United States and the former Soviet Union appear to have capped and even reversed the nuclear arms race, while the Cold War has ended with the collapse of communism and the Soviet empire. In their 1992 "Camp David Declaration on New Relations," President George Bush and President Boris Yeltsin declared that "Russia and the United States do not regard each other as potential adversaries." This was truly a remarkable statement. To have merely said that the United States and Russia were no longer enemies would have been significant. But to state that there is not even the potential for animosity was truly a victory for a *new world order* in which military conflict is irrelevent for resolving most differences among both advanced and struggling industrial countries alike.

The Cold War was not a war in the traditional sense. During the almost five decades in which they were mortal enemies, the United States and Soviet Union never directly fought each other. Deterrence, not conquest, was the heart of the Cold War. When the Soviet empire and communism crumbled, no American troops swept triumphantly into Moscow and the other former Soviet capitals.

New Conceptions of War, Peace, and National Security

The Cold War's end did inaugurate the beginning of a "new world order." While power is still the currency of international relations, the nature of the conflicts and the means by which states assert their interests is rapidly changing. National security traditionally meant freedom from the threat of foreign attack. Today, and into the future, an ever smaller fraction of international conflicts will be over territory and ideology. Although war is unlikely to ever become obsolete, an increasing number and percentage of wars will be civil rather than international. Edward Luttwak is among those who sees profound changes in the nature of international conflict in the post-Cold War era:

*Except in those unfortunate parts of the world where armed confrontations or civil
strife persist for purely regional or internal reasons, the waning of the Cold War is
steadily reducing the importance of military power in world affairs.   .   .   .
Everyone, it appears, now agrees that the methods of commerce are displacing
military methods—with disposable capital in lieu of firepower, civilian innovation
in lieu of military-technical advancement, and market penetration in lieu of
garrisons and bases.[3]*

The Triumph of Liberal Democracy

Since 1815, liberal democracies have never gone to war. Thus the more countries that
achieve liberal democracy, the less chance for war. Mixing Hegel's notion that history
moves by the clash of ideas with Kant's notion of perpetual peace, Francis Fukuyama
writes: "the triumph of the West, of the Western idea, is evident .   .   . in the total exhaustion of viable systematic alternatives to Western liberalism."[4] According to
Fukuyama, liberal democracy has emerged triumphant from 7,000 years of a dialectical
struggle between different ideologies. History is ending in a Hegelian sense and bringing with it an unprecedented and unending era of peace among humanity.

Liberal democracy is solidly rooted in North America, Europe, and Japan, and is
developing in virtually all other regions around the world. What explains the democratic revolutions of the 1980s? How enduring are they? Is democracy for everyone or are
there cultural prerequisites for a lasting democracy?

Certainly there is a link between economic prosperity and political freedom. When
people have one, they inevitably desire the other. While most cultures do not have democratic values of political equality and liberty, democracy has become a universal
good. Virtually every regime, even the most despotic, claims to be democratic in some
ways. And as Fukuyama and others have pointed out, there is no universal alternative to
democracy.

Interdependence and Integration: Sovereignty at Bay

Many believe that the global system is undergoing changes as profound as those which
followed the 1648 Treaty of Westphalia that inagurated the nation-state system. With
the Cold War's end, the United Nations has embarked upon an unprecedented series of
peace keeping ventures. Meanwhile, the world becomes ever more tightly knit economically, politically, environmentally, and socially. Regional political economic communities like the European Union (EU) and the North American Free Trade Association
(NAFTA) gain more members and more extensive ties.

Even states which are not members of such international communities find their
national sovereignty eroding as the world becomes more interdependent. Governments
are finding it increasingly difficult to keep out foreign influences such as goods, services,
investments, immigrants, drugs, pop culture, pollution, disease, money, and so forth,
and to stem the outflow of technology, skilled workers and scientists, money, and secrets. International law, morality, and opinion are increasingly important constraints on
state behavior. Mass communications have put every government, even the most

oppressive, in media fishbowls, in which their gaffs and crimes are inevitably exposed to the world.

Is sovereignty increasingly an anachronism in an increasingly interdependent world? Could the United Nations develop into the global political government?

Disintegration and Discord

While some states are integrating others are disintegrating. Fifteen states achieved independence in 1991 alone, while dozens of regions are declaring themselves autonomous from central governments, the first step toward eventual independence.[5] National sovereignty is the biggest obstacle to the success of international organizations. States can always refuse to accept the resolutions of the organizations of which they are members. Within a century there may well be twice as many states as today. Yet while nation-states will be more numerous, their sovereignty will be significantly curtailed.

GEOECONOMIC CONFLICT AND COOPERATION

In the almost five centuries since its creation, the global political economy has proven enormously resilient. During the twentieth century, the global political economy was battered and emerged stronger from a succession of crises, including World War I, the Great Depression, World War II, the Cold War, and the breakup of the empires.

Industrialization Revolutions

The industrial revolution has evolved through several distinct stages, each centered around a distinct interrelated cluster of new technologies and mass production industries. The first revolution began in England in the late eighteenth century and centered on the use of new farming techniques, coal and iron production, steam power, and mass textile production techniques. The second phase emerged during the mid-nineteenth century in England, France, the United States, and a generation later, in Germany and Japan. This phase was built around the railroad, telegraph, steamship, chemicals, and farm machinery. The third phase emerged in the early twentieth century with the automobile, electric and gas power, and the telephone. The fourth phase started with World War II and included petrochemicals, nuclear power, electronics, air transportation, computers, and new plant hybrids. In the 1970s, we entered a fifth phase centered around microelectronics, supercomputers, biotechnology, electronic mail, and virtual reality. Each phase both stimulated and was stimulated by a transportation and communications revolution—canals in the first phase; the railroads, steamships, and telegraphs of the second phase; automobiles, airplanes, and telephones in the third phase; jet planes and huge cargo ships in the fourth phase; and fax machines and computer networks in the fifth phase. Wars proved the catalyst for many of the new inventions and production techniques which fueled each phase of the industrial revolution. America's industrialization took off with the Civil War and World War II pushed the country into a fourth industrial stage.

Nations did not always capitalize on the inventions occuring within their borders. For example, a German invented the automobile but it was American entrepreneurs that transformed the technology into a mass industry. Americans invented the transistor and microchip, but Japanese entrepreneurs built those inventions into high quality, low cost consumer goods and have reaped hundreds of billions of dollars selling them around the world.

Each industrial phase transformed the nations that pioneered it, the nations to which it spread, and eventually the global political economy. For example, the enormous mobility that came with the automobile allowed for the growth of suburbs and the decentralization of economic and political power to the new homes and businesses in the suburbs. Urbanization and suburbanization accelerated. Of industrial countries, as much as 80 to 90 percent of the population lives in cities which are fed by an increasingly smaller farm population—about 2 percent in the United States and 5 to 7 percent in the other democratic industrial countries.

White-collar office production has replaced blue-collar factory production as the economy's dynamic core. In the United States, about 75 percent of workers are in offices, 20 percent in factories, and about 5 percent on farms, in forests, or in fishing boats. Although many white-collar workers are manufacturing things like software, books, and music, most are producing services like banking, insurance, travel, and education.

Industrialization has brought ever higher living, work, and health standards. The industrial horrors revealed by writers like Charles Dickens and Upton Sinclair have been largely eliminated in the advanced democratic industrial societies. Work weeks are 35 to 40 hours, with a bonus for overtime, the workplace safety and health is regulated. Factory workers are middle class rather than poor. White and blue-collar workers alike have become increasingly specialized and skilled. Virtually everyone has become a specialist on some relatively minute type of production.

Union power, however, is diminishing with factory style mass production. In the United States, union membership among non-farm workers dropped from its height of 35 percent in the 1950s to about 12 percent in the early 1990s! Union membership as a percentage of workers has also fallen in most other democratic industrial countries, although not as dramatically as in the United States. In Japan the percentage of unionized workers remained 25 percent in the early 1990s, in Germany 40 percent, Britain 45 percent, and Switzerland 35 percent.

Industrialization means greater interdependence within and between countries. Production has become increasingly spread across many nations. Corporations build factories overseas to capture local market which are protected from competitive imports, to take advantage of cheap labor or natural resources. The world's once diverse range of economic systems are steadily converging. The extremes of free market and state capitalism have been largely rejected in favor of some middle ground of managed market capitalism.

Policy, Trade, and Investment Conflicts

There are some significant problems and conflicts. While the global economy is increasingly integrated, some countries use predatory neomercantilist strategies to enhance their own wealth and power at the expense of others. Japan has been the most notorious neomercantilist country. Japan has surpassed the United States as the world's leading financial, technological, and manufacturing power by most indicators. Yet unlike the United States, Japan has refused to genuinely open its markets to free competition, halt the dumping by its corporations of products in foreign markets to destroy their foreign rivals, or untie its foreign aid and donate amounts commensurate with its economic power. In 1992, Japan's payments surplus surged 61 percent from $72.9 billion to $117.6 billion and its trade surplus from $103.9 billion to $132.6 billion! In contrast, the United States and European Community suffered trade deficits of $86.1 billion and $54.9 billion, respectively, most of which was with Japan.

Related to the inbalance in global trade among the economic superpowers is the possibly growing clashes between rival trade blocs. The EC and NAFTA are increasingly consolidating formal integration within their respective ranks while Japan is forging an informal but no less powerful East and Southeast Asian bloc. These regional blocs will undoubtedly strengthen in the decades ahead. Yet trade between the blocs will remain vital to the prosperity of all. The greater the interdependence between blocs, the most destructive a trade war would be to all concerned. There would no true victors, only losers in a global trade war. However, these blocs will increasingly manage trade to ensure that the benefits are evenly distributed. For example, the EU and NAFTA may eventually insist that Japan import as much as it exports to them.

Dilemmas of Development

Underlying the geoeconomic conflicts among the advanced industrial states or between them and the Third World are deep psychological conflicts over the nature of development itself. While enjoying unprecedented affluence and comfort, many people living in modern industrial countries at times feel overwhelmed and imprisoned by vast economic, political, and social institutions and forces beyond their control. At times, it is not clear whether development exists for the sake of humanity, or humanity for the sake of development.[6]

The *Faust* story best illustrates this modern dilemma. Living on the cusp of the industrial revolution, Faust is a Renaissance Man—a doctor, philosopher, scientist, and professor—but as the story opens he is locked in his room and is experiencing a mid-life crisis. Something is missing from his life. He is empty at the core, and he is contemplating suicide. Church bells that remind him of his lost, beautiful childhood save him as he recognizes that something magical exists beyond the sterile world of his study. Berman summarizes Faust's transformation:

> *In his first phase, he lived alone and dreamed. In his second period, he intertwined his life with the life of another person, and learned to love. Now, in his last incarnation, he connects his personal drives with the economic, political, and social forces that drive the world; he learns to build and to destroy. He expands the horizon of his being from private to public life, from intimacy to activism, from communion to organization. He pits all his powers against nature and society; he strives to change not only his own life but everyone else's as well. Now he finds a way to act effectively against the feudal and patriarchal world: to construct a radically new social environment that will empty the old world out or break it down.[7]*

To accomplish his dreams, he teams up with Mephistopheles and his supernatural powers. Their talents complement each other—Faust the visionary and organizer, Mephistopheles the cynical, selfish, scrupleless hit man.

The same spirit to destroy and create has driven all the great developers, whether their projects have been successful or not. Stalin dreamed of achieving a communist utopia. To achieve his goal, Stalin had tens of millions of people murdered or imprisoned in his drive to collectivize and centrally plan the Soviet economy. In the end, all of his scheme were abject failures. In the United States, Roosevelt's Manhattan Project to create an atomic bomb, Kennedy's Apollo Project to put a man on the moon, and Reagan's Strategic Defense Initiative to create an anti-nuclear shield over the United States were all animated by the vision to transform the world.

Nothing illustrates the Faustian dilemma of modern man greater than nuclear power. Alvin Weinberg, the director of the Oak Ridge Laboratory captured this dilemma: "We nuclear people have made a Faustian bargain with society. On the one hand, we offer—in the catalytic nuclear burner—an inexhaustible source of energy. . . . But the price we demand of society for this magical energy source is both a vigilance and a longevity of social institutions that we are quite unaccustomed to."[8]

Global Environmental Crises and Cooperation

In an increasingly interdependent world, "national security" and "world security" become increasingly indistinguishable, particularly in environmental issues. On April 22, 1990, tens of millions of people around the world celebrated the twentieth anniversary of Earth Day. Celebrants had cause to cheer and mourn. Over the previous two decades, there had been a growing awareness of the steps needed to counter a range of interrelated environmental crises that threatened humanity's future. At the same time these crises worsened and seemed insurmountable. Increasing numbers of individuals and governments are mobilizing to counter a much more insidious form of global destruction than the threat of nuclear war—the greenhouse effect and ozone layer depletion brought on by the unbridled growth of population, industrialization, desertification, and deforestation.

Malthus ultimately may be right about the earth's inability to sustain a continually swelling population. All human activities have an environmental impact, some relatively benign and others destructive. Every ecosystem has a particular "carrying capacity" or threshold beyond which too many humans or animals living there will destroy it. As the greenhouse effect, ozone depletion, deforestation, desertification, and other environmental calamities reveal, the world's population has already exceeded the earth's carrying capacity. Can we any longer speak of national interests in an age of a deteriorating environment?

For decades, grass roots environmental organizations in the United States, Europe, and elsewhere have struggled to make environmental problems a global priority. The Cold War's end has finally brought environmental issues to the center of the world's political stages. The 1992 Rio de Janeiro Earth Summit, attended by representatives of 178 countries, created a nearly unanimous global consensus on the environmental crises and how to address them. The heart of the conference was a nonbinding "Agenda 21," an 800 page set of analyses and proposals.

The trouble was not in creating a consensus on what was wrong and how to fix it, but acquiring the political will to act on that understanding. The estimated cost of enacting the agenda was $125 billion a year, three times the size of the world's combined foreign aid budgets and equal to 1 percent of the advanced industrial countries' GNPs. Few governments are willing to make the short-term sacrifices vital for the planet's long-term survival.

The United States in particular was harshly criticized and isolated for its "spoiler" role at the conference. Rather than leading the conference, President Bush seemed more intent on obstructing and watering down its treaties and messages. Against all contrary evidence, the Bush administration clung to the idea that there was a trade-off between environmentalism and business. The White House succeeded in tabling a proposal that would have required the advanced industrial countries to pledge 0.7 percent of their GNP in "green" aid to the Third World.

Meanwhile, most Third World countries see environmentalism as a potential means of reaping more foreign financial and technological aid. They argue that environmental treaties place an unfair financial burden on them, and that the wealthier nations should pay for the antipollution technology and related costs that the poorer countries are required to adopt.

CONCLUSION

On October 12, 1992, the 500th anniversary of Columbus' journey to the western hemisphere, NASA pointed huge radio interceptors toward the Milky Way in hopes of picking up an intergalactic message from a distant civilization. From the first recorded thoughts through today, people have wondered whether there was another presence in the universe. Now we have the means to find out. Someday intergalactic relations may become as important as international relations today.

Meanwhile, the world's inhabitants must find better ways of dealing with ever worsening environmental crises, along with such perennial problems as war, economic conflict, disease, immigration, drugs, exploitation, and poverty, to name some of the more prominent. Yet international relations occur in a system which is still largely characterized by:

> *few restraints on the behavior of individual actors; mutual suspicion and competition; the need to provide for one's own security; self-interest as a guide to policy; the duty to protect one's citizens; the pain associated with miscalculation; the reluctance to depend on others; and difficulties pertaining to the judgment of what is morally proper in an international context.*[9]

Henry Kissinger captured the essence of these problems when he declared that we "are stranded between old conceptions of political conduct and a wholly new conception, between the inadequacy of the nation-state and the emerging imperative of global community."[10]

Despite the deepening interdependence among all peoples, can we ever truly know another? Cultures, just like individuals, are unique and endless complexes of values, perceptions, and behavior which we can never truly know. Theodore Von Laue argues that there are "no cultural universals providing a common language for transcultural understanding; like poetry, cultures are not translatable. We have no choice but to interpret the others by our own lights."[11] And therein lies most of the dilemma.

ENDNOTES

1. Taken from George Modelski, "Is World Politics Evolutionary Learning?" *International Organization,* vol. 44, no. 1, Winter, 1990, 2–24. Immanuel Kant distinguished between the warlike tendencies of democratic and authoritarian countries almost two hundred years ago when he argued that democratic nations, tied together by trade and a respect for international law, would be unlikely to go to war. In his 1795 essay entitled "Perpetual Peace," Kant asserts that "if the consent of citizens is required in order to decide that war should be declared . . . , nothing is more natural than they would be very cautious in commencing such a poor game, decreeing for themselves the calamities of war . . . In a constitution which is not republican, and under which the subjects are not citizens, a declaration of war is the easiest thing in the world to decide on." Immanuel Kant, "Perpetual Peace," in Peter Gay, ed., *The Enlightenment* (New York: Simon & Schuster, 1974), 790–792. For a fuller discussion of the changes and continuities of international relations from which some of the following material and ideas have been taken, see William Nester, *American Power, the New World Order, and the Japanese Challenge* (New York: St. Martin's Press, 1993).

2. Richard Rosecrance, *The Rise of the Trading State: Commerce and Conquest in the Modern World* (New York: Basic Books, 1986), 62.

3. Edward Luttwak, "From Geopolitics to Geoeconomics," *National Interest,* vol. 20, Summer 1990, 17.

4. Francis Fukuyama, "The End of History?" *The National Interest,* no. 16, Summer 1989, 3.

5. See Daniel Patrick Moynihan, *Pandemonium: Ethnicity in International Politics* (New York: Oxford University Press, 1993). See also Zbigniew Brezezkinski, *Out of Control: Global Turmoil on the Eve of the Twenty-First Century* (New York: Charles Scribner's , 1993); Al Gore, *Earth in the Balance: Ecology and the Human Spirit* (New York: Houghton Mifflin, 1992).

6. For a brilliant discussion of these and related questions, see Marshall Berman, *All That Is Solid Melts Into Air: The Experience of Modernity* (New York: Simon & Schuster, 1982).

7. Ibid, 61.

8. Quoted in Ibid, 84.

9. John Rothgeb, *Defining Power: Influence and Force in Contemporary International System* (London: St. Martin's Press, 1993), 65.

10. Henry Kissinger, *The White House Years* (Boston: Little, Brown, 1975), 12. Some recent books and articles that have addressed the changes and continuities in international relations into the 1990s and beyond include : Michael Brecher and Patrick James, *Crisis and Change in World Politics* (Boulder, Colo.: Westview Press, 1986); Ernst-Otto Czempiel and James Rosenau, eds., *Global Changes and Theoretical Challenges: Approaches to World Politics for the 1990's* (Lexington Books, Mass.: Lexington Books, 1980); Charles F. Doran, *Systems in Crisis: New Imperatives of High Politics at Century's End* (Cambridge: Cambridge University Press, 1991); Robert Jervis, "The Future of World Politics: Will It Resemble the Past?" *International Security,* vol. 16, Winter 1991–1992, 39–73. Charles Kegley and Eugene Wittkopf, eds., *The Global Agenda. Issues and Perspectives* (New York: McGraw-Hill, 1992). James Rosenau, *Turbulence in World Politics: A Theory of Change and Continuity* (Princeton, N.J.: Princeton University Press, 1990); Tad Szule, *Then and Now: How the World Has Changed Since World War II* (New York: Morrow, 1990); Paul Kennedy, *Preparing for the 21st Century* (New York: Random House, 1993).

11. Theodore Von Laue, *The World Revolution of Westernization* (New York: Oxford University Press, 1987), 376.

INDEX